THE
IRISH STONE AGE

THE IRISH STONE AGE

ITS CHRONOLOGY, DEVELOPMENT & RELATIONSHIPS

by

HALLAM L. MOVIUS, JR., PH.D.
Assistant Curator of Palaeolithic Archaeology,
Peabody Museum, Harvard University

GREENWOOD PRESS, PUBLISHERS
NEW YORK

Reprinted by permission
of the Cambridge University Press

First Greenwood Reprinting, 1969

Library of Congress Catalogue Card Number 69-14008

SBN 8371-1152-8

PRINTED IN UNITED STATES OF AMERICA

To

EARNEST ALBERT HOOTON

an able teacher and a loyal friend
who created the Harvard Irish Survey
and whose inspiration and guidance
led to the writing of this book

CONTENTS

Foreword PAGE xiii

Preface xv

Introduction xxi

Part One

THE CHRONOLOGY OF THE LATE-GLACIAL AND EARLY POST-GLACIAL PERIODS IN NORTHERN AND WESTERN EUROPE

Chapter I. The Chronology of Northern Europe 1

Introduction; The recession of the last ice-sheet; Geochronology; Changes of level: Delevelling; Water bodies in the Baltic Basin; Climatic phases; Pollen analysis: Palaeobotany; Summary (with Table 1).

Chapter II. The Late-Glacial Sequence in Britain and Ireland 25

Introduction; The Old Drift Glaciation; The raised beach of the Third Interglacial Period; The stratigraphy of the Late-Glacial Period; Deposits of the Interstadial Period between the Old and the New Drift Glaciations (W_I/W_2); The New Drift Glaciation; The age of the New Drift Glaciation (with Table 2); The recession of the last ice-sheets (with Table 3); Deposits of the Late-Glacial Sea; Correlations with Fennoscandia (with Table 4); Late-Glacial peats and laminated clays (with Table 5); The earliest occupation of Northern Britain and Ireland after the retreat of the ice.

Chapter III. Early Post-Glacial Chronology in Britain and Ireland 75

Introduction; Submerged forests and raised beaches; Raised beaches: general discussion; The Post-Glacial land-bridge; Climatic phases; Palaeobotany; Correlations with Fennoscandia (with Table 6).

Part Two

THE STONE AGE CULTURES OF IRELAND

Chapter I. The Antiquity of Man in Ireland 105

General aspects and nature of the problem; Rosses Point and other sites, County Sligo; Kilgreany Cave, County Waterford; The Old Stone Age in Ireland: Summary; Lough Neagh, County Londonderry.

CONTENTS

PAGE

CHAPTER II. The Mesolithic Culture of the Irish Raised Beaches 121

Distribution and method of approach; Stratigraphy; Chronology (with Table 7); Archaeological material; Summary and Conclusions.

CHAPTER III. The Origin and Affinities of the Larnian Culture 175

Introduction; The Mesolithic of Scotland; The Mesolithic of England; Other considerations; Mesolithic navigation; The earliest settlers in Ireland.

CHAPTER IV. Post-Larnian Developments 211

Introduction; The Campignian sites; The age and cultural affinities of the Irish Campignian; The Bann culture; The Sand Hills; Summary.

CHAPTER V. Conclusions 257

APPENDIX I. The Raised Beach of the Third Interglacial Period 265

II. Deposits of the Interstadial Period between the Old and the New Drift Glaciations (W_1/W_2) in England and Scotland 266

III. The New Drift Glaciation 207

IV. The Recession of the Last Ice-Sheets 273

V. Deposits of the Late-Glacial Sea 284

VI. Submerged Forests and Raised Beaches in Britain and Ireland 288

REFERENCES CITED IN THE TEXT 295

List of Abbreviations 295

List of Works 296

CLASSIFIED LIST OF REFERENCES TO CAVE RESEARCH AND STONE AGE ARCHAEOLOGY IN IRELAND 317

ADDENDUM 320

INDEX 321

ILLUSTRATIONS

TEXT FIGURES

PAGE

1. The Stages in the Recession of the Last Ice-Sheet in Northern Europe. (After De Geer, with later additions.) 5
2. Map illustrating the Depression of Fennoscandia under the Weight of the Last Ice-Sheet. (After Daly.) 9
3. Map of the Litorina Sea with the Isobases of the Litorina Strand-Lines in metres. (After Daly.) 10
4. Deposits of the Interstadial Period (W_1/W_2) between the Old and the New Drift Glaciations in Britain and Ireland. 35
5. Archaeological and Palaeontological Sites of the Late-Glacial Period. 42
6. The New Drift Glaciation of Britain and Ireland and the Stages in the Retreat of the Last Ice-Sheets. 52
7. Late-Glacial and Early Post-Glacial Isobases in Britain and Ireland. (Based on Wright, 1937, Fig. 127.) 58
8. Tentative Chronology of the Late-Glacial Period in Northern and Western Europe. *facing* 60
9. Localities contemporary with the Retreat of the Last Ice-Sheets in Britain and Ireland. 66
10. Southampton S.R. Graving Dock Section, 1932. (After Godwin.) 78
11. Distribution of Post-Glacial Coastal Deposits in Britain and Ireland. 79
12. Land and Water in Northern and Western Europe during the Early Post-Glacial Period. 88
13. Diagram showing the Percentage Pollen Composition of Peat Samples of Late Boreal Age from Sites in Britain and Ireland. (After Godwin.) 97
14. Diagram showing the Percentage Pollen Composition of Peat Samples of Early Atlantic Age from Sites in Britain and Ireland. (After Godwin.) 97
15. Map showing the Location of Archaeological Sites in Ireland and Neighbouring Regions. 110
16. Lower Palaeolithic Implement(?) found *in situ* in Glacial Gravel, Drumfresky, Dun River, County Antrim. (After Burchell and Moir.) 112
17. Massive Flake Implements of Limestone from Rosses Point, County Sligo. (After Burchell, Moir, and Dixon.) 113
18. Flint Industry from below Late Boreal Peat on the North-Western Shore of Lough Neagh, County Londonderry. (After Whelan.) 119

ILLUSTRATIONS

PAGE

19. Section through the Deposits at The Cloney, Glenarm, County Antrim. 138
20. Section showing the Early Post-Glacial Deposits at Rough Island, County Down. 138
21–25. Early Larnian Flints. 150–56
26–32. Late Larnian Flints. 160–69
33. Map showing the Location of Sites mentioned in the text. *facing* 176
34. Early Larnian Flints from the Litorina Raised Beach at Campbeltown. (After Breuil.) 179
35. Obanian Flints from the Caisteal-nan-Gillean Kitchen-Midden, Oronsay. (After Breuil.) 182
36. Obanian Stone Implements from the Caisteal-nan-Gillean Kitchen-Midden, Oronsay. (After Breuil.) 184
37. Obanian Bone Implements from the Caisteal-nan-Gillean Kitchen-Midden, Oronsay. (After Breuil.) 186
38. Obanian Harpoons of Bone and Horn. (After Breuil.) 187
39. Azilian Implements from Victoria Cave, near Settle, Yorkshire. (After Breuil.) 189
40. Implements of Sandstone and Schist, probably Azilian, from Victoria Cave, near Settle, Yorkshire. (After Breuil.) 190
41. Implements of Horn and Bone, probably Magdalenian, from Victoria Cave, near Settle, Yorkshire. (After Breuil.) 191
42. Perforated Antler Axe-Hammer from Meiklewood Estate, near Stirling. (After Munro.) 192
43. Tardenoisean Flints from Shewalton Moor, Ayrshire. (After Lacaille and Clark.) 195
44. Neolithic Flints from Glenarm, County Antrim. 215
45. Neolithic Flints from Glenarm, County Antrim. 217
46. Neolithic Flints from Glenarm, County Antrim. 218
47. Neolithic Flints from Cushendun, County Antrim. 220
48. Neolithic Flints from Rough Island, Strangford Lough, County Down. 221
49. Neolithic Stone Axes from Tievebulliagh, near Cushendall, County Antrim. (After Knowles.) 225
50. Neolithic Stone Implements from Tievebulliagh, near Cushendall, County Antrim. (After Knowles.) 226
51. Neolithic Stone Implements from Tievebulliagh, near Cushendall, County Antrim. (After Knowles.) 227
52. Neolithic Implements of Flint and Stone, and Pottery from Ballynagard, Rathlin Island, County Antrim. (After Whelan.) 230

PAGE

53. Neolithic Flints and Pottery from Le Campigny, Seine-Inférieure. (After Salmon, Du Mesnil, and Capitan.) 236
54. Pollen Diagram from the Excavated Site at Newferry, County Londonderry. (After Jessen.) 241
55. Flint Implements typical of the Bann Culture from the Sub-Diatomite Hearths excavated at Newferry, County Londonderry. 243
56. Flint and Stone Implements typical of the Bann Culture from the Sub-Diatomite Hearths excavated at Newferry, County Londonderry. 245
57. Neolithic Pot from the Base of the Diatomite at Newferry, County Londonderry. 246
58. Implements of Flint and Stone from the Lower Bann Valley. (After Whelan and Hawkes.) 248
59. Chart showing the Post-Larnian Developments in Ireland. 255

PLATES

I. Kilgreany Cave, County Waterford *facing* 114

Upper: General view of the present mouth of the cave. *Lower:* Section through the deposits in the second chamber of the cave.

II. Cushendun, County Antrim *facing* 126

Upper: General view of the mouth of Glendun looking north-west, showing the Dun River, the excavated site, and the 35-foot (Early Post-Glacial) terrace. *Lower:* Section through the deposits at the excavated site.

III. Glenarm, County Antrim *facing* 130

Upper: General view of the site, showing the upper end of the Litorina raised beach. *Lower:* Typical section through the deposits.

IV. Larne, County Antrim *facing* 132

Upper: Larne Lough, Island Magee, and Curran Point showing the location of the site. *Lower:* The stratigraphy of the excavated pit.

V. Rough Island, Strangford Lough, County Down *facing* 140

Upper: The Island at high tide. *Lower:* Section through the deposits: (A) Deposit A; (B) Deposit B; Sand, Deposit C.

VI. Newferry, County Londonderry *facing* 240

Upper: General view of the excavated site. *Lower:* Section through the deposits, showing two large hearths associated with Deposit D and projecting into the base of the Diatomite.

VII. Newferry, County Londonderry *facing* 246

Sherds from the base of the Diatomite: A. Interior. B. Exterior showing horizontal lug.

TABLES

PAGE

1. Chronological Chart of Northern Europe during the Late-Glacial and Early Post-Glacial Periods. (After De Geer, Jessen, Clark, Daly, and Wright.) 23
2. The Late-Glacial Sequence in Britain and Ireland, and the Continental Equivalents. 44
3. Tentative Chronology of the Recession of the Last Ice-Sheets in Britain and Ireland. 56
4. Late-Glacial and Early Post-Glacial Chronology in Northern and Western Europe. 63
5. Glacial Stages and the Climatic Development in Northern and Western Europe. 70
6. The Chronology of the Late-Glacial and Early Post-Glacial Periods in Britain and Ireland. *facing* 102
7. The Post-Glacial Chronology and Archaeological Sequence in North-East Ireland. 143

FOREWORD

The participation of Harvard University in Irish archaeology came about as the result of a five-year research programme inaugurated and directed by Professor E. A. Hooton, Chairman of the Division of Anthropology at Harvard. This project, known as the Harvard Irish Survey, dealt with the physical anthropology, sociology and archaeology of Ireland.

The work in physical anthropology was directed by Professor Hooton and the work in the field was conducted by Dr C. Wesley Dupertuis, now of the Presbyterian Hospital, New York. Some 10,125 adult male individuals were measured, and the results of this study are now being prepared for publication by Professor Hooton. The sociological survey was initiated by Professor W. Lloyd Warner, now of Chicago University, and was carried on by Professor Conrad M. Arensberg, now of Brooklyn College. The work of the sociologists, concentrated in County Clare on the west coast, has been published in two books, *The Irish Countryman* by Professor Arensberg (Macmillan & Co., New York, 1937) and *Family and Community in Ireland* by Professor Arensberg and Dr Solon T. Kimball (Harvard University Press, 1940).

The archaeological field-work was carried out by the Harvard Archaeological Expedition to Ireland from 1932 to 1936. Its work was conducted with the generous financial assistance of the governments of Eire and Northern Ireland, and with grants from the American Council of Learned Societies, the American Philosophical Society, the Milton Fund and the Division of Anthropology at Harvard University, as well as by numerous private subscriptions. Fifteen sites were fully excavated, covering nearly every cultural phase from the beginning of the Irish Stone Age to the eleventh century A.D. The site reports are being published by the Royal Irish Academy and the Royal Society of Antiquaries of Ireland, and at the present time all but two have appeared or are in the press. The material excavated in Eire is deposited in the National Museum of Ireland and that from Northern Ireland will be returned when possible to the Belfast Municipal Museum and Art Gallery. These two museums and their staffs generously provided every facility to the Expedition for work and study.

FOREWORD

The activities of the Expedition were divided into two parts, one dealing with the Stone Age and the other with the later periods. The Stone Age excavations were in charge of the Assistant Director of the Expedition, Dr H. L. Movius, Jr., who is also Assistant Curator of Palaeolithic Archaeology in the Peabody Museum of Harvard University. The present volume embodies a consideration of Late-Glacial and Early Post-Glacial chronology in Ireland, Great Britain and Scandinavia, a study of the natural environment of Stone Age man in Ireland, and a comprehensive treatment of the results of six excavations conducted there by Dr Movius.

H. O'NEILL HENCKEN

Director of the Harvard Archaeological Expedition to Ireland

PREFACE

As stated in the foreword the principal aim of the Harvard Irish Survey was to embody in the field three of the techniques of modern anthropology—physical anthropology, social anthropology and archaeology—directed towards research on the same problem: *the origin and development of the races and cultures of Ireland*. One particular aspect of the archaeological work, the scope and general character of which will be summarized in the introduction, is included in this book; the original version was presented in partial fulfilment of the requirements for the degree of Doctor of Philosophy at Harvard University in May 1937. Here I shall take the opportunity of thanking the scholars of several countries whose learning and generous assistance in many ways have made this work possible.

At the outset I wish to express my gratitude to Dr H. O'Neill Hencken, Director of the Harvard Archaeological Expedition to Ireland. Dr Hencken's helpful advice, close co-operation and friendship during the entire programme are reflected in a large measure by the degree of success achieved. A total of six Stone Age sites was investigated by the Expedition, five of them in Northern Ireland. During the 1934 season excavations were conducted at Kilgreany Cave, County Waterford (*Jour. Roy. Soc. Ant. Ireland*, LXV (1935), 254–296); Newferry, County Londonderry (*Proc. Roy. Irish Acad.* XLIII (1936), 17–40); Glenarm, County Antrim (*Jour. Roy. Soc. Ant. Ireland*, LXVII (1937), 181–220); and Cushendun, County Antrim (*Proc. Roy. Irish Acad.* XLVI (1940), 1–84). In 1935 an excavation was made at Curran Point, Larne, County Antrim, and it is hoped that the report covering this work will be published in 1942. A site on Rough Island, in Strangford Lough, County Down (*Jour. Roy. Soc. Ant. Ireland*, LXX (1940), 111–142), was investigated in 1936 to complete the field-work. In Eire the Expedition has worked in close conjunction with the National Museum, of which Dr Adolf Mahr, M.R.I.A., is Director, and with the Ancient Monuments Committee, with H. G. Leask, M.R.I.A., as Chairman. Mr Anthony Farrington, Secretary of the Royal Irish Academy, and Justice Liam Price, M.R.I.A., Editor of the *Journal of the Society of Antiquaries of Ireland*, have given much helpful advice. Professor R. A. S. Macalister, M.R.I.A., of the

National University, and Dr R. Lloyd Praeger, M.R.I.A., have likewise helped in many ways. In Northern Ireland, where the majority of the Stone Age sites are located, the Ancient Monuments Advisory Committee, of which the late Very Reverend Dean Carmody, M.R.I.A., was the former Chairman, and Dr D. A. Chart, I.S.O., M.R.I.A., Vice-Chairman, readily gave us permission to excavate and helped in every way to facilitate the work. Likewise the Belfast Municipal Museum and Art Gallery, Mr Arthur Dean, M.R.I.A., Curator, and Mr J. A. S. Stendall, M.R.I.A., Deputy Curator, has extended many courtesies. Professor J. K. Charlesworth, M.R.I.A., of Queen's University, whose important geological papers are frequently referred to in this book, has offered many helpful suggestions.

In the actual field-work I have been assisted by Messrs Amory Goddard of Sharon, Massachusetts, F. T. Riley of Dublin, and F. L. W. Richardson, Jr., of Harvard University, all in 1934; in 1935 at Larne, Miss Dorothy Newton, formerly of the Peabody Museum at Harvard, and my wife ably helped with the management of the digging; while during the 1936 season, Mr J. Raftery of the National Museum, Dublin, assisted in supervising the Rough Island excavation. Although not a member of the staff, Mrs Nora Fisher McMillan, Free Public Museums, Liverpool, has carried out the important work of identifying the marine fauna. Professor Glover Allen of Harvard University, Mr A. W. Stelfox, M.R.I.A., of the Natural History Division of the National Museum, Dublin, and Dr J. Wilfred Jackson of the Manchester Museum, have examined and identified the animal and fish bones, and the important task of identifying the charcoal was done by Mr J. Cecil Maby, F.R.A.S. Professor V. Gordon Childe of Edinburgh University reported on the pottery recovered at Newferry; in 1934 several very pleasant days were spent with Professor Childe while in Scotland on a survey of Mesolithic sites and collections.

In 1934 a Committee for Quaternary Research was formed in Ireland, and the Danish geologist and palaeobotanist, Professor Knud Jessen, Director of the Botanical Gardens, Copenhagen, came to Ireland for two consecutive years to conduct research on the Irish bogs. Both Professor Jessen and his assistant Dr H. Jonassen visited all the sites containing polleniferous deposits excavated in Northern Ireland, and their reports on the pollen analyses are summarized in the text. Dr Jessen's extensive background concerning Early Post-Glacial deposits in the Baltic, acquired while he was a member of the Danish Geological Survey, has made the geological interpretation of the sites far clearer. I visited Denmark in 1934 and was shown many important Litorina deposits around Roskilde Fjord in the Island of Zealand by Professor Jessen, as well as several Mesolithic stations. Since the geological situation in Ireland closely parallels that of the Baltic region, this experience has proved invaluable. At the National Museum, Copenhagen, Dr Therkel Mathiassen placed at my disposal the rich collections from the Mesolithic sites in Denmark, and thereby I have obtained a clearer impression of this material at first hand than I could ever have had otherwise. In 1932 Dr G. Schwantes and Professor H. Obermaier visited Ireland, where they examined several important collections, and they both made valuable suggestions concerning the Irish Stone Age at that time, as well as subsequently by correspondence. In England some of the excavated material was examined by Professor D. A. E. Garrod and Mr Miles Burkitt, F.S.A., both of whom have offered helpful remarks. The book itself, however, was inspired by Dr J. G. D. Clark's recent work—*The Mesolithic Settlement of Northern Europe* (Cambridge University Press, 1936). Its writer, who is an accepted authority on the Mesolithic, critically read my Part II in manuscript and offered many very practical comments on the subject-matter dealt with. Throughout I have endeavoured to base the method of presenting my material on the admirably full and concise way in which he has treated his. While still in manuscript form, Part I was read by Professor P. G. H. Boswell, F.R.S., of the Imperial College of Science and Technology, London; Dr H. Godwin of the Botany School, Cambridge, England; and Dr F. E. Zeuner of the British Museum of Natural History. I am most profoundly indebted to these scholars for their many helpful suggestions and much in the way of constructive criticism with regard to my handling of various problems. Throughout, both Dr Hencken and my wife have helped me in innumerable ways with the actual organization of the text and with making my presentation of it clear and correctly expressed. Others who have offered valuable comments include: Professor H. Breuil of Paris; Mr J. P. T. Burchell, F.S.A., of London; Mr C. F. C. Hawkes, F.S.A., Assistant Keeper of British Antiquities, British Museum; Mr A. D. Lacaille, F.S.A., of London; Dr W. J. McCallien of Glasgow University; and Dr R. E. M. Wheeler, F.S.A., Keeper of the London Museum.

No small share of the credit for the accomplishments achieved during my three seasons of field-work on the Irish Stone Age sites is due to the co-operation of Mr C. Blake Whelan, M.R.I.A., of Belfast. Since the beginning of the century interest in Irish Prehistory had declined; nevertheless, as a result of Mr Whelan's efforts, it was again revived in 1930. In 1933 two enjoyable weeks were spent with him surveying the coasts of Counties Antrim and Down, as well as visiting the inland sites of Lough Neagh and the Lower Bann Valley. At this time plans for the future were made, as Mr Whelan willingly placed all his sites at the disposal of the Expedition for consideration. In addition, a small Neolithic station on Rathlin Island, County Antrim, was dug in 1934 as part of the programme (Whelan, C.B., *Proc. Roy. Irish Acad.* XLII [1934], 121–143). It has been largely Mr Whelan's unselfish attitude that has led to the successful results of many of the excavations.

It is difficult for me adequately to express my gratitude to my professors at Harvard. To some degree I count all whose names appear above as my teachers, but it is to the Division of Anthropology, including Professors E. A. Hooton (Chairman), Mr A. M. Tozzer, and the late Mr R. B. Dixon, as well as Professor K. Bryan of the Department of Geology, that I owe my basic training. Also I wish to thank Dr V. J. Fewkes of the University of Pennsylvania, and Dr T. D. McCown of the University of California, under whose direction I did my first work in the field of Old World archaeology—both in Central Europe and the Near East—before joining Dr Hencken in Ireland. Although not one of my teachers, I must mention Mr Donald Scott, Director of the Peabody Museum of Harvard University, whose generous support and sympathetic understanding made it possible for me to rewrite this book from the form in which it was originally submitted as a thesis. Of the others who have assisted in many ways, and among whom I include the tutors and lecturers in the Department of Anthropology, as well as the staff of the Peabody Museum, I should like to refer again to Dr Hencken. The five seasons spent with him in Ireland were among the most enjoyable and interesting of my life, and the experience gained from contact with him will always be remembered.

I am profoundly grateful to the following authors, who have very kindly given me permission to make use of illustrations from their publications:

Professor H. Breuil; Mr J. P. T. Burchell, F.S.A.; Professor V. Gordon Childe, F.S.A.; Dr J. G. D. Clark, F.S.A.; Professor R. A. Daly; Dr H. Godwin; Mr C. F. C. Hawkes, F.S.A.; Professor K. Jessen; Mr A. D. Lacaille, F.S.A.; Mr J. Reid Moir, F.R.S.; Dr R. Lloyd Praeger, M.R.I.A.; and Mr C. Blake Whelan, M.R.I.A. I am likewise indebted to the courtesy of the following publishers and learned societies for their permissions, in all cases readily granted, to reproduce illustrations: the Council of the Royal Irish Academy, the Council of the Royal Society of Antiquaries of Ireland, the Editor of *The Irish Naturalists' Journal*, the Council of the Society of Antiquaries of Scotland, the Council of the Royal Society of London, the Society of Antiquaries of London, the Executive Committee of the Royal Anthropological Institute of Great Britain and Ireland, the Editor of *The Archaeological Journal*, the Editors of *The New Phytologist*, the Executive Committee of the Prehistoric Society (formerly the Prehistoric Society of East Anglia), the Cambridge University Press, Macmillan & Co., Ltd., London, and the Yale University Press. As a result of the war, permission to reproduce the drawings of objects from Le Campigny, shown in Fig. 53, could not be obtained from the Editor of the *Revue Mensuelle de l'École d'Anthropologie de Paris*. Therefore we are proceeding in this matter on the assumption that, were it not for the present chaotic state of world affairs, this permission would have been forthcoming.

It is a pleasure to thank all those who have assisted with the original illustrations included in this book. These represent hours of painstaking work to which the following have contributed: Messrs Elmer Rising of the Peabody Museum, Ferdinand R. Iwasko of Cambridge, Massachusetts, and Robert Bremer of Milton, the Misses Helen Cabot of Jamaica Plain and Mary-Eily de Putron of Terenure, Dublin, as well as my wife. It is to my wife for the drawings of the implements from Cushendun, Rough Island and Larne, and to Messrs Rising and Iwasko for the maps, plans and sections that I am especially indebted.

Finally I should like to acknowledge my gratitude to those who have made the publication of this book financially possible. A substantial share of the cost was very kindly undertaken by the Peabody Museum and the Division of Anthropology of Harvard University, while the balance was most generously contributed partly by my father-in-law, Sir Constantine T.

Champion de Crespigny of Adelaide, South Australia, and partly by my aunt, Mrs Richard M. Saltonstall of Chestnut Hill, Massachusetts.

With regard to the actual work of printing and publishing this book, I wish in conclusion to express my sincere thanks to the Cambridge University Press for the magnificent manner in which they have carried on with the job in spite of the war. Although several letters and one batch of proofs were lost "due to enemy action", the publication date has only been delayed by several months. This is largely a result of the prompt and understanding manner in which the officials of the University Press have handled numerous difficult situations arising not only from losses of correspondence, but also from working with a reduced staff. I wish to express my thanks to them for their many courtesies and efficient co-operation.

HALLAM L. MOVIUS, Jr.

SOUTH SUDBURY,
MASSACHUSETTS, U.S.A.
AUGUST 1941

INTRODUCTION

The primary purpose of this book is to present in a comprehensive manner the results of the writer's research into the problems of the Irish Stone Age. The area is limited to the North-Eastern Irish coast, which witnessed a local development of culture in the Mesolithic Period during Early Post-Glacial times, and includes Counties Antrim and Down westward to the valley of the Lower Bann River. Between the littoral of this region, and the inland valley of Lough Neagh and the Bann, a highland zone occurs, formed by a plateau of Cretaceous chalk overlain by Tertiary basalt, and rising to an average height of 1000 feet above the sea. A ready and almost inexhaustible supply of flint was available in the chalk of this region, which was exploited throughout the Stone Age, and which doubtless was an important factor in attracting settlers.

For the most part the previous attempts to trace the origins and development of the Stone Age cultures of Ireland have been made from a typological point of view; however, it is a commonplace to state that even more important than the typology of a culture is its chronological position and its relation to comparable developments in other regions. Although recent excavations in Counties Antrim and Down have revealed prolific Mesolithic and Neolithic material at several sites, no Palaeolithic remains were discovered. The reason for this is obviously connected with the geological history of the area, and an examination of the published material has disclosed a wealth of disconnected but extremely important data, the clarification of which answers the question of the date of the earliest settlement in Ireland. The results of this investigation are incorporated into Part I of this book, and an attempt has been made to bring the material together with a definite purpose in mind: that of stimulating further work. Future research will doubtless show that some of the geological interpretation is incorrect in detail, nevertheless it is hoped that the data have been presented in a sufficiently comprehensive manner to be of use to other workers. The writer, trained as an archaeologist and approaching the problem from the purely objective viewpoint of an outsider, sees no valid reason for doubting an intimate relationship between Britain and Ireland on the one hand and Northern Europe on the other during Late-Glacial and Early Post-Glacial times. With the background of Part I, the problems of the Irish Stone Age are more clearly defined, and the environmental conditions which governed the growth and development of the Early Post-Glacial cultures may be more vividly depicted. Likewise the age of the stratified deposits containing the archaeological material becomes firmly established.

"The last ten years have witnessed an extraordinary increase in the data available to the prehistorian, and a remarkable expansion of the fields he must survey" (Childe, 1936 [*b*], p. 1). During this period, archaeology has taken on a new function, as Professor Childe clearly points out: that of carrying "natural history forward from the point where geology and palaeontology would leave it". But, with the exception of the primary rule of stratigraphy, the laws of the natural sciences are far too rigid to provide an adequate interpretation of human culture, which must always be regarded as the product of man in his struggle to adapt himself to his environment, and ultimately to seek the control of it. The fact that this interplay has always existed, everywhere that man has settled, makes it of paramount necessity for the archaeologist to strive for as detailed a reconstruction as possible of the geographical setting of prehistoric cultures. With respect to this concept, ethnology has made many important contributions. The late Professor R. B. Dixon, referring to modern food-gathering peoples, states: "the extent of the dependence of culture on environment and the closeness of the correlation between them is greatest in the lower stages of cultural growth" (1928, p. 31). This applies with equal force to archaeology, which alone is capable of introducing the time-factor and makes it clear that environment, including climate, soil, flora, fauna, natural resources and topography, represents in its totality the physical background of all human activity. Divorced from this background, archaeology is too abstracted from reality to be considered a science. In this book an attempt has been made to approach the problem of the Stone Age cultures of Ireland with a view to their identification and interpretation in the light of the natural history of the area at the time of the first settlement.

During the Mesolithic Period, the basic economy was food gathering—hunting, fishing, fowling and collecting—and in this regard the cultures referable to this phase are comparable with the Palaeolithic cultures of the Glacial Period, as Dr Clark has pointed out (1936, p. xiv). Because of this fact, the question of the classification of backward or retarded cultures surviving in peripheral regions has long been under dispute, and there still exist differences of opinion as to the most satisfactory nomenclature to embrace them collectively. Thus they are classed as "Epi-Palaeolithic" by those who would emphasize their connection with the Upper Palaeolithic, while others, who regard the axe as indicative of a new era, prefer the term "Proto-Neolithic". A few workers recognize both groups and would subdivide the Mesolithic into an early phase: "Epi-Palaeolithic", and a later phase: "Proto-Neolithic". Even this is inadequate, however, since the two existed side by side and even influenced each other or were combined in some cases. Professor Menghin, in his *Weltgeschichte der Steinzeit*, has advocated substituting "Epimiolithic" and "Opsimiolithic" to describe backward cultures preserving the food-gathering economy of the Palaeolithic into Neolithic times. But his system of isolating culture cycles from the environment to which they are adapted seems to disregard utterly their function. As Professor Childe remarks (1936 [*b*], p. 14), an axe to Menghin is "an expression of a historical tradition and not an implement for felling trees". Whereas it cannot be denied that several distinct cultures are present at this time, it seems clear that the old term Mesolithic, properly understood as forming a separate period during which cultures flourished between the Old and the New Stone Ages in point of time, but in no way forming an evolutionary stage between the two, still meets with wide approval. In a positive sense the Mesolithic defines a stage in cultural development, basically founded on the economy of the Upper Palaeolithic, but profoundly modified by the changes in environment induced by the recession of the ice at the close of the Glacial Period. It is in this sense that the term is used here, since with the coming-in of the new food-producing Neolithic civilization, bringing its associated elements—pottery, domestication of animals, agriculture and polished stone—there is a break in the sequence. Certain elements from the earlier phase, however, continued in use, as no new forms displaced them, but these cannot be regarded as evolutionary. Instead they represent the survival of types of implements for which there was still a need, and in place of which no innovations were introduced by the new culture.

During Early Post-Glacial times, new elements entered Europe from the south, and these, together with the Forest cultures which developed on the North European Plain, penetrated the Lowland Zone of Britain. But the Highland Zone of the north and west was only very indirectly affected from this source. Indeed North-East Ireland and South-West Scotland, isolated by the mountainous backbone of Britain, formed a refuge area where a fundamentally Upper Palaeolithic stock survived after the retreat of the ice. The early phase of the Mesolithic in this region was an outgrowth of the Creswellian of Southern Britain, under influence from the Azilian of the Continent, as well as environmental factors. Geographical events of the first order led to further specialization, after the transgression of the Litorina Sea, which profoundly modified the earlier flint industry. By utilizing and synthesizing the evidence deduced from a study of the natural sciences, it is possible to reconstruct the conditions which led to these changes, and to visualize the cultures themselves as entities, functioning in the environment to which they were adapted. Of all the prehistoric periods, the Mesolithic lends itself particularly well to this approach. By such methods as the interpretation of the stratigraphy of the archaeological sites, the evidence of geology, pollen analysis and the identification of the associated fauna, the Irish Stone Age may be regarded as a living, functioning organism, and not a conglomeration of isolated traits and techniques for making stone tools.

The time-span of the Mesolithic varied in proportion to its relative remoteness from the early centres of food production. The art of crop cultivation was slow in diffusing through Northern and Western Europe, as a result of which the Mesolithic lasted longer here than elsewhere. It is now generally held that the Magdalenian persisted in this region until ±8000 B.C., and that the earliest Neolithic does not antedate 2500 B.C. Hence, at the maximum, the Mesolithic Period covers an interval of roughly 5500 years, a period longer than the entire remainder of prehistoric and historic time combined. But with the advent of agriculture, the earlier food-gathering economy did not come abruptly to an end. In many regions a basically Mesolithic mode of life still survived, and this was particularly true on the periphery. Insular isolation in the case of Ireland, coupled with her peripheral position, led to a considerable time-lag from point of view of the diffusion of new ideas. Thus we find cultures, based on hunting, fishing and collecting, persisting well into the Metal Age and even Early Christian times, although strongly influenced and modified by contact with more advanced sources. Therefore it may be emphasized that, whereas the doctrine of survival is apparent in later periods of Irish archaeology, it is especially applicable to the Stone Age. In fact the descendants of the original Early Post-Glacial settlers form the basic stock in certain sections of Ireland at the present day.

Part One

THE CHRONOLOGY OF THE LATE-GLACIAL & EARLY POST-GLACIAL PERIODS IN NORTHERN AND WESTERN EUROPE

Chapter I

THE CHRONOLOGY OF NORTHERN EUROPE

1. INTRODUCTION

The recession of the last ice-sheets in Europe induced changes of far-reaching effect, which materially altered the shape and climate of the area, thus modifying the environment for plants, animals and man. The geographical events were of the first order, since they opened up and made available new land for human settlement, but the prime factor was climatic. In this changing world the Mesolithic cultures arose in Northern and Western Europe. One of them, which was chiefly centred in North-East Ireland, forms the main subject of this book. Therefore, if the archaeological data relating to this development are to be understood, the natural history of the area at the time of settlement must be established. This is the primary concern of the archaeologist, since therein rests the key to the interpretation of the material culture traits brought to light by excavation. But the problem is even more complex. It is also necessary to know the date of occupation in order that it may be fitted into the existing chronology of contiguous areas. Such a chronology has been established for Late-Glacial and Early Post-Glacial time in Northern Europe, but its extension into Western Europe—Britain and Ireland—has always rested on a somewhat nebulous foundation. The full picture that shows the close degree of similarity which exists between these two areas throughout the periods under discussion has not yet been reconstructed. It is not proposed to deal here extensively with the techniques which have been developed in order to compile the data; such discussions are better left to the specialist. However, the evidence itself, which offers the necessary chronological background for dating the archaeological sequence, will be outlined. In this chapter a brief summary of the history of Northern Europe during the Late-Glacial and Early Post-Glacial Periods is given, since this forms a basic pattern for the interpretation of the material in the two following chapters.

2. THE RECESSION OF THE LAST ICE-SHEET

During the peak of the last glaciation there were five independent centres of ice-dispersal in Northern and Western Europe: Novaya Zemlya and the North Urals, Fennoscandia, the Alps, the Pyrenees, and Great Britain and Ireland. In the latter region there were actually two principal independent sheets, but at the period of maximum advance these were confluent with each other. Thanks to the work of De Geer, Munthe, Sauramo, Tanner, and others, the data on the Fennoscandian Ice are particularly full and may be briefly summarized.

The ice did not retreat everywhere uniformly, as the edge was irregular and the recession was interrupted by pauses or even moderate readvances, as shown in Fig. 1. At the time of maximum advance the southward extension of the ice covered North-East and North Central Germany, and Denmark except the south-western portion of Jutland. The relic of this advance is known as the Brandenburg End-Moraine. During the first retreat period, known as the Daniglacial, or German substage, Denmark and most of North Germany were freed of ice. The first major halt is marked by the Baltic or Pomeranian End-Moraine, and during the next stage, the Gotiglacial, made up of the Danish and Scanian substages, the ice withdrew from Götland to approximately 59° North latitude, and uncovered Southern Sweden. There is evidence for a minor oscillation at this time in Southern Sweden where the Scanian Moraine was formed (Daly, 1934, p. 54). The Fennoscandian End-Moraine, which marks the second major pause in the recession, affords evidence of a slight readvance, and is made up of the Inner Ra Moraines in South Sweden and the Inner Salpausselkä Moraines in Finland. During the ensuing retreat, the Finiglacial, or Bothnian substage, the greater part of Finland was uncovered, and the ice was reduced to two separate lobes in Scandinavia. The split between the lobes occurred at Ragunda in Jämtland. Scandinavian geologists regard this as marking the end of the Glacial Epoch and the beginning of Post-Glacial time in this area.

In the Alpine region, three main series of end-moraines have been found, representing stadia in the retreat of the last ice (Penck and Brückner, 1909, pp. 948–53), which is known in this region as Würm II. Similarly, three stages in the recession of the last ice-cap in the Pyrenees have been traced by Obermaier (1906, p. 299 and p. 244). These phenomena, together with the

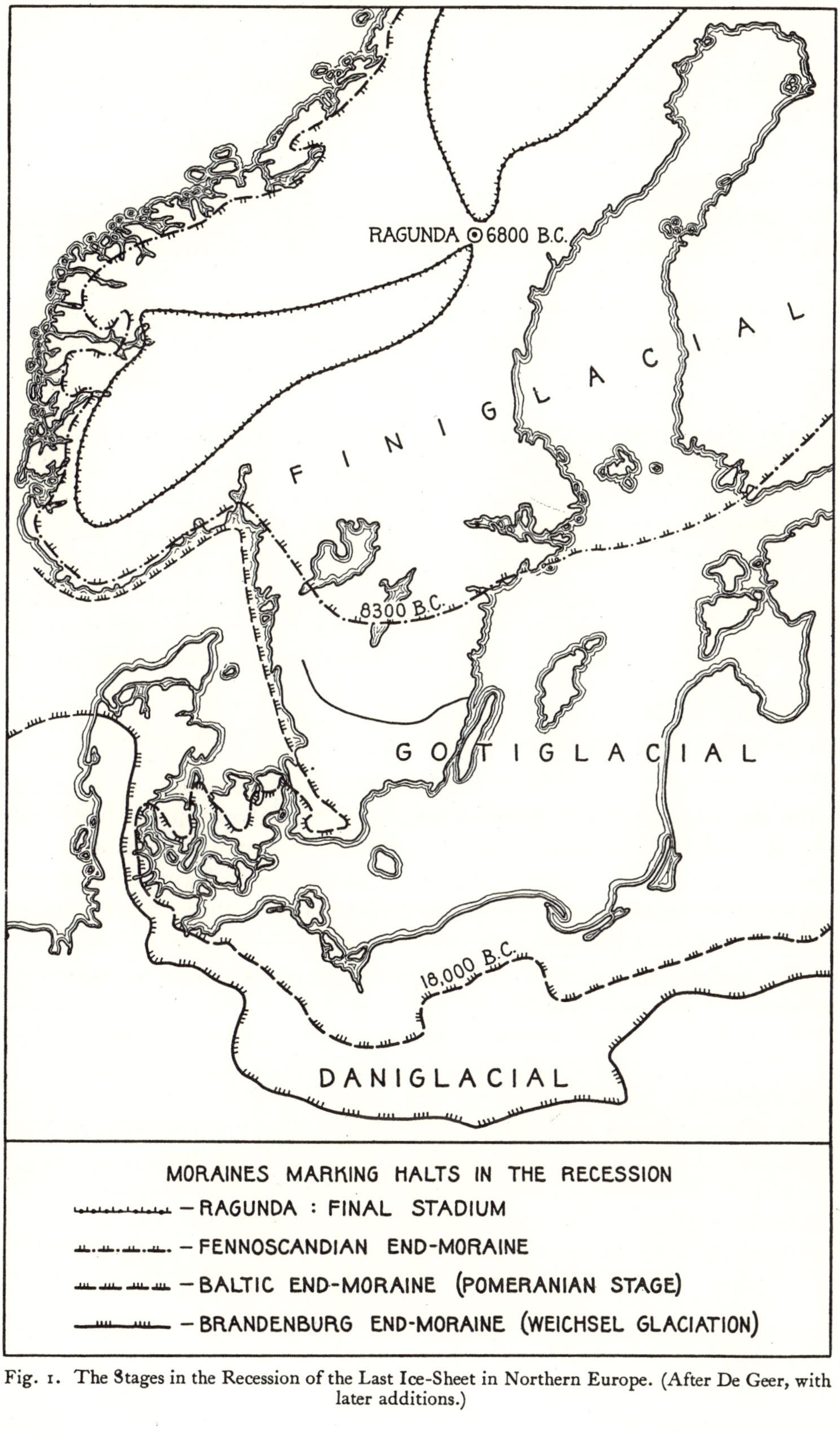

Fig. 1. The Stages in the Recession of the Last Ice-Sheet in Northern Europe. (After De Geer, with later additions.)

three stages of retreat, which will be shown in the next chapter to exist in the British Isles, strongly suggest the assumption that such major oscillations could not have had merely local causes; hence contemporaneity becomes a more plausible explanation. While admitting that actual proof is not possible, Clark (1936, p. 2) suggests the following correlation of the North European and Alpine ice-sheets.

SCANDINAVIA (De Geer)	THE ALPS (Penck and Brückner)
4. *Post-Glacial Period*	4. *Post-Glacial Period*
Final Stadium: bipartition of the ice at Ragunda	Daun Stadium: snow-line 300 m. below present level
3. *Finiglacial Period*	3. *Geschnitz-Daun Period*
Fennoscandian End-Moraine	Geschnitz Stadium: snow-line 600 m. below present level
2. *Gotiglacial Period*	2. *Bühl-Geschnitz Period*
Baltic End-Moraine (Pomeranian Stage)	Bühl Stadium: snow-line 900 m. below present level (Würm III)
1. *Daniglacial Period*	1. *Achen Retreat Period*
Maximum Advance (Weichsel). Brandenburg End-Moraine	Maximum Advance (Würm II)

The importance of the retreat to archaeology is obvious, as a maximum date can thereby be fixed for any site within the glaciated area. The indirect importance is likewise at once apparent, because the changes induced in sea-level, climate, vegetation and fauna had a marked effect on the development of the successive cultures which occupied the region. Before considering these changes, the method of arriving at an absolute dating for the recession will be presented.

3. GEOCHRONOLOGY

The chronology of the recession was established by De Geer (1910, p. 252), who counted the annual varves deposited in the lakes formed of melt-water in the depressions left by the northward receding ice-front. Varves are formed in lacustrine sediments which are composed of silt, clay and sand. A periodic deposition of materials is fundamental for their formation resulting from a large supply of sediments in summer and little or none in winter. Precisely such conditions are found near the margin of an ice-sheet, where the summer melt-waters bring their annual loads into the lakes. Here the heavier materials, sand and coarse silt, are deposited first, and the finer particles, clay and fine silt, remain in suspension until winter. They are then laid down in the quiet waters of the lakes, whose surface would be frozen over. This alternation forms distinct coarse laminae or varves, which range in thickness from about 0·2 cm. to 3·0 cm., each being made up of (*a*) a lower or summer layer which is thicker and contains more sandy material, and (*b*) an upper or winter layer, which is thinner, darker in colour, and composed of fine clays and silts. At no single place does a complete section of varves occur between two stages of the ice-retreat; but De Geer counted overlapping sections at one kilometre intervals from Scania to Ragunda, and thereby established an absolute chronology for the last sixteen millennia. The importance of De Geer's work in the light of Late-Glacial and Early Post-Glacial archaeology can hardly be overestimated.

On the basis of the geochronological dating established in Scandinavia, the ice reached Ragunda about 6800 B.C., as shown on the map (Fig. 1), and this point is regarded by geologists as marking the beginning of Post-Glacial time (De Geer, 1910, p. 252; 1927, pp. 422–5). It took approximately 11,000 years for the retreat from the Baltic End-Moraine, or Pomeranian stage (± 18,000 B.C.), to Ragunda. The first authentic date, according to De Geer (1928, p. 312), is ± 14,800 B.C., which marks the beginning of the Gotiglacial Period; the earliest stage of the Fennoscandian halt has been fixed at ±8300 B.C., and the Finiglacial Period began ±7800 B.C. In the absence of varves, allowing approximately an equal time for the Daniglacial Retreat stage, the recession from the line of maximum advance probably began ± 30,000 B.C. On the basis of Milankovitch's solar radiation curve, however, which places the last ice-advance at 72,000 B.C. (Zeuner, 1938, p. 56), this figure seems absurdly low.[1] Whether or not the Milan-

[1] It should be pointed out that those who use the solar radiation curve for dating Pleistocene events argue that there is a close agreement between De Geer's date (± 18,000 B.C.) and Milankovitch's date (± 23,000 B.C.) for the Pomeranian stage (Würm III of the Alpine sequence), if allowance is made for the inevitable time-lag (in this case 5000 years) between cosmic cause and geological effect (Clark, 1939, p. 139). Before the Milankovitch system can be accepted, however, several fundamental points remain to be proved:

(*a*) That a decrease in solar radiation is the direct cause of glaciation. This is the basic assumption made by those geologists who have accepted Milankovitch's curve of radiation as a means for dating Pleistocene events.

(*b*) That an extension of the curve (calculated by the same method as that apparently established for the Pleistocene) to cover the Tertiary Period be made as well. If similar amplitudes can be demonstrated for other periods (e.g. the Eocene) in Western Europe, then the whole question of the alleged coincidence between the solar radiation and glacial curves for the Pleistocene will have to be reinvestigated.

kovitch system will prove to be absolute, we have the established geochronological date of ±14,800 B.C. for the beginning of the Gotiglacial Retreat, and earlier than this, time-scale computations are based on a different approach, although it appears likely that the Pomeranian stage can be assigned to ±18,000 B.C. After the Pomeranian stage, there was considerable acceleration in the recession, due principally to two factors: first, the thinning of the ice-cap, because the thinner it became the faster it melted, and second, as the area covered by the ice was reduced, the climate became more moderate, since an ice-cap creates its own unfavourable environment. In spite of the continued existence of some ice, the climate was definitely ameliorating, as seen by the plant remains near the ice-front. With the beginning of the Finiglacial, this change was especially marked.

Independent work on the varve clays of Finland has shown that they correlate very closely with those of Sweden (Clark, 1936, p. 6). Since a margin of error of not over a few centuries exists, the natural system of chronology for the last sixteen millennia in Scandinavia may be taken as very nearly absolute for geological and archaeological purposes. This degree of accuracy is not even approached by any system based on the development of early human history. Outside the Baltic, the earliest index of time is the rather dubious northward extension of Egyptian and Near Eastern chronology, which is not practicable before *ca.* 2000 B.C. (Burkitt and Childe, 1932, p. 186). Geochronology is of special importance, therefore, since it furnishes us with fairly reliable prehistoric dates and may form the basic chronological framework in other areas as well.

4. CHANGES OF LEVEL: DELEVELLING

During the last ice-advance there is no doubt that the Scandinavian region was basin-shaped, in consequence of the downward pressure produced by the superposition of the great weight of ice. Corresponding to this basining, or sinking, of the land, there was an emergence in the zone about and beyond the edge of the ice-sheet, which is known as the peripheral bulge. In Scandinavia very complete data, relating to the recoil of the land after the recession of the ice, have been compiled from the study of high-level strand-lines. Since the melting of the ice affected the mutual relations of both land and sea, the study of delevelling is complicated, and will be only briefly outlined here (compare Daly, 1934, Chapters I and II; Wright, 1925 and 1934).

The crustal recoil of the land, isostasy, may be a primarily local phenomenon with local uplift, or general subsidence of the earth's crust as the

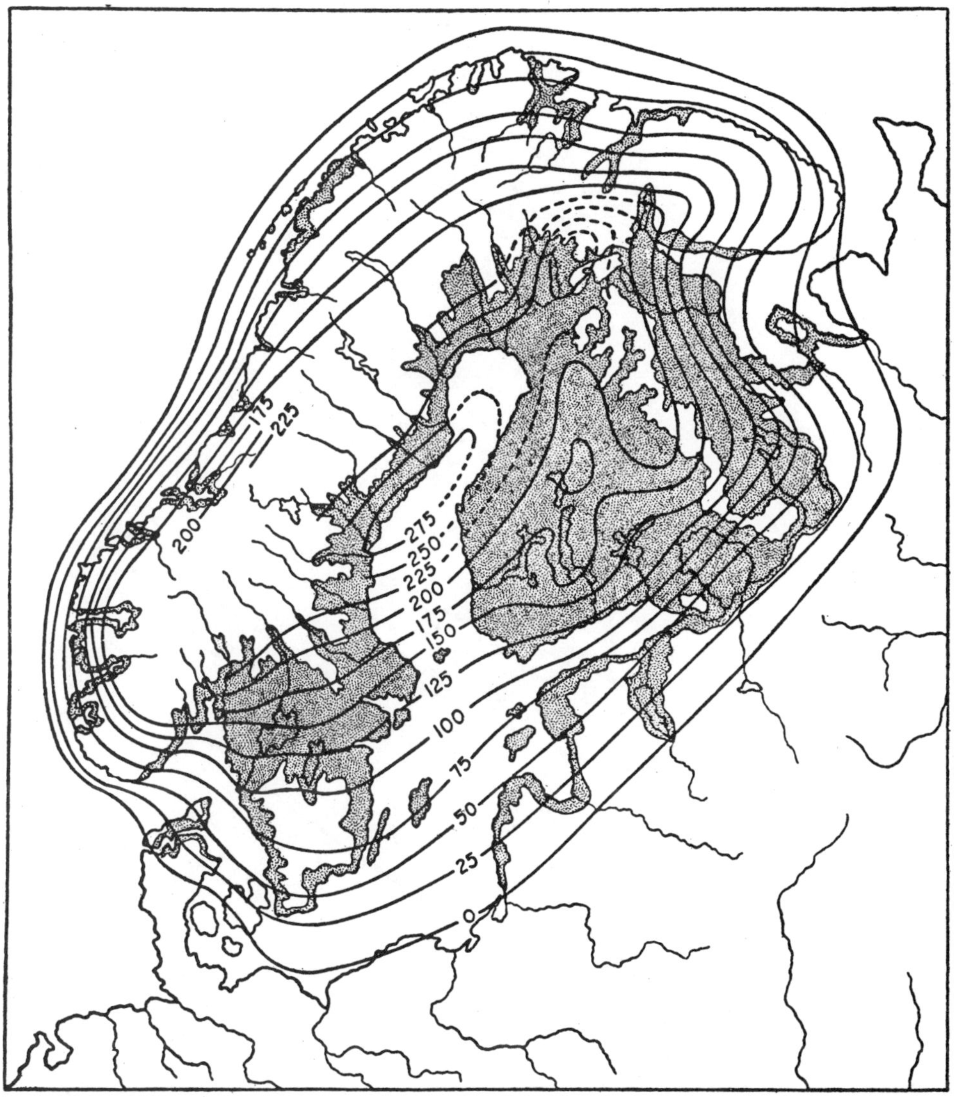

Fig. 2. Map illustrating the Depression of Fennoscandia under the Weight of the Last Ice-Sheet. The contours of the depression, or isobases, represent in metres the Late-Glacial and Early Post-Glacial uplift of the highest strand-lines of the ocean. The area covered by the Yoldia Sea is shown by stippling. (After Daly.)

principal cause. In Fennoscandia, elevated sea beaches and submerged peats, the age of which is determined from fossils and pollen grains, prove that there has been a general isostatic uplift of the whole area. By carefully mapping the points above which there has been no Post-Glacial wave action, the contours or isobases of the depression are produced (Fig. 2). The

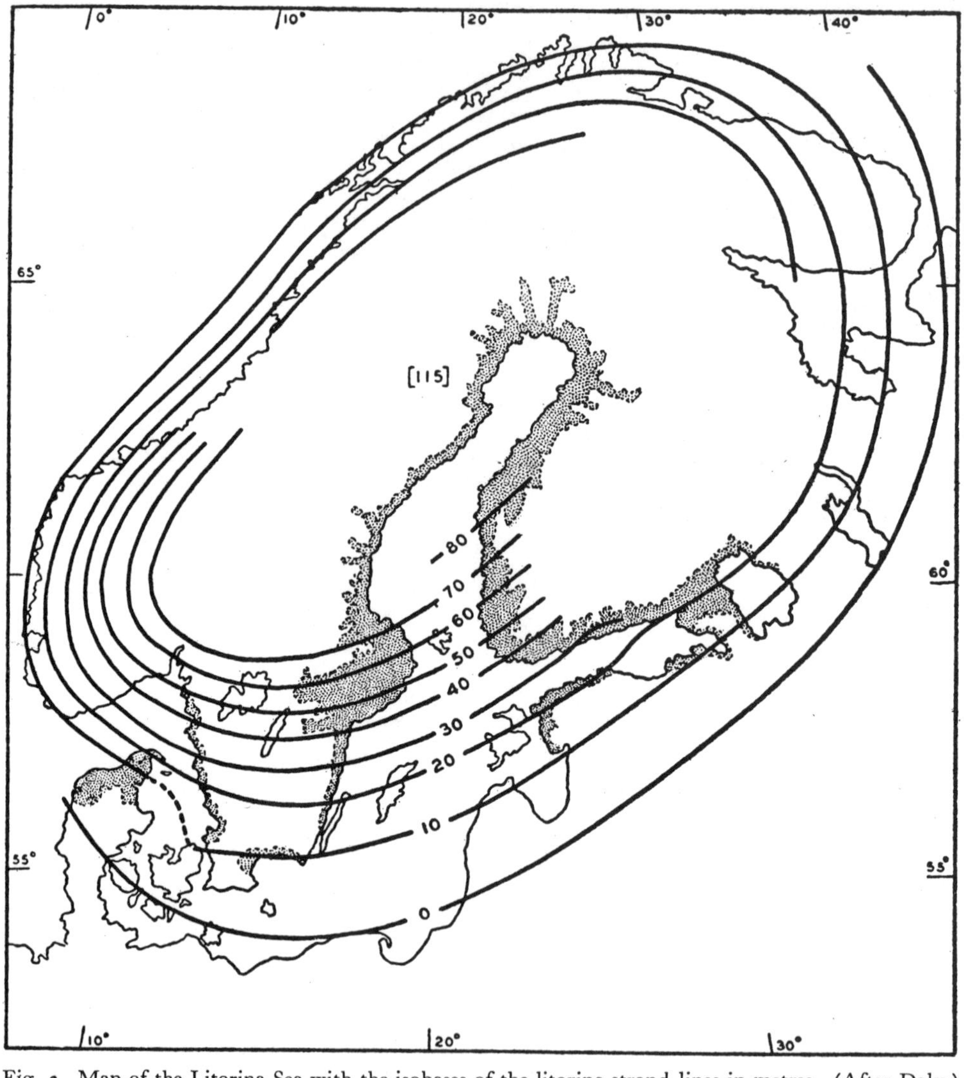

Fig. 3. Map of the Litorina Sea with the isobases of the litorina strand-lines in metres. (After Daly.)

area of greatest depression thus defined may be taken as the centre of greatest ice-dispersal. The present o-isobase of the Late-Glacial uplift is close to the line marking the o-isobase in Early Post-Glacial time (Fig. 3). South of this line the land has been sinking, as proved by submerged land surfaces and drowned valleys, whereas tide-gauge records prove that uplift is taking place at the present day to the north of it. The total amount of warping and its changes of rate cannot, however, be accurately measured, since the recoil of the earth was accompanied by a shift of sea-level, resulting from the release of water by the melting ice. This rising of the sea-level, eustasy, may be world-wide in the same positive or negative sense all over the ocean, or over hemispheres or alternating zones of the globe where sea-level is rhythmically displaced up and down in tune with the advances and retreats of the ice-sheets. In general, the trend is towards greater intensity of both isostatic and eustatic factors in regions proximal to the ice-margins, since in these areas the land, after a rapid initial uplift, gradually subsided only to regain at a later period part of its former height. The history of these changes in mutual level of land and sea are of importance to archaeology, since much of the material to be described in this book occurs in high-level beaches—in the form of inland beach shingle, and other sand and gravel deposits—as well as in submerged forests, and marine clays and silts at present above low-water level. The conditions of formation of beach and long-shore deposits are indicated by:

1. Marine molluscs: shells (invertebrates).
2. Crustaceans: crabs and their relatives (invertebrates).
3. Marine vertebrates: fish and other sea animals.
4. Foraminifera: mainly marine except a few species which inhabit brackish water (microscopic unicellular invertebrates).
5. Diatoms: microscopic unicellular plants, some of which grow in fresh and others in salt water.

Before a decision can be reached on the age of a horizon in a raised beach, the archaeologist will almost certainly find it necessary to consider as many of these factors as possible. To the prehistorian in particular, a background of the geological history of the localities in which work is being done is essential, if accurate results are to be obtained.

5. WATER BODIES IN THE BALTIC BASIN

The facts outlined above have been correlated by specialists, and while much remains obscure, due to the complexity of the problem, certain important conclusions, relating to the contemporary water bodies in the Baltic

Basin and their history, may be deduced. These are of great significance for chronological purposes and are briefly summarized below:

1. The Baltic Ice-Lake (?—±7800 B.C.)

During the Gotiglacial Period, when the ice-sheet commenced to retreat from the Baltic End-Moraine, the southern and south-western parts of the Baltic Basin stood somewhat higher than at present with respect to sea-level. Denmark at this time was joined to South Sweden, and this land mass, together with the retreating ice-front on the north, shut the North Sea out of the Baltic region, and formed a lake. Melting ice and local precipitation raised the level of this lake until it overflowed into the ocean, first across the Jutland-Scanian land-bridge, and later across South Sweden. Whereas this ice-lake was confined to the Baltic Basin, outside this area the sea transgressed the ice-free portions of the coast during this period. Thus extensive clay deposits laid down by the Late-Glacial Sea are found in South Sweden in the region of the Cattegat and the Skager Rack (Wright, 1937, pp. 335–43), which are contemporary with minor stages in the Gotiglacial Retreat. In other words, marine deposits outside the Baltic are the same age as lacustrine sediments within the basin itself. As a result of the land-bridge, the lake had a maximum height of 17 m. above the sea-level of the period.

2. The Yoldia Sea (±7800—±7300 B.C.)

This was formed in early Finiglacial times, and when the ice had melted from the broad belt of country north of Mount Billing, between Lakes Vener and Vetter, in South Sweden. The sea was thereby let in, since, despite the recoil of the earth's crust, the belt was below sea-level. The Danish-Swedish land-bridge continued, the East Baltic region emerged to a considerable extent, and Denmark and North Germany were still relatively high above the existing level. Marine diatoms and molluscs are common in the sediments laid down at the time. The limits of this sea are indicated in Fig. 2, and its name is derived from the characteristic mollusc, *Yoldia arctica*. Outside the Baltic the areas immediately peripheral to the ice-sheet were under water as in the previous period. This is revealed by high-level strand-lines associated with retreat phenomena of the ice.

3. The Ancylus Lake (± 7300—± 5600 B.C.)

In late Finiglacial time the region north of Mount Billing began to rise because of the continued recoil of the earth's crust, and free communication with the sea was broken. Lacustrine conditions were thereby revived, and fresh-water diatoms and molluscs once again throve, including among the latter the type-fossil bivalve, *Ancylus fluviatilis*. This lake first drained by way of Southern Sweden, since the land-bridge across the Cattegat was still in existence. Later drainage was, however, through the Cattegat itself, since the eustatic rise of sea-level caused the North Sea and the Ancylus Lake, the level of which had risen with melt-water and local drainage, to join at this point.

4. The Litorina or Tapes Sea (± 5600—± 2500 B.C.)

Once the Jutland-Scanian connection was broken, the history of the Baltic as a lake came to an end. The name of the next body of water to occupy the Baltic Basin is again derived from its type fossil, the periwinkle, *Littorina littorea*, which is commonly found, along with *Tapes decussatus*, among the salt-water mollusca in the raised beaches at this period. Because of the delay in the crustal recoil of the earth, the Litorina Sea was a much vaster body of water than the Baltic to-day, as shown by Fig. 3, both in depth and extent. Its greater depth, due in part, presumably, to the general eustatic rise caused by the melting of the North American and Antarctic ice, is regarded as the probable cause of its greater salinity than the present Baltic. During this period, the region from Central Scandinavia northwards, including Finland, continued to rise above the waters. The marine transgression of the Litorina Sea reached its maximum about 4500 B.C. (Jessen, 1935, p. 41), and since that time Fennoscandia has continued to recoil from the Late-Glacial depression.

Exclusive of the Baltic region and Great Britain and Ireland, there is abundant evidence for the marine transgression (Clark, 1936, p. 12). In the Oslo area there was an early phase of depression followed by continued rising of the land, and as far north as Finnmark, on the Norwegian coast, there are earlier beaches at higher levels than the younger ones. In the North Sea, dredging has revealed that formerly a greater extension of land existed there along the seaboard, from Jutland to Holland (Jessen, 1935, p. 56). At many places out of sight of land, as well as on the English coast itself, there is striking evidence for a Post-Glacial rising of the land, and subsequent submergence; in fact, during the Early Post-Glacial Period the region of the Dogger Bank was dry land. The proof of this fact will be presented later, as it is important archaeologically with regard to the diffusion of culture across the North German plain. At many inland sites in North-Western Germany, evidence for the subsequent marine transgression has been revealed by borings. In several instances peat has been found below sea-level, overlain by Litorina clays and other marine deposits. Similar evidence is also available on the north coast of France (Day, 1866, p. 111), but the data are somewhat unsatisfactory, since there is absolutely nothing to prove that the Early Post-Glacial submergence in France was the same age as the Litorina transgression, as Clark points out (1936). However, the sequence of events in both regions is broadly similar, but it is probable that the crustal recoil after the last ice-sheets would have been somewhat earlier in Northern France, a peripheral area.

6. CLIMATIC PHASES

During the Post-Glacial Epoch climatic changes or fluctuations occurred in Northern Europe which involved both precipitation and temperature. The evidence for these changes has been deduced from the study of peat bogs and the analysis of contained flora, as well as from the identification of the land and marine fauna associated with datable horizons. After a period of fluctuating Late-Glacial conditions, and a transitional Early Post-Glacial phase (Pre-Boreal), the climate of this area underwent a twice-repeated cycle of (*a*) cold and dry: continental phase (Boreal and Sub-Boreal); (*b*) warm and damp: oceanic phase (Atlantic and Sub-Atlantic). Thus the "standard" succession is as follows: (1) Pre-Boreal, (2) Boreal, (3) Atlantic, (4) Sub-Boreal and (5) Sub-Atlantic. This sequence of events is based on the detailed stratigraphy of peat bogs, especially in Sweden and Denmark, and it has been fitted into similar evidence in other Baltic countries as well as elsewhere. Even in Central Europe a comparable succession has been observed (Erdtman, 1931); similarly in the Auvergne district of France, Dubois (1932, p. 288) has established a corresponding series of climatic periods. In the Baltic region these fluctuations are connected to some extent with the contemporary geographical changes. Thus the Boreal Period roughly corresponds with the phase of relative land elevation—the Ancylus Lake, and the Atlantic with the period of marine transgression—the Litorina Sea. The Post-Glacial temperature curves for this region show a steep rise after the ice-retreat to a maximum at the time of the Litorina Sea, and then subsequent recession to the present level. After a slight rise in the Pre-Boreal Period, there was a rapid climb in Boreal times to the climatic optimum of the Early Atlantic. During this phase of maximum warmth the average July temperature was 2–3° C. higher than at present in the Baltic area. As will be presently discussed, this increase is documented by the analysis of pollen contained in the peat bogs. In the Pre-Boreal Period the traces of forest trees are not numerous, and the forms represented are indicative of cold temperate conditions. During Boreal times forest forms are dominant, and the sequence of development implies a progressive increase in temperature until the Atlantic phase. At this stage the climatic optimum witnessed the maximum development of deciduous trees (Oak, Elm, Lime, etc.), which flourished in a climate warmer than that prevailing at present in the Baltic. The former distribution of flora is in agreement with this evidence, and it is based on two kinds of data: (*a*) *horizontal*, over wide geographical regions which reveals that present-day southern forms once existed farther north than at present, and that since the warmth maximum this distribution has contracted; and (*b*) *vertical*, on the slopes of mountain systems where it has been found that the tree limit was higher during the Atlantic Period than at present.

The study of fauna, however, has an even more critical bearing on the development of climate. This is particularly true of conchology, because of the rapid reaction of molluscs to environmental factors, especially near the northern periphery of their distribution. Here a very slight change will produce either a decrease or increase in numbers or a difference in relative size or development. The Boreal Period witnessed a gradual invasion of southern forms, and several species, which have now withdrawn to warmer waters, were present at the time of the Early Atlantic climatic optimum. On the basis of molluscs the estimated average temperatures for July in Denmark, as given by Clark (1936, pp. 25–6), are as follows: Pre-Boreal, 8° C.; Boreal, 14° C.; and Atlantic, 16–17° C. These figures are substantiated by the study of foraminifera, fresh-water molluscs, and the land fauna. Whereas the latter are by no means such critical indicators of climate as molluscs and foraminifera, they none the less show a definite transition which reflects the marked improvement in conditions during Early Post-Glacial times. Thus the end of the Late-Glacial Period is heralded by the arrival of forest forms and a gradual displacement of cold-loving tundra and steppe species by temperate forest-dwelling forms. While the change is slow, as in the case of the forests themselves, it is none the less sweeping: the Late Upper Palaeolithic and Mesolithic sites yield very few species in common (compare Clark, 1936, pp. 48–51; 1938, pp. 160 and 166; Jessen, 1935, pp. 61–2). In general the fauna of the Pre-Boreal Period is made up of mixed tundra and forest forms: that of Boreal times is typical of forests and lakes; in the Atlantic Period most of these hold over and are supplemented by additional warm forms (i.e. the fresh-water Tortoise) and aquatic types which show the changing environment. A study of the fauna is often the only key to the climatic succession in cave deposits, and therefore provides an indication of age in sites where reference to other dating methods is lacking.

7. POLLEN ANALYSIS: PALAEOBOTANY

This particular branch of the science of palaeobotany was developed in Scandinavia, based upon early studies on the stratification of peat bogs, and it has diffused to almost every country in Europe (Erdtman, 1927[*a*]). Work is now being carried out along extremely accurate and precise lines, which deal mainly with the microscopic identification of pollen grains found preserved in certain natural deposits. These consist in the main of waterlogged and unaerated deposits such as peats, clays and silts. By far the greatest sources for pollen grains available for study are the extensive peat bogs of Northern and Western Europe. These may be divided into three types: (1) *topogenous*, which depend for their origin and development on topographical features such as filled-up lakes; (2) *ombrogenous*, which are due primarily to surface precipitation, e.g. raised bogs (German = "Hochmoor"); and (3) *soligenous*, which are produced either by surface water flowing into the bog area from surrounding country, or by ground water rising up to the surface layers of the ground (Erdtman, 1928, p. 126; von Post, 1937, pp. 218–23). Forest trees do not normally grow near such deposits, but pollen grains are blown great distances and incorporated into the peat. Pollen may also be transported by water (Godwin, 1934, p. 301). Moisture is an essential factor in the formation of peat, but even intense precipitation or periodic flooding is not sufficient to cause pollen downwash through a peat layer. Thus any given horizon in a bog yields a fairly reliable representation of the forest forms extant at the time of formation. By studying a series of these horizons at regular intervals through a polleniferous deposit, it is possible to express, in terms of percentage, the relative frequency of the forest forms present, the results of which are given diagrammatically. A series of these diagrams in an intensively worked region may then be compiled in a generalized form, and by comparing these with similar diagrams from other areas, it is possible to reconstruct the forest history in certain countries for the Post-Glacial Period. At present such diagrams exist for most of the Baltic region, and, as a result, any vertical series in time may be fixed with respect to the general forest development. It is also possible to correlate series from different regions with a fair degree of accuracy, and to fix given points in a vertical series into the general scheme established for the region.

The conclusions have been summarized by Clark (1936, p. 36) as follows:

(*a*) "Any phenomena, whether geological, archaeological, or zoological, which can be related to polleniferous deposits, can be dated in terms of phases of local forest succession, and can, therefore, be arranged in chronological succession within a given area."

(*b*) "Similar phenomena, even when widely separated over Northwestern Europe, can, when found in association with a polleniferous deposit, be related to the general history of forest development and may, within certain limits, which future work will narrow, be synchronized."

Therefore, the importance of palaeobotany to any of the natural sciences concerned with the Post-Glacial Period can hardly be exaggerated, and numerous examples of the mutual assistance of archaeology and pollen analysis to our present knowledge of the development of early culture could be cited. In Northern Europe the amelioration of the climate after the retreat of the last ice made possible a rapid spread of forests, certain major drifts in the development of which have been established by palaeobotanists. These drifts reflect in a striking manner the known trends of Late-Glacial and Post-Glacial climate, and afford in themselves conclusive proof that climate has been the chief agent in moulding their history. They are applicable in the main for the whole of Northern and Western Europe, which furnishes archaeology with a dating technique of the utmost importance. In Denmark recent research has made it possible to divide the bog sequence into a series of zones, which have been synchronized with the established climatic periods (Jessen, 1935[*a*]; 1938[*a*]), and this evidence has been incorporated into the following summary:

A. Late-Glacial Period. Three Late-Glacial climatic periods, which demonstrate one amelioration and one deterioration of the climate contemporary with the retreat of the ice, have been recognized:

1. *Early Dryas Period*: Zone I. Tundra conditions prevailed as indicated by traces of pollen of *Dryas octopetala*, *Myriophyllum alterniflorum*, *Salix herbacea* and *Betula nana*, together with various mosses, from the Lower Dryas Clays of Denmark. There was no local growth of Pine at this time, although Pine pollen blown in from the south is commonly found in these clays. Deposits referable to this period frequently afford evidence of solifluction,[1] showing that an intense Arctic climate existed along the edge of the ice-sheet. The Late Upper Palaeolithic—Hamburg culture—of Northern Germany belongs to this zone (Clark, 1938, p. 160).

2. *Allerød Period*: Zone II. The Allerød oscillation occurred during this zone, which is also known as the Late-Glacial Birch Period. No evidence of solifluction is found in Allerød deposits; these are usually composed of mud rather than clay. The occurrence of Birch (*Betula pubescens*), Willow (*Salix* sp.) and Pine-wood (*Pinus sylvestris*) afford conclusive proof of an amelioration in the climate during this phase. It has been demonstrated that during the Gotiglacial Period, the recession was interrupted by many halts and fluctuations, and that the Allerød oscillation belongs to this period of the fluctuating ice-front (Brooks, 1917, p. 304; Antevs, 1928, pp. 157–60). It has been provisionally dated on the basis of geochronology as beginning ± 10,000 B.C. and ending ± 8300 B.C. (compare Gross, 1938, p. 88).

3. *The Upper Dryas Period*: Zone III. A second solifluction layer, consisting of clay and indicating a temporary return of Arctic conditions, overlies the deposits of Zone II. The flora associated with the Upper Dryas Clays is in the main similar to that of Zone I, but the pollen grains are more numerous. It seems probable that this period is synchronous with the halt of the ice at the Fennoscandian End-Moraine: ± 8300 to ± 7800 B.C. (compare Gross, 1938). The Early Mesolithic—Ahrensburg culture—has been found in deposits referable to the lower part of this zone in Northern Germany (Clark, 1938, p. 166).

[1] A solifluction deposit is produced by the sludging or slow, massive movement of the upper few feet of surface deposits over the frozen subsoil. This movement is caused by alternate freezing and thawing during certain seasons of the year in regions proximal to an ice-sheet.

B. Post-Glacial Period. This consists of five climatic periods divisible into six zones; these indicate a steady improvement in the climate until the Post-Glacial climatic optimum, which was followed by a slight deterioration:

1. *Pre-Boreal Period* (± 7800 to ± 6800 B.C.): Zone IV. The beginning of Post-Glacial time is synchronous with the beginning of this zone, according to Jessen (1935[*a*], p. 187); it is also known as the Birch-Pine Period. Cold temperate conditions are revealed by Pre-Boreal pollen diagrams, which show a maximum for the Birch curve (especially *Betula pubescens*), the gradual ascent of the Pine curve (*Pinus sylvestris*), the coming in of Hazel (*Corylus avellana*) and the presence of Aspen. Thus the initial stages of the Post-Glacial rise of temperature are reflected by the prevalent forest forms. The Early Pre-Boreal Period coincides with the phase of relative submergence in the Baltic which resulted in the formation of the Yoldia Sea; in Late Pre-Boreal times the sea-level was lower with respect to the land and the Baltic Basin was occupied by the Ancylus Lake, while the southern part of the North Sea was dry land which connected Jutland and England (Jessen, 1935, p. 56). Finds of the Early Mesolithic—Lyngby culture—are referable to Zone IV (Jessen, 1935[*a*], p. 187; Clark, 1936, p. 83), during which the North European Ice-Sheet retreated to Ragunda. On this basis the Pre-Boreal is contemporary with the Finiglacial Period (see p. 21).

2. *Boreal Period* (± 6800 to ± 5600 B.C.): Zones V and VI. Zone V is Early Boreal and witnessed the dominance of Pine in the Danish forests, whereas in Zone VI, Late Boreal, a very high Hazel maximum is represented. The zone boundary V/VI has been fixed at the rational border[1] of the Alder curve (*Alnus glutinosa*), according to Jessen (1938[*a*], p. 124). The marked rise in the temperature at this time led to the introduction of new deciduous trees from the south, Oak (*Quercus robur*), Elm (*Ulmus glabra*) and Lime (*Tilia cordata*), which make their first appearance in these zones. The Boreal Period is contemporary with the main development of the Ancylus Lake in the Baltic Basin when the average height of the land relative to the sea was ± 150 feet greater than at present. In the upper part

[1] The "rational border" may be defined as the point at which the curve, showing the percentage frequency of a given forest form on a pollen diagram, swings away from the ordinate—the vertical axis of the diagram. In other words the "rational border" of this type of curve is the inflection point. This point marks the actual colonization rather than the earliest immigration of a given forest form in the region. If a total of one thousand grains instead of one hundred were counted in each sample, the picture would probably be somewhat modified, although the main trends of the curves would be essentially the same.

of Zone VI the Pine curve falls off, and the boundary between Zones VI and VII has been placed at the point of intersection between the ascending curve of the Oak-Mixed-Forest (OMF: Oak+Elm+Lime), and the descending Pine curve (Jessen, 1938[*a*]). As Jessen has clearly established (1935), the Maglemosean culture flourished during this period, when the first deciduous trees were colonizing on the North European Plain, and when the average summer temperature in Denmark was very like the present.

3. *Atlantic Period* (±5600 to ±2500 B.C.): Zone VII. This zone covers only the Early Atlantic Period, and as the lower boundary of the succeeding Zone VIII has not been established in relation to either changes of level or the archaeological sequence (Jessen, 1935[*a*], p. 188), it is not possible to synchronize precisely the pollen-diagrammatical zones with the climatic periods at this point. In the first half of the Atlantic Period, which covers the maximum of the Litorina transgression in the Baltic, the Post-Glacial climatic optimum occurred. Except in the Alpine and very northernmost regions of Scandinavia, warmth-loving trees, including Alder, the newly introduced Maple (*Acer platanoides*) and the Ash (*Fraxinus*), as well as Oak, Elm and Lime—the three components of the Oak-Mixed-Forest—predominated. These deciduous trees occupied the region to the almost total exclusion of the conifers and Birch; in Zone VII the maximum for the OMF curve is found. The Kitchen-Midden culture (Ertebølle) developed in Denmark on the shores of the Litorina Sea during the Atlantic Period.

4. *Sub-Boreal Period* (±2500 to ±400 B.C.). The period falls within Zone VIII, but as stated above this zone also includes Late Atlantic time. It is characterized by a marked decrease in the OMF curve, a second maximum of Pine, an increase in the values of Oak and Hazel, the introduction of Hornbeam (*Carpinus*) and a high frequency of Beech (*Fagus*). During the Sub-Boreal there was recrudescence of cold, dry conditions, and according to Brooks (1931), the precipitation was about one-half that of the present day. Many surface peat bogs dried up at this time, the lakes decreased in size, some to below their level of outlet, and the Neolithic and Bronze Age cultures spread into Northern and Western Europe.

5. *Sub-Atlantic Period* (±400 B.C. to present): Zone IX. An increase in rainfall caused a suppression of tree growth, and the return to an Atlantic type of climate, which was conducive to the rapid formation of *Sphagnum* peat over the Sub-Boreal forests. This was accompanied by a general rise in lake level, beginning in the Early Iron Age in Denmark.

As indicated in the above outline, the established phases of forest development have been related to the absolute Post-Glacial time-scale based on geochronology, and to the geological changes involving the mutual level of land and sea in the Baltic. This applies to the early periods, since from the introduction of the Neolithic onwards, the dates are based on archaeological evidence. However, the close degree of accuracy with which Mesolithic sites can be dated by these indices makes the correlation of paramount importance to Stone Age archaeology. Thus the science of palaeobotany makes it possible to fix the upper and lower dating limits of any site referable to Early Post-Glacial polleniferous deposits, and in addition it establishes the end of the Late-Glacial Period. Geologists have maintained that this point could be fixed by the bipartition of the ice at Ragunda (± 6800 B.C.). But this assumption rests on a purely arbitrary basis, which does not take into consideration the evidence of the climate as determined by a study of the fauna and flora of the Baltic. According to these data, the beginning of the Post-Glacial Period is synchronous with the end of the last solifluction layer in the Danish Bogs, represented by the Upper Dryas Clays of Zone III (Jessen, 1935[*a*], p. 187). As previously stated, it seems very probable that this zone was formed during the halt of the ice at the Fennoscandian End-Moraine, which implies that Post-Glacial time commences with the beginning of the Finiglacial stage—± 7800 B.C., according to the De Geer system (see p. 7). In Denmark the Pre-Boreal Period (Zone IV) seems to correspond with the Finiglacial. This definition is given precision in the field by the markedly improved climate during Pre-Boreal times. Arctic forms such as the Lemming disappeared, a temperate fauna and flora were introduced from the south and a true forest sequence was initiated. For purposes of this book the Late-Glacial–Early Post-Glacial boundary will be regarded as contemporary with these natural changes, and this line agrees in a striking manner with the archaeological evidence. Thus the main Mesolithic development falls in the Post-Glacial Period, but the presence of the Ahrensburg culture in deposits of the Upper Dryas Period (see p. 18) demonstrates that new influences were already penetrating Northern Europe at the very end of Late-Glacial times. Possibly future research will establish even earlier Mesolithic traits contemporary with the Allerød oscillation. There are as yet, however, only a few stray finds which may be assigned to this phase.

8. SUMMARY

In Northern Europe five firmly established sciences have been developed for dating Late-Glacial and Early Post-Glacial archaeological deposits. These are as follows:

1. *Geology*: the relation of archaeological sites to the ice-front at various stages, and to deposits which were formed as a result of changes in the mutual relation of land and sea.

2. *Geochronology*: an absolute time-scale based on natural phenomena induced by the retreating ice.

3. *Climatology*: established cycles, involving fluctuations in rainfall and temperature, which have a direct effect on the flora and fauna.

4. *Palaeontology*: the identification of both aquatic and land fauna, thereby deducing information regarding prevailing conditions at the time the species were extant.

5. *Palaeobotany*: the microscopic study of polleniferous deposits, and tracing the major drifts in forest development at given periods over broad areas.

All of these sciences are intimately associated with each other as well as with archaeology, and the data furnished by each may be woven into a coherent pattern as shown on the accompanying chronological chart (Table 1). In prehistoric archaeology, a knowledge of all of these allied sciences is of paramount importance for establishing the relationship of cultures in time and space, as well as from the point of view of interpretation of cultural phenomena. In a vital sense environment exerted a powerful influence on the Late-Glacial and Early Post-Glacial food-gathering peoples in Northern Europe both indirectly, through its effect on the flora and fauna, and directly by affecting both human settlement and culture. During the period under discussion a gradual shift from the cave occupation of the Upper Palaeolithic into the open took place. Whereas some of the sites of the Boreal Period on the North European Plain reveal seasonal occupation only, the Ertebølle sites of Atlantic times were occupied all the year round, thus reflecting the more equable climate. Climatic influences on the development of culture were felt throughout the Mesolithic Period, and new implements, such as axes and adzes, were evolved to cope with the forest conditions. By applying the combined evidences of the five sciences listed

(after De Geer, Jessen, Clark, Daly and Wright)

Approximate Dates (after De Geer)	Periods	Stages in the Recession of the Ice	Land Movement	Water Bodies in the Baltic	Climatic Phases	Zones in Denmark	Forest Development	Fauna	Archaeology
B.C. 2500 3000	Post-Glacial		Emergence	Baltic as at present	Sub-Boreal Cold and dry: Continental climate	VIII	Beech and Horn-beam coming in Pine curve ascending OMF diminishing	Domestic animals	Neolithic
4000 4500 5000			Submergence	Litorina Sea	Cooler at end Warm and moist: Oceanic climate Atlantic Climatic optimum July temperature 17° C.	VII	Oak-Mixed-Forest (Oak, Elm, Lime) dominant Maple and Ash coming in	Dog Forest, lake and sea forms Elk rare Reindeer absent	Mesolithic: Period III — Kitchen-Midden Culture (Ertebølle)
5600 6000 6800		Ragunda:	Emergence	Ancylus Lake	Late: July temperature 16 to 17° C. Boreal	VI	Pine diminishing Hazel maximum Alder curve begins	Dog Forest and lake forms Elk very common Reindeer survived	Mesolithic: Period II — Maglemosean Culture
7000		Final Stadium			Early: Cold and dry: Continental climate July temperature 12 to 14° C.	V	Oak-Mixed-Forest coming in Pine maximum		
		Finiglacial Period		Yoldia Sea	Pre-Boreal Gradual then rapid rise of July temperature from 8 to 12° C.	IV	Birch-Pine Period Hazel coming in Birch (*B. pubescens*) Pine (*P. sylvestris*) Aspen	Mixed tundra and forest forms Lemming absent	Mesolithic: Period I — Lyngby Culture
7800	Late-Glacial	Fennoscandian End-Moraine	Submergence	Baltic Ice-Lake / Late-Glacial Sea outside the Baltic	Arctic	III	Upper Dryas Period		Ahrensburg Culture
8300		Gotiglacial Period			Sub-Arctic	II	Allerød Oscillation *B. pubescens* *P. sylvestris*	Tundra and steppe forms: Reindeer, Horse, Lemming, Glutton, etc.	Late Upper Palaeolithic Hamburg Culture
10,000 14,800		Pomeranian Stage Baltic End-Moraine							
18,000		Daniglacial Period		Ice receding to the Baltic	Arctic	I	Lower Dryas Period *Dryas octopetala* *Salix herbacea* *Betula nana*		
		Weichsel Glaciation Brandenburg End-Moraine							

above, Dr Clark has divided the Mesolithic of Northern Europe into three main periods, and these are indicated I, II and III respectively in their proper context on the chart. With this background, the data available from Britain and Ireland will now be examined, in order to determine whether or not they reveal a sufficient degree of uniformity with Northern Europe to warrant correlation with this area, where chronology rests on such a solid basis of fact.

Chapter II

THE LATE-GLACIAL SEQUENCE IN BRITAIN & IRELAND

1. INTRODUCTION

Although this chapter, including the Appendices which go with it, is entirely a bibliographical study, not based upon actual field work, the material is presented in the hope that it will provide a tentative chronology for the Late-Glacial Period and lead to further research into the numerous problems involved. The writer was forced to embark upon this investigation to establish the necessary background, as determined by natural history, for the Stone Age settlement of Northern Britain and Ireland, and to work out provisional dates for the various events, so far as possible, on the basis of the North European sequence. In Britain there is an urgent need for broad-scale chronological mapping of the drift sequence for the assistance of archaeologists, as Sandford points out (1935, p. 503). The limits of glaciation have been known in England for a considerable period (Wright, 1914, p. 49), and it has long been an established fact that Ireland was entirely covered during the period of maximum advance. Notwithstanding the wealth of material on this subject, such loose statements as "at the maximum of the last ice all the British Isles were covered north of approximately latitude 52°" (Coleman, 1929, p. 34) are still made, and a glance at Dubois' maps (Daly, 1934, p. 77) reveals how inadequately the recession of the last ice-sheet in the region under discussion is generally understood. For the most part, hastily compiled information has led to a misrepresentation of the facts, and even Antevs' correlations (1929, pp. 663–7), although they reflect the advances made in this subject during the last ten years, are far from reliable. Before any really marked advance is made in British glacial geology, however, a uniform nomenclature for individual glaciations over the whole country must be evolved, as Harrison has stated (1937, p. 235). As yet no general system of this sort exists and in each district one finds a different set of labels for contemporary deposits. Whereas no complete synthesis of these data has yet appeared, the following is an attempt to outline the salient features and to offer a plausible interpretation based upon known facts. Certainly much remains to be done to fill in the gaps in our existing knowledge, since the region offers limitless possibilities for future research. Therefore, this summary and suggested correlation with the established Continental sequence can be no more than tentative, and they are presented in this light. In the case of Sections 3, 5, 6, 8 and 9 much, or in certain instances all, of the detailed evidence will be found in the form of Appendices at the end of the book. In so far as possible an effort has been made to make the text comprehensive. The Appendices are designed to supplement the text and to furnish the specialist with a completely documented account of certain portions of the material covered only in a very general fashion in this chapter.

2. THE OLD DRIFT GLACIATION

The following sequence and correlation with the Continent has been established for the eastern and northern portions of England and is generally accepted (Boswell, 1931, 1932, 1936; Sandford, 1932, 1933 and 1933[*a*]; Zeuner, 1937, 1938):

England	Alps	Northern Germany
Scottish Readvance (only in the north)	Würm III	Pomeranian Stage
Hunstanton-Hessle Boulder Clay (New Drift Glaciation)	Würm II	Weichsel
Upper Chalky Boulder Clay (Old Drift Glaciation)	Würm I	Warthe
Great Chalky Boulder Clay	Riss	Saale
North Sea Drift	Mindel	Elster
Later Crag Deposits	Günz	

Here we are only concerned with the deposits from the Upper Chalky Boulder Clay, or the Purple Drift of Yorkshire, onwards. In East Anglia this stage is also referred to as the Little Eastern Glaciation (*B.R.G.*[*a*], p. 54: Solomon, 1932, p. 267), and embraces (*a*) the sandy brickearths, and (*b*) the Cromer Ridge gravels. It has been suggested (Sandford, 1933[*a*], p. 864) that the term New Drift be employed with reference to deposits of this glaciation as well as to those of the Hunstanton-Hessle phase, but for purposes of this book the New Drift is considered in a more limited and conventional sense, embracing no more than the Hunstanton-Hessle and equivalent deposits of the last major glacial episode. Thus the writer has adopted the definition of the term New Drift recently advocated by Wright (1937, pp. 91–2), which seems to have much to commend it. By the term Old Drift is meant deposits referable to the Upper Chalky Boulder Clay stage *only*, although actually the Old Drift embraces drifts of earlier glaciations as well. Thus the term is ambiguous, since in East Anglia and South Central England this label has been attached by geologists to all glacial drifts demonstrably older than the New Drift. For this reason the present use of "Old Drift" with reference to a specific glacial episode—the one immediately preceding the New Drift Glaciation—is bound to meet with objections. It may be pointed out, however, that in this instance the difficulty of nomenclature is only too apparent. In defence of the present usage it is well to bear in mind that within much of the region under discussion—Wales (Jehu, 1904, 1909; Williams, 1927; Griffiths, 1939; *B.R.G.*[*e*], p. 103), Scotland (McCallien, 1937, p. 180; Bremner, 1934[*a*], p. 47) and Ireland (Charlesworth, 1930, p. 379; Farrington, 1939)—no earlier glaciations have as yet been recorded. Therefore in these latter areas the Old Drift is synonymous with the maximum glaciation, or first ice-sheet of which any record has been preserved.

In Ireland a shelly boulder clay along the south coast proves that this glaciation completely covered the country and passed out to sea to a line corresponding to the 50-fathom isobath (Charlesworth, 1930, p. 379). This fact is also demonstrated by the direction of the striae in Southern Ireland (Wright and Muff, 1904, Pl. XXXI), although Farrington feels that the evidence for the complete glaciation of Ireland is uncertain (1932, p. 66). Only a small area in Southern Britain escaped glaciation; at this stage England probably formed part of the Tundra Zone, but no true loess deposits are known as yet (Zeuner, 1937[*b*], p. 394). The line of the Old Drift (Fig. 8, facing p. 60) passes along the northern coast of the Bristol Channel, around the northern end of the Cotswolds, and from Oxfordshire south to the northern edge of the Thames Valley, where it pursues a sinuous course eastward and passes out to sea in the vicinity of Harwich (Wright, 1937, Fig. 35, p. 61). This ice-sheet was confluent with the Scandinavian Ice which attained a considerable development in the North Sea during this period (Harrison, 1937, p. 243; MacClintock, 1933, Fig. 4, p. 1051). Erratics from Norway and Sweden are of common occurrence in the Upper Chalky Drift of East Anglia and other sections of Eastern England and Scotland. Indeed this fact suggests that the earliest glaciation of Scotland may also be of Upper Chalky age. Many Scottish geologists, however, consider that the Glacial Period, i.e. the Pleistocene, begins with the earliest glacial episode in that country, and that any events antedating the first apparent glaciation are accordingly Pliocene. Actually all the glacial episodes present in this area appear to be referable to the various Würm phases of the Alps, as outlined above. It seems evident that records of earlier glaciations existed, but were destroyed by Late Pleistocene Ice which pushed down from the Highlands and obliterated all former deposits, except in the morainic regions of South-Eastern and Central Britain. In this sense the high-level marine deposits at Clava, Nairnshire (Fraser, 1869), and the enigmatical shell beds of the Clyde Basin and Campbeltown, Kintyre (Wright, 1937, p. 368) may be referred to as "Pre-Glacial". Probably the deeply buried river channels of the Midland Valley of Scotland, indicating that the sea-level was once ± 300 feet lower than at present (McCallien, 1937, pp. 176–7), also belong to an earlier stage. These localities afford definite evidence for periods at which the mutual relations of land and sea differed greatly from those of to-day, and they all seem to be older than the earliest glacial records in Scotland.

In North-East Scotland the earliest glaciation is documented by the local grey boulder clay (Bremner, 1915, pp. 335–6; 1936, p. 378) as well as by a dark shelly drift (Bremner, 1935, p. 268). The shells in the latter deposit, which is found only at a few localities on the east coast (Bremner, 1934, p. 18), are sometimes striated and indicate that the Scandinavian Ice, after crossing the bed of the North Sea, invaded the coastal regions of the Scottish mainland (Bremner, 1934[*a*], p. 48). At one locality the shelly drift and the grey boulder clay are associated, but no Scandinavian erratics have as yet been found actually in the shelly drift, although they have been recorded at several surface stations on the mainland (Read, Bremner *et al.* 1923; Bremner, 1934, p. 18; 1935, p. 268), and in one instance a Scandinavian boulder has been found in the grey boulder clay (Bremner, 1934[*a*], p. 48). The main ice-sheet in North-East Scotland, whose centre was in the Highlands west of the Great Glen (Bremner, 1934[*a*], p. 53), was confluent at this period with the Scandinavian Ice and both moved in a general south-easterly direction (Bremner, 1934, p. 17). No trace of deposits of this age has been found in the Orkneys and Shetlands (Bremner, 1934[*a*], p. 48). In Caithness the lowest boulder clay is the equivalent of the basal boulder clay of the Moray region. The associated striae indicate a general north-easterly movement, since the pressure of the Scandinavian Ice caused the

Highland Ice to split in the Moray region, one stream flowing south and the other north (Bremner, 1934[*a*], p. 50). This episode in the glaciation of Scotland is usually referred to as the Early Scottish Glaciation (McCallien, 1937, pp. 179–80); it is the Scottish counterpart of the Old Drift Glaciation. It might be argued that the basal boulder clay of Northern and Eastern Scotland belongs to an even earlier glacial episode when ice from Scandinavia invaded the British coasts. But the data presented in this chapter (Sections 4–8 inclusive) relative to the age of the overlying beds are not in accord with an early dating of these deposits. Farther south, the coming of this ice-sheet was heralded in the ice-free regions by the appearance of cold fauna on the Upper Flood Plain Terrace, Stage I (Ponders End stage) of the Thames (King and Oakley, 1936, pp. 65–7), but there are no faunal remains in Scotland and Ireland which can indisputably be assigned to this period.

3. THE RAISED BEACH OF THE THIRD INTERGLACIAL PERIOD

(Appendix I)

Before the advent of the Old Drift Glaciation (=Upper Chalky Boulder Clay of East Anglia), the coastlines of Britain and Ireland must have been almost identical with those of the present day. This can be definitely established by a marine platform found south of the line indicated on the map (Fig. 7, p. 58), which dates from the Third Interglacial Period (Riss-Würm). This period witnessed the introduction of the Mousterian culture into Western Europe. Over three-quarters of the area of Ireland is included in the distribution of this raised beach, since it extends from Achill Island, County Mayo, around the south and east coasts to Ardglass, County Down (see Appendix I, p. 265). It is also found in the Isle of Man, and in England south of a line between Ravenglass in Westmorland and Whitby in Yorkshire; it is especially well developed along the south coast of Wales, and in Devon and Cornwall. The counterpart of this beach is found in the Channel Islands and along the northern coast of France. That its age is Third Interglacial is established by the fact that everywhere it is overlaid by a rubble head or ancient talus, resulting from the degradation of the old cliff, which contains derived implements of Middle Palaeolithic type (Dewey, 1913; Wright, 1937, p. 121), and the overlying deposits are composed of either drifts or solifluction layers referable to the period of the Würm ice-sheets of the Continent. Furthermore, at localities where a Pleistocene mammalian fauna has been found, the assemblage suggests a Third Interglacial dating. For the most part this platform occurs at a uniform height of 10–12 feet above present sea-level, but in Western Ireland and the Channel Islands it has been recorded at elevations of 20 and 25 feet respectively. Although the period of this beach lies outside the scope of this book, the distribution is mentioned here in order to avoid confusion with the later beaches to be presently described. Furthermore, its 0-isobase corresponds approximately with the line north of which the land appears to have been rising in Post-Atlantic times, while a slight sinking has taken place to the south, as discussed in Chapter III. Whereas this is not of direct importance, a glance at the map (Fig. 7, p. 58) will reveal that the regions of low-level very roughly correspond with the present limit of distribution of the Post-Glacial raised beach. It should therefore be used as a datum to which all subsequent oscillations may be referred, because its remarkably uniform height, as Dr Wright points out (1914, p. 422), precludes the possibility of Late- or Post-Glacial folding or faulting.

4. THE STRATIGRAPHY OF THE LATE-GLACIAL PERIOD

Thus far the data have been presented horizontally over the entire area in order to provide a base-line to serve as the foundation for the stratigraphic study of Late-Glacial deposits in Britain and Ireland. Before discussing these stratified deposits, it is necessary to consider the evidence from six key localities where the vertical sequence is well established, following which it is proposed to revert to a horizontal consideration of the material as a whole and present the arguments for the contemporaneity of Late-Glacial events in the various regions. The key localities are: (*a*) East Anglia, (*b*) the Lincolnshire coast, (*c*) West Yorkshire, (*d*) Northern England, (*e*) North-East Scotland and (*f*) North-East Ireland. In each of these areas deposits, referable to the second and in some cases to the third Würm phases, are found overlying the drifts and boulder clay described above.

(*a*) EAST ANGLIA. The standard sequence for the Glacial Period in England has been established here, as given on p. 26. Between the Upper Chalky and the Hunstanton Brown Boulder Clay weathered soils (MacClintock, 1933, p. 1049) and the raised beach at Morston (Solomon,

1932, p. 251) occur. No glacial deposits later than the second Würm stage of the Alps have been recorded.

(*b*) THE LINCOLNSHIRE COAST. Overlying the Purple Boulder Clay (=Würm I) at Kirmington Pit, the following section has been established (MacClintock, 1933, p. 1047):

	Feet
8. Weathered Gravel	2
7. Hessle Boulder Clay (New Drift)	0–1½
6. Sand and Gravel	3
5. Silt and Clay containing undisturbed marine shells	8
4. Peat	½
3. Clay containing vegetation	1½
2. Rusty-Brown Sand	3
1. Purple Boulder Clay (Old Drift)	—

This section corroborates the East Anglian evidence and indicates that between the Old and the New Drift the climate ameliorated sufficiently to permit the formation of peat. Presumably the marine clay (Layer 5) is the equivalent of the Morston raised beach.

(*c*) WEST YORKSHIRE. The Upper Purple Boulder Clay in this area is the equivalent of the Hessle Boulder Clay of the coast (Raistrick, 1933[*a*], pp. 201–2). In the eastern part of the Dales, the Old Boulder Clay (Lower Purple) of the maximum (Old Drift) glaciation is overlain by sands and occasionally by laminated clays. Above this occurs Upper Purple Clay (Raistrick, 1933, p. 264) of Würm II age.

(*d*) NORTHERN ENGLAND. Outside of East Anglia this is the best known region in England with respect to the chronology of the Late-Glacial Period. Here Trotter and Hollingworth have established the following sequence (*M.G.S.* England and Wales, 1932, p. 146):

Deposits		Interpretation
Episode 3	Upper Sands and Gravels	Retreat of Scottish Readvance Ice
	Upper Boulder Clay	Scottish Readvance Glaciation
Episode 2	Middle Sands and Gravels with Laminated Clays	Retreat of Ice of the Main Glaciation
	Lower Boulder Clay	Second or Main Glaciation
Episode 1	Sands and Laminated Clays	Retreat of Early Scottish Ice
	Basal Boulder Clay	Early Scottish Glaciation

Each episode represents the waxing and waning of an ice-sheet. On this basis the following interpretation may be suggested: (1) that the Basal Boulder Clay is probably the equivalent of the Old Drift or Upper Chalky Boulder Clay of East Anglia (Würm I); (2) the Lower Boulder Clay = the Hunstanton-Hessle or New Drift Boulder Clay (Würm II); and (3) the Upper Boulder Clay = the Scottish Readvance as indicated above (Würm III). In the Isle of Man an identical sequence has been established by Dr Bernard Smith (1930, p. 21).

(*e*) North-East Scotland. This area furnishes definite evidence for three distinct glaciations, which have been summarized by Bremner (1928, 1934) as follows:

1. *First Ice-Sheet*: on the basis of the distribution of the erratics, the direction of the striae and the contents of the ground moraine, this ice-sheet moved from north-west to south-east. It was confluent with the Scandinavian Ice, which deposited shelly drift along the coast as previously described.

2. *Second Ice-Sheet*: the Strathmore Glaciation which, because of influence from Scandinavian Ice in the North Sea, was compelled to flow northward and westward depositing a red boulder clay and southern erratics. The reasons for equating this ice-sheet with Hessle-Hunstanton Glaciation of England are given on p. 41.

3. *Third Ice-Sheet*: the Scottish Readvance or Highland Glaciation, which moved in a general easterly direction, only reached the coast in a few localities, as will be shown presently. This stage is the equivalent of Würm III of the Alps and the Pomeranian End-Moraine of North Germany.

Following the Third Ice-Sheet there is abundant evidence in Scotland for a fourth glacial stage. This is known as the Valley, District or Morainic Glaciation, and it seems to be the counterpart of the Alpine Geschnitz stage and the Fennoscandian End-Moraine of Northern Europe.

(*f*) North-East Ireland. In Counties Antrim and Down the sequence given below has been established by Dwerryhouse (1923, pp. 417–20):

1. *First stage*: at this period the dominant agent in the glaciation of this region was the Firth of Clyde Ice, whose origin was in the Highlands of Scotland. As stated above it appears likely that Ireland was completely overridden by ice during this (Old Drift) glaciation.

2. *Second stage*: much of the country formerly covered by Scottish Ice was now glaciated from the west by ice from the Donegal Mountains. This local Irish Ice or the Ivernian Ice-Sheet was in contact with the Highland Ice on the east (New Drift).

3. *Third stage*: by this time the Ivernian Ice-Sheet had withdrawn to the region west of the Lower Bann Valley, and the coastal portions of Counties Antrim and Down were invaded by Scottish Ice (Scottish Readvance).

The evidence furnished by these six areas is unanimous in its implications, but it is necessary to consider in some detail the extent of the deposits and the evidence of their age in order to establish the Late-Glacial sequence in Britain and Ireland on a firm basis.

5. DEPOSITS OF THE INTERSTADIAL PERIOD BETWEEN THE OLD AND THE NEW DRIFT GLACIATIONS (W_1/W_2)

(Appendix II)

Remains of fauna, flora and man within the area covered by the New Drift clearly indicate an old land surface following the Old Drift Glaciation. Most of this old land surface is now covered by either the boulder clay of the last ice or surface deposits showing the effects of solifluction during the last glacial maximum. That the latter period was preceded by a retreat of the ice is borne out by the state of the drift outside the end-moraine of the New Drift, which is far more heavily weathered than that within it, and also by the presence of sands and gravels between the Old and New Drifts in Wales (compare Jehu, 1904, 1909; Williams, 1927; Charlesworth, 1929, p. 350; Griffiths, 1939). Similar "interval" deposits are known in East Anglia, Northern England, Scotland and Ireland. Comparatively warm fluviatile and marine mollusca in beds of this period on the coast of Eastern England prove, as Baden-Powell points out (1934, p. 215), that a cool temperate climate prevailed. Evidence based on soil analysis suggests humid conditions with chemical weathering between Würm I and Würm II deposits on the Continent (Zeuner, 1937[*a*], p. 37), and Boswell (1936, p. 159) indicates that during this phase the climate was mild. This interval is usually regarded as marking an oscillation, called the "Aurignacian oscillation" by Charlesworth (1929, p. 351), in the Late-Glacial sequence. The data, a summary of which is presented below,[1] indicate, however, that it was of full

[1] A somewhat more detailed account of the English and Scottish evidence on which this summary is based will be found in Appendix II; the Irish material appears only in the text.

interstadial magnitude with a climate approaching that of the present day. In Northern Britain and Ireland it was not a true Interglacial Period, as it was of relatively short duration and the ice does not seem to have disappeared completely. But Jessen and Milthers (1928, p. 376) maintain that in North-West Germany and South-West Jutland, the Warthe-Weichsel Period must be regarded as an Interglacial and not merely an Interstadial Period. The fresh-water peats laid down at this time reveal that at the interglacial maximum there is evidence for a marine transgression, represented by the Eem Sea, and a temperate climate with a summer temperature probably as high as it was during the Post-Glacial climatic optimum. In an Interstadial Period it seems unlikely that this would have occurred. Gams, who has recently summarized the Late-Glacial sequence in Northern Europe, agrees that the Eem Interglacial falls between the Fläming (Warthe) and the Brandenburg (Weichsel) End-Moraines (1938, p. 76).

Now the British equivalent for the Eem Sea is documented by the March-Nar raised beach gravels, sands and clays (Harrison, 1935), which are found on the east coast from Norfolk to Durham. Fortunately at several of the localities such valuable climatic indicators as pollen and molluscs have been preserved. Thus in the peat layer at Kirmington (Fig. 4; see p. 31 for section) Alder, Birch, Pine, Spruce, Oak, Elm, Lime, Holly, Ash (?) and Hazel have been found, demonstrating a cool temperate climate. The overlying silts and clays contain shells typical of present-day waters in the region of the Baltic. This evidence is confirmed by marine deposits at Easington in Durham (Fig. 4), where there is a raised beach 60 feet above present sea-level, and at March in the Fenland (Fig. 4), both of which sites have yielded shells; a few forms are listed in Appendix II, p. 267. The foraminifera from March prove that a mild climate prevailed during this period. At Morston in Norfolk (Fig. 4) a raised beach ± 20 feet above the sea represents the southern limit of the deposits referable to the March-Nar submergence. In river gravels of comparable age in the Valley of the Trent near Derby, in the vicinity of Cambridge (Upper Barnwell Village Beds) and in the March area, all shown on the map (Fig. 4), the remains of Mammoth, Rhinoceros, Red Deer, Roebuck, Wild Ox and Wild Horse have been found, although not all at the same locality. The evidence from Eastern England therefore proves that during the interval between the Old and the New Drift Glaciations the climate improved considerably and that conditions were similar to those prevailing at present. With this period the

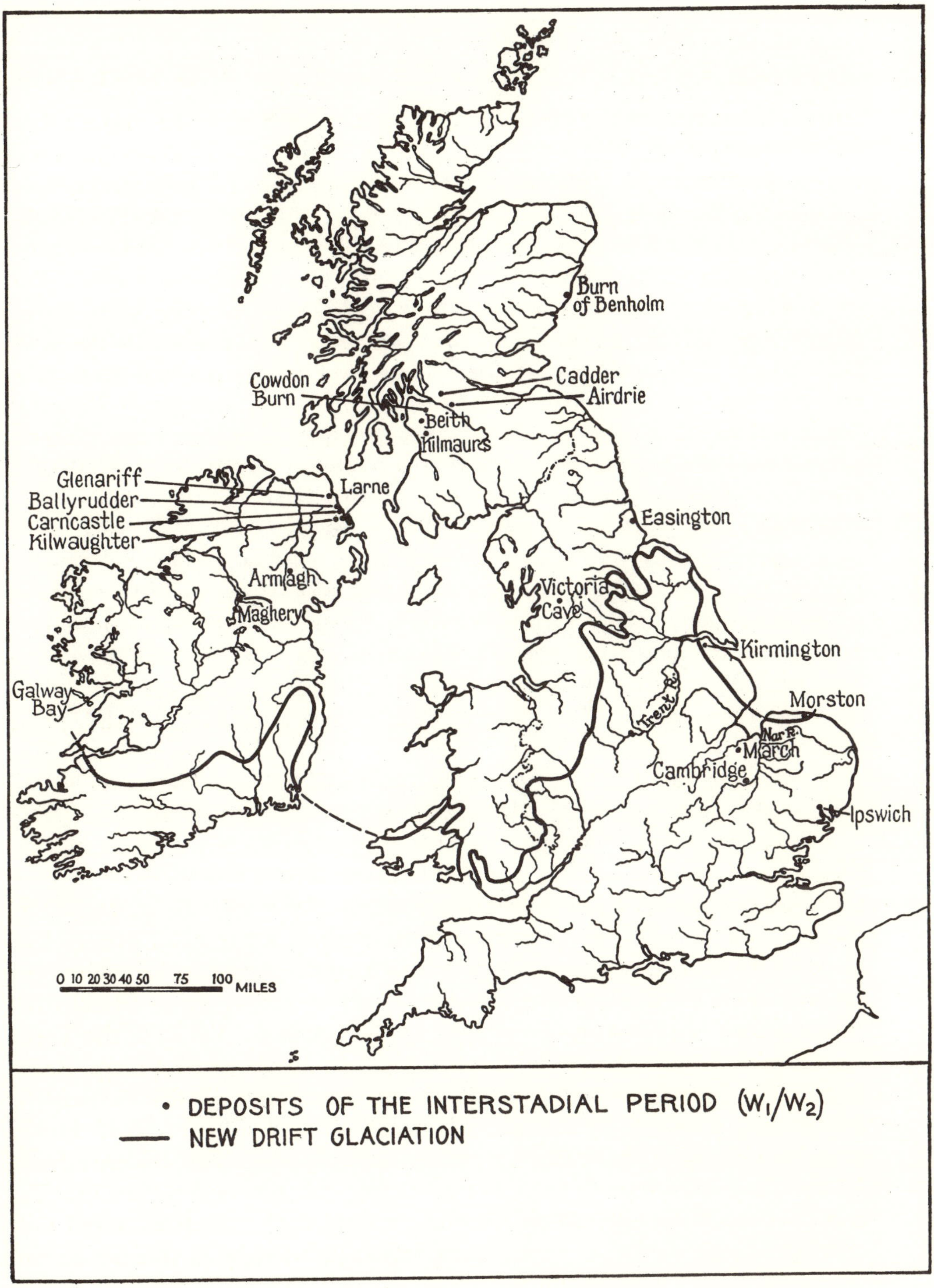

Fig. 4. Deposits of the Interstadial Period (W_1/W_2) between the Old and the New Drift Glaciations in Britain and Ireland.

main development of the Aurignacian culture in Western Europe may be correlated.

In the southern portion of the Irish Sea Basin there is no evidence at present of a submergence at this time. In Western Scotland, however, there are two sites (shown on Fig. 4), which demonstrate a marine transgression prior to the advent of the New Drift Glaciation. At Kilmaurs, near Kilmarnock in Ayrshire, there is a marine deposit (Bed 4, see p. 268 for section) containing an Arctic fauna at a height of 40 feet above present sea-level, and at Chappel Hall, near Airdrie in Lanark, a similar deposit has been reported. Both these sites are described in Appendix II. Underlying the marine layer at Kilmaurs are fresh-water clays in which seeds of cold temperate plants, beetle remains, as well as bones and teeth of Mammoth and Reindeer, have been discovered. To this list may be added Woolly Rhinoceros known from an horizon of the same age near Cadder, Dumbartonshire, just north of Glasgow (Fig. 4). The Reindeer also occurs in an horizon overlain by New Drift at Croftamie near Cowdon Burn, Ayrshire, while from Cowdon Burn itself (Fig. 4) in a thick series of lacustrine sediments containing peat of this period Wild Ox, Wild Horse, Irish Elk (?) and Red Deer have been documented (see Appendix II, pp. 268–9). In the peat an imposing list of thirty-one plants and trees, including Birch, Willow and Pine, have been identified. Near Beith, in Ayrshire, Hazel is known from interstadial clays, and from a peat layer between the Old and the New Drift at Airdrie, Lanark, Dunlop (1888) has collected the remains of Birch, insects (beetles and weevils) as well as mosses (Fig. 4). In the Burn of Benholm in Eastern Scotland (Kincardineshire) a polleniferous peat bed has been described by Campbell (1934, 1934[*a*]). It is overlain by deposits of the New Drift or Strathmore Ice-Sheet and rests in turn upon the basal grey or Old Drift Boulder Clay. The two most important forest forms from this locality, shown on Fig. 4, are Birch and Pine, Pine being dominant in the lower part of the peat layer while the pollen frequency for Birch runs over 60 per cent in the upper portion of the profile (see p. 269). In addition Alder and Oak are found throughout; the upper layer is characterized by the appearance of Elm and Hazel. Palaeobotany in Scotland therefore not only corroborates the data from the east coast of England, but it also supports Ritchie's conclusions (1929, pp. 189–90) that "the known ingredients of the first Scottish glacial fauna, then, compel us to place it in the Würm ice-period of continental workers" by demonstrating that the ice withdrew sufficiently far into the Highlands to permit the invasion of Scotland by a Late Pleistocene fauna during Würm I–II times.

In Western Scotland the climate was not as mild during this period. Both here as well as in Northern Ireland cooler conditions prevailed, suggesting that a certain amount of ice remained in the Highlands. The evidence from Kilmaurs and Airdrie for the existence of an Arctic sea is substantiated at Ballyrudder, north of Larne on the County Antrim coast (Praeger, 1893, pp. 518–25). The deposit, the surface of which is 47½ feet above high-water mark, is 27½ feet thick and composed mostly of gravel, sands and clays. It occurs below 36 feet of New Drift, and it has yielded a cold fauna—*Astarte borealis*, *Mytilus edulis*, *Puncturella noachina*, *Buccinum undatum* and *Mya truncata* being among the forms represented. Thus the Kilmaurs, Airdrie and Ballyrudder beds prove that colder conditions prevailed in the region of the North Channel than on the east coast of Britain. It seems very probable that the layer of marine sands and silts found between deposits of the Old and the New Drift Glaciations in the Isle of Man (Smith, 1930, p. 21) was formed at the time of this transgression.

In Ireland the fauna, documented from deposits of the Interstadial Period between the Old and the New Drift in the Midland Valley of Scotland, is represented only by stray finds of *Elephas primigenius* (Charlesworth, 1928, p. 323). Teeth and, rarely, bones of Mammoth have been recorded either in or below the New Drift from the following Irish localities along the Antrim Coast—Larne, Ballyrudder, Carncastle, Kilwaughter and Glenariff—as well as from Galway Bay, and Maghery, Belturbet, County Cavan. All these localities are shown on the map (Fig. 4). It is possible that the peat beds mentioned by Brooks (1917, p. 329) at Newtown Colliery and near Armagh also date from this phase, but the question needs further investigation (compare Praeger, 1928, p. 100). In addition to the Mammoth, this period witnessed a further introduction of fauna, according to Charlesworth (1930, p. 380). He suggests that an almost complete landbridge, affected by an isostatic uplift of the land at an early stage following the retreat of the Old Drift Ice, permitted forms to migrate to Ireland with comparative ease. It is highly improbable, however, that a direct land connection was in existence, and since the subsequent ice-advance must have largely obliterated the now submerged valleys and land surfaces formed at this time in the region of the Irish Sea (Charlesworth, 1936, p. 1041), the data on this point will be difficult to obtain. As previously stated, the evidence in England and Scotland indicates that a submergence occurred during this interstadial, nevertheless there is no reason why this marine transgression could not have been preceded by an emergence, as was the case during the Post-Glacial Period (see p. 83). That the fauna under discussion can date from an earlier interglacial episode preceding the Old Drift Glaciation is precluded by the fact that Ireland was completely overridden by this ice-sheet. Furthermore, this possibility is not indicated by the forms represented. It is therefore apparent that mammals entered the country during some part of the Interstadial Period (W_1/W_2), when a favourable temperate climate prevailed, and survived the last ice-advance. Although the Mammoth definitely must have been introduced before the advent of the last ice-sheet (see p. 37), it is quite possible, as Charlesworth points out (1928, p. 322), that some of the "cold" fauna may have migrated later over the Irish Sea Ice. Possibly this would account for the restricted number of genera in a country so full of Carboniferous limestone caves. The list of typical cave types in the following table is based on Charlesworth (1930, p. 381) and it establishes that the animals were present at the time of the last ice-advance, since in all cases the sites lie south of the end-moraines of the New Drift Glaciation (see Fig. 5, p. 42).

	Mammoth	Cave Hyaena	Arctic Lemming	Scandinavian Lemming	Irish Elk	Reindeer	Bear (*Ursus arctos*)	Arctic Fox
Shandon Cave, Dungarvan, County Waterford	+	.	.	.	+	+	+	.
Ballinamintra Cave, Cappagh, County Waterford	.	.	.	.	+	.	.	.
Kilgreany Cave, Cappagh, County Waterford	.	.	+	.	+	+	+	+
Doneraille, or Castlepook Cave, County Cork	+	+	+	+	+	+	+	+
Killavullen Caves, County Cork (Leask, 1934, p. 410)	.	.	+	.	+	+	+	+

This fauna bears the unmistakable stamp of the Late-Glacial Period: its contemporaneity with the last ice-sheet is obvious, since no strictly southern forms are present. With the age of the introductions of these mammals established, this evidence is of great importance, and it strengthens the contention that the Old and the New Drift Glaciations, as defined on p. 27, are contemporary in Great Britain and Ireland. With a few exceptions in both regions, which will be discussed later, the Late-Glacial cave fauna is not found north of the line of the southernmost extension of the New Drift. This can only mean that all the area north of the line was covered by ice.

It is obvious that a restricted flora must have existed to support these animals. In Ireland this flora consisted mainly of Arctic and Alpine forms, some of which survive to the present day, together with the small Lusitanian element which was probably present (Charlesworth, 1930, p. 381). It is not the question, however, of whether or not this flora survived the last glaciation, which is admitted by Jessen (with Farrington, 1938, p. 239) and Walton (1933, p. 142), but it is whether or not it could have survived the earlier glaciation when all Ireland appears to have been covered by ice. In particular this applies to certain groups of Southern and American plants and invertebrate animals (Praeger, 1934, pp. 127–8), which puzzle Irish botanists and geologists. Praeger maintains (1934, pp. 129–30) that these relic species have survived from "Pre-Glacial" times, but Charlesworth (1930, pp. 380–2) feels that the flora became extinct at the time of maximum glaciation and was reintroduced later. According to him, it is just possible that a few extremely hardy Arctic species could have survived from the preceding warm period, had a land mass existed off the South Irish coast during the period of maximum glaciation. That such was the case cannot be definitely established. In this regard Farrington (1932) has advanced the interesting theory that the flora was not exterminated, since the influence of solar radiation on the Irish ice-sheets would be such that glaciation in the north and south of the island would not be contemporaneous. Thus there would always be ice-free areas. Exactly how this situation could have occurred in an area as small as Ireland is difficult to understand. But evidence from Greenland, Spitsbergen and elsewhere shows that the survival of both plants and animals in unglaciated tracts on nunataks within the glaciated area is to be expected, as Antevs (1928, pp. 27–8) points out, and this is Praeger's conclusion regarding Ireland (1934, p. 143). Although this problem lies outside the scope of the present book, it is introduced to show the pressing necessity for a careful checking of the geological data, especially in that area of South Ireland not covered by New Drift. On the whole the evidence favours the doctrine of survival.

Reviewing the facts presented above, it seems difficult to escape the conclusion that a mild Interstadial Period with a climate similar to the present is indicated by the interval between the Old and the New Drift Glaciations. As compared with earlier interglacial episodes, it was of short duration. During it Great Britain and Ireland experienced (*a*) a period of relative emergence during which a partial land connection probably existed between Ireland and England, and (*b*) a period of relative submergence represented by the Morston raised beach, the March-Nar gravels, and associated deposits. Marine molluscs and foraminifera from these gravels and silts, as well as the immediately underlying Kirmington peat bed, reveal that present-day conditions prevailed. That the ice retreated far up into the Highlands of Scotland is attested by peat beds yielding a temperate flora in the Midland Valley, and the Burn of Benholm, Kincardineshire, as well as by the peat incorporated in the moraines of the next glaciation in the Aberdeen district (see p. 269). The Mammoth, Woolly Rhinoceros and other mammals roamed north as far as the Scottish Midland Valley, and the Mammoth at least crossed to Ireland probably via the partial land-bridge. In this region, before the next ice-advance (New Drift Glaciation), there is evidence from three sites bordering on the North Channel and the Clyde Estuary for a marine transgression. The deposits in question contain a typically cold fauna, suggesting that the climate of the Western Highlands as well as that of Northern Ireland was directly influenced as a result of the presence of ice in the mountains. If the interpretation regarding the age of the deposits described in this chapter is correct, it is difficult to conceive of these events taking place during a mere oscillation of the ice. Thus it seems reasonable to conclude that a temperate Interstadial Period, during which conditions approached those of a true Interglacial stage, intervened between the last two major ice-advances in the north of Great Britain and Ireland. This conclusion is confirmed by the evidence in the Baltic, where the Warthe-Weichsel Period is regarded as a true interglacial of relatively short duration, the counterpart of the Würm I–II oscillation in the Alps. The difference between an interstadial and an interglacial stage is, however, only a matter of degree. In Northern Britain and Ireland faunistic and vegetational criteria demonstrate that we are dealing with a period of interstadial rather than interglacial magnitude. But in regions farther removed from the main centres of ice-dispersal, such as Southern England and the Baltic, it is to be expected that the same period would have been sufficiently long to permit true interglacial conditions to become established.

6. THE NEW DRIFT GLACIATION
(Appendix III)

Subsequent to the Interstadial Period (W_1/W_2), described in the last section, the ice advanced to the York Line, shown on Fig. 5. This advance is represented by the New Drift–Hunstanton or Hessle Boulder Clay (Boswell, 1932). Solomon has advocated the name Hessle Glaciation for this episode (1932, p. 267), and Little Eastern Glaciation for the preceding (Old Drift) stage, but since these terms have not yet been generally adopted outside of Eastern England, for the purposes of this book the question of nomenclature is being left open. The urgent necessity for a general terminology is, however, only too apparent. Cheviot erratics on the east coast of England in the Hessle-Hunstanton deposits prove that the ice-flow was from the north (Solomon, 1932, p. 251). "The distribution of the Younger Drift in the east of England seems to leave little doubt that the glacier which produced it was in contact with ice originating from Scandinavia", according to Dr Wright (1937, p. 93). This is confirmed by the evidence in the Cleveland Hills (Kendall, 1902) and East Anglia (MacClintock, 1933, Fig. 4, p. 1051), and it affords a very strong argument for correlating the Strathmore Ice-Sheet of North-East Scotland with this glacial stage in England, as indicated on the map (Fig. 6, p. 52). Of the various centres of ice-dispersal in Britain and Ireland, the chief component was furnished by the Highlands of Scotland during the New Drift Glaciation. In general the ice during this period spread out fanwise from the Highlands (*B.R.G.* [*l*], pp. 72–3), except in Eastern and North-Eastern Scotland, where the direction of flow was from south to north, a direct result of the pressure exerted by Scandinavian Ice lying off the coast (Bremner, 1934[*a*], p. 53). Indeed this fact, together with the identical age of the underlying deposits in both cases, identifies the Strathmore Ice-Sheet as part of the New Drift Glaciation of Scotland—the equivalent of the Hessle-Hunstanton stage in Eastern England.

As shown in Fig. 6, the major portion of Ireland was covered by local Ivernian Ice, which was an immense sheet formed on the plains by the confluence of numerous glaciers from Counties Donegal, Sligo, Leitrim, Mayo and Galway in the north-west (Charlesworth, 1930, p. 360). The flow was generally radial over the Central Plain; the trend was from the north-west or north-north-west. On the east the Ivernian Ice was united

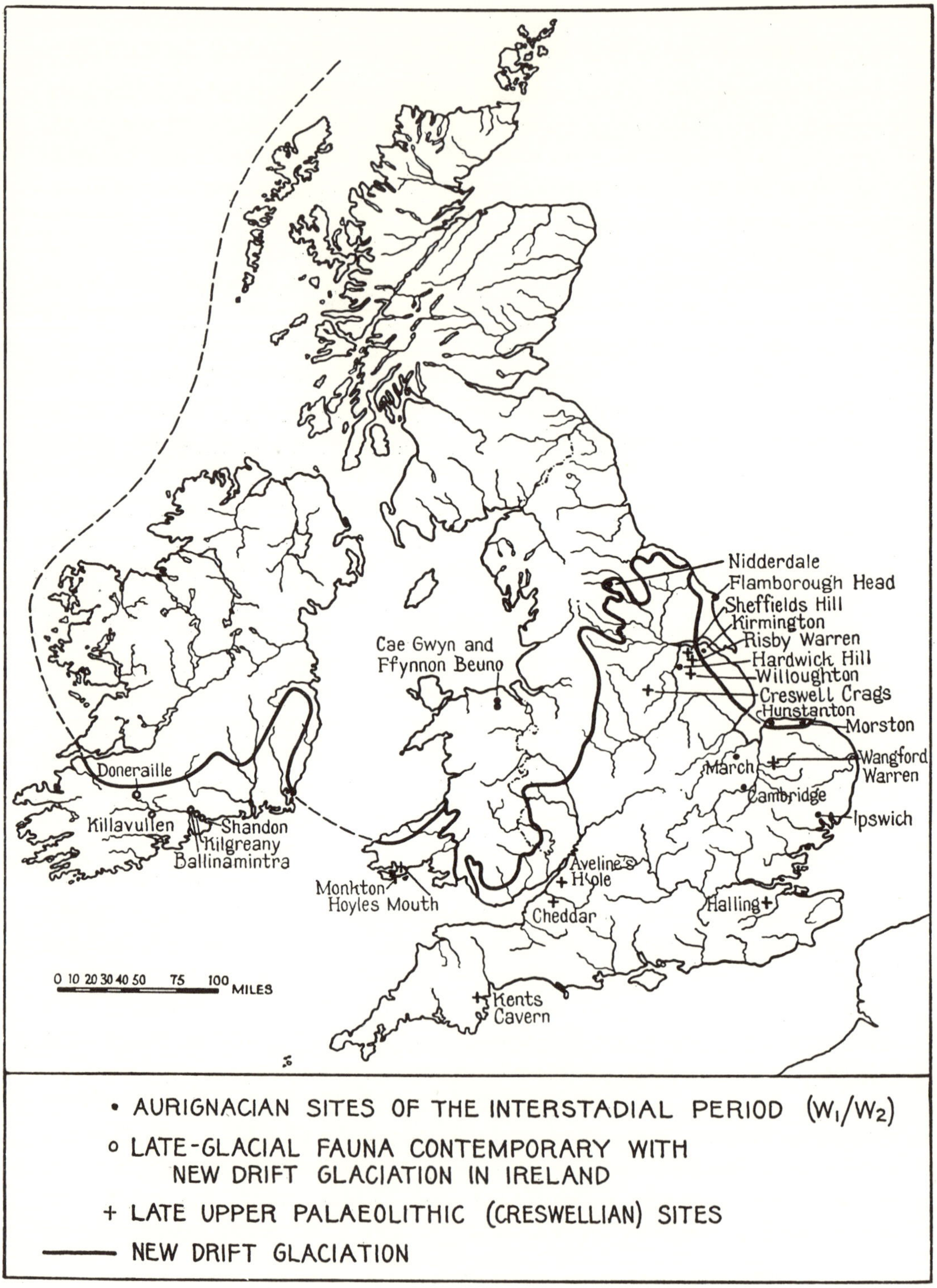

Fig. 5. Archaeological and Palaeontological Sites of the Late-Glacial Period.

with the Irish Sea Ice whose ultimate source was in Scotland and Northern England. The distribution of the Irish cave fauna, described on p. 38, suggested to Professor Charlesworth as a working hypothesis that the end-moraine of the New Drift ran somewhere to the south of the Central Plain, and he has traced its 310-mile course in detail from the Irish Sea to the Atlantic (Charlesworth, 1928). The line is shown in Fig. 6. It will be noted that in the east of Ireland the ice-front swings in a broad U around the northern flanks of the Wicklow Hills. It was originally Charlesworth's opinion that, contemporaneously with the last advance of the Ivernian and Irish Sea Ice-Sheets, local centres of glaciation existed in Ireland (1928, pp. 300–4). But recent work in the Wicklow Mountains (Farrington, 1934, pp. 199–205; Charlesworth, 1937, pp. 30–1) has conclusively shown that on the basis of the stratification and distribution of the drifts, the local glaciation of this region was later than the main ice-advance. As Charlesworth points out (1937, p. 35), it scarcely seems credible that while ice-sheets covered over two-thirds of Ireland and encircled the Wicklow Mountains, except on the south, these mountains—over 3000 feet high and in the path of moisture-bearing, westerly winds—bore no glaciers of their own. This suggests that different factors were involved with regard to the formation of the local Irish glaciers from those controlling the main ice-sheet. Furthermore, it also suggests that local glaciation elsewhere in Ireland was later and probably contemporary with the last glaciation in Wicklow. These local glaciations are discussed on p. 54, as from present evidence they appear to be definitely later than the maximum of the New Drift Glaciation.

The foregoing facts may now be summarized. The New Drift in England, Wales and Ireland (north of the South Irish End-Moraine) represents the maximum advance of the last ice-sheet and is Late Pleistocene in age. It was preceded by an Interstadial Period during which the ice must have receded far into the Scottish Highlands and the mountains of North-West Ireland. This glaciation had an important effect on the Pleistocene fauna, as both Hinton (1926, p. 342) and Hopwood (1936, p. 188) clearly point out—the cold steppe forms, such as Mammoth, Woolly Rhinoceros, etc., were replaced by Arctic types, and became extinct probably as a result of the abrupt change in climate, since they never returned to Northern and Western Europe in the Post-Glacial Period. The Upper Flood Plain Terrace, Stage 2, of the Lower Thames Valley (King and Oakley, 1936, pp. 67–8) was formed during the New Drift Glaciation. The Continental equivalents for this stage are the Weichsel in Northern Europe and Würm II in the Alps. The presence of the Scandinavian Ice-Sheet in the North Sea strongly influenced movement of local ice-sheets in Eastern England and Scotland.

7. THE AGE OF THE NEW DRIFT GLACIATION

Whereas absolute proof that the New Drift Glaciations in England and Ireland are contemporaneous is lacking, it seems, on the basis of the confluence of the Ivernian and Irish Sea Ice-Sheets during the last glacial maxima, that this must be accepted as a statement of fact. This is rendered all the more definite by the nature of the moraines and marginal drainage channels associated with the last ice in both regions; these features exhibit identical characteristics according to Charlesworth (1928, p. 319). Once admitted, this correlation implies that the first advance of the last ice-sheets, represented by the Old Drift, was contemporary also. The same argument holds for Scotland. Here the data, as discussed on p. 41, strongly favour the view that the Strathmore Ice-Sheet is the Scottish counterpart of the Hessle-Hunstanton stage in Eastern England, and that the Old Drift of Aberdeenshire and elsewhere corresponds to the Upper Chalky Boulder Clay of East Anglia. The counterparts of these glaciations on the Continent are reasonably clear. Evidence will be given below showing that the following chart (Table 2) is in the main valid for Northern and Western Europe, although the peaks may not be absolutely contemporary in all instances.

TABLE 2. The Late-Glacial Sequence in Britain and Ireland, and the Continental equivalents

ENGLAND (Boswell, Harrison *et al.*)	SCOTLAND (Bremner)	IRELAND (Charlesworth)	ALPS (Penck and (Brückner)	NORTH GERMANY (Jessen and Milthers)
New Drift (Hunstanton-Hessle and Associated Boulder Clays—Late Upper Palaeolithic Cultures)	Strathmore Ice-Sheet (Red Boulder Clay)	New Drift (Southern Irish End-Moraine)	Würm II	Weichsel (Brandenburg Stage)
Interstadial Period (March-Nar Submergence—Early Upper Palaeolithic Cultures)	Interstadial Period (Mammoth fauna and Burn of Benholm peat)	Interstadial Period (Mammoth fauna and (?) peats)	Oscillation (Laufen?)	Interglacial Period (Eem Submergence)
Old Drift (Upper Chalky Boulder Clay and Associated Deposits only)	Old Drift (Basal Grey Boulder Clay)	Old Drift (Indurated Boulder Clay)	Würm I	Warthe (Fläming Stage)

As first pointed out by Charlesworth (1929, p. 351), proof for the above is furnished by archaeology, which affords an important base-line for geological dating in this instance. During the Interstadial Period between the Old and the New Drift Glaciations the Aurignacian culture appeared in England, and it was in part coexistent with the surviving Late Mousterian and Levalloisean cultures. The following critical facts establish beyond all reasonable doubt that the age of the last ice-advance was contemporary with the latter part of the Upper Palaeolithic. In each case the sites referred to are shown on the map (Fig. 5).

1. At the caves of Ffynnon Beuno and Cae Gwyn in the Vale of Clwyd, Flintshire, North Wales (Garrod, 1926, pp. 104–17; *B.R.G.* [*f*], p. 83), within the area covered during the last ice-advance, Aurignacian implements have been found below deposits of the New Drift. The New Drift is therefore Post-Aurignacian.

2. In Nidderdale (at Gouthwaite Reservoir), Yorkshire, Major Collins (1932, p. 77; 1933, p. 185) has reported Aurignacian implements from an old land surface below the outwash material of the end-moraine of the last ice-sheet, which advanced in this region to near Ripley (Tillotson, 1933, p. 223).

3. At several sites near Ipswich, Suffolk, implements of Middle Palaeolithic type occur in the Upper Chalky (Old Drift) Boulder Clay, which implies an Upper Palaeolithic dating for the New Drift (Moir, 1920, p. 135).

4. In deposits of the Interstadial Period (W_1/W_2) near March, Cambridgeshire, Upper Palaeolithic and Late Levalloisean[1] material has been described by Baden-Powell (1934, p. 216), and definite Upper Palaeolithic tools are known from the interstadial gravels at Elfleda House, near Cambridge (Marr, 1919, pp. 222–4 and p. 242). These beds are described on p. 267.

5. From the interstadial raised beach at Morston, Norfolk (see p. 30), Aurignacian and Late Levallois type implements have been recovered (Solomon, 1931, p. 275). Likewise Armstrong has described rolled Aurignacian artifacts from a raised beach, ± 50 feet above O.D., at Hardwick Hill, on the east side of the Trent Valley, Lincolnshire (1932 [*a*], p. 130)—this beach was probably formed during the March-Nar submergence, although possibly it dates from the last glacial maximum. In any case Upper Palaeolithic man was in this region, as well as at Morston, prior to the last ice-advance.

6. Near Ipswich, Suffolk, in the Valley of the River Gipping, Aurignacian and Proto-Solutrean levels are overlain by hillwash deposits (Moir,

[1] In part contemporary with Aurignacian and influenced by it.

1917, pp. 394–407), which owe their origin to solifluction contemporaneous with the last glaciation (Moir, 1917, p. 412; *B.R.G.*[*a*], p. 64).

7. At South Hunstanton, Norfolk, Upper Palaeolithic implements have been found *in situ* in the Brown Boulder Clay (Moir, 1930, pp. 366–8; 1931, p. 307; see also Boswell, 1931, p. 98; 1935, p. 367; Sandford, 1932, p. 10).

8. In the underlying gravel and extending up into the base of the Hessle Boulder Clay at several sites at Flamborough Head in Eastern Yorkshire, Burchell has discovered Late Levallois and Aurignacian implements (1930, pp. 374–80; 1930 [*a*], p. 226; 1931, p. 267).

9. In Late-Glacial deposits overlying Layer 5 at Kirmington, Lincolnshire (Burchell, 1931 [*a*], p. 264; 1933, p. 286), artifacts of Upper Palaeolithic type occur (see p. 31 for the Kirmington section). Similar material is known from a corresponding horizon at other sites in the region of the Humber Estuary (Burchell and Moir, 1935, pp. 130–2).

10. At Creswell Crags, Derbyshire, there is a sequence from Mousterian through the Mesolithic Period (Garrod, 1926, pp. 122–50). This site, the type station for the Upper Palaeolithic of Britain, is south of the end-moraine of the last ice, but inside the area covered by the Old Drift.

11. At the key site for the Late-Glacial stratigraphy in relation to Upper Palaeolithic development in England—Pin Hole Cave, Creswell Crags—the following section has been established for the upper portion of the deposit by Armstrong (1931, p. 332):

<table>
<tr><th colspan="2">STRATIGRAPHY
(after Armstrong)</th><th>CULTURE
(after Armstrong)</th><th>INTERPRETATION</th></tr>
<tr><td>(*c*) Stalagmite</td><td colspan="2">Sterile (prolonged cold period)</td><td rowspan="2">New Drift Glaciation (Würm II)</td></tr>
<tr><td rowspan="3">(*b*) Upper Cave Earth</td><td>3. Upper Zone (cold fauna)</td><td>Developed Aurignacian (Magdalenian in Age)</td></tr>
<tr><td>2. Intermediate Zone (temperate fauna)</td><td>Font Robert Level
Upper Aurignacian and Proto-Solutrean</td><td>Interstadial Period</td></tr>
<tr><td>1. Basal Zone (cold fauna)</td><td>Late Mousterian</td><td>Retreat of the Old Drift Ice</td></tr>
<tr><td>(*a*) Slab Layer</td><td colspan="2">Sterile (intense cold)
(Würm II according to Armstrong)</td><td>Old Drift Glaciation (Würm I)</td></tr>
</table>

The above correlation is confirmed by the evidence from the other British sites mentioned in this chapter. Deposit (*a*), a slab layer, was formed during glacial conditions (Armstrong, 1931, p. 331); this certainly corresponds to the Old Drift Glaciation, when the area was covered with ice. During the following Interstadial Period (W_1/W_2) the cave was reoccupied first by Late Mousterian and then by Upper Palaeolithic man until the maximum of the New Drift Glaciation. Since the site lies south of the end-moraine of this ice-sheet (see Fig. 5), the interpretation is in accord with the geological facts.

12. All of the Late Upper Palaeolithic stations of Britain—Hoyles Mouth, Pembrokeshire (Garrod, 1926, pp. 70–5); Monkton, near Pembroke (Grimes, 1932, p. 382); Avelines Hole, Somerset (Garrod, 1926, pp. 80–90); Cheddar, Somerset (*ibid.* pp. 90–7); Kents Cavern, South Devon (*ibid.* pp. 25–47); Wangford Warren, Norfolk (*ibid.* pp. 185–6; Halling, Kent (*ibid.* pp. 161–7); Sheffields Hill, Lincolnshire (Armstrong, 1931[*a*], 1932); Willoughton and Risby Warren, Lincolnshire (Armstrong, 1932 [*a*])—lie outside the area of the New Drift.

In spite of persistent doubts concerning the authenticity of some of the finds enumerated above, the evidence is overwhelmingly in favour of a Late Palaeolithic age for the New Drift Glaciation, and an Aurignacian age for the preceding Interstadial Period. It is therefore possible to make certain deductions which are not likely to be seriously modified by further work. The Aurignacian Period in England is universally accepted to be contemporary with the Continental Aurignacian; the fact that a similar fauna is found associated with it in both areas bears out this contention. In France (Burkitt, 1933, p. 148) and Central Europe (Zeuner, 1935, pp. 367–71; 1937[*a*], pp. 37–8) the Aurignacian appears in the Würm I/II Period, which affords additional proof of the validity of the above table. In Upper Aurignacian times in England the Proto-Solutrean appears; it is found below hillwash deposits in East Anglia developed by solifluction during the last glacial maxima, and in the Intermediate Zone of the Upper Cave Earth at Pin Hole Cave, Derbyshire. The full Solutrean held sway in Western Europe at the time of the Würm II Glaciation, but England was only slightly influenced by this intrusive culture. In the latter region the Creswellian developed as an evolved Gravettian (Upper Aurignacian) facies (Garrod, 1926; 1938, p. 23); this together with the Magdalenian of the Continent witnessed the closing stages of the last ice-advance, followed by a steady amelioration of the climate, at the end of which new cultural influences penetrated Europe (Clark, 1936, p. 47).

Until recently no glacial deposit in Scotland was known to have yielded human implements (McCallien, 1937, p. 175), in spite of Ludovic Mann's claim for the presence of palaeoliths in the Pleistocene deposits of Shetland (1936, p. 512). But Professor Breuil (1937, p. 464) has at last discovered what appears to be a genuine artifact from what may represent an interstadial deposit near Comrie, Perthshire (Fig. 9, p. 66). The object is an oval flake of Levallois type. It was discovered in a sand and gravel layer overlain by boulder clay, but the age of the boulder clay is unknown. Since the ice of the Highland Glaciation advanced to a line east of Comrie (see p. 53), it may be suggested that the implement is later than the New Drift maximum. On this basis the object dates from the interval between the New Drift Glaciation and the Scottish Readvance, rather than from the Interstadial Period (W_1/W_2). The evidence for this suggestion will be presented later. Accordingly this flake is probably later than the fauna of the Midland Valley and the Burn of Benholm peat bed previously described. Thus far there are no definite human remains associated with the mammoth fauna in either Scotland or Ireland, hence it does not seem probable that during this Interstadial Period, Aurignacian man followed the retreating ice north. This may be due to the fact that Southern Scotland is singularly lacking in flint available for the manufacture of implements, but it appears more likely that the Aurignacian population of England was not sufficiently dense to render necessary a periodic migration of roving bands of hunters into this area for purposes of subsistence. Had there been a strong Aurignacian invasion of Britain the situation might have been different, since the flint region of North-East Ireland must have been ice-free and therefore available for exploitation. In spite of all the apparent improbabilities, however, Late Mousterian or even Aurignacian deposits may some day be discovered in these areas.

Essentially the same argument holds for that region of Southern Ireland which was not glaciated during the last ice-advance, on the basis of present data. Here flint occurs only very sporadically as erratics in the glacial deposits, and raw material in quantity for implements and weapons is practically lacking. Whereas it is not impossible that wandering groups of Upper Palaeolithic hunters came in during the Interstadial Period of Aurignacian times, or even later during the last ice-advance, no remains have as yet been found. Professor Charlesworth emphasizes (1928, p. 322) that the absence of Upper Palaeolithic remains in Ireland is due to the proximity of the ice-sheets, and that man was kept out by the severe environment, which must have been like that of Greenland to-day. The fact that Hoyles Mouth (Garrod, 1926, pp. 70–5) and Monkton (Grimes, 1932, p. 382), both in Pembrokeshire, were probably occupied throughout Upper Palaeolithic times in Britain would seem to indicate that additional factors must have been responsible for the absence of Upper Palaeolithic man in Ireland. It should be noted that Hoyles Mouth and Monkton are situated in a relatively small unglaciated region of South-West Wales, Fig. 5, p. 42. Rocks other than flint could have been used in Southern Ireland, but it does not seem probable that man would have left the rich flint country of South Britain and traversed the Highland Zone, to migrate to a region where the flint supply was far too meagre to encourage settlement, especially since there was no apparent pressure to force him to leave his peripheral habitat. Even in the Mesolithic, when such pressure did exist, there was no settlement except on the Antrim and Down coasts and in the Lower Bann Valley; on the basis of existing data, it was not until Neolithic times that Southern and Central Ireland were occupied.

8. THE RECESSION OF THE LAST ICE-SHEETS

(Appendix IV)

When actual retreat began the confluent ice-sheets which advanced to the York Line and the Southern Irish End-Moraine during the New Drift Glaciation did not withdraw uniformly to their respective centres of dispersal. Careful and detailed research in the key glaciated areas has led to the recognition of phenomena which mark prolonged halts and even major periods of readvance along the ice-fronts as they receded stepwise towards the north. These stages, which break up the recession into three periods of retreat, are of the utmost importance not only for establishing a basis for correlating similar events in Ireland, England and Scotland, but also for fitting the Late-Glacial chronology of these areas into the accepted and long-established North European sequence. This has a direct bearing on the Irish Stone Age. It fixes a maximum date for occupation in over three-quarters of the country, and it substantiates the Post-Glacial chronology which in turn provides the background for the Mesolithic Period in Ireland. It is proposed to present here in the text only a brief summary of the most important Late-Glacial events which have led to the definition of the three retreat stages mentioned above. Appendix IV, which contains the documented evidence on which this summary is based, will be found on p. 273; it includes a complete account of the writer's conclusions regarding the period under consideration and may be read by the specialist quite independently of the material presented below.

Everywhere along the ice-fronts, even during the period of maximum advance, oscillations occurred. Neither these nor the minor pulsations, which have been recorded for the recession, seem to be of direct importance, however, for establishing the chronology of the Late-Glacial Period. Hence they are not considered here. In Central and Southern Ireland the First Retreat Period was marked by the withdrawal of the Irish Sea Ice from the east coast. The Wicklow Hills, which were not glaciated at this time, acted as a pivot for the local Ivernian Ice as it receded in a series of tangential curves from the Southern Irish End-Moraine. As shown on the map, Fig. 6, a minor readvance of the Ivernian Ice during an early stage of its retreat has been documented in the Carlingford district. Varved sediments formed at this time have been counted in Silent Valley (Charlesworth, 1939, p. 270; see Fig. 9, p. 66), but until other diagrams of comparable age from other parts of Britain and Ireland are available, it is impossible to determine the position of the Carlingford Readvance in the Late-Glacial sequence by this approach. As the main retreat progressed, the Ivernian Ice split into three great lobes which issued from the mountains of Donegal, Leitrim, Mayo and Galway. In the region of the Central Plains the first halt took place. This is indicated by the extensive moraines and other marginal deposits which have been traced from Virginia, Kells and Navan in County Meath, to Kinnegad, County Kildare, Tyrrellspass, County Westmeath, the Shannon Valley north-west of Cloghan, County Offaly and thence to the sea at the head of Galway Bay (Fig. 6). In County Meath on the west there is evidence suggesting that a readvance occurred.

In England the main movements during the First Retreat Period were towards the north and west. The phenomena connected with the withdrawal of the Cheviot, Scottish, Lake District and Irish Sea Ice-Sheets have been worked out in great detail. This stage, which witnessed the disappearance of the Scandinavian Ice from its position off the east coast of Britain, forms part of Episode 2 in the Late-Glacial sequence of Northern England (see p. 31).

At this time a temperate climate prevailed in the ice-free area, but as the direct result of the return of Arctic conditions, the ice readvanced. This event is known as the Scottish Readvance, and it may be correlated with the Pommeranian stage of Northern Europe and Würm III in the Alps (Boswell, 1936, p. 159; Zeuner, 1937, p. 139). The glaciers responsible for this reinvasion of Northern England came from the Southern Uplands of Scotland; as shown on the map, Fig. 6, it completely covered the Carlisle Plain with ice. At St Bees in Cumberland (Fig. 9) a peat bed formed during the First Retreat Period is overlain by Scottish Readvance drift. The flora identified from the peat suggests a climate similar to that of the present day in the Lake District. A second important section is recorded at Holmpton (Fig. 9) on the Holderness coast. Here a temperate peat deposit of the same age as the St Bees layer and resting on Hessle Boulder Clay (New Drift) is overlain by an Arctic bed dating from the time of the Scottish Readvance. Thus this glacial episode must have been accompanied by a severe climatic oscillation in order to explain the abrupt change in the flora of a region approximately 150 miles away from the ice-front. At Botcherby, near Carlisle (Fig. 9), a deposit of laminated clay overlain by drift of the Scottish Readvance has been studied by De Geer. Fifty-nine varves are present, but since varves of comparable age are unknown in Northern Europe, it is impossible to date the Botcherby series. At several other sites in the same region Pre-Scottish Readvance varved clays have also been discovered.

From the Cumberland coast the line of the Scottish Readvance swings across the Irish Sea via the northern plain of the Isle of Man. It reappears in North-East Ireland on the coast of County Down (Fig. 6). During the First Retreat Period the ice from Scotland withdrew from both these areas, but with the return to Arctic conditions, partial glaciation resulted. The north-eastern coast of Ireland was completely overridden, as shown on the map, and ice-dammed lakes were formed in all the principal Antrim Glens. The varved sediments laid down by Glacial Lake Belfast have been counted by Charlesworth (1939, p. 270) at Martin's Brickyard near Belfast (Fig. 9), but the diagram has not been compared with other records of the same period in neighbouring regions. At this time the Scottish Ice did not establish contact with the local Ivernian Ice, which had receded to a line west of Armagh and Londonderry (see Fig. 6). As Charlesworth has suggested (1928, p. 341), it seems very probable that the Central Plains Moraines represent

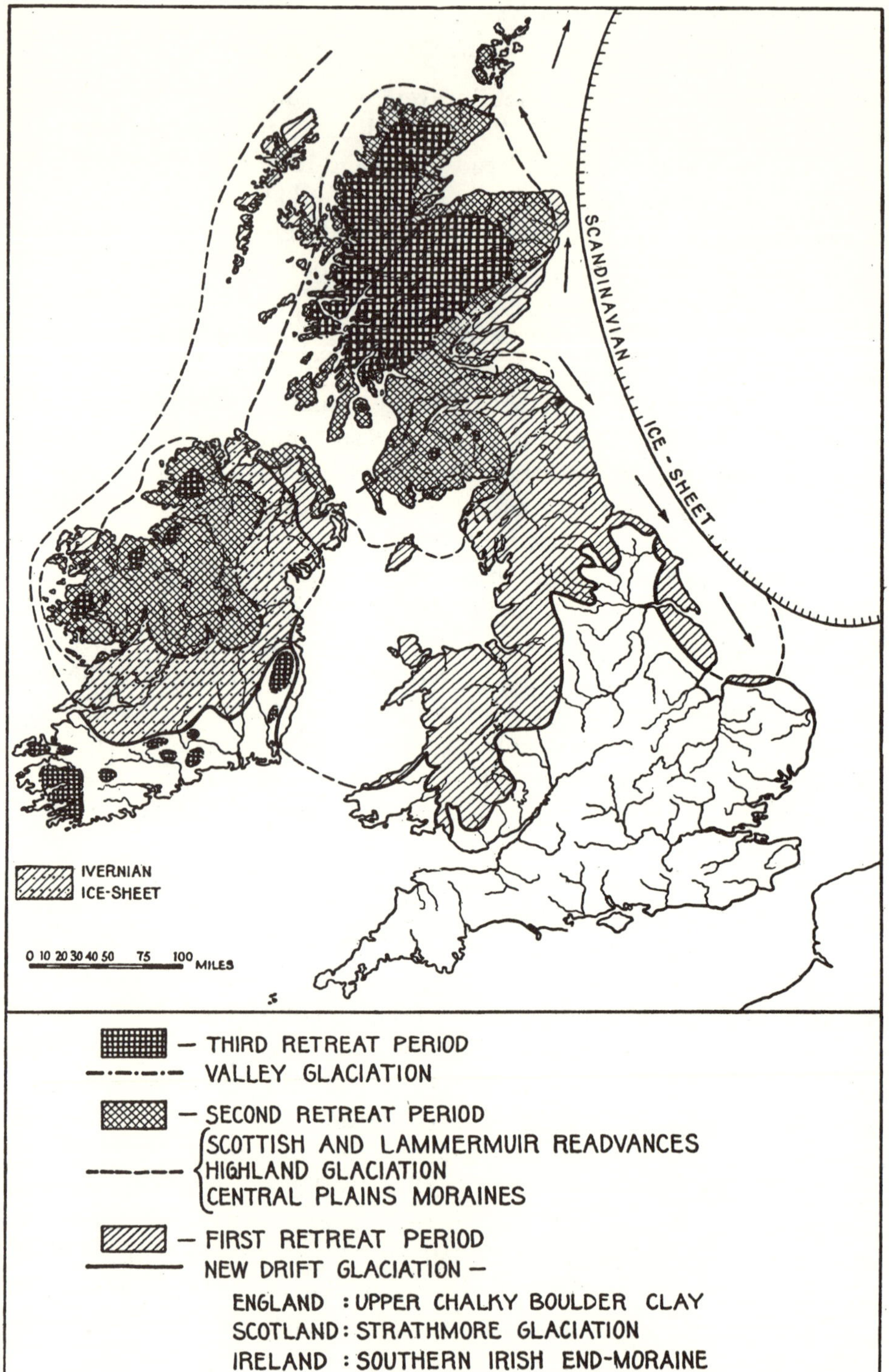

Fig. 6. The New Drift Glaciation of Britain and Ireland and the Stages in the Retreat of the Last Ice-Sheets.

the extent of the Ivernian Ice-Sheets at the time of the Scottish Readvance of North-East Ireland, North-West England and the Isle of Man.

In North-Eastern England and South-Western Scotland there is no evidence demonstrating the presence of ice during the time of the Scottish Readvance on the Carlislé Plain. Actually the limit of this ice from the Southern Uplands has not been traced north of Brampton in Cumberland, but the absence of ice in the Cheviots indicates that during this period this section was ice-free. The limits of the Highland Ice, however, are fixed by the Lammermuir-Stranraer Readvance Moraine. In South-Western Scotland this ice was confluent with the Southern Uplands Glaciers except on the north (see map, Fig. 6). Moraines in the vicinity of St Abbs Head in the east may be traced via the northern flanks of the Lammermuir Hills and connected with similar moraines near Stranraer and in the Rhinns of Galloway region on the west. In Southern Ayrshire there is a break resulting from union with the Southern Uplands Ice. The Lammermuir-Stranraer Moraine therefore marks the position of the Highland Ice at the time of the Scottish Readvance in Northern England.

North of the Midland Valley of Scotland this event is known as the Highland Glaciation. As shown on the map (Fig. 6), the extent of the Highland Ice during this stage is well established in Eastern Scotland. The main movement in this area was from west to east, and the ice was still sufficiently powerful to reach the sea at several places. It is probable that the Stone Age implement found by Breuil near Comrie (see p. 48, and Fig. 9, p. 66) comes from deposits laid down during the First Retreat Period, and that the overlying boulder clay is the age of the Highland Glaciation. At this time the Moray Firth was completely filled with ice, one-half of the Caithness Plain was glaciated and there was local ice in several islands of the Orkney, Outer and Inner Hebrides groups. In the west of Scotland the glaciers were in contact with the sea, which was also the case in certain unglaciated sections along the east coast.

The data presented thus far seem to indicate fairly conclusively that, following the First Retreat stage of the ice-sheets responsible for the New Drift Glaciation, a major halt or even a readvance occurred. In Britain and Ireland this is represented by (*a*) the Central Plain End-Moraine of Ireland; (*b*) the Scottish Readvance of North-East Ireland, the Isle of Man and Cumberland; (*c*) the Lammermuir-Stranraer Readvance of Southern Scotland and (*d*) the Highland Glaciation of Central and Northern Scotland

—all of which may be considered contemporary, although the maxima may not be precisely synchronous in each case.

The final withdrawal of the Scottish Ice from the North-East Irish coast occurred during the Second Retreat Period. At the same time the three lobes of the Ivernian Ice split up and receded from the Central Plains to the mountains of North-Western Ireland, Mayo and Connemara. In the Sperrin Mountains of County Londonderry five stages of retreat have been recognized, each marking an oscillation of the ice-front. By the end of this period the major portion of Ireland was free of ice, but before its final disappearance Arctic conditions returned temporarily, causing the last phase of glaciation. This is known as the Valley Glaciation stage. In Galway, where there is good evidence for a readvance at this time, the ice was centred in the mountains of Connemara. Small corrie glaciers existed in the Ox Mountains of Mayo, and in Donegal and Sligo similar conditions pertained. That a marked climatic oscillation occurred along with this event is confirmed by the palaeobotanical data presented in Section 11 of this chapter (pp. 65–69).

The last ice-advance in Wicklow may be assigned to the period of Valley Glaciation recognized in the mountains of Northern and Western Ireland. Intensive work on the Late-Glacial stratigraphy of the Wicklow region has revealed that the most recent maximum of the Wicklow Ice was subsequent to the retreat of the three Ivernian lobes from the Central Plains. This fact has been substantiated by palaeobotany, which proves that the same oscillation which coincides with the final glacial episode in the mountains of Galway, Mayo, Sligo and Donegal may be even more directly correlated with the strictly local glaciation in Wicklow (see Section 11). Furthermore, although absolute proof is lacking, it seems probable that the last glacial phase in South-West Ireland, which was centred south of Macgillicuddy's Reeks in County Kerry, may also be referred to this period. Other mountainous regions in Southern Ireland which appear to have supported local ice include Mount Leinster, Blackstairs Mountain, the Comeraghs, Knockmealdowns, Galtees and Boggeraghs, as well as Slievenamon. On the basis of the Wicklow evidence, it may well be that the last advance in Wales (see Appendix IV, p. 281) should be likewise assigned to the Valley Glaciation stage.

During the Second Period of Retreat the Scottish Readvance Ice withdrew from the Carlisle Plain in Cumberland. As in the Sperrin Mountains, five minor recessional stages have been recognized in the Southern Uplands of Scotland, the most important of which—the Kircowan stage (Fig. 6)—marks a slight readvance. The counterpart of this oscillation in the case of the Highland Ice has also been recorded, and it is represented by the Pentland-Carstairs-Maybole Moraine, also shown on the map (Fig. 6). This was formed during the retreat following the Lammermuir-Stranraer Readvance. Subsequently the ice-sheet of Highland origin split up into local glaciers as it receded in stepwise fashion into the mountains. In both Scotland and Ireland therefore during the Second Retreat Period a number of minor oscillations took place along the margin of the ice-front. Lacustrine sediments at Corstorphine, near Edinburgh (Fig. 9, p. 66), formed at this time have yielded a Late-Glacial fauna (Irish Elk and Arctic Lemming) associated with an Arctic flora. At a second site of this period—Portobello, also near Edinburgh (Fig. 9)—remains of Wolf have been found in marine deposits. The documentation on these important localities is given in Appendix IV, p. 282. During the period of Valley Glaciation only small corries existed in the Southern Uplands of Scotland.

North of the Scottish Midland Valley and in much of Eastern Scotland the ice retreated into the mountains in a general westerly or north-westerly direction. At several localities it has been demonstrated that as the movement advanced away from the coast, the land was transgressed by the Late-Glacial Sea. The Valley Glaciation of Scotland was more severe than elsewhere in Britain and Ireland, and it marks the last glacial episode in that region. In every Highland glen and strath there are moraines showing the limits of the ice at this period when a halt or even a minor readvance occurred. As shown on the map, Fig. 6, nearly all the land bordering on the Highlands above +1250 feet O.D. seems to have been covered by ice. Only in the valleys did the glaciers descend to lower levels. In the Loch Lomond depression and the Upper Forth Valley there is clear evidence for a readvance at this time. These stages are contemporaneous and may be equated with the Valley Glaciation of Scotland. In the north-western and western portions of the area this stage is likewise documented. Along much of the coast the ice was in contact with the Late-Glacial Sea, and, as stated in Section 9, the moraines are in many cases associated with contemporary high-level raised beaches. It seems fairly evident from the excavations in the Reindeer Cave, near Assynt in Sutherland (Fig. 9, p. 66), that man had already temporarily occupied the north of Scotland during the Second Retreat Period prior to the Valley Glaciation stage (see pp. 71–73).

By the end of the Third Retreat Period the ice was completely melted. During the final waning of the glaciers the erosion of corries was active, and in many regions numerous ice-dammed lakes were formed. As will be presently discussed, the Post-Glacial forests became established in Britain and Ireland at an early stage during this recession.

The data presented in this section can best be outlined in tabular form, Table 3. In Britain and Ireland the last ice-sheet receded in three clearly

TABLE 3. Tentative Chronology of the Recession of the Last Ice-Sheets in Britain and Ireland

GREAT BRITAIN	IRELAND
By the end of this period the ice was completely melted **Third Retreat** BEGINNING OF POST-GLACIAL PERIOD	**Third Retreat**
VALLEY GLACIATION MINOR READVANCE OF HIGHLAND ICE 1. Loch Lomond and Upper Forth Valley Stages 2. Local Corrie Glaciers in Southern Uplands 3. Glaciation (?) in the Mountains of Wales	VALLEY GLACIATION LOCAL GLACIATION IN MOUNTAINS: Donegal, Sligo, Leitrim, Mayo, Galway, Wicklow, Kerry, and the principal ranges of Southern Ireland
Second Retreat Moraines of the Central Lowlands of Scotland 1. Pentland—Carstairs—Maybole Moraine 2. Kircowan Stage of the Southern Uplands	**Second Retreat** Withdrawal of Ice from Central Plains and North-East Ireland Five Stages in Sperrin Mountains
SCOTTISH READVANCE HIGHLAND GLACIATION CUMBERLAND—ISLE OF MAN—NORTH-EAST IRELAND END-MORAINE LAMMERMUIR-STRANRAER READVANCE	CENTRAL PLAINS MORAINES (Ivernian Ice in three lobes) READVANCE OF SCOTTISH ICE IN NORTH-EAST ULSTER
First Retreat Withdrawal of Ice-Sheets from England and Scandinavian Ice from the East Coast St Bees and Holmpton peats	**First Retreat** Withdrawal of Scottish Ice Recession of Ivernian Ice to Central Plains
MAXIMUM ADVANCE OF THE LAST ICE NEW DRIFT GLACIATION: YORK LINE (ENGLAND) STRATHMORE ICE-SHEET (SCOTLAND)	NEW DRIFT GLACIATION (Southern Irish End-Moraine)

defined, major stages separated by two halts or even readvances in some cases; the first of these was far more severe than the second. The beginning of the Third Retreat stage was synchronous with the end of the Late-Glacial Period, or conversely, Post-Glacial time commenced after the last readvance. The evidence on which this statement is based is discussed on pp. 65–69.

9. DEPOSITS OF THE LATE-GLACIAL SEA

(Appendix V)

As a result of the basining of the land under the weight of the last ice-sheet, high-level marine beaches and wave-cut platforms were formed contemporaneously with the later stages of the glacial retreat. The distribution of these beaches, shown on the map (Fig. 7), reveals the isobases of the depression caused by the last ice as they are known at present. Ranging from 50 feet above sea-level in North-East Ireland and South-West Scotland, these ancient strand-lines converge on Colonsay, where huge shingle beaches have been recorded at a height of 135 feet above O.D. (Wright, 1911, p. 100). According to Wright, this very high beach is confined to Mull, Islay, Colonsay and the Treshnish Islands. Hitherto this plain of marine erosion has been considered "Pre-Glacial", its surface being everywhere ice-moulded and in some cases striated and covered with boulder clay. As pointed out on p. 279, however, the glaciation responsible for the overriding of the 135-foot beach was almost certainly the Scottish Readvance or Highland Glaciation, hence the high-level beaches of the Western Isles of Scotland are Late-Glacial in age. Simpson's work in the Perth region conclusively proves that the Late-Glacial Sea was present at this stage (1933, p. 635), since the Perth Readvance reached the then-existing sea between Methven and Crieff during the Highland Glaciation (Appendix IV, p. 278). Furthermore, near Kilwinning, North Ayrshire, the raised beach is absent above 40 feet O.D., and it is cut into glacial deposits at this height (*M.G.S.* Scotland, 1930, p. 342). Since there is abundant evidence elsewhere in Ayrshire for a 100-foot raised beach at this period (see Appendix V), this fact indicates that it was the ice of the Highland Glaciation which prevented the sea from cutting platforms at higher levels, as Ayrshire was ice-free after the Second Retreat Period. On the other hand, it is perfectly clear that in the lochs of the west coast of Scotland the Late-Glacial Sea was contemporary with the much later Valley or Moraine Glaciation (Wright, 1937, p. 373; McCallien, 1937, p. 190) for the following reasons: (1) Late-Glacial raised beach deposits merge into or are buried beneath fluvio-glacial sands and gravels formed by the melt-waters of the valley glaciers; (2) raised beach deposits are entirely absent in many large lochs, although they are present in neighbouring smaller valleys, since the large valleys were filled with ice at that time, which excluded the sea; and (3) the Late-Glacial raised

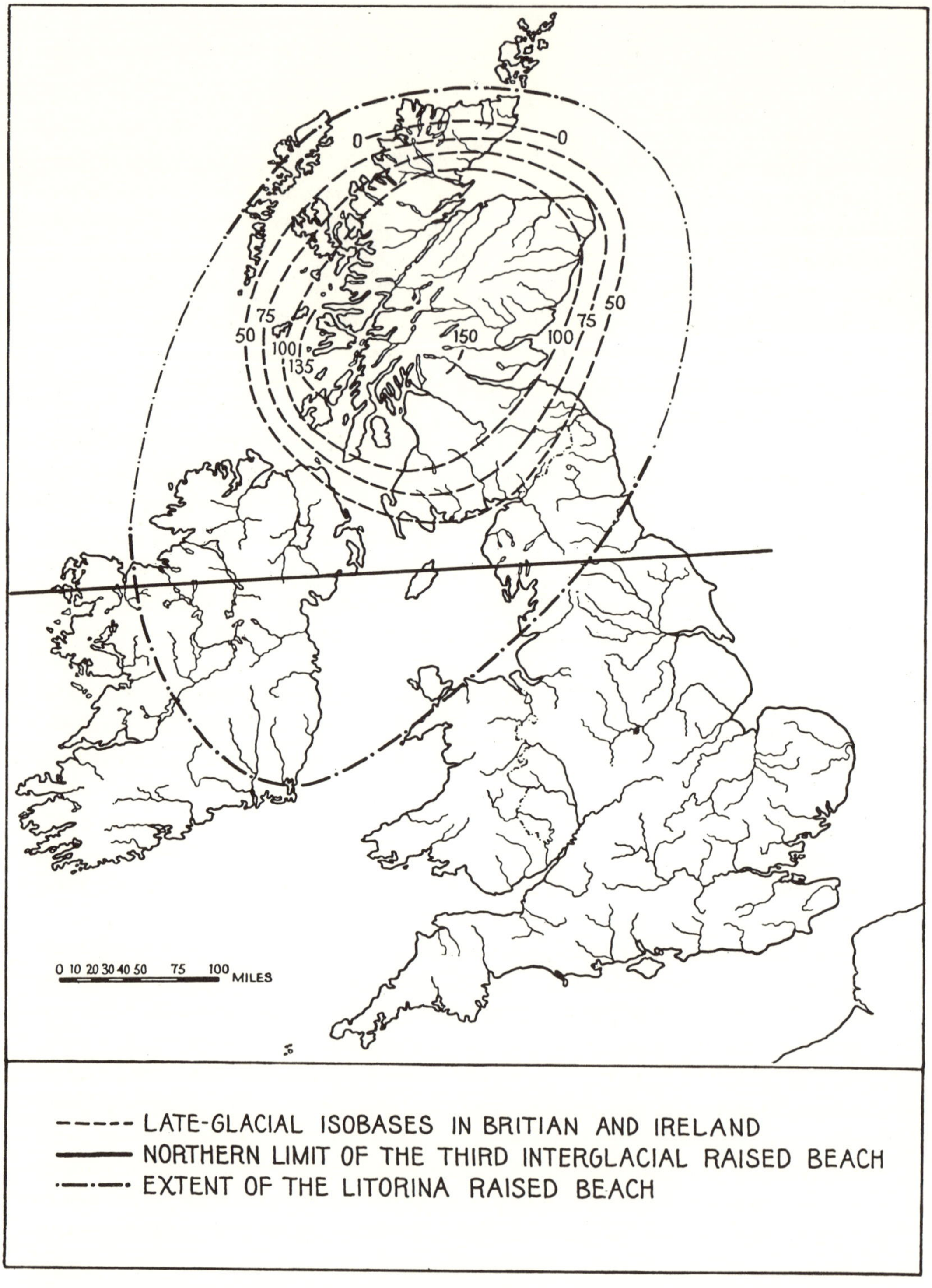

Fig. 7. Late-Glacial and Early Post-Glacial Isobases in Britain and Ireland. (Based in part on Wright, 1937, Fig. 127.)

beaches are often absent in the upper part of the Highland Valleys, but present in the lower part. Thus the Late-Glacial Sea seems to have appeared at two different periods. Actually, immediately following the glacial retreat, it transgressed the land, which was depressed under the weight of the ice. *It may be correlated with that particular stage in the recession during which the region where it occurs became ice-free.* In other words the sea invaded the land, which was basined as a result of isostatic factors connected with the weight of the ice-load, as soon as the ice receded from the coast. Thus Late-Glacial raised beaches are not necessarily the same age in all parts of the country, but since their relation to the various stages in the retreat of the last ice is so little known, they must be considered as being more or less contemporary. As long as this point is clearly understood the heights of the Late-Glacial sea beaches may be discussed, because irrespective of age they show the extent of uplift which has taken place since the Late-Glacial Period. For the immediate purpose of fixing the isobases of the depression, these raised beach deposits may be considered synchronous.

In Appendix V the detailed material on which the following statements are based will be found. The region best documented from the point of view of the distribution of Late-Glacial raised beaches and associated deposits in Britain and Ireland is Scotland, but further research in North-West Ireland should reveal important data. On the basis of present evidence this beach is found 50 feet above present sea-level in Southern Scotland and North-East Ireland, but northward in Ayrshire as well as along the east coast this marine terrace is found at progressively higher levels up to 100 feet above the sea. In the Forth Valley above Stirling, Dinham (1927, p. 488) reports that inland the height of the raised beach increases in excess of this figure, since at the head of the valley it occurs at +155 feet, whereas near Stirling itself it is found at the 100-foot level. This shows that the greatest amount of recoil or uplift has taken place in the Highlands—near the main centre of ice-dispersal during Late-Glacial times. Evidence of this nature is, however, difficult to obtain, because in most cases the sea which formed these strand-lines was excluded from the upper reaches of the Scottish lochs, especially on the west, due to the presence of ice. But platforms at progressively lower levels are frequently found marking stages in the recovery of the land after the retreat of the ice. In North-East Scotland the raised beach occurs at 100 feet above present sea-level; in Sutherland its elevation decreases to 75 feet, and in the extreme north—Caithness and the Orkneys—this feature is absent. Thus the o-isobase has been established here as shown in Fig. 7.

That the mutual relations between land and sea after the retreat of the ice in Late-Glacial times differed from the present is further attested in Scotland by extensive deposits of marine clays. Especially fine sections occur in the Clyde, Forth and Tay Estuaries. In addition to typical "cold" molluscs, including *Cyprina islandica*, *Astarte borealis*, *Yoldia norvegica* and *Tellina calcarea*, these deposits frequently yield Arctic Seal remains. It seems reasonably clear that the period of submergence responsible for the deposition of these clays, as well as the formation of the Late-Glacial raised beaches, is the British and Irish counterpart of the Yoldia Sea of the Baltic. In both cases contemporaneity with the later stages in the retreat of the ice may be demonstrated.

10. CORRELATIONS WITH FENNOSCANDIA

In spite of many difficulties, it seems obvious that connections between the phenomena relating to the retreat of the last ice in Britain and Ireland on the one hand and Fennoscandia on the other must exist. Events of the magnitude of those described in this chapter cannot have been purely local; they must have extended over a much larger region. Previous attempts to correlate Late-Glacial episodes in these two regions are, however, somewhat difficult to follow (compare Brooks, 1917; Osborn and Reeds, 1922). The late Dr W. B. Wright (1937, p. 458) proposed a basis on which the British and Continental successions may be compared, but in spite of the fact that the Scottish Readvance has been recognized for almost ten years (see p. 26; also Boswell, 1932, p. 88; Zeuner, 1938, p. 36), Wright did not consider it to be of major importance. The most satisfactory data have been suggested by Charlesworth (1931, pp. 76–8), and on his tentative reconstruction of some of the ice-margins in Britain, Ireland and Northern Europe, a part of the following correlation is based. This scheme has also been followed by McCallien (1937, p. 193). The critical facts enumerated below, and the map (Fig. 8), will perhaps help to clarify the situation and afford a provisional basis for comparison between the areas in question.

1. It has been shown above that the New Drift in England, marked by the York Line, and in Ireland indicated by the Southern Irish End-Moraine, is of the same period, and that the Upper Diluvium of the last ice, laid down

important. Likewise in North-Western Ireland five oscillations occurred during this stage in the recession of the ice. The association of these phenomena, some of which mark readvances, with the Second Retreat Period in three separate regions would seem to be more than pure coincidence.

7. The Fennoscandian Moraine marks the end of the second stage of the retreat in the Baltic. In Scotland the Valley Glaciation indicates a halt or even a slight readvance of the ice at this time, and in Ireland local ice was present in the principal mountain ranges, especially in the north-west and Counties Wicklow and Kerry.

8. The Late-Glacial Sea of Scotland and Ireland was synchronous with the Highland Glaciation and later with the Valley Glaciation. This forms the counterpart of the Baltic Ice-Lake and the Yoldia Sea. The Late-Glacial Sea was caused by isostatic and eustatic factors; it transgressed the land as soon as the present coast was ice-free. In many Highland fjords the sea was in contact with the ice-front, paralleling the history of the early water bodies in the Baltic. Similarity in all respects with regard to this marine transgression therefore strengthens the argument for the contemporaneity of the two areas.

9. The Finiglacial Period witnessed the withdrawal of the ice to Ragunda in Sweden, and the final melting of the British and Irish Ice-Sheets. With the beginning of this retreat period the Post-Glacial forests established themselves in the Baltic, Britain and Ireland.

The available Late-Glacial geological data have now been summarized, and they are set out on the accompanying chart (Table 4). Although much field work remains to be done, the material from Ireland and Britain published to date offers a plausible basis for fitting the chronology of this area into that of Fennoscandia. There the chronology has long been established as the result of very thorough and conclusive investigations over many years. Whether world-wide pulsations of climate do, or do not, exist is outside the scope of this book, but it is not surprising to find such a close degree of correlation between these neighbouring regions of North-West Europe. It is hoped that this attempt to assemble the English and Irish material will lead to further research directed towards filling in the obvious gaps. Much of the old work needs rechecking in the light of modern knowledge. For our present purposes, however, there are adequate data on which to build a framework, and with this framework satisfactorily established, the archaeological facts may be more readily understood. Furthermore, since Northern Ireland was covered with ice during Late-Glacial times, the explanation for the apparent absence of Late Upper Palaeolithic remains in this region, as well as for the earliest possible date of occupation, now becomes clear.

TABLE 4. Late-Glacial and Early Post-Glacial Chronology in Northern and Western Europe

APPROXIMATE DATES (after De Geer)	PERIODS	FENNOSCANDIA	WATER BODIES IN THE BALTIC	BRITAIN	IRELAND
B.C.	Post-Glacial	FINAL STADIUM Ice at Ragunda	ANCYLUS LAKE	By the end of this period the ice was completely melted	
6,800	Post-Glacial	FINIGLACIAL PERIOD (Bothnian Substage)	YOLDIA SEA	**Third Retreat**	**Third Retreat**
7,800	Late-Glacial	FENNOSCANDIAN END-MORAINE Inner Ra and Salpausselkä Moraines	BALTIC ICE-LAKE / LATE-GLACIAL SEA OUTSIDE BALTIC	VALLEY GLACIATION Minor Readvance of Highland Ice	VALLEY GLACIATION Local Glaciation in Mountains
8,300	Late-Glacial	GOTIGLACIAL PERIOD (Scanian Substage) Outer Ra and Salpausselkä Moraines	BALTIC ICE-LAKE / LATE-GLACIAL SEA OUTSIDE BALTIC	**Second Retreat** Moraines of the Central Lowlands, and Southern Uplands of Scotland	**Second Retreat** Recessional Moraines of North-West Ireland
				LATE-GLACIAL SEA (Third Retreat to Highland Glaciation)	
14,800	Late-Glacial	POMERANIAN STAGE BALTIC END-MORAINE (Würm III in the ALPS)		HIGHLAND GLACIATION READVANCE OF SCOTTISH ICE-SHEETS	CENTRAL PLAINS MORAINES
				Cumberland—Isle ot Man—North-East Ireland End-Moraine	
18,000	Late-Glacial	DANIGLACIAL PERIOD (German Substage)		**First Retreat**	**First Retreat**
		WEICHSEL GLACIATION BRANDENBURG END-MORAINE (Würm II in the ALPS)		NEW DRIFT GLACIATION Advance of Ice to the York Line Strathmore Glaciation of Scotland	Glaciation to the Southern Irish End-Moraine

11. LATE-GLACIAL PEATS AND LAMINATED CLAYS

The Late-Glacial peats investigated in Ireland and Britain bear a striking similarity to the established succession for Scania, Southern Norway, Denmark and Northern Germany; this supports the correlation of these regions as outlined above. In Jutland the zones into which the Late-Glacial pollen sequence is divisible, according to Jessen (1935[*a*]), are outlined on pp. 18–20, and the evidence of the Allerød oscillation (Zone II) shows that during this period the climate began to improve. But before the beginning of the Post-Glacial Pre-Boreal Period, the reappearance of *Dryas flora* in Zone III indicates that a deterioration occurred. The relation of Zones I, II and III to the stages in the recession of the last Scandinavian Ice-Sheet is made clear on the chart (Table 1, p. 23). Recently Gross (1938) has identified Allerød deposits in East Prussia, and in the Hamburg area of North-West Germany it has been possible to correlate archaeological deposits with the above succession (Clark, 1938; Gams, 1938, p. 40). The sequence established by the Meiendorf section is given by Clark, and it reveals the following horizons:

<table>
<tr><th>Stratification</th><th colspan="2">Interpretation
(based on Jessen)</th></tr>
<tr><td>7. Brushwood Peat
6. Reed Peat</td><td colspan="2">Post-Glacial
Zone IV</td></tr>
<tr><td>5. Mud with tundra flora: Arctic conditions
Early Mesolithic—Ahrensburgian Culture Layer</td><td>Zone III</td><td rowspan="3">Late-Glacial</td></tr>
<tr><td>4. Sedge Peat with pine wood: Allerød Oscillation
3. Sand: thin layer</td><td>Zone II</td></tr>
<tr><td>2. Calcareous Mud with tundra flora: Arctic conditions
Late Upper Palaeolithic—Hamburgian Culture Layer
1. Late-Glacial varved Clays</td><td>Zone I</td></tr>
</table>

In England no Allerød deposits are known at present, since the temperate peats at St Bees, Cumberland, and Holmpton, Yorkshire (see p. 51 and Fig. 9), are older. This is demonstrated by the fact that the St Bees peat layer is overlain by drift of the Scottish Readvance, and is therefore earlier than the Pomeranian stage of the Baltic. The Arctic layer at Holmpton, overlying the temperate bed, is probably to be correlated with Zone I of Northern Europe. But both these sections should be thoroughly investigated by a palaeobotanist before definite conclusions are drawn. In the meantime the above must be regarded as tentative only, although evidence from the Isle of Man, where an Allerød level occurs, indicates that the interpretation is probably correct. According to Jessen (with Farrington, 1938, p. 247), the following section has been recorded from near Ballaugh (see Fig. 9):[1]

STRATIGRAPHY	INTERPRETATION	
6. Peat	Post-Glacial	
5. Sand without fossils 4. Sandy Silt with *Salix herbacea* and *Apus glacialis*	Zone III (after Jessen)	LATE-GLACIAL
3. Loamy Peats with water plants	Zone II: Allerød Layer (after Jessen)	
2. Gravel without fossils	Scottish Readvance (see p. 51)	
1. Chara Mud with Irish Elk and water plants	First Retreat (Age of St Bees peat?)	

Thus it seems very probable that the Allerød layer (Zone II) is contemporary with the Second Retreat Period (Gotiglacial), which is in accord with the Scandinavian sequence. On this basis Zone III is the age of the Valley Glaciation of the Highlands, when the temporary return to glacial conditions resulted in the formation of the Fennoscandian End-Moraines of Northern Europe, and a second Arctic peat horizon. Following this the Post-Glacial forest development commenced.

Thus far the interpretation given for the Late-Glacial peats in England and the Isle of Man, based on existing evidence, must be regarded as somewhat speculative until checked by thorough palaeobotanical research. The same applies to Scotland, where the Late-Glacial and Early Post-Glacial peat stratigraphy has been investigated by Lewis (1905, 1906, 1907, 1910). Whereas it is possible that Lewis' Lower Forest Bed in the Southern Uplands (1905, pp. 708–9) is the equivalent of the Allerød Period of the Baltic, the sections must be carefully investigated before the evidence can be accepted. In Ireland, however, as a result of recent work by Farrington and Jessen (1938), the Late-Glacial succession has been established, and it fits the North European evidence in every respect. The standard succession has been worked out in the north-western bog at Ballybetagh, approximately

[1] C. Reid, *The Origin of the British Flora*, London, 1899. (This book was not available.)

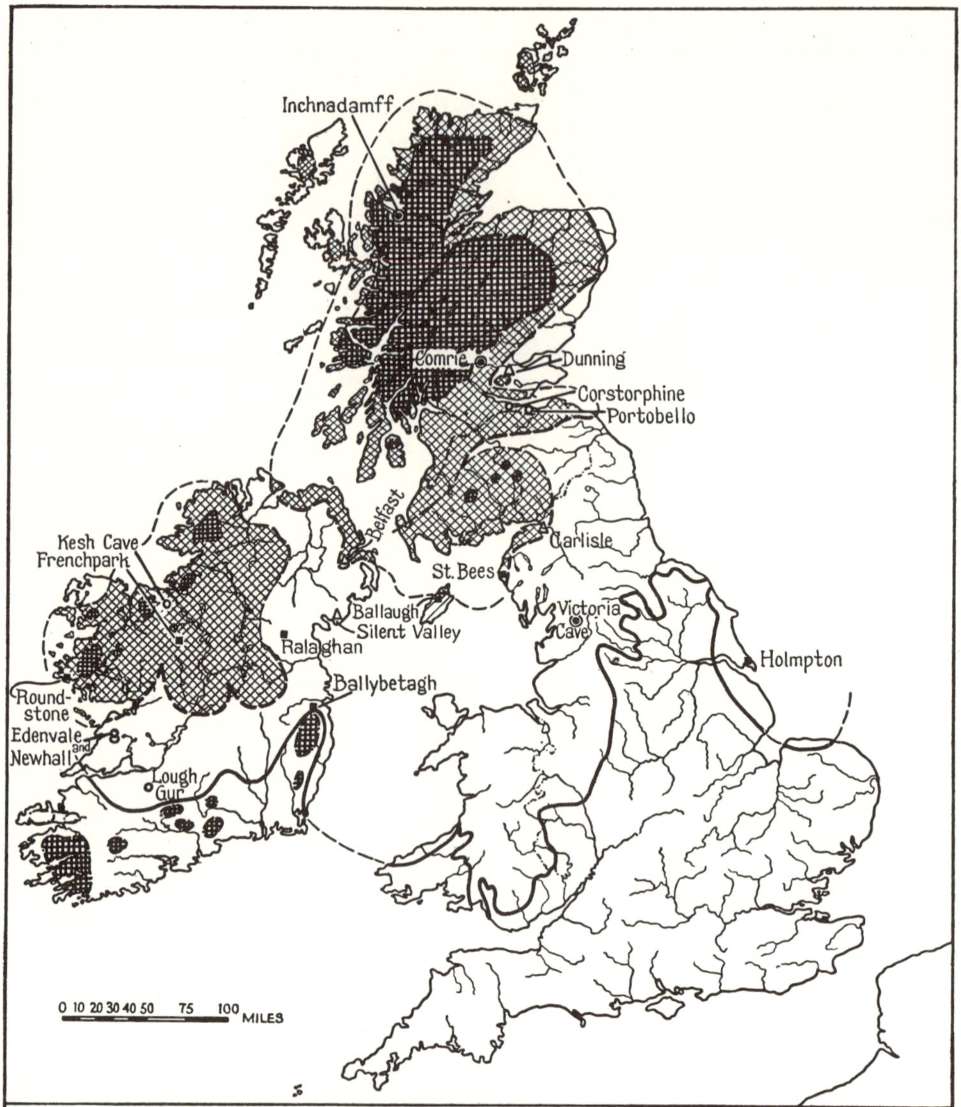

- ◦ LATE-GLACIAL FAUNA CONTEMPORARY WITH THE RETREAT OF THE LAST ICE-SHEETS
- ◉ SITES WITH ARCHAEOLOGICAL MATERIAL DATING FROM THE END OF THE GLACIAL PERIOD
- ▪ LATE-GLACIAL PEATS
- △ LATE-GLACIAL VARVED CLAYS
- —— NEW DRIFT GLACIATION

NOTE: THE RETREAT STAGES AND MORAINES ARE THE SAME AS THOSE SHOWN IN FIGURE 6.

Fig. 9. Localities contemporary with the Retreat of the Last Ice-Sheets in Britain and Ireland.

7 miles south-south-east of Dublin, shown in Fig. 9. The bogs, of which there are three, lie in a hollow between two foothills at the northern end of the Wicklow Mountains; they have been known to collectors of Irish Elk bones since 1847. Stelfox (1927, p. 781) and Erdtman (1928, p. 169) did the first palaeobotanical researches on the Ballybetagh peats, which occur at a height of approximately 750 feet O.D. According to Charlesworth (1937, p. 33), the hollow in which the bogs are situated served as a Late-Glacial overflow channel, but the original valley probably dates from an earlier period (Farrington, with Jessen[1], 1938, p. 216). This locality is 3 miles to the north of and well outside the moraines marking the last advance of the local ice in the Wicklow Mountains, which occurred at a later period than the maximum of the New Drift Glaciation (see p. 54). The latter invaded the region and its moraines are present near Ballybetagh at a height of 1000 feet O.D.

According to Farrington and Jessen (1938, p. 213, and pp. 217–21), the following section has been established for the north-western bog at Ballybetagh:

Stratigraphy		Interpretation (after Jessen)	
6. Layers A–C	Post-Glacial Peat	Zones V and VI	Post-Glacial
5. Layer D	Light-Brown Chara Mud	Zone IV	Post-Glacial
4. Layer E	Alternating layers of grey clayey sand and stony clay, showing the effect of solifluction Sub-Arctic flora: rich in herbaceous plants, *Salix herbacea* and *Oxyria digyna*	Zone III	Late-Glacial
3. Layer F	Light Yellow Mud Valley filled with a small lake Irish Elk and Reindeer Woody plants: *Betula, Salix, Juniperus* and *Empetrum*. Stomata of *Pinus*, herbs and ferns *Myriophyllum verticillatum* and *Potamogeton*	Zone II	Late-Glacial
2. Layer G	Solifluction Earth: Arctic conditions	Zone I	Late-Glacial
1. Layer H	Undisturbed Boulder Clay	New Drift	

[1] Cited hereafter under the individual author quoted—i.e. (Jessen, 1938) or (Farrington, 1938).

Thus after a long period without solifluction (Zone II) there was a return to an Arctic-Alpine climate. Jessen states (1938, p. 222) that the Post-Glacial Period begins at the cessation of the solifluction layer (Zone III) causing the formation of Layer E. That a marked amelioration in the climate occurred in Zone II is shown by the flora as well as by the insect remains from this horizon, which includes the beetle *Calathus cisteloides*. The appearance of such a remarkably southern form in a Late-Glacial bed suggests comparison with the Allerød Period of the Baltic, according to Jessen (1938, p. 241). Now Layer E (Zone III) is contemporary with the last glaciation of the Wicklow Mountains (Farrington and Jessen, 1938, p. 245). Therefore the climate improved considerably between the retreat of the New Drift Ice from the region and the advance of the Valley Glaciers. Evidence from elsewhere in Ireland given below indicates that the comparatively warm deposits, represented by Zone II, were formed during the latter part of the Second Retreat Period. Hence the last Wicklow advance must be of the same age as the Valley Glaciation of North-West Ireland.

As well as at Ballybetagh, a succession of alternating mud and clay layers has been found in three other Irish bogs: Ralaghan, County Cavan; Frenchpark, County Roscommon; and Roundstone, County Galway (Farrington and Jessen, 1938, pp. 242–4). The locations of these sites with respect to the stages in the retreat of the last ice-sheets is given in Fig. 9. The examination of the material from Frenchpark and Roundstone is not yet complete, but it will be noted that both lie within the area covered by ice until after the Second Retreat Period. Roundstone is on the coast and was unglaciated at an early stage during this period; Frenchpark on the other hand falls within the area glaciated by ice from Leitrim, but during this stage the Leitrim Lobe appears to have withdrawn comparatively fast (Charlesworth, 1928, p. 340). Thus the Late-Glacial bog development at both these sites probably commenced at approximately the same time as at Ballybetagh. The succession at Ralaghan, situated just outside the Central Plains Moraines approximately 4 miles north-east of Bailieborough, is very similar to Ballybetagh with the exception that Layer G (Zone I) is composed of clay at the former locality. The section is given on p. 69 (Farrington and Jessen, 1938, pp. 242–4).

Here there is evidence for one period of amelioration, Layer F, and one of deterioration, the solifluction deposit, Layer E, before Post-Glacial conditions were established, confirming the Ballybetagh sequence. As Jessen points out, Zone III at Ralaghan, Frenchpark and Roundstone must be the same age as Zone III at Ballybetagh (1938, p. 246). Now it has been shown that at the latter locality Zone III is synchronous with the last glaciation of Wicklow, an event which occurred subsequent to the recession of the Ivernian Ice from the Central Plains (see p. 280). Since the Frenchpark and Roundstone bogs are both situated behind the Central Plains Moraines, the deposition of polleniferous layers at these sites could not have begun until during

Stratigraphy		Interpretation (after Jessen)	
6. Layers A–C	Post-Glacial Peat	Zones V and VI	Post-Glacial
5. Layer D	Olive-Brown Mud	Zone IV	
4. Layer E	Clayey and stony layer Arctic conditions Solifluction deposit Arctic-alpine flora with *Salix hervacea*	Zone III	Late-Glacial
3. Layer F	Brown Mud with Clay Flora of northern type including *Pinus sylvestris*	Zone II	
2. Layer G	Grey Lacustrine Clay Late-Glacial lake deposit Arctic conditions	Zone I	
1. Layer H	Boulder Clay	New Drift	

the Second Retreat Period. If Zone III at these localities should be younger than the Ballybetagh Zone III, one would expect evidence for a deterioration in the climate for a second time in Zone IV at Ballybetagh; according to Jessen, there is no indication of this. The data point to a conclusion, expressed elsewhere, that Zone III was formed during the Valley Glaciation stage, and that the last glacial maxima in the Wicklow Mountains is of this age.[1]

[1] Mr Mitchell's recent investigations in the large bog partly on the townland of Lagore east of the village of Dunshaughlin, ±20 miles north-west of Dublin in County Meath, have revealed the existence of Late-Glacial Zones I—III at the base of the deposits in the centre of the basin, showing the local response to the contemporary development documented at Ballybetagh (Mitchell, 1940, pp. 18–19). At Dunshaughlin, however, there is no trace of the severe solifluction in Zone III found at Ballybetagh and Ralaghan. This reflects not only the local topography, as Mitchell (1940, pp. 30–31) points out, but also the fact that this region of County Meath was far removed from the ice-front during the Valley Glaciation stage.

TABLE 5. Glacial Stages and the Climatic Development in Northern and Western Europe

APPROXIMATE DATES (after De Geer)	PERIOD	GLACIAL STAGES		ZONES	CLIMATIC PHASES (after Jessen)	
		NORTHERN EUROPE	BRITAIN AND IRELAND		NORTHERN EUROPE	IRELAND
B.C. 6,800 —	POST-GLACIAL	Ragunda: Final Stadium **Third Retreat** FINIGLACIAL PERIOD	Final melting of Ice-Sheets **Third Retreat**	IV	PRE-BOREAL Birch-Fir Period	PRE-BOREAL Birch Period
7,800 —	LATE-GLACIAL	FENNOSCANDIAN END-MORAINE	VALLEY GLACIATION Local ice in Wicklow, Donegal, Scottish Highlands, etc.	III	LATE DRYAS PERIOD Arctic Flora	SECOND SOLIFLUCTION LAYER *Salix herbacea* Zone
8,300 — 10,000 —		**Second Retreat** GOTIGLACIAL PERIOD	**Second Retreat** I←Dunning varves	II	ALLERØD LAYER Warm Oscillation	MUD *Betula pubescens* *Pinus sylvestris*
14,600 — 18,000 —		POMERANIAN STAGE BALTIC END-MORAINE (WURM III OF THE ALPS)	BRITAIN: Readvance of Scottish Ice-Sheets Highland Glaciation IRELAND: Central Plains Moraines Scottish Readvance in North-East Ulster	I	EARLY DRYAS PERIOD Arctic flora	FIRST SOLIFLUCTION LAYER and LATE-GLACIAL CLAYS Arctic flora

Palaeobotany therefore demonstrates that the Allerød deposits in Ireland must be assigned to the Second Retreat Period, which supports the view that this phase is the counterpart of the Gotiglacial Period in the Baltic. Table 5 is an attempt to synchronize the geological and palaeobotanical sequence in the areas under discussion.

Recent research on the varve clays of Scotland (De Geer, 1935, 1935[*a*]) mark the first attempt to build up a geochronological time-scale for the area (compare McCallien, 1935, p. 67), and indicates the proper method of approaching the problem of Late-Glacial and Early Post-Glacial times. The results afford almost conclusive proof that the correlation with Fennoscandia is valid. Near Dunning (see Fig. 9), in the valley of the Earn River, 7½ miles south-west of Perth, a section, discovered by Simpson (1933, p. 637) and composed of fifty-nine varves, was examined by De Geer (1935[*a*], pp. 23–6). The variation of thickness displayed by these varves is very marked, as shown in the diagram (De Geer, 1935[a], p. 25), and they compare almost exactly with the corresponding part of the curve from Lyngby, approximately 3½ miles north-north-west of Copenhagen. According to De Geer, the key varves occur at exactly equivalent intervals in the two curves which certify that the Dunning-Lyngby teleconnection is satisfactory. Thus the Dunning series dates from 4313 to 4371 years before 0 (6800 B.C.), or 11,113 to 11,171 B.C., establishing an Early Gotiglacial date for the ice at this stage, as indicated on Table 5. Such a date is in exact accord with the chronology outlined in Section 10, and provides a firm basis for comparison between Britain and the Baltic. Dunning and Lyngby, as shown on the map, Fig. 8, facing p. 60, are similarly situated with relation to end-moraines in Scotland and Denmark—the former being just outside the limits of the Highland Glaciation and the latter immediately inside the line of the ice-front during the Pomeranian stage. Since it has been demonstrated that these glacial stages are contemporary, De Geer's teleconnection must be recognized as the first step towards establishing absolute dates in Britain on the basis of the existing North European time-scale.

12. THE EARLIEST OCCUPATION OF NORTHERN BRITAIN AND IRELAND AFTER THE RETREAT OF THE ICE

At the end of the Late-Glacial Period in Britain man seems to have followed the retreating ice northward, but thus far very little has come to light to prove this point. At Victoria Cave, Yorkshire, indications of a Late Magdalenian industry have been found (Breuil, 1922, p. 275). The exact horizon of these finds, which include two fragments of points made of Reindeer antler and a bone borer (Fig. 41, p. 191), is somewhat difficult to establish, but they are probably from the upper part of the stiff grey clay which separates the upper and lower cave earths, as suggested by Professor Garrod (1926, p. 120). The stiff grey clay seems to be of glacial origin (see Appendix II, pp. 267–8), and since this site lies within the area covered by the New Drift Ice-Sheets (Fig. 9) the Magdalenian occupation could not have occurred until during the First Retreat Period. The stone implement found by Professor Breuil at Comrie may possibly date from this time, as previously mentioned (see p. 53), but from elsewhere in Northern Britain no human artifacts of this period have been recorded, with the exception of several suspicious specimens described by Breuil (1937) from Perthshire. During the Second Retreat Period, however, man appears to have settled in Northern Scotland, since excavations at the Reindeer Cave at Inchnadamff, 3 miles south of Assynt, Sutherland (see Fig. 9), have brought to light a human artifact in deposits probably referable to the Valley Glaciation (Callander, Cree and Ritchie, 1927; Cree, 1927; Ritchie, 1929). In all there are four caves in the Inchnadamff Valley, situated at the base of a limestone cliff at an elevation of ±1000 feet above sea-level. One of these, the Bone Cave, was excavated in 1889 by Drs Peach and Horne, and it is necessary to review the Bone Cave sequence in order to understand the horizon of the implement from the Reindeer Cave, since only preliminary reports on the latter are available. The following section was established by Peach and Horne (1917, pp. 338–42):

STRATIFICATION	INTERPRETATION
6. Peaty layer containing sheep excrement 5. Whitish Marl containing land snails	Recent
4. Red Clay or Cave Earth containing abundant remains of mammals and birds, including Lynx, Reindeer, Red Deer, Otter, Frog and Toad(?)	Third Retreat Period
Evidence of occupation by man: hearths and firestones, split and burnt bones, Reindeer antlers sawn off, but no implements	Early Post-Glacial
3. Fine Grey Clay containing quartzite boulders—pushed into the cave from outside by ice	Valley Glaciation
2. Limestone Fragments containing bones of mammals and birds, including Arctic Lemming, Field Vole, Rat Vole, Reindeer, Cave Bear, Ptarmigan (very numerous), Red Grouse, Ducks, Little Auk and Puffin	Second Retreat Period
1. Gravel accumulated while ice occupied the valley	Highland Glaciation

Although the accounts of the sequence in the Reindeer Cave vary somewhat in detail, the sections given by Cree (1927, pp. 219–20), Callander, Cree and Ritchie (1927, pp. 170–1) and Ritchie (1929, pp. 192–3) are very similar to the above, but Layers 5 and 6 are apparently absent. According to the excavators, the following deposits in descending order occurred in the Reindeer Cave:

4. *Upper Bone Layer*: composed of cave earth and containing mammal and bird bones of extant forms; the remains of Bear, however, indicates a considerable antiquity for this deposit. Two human artifacts—a bone awl 4 inches long, and a bone pin with a large loop at the head—were found. The pin was associated with a fragmentary "ceremonial" burial of a dolichocephalic individual who had been placed in an enclosure, formed by two flat stone slabs and the cave walls, in a small recess at the rear of the cave. It is stated that a second skeleton was discovered in this layer (Callander, Cree and Ritchie, 1927, p. 171), but the circumstances of this find are not discussed. This horizon appears to correspond to Layer 4 at the Bone Cave and to be of the same age.

3. *Intermediate Layer*: 18 inches to 2 feet of water-worn gravel washed into the cave by a marginal or surface stream composed of melt-water from a glacier, the surface of which stood at about the level of the cave's mouth. This deposit seems to be the equivalent of Layer 3 at the Bone Cave.

2. *Lower Bone Layer*: red cave earth containing fossilized bones of Reindeer, Cave Bear, Arctic Fox, Wolf, Lynx and many Arctic Rodents. The association of Cave Bear and Reindeer suggests that this deposit very probably corresponds to Layer 2 at the Bone Cave. It is after this horizon that the cave takes its name: an enormous number of shed antlers of young Reindeer were found. These were mostly broken, nevertheless they represented over 400 individual animals. Several are artificially cut, probably by man; human occupation is also attested by fragments of charcoal from this level.

1. *Basal Gravels*: deposited during the Highland Glaciation as in the case of Layer 1 at the Bone Cave.

Between the rear chamber and the front of the cave a small implement made of Reindeer antler was discovered in a layer of redeposited gravel and sand. Since this layer is of glacial origin, it probably was formed at the time of the Valley Glaciation. The implement, which is 2 inches long and displays definitely human workmanship, appears to have been associated with Reindeer antlers and remains of Cave Bear (*Ursus spelaeus*), as well as Arctic Fox (*Canis lagopus*). This together with the cut antlers and charcoal from the Lower Bone layer therefore indicates that man was in Northern Scotland in Late-Glacial times contemporary with the final glacial stages. Breuil, who has seen the find, agrees with this conclusion and has suggested to the writer that the scarcity of cultural remains, and the presence of shed horns of young Reindeer, infers temporary occupation of the cave, probably during the summer only. If the interpretation given above is correct, it seems evident that the region was occupied by Late Stone Age hunters during the Second Retreat Period. In the meantime the final report on this site, together with illustrations of the archaeological material and a description of the burials, will be eagerly awaited.

On the basis of present data, Ireland was not inhabited by man until the Post-Glacial Period which began after the Valley Glaciation, *ca.* 7800 B.C. following Northern European chronology (see p. 21). But the fauna which entered Ireland during the Interstadial Period (W_1/W_2), as well as that which came in during the maximum of the last ice-advance, survived into later times, as proved by its occurrence within the area of the New Drift. Recent excavations by Ó'Ríordáin at the Red Cellar Cave, Lough Gur, County Limerick, have yielded Arctic Lemming, Irish Elk and Bear (Leask, 1938, p. 314). At Edenvale and Newhall Caves, County Clare, the same forms, in addition to Reindeer, are present (Charlesworth, 1928, p. 323), and at Kesh Cave, County Sligo, Reindeer, Bear and Lemming have also been found (*ibid.*). The Late-Glacial fauna of Ireland therefore definitely survived the last glacial maximum and followed north with the retreat of the ice. These sites are shown on the map (Fig. 9). Evidence that the Irish Elk (Scharff, 1926) persisted until Early Post-Glacial times (compare Stelfox, 1934, 1938) will be presented in the next chapter.

Chapter III

EARLY POST-GLACIAL CHRONOLOGY IN BRITAIN & IRELAND

1. INTRODUCTION

The degree of correlation between the British Isles and Fennoscandia, revealed by the summary of Late-Glacial events presented in Chapter II, is closer than heretofore established. With Late-Glacial varve clays, fauna, peats, raised beaches and archaeological horizons to work on, the lacunae should be filled in the future. Similarly, the Post-Glacial phenomena reflect the Scandinavian sequence dealt with in Chapter I. As the aim of archaeology is to establish cultures in their true chronological position, these phenomena must now be considered with respect to dating, as well as to the environment in which Mesolithic man lived in Ireland. The relative importance of rise and fall of the land and alterations in the volume of the ocean in producing changes in the mutual relation of land and sea at various periods is not considered here. Thus the terms "submergence" and "emergence" are used throughout this book without any attempt to distinguish between eustatic and isostatic factors.

2. SUBMERGED FORESTS AND RAISED BEACHES (APPENDIX VI)

A. ENGLAND & WALES. In this area there are particularly full data concerning the Post-Glacial oscillation of land and sea. The material is far clearer and more obvious than the similar fragmentary evidence of the Late-Glacial Period. The most striking proof of an emergence of the land is afforded by a study of the peat deposits of the Dogger Bank, which are known as moorlog. This usually occurs at a depth of 22–3 fathoms, and great fragments of it are frequently dredged up (Reid, 1913, pp. 41–7). Beetle elytra and plant remains show that the deposit was laid down in a fresh-water fen somewhat removed from the sea. The pollen has been studied by Godwin (1934, p. 340) and Erdtman (1924, pp. 677–8). The published analyses of a total of twenty samples agree in a striking manner, and in fact all but two are almost identical. Birch and Pine are the dominant forest forms in all cases, and this fact indicates a Late Pre-Boreal or Early Boreal date. The two aberrant analyses may be interpreted as indicating the advent of Oak and Hazel in Boreal times. On the margins of the North Sea there are later peats with a spectrum consisting largely of Oak-Mixed-Forest forms indicative of the Early Atlantic Period. The moorlog was therefore formed during Early Post-Glacial time, and the fact that wide areas of land, now submerged, were then available for settlement, is important in explaining the homogeneity of the contemporary Mesolithic cultures on the North European Plain.

That the Post-Boreal submergence was probably rapid is evidenced by the following facts: nowhere do clays overlie the moorlog (Godwin, 1934); for the most part the moorlog occurs at a fairly uniform depth, suggesting that no peat formed during the subsidence; the sudden termination of all moorlog spectra; and the intact and undisturbed nature of the deposits (Clark, 1936, p. 37). At this period the English Channel was either a narrow lake, an arm of the sea, or a land-bridge, but marine erosion has altered the floor to such an extent that it is difficult to state which definitely was the case (Clark, 1936[*a*], p. 239). Even after the submergence had taken place, there was probably a narrow strait for a long time (possibly as late as Neolithic or Early Metal Age times) across which animals could swim. This was enlarged by tidal scour, a process which is still in operation to-day (Reid, 1913, pp. 68–9; compare Peake and Clark, 1938, 1938[*a*]; Fox, 1938, p. 26). As Wright has suggested (1937, p. 295), the actual cutting of the strait itself was probably intermittent, and went on over a long period *in tempo* with the changing of the mutual relations of land and sea during the Pleistocene—a result of the rhythmic displacements connected with advances and retreats of the ice-sheets. Thus during the Early Post-Glacial Period, the land-bridge in this region very likely consisted of a valley, the floor of which was filled with alluvium. During the submergence, erosion set in which is still going on at present.

Confirmation of a Late Pre-Boreal–Early Boreal dating for the land connection between England and the Continent has recently been demonstrated by zoogeography, as Ullyott (1936, 169–77) has shown that the present distribution of flatworms in Northern and Western Europe took place after the average summer temperature had exceeded 12° C. and before it reached 16° C. On the basis of the mean summer temperature curves for the Post-Glacial Period, this proves that direct connections must have been severed during Late Boreal times before the climatic optimum, since these worms migrate only in fresh water. Further evidence is afforded by archaeology, as Maglemosean harpoons of Baltic type have been found at several sites in Britain as well as in the moorlog itself (Godwin, H. and M. E., 1933, pp. 38–43), and in Denmark, Germany and Esthonia, the Maglemosean or Mullerup culture is referable to the Boreal Period (Jessen, 1935). The later types of the Maglemosean, however, found in the Late Boreal sites of Zealand, are absent in Britain, and this points to a break in cultural connections between the two areas in Late Boreal times; by Atlantic times the cultures of Period II in Northern and Western Europe had diverged to a pronounced degree (Clark, 1936[*a*]).

Submerged peats, not all of which have been studied palaeobotanically, but which seem to belong to the Early Post-Glacial Period, have been recorded at numerous localities elsewhere in England and Wales (compare Boyd Dawkins, 1880, pp. 248–55; Reid, 1913). Here in the text only a summary of the material is presented; in Appendix VI a somewhat more detailed and completely documented account of the evidence of each locality will be found. Along the south coast of Britain there are submerged peat beds 40–50 feet below present sea-level, whereas submerged valleys have been traced off the South Devon coast to a depth of ±100 feet. An old land surface at Southampton, 20 feet below high-water level, has been studied by Dr Godwin (1935, pp. 211–12), and the pollen diagram, Fig. 10, shows that the peat layer associated with it began to form in the Pre-Boreal Period and continued its accumulation during Boreal times. In the Bristol region there is a buried channel ±100 feet deep near the present mouth of the Severn, and in Swansea Bay there is evidence that the land formerly stood ±150 feet higher than at present. Several localities in Wales revealing up to three superimposed peat beds suggest that the sinking has been intermittent; palaeobotanically the lowest peats are apparently Late Boreal in age. The evidence from these Welsh localities as well as that from the south English coast demonstrates that the last movement has been a sinking of the coastline. Farther north the existence of former land surfaces, now submerged, is clearly indicated by peat deposits along the Flintshire, Cheshire and Lancashire coasts; near Workington in Cumberland the lower horizon is found at an approximate depth of 60 feet below sea-level. In the Solway region, vicinity of Silloth, the Post-Glacial raised beach which overlies the Pre-Boreal and Boreal submerged peats, attains a height of 15 feet 6 inches. Southward along the coast it gradually loses elevation until in North-West Wales it approaches sea-level. Its 0-isobase has been established in this region (Wright, 1937, p. 369, Fig. 127), as indicated in Fig. 11.

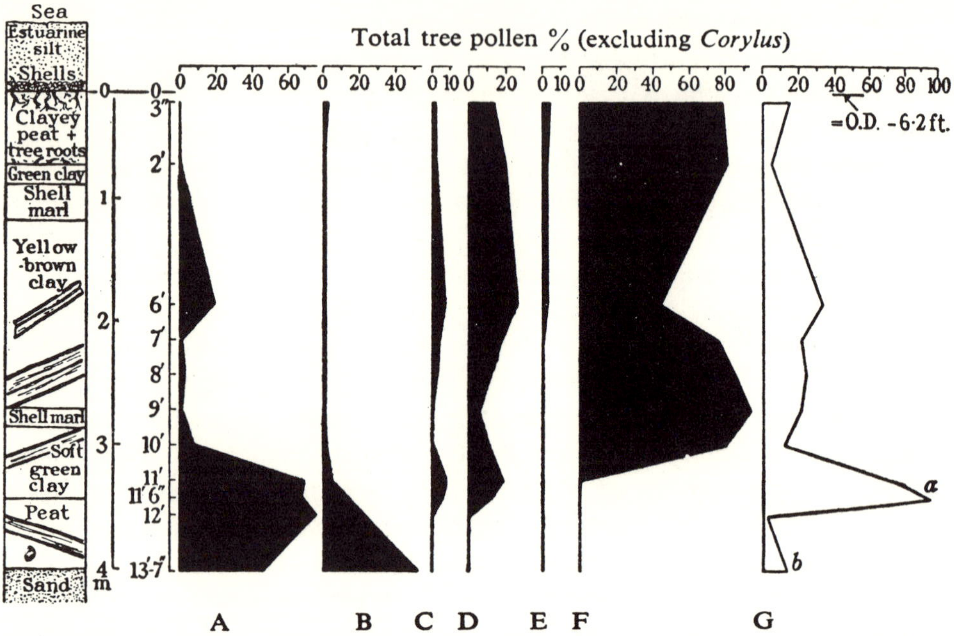

Fig. 10. Southampton S.R. Graving Dock, 1932. A, *Pinus* (pine); B, *Betula* (birch); C, *Ulmus* (elm); D, *Quercus* (oak); E, *Tilia* (lime); F, *Alnus* (alder); G, *Corylus* (hazel); *a*, *Myriophyllum* + *Salix* 10 per cent; *b*, *Myriophyllum* 12 per cent, *Salix* 10 per cent. (After Godwin.)

In Eastern England Post-Glacial deposits proving a period of relative emergence followed by successive stages of submergence, which began at the end of Boreal times, are found south of the Durham coast. According to Dr Wright (1937, p. 369), the 0-isobase of the Post-Glacial raised beach, shown in Fig. 11, occurs near Sunderland. Off the coasts of Durham, Yorkshire and Lincolnshire submerged peats occur at depths varying from 25 to 35 feet below present sea-level. The recent very thorough palaeobotanical work by Godwin and Clifford (1938) in the Fenland (see Fig. 11) furnishes the key to the Post-Glacial forest succession in Southern Britain in relation to

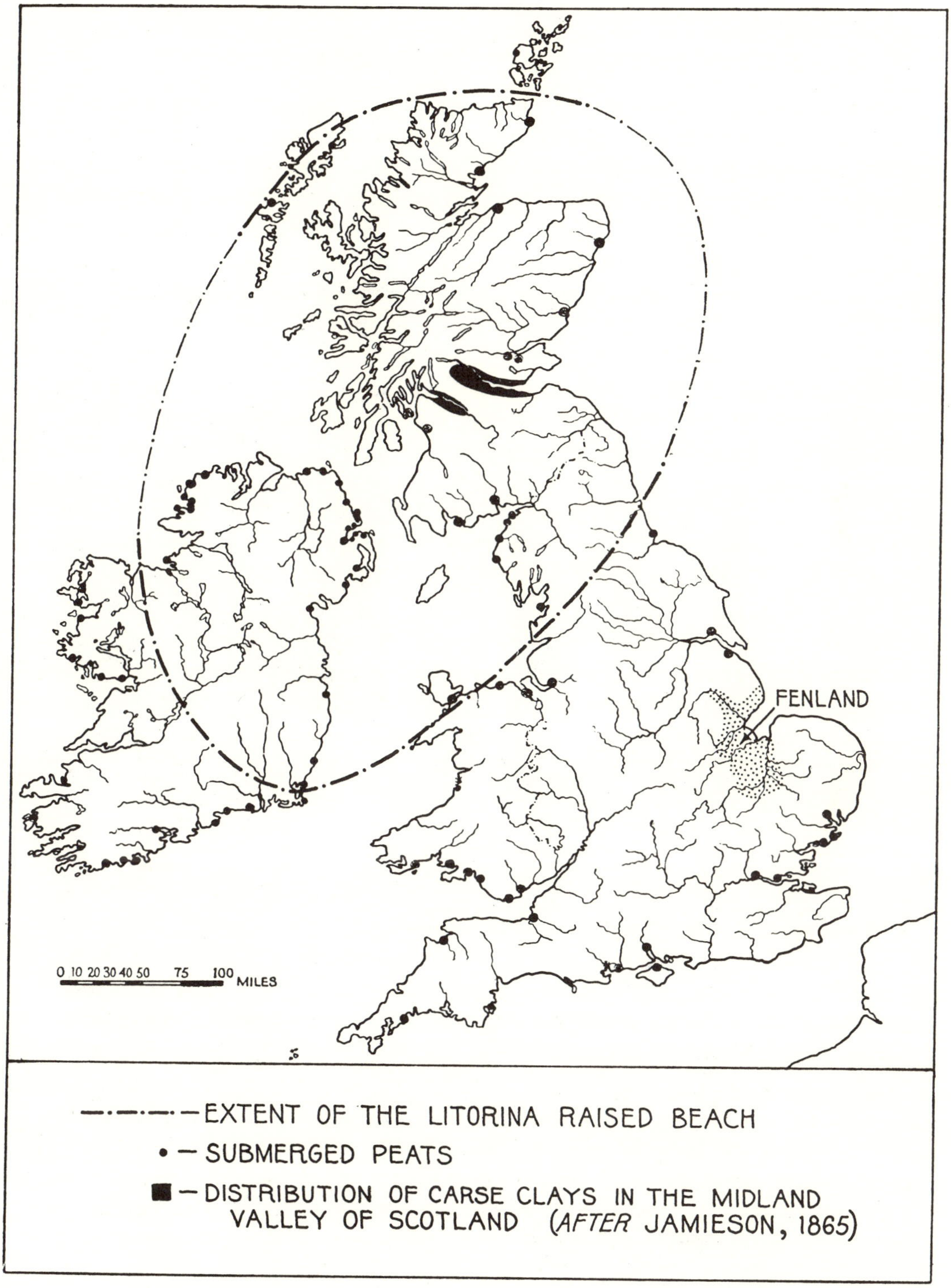

Fig. 11. Distribution of Post-Glacial Coastal Deposits in Britain and Ireland.

archaeology as well as to relative movements of land and sea (see also Godwin, 1940). Several very fine sections revealing submerged peats and estuarine deposits also exist in the Thames Valley, although the contained pollen has never been analysed. But at Lower Halstow in the Medway Valley, North Kent, Burchell (1931, pp. 296–9) has discovered a Mesolithic floor (see p. 204) overlain by deposits of peat and clay; the peat layer which directly overlies the archaeological horizon belongs to the Early Atlantic Period. In spite of the fact that only a few localities have been scientifically investigated, however, there seems to be very little doubt that the south coast of Britain has been sinking intermittently since the Early Post-Glacial Period. This is also confirmed by the archaeological evidence from several coastal stations, mentioned in Appendix VI, where material typical of successively later cultures has been discovered in association with superimposed layers of peats and clays. On the other hand, the region north of the 0-isobase of the Post-Glacial raised beach apparently has not been seriously affected by this movement, as the beach itself is well developed and in most cases unmodified by extensive marine erosion since the period of emergence. In fact at some localities the modern beaches represent a continuation of the cycle of deposition which was initiated during the Early Post-Glacial marine transgression at the beginning of the Atlantic Period.

B. SCOTLAND. In Scotland there is abundant evidence for a Boreal land surface overlain by deposits of the marine transgression of the Atlantic Period. The old land surface, which clearly represents a phase of relative emergence, separates the Late-Glacial raised beaches from those of Post-Glacial age. It may be correlated with the Ancylus Lake stage of the Baltic, according to Wright (1937, p. 457), and there are numerous data on which to establish this correlation (compare Geikie, J., 1881, p. 405). Jamieson (1865) records sections at Kilchattan Brickyards on the Island of Bute, Clyde district; Blair Drummond, in the Forth Valley; Errol, Perthshire; the Valley of the Ythan, Aberdeenshire; and elsewhere on which the following generalized section is based:

(5) Peat.
(4) Estuarine deposits ("carse" clays) of the "25-foot" raised beach containing "warm" molluscs.
(3) Submerged peat—old land surface.
(2) Late-Glacial marine beds with an Arctic fauna.
(1) Glacial Boulder Clay.

A similar sequence has been reported by Howden (1868) near Montrose, in the Estuary of the South Esk. In the Post-Glacial clays skeletons of stranded Whales, and in some cases Seals, are commonly found (Jamieson, 1865, p. 189; Dinham, 1927, p. 490; *M.G.S.* Scotland, 1930, p. 344). These sediments are commonly known as "carse" clays. The above sections establish beyond doubt that, following the submergence represented by the Late-Glacial Sea, there was a period of land emergence. This was followed by a marine transgression, during the time of which the "25-foot" raised beaches and the carse clays were formed, before the subsequent rising of the land to its present level. Extensive deposits in Northern England, Scotland and Ireland prove that the "25-foot" submergence was an event of considerable magnitude. As McCallien points out (1937, p. 196), striae of glacial origin have been preserved at many places along the coast, although exposed to weathering and wave action since the Late-Glacial Period. During the time of the Post-Glacial maximum of depression, however, rock-cut platforms up to 100 yards in breadth were made, and huge caves were formed in the cliffs of Northern Ireland and Scotland (compare Hull, 1866; Gregory *et al.* 1930, p. 248; Maxwell, 1934), some of which contain archaeological deposits dating from the period of the last emergence.

The distribution of submerged peats, raised beaches and associated deposits in Scotland, discussed in Appendix VI, is of interest since it helps to establish the isobases of the Post-Glacial uplift. In Southern Scotland these are extensively developed, in fact both Glasgow and Edinburgh are in part built on the "25-foot" marine terrace. On the west coast between Loch Linnhe and the Firth of Clyde the Post-Glacial raised beach is found at a maximum height of just over 40 feet (McCallien, 1937, p. 198). In the east, in the Upper Forth Valley as well as in the Tay Valley, deposits of this period are found up to the 50-foot contour-line (Geikie, J., 1881, p. 383; Dinham, 1927, p. 490; Simpson, 1933, p. 640). Thus the greatest uplift in Central Scotland has occurred in the upper reaches of the Scottish lochs and firths which border on the Highlands—the main centre of ice-dispersal during Late-Glacial times. In Caithness in the extreme north of Scotland, however, the level falls abruptly to between 8 and 5 feet above sea-level (*B.R.G.*[*n*], p. 96), whereas in the Orkneys the raised beach is absent (Flett, 1920, p. 49). This indicates that the 0-isobase limiting the northern extent of this feature should be drawn just north of John O'Groats, as in Fig. 11. By connecting this line with its equivalent in Northern England and Wales it is possible to establish the o contour-line, or isobase, for the Post-Glacial raised beach in Britain.

Professor Erdtman (1928, pp. 181–2) has demonstrated that the submergence which resulted in the formation of the Post-Glacial raised beaches and carse clays in Scotland occurred during the Atlantic Period: it represents the British equivalent of the Litorina transgression of the Baltic. As previously stated, the carse clays consist of estuarine deposits up to 18 feet in thickness, and in all the principal firths on the east coast, as well as in the Clyde Estuary on the west, they form the counterpart of the so-called "25-foot" raised beaches found elsewhere in Scotland. Now the carse itself is unpolleniferous, but it is underlain at many localities by Boreal peats whereas the overlying *Sphagnum* peats reveal spectra typical of the Sub-Boreal Period, as discussed in Appendix VI (p. 291). Submerged peats found below the raised beaches are likewise Boreal in age, indicating that these deposits were also formed, as elsewhere in Britain, during Atlantic times. As yet there is no direct evidence that Scotland was occupied when the submerged peats were forming, except possibly that afforded by the upper levels of the Inchnadamff Caves in the extreme north. The date of the overlying raised beaches, however, is of great importance because at Campbeltown, Oban, and elsewhere in Scotland, archaeological material has been found associated with them. Other evidence deduced from a study of these deposits has a direct bearing on the interpretation of archaeological data. In the Midland Valley carse clays are found up the Forth as far as Gartmore in Perthshire (Jamieson, 1865, p. 189), and in the Clyde Valley these deposits also have an extensive distribution (Jamieson, 1865, Fig. 1, p. 163). Thus, as Erdtman points out (1928, p. 181), at the maximum of the Litorina transgression in Scotland, the Central Highlands were only connected to the rest of Great Britain by a narrow isthmus, indicated on the map (Fig. 11), a fact which helps to explain the localized, peripheral, cultural development of the Mesolithic in North-Eastern Ireland and South-Western Scotland. The nature of this development will be discussed later. At the moment it is significant to note that the geography of Atlantic time established by geological and palaeobotanical data may be used in the interpretation of archaeological material of this period.

C. Ireland. The published material with respect to the Early Post-Glacial deposits in North-East Ireland is particularly complete (compare Praeger, 1896[*a*]), and the evidence reproduces very closely the sequence of events established in England and Scotland. Praeger, whose work on the estuarine clays (1892) and raised beaches (1896) has not received its full measure of attention, has reached conclusions, of which the following statement is a synthesis. On the boulder clay of the New Drift, marine sand and gravel with an Arctic fauna is often found. This deposit is the equivalent of the beds laid down by the Late-Glacial Sea in Scotland, which as has been previously shown is the time-equivalent of the Yoldia Sea in the Baltic area. Overlying these beds, but below high-tide level, is a layer of peat. It lies 27 feet below the level of high water at Alexandra Dock, Belfast (Praeger, 1888), and approximately 31 feet below the top of the section at Milewater Dock, Belfast (Charlesworth and Erdtman, 1935), but its relation to sea-level at this latter site is unknown. Elsewhere along the Antrim and Down coasts, as well as within Belfast Lough (Praeger, 1904), it occurs at a fairly uniform height between tide marks, except at Downpatrick and Newcastle, County Down (Praeger, 1892, pp. 239–40). At the former locality, in the Quoile Estuary, the submerged peat is over 30 feet below high-water level; at Newcastle, Dundrum Bay, it underlies 4 feet of estuarine clay, the surface of which is near the low-water mark. Therefore within North-East Ireland the level to which the Early Post-Glacial land surface has been submerged varies considerably, which suggests that the movements since the time of formation may not have been uniform at all localities. The age of the submerged peat in North-East Ireland has been determined at two localities: Milewater Dock, Belfast (Charlesworth and Erdtman, 1935; Praeger, 1935), and Cushendun, County Antrim (Jessen, 1940, p. 42). According to Jessen, the pollen analysis of the Belfast samples indicates a Boreal age, whereas this layer at Cushendun is somewhat later, and may be assigned to the transition between the Boreal and Atlantic Periods. In both cases, however, the pollen spectra fall within the so-called Boreal Hazel maximum (Zone V*b* in Ireland), hence these submerged peats in North-East Ireland agree quite well with the established age of comparable deposits in South-Eastern England and the Baltic (Jessen, 1940, p. 45). In addition to plants and pollen, the peat has produced elytra of beetles and the bones of Red Deer (*Cervus elaphus*), Wild Boar (*Sus scrofa*), and Irish Elk (*Cervus megaceros*). In general the peat is contemporary with the coming in of temperate conditions in Early Post-Glacial times, and it reveals that at this period the coast was considerably higher than at present. Subsequently the land was transgressed by the sea during a period of relative submergence, since extensive deposits of marine origin occur overlying the peat. In places these are in the form of estuarine clays found in the present bays and estuaries. These beds are rich in marine shells; invariably the marine animals, including mollusca and foraminifera, lived in the site of deposition, so that a marine invasion must be admitted. Dr Praeger studied deposits of this clay in over eighteen localities from Lough Foyle around the Antrim and Down coasts to Dundrum Bay, and he recorded nine forms and forty-two species (1892, p. 219). The clay is divided into two principal zones (compare Stewart, 1871), distinguishable by their lithological and faunal characteristics—a lower bed (*Scrobicularia* Zone), which was laid down under littoral conditions, and an upper bed (*Thracia* Zone).[1] The latter was deposited in at least 5 fathoms of water and coincides with the Post-Glacial climatic optimum. At this period there was a dominance of southern forms not found in the present Irish Sea, as revealed by the percentages in the following table:

		Arctic	Northern	Southern
1. Glacial Clays		13	5	3
2. Estuarine Clays	(*a*) Lower Zone	0	2	6
	(*b*) Upper Zone	0	3	9
3. Present Seas		0	4	3

At many localities beach shingle and storm-beach accumulations formed by the sea during the submergence are also found. These tend to be the characteristic deposits along the less sheltered portions of the coast. Often they rest on the lower bed of the estuarine clay and are contemporaneous with the *Thracia* Zone, but in other cases they rest directly on the submerged peat. Abundant archaeological material occurs in such gravel deposits. The subsequent emergence has elevated them to an average present-day height of 25 feet O.D. Actually the term "raised beach" as referable to these deposits is ambiguous, since not in all instances do they comprise true beach formations. In many cases they are made up of submarine gravels, which once formed sea beds rather than true beaches, as proved by the contained mollusca.

[1] An intermediate zone formed in 2–3 fathoms of water is also present at some localities, see p. 145.

Southward along the east coast of Ireland, the Post-Glacial raised beach, its height steadily decreasing as discussed in Appendix VI, has been traced as far as Wexford Harbour. Here the 0-isobase has been drawn, Fig. 11. Numerous deposits of submerged peat off the south coast suggest that the sea has been encroaching on the land in Post-Atlantic times. The Rostellon Dolmen in County Cork and the Ardmore Crannog in County Waterford, both submerged at high tide, prove beyond reasonable doubt that the south coast of Ireland has been sinking in comparatively recent times. This not only parallels the situation in England and Wales south of the 0-isobase of the Post-Glacial raised beach, discussed in Appendix VI (p. 288), but it also accords with the fact that in Brittany there are many sites which clearly demonstrate a Post-Megalithic subsidence (Munro, 1898, pp. 263–6). Submerged peats in South-Western and Western Ireland also indicate that formerly there was a greater extension of land in this area. In the north-west the Early Post-Glacial raised beach is again found; on the map, Fig. 11, its 0-isobase has been drawn through the south-western part of County Sligo and connected with the line established in County Wexford in the south-east. Within North-East Ireland numerous localities are known, and, as previously mentioned, most of them have yielded archaeological material. The study of this material in the light of its geological age, and the environment under which it was produced, forms the subject of the second part of this book.

3. RAISED BEACHES: GENERAL DISCUSSION

By far the most clearly marked feature of the Post-Glacial landscape of the North-East Irish and Scottish coasts are the Post-Glacial raised beaches. It has been shown that these deposits have this essential difference from the submerged forests: the latter are widely distributed, while the former are grouped around a centre in Scotland—the main region of ice-dispersal during the last glaciation. The reason for this is connected with isostatic factors, since the land outside the area of the present distribution of the Post-Glacial raised beach seems to have been sinking intermittently since the Atlantic Period. For the most part the actual term "raised beach" has been found to be a misnomer, as only in certain cases are the deposits thus described true beaches. Rather, many of them represent either wave-cut platforms with a low erosion scarp limiting their inland extension, or long-shore marine accumulations laid down under conditions of a sinking coastline. Actually the term "beach" implies deposits which have been thrown up into their present position either during a period of equilibrium or when the land was rising. This distinction between sediments is of obvious importance for purposes of fixing their age, i.e. whether they were formed during (1) the period of submergence; (2) the time of maximum subsidence; or (3) the time of emergence. As in the Baltic, however, this is generally understood by scientists, and hence the term "raised beach" has been retained. In order to distinguish these deposits from those of the Late-Glacial Period, the phrase "25-foot Raised Beach" came into use, because this feature coincides in part with the 25-foot Ordnance Survey contour-line. But since its elevation varies from 0 to 50 feet above sea-level, this name has been discarded. In 1928 Wright proposed the term "Early Neolithic Beach", because at that time the archaeological material was thought to date from this period (1928, p. 99). That this is not the case in any respect will be presently made clear, and in addition such a term, confusing as it does archaeological with geological phenomena, is not practical. For the same reason McCallien's proposal, "Mesolithic Raised Beach" (1937, p. 196), has been rejected, although the archaeological material found in it is Mesolithic in a very real sense of the word. Therefore for purposes of this book it is proposed to call it the LITORINA RAISED BEACH after its counterpart the Litorina Sea in the Baltic, because in both cases the Periwinkle, *Littorina littorea*, is the characteristic fossil. In general the Litorina raised beach is more heavily eroded than the present coast, but not to the same degree as the older Late-Glacial deposits. For this reason it is fairly certain that its formation occupied a period comparable with that which has elapsed since it was raised to its present position. As it presents the most prominent cliffs associated with any of the shores, it is easily identified. The maximum recorded height is approximately 50 feet above high-water level in the Tay region and the Upper Forth Valley of Eastern Scotland; between Loch Linnhe and the Clyde Estuary on the west it is just over 40 feet (see p. 81). It is of significance to note that this area of greatest height coincides exactly with the highest isobases of the Late-Glacial Sea, which agrees precisely with the evidence from Fennoscandia (see Figs. 2 and 3, pp. 9 and 10). In the latter area the Post-Glacial submergence occurred in the Atlantic Period, and on the basis of present information, the evidence in the British Isles seems to be in unanimous accord with this date.

4. THE POST-GLACIAL LAND-BRIDGE

It has been shown above that the Late-Glacial and the Litorina transgressions were separated by a period of relative elevation of the land, and that at the time England was connected with the Continent. This period of elevation coincides in the main with the Boreal climatic phase, and it is probable that during it a large area of the present Irish Sea was dry land. That the land-bridge existed and was eventually submerged is indicated by the occurrence of drowned valleys, submerged peats, and the discontinuous distribution of present-day Irish flora and fauna with that of Britain (Charlesworth, 1930, pp. 384–8). This point, however, is very difficult to prove, although on the basis of present data an extremely strong case for the former existence of a land-bridge can be made. As mentioned in Appendix VI, p. 288, north-east of Gower in the Valley of the Tawe River, Glamorganshire, Jones (1934, p. 306) has reported a buried river channel at a depth of ±150 feet below present high-water level, but since the submerged peats on the Welsh coast demonstrate that this region has been sinking in comparatively recent times, this figure is probably somewhat high. Recent work in the south-eastern portion of the Irish Sea Basin has furnished more satisfactory data. Gresswell (1936, pp. 347–8) has shown that, in spite of the intricacy of the submarine contours off the Lancashire and Cheshire coasts, the Early Post-Glacial estuaries of the Ribble, Mersey and Dee Rivers may be traced to between the 16- and 25-fathom lines. Indeed the former valleys of the Mersey and Dee appear to unite at a depth of 25 fathoms, and submerged peats on the Formby and Wirral coasts suggest that the land stood 120 feet higher at the time they were formed (Gresswell, 1936). These data are in striking agreement with De Rance's observations (1870, p. 666) that during the period of the Early Post-Glacial emergence the Ribble excavated a gorge 20 miles long and 150 feet deep in the glacial deposits of Lancashire. This gorge was subsequently filled with deposits of silt, clay and peat. Present evidence therefore makes it appear more than likely that the 20-fathom line represents a safe figure for indicating the amount of the uplift, although according to some authorities this estimate may be high (compare Fox, 1938, p. 23). Fig. 12 reveals the present extent of the land if such an elevation were effected, but marine erosion and tidal scour have so materially altered the floor of the Irish Sea since the submergence that it is impossible to reconstruct a true picture of the coastlines during this period of Early Post-Glacial time. It is probable that this area was once thickly covered with glacial deposits, and that the contours were quite different from those at present. Nevertheless, if the land were uplifted

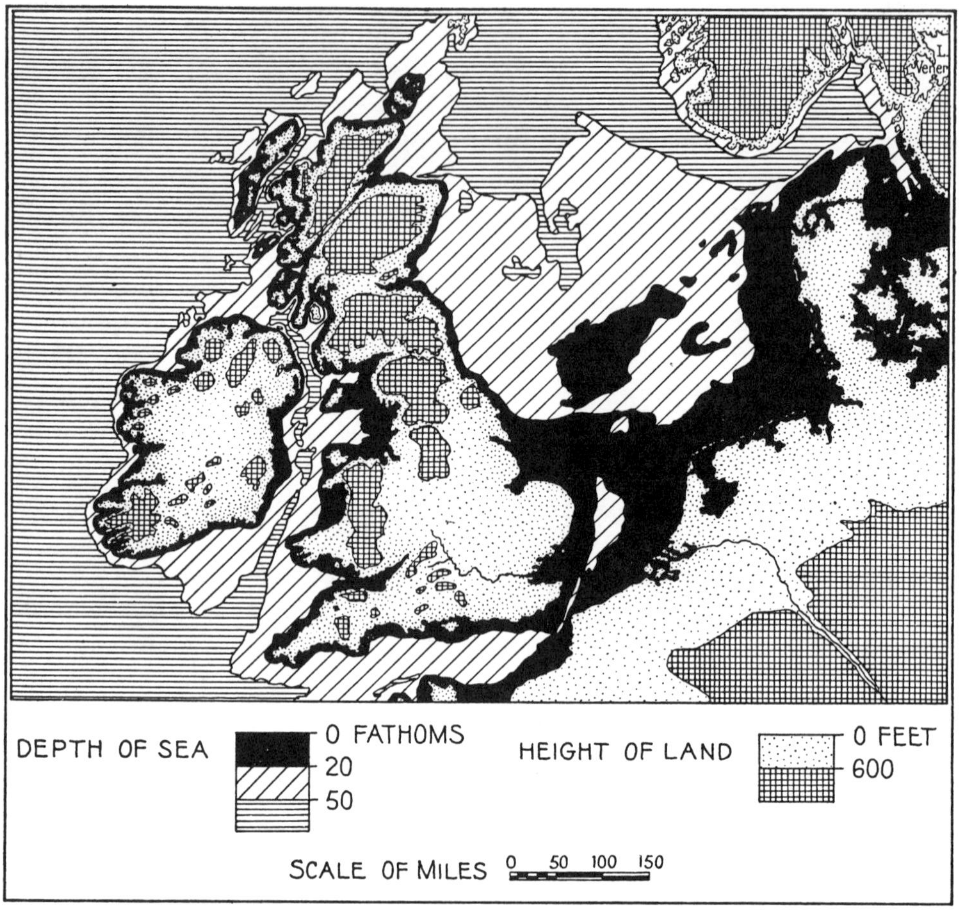

Fig. 12. Land and Water in Northern and Western Europe during the Early Post-Glacial Period. At this time the present North and Irish Sea floors were land, at least as far as the 20-fathom line.

to the 20-fathom line during the Boreal Period, Lambay Island and the Isle of Man would have been joined to the mainland, and the whole or at least a part of Cardigan Bay would have been dry land (Fox, 1938, Fig. 10). It is certain, however, that at no time was the whole of the area dry land, because even during the maximum of the emergence the sea must have been present, although it was restricted to a great river or an estuary separating

Britain and Ireland. This river, the "Irish Channel River", received the drainage of the surrounding land (Charlesworth, 1930), but since then the sea floor has been so extensively changed that its course can only be postulated. As will be seen later, the existence of this partial connection between England and Ireland played an important role in the diffusion of culture during the Early Post-Glacial Period, and it is almost certain that the area, which must have had a favourable environment, was settled. Conditions similar to those of the present day resulted from the marine transgression of the Atlantic Period, which was responsible for the cutting off of this connection and the submergence of large tracts of land. The development of culture reveals that in the two regions important local variations took place after this event. In Atlantic time large areas of the present coast were submerged, and Scotland was only joined to England by a narrow isthmus.

The material effect of the Post-Glacial emergence of the land must have been considerable (Charlesworth, 1930). The low flat plains of the present coastline would have been extended far beyond their present limit, and two partial land-bridges would have existed following the shallows of the present sea floor. The first and more southernly of these would have been from Anglesey, the Lleyn Peninsula and the northern part of Cardigan Bay to the coastal portion of the Dublin area; and the second from Scotland via the shallows between Islay, Inishowen and the North Irish coast (compare Charlesworth *et al.* 1935, p. 483). In neither case were these bridges completely intact, since the northern one would have been broken by the Sound of Jura, and the Dublin-Wales connection interrupted by a narrow strait or a wide river west of Anglesey. But this could not have altered the general effect, since British flora and fauna came into Ireland during the Boreal emergence, and a restricted number of new forms were widely dispersed. According to existing data, it was at this time that man made his first appearance in Ireland, when the Post-Glacial amelioration of the climate resulted in the development of extensive forests and the favourable conditions of this new region for settlement.

5. CLIMATIC PHASES

On the whole the evolution of the climate during the Early Post-Glacial Period in Britain and Ireland duplicates the established Baltic sequence, although it is difficult to determine at present precisely how the Blytt-

Sernander system applies throughout the British Isles. Nevertheless Dr Praeger's comparisons of the marine mollusca from different localities in North-East Ireland (1896, pp. 47–8) clearly demonstrate a slow but steady rise in temperature, which followed in time the retreat of the ice, and which culminated in the Post-Glacial climatic optimum (see p. 15). During the period of maximum warmth southern forms predominated, as shown by the table on p. 84, and in Ireland as well as in the Baltic the climatic optimum seems to be approximately synchronous with the maximum of the Litorina transgression. It seems unlikely that an event of this magnitude could have occurred in these two regions at different periods, therefore it may be safely assumed that the development has been uniform in both instances. As in Northern Europe, the Post-Glacial rise in temperature is reflected in the forest development. The approach of the warm period is characterized by the appearance and initial increase of the various heat-loving deciduous trees, which rose to dominance during Atlantic times, whereas after the period of the Litorina submergence very few new forms were introduced. Therefore the study of the forest history of this area is very complex (Godwin, 1934, p. 351). For the Pre-Boreal and Boreal Periods, however, the horizons are as clear in Britain and Ireland as elsewhere, and the parallelism in development with the established Continental sequence may be regarded, according to Godwin, as sufficient evidence for contemporaneity. From the end of Atlantic times onward the climatic phases in Western Europe are in the main analogous with those of the Baltic region. Thus in the Sub-Boreal Period, Pine was important, especially in Ireland and Scotland where beds of decomposed Pine stumps or "stools" are found. The transition to the Sub-Atlantic was sudden, and marked by the appearance of a cold moist climate, probably due to solar radiation (Erdtman, 1929, p. 120). Although no Early Post-Glacial temperature curves have yet been worked out for Britain and Ireland, the evidence of the marine molluscs and the forest development indicate that, in spite of regional variations due to certain factors, essentially the same conditions pertained here as in Northern Europe during this period. Therefore it seems apparent that the established Baltic chronology may be extended into Western Europe, and this view is in accord with the geological data summarized in a previous section of this chapter.

As yet very little is known about the Early Post-Glacial land fauna in Britain and Ireland, hence this evidence can only be put forward in generalized form to support the argument for parallelism. As in the case of the forest development, the advent of the climatic optimum is heralded by the arrival of new types. This led to a change, but the transition was not abrupt—the Late-Glacial fauna was gradually replaced by temperate, forest-loving species. Certain forms such as the Arctic Lemming became extinct with the final disappearance of the ice, but survival well into Post-Glacial times was the rule, which complicates the picture. Remains of Irish Elk (*Cervus megaceros*), characteristic of the Late-Glacial Period, have been reported from the submerged peats of Belfast Lough by Praeger (1888, 1892, pp. 268–9), Young (1894, p. 77) and others, although there is no evidence that this animal survived later than the Late Boreal phase. In Northern Scotland, the Reindeer (*Rangifer tarandus*) lingered in Caithness until the twelfth century (Hinton, 1926, p. 343).[1] In addition the Wild Ox (*Bos primigenius*) appears to have been present (Jones, C. B., 1932, p. 152); this animal, the Aurochs, is known from several Post-Glacial localities in Scotland (Gregory and Currie, 1928, pp. 8–9), but disappeared before Roman times (Gregory, 1927, p. 372). New forms which commonly occur include Red Deer (*Cervus elaphus*) and Wild Boar (*Sus scrofa*), and they are found in Post-Glacial deposits at many localities in England, Wales, Scotland and Ireland (compare Fox, 1938, p. 59). In Scotland the earliest appearances of Horse (*Equus caballus*) and Elk (*Alces machlis*) are in the Early Post-Glacial Period (Gregory and Currie, 1928, pp. 8, 9–12). Jamieson (1865, p. 187) records Irish Elk, Red Deer and Aurochs from Post-Glacial marls at Maybole, Ayrshire, and in addition to the above, Wolf, Bear and Beaver are typical forms of this period in Scotland (Jamieson, 1865, p. 195). In Ireland the Wolf (*Canis lupus*) definitely survived from Late-Glacial times, since its remains are found in Iron Age sites. The date of the introduction of true cattle (*Bos longifrons*) must be left an open question; at several sites in Ireland and Scotland bones, identified as this species, have been reported from deposits associated with Mesolithic material. Specific information regarding the first appearance of the temperate animals is virtually non-existent. This is due in the main to the small number of primary settlement sites which have thus far come to light, as compared with the enormous wealth of excavated material in Northern Europe. Thus actual Early Mesolithic occupation within the area covered by the New Drift is known

[1] According to Gregory and Currie (1928, pp. 5–6) the evidence for Reindeer as late as the Christian Period in Scotland is inconclusive. These authorities feel that the presence of Reindeer bones in the Scottish brochs is no proof of contemporaneity, since they may have come either from Scandinavia or from older deposits, such as the Inchnadamff Caves. This question can only be settled by further excavation.

only from the upper deposits at Victoria Cave, Yorkshire (Garrod, 1926, p. 118), where the stratigraphy had been disturbed, and from the Inchnadamff Caves, Sutherland (Peach and Horne, 1917; Cree, 1927), where the latest settlement appears to date from early in the Post-Glacial Period (see p. 73). Nevertheless, on the basis of the fragmentary evidence outlined above, it is clear that as the climate ameliorated new types gradually replaced the old, which survived on the periphery and in areas of isolation into comparatively recent times.

Whereas the close similarity in Post-Glacial development between Britain and Ireland on the one hand with Northern Europe on the other has been constantly referred to above, the following synthesis of the climatic and geologic evidence may perhaps establish more clearly the close degree of relationship prevailing in the two regions. Since the palaeobotanical zone system has not as yet been established in Western Europe on the same detailed basis as in the Baltic, the Blytt-Sernander climatic periods of Post-Glacial time have been retained. At present this seems to be the most practical method of comparing the two areas.

1. *Pre-Boreal.* Although remnants of the last ice-sheet were still present in Scotland and Ireland, this period (Zone IV in Ireland) marks the beginning of Post-Glacial time (compare Jessen and Farrington, 1938, p. 222). The land has not yet fully recovered from the depression caused by the weight of the last ice-sheet, and the Late-Glacial Sea existed in Northern England, Scotland and Ireland. By the end of this period the isostatic uplift was complete in the southern portion of the area, and Britain was connected by a land-bridge to the Continent. The gradual amelioration of the climate resulted in the coming in of Pine; Birch and Willow were more widely dispersed. Hazel was introduced towards the end of this phase. In all essential features this forms the precise counterpart of the Pre-Boreal Period in Northern Europe.

2. *Boreal.* This was a period of relative land emergence: the Ancylus Lake was formed in the Baltic region; the Dogger Bank, most of the present English Channel and much of the Irish Sea were dry land. Temperate conditions are reflected in the fauna in both regions: Wild Pig, Red Deer, etc. being typical, and the Irish Elk, the Wolf and the Reindeer also survived. The Lemming became extinct. The forest history reveals the rise to dominance of Pine, although a marked Hazel maximum is characteristic of the British Isles; Oak, Elm and Alder are present. As in Northern Europe

this period was favourable to the spread of new types into Britain and Ireland, in which areas the oldest submerged peats were being formed. Archaeological evidence also points to contemporaneity with the extension of the Maglemosean culture into South-Eastern England.

3. *Atlantic.* The marine transgression led to the formation of the Litorina Sea in the Baltic, the severing of English-Continental land connections and the submergence of the Irish Sea Basin. During this phase the coastal portions of Northern and Western Europe were under water, and Scotland was only connected with England by a narrow isthmus. There is some evidence that the sinking of the land was a comparatively sudden event. In Ireland, Scotland, Northern England and the Baltic, extensive raised beach deposits mark the limits of the Litorina Sea, and it is proposed to refer to these deposits as Litorina Raised Beaches (see p. 86). In parts of North-East Ireland and Scotland, clays and other sediments corresponding to the beaches were laid down in the fjords, bays and estuaries. The Post-Glacial climatic optimum is synchronous with the maximum extent of this sea in both regions since, on the basis of the marine fauna, the warmth maximum can be shown to have occurred at this time in Ireland and in Northern Europe. A steady amelioration of the climate up to this point was in progress. It is probable that the Irish Elk became extinct at this time, though the Reindeer still survived in Scotland. The Atlantic Period witnessed the rise to dominance of the Oak-Mixed-Forest after the introduction of Lime; from palaeobotanical evidence the maximum of the Litorina transgression occurred towards the end of this phase, and the emergence of the land began. In England the point at which the advancing curve for Alder crosses the decreasing Pine curve is usually taken as the beginning of the Atlantic Period. Since Alder is comparatively rare in Ireland, this boundary is not clearly defined there.

4. *Sub-Boreal.* In the Baltic and the British Isles this period is marked by a second Pine maximum, but the almost complete absence of new forest forms in the latter region makes determination of the Sub-Boreal by pollen analysis difficult. It is probable that their failure to disperse may be accounted for by the Litorina submergence which cut these islands off from Western Europe. The beginning of this period is marked by the sudden appearance of forest peat beds with "Pine stools" in Ireland and Scotland, which indicates a comparatively sudden change, and the recrudescence of a cold, dry Continental climate. During the Sub-Boreal, the Neolithic and Early Metal Age cultures spread into the British Isles.

5. *Sub-Atlantic*. The transition from the Sub-Boreal phase to the cold, wet, oceanic conditions of Sub-Atlantic times is clear only in the northern part of the British Isles. *Sphagnum* peat deposits were extensively developed at this time, but since these formed in England, during earlier periods as well, the beginning of this phase is difficult to fix. In the Fenlands of East Anglia, however, the Sub-Boreal–Sub-Atlantic boundary is marked by the rapid increase of aquatic forms (Godwin and Clifford, 1938, p. 390). Submerged forest beds on the Essex, Hampshire and Glamorganshire coasts and elsewhere of Sub-Boreal–Sub-Atlantic age, in addition to the drowned valleys of Southern England and Ireland, prove a Post-Litorina sinking of the land paralleling Northern Europe.

On the basis of the above it can be seen that in the main the Post-Glacial climatic cycles established in Scandinavia may be extended into Britain and Ireland within certain limits, which will be narrowed by future research. Therefore we are now in a position to date approximately the changes of level described in the first part of this chapter in terms of Baltic chronology. For archaeological purposes the importance of this can hardly be overstressed. Especially in Ireland is it of paramount necessity to fix the age of the Stone Age cultures by as many different indices as possible—geology, palaeontology, climatology and palaeobotany. Early workers made the common mistake of attempting to date the various levels solely with the aid of the contained industries, which is a practical method for checking results only where the archaeological sequence rests on a firm foundation. Since the Irish Mesolithic represents a new and indigenous culture, it cannot be studied on this basis alone until the relative chronology, as revealed by the key stratified sites, has been worked out. Likewise an interpretation of the material itself can only be extended along superficial lines unless the background of geographical factors is understood. This had a profound influence on the cultural development, especially with respect to the new needs conditioned by the changing climate, which in turn had a marked effect on the fauna and flora of the region. Also the changes in the mutual relations of land and sea had a far-reaching influence on the evolution of culture. The Late Pre-Boreal–Boreal uplift of the land resulted in the availability of larger areas for settlement by Mesolithic man. With respect to Northern and Western Europe this led to cultural unity on the North European Plain, and the beginning of intensive occupation in Ireland and Scotland. Submergence during the Atlantic phase was the cause of regional specialization of culture, and the effect of the climatic optimum may be noted in the evolution of new tools. At the moment, however, the main point to be emphasized is that, on the basis of all available geological and other data, the established Baltic chronology holds for the British Isles. Thus the synchronisms, first, of the submergence of the coastal peats with the transgression of the North and Irish Seas, secondly, of the subsequent maximum of the submergence with the Post-Glacial optimum climate, and finally, the emergence of the land to its present level, prove beyond much doubt that the dates fixed by geochronology may be applied with a reasonable degree of accuracy in our region. Therefore, the upper time-limit at which the Mesolithic Period, except for certain peripheral survivals, came to an end, and the first waves of Neolithic culture were slowly diffused into Britain, Ireland and Scandinavia, corresponds in the main with the beginning of Sub-Boreal times in the second half of the second millennium B.C.

6. PALAEOBOTANY

Palaeobotany demonstrates that there is a close measure of agreement between the relative frequencies of the various forest forms and the sequence set forth in the last section as established by climatology and geology. The first really serious attempt to extend the established method of pollen analysis into Britain and Ireland was made by Erdtman (1928), but recent intensive work in both countries has revealed that the sequence is far more complex than at first suspected. This is partly due to insular isolation, effected by the Litorina transgression when the land connection with the Continent was severed. After this event the dispersal of forest forms is not apparent, and Spruce and Fir, which in substantial amounts are indicators of a Post-Boreal date in Northern Europe, are absent (Godwin, 1934, p. 351). The same is true to a certain extent of Beech and Hornbeam, which have a restricted distribution mainly in South-Eastern Britain according to Godwin; whereas the former seems to be entirely lacking in Ireland (Erdtman, 1927), traces of Hornbeam have recently been reported in County Kildare (La Touche, 1936). Another important determining factor of Post-Glacial forest history in these islands is the strong influence exerted on tree growth by the North Atlantic oceanic climate. During certain periods this was dominant and tended to offset new influences from the Continent. The picture is further complicated by modifications in normal development resulting from the local conditions under which the bogs themselves were formed—each locality investigated displays definite individual characteristics which make broad-scale comparisons difficult. It is therefore desirable to fix the horizons established by pollen analysis to as many independent indices as possible, and in this regard particularly satisfactory results are being given by archaeological, climatological and geological data (compare Godwin and Clifford, 1938). With regard to the later Post-Glacial phases which are those most difficult to interpret from the point of view of palaeobotany, archaeology affords a reliable check, and in the case of dated finds from polleniferous deposits, accurate results are being obtained. For the early periods the situation is more obscure. In spite of the many variables mentioned above, however, the main drifts of forest development can be determined, and when these are considered in the light of climatic phases and changes in the mutual relations of land and sea, it is possible to synchronize the sequence during Early Post-Glacial time in terms of Scandinavian chronology.

Until the end of the Boreal Period, Britain and Northern Europe underwent a very similar development, as previously stated. Up to this point the continued existence of the land connection between England and the Continent, and the partial connection between Ireland and Britain,[1] led to the introduction of the warmth-loving, deciduous trees, after the rapid spread of Hazel and the suppression of Pine. Thus the Early Post-Glacial rise in temperature induced changes of a comparable order in Northern and Western Europe, which Godwin has graphically shown (Figs. 13 and 14). As is generally accepted, the intersection of the falling Pine and rising Alder pollen curves has been taken by Godwin to indicate the Boreal–Atlantic boundary; this horizon is clearly shown on the diagram from Southampton (Fig. 10, p. 78). On the maps (Figs. 13 and 14) the percentage of the pollen of each tree genus is shown by the size of a sector of the circle, marked distinctively at each site. In the one case Pine reveals a high frequency, Fig. 13, and Alder in the other, Fig. 14. Five Boreal sites yield a Hazel maximum greater than 100 per cent, whereas by Atlantic times there is no instance of 100 per cent Hazel pollen. Other features are the general drift, and the regional parallelism in development—in the Boreal Period there was a preponderance of Birch in Scotland, but in the south higher

[1] The possibility of survival must also be reckoned with; some trees may have survived the period of the last ice advance in the unglaciated sections of Southern Britain and Ireland, but direct proof is lacking. If this is demonstrated it is obvious that a Post-Glacial introduction from the Continent need not be postulated to account for their presence in the area under discussion.

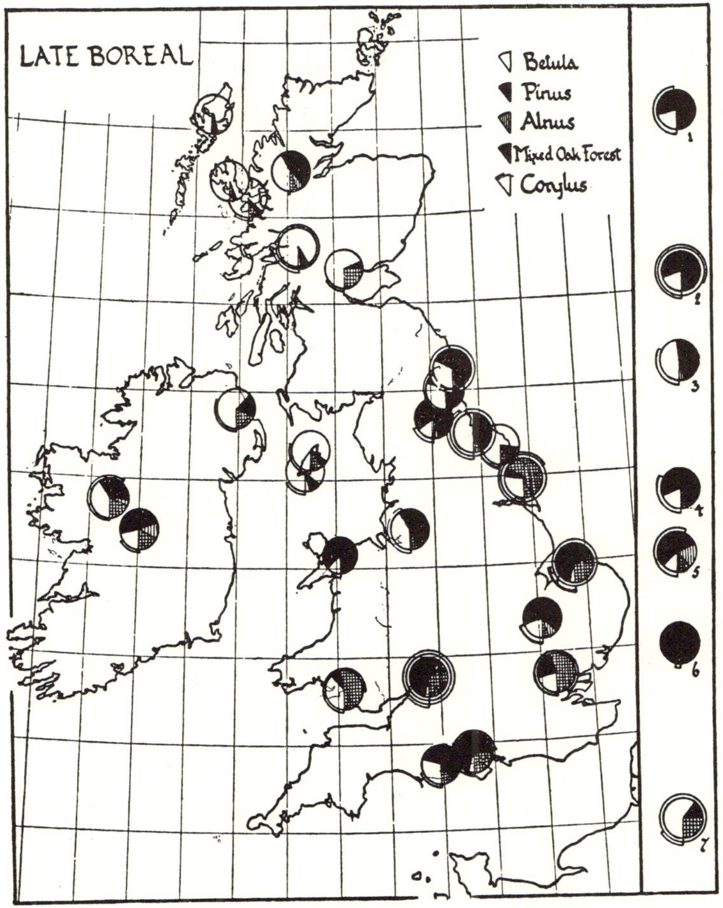

Fig. 13.

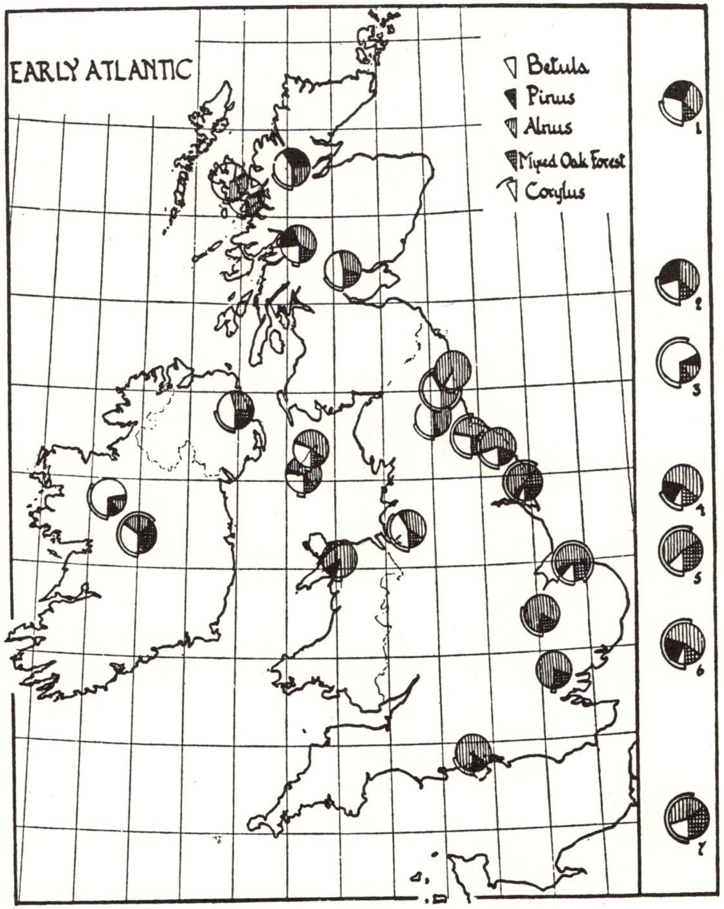

Fig. 14.

Figs. 13, 14. Diagrams showing the Percentage Pollen Composition of Peat Samples of Late Boreal (Fig. 13) and Early Atlantic (Fig. 14) Age from Sites in Britain and Ireland. The intersection of the falling Pine and rising Alder curves has been taken as the criterion of the Boreal–Atlantic transition. The percentages of the different types of pollen shown are indicated always in the same clockwise order, and the size of each sector is proportional to the percentage of each type of tree pollen present. Hazel pollen, which is reckoned separately, is expressed as a percentage of the total tree pollen. The columns on the right of each figure are analyses of comparable age from lowland stations on the North Sea border of the Continent and each is shown approximately at its proper latitude. (After Godwin.)

values of the Oak-Mixed-Forest are present. In the Early Atlantic phase, Birch is almost absent in the southern sites, and Pine in substantial amounts is limited to Scotland. In the right-hand column are corresponding analyses from lowland sites on the margin of Continental Europe. Each is set approximately at its proper latitude and covers the range from Southern Belgium to Göteborg in Sweden. To a remarkable degree these are in agreement with the British results. The lacunae in these maps are apparent, but nevertheless they show tentatively the general situation during the period when the Post-Glacial climatic optimum was approaching.

In England it is not absolutely clear at present precisely how the pollen diagrams may be zoned[1], and whether or not these fit the zones into which the Danish bogs are divisible, as outlined in Chapter I. This work has been extended into Western England (Hardy, 1939) and Wales (Godwin and Mitchell, 1938), but during the last ten years there has been little progress in the science of palaeobotany in Scotland. In Ireland, however, rapid strides have been made under the auspices of a Committee for Quaternary Research (Praeger, Farrington, Jessen, Whelan, and others, 1934), and valuable results are being obtained. Following the early work of Erdtman (1927, 1928), and certain general conclusions concerning the climatic and geological factors which have determined the main distribution of Irish peats suggested by Charlesworth (1932), Professor Jessen has undertaken an extremely thorough and detailed investigation of the bogs in Ireland. This work is not as yet sufficiently advanced to permit of more than a brief summary of the results to date, on the basis of tentative conclusions arrived at by Jessen. *These apply to Ireland only.* Thus far the work has been concentrated on the early periods. The data pertaining to the Late-Glacial Zones (I–III) have already been summarized in Chapter II; from material published to date (Jessen, 1936, 1940; Jessen and Farrington, 1938) it is possible to outline the development from Pre-Boreal times onward as follows:

1. *Zone IV.* Post-Glacial Birch Period. At this time Birch is dominant, and it reaches a maximum in the upper part of the zone, whereas the greatest frequencies for Pine and Willow are in the lower part. The top of IV is marked by the rational border[2] of the Hazel curve. This development closely parallels that of the Pre-Boreal (Zone IV) in the Baltic (see p. 19).

[1] Dr Godwin (1940, pp. 243–8) has recently proposed a series of numbered zones into which the Fenland diagrams may be divided, but it has not yet been determined how generally applicable these are even within the eastern section of Britain.

[2] See footnote, p. 19.

2. *Zone V.* This contains the so-called Boreal Hazel maximum. At this time the first Post-Glacial high forests came into Ireland in which Pine, Elm and Oak were the leading forms. Ash (*Fraxinus*) was introduced during Zone V, but it is rare. The boundary V/VI is marked by the rational border for Alder. Zone V is divisible into two sub-zones (*a*) and (*b*):

(*a*) *Zone Va.* In this horizon Hazel is coming in; the Birch curve tends to fall; Willow is falling, and Pine begins to rise.

(*b*) *Zone Vb.* The Hazel maximum occurs here, and this attains a frequency of over 800 per cent in some diagrams. The curve for Pine continues to rise, and in the upper part of V*b* it displays two distinct maxima. Willow is rare; the Birch curve swings in; a high frequency of Elm is present in the lower part of this zone; Oak is rising, and in the upper part of V*b* it is dominant over Elm. Only traces of Alder are found here. In the upper part of this zone the Hazel curve swings in.

As yet it is not possible to fix in detail exactly how Zone V in Ireland fits into the Danish sequence. It seems probable, however, that V*a* is Early Boreal and is therefore roughly the equivalent of Zone V in Denmark. Tentatively Jessen has placed the Boreal–Atlantic transition in Ireland at the point in Zone V*b* where the Hazel curve falls from the maximum (1940, p. 46); the comparative absence of Alder in Ireland at this time makes this point more difficult to determine than elsewhere. According to this view the lower part of Zone V*b* is Late Boreal (Zone VI in Denmark), whereas the upper part is Early Atlantic (roughly corresponding to the Danish Zone VII). When the final results from Jessen's investigations in North-East Ireland are available, greater precision for the extension of the Danish Zone sequence into that region will be possible. On the County Antrim coast polleniferous horizons, which can be geologically dated in relation to the Litorina submergence, have been studied, and at present it appears likely that on this basis the marine transgressions in Ireland and the Baltic are contemporary.

3. *Zone VI.* This is the first period in which Alder becomes dominant. Hazel is comparatively rare, and its curve falls to a minimum in the lower part of this zone. Elm and Oak tend to fall off; Birch is present; and at the top of VI the curve for Pine stops.

The boundary between Zones VI and VII is a very important level in the Irish bogs, and it is marked by an increase in rainfall which must have been due to a change in climate according to Jessen (in Mahr, 1937, pp. 276–7). This recurrence surface, or *Grenzhorizont*, can be placed archaeologically between Middle and Late Bronze Age times in Ireland. It therefore seems almost certain that Zone VI in Ireland is synchronous with Zone VIII in Denmark and is accordingly Late Atlantic–Sub-Boreal, in terms of the established Continental sequence. This is supported by the view that a change in climate of the magnitude responsible for the formation of this recurrence surface was not a purely local phenomenon; such a change also occurred in Denmark at the end of Sub-Boreal times. In Ireland the maximum of the Litorina transgression is registered at three sites which have been dated by pollen analysis to the middle of Zone VI (Jessen, 1940, p. 44); therefore the emergence did not commence until near the end of the Atlantic Period in that region. In the upper part of Zone VI, Jessen (1938, p. 256) has placed the Neolithic culture of the Lower Bann Valley, which belongs to the Late Atlantic–Early Sub-Boreal transition period (Jessen, 1936, p. 36). Whereas the Atlantic Period was a time of rapid peat formation in Ireland, which indicates heavy rainfall, the Sub-Boreal seems to have been comparatively dry (compare Brooks, 1927). During this phase many lakes sank to below their level of outlet and forest peat is found beneath the present water-level, as first recognized by Wright (1912, p. 116). These submerged peats have been assigned to the Sub-Boreal Period by Erdtman (1928, p. 165). Since Jessen has confirmed this and also demonstrated the return to wetter conditions in Zone VII (Sub-Atlantic), it would seem that the climatic sequence in Ireland, from Late-Glacial times onward, follows very closely the established Baltic succession. It is not altogether clear, however, where the Atlantic–Sub-Boreal boundary occurs within Zone VI in Ireland. Likewise Zone V presents difficulties, as the Boreal–Atlantic horizon is not yet as firmly established here as elsewhere from the point of view of the pollen diagrams. It is, therefore, fortunate that for dating archaeological deposits referable to this period such a wealth of geological and palaeontological evidence exists. For purposes of checking the results of these sciences palaeobotany provides an extremely important base-line which is obvious in the second part of this book.

7. CORRELATIONS WITH FENNOSCANDIA

The close measure of uniformity demonstrated in Chapter II in the behaviour of the last ice-sheets in Northern and Western Europe has been confirmed by recent investigations of Late-Glacial peats in Ireland and the Baltic;

doubtless this will be strengthened by detailed work in other areas. The synchronism of events in both regions is also borne out by geochronology, and further research along these lines is urgently needed to elaborate the present efforts of dating by Late-Glacial varves. The Late-Glacial correlation makes subsequent comparisons seem much more plausible, since if glaciation in the British Isles resulted from the cooling effect induced by the Fennoscandian Ice, it follows that, as a result of the withdrawal of the ice, the Post-Glacial climatic succession must to some extent be uniform in both areas. This is reflected by the not strictly parallel but comparable forest history. Likewise the sequence of the land and marine fauna, particularly the latter, which have been intensively studied in Ireland, reveal a uniform development in both the British Isles and the Baltic region. Throughout the archaeological data are in complete accord with these conclusions.

Perhaps the strongest argument for the contemporaneity of the Late-Glacial and Early Post-Glacial Periods in Northern and Western Europe is afforded by the geological evidence. Both regions were basined as a result of the weight of the ice-load, but uplift began soon after the retreat was well under way. It was always more advanced in the peripheral areas than in those proximal to the centre of ice-dispersal (compare Wright, 1934). In Scandinavia the uplift was far more extensive because of the greater weight of matter incorporated into the ice. But the Late-Glacial Seas of Northern Britain, Ireland and Fennoscandia are contemporary, and deposits of this period in these regions contain an identical fauna. At this time the area of the present Baltic was occupied first by an ice-dammed lake and later, when the ice had retreated farther northward, by the Yoldia Sea. The first Post-Glacial land movement was apparently rapid, and resulted in the elevation of the land above its present level relative to the sea. During the emergence, which occurred in Late Pre-Boreal–Boreal times, forests flourished which are now submerged beneath the sea, and there was a greater extent of the land throughout the whole of Northern and Western Europe. At the peak of the uplift, climatic and geographic conditions were more favourable for the wide dispersal of forest trees than at any other time in the Post-Glacial Period. A phase of relative submergence, the Litorina, followed: the almost simultaneous transgression of extensive land surfaces between the British Isles and the Continent is in itself sufficient proof that the Post-Glacial history of these regions is intimately connected. The steady amelioration of the climate after the recession of the ice culminated in a phase of maximum warmth called the Post-Glacial climatic optimum, which is synchronous with the greatest extent of the Litorina Sea in Ireland as well as in the Baltic. This falls in the Atlantic climatic phase. The sea was then dominant, and Litorina raised beaches, marine deposits and erosion features indicate its extent. In this regard it is an important fact that the highest level Litorina beaches coincide almost exactly with the region of greatest Late-Glacial depression. Then, towards the end of the Atlantic Period, a change in the climate occurred which resulted in the return of cold, dry, Continental conditions. Phenomena operating to restore equilibrium after the sinking set in at this time, and an emergence, or a period during which the land was dominant, took place. The recovery has been slow and it is still in progress. South of the 0-isobase of the Litorina beaches there seems to have been secondary sinking up to the present, whereas in the north the movement appears to have ceased. As pointed out on p. 30, the general tendency is to approach the sea-level of the Third Interglacial Period.

All the most important phenomena that serve as time-indices to phases of Late-Glacial and Post-Glacial Periods have been examined in Great Britain and Ireland, and they show a striking measure of agreement in their conclusions, which have been summarized in the accompanying chart (Table 6). It has been shown that not only are the pollen sequences of Britain and Ireland on the one hand and the Baltic on the other divisible into the Blytt-Sernander climatic periods on the basis of the succession of forest phases, but also that this sequence may be correlated with important geological events common to all three areas. The chronological significance is apparent, for it is now possible to extend the long-established North European time-scale into Britain and Ireland, and to reconstruct with reasonable certainty the natural history of the area of settlement. Many problems still remain to be solved, but the extraordinary wealth of existing data are unanimous in their implications. This is of special importance with regard to fixing the age of archaeological deposits, especially in Ireland where the material cannot be dated through direct cultural affinities with the Continent. Thus the Irish Stone Age may now be placed in its proper context with relation to contemporary cultures in other regions. With a tentative time-scale thus fairly definitely established, the archaeological subject-matter of this book may be considered.

TABLE 6. The Chronology of the Late-Glacial and Early Post-Glacial Periods in Britain and Ireland

TENTATIVE DATES (after De Geer)	PERIODS	GLACIAL ERAS	LAND MOVEMENT	LAND MOVEMENT: BALTIC	LAND MOVEMENT: NORTH SEA	LAND MOVEMENT: IRISH SEA	LAND MOVEMENT: SCOTLAND	CLIMATIC PHASES	FOREST DEVELOPMENT IN IRELAND (K. Jessen): ZONES	FOREST DEVELOPMENT IN IRELAND (K. Jessen)	FAUNA
B.C.	POST-GLACIAL		EMERGENCE	CONDITIONS AS AT PRESENT				SUB-BOREAL Cold and dry: Continental climate	VI	Pine curve stops Alder dominant Oak, Elm, Pine, Birch Hazel comparatively rare Alder curve starts	Domestic animals introduced
2,500 3,000 4,000			SUBMERGENCE	LITORINA SEA	TRANSGRESSION OF THE NORTH SEA BED	LITORINA RAISED BEACHES Submerged Gravel and Marine Clay Deposits Caves formed at Oban and elsewhere TRANSGRESSION OF IRISH SEA BED Invasion of Valleys by the Sea	Scotland separate from England except for a narrow isthmus	Cooler at end Climatic optimum ATLANTIC Warm and moist: Oceanic climate			Red Deer Wild Boar Aurochs Wolf and Bear? Beaver Reindeer survived Irish Elk absent
5,000									Vb UPPER	Pine: two maxima Alder: traces only Oak dominant over Elm Hazel diminishing	
5,600 6,000			EMERGENCE	ANCYLUS LAKE	MOORLOG FORMING Land Connection between Britain and the Continent	SUBMERGED PEATS FORMING Partial Land-Bridge between Britain and Ireland		BOREAL, LATE Warmer at end	Vb LOWER	Hazel maximum Elm dominant over Oak Pine curve rising	Forest forms: Irish elk and Reindeer survived Lemming absent
		RAGUNDA: FINAL STADIUM						BOREAL, EARLY Cold and dry: Continental climate	Va	Hazel curve starts Birch and Willow comparatively rare Pine increasing	
6,800		FINIGLACIAL PERIOD **Third Retreat**	SUBMERGENCE	YOLDIA SEA LATE-GLACIAL SEA OUTSIDE THE BALTIC	LATE-GLACIAL SEA			PRE-BOREAL Gradual then rapid rise in temperature	IV	Birch dominant Pine and Willow common	Mixed tundra and Forest Lemming?
7,800	LATE-GLACIAL	FENNOSCANDIAN MORAINES VALLEY GLACIATION		BALTIC ICE-LAKE				ARCTIC	III	SOLIFLUCTION EARTH	Tundra forms: Reindeer Bear Irish Elk Arctic Fox Lemming Wolf
8,300		GOTIGLACIAL PERIOD **Second Retreat**						SUB-ARCTIC	II	ALLERØD DEPOSITS	
10,000 14,800		POMERANIAN STAGE READVANCE OF SCOTTISH AND IVERNIAN ICE			ICE RECEDING FROM SEA BEDS			ARCTIC	I	SOLIFLUCTION EARTH	
18,000		DANIGRACIAL PERIOD **First Retreat**									
		MAXIMUM ADVANCE		COVERED WITH ICE	PARTIALLY COVERED WITH ICE		COVERED WITH ICE				

[To face p. 102

Part Two

THE STONE AGE CULTURES OF IRELAND

Chapter I

THE ANTIQUITY OF MAN IN IRELAND

1. GENERAL ASPECTS AND NATURE OF THE PROBLEM

The final disappearance of the last ice-sheet, at about the beginning of the seventh millennium B.C., appears to represent the earliest date for the settlement of Ireland on the basis of existing data. Although the evidence from Inchnadamff, discussed on pp. 71–73, demonstrates that Scotland was already occupied by wandering groups of hunters at the very end of the Late-Glacial Period, there is no proof that man immigrated to Ireland until Early Post-Glacial times. During the Boreal Period a partial land-bridge across the Irish Sea (see pp. 87–89) made possible the dispersal of new forest forms from the Continent via Britain, as well as a temperate fauna and man, but up to the present no clear association of human remains or artifacts with glacial deposits has been established in Ireland. However, various claims have been made for the existence of an Irish Palaeolithic; these have been based on wholly unreliable data. In several cases the typological convergence of certain large coarse Mesolithic implements upon some of the established Lower Palaeolithic forms has led to confusion in this regard, whereas in other cases the claims have resulted from a misinterpretation of the facts. The material published by the Reverend Frederick Smith (1909, pp. 308–32) from Killiney Bay, County Dublin, is a good example of a claim in the latter category. In the first place, all of the illustrated specimens appear to be natural—it is only necessary to look over the examples of so-called Lower Palaeolithic implements shown by the Reverend Mr Smith from Northern Britain and Scotland to be convinced of this point. Not even the most ardent supporters of Palaeolithic man in Ireland have considered the Killiney series. Nor has the material from the Arctic beds at Ballyrudder, near Larne, County Antrim (see p. 37), ever been accepted as human, although Knowles (1892) submitted a series from this locality as evidence of an interglacial occupation of Ireland.

In the second category, the claims concern certain crude, very heavily rolled, coarse implements, which are Mesolithic in age, although to some degree reminiscent of certain Lower Palaeolithic types. In some cases they display surface scratches which resemble glacial striae, but which are a result of severe wave action. They occur in the Litorina raised beaches of North-East Ireland, on the modern foreshore near these deposits, and in a few river valleys, and are often associated with comparatively fresh and unrolled material. They form a noteworthy component of the Irish Mesolithic, especially at the classic site, Larne, County Antrim. Many theories have been advanced to explain the presence of these forms in Post-Glacial deposits, the most prevalent one being that they represent survivals of Palaeolithic forms into later times (Knowles, 1897) However, several authorities (Smith, R. A., 1911, p. 141; Knowles, 1914, pp. 119–21) have also contended that they were Palaeolithic in age, as well as in ancestry, and that the earlier series had been derived from glacial drifts and incorporated into the Litorina raised beach along with later material. Recently a more rational view of the situation was adopted (Macalister, 1928, pp. 30–6), but the case for remote antiquity has lately been opened anew (Burchell and Moir, 1932). This claim was based on the contention that many of the implements were Lower Palaeolithic, or even earlier in type, and that they were derived from deposits of the Glacial Period. Likewise a recrudescence of earlier forms in Post-Glacial times was recognized. Since this has an important bearing on the problem of the antiquity of man in Ireland, the evidence on which this claim is based must be considered. Burchell and Moir have identified the following types: (1) typical Harrisonian eoliths; (2) other forms of eoliths, transitional in type between true eoliths and rostro-carinate; (3) rostro-carinates; (4) rostrate hand axes, transitional in type between rostro-carinates and Early Chellean hand axes; (5) Early Chellean hand axes; (6) flakes of Cromerian type; and (7) flake implements and choppers of Clactonian type.

The mere assemblage of industries indicated by the above list is extraordinary. In Southern England and France, where true Lower Palaeolithic occurs in abundance, such a variety of forms, representing different and mutually distinct cultures, is seldom found in association with each other. The reported sites are all in County Antrim, and the finds are as follows: (1) *Carey River*, near Ballycastle: ten implements from the modern gravel spread in the base of the valley. Types 1, 2, 4, 5, 6 and 7; (2) *Ballyvoy*, Carey River Valley: one implement from glacial gravel between boulder clay. Type 3; (3) *Glendun*, Cushendun: one implement from the Post-Glacial gravel. Type 3; (4) *Drumfresky*, Dun River, near Cushendun: one implement from the boulder clay. Type 4; (5) *Closeburn Bay*: one implement from the foreshore. Type 5; (6) *Larne*: one implement from the foreshore. Type 5; (7) *Island Magee*: five implements from the lower estuarine clay. Types 3 and 5. The Ballyvoy and Drumfresky specimens, classified as rostro-carinate and rostrate hand axe forms, are both striated and heavily rolled. The patination is grey to putty colour. These are the only supposed Lower Palaeolithic or older implements found *in situ* in the region. In the writer's opinion the flake facets on both the former (Burchell and Moir, 1932, Fig. 6, p. 22) and the latter, shown in Fig. 16, are natural; such forms are common in Irish glacial drifts. Even if human origin could be established, the deposits in both instances date from the Late-Glacial Period, or the first advance of the last ice, at the earliest (Dwerryhouse, 1923, pp. 359 and 364). Hence on both geological and archaeological grounds the Lower Palaeolithic claim is disproved.

The specimens from the Carey River gravels display an ochreous patination; in some cases lines or scratches can be detected on the surface resulting from abrasion and heavy rolling. These marks, however, are described as glacial striae. The implements are supposedly derived from the glacial and interglacial deposits through which the river has cut its course, but direct proof is lacking on this point. Even if this could be proved, it would imply a Late-Glacial age as has been mentioned above. All the types are of frequent occurrence in the Litorina raised beach deposits of the Antrim coast, where the usual patination is a chalky white, and the degree of resemblance between the alleged ancient specimens is overwhelmingly greater when compared with a Late Mesolithic series than it is with types of the Lower Palaeolithic. The ochreous colour of the so-called Palaeolithic forms has developed as a result of the presence of iron oxide in solution in the waters of the Carey River, whose source is in the Tertiary basalt plateau south-west of Ballycastle, and which has a high iron content. Indeed, in the Litorina raised beaches of the County Antrim coast more heavily rolled forms are frequent, many of which, especially in the superficial layers, are patinated an even deeper ochreous colour than the Carey River "Palaeoliths". Thus, in the writer's opinion, the ancient appearance of these specimens is solely a result of recent steam erosion. The implements from Larne, Glendun and Closeburn Bay include forms similar to those from the Carey River. This fact is put forward as proof of the survival, or recrudescence (?), of the Lower Palaeolithic technique in Post-Glacial times, while on the other hand, the artifacts from the lower estuarine clay, Island Magee, are admitted to be of later age. Although the types are identical in every respect, the tradition of the early part of the Old Stone Age is declared to have persisted into the Post-Glacial Period at this site.

Since the entire foundation for the above claims of an Irish Palaeolithic rest on whether or not human implements occur in the glacial deposits of that area, the writer examined flints from this horizon at several localities visited while excavating Mesolithic sites in North-East Ireland (1933–6). All of these were of natural origin; yet the implements which are alleged to be derived from these drifts are found in great profusion in the Litorina raised beach. In view of this fact one would expect to find numerous sites where the older material still remains *in situ*. But no such locality has yet been reported either on the coasts of Counties Antrim and Down, or elsewhere in Ireland. Therefore the conclusions based on the present evidence are clear: the material in question dates from Post-Glacial times, and during this period forms were evolved in Ireland which converge on certain Lower Palaeolithic and older types in other regions. These are not a result of survival, but represent new types which developed in response to the changing environment of Post-Glacial times. This will be further discussed in the next chapter. At the moment, however, it is necessary to mention that the degree of rolling displayed by implements from the Litorina raised beaches and from the present foreshore is not a valid criterion for remote antiquity, since, at many sites in North-East Ireland, Late Mesolithic artifacts have been rolled almost beyond recognition. Thus the above claims may be dismissed as conclusive evidence of a Palaeolithic occupation of Ireland. Several other sites in Counties Sligo and Waterford must be considered before the Early Post-Glacial cultures, which are abundantly represented, are described.

2. ROSSES POINT AND OTHER SITES, COUNTY SLIGO

The announcement was made by Mr Burchell in 1927 that definite Palaeolithic implements had been found in County Sligo, North-West Ireland (Burchell, 1927[*a*], p. 260). It was declared that these were of Early Mousterian type. They consist of very heavy crude flakes, rarely worked, and made either of limestone or quartzite. During the following two years over forty papers were published concerning these implements, until the controversy was finally settled by Professors Charlesworth and Macalister (1930, pp. 18–32). Although few would reject the implements on the grounds that they are not human, the question of their age must be considered.

1. The Sites. At three sites on the Sligo coast, shown on the map, Fig. 15, Burchell discovered possible evidence for early human occupation.

(*a*) *Rosses Point.* On the west side of the end of a long promontory extending seaward on the north side of Sligo Bay, remains of a limestone rock shelter were reported (Burchell *et al.* 1929, pp. 1–4). The former existence of this shelter was, however, based on pure speculation, since actually only the fallen blocks of what was supposed to have been a rock shelter were found (compare Welch, 1928, Pl. IV; Jones and Boswell, 1928, p. 861). Above this level (± 8 feet above high-water level) is a Litorina raised beach consisting of powdered shells to a depth of 1 foot. Although it is alleged that the roof of the supposed shelter fell as a result of the weight of boulder clay deposited by the ice, the jointing planes in the limestone are such that they would have prevented the formation of any sort of a cave, and the fallen blocks were almost certainly produced by wave action. Below these blocks were found more than one hundred unrolled flakes and implements of limestone considered to be of Levalloisean technique. It is difficult to reconcile the comparatively fresh state of these with the violent erosion to which this portion of the coast has been subjected, exposed as it is to the full force of North Atlantic storms. Moreover, the effect of water rolling is particularly apparent on limestone.

(*b*) *Coney Island.* This island is situated in the centre of the mouth of Sligo Bay, and is approximately a mile long. According to Burchell (Burchell *et al.* 1929, pp. 4–6) abundant archaeological material was recovered for a distance of ½ mile along the north-eastern foreshore. It was originally contended that the implements had been derived by the sea from a huge cave, but this view was subsequently abandoned and the layer between the upper and lower boulder clay was held to be the archaeological horizon (Charlesworth and Macalister, 1930, p. 24). The small cave that does exist is definitely the result of recent erosion by the sea (Jones and Boswell, 1928, p. 682); this is still actively in progress. About a dozen artifacts were found, and they are of the same type as those from Rosses Point. Since they are unabraded, the same argument in favour of recent origin applies here, where the marine erosion is likewise severe at the present time.

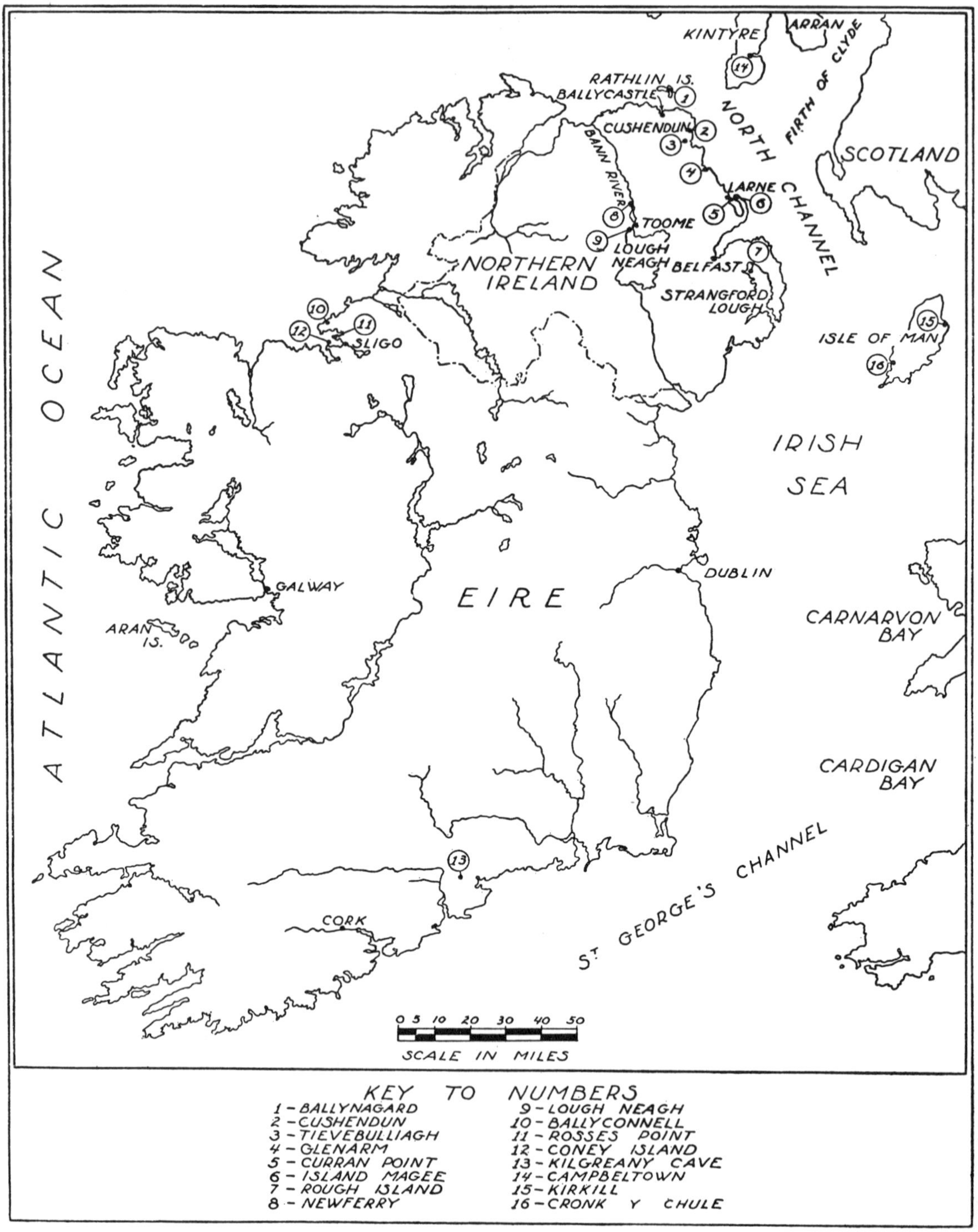

Fig. 15. Map showing the Location of Archaeological Sites in Ireland and Neighbouring Regions.

(*c*) *Ballyconnell.* At this site on the eastern side of Drumcliff Bay, approximately 5 miles north-west of Rosses Point, three limestone flakes were found (Burchell *et al.* 1929, pp. 6–8). Two of these were embedded in the boulder clay 39 feet below the surface, and the other came from the base of a gravel deposit some 20 feet away, at a depth of 7 feet 8 inches. The composite section is as follows:

(1) Peat	6 inches
(2) Upper Boulder Clay	6 feet
(3) Gravels, Sands and Loams	4 feet
(4) Lower Boulder Clay	28 feet 6 inches
(5) Carboniferous Limestone	Thickness undetermined

These artifacts are regarded as of the same age, definitely human, and conclusive proof of the antiquity of the Rosses Point and Coney Island material. Whereas each displays conchoidal fracture, there is no suggestion of secondary working. A few definite patches of patination occur. All are limestone and from deposits admittedly of glacial age. The question of whether or not the alleged Sligo implements date from the Glacial Period, therefore, rests on the evidence from this site.

2. Discussion. In County Sligo, especially along the portion of the coast with which we are dealing, there is evidence of severe glaciation (Charlesworth and Macalister, 1930, p. 29), and signs of excessive glacial plucking are everywhere apparent. In the boulder clay many broken and angular pieces of limestone and quartzite occur (compare Jones and Boswell, 1928, p. 861), among which if carefully sorted many examples could be found analogous in all respects with the Ballyconnell specimens. These finds must, therefore, be rejected as conclusive evidence for a Palaeolithic settlement of Ireland, since the so-called implements from Ballyconnell are natural. If, on the other hand, further research should bring to light additional specimens of demonstrably human origin, then man must have been in Ireland during the last Interglacial Period prior to the deposition of the boulder clay. The present evidence is definitely against this view.

The Rosses Point and Coney Island implements are, however, somewhat different. They exhibit the same characteristic fracture as the Ballyconnell material, which is peculiar to limestone and quartzite, but they are fresh and unpatinated. Those examined by the writer seem to be definitely human artifacts of which the two specimens illustrated in Fig. 17 are typical. A flat bulb of percussion, indicated by a white shattering mark at the point of impact, is clearly visible on many of the flakes. The striking platforms are

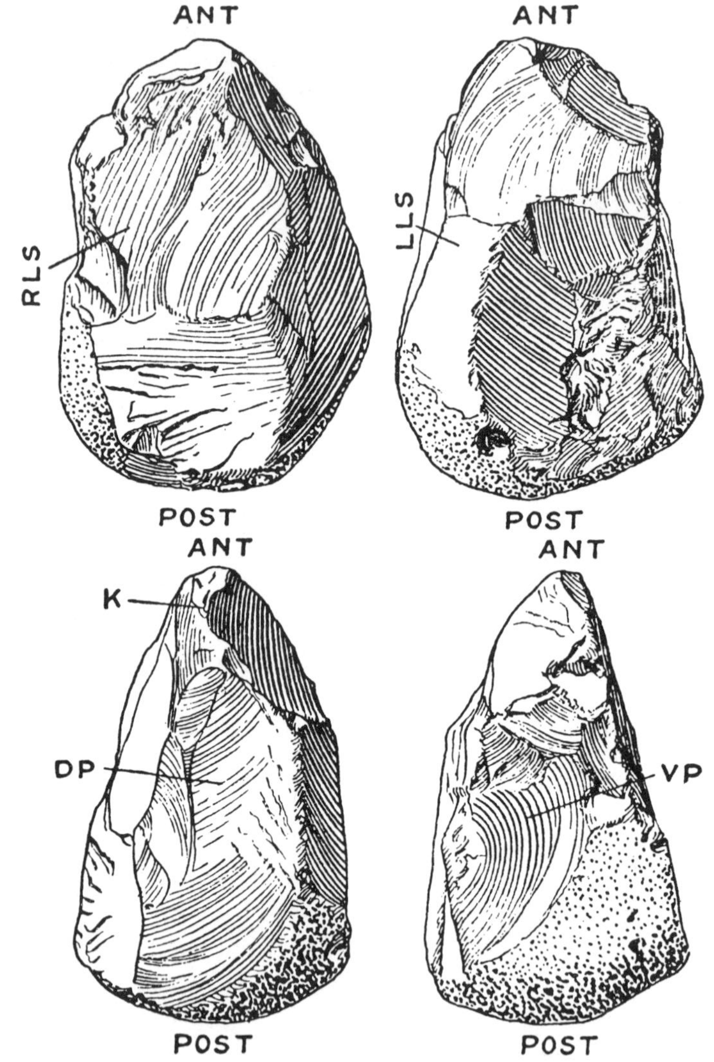

Fig. 16. Lower Palaeolithic Implement (?) found *in situ* in Glacial Gravel, Drumfresky, Dun River, County Antrim. ANT=anterior; POST=posterior; RLS=right lateral surface; LLS=left lateral surface; K=keel; DP=dorsal plane; VP=ventral plane. (After Burchell and Moir.) Scale: 1/1.

plain in most cases, although a few examples of faceting occur; secondary working is rare. When present, it is haphazard, probably the result of recent

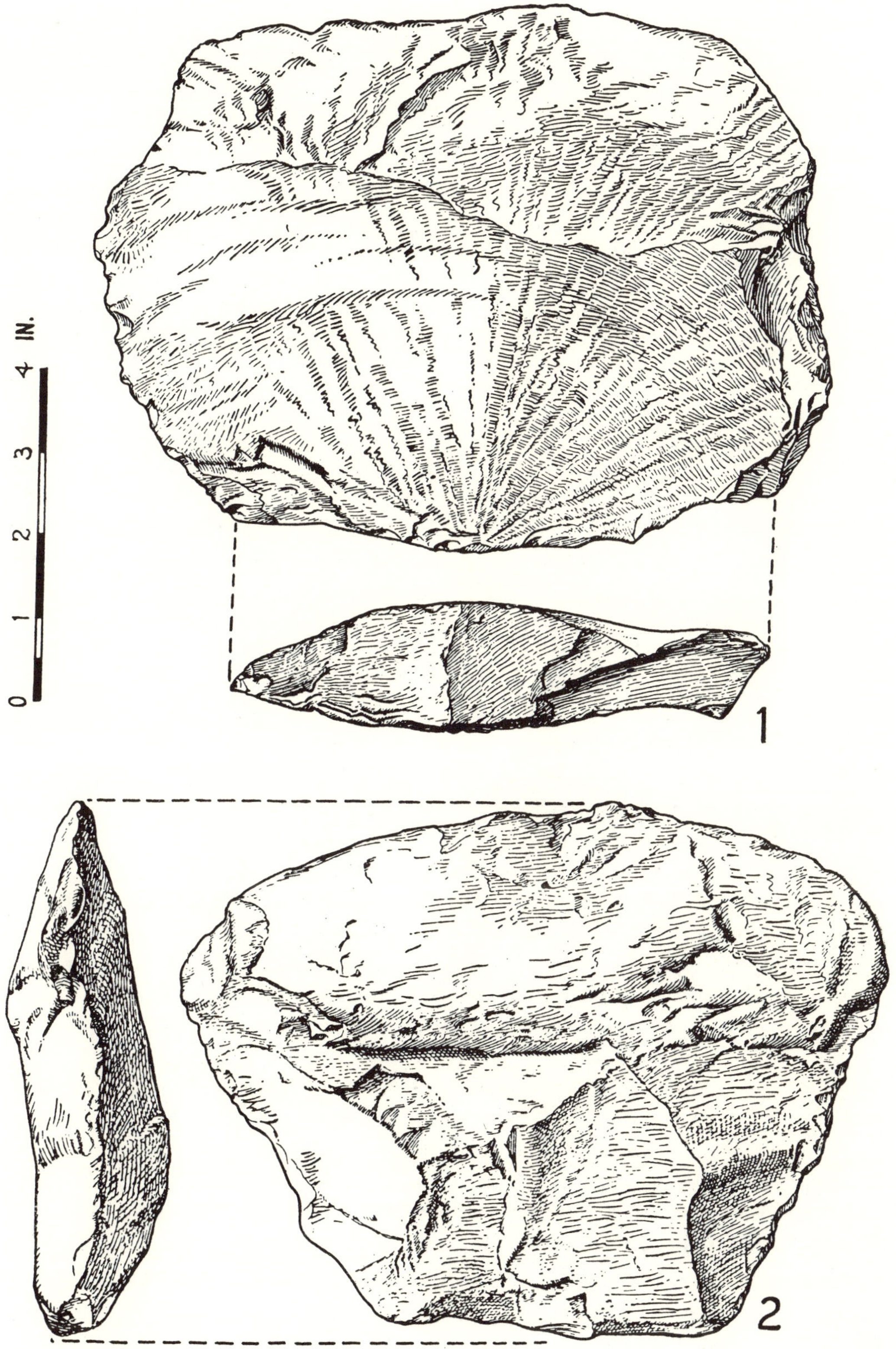

Fig. 17. Massive Flake Implements of Limestone from Rosses Point, County Sligo. No. 1, pseudo-Levallois flake with faceted striking platform; no. 2, fan-shaped flake struck from a prepared core. (After Burchell, Moir and Dixon.) Scale: 1/2.

sea action. The implements must, however, be regarded as modern, since none of them display signs of the severe marine erosion to which this portion of the coast has been subjected since the Late-Glacial Period, and both sites are well within the reach of the sea. It is quite possible that the material represents the refuse from chipping stone anchors or scapling waste from quarrying. The active fishing industry in the district favours the former explanation, though the latter is supported by a concrete foundation near the site on the Coney Island foreshore, and the golf links on the Rosses Point promontory.

3. SUMMARY AND CONCLUSIONS. If Ireland were occupied during the Palaeolithic Period, these sites cannot be accepted as proof of it, since the evidence is unsound and inconclusive. The whole Sligo controversy issues a definite warning to those who attempt to deduce archaeological facts on purely typological grounds with complete disregard for the geological data.

3. KILGREANY CAVE, COUNTY WATERFORD

Cave research in Ireland has produced abundant remains of Late-Glacial fauna from Counties Waterford, Cork, Clare and Sligo, as mentioned in Chapter II of Part I, and a bibliography covering this work is given on p. 316. By far the most intensive excavations have been carried out near Cappagh, approximately half-way between Dungarvan and Cappoquin, County Waterford, but it cannot as yet be proved that the extinct fauna is contemporary with remains of man. At Ballinamintra Cave, Cappagh, County Waterford, broken bones of Irish Elk and Bear were found in an horizon which yielded implements and human skeletal material (Adams *et al.* 1881). It was alleged that the animal bones were split by man for the extraction of marrow, but since the deposits at this site were somewhat confused, this evidence has not been accepted as conclusive proof that man was present in Ireland during Late-Glacial times. However, in 1928 a skeleton believed to be of importance was discovered at Kilgreany Cave, also near Cappagh, County Waterford (Plate I), on the north side of the valley of the Brickey River (Tratman, 1928). This skeleton, Kilgreany B, came from a stratum yielding Late-Glacial fauna, and hence an Upper Palaeolithic dating was suggested for it. Recently Dr Tratman (1937) has qualified this by stating that the burial belongs to the final Pleistocene, a period which he dates as late as ±4000 B.C. in England and Ireland. Since a large part of the deposit

KILGREANY CAVE, COUNTY WATERFORD

Upper General view of the present mouth of the cave.

Lower Section through the deposits in the second chamber of the cave.

was left unexcavated in 1928, it was decided in 1934 to undertake further investigations at Kilgreany as part of the programme of the Harvard Archaeological Expedition to Ireland. Great hopes were entertained that important evidence would be obtained for definitely establishing a Palaeolithic occupation of Ireland, but the results (Movius, 1935) were of a negative character.

Since the Kilgreany B skeleton was embedded in a discontinuous stratum of stalagmite, consisting of an upper tufaceous layer and a lower crystalline portion, particular attention was paid to this horizon. The burial was associated with a hearth, traces of which were found in the clearly defined stalagmite deposit adhering to the cave walls on three sides of the pit excavated in 1928. The most significant points established in 1934 may be summarized as follows: (1) The charcoal from the hearth with which the burial was associated was Post-Glacial and yielded Oak, Ash and Hazel. (2) Approximately 1 m. from the place where Kilgreany B was discovered a small amber bead was found embedded in the upper tufaceous portion of the lower stalagmite. This bead is probably not earlier than the Bronze Age, according to Professor Macalister (1928, pp. 91–2). (3) Bones of domestic Ox were found in the lower stalagmite near to the position of the skeleton and in the same horizon. (4) In all parts of the cave where the Late-Glacial fauna occurred, including the basal layers, it was associated with Ox, Sheep or other domestic animals, as well as with fragmentary remains of man. Indeed, the latter were present throughout the layer, and in every instance where they were found in deposits containing extinct mammals, remains of domestic animals were recovered as well. (5) Everywhere throughout the Kilgreany section evidence of great disturbance was apparent. In fact modern objects—glass, iron, pottery, etc.—were frequently associated with the Late-Glacial fauna. This evidence in itself is sufficient to cast serious doubt on the claim of a Late Palaeolithic occupation of Ireland based upon the finds from this site. (6) In the second chamber of the cave below 56 cm. of stalagmite, which formed a sort of boss supported by rocks and resting on the basal clay of the cave floor, a group of Neolithic potsherds of Windmill Hill type was found. Nearby, in the same horizon, remains of Irish Elk, Bear, Reindeer, and other extinct mammals occurred. (7) Not a single Palaeolithic implement has ever been found at the site, nor do any of the bones of the Late-Glacial group display evidence of working. (8) Finally, the anthropological data do not support the claim for assigning the skeleton to the Upper Palaeolithic Period. The measurements for Kilgreany A, a later skeleton found above the stalagmite in what is probably a Late Neolithic–Early Bronze Age stratum, compare very closely with those given for Kilgreany B. Sir Arthur Keith (1931, p. 431) points out that the former may well represent the female counterpart of Kilgreany man, and states that there is nothing intrinsically primitive in the morphology of the latter. This evidence strongly suggests that Kilgreany man cannot be placed earlier than the Neolithic, which substantiates the archaeological finds, since the Neolithic A sherds were the earliest datable objects recovered at the site.

On the basis of the above it appears certain that Kilgreany man is definitely Post-Glacial. The fact that this skeleton was found in a stalagmite layer with an extinct fauna with which were associated modern forms is no proof of antiquity, even when the evidence from the area excavated in 1928 alone is considered. This view has been accepted by Jackson (1936), Clark (1936[*b*]), and Mahr (1937, pp. 281–2), although Tratman (1937, p. 124) has recently stated that, since the section excavated by him was undisturbed except for the admitted intrusion of domestic Ox, the human skeleton must be accepted as "final Pleistocene". However, until more satisfactory evidence is available, the writer feels more than reluctant to admit that man was extant in Ireland while such forms as the Arctic Lemming, present at Kilgreany, still survived. In any case, natural forces had so completely disturbed the deposits at Kilgreany Cave, that precise dating of the material was impossible. The most important finds include a mandible and several fragmentary bones of Lynx, the first recorded in Ireland (Stelfox, 1937), and a very fine eighth-century art object. The latter was silver-plated and decorated in the characteristic animal style of the Early Christian Period; it was found in the superficial deposits in the second chamber of the cave.

4. THE OLD STONE AGE IN IRELAND: SUMMARY

The data from the sites described above point clearly to the same conclusion. If Palaeolithic man did reach Ireland, there is no valid evidence that it was during the Glacial Period. When all the material which has thus far come to light in support of an Old Stone Age occupation of this area is considered as a whole, it is untrustworthy and therefore must be discarded. Whereas the possibility that in Late-Glacial times wandering bands of Upper Palaeolithic hunters crossed on the ice from Britain in pursuit of game cannot be ruled out, there are no facts as yet to substantiate such an argument. Lack of pressure, the barrier of the ice-covered Highland Zone of Britain, and the absence of an available flint supply in the unglaciated portion of Southern Ireland, however, make this highly improbable. Thus in spite of the wealth of limestone caves in the latter region, the incentives to migrate to such an isolated insular region on the periphery of Western Europe were lacking. Furthermore the adverse climatic conditions which prevailed in Ireland at this time were probably anything but conducive to settlement. The situation was very different in the Early Post-Glacial Period. Following the retreat of the ice, man moved northward from Southern and Central Britain and settled in North-East Ireland and South-West Scotland under extremely favourable climatic conditions. The sites of this period on the coasts of Counties Antrim and Down, which form the major subject of this book, will be discussed in the next chapter. Before considering these coastal stations, one inland site, which has yielded the earliest datable archaeological material of unquestionably human origin thus far discovered in Ireland, will be described.

5. LOUGH NEAGH, COUNTY LONDONDERRY

The great significance of this site lies in the fact that it definitely establishes occupation in Ireland during the Boreal Period. In addition it is the only Early Post-Glacial station hitherto reported from the interior of the island. Whereas Mesolithic material is abundantly represented in the Litorina raised beach and estuarine clay deposits of the north-eastern coast, it is always in a secondary position, but here the implements are *in situ*. Since they are sealed below Boreal peat, they afford important evidence which is pertinent to the question of the antiquity of man in Ireland. Mr C. B. Whelan (1930[*a*]) discovered the site (see p. 317 for bibliography), located approximately three-quarters of a mile south-south-west of Toome, on the north-western shores of Lough Neagh near the point where the Lower Bann River flows out of the lough (Fig. 15). It has never been thoroughly excavated, although Mr Whelan made a careful investigation in 1932. Until recently the area was under water, but since the Bann Drainage Project went into operation it has been easily accessible.

Just above the water level of the lake, which is approximately +54 feet O.D., an eroded peat surface has been exposed. This proves that at the time of the formation of the peat, the surface of the water must have been at least 1 m. below its present level. At the point investigated by Mr Whelan the following section was recorded:

(A) Yellow Lacustrine Sand	40·5 cm.
(B) Forest Peat	28 cm.
(C) Dark Greenish-Grey Sand	Thickness undetermined

Water level now occurs approximately 10 cm. below the base of the peat, Deposit B, hence the underlying sand could not be thoroughly examined, but the portion exposed is a fine quartzose sand, and it grades into coarser material containing gravel. The peat was studied by Erdtman (1932, p. 106; Whelan, 1933[*a*], p. 150), and on the basis of pollen analysis it contains Alder 4 per cent, Birch 52 per cent, Pine 7·5 per cent, Oak 19·5 per cent, Elm 17 per cent, Hazel 13 per cent, and Willow 1 per cent. According to Jessen (1940, p. 51), this layer is older than the earliest implementiferous horizon at Cushendun, County Antrim (see p. 128). Thus it must belong to the lower part of Zone V*b* in Ireland, which confirms Erdtman's conclusions that it may be assigned to the very end of the Boreal Period. Peaty layers are present in the base of the overlying deposit of yellow lacustrine sand, indicative of fluctuating conditions at the beginning of Atlantic times. The upper part of this sand is probably quite recent. The peat itself appears to be archaeologically sterile. Quantities of artifacts, however, as well as bones of Red Deer, occur on the surface of the lower sand, Deposit C, and several implements have been found *in situ* in this layer at points where the overlying peat layer still exists. It must be concluded therefore that the sand once formed a land surface along the edge of the lake where a Stone-Age settlement of the Early Post-Glacial Period was situated. This has been sealed by the overlying layer of Late Boreal peat.

The flint implements from this site are fresh, sharp and unrolled; the patination varies from dark olive-green to dark brown. Small forms predominate, the retouching is carefully executed, and the flakes are well struck. The leading types, as illustrated by Fig. 18, include steep scrapers or planes, nos. 2–8; small end-of-blade scrapers, no. 13; perforators, no. 14; utilized blades, no. 12; gravers or burins, nos. 9–11; small picks, no. 1; cores with plain striking platforms, no. 15; and small hammerstones, no. 16. As a whole this assemblage suggests an Upper Palaeolithic derivation; the technique is basically Aurignacian in tradition. However, the cultural

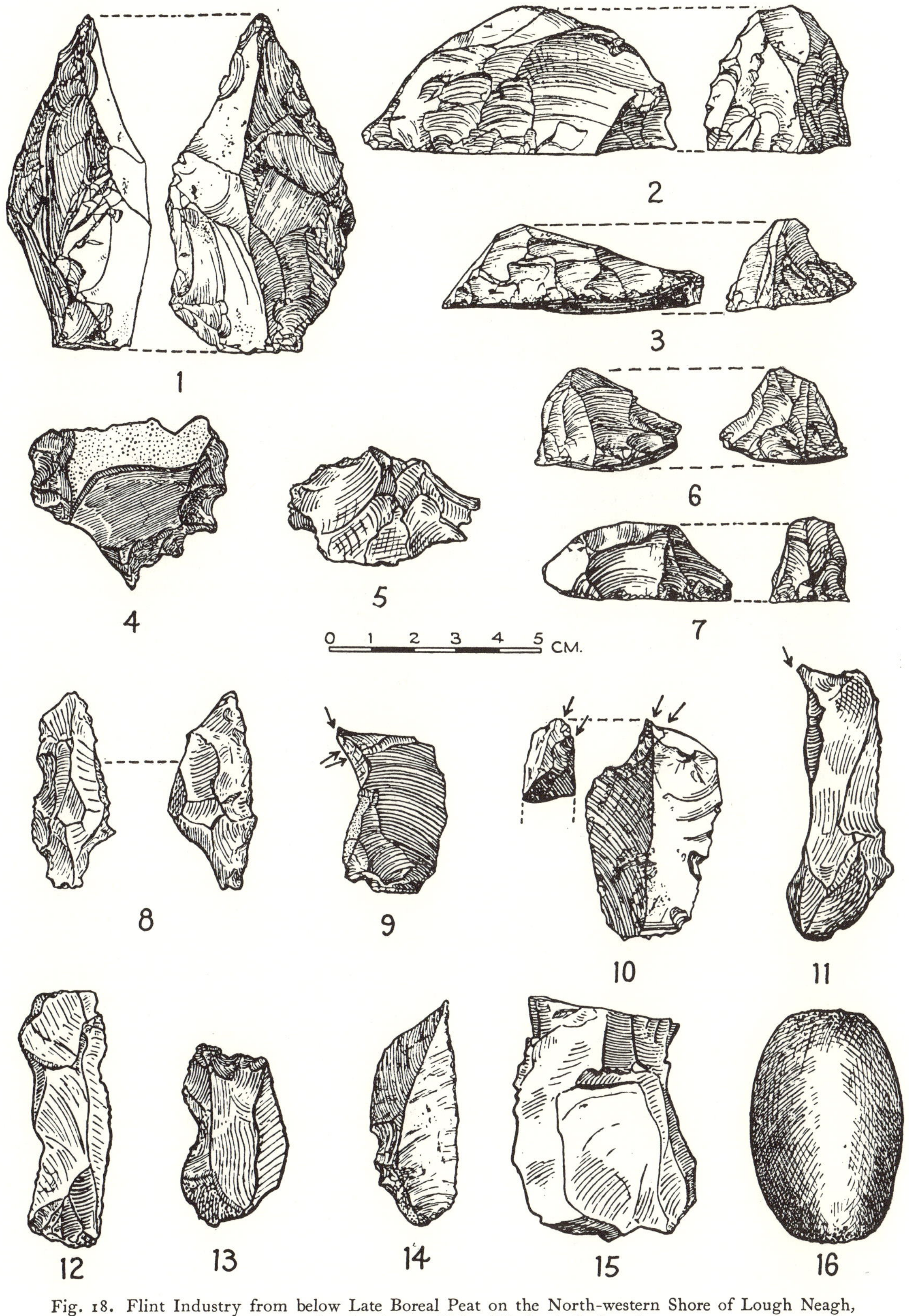

Fig. 18. Flint Industry from below Late Boreal Peat on the North-western Shore of Lough Neagh, County Londonderry. (After Whelan.) Scale: 2/3.

affinities of this inland site will be considered in the next chapter, since the industry is closely related to the Early Mesolithic found in marine deposits on the coast of Counties Antrim and Down. This station, therefore, affords conclusive proof of an Early Post-Glacial occupation of Ireland prior to the transgression of the Litorina Sea.

As will be discussed later, the first settlers in Ireland of whom we have any record were the descendants of Upper Palaeolithic hunters who migrated northwards in Mesolithic times and occupied the new land made available after the retreat of the ice. Although at present direct evidence is lacking, the possibility that Pre-Boreal sites in Ireland may eventually be discovered must be considered. It seems probable that during this period Scotland was occupied, but the existence of the Late-Glacial Sea would have prevented man from reaching Ireland unless boats had already been introduced. There are, however, no finds in Northern or Western Europe demonstrating the use of boats until Boreal times (see p. 206). Nevertheless the question of Pre-Boreal settlements in Ireland cannot be dismissed on these grounds; such sites if they exist would have an extremely important bearing on the origins of the Irish Mesolithic. In conclusion it may be stated that there are as yet no valid data to prove that this region was inhabited prior to the Boreal Period, ±6800–5600 B.C. on the basis of Scandinavian chronology, which further answers the question of the antiquity of man in Ireland.

Chapter II

THE MESOLITHIC CULTURE OF THE IRISH RAISED BEACHES

1. DISTRIBUTION AND METHOD OF APPROACH

The sites of this period occur in abundance along the coast of North-East Ireland, from Carlingford Lough around to the mouth of the Lower Bann River, and in all cases they are associated with Post-Glacial marine deposits. Prior to 1930 only one of these, Curran Point, Larne, County Antrim, had been scientifically excavated (Praeger, 1890; Gray, W., 1890; Coffey and Praeger, 1904). Therefore, the problem of the Harvard Archaeological Expedition was to select key stations where the archaeological sequence could be established, since in spite of the wealth of material in the Dublin and Belfast Museums, the origin and development of the Irish Stone Age had never been completely worked out. In selecting the four sites which were excavated in 1934–6, the expedition was given much helpful advice by Mr C. Blake Whelan, M.R.I.A., of Belfast, who together with Mr J. P. T. Burchell, F.S.A., of London, has been untiring in his efforts to further the cause of Irish prehistory in recent years. During the last century Dr Praeger (1892, 1896) established the Post-Glacial stratigraphy of Northern Ireland, based on a detailed geological study of the coastal deposits with special reference to the fauna which they contained. But the archaeological sequence has never been fitted into this succession, nor have the beds been thoroughly investigated from a palaeobotanical point of view. In this regard the expedition worked in conjunction with the Committee for Quaternary Research in Ireland, and Professor K. Jessen was able to examine each site where polleniferous deposits were uncovered. At two of the localities, Cushendun and Glenarm, County Antrim, the recent physiographic history of the region as a whole was studied by F. L. W. Richardson, Jr., of Harvard, and the important work of identifying the marine fauna was undertaken throughout by Mrs N. F. McMillan of Liverpool. The conclusions of each of these specialists is contained in the discussion of the excavations in the first part of this chapter. Before considering this information, however, the composite section, as originally produced by Praeger (1892, p. 213;

1896, p. 43), will be presented. This provides the basis of the archaeological sequence, and the evidence has been confirmed by excavation and pollen analysis. The results from each independent line of research are in strict accord with one another, and the compilation and correlation of this material provides the key to the Mesolithic succession in Ireland. The actual typology of the Irish Mesolithic will be described in a later section of the chapter.

Although at no one site have all the deposits listed below been recorded, the Post-Glacial stratigraphy of North-East Ireland may be summarized as follows:

(A) SURFACE. Recent humus which usually contains Neolithic material.

(B) RAISED BEACHES. These are composed of coarse material—sand, gravel and large stones—which yields Mesolithic implements. They were formed during the period of the transgression and subsequent regression of the Litorina Sea. Sometimes estuarine clays (Deposit C) underlie them, and their height varies from 10 to 30 feet above present sea-level. Actually the term "raised beach" is ambiguous, as in many cases these deposits were laid down under water; technically, therefore, the majority of them are raised sea beds. Nevertheless the name "raised beach" has been retained, but since their height is extremely variable, and since they contain distinctive archaeological material, the term "Litorina Raised Beach" has been introduced (see p. 86) in place of "25-foot Raised Beach" or "Early Neolithic Raised Beach". Recent marine erosion has affected the seaward portion of the Litorina raised beaches at some localities.

(C) ESTUARINE CLAY. Also laid down during the Litorina submergence. This consists of three zones:

(1) *Upper or Thracia Zone*. Deposited in at least 5 fathoms of water and characterized by the great variety of warm molluscs and foraminifera which it contains. Of these *Thracia convexa* is typical. This clay is light blue in colour, pure and unctuous. The zone coincides with the Post-Glacial climatic optimum.

(2) *Intermediate Zone*. Similar to the *Thracia* Zone, and containing a rich marine fauna which includes warm forms not found in the present seas. These clays were deposited in 2–3 fathoms of water.

(3) *Lower or Scrobicularia Zone*. For the most part this is a brownish-blue, somewhat sandy clay, which is characterized by a great many littoral shells. These belong to a comparatively limited number of species, and

indicate that present-day conditions pertained at the time of deposition. In addition an abundance of roots of the Grass Wrack (*Zostera marina*) occur.

The Litorina raised beaches (Deposit B) are in the main contemporaneous with the deep water *Thracia* clays, and they frequently overlie clays of either the Intermediate or the *Scrobicularia* Zones. At some localities, however, no clays were deposited during the submergence: the raised beach has been formed on top of gravels, which were laid down during the marine transgression. In other cases both gravels and clays are found dating from this period. Local conditions therefore have determined the sedimentation, so that it is difficult always to be certain of the precise age of any given horizon in this series on the basis of its composition alone. In such circumstances it is necessary to utilize as many different kinds of dating evidence as possible.

(D) Submerged Peat. This is usually visible on the coast between tide marks, but at the head of Belfast Lough, near Downpatrick, and in Dundrum Bay, it is found down to a depth of 31 feet below high-water level (see p. 83). At these localities the thickness varies from 1 foot 6 inches to 3 feet, but elsewhere the average is under 6 inches. It is dark brown in colour, tightly compressed, and overlain by Litorina deposits. The pollen spectra vary within certain limits, but in general they indicate the Late Boreal, or Boreal–Atlantic transition Period (Zone V*b*), since a maximum of Hazel, in addition to Birch, Pine, Willow, Alder, Oak and Elm are represented. Marsh plants—sedges, flags and rushes—are characteristic, and elytra of beetles, as well as mammalian remains, are often found. The latter include Irish Elk, Red Deer and Wild Boar. This is the first bed in the Post-Glacial series to show the arrival of temperate conditions. Furthermore, it indicates that the land in the region of the North Irish Sea stood higher in relation to sea-level during this period.

(E) Sands and Gravels. These are marine, as attested by a few worn foraminifera, and were probably laid down by the Late-Glacial Sea.

(F) Resorted Boulder Clay. This appears to represent an old land surface formed after the retreat of the ice.

(G) Laminated Clay. This deposit is found in isolated instances. The sediments were formed in the extra-glacial lakes impounded by the ice during its retreat in certain of the bays and inlets along the coast.

(H) Boulder Clay. Glacial drift or boulder clay covers all of Northern Ireland, containing striated flint pebbles which often exhibit natural flake facets. It is also referred to as glacial till.

This is the standard section for North-East Ireland from Late-Glacial times to the beginning of the Sub-Boreal climatic phase, and it furnishes a framework into which it is proposed to fit the archaeological succession of the coastal Mesolithic sites. It is regrettable that in this area all the early material recovered thus far comes from secondary sources; it has been derived by the sea and washed into deposits along the present coast. These date from the time of the transgression of the Litorina Sea. The only undisturbed occupation site of a period prior to the maximum of the submergence is the inland station on the northern shore of Lough Neagh, described in the last chapter (see p. 117). This provides important data bearing on the problem of the earliest occupation of Ireland, which cannot definitely be established from the evidence of the coastal stations. When archaeological, geological and climatological factors are considered, however, it will be shown that settlement probably was effected on the coast during the Boreal Period when the existence of a partial land-bridge made migration comparatively easy. This question will be further discussed in the next chapter, but until Mesolithic occupation sites are found in Counties Antrim and Down establishing this point, it is possible to arrive only at tentative conclusions. Whereas some sites of this period exist in Scotland and Northern England, they contribute only very indirectly to the problem.

During Mesolithic times the principal focus of settlement in this area was in North-East Ireland, where, along the coast in the Cretaceous chalk, there is an almost inexhaustible and easily accessible supply of flint. The deposit is contained in the Tertiary basalt uplands of County Antrim, and extends the entire length of the north and east Antrim coasts to near Lisburn, County Down. These uplands, which rise to ±1000 feet O.D., do not appear to have been occupied during the Mesolithic Period, a fact which suggests that for purposes of subsistence, the coastal lowlands offered a greater inducement to settlers. This may also explain the comparative absence of inland sites. The most important localities where implements have been reported in the raised beaches and other Litorina deposits are as follows:

1. *Greenore*, Carlingford Lough, County Louth (Praeger, 1896, p. 31; Martin, 1930, p. 494).
*2. *Rough Island*, Strangford Lough, County Down (Whelan, 1933, p. 1216; 1938, p. 124; Movius, 1940 [*a*]).
3. *Strangford Lough*, County Down. Many unpublished sites in the vicinity of Newtownards and on the Ards Peninsula.

4. *Groomsport and Sandeel Bay*, County Down (Angus MacDonald Collection in the Belfast Municipal Museum and Art Gallery).
5. *Ballyholme Bay*, County Down (Du Noyer, 1869[*a*], p. 169).
6. *Kinnegar, Holywood*, Belfast Lough, County Down (Praeger, 1896, p. 34; Holme, 1912).
7. *Cultra*, County Down (Gray, W., 1893, p. 556).
8. *Vicinity of Belfast* (Young, 1877).
9. *Kilroot*, Belfast Lough, County Antrim (Knowles, 1914).
10. *Greencastle*, Belfast Lough, County Antrim (Gray, W., 1880, p. 112).
11. *Greenisland*, Belfast Lough, County Antrim (McMillan, 1938; 1938[*a*]).[1]
12. *Carrickfergus*, Belfast Lough, County Antrim (Du Noyer, 1869, p. 48; 1869[*a*], p. 169).
13. *Island Magee*, County Antrim (Knowles, 1914; Burchell, 1931, pp. 270–81; 1934).
*14. *Curran Point*, Larne Harbour, County Antrim (Praeger, 1890; Coffey and Praeger, 1904).
15. *Vicinity of Larne Lough*, County Antrim. Many sites (Knowles, 1914; Du Noyer, 1869).
16. *Closeburn Bay*, County Antrim (Burchell, 1931, p. 295).
*17. *Glenarm*, County Antrim (Whelan, 1930, p. 178; Movius, 1937).
18. *Carnlough*, County Antrim (Gray, W., 1880).
*19. *Cushendun*, County Antrim (Burchell, 1931, p. 282; Movius, 1940).
20. *Ballycastle*, County Antrim. Modern gravel spread of the Carey River (Burchell, 1932, p. 19).
21. *Ballintoy*, County Antrim. Basal levels of several caves cut by the Litorina Sea (Jackson, 1933; 1936[*a*]; 1938).
22. *White Park Bay*, County Antrim (Coffey and Praeger, 1904, pp. 191–2).
23. *Portrush*, County Antrim (Simpson, W., 1889, p. 76; Patterson, 1896; 1896[*a*].
24. *Portstewart*, County Londonderry (Coffey and Praeger, 1904).

* Sites excavated by the Harvard Archaeological Expedition to Ireland 1934–6.

The wealth of material from these sites is amazing, arguing in favour of an intensive occupation of the littoral of North-East Ireland during Mesolithic times. This emphatically applies to the Late Mesolithic, to which phase the major portion of the localities listed above may be assigned.[2] Doubtless

[1] Although the geological and palaeontological evidence suggests that this site is Mesolithic, the archaeological material is very disappointing.

[2] As an example of the evidence on which this statement is based, the Litorina gravels at Curran Point, Larne, may be cited. The deposit covers an area of over 1 square mile and attains an average thickness of approximately 10 feet (see p. 132). Late Mesolithic implements occur in profusion throughout these gravels. Indeed literally tons of them have been collected during the last seventy-five years, and wherever an excavation is made for a building or other purposes hundreds more specimens are brought to light. Since the position of the implements is secondary, such a concentration of material would only be possible

the material from many of the early sites was completely lost during the first stages of the transgression of the Litorina Sea. But enough has been recovered to recognize two phases—early and late—in the development within this area. The complex revealed by a close study of large series of implements from stratified sites in Counties Antrim and Down has been identified as an independent Mesolithic culture, and it is well to make clear at the outset that for this complex the name LARNIAN, after the classic site at Larne, has been proposed (Movius, 1940, p. 75). The sites which provide the stratigraphic background of the Larnian will be summarized, and the archaeological horizons in each grouped on a chronological basis, before the typology of its various phases is discussed as a whole.

2. STRATIGRAPHY

A. CUSHENDUN, COUNTY ANTRIM

This site was first recorded by Dwerryhouse (1923, pp. 364–6) and a preliminary archaeological investigation was made in 1931 by Burchell and Whelan (Burchell, 1931, pp. 282–7). It is situated on the left bank of the Dun River, approximately 55 miles north of Belfast, see Fig. 15, and was excavated in 1934 by the Harvard Archaeological Expedition to Ireland (Movius, 1940). The village of Cushendun itself is situated on the Early Post-Glacial Terrace, ±35 feet O.D., which is well exposed 150 yards west of the town, and here the following section was recorded (Plate II):

(A)	Humus	(Horizon 4)	50 cm.
(B)	Upper Gravel	(Horizon 3)	3·15 m.
(C)	Upper Lagoon Silt		77 cm.
(D)	Lower Gravel	(Horizon 2)	3·58 m.
(E)	Lower Lagoon Silt	(Horizon 1)	46 cm.
(F)	Swamp Peat		10 cm.
(G)	Resorted Boulder Clay		30 cm.
(H)	Laminated Clay }		Thickness undetermined
(I)	Boulder Clay }		

(A) HUMUS. For the most part this has accumulated since the emergence of the land in the Late Atlantic Period. In this deposit a few flint

if numerous occupation sites had existed along the foreshore contemporary with and prior to the Litorina submergence when the gravels themselves were laid down. As will be presently discussed the actual time-span during which this industry flourished was not of long duration. Therefore the occupation itself must have been fairly intensive. In the writer's opinion Larne is among the richest secondary archaeological localities in Europe.

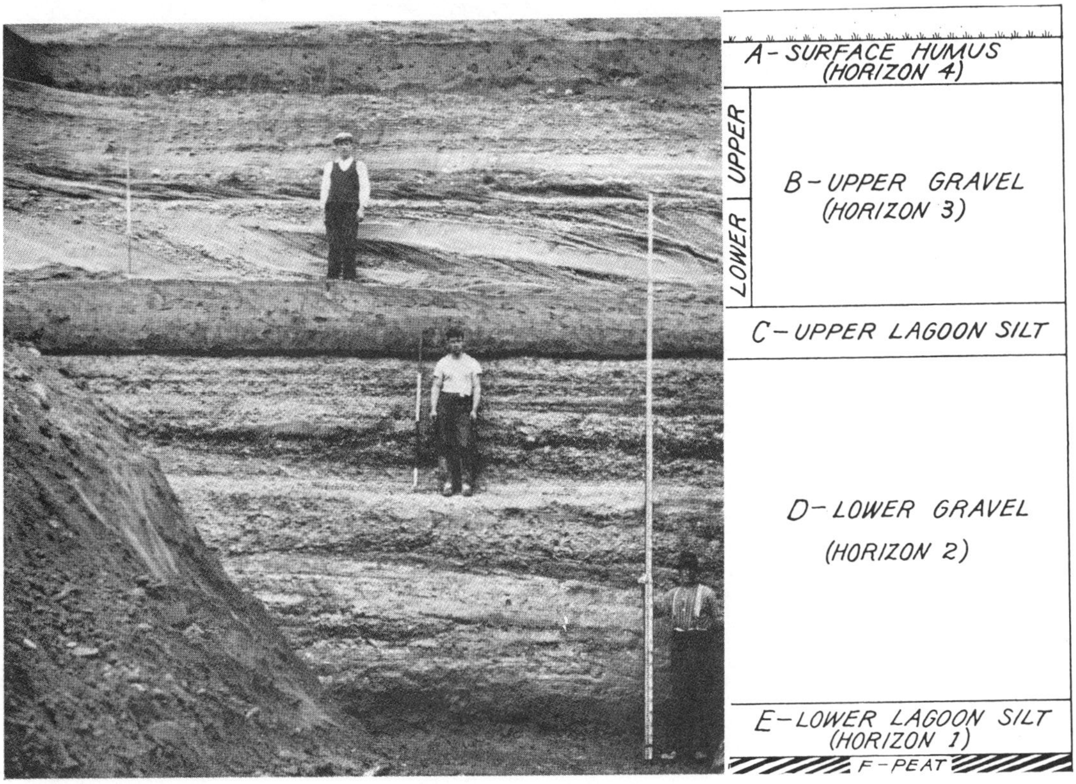

CUSHENDUN, COUNTY ANTRIM

Upper General view of the mouth of Glendun looking north-west, showing the Dun river, the excavated site, and the 35-foot (Early Post-Glacial) terrace.

Lower Section through the deposits at the excavated site.

implements were found in association with a hearth (Horizon 4); the material, described in Chapter IV, is typical of the industries of Neolithic age which occur at many surface stations in Counties Antrim and Down.

(B) UPPER GRAVEL. The upper portion of this deposit is a typical storm beach formed by the sea during the emergence. Layers of medium-sized boulders occur at intervals, indicating severe wave action; these beds slope gradually in the direction of the present strand. The lower part of the upper gravel is made up of inclined beds, formed during the maximum of the submergence, as a result of the interaction between waves and currents at the mouth of a tidal inlet. Implements are not common on this deposit. They are mainly concentrated in the coarser layers of the horizontal beds, and consist of the crude, much rolled flakes, which belong to the Late Larnian culture (Horizon 3).

(C) UPPER LAGOON SILT. This is sterile archaeologically, but since it seals in Deposit D and contains pollen as well as molluscs, it is important for dating purposes. Professor Jessen has assigned this layer to the palaeo-botanical Zone V*b* in Ireland (1940, p. 44); it contains Elm, Oak, Birch, Pine, Hazel, and a small amount of Alder pollen. According to Mrs McMillan, the following shells occur: *Cardium edule* (90 per cent) and *Scrobicularia plana* (10 per cent), and the presence of only two forms makes it possible to establish the conditions which prevailed at the time of deposition (1940, pp. 37–8). Both thrive from low water to a depth of a few fathoms, hence this layer was formed in a relatively shallow tidal lagoon or estuary, existing in the valley during this stage of the submergence.

(D) LOWER GRAVEL. The lower gravel is stratified horizontally, is coarser than Deposit C, and far less rolled. A sinking of the land of ± 4 m., during which the deposition was *in tempo* with the subsidence, accounts for this deposit, which was laid down by the sea during Early Atlantic times. It is very prolific throughout of flint implements (Horizon 2), but contains no trace of either bone or shell. The archaeological material is sharp and practically unrolled, which indicates that the sea rapidly invaded occupation sites along the coast and swept up the refuse material, transporting it by swift currents to a position farther inland. All of this material was in a secondary position, no evidence of occupation being found in the lower gravel. The large series of implements recovered from this horizon belongs to the Early Larnian, in which well-struck blade implements are typical.

(E) Lower Lagoon Silt. High-water level coincides with the basal part of this layer, which contains peaty material, fine sand, and silt. An abundant marine fauna, including *Littorina littorea*, *L. saxatilis*, *L. littoralis*, *Nucella lapillus*, *Ostrea edulis*, *Cardium edule*, *Paphia pullastra* and *P. decussata*, is present, according to Mrs McMillan (1940). These forms prove that the deposit is a typical lagoon accumulation laid down under relatively quiet conditions between tide marks. *Paphia decussata*, a southern form now absent on the coast of North-East Ireland, points to a milder climate at this period. Remains of Codfish (*Gadus morrhua*) and Wild Boar (*Sus scrofa*) have been recorded. The pollen analysis shows that Deposit E belongs to the lower part of the Irish Zone V*b*, which contains the so-called Boreal Hazel maximum, an absence of Alder, and a decline of the Pine curve (Jessen, 1940). However, the Hazel frequency is somewhat lower here than in a typical pollen spectrum of the Boreal Period, therefore Professor Jessen has suggested that this layer corresponds to the Late Boreal–Early Atlantic transition phase of the Baltic. A few unrolled implements occur in the basal portion of the deposit; these are of Early Larnian type (Horizon 1).

(F) Swamp Peat. This layer is very tightly compressed, and represents the old land surface which existed in the valley during the Early Post-Glacial emergence. Although very little pollen is present in Deposit F, it also belongs to the early portion of Zone V*b*—Boreal–Atlantic transition—and was accumulated under swampy conditions, as demonstrated by the high frequency of Common Reed (*Phragmites communis*) which it contains. It seems very probable that the archaeological material from Deposits D and E is the refuse from occupation sites in the vicinity of the mouth of the present Cushendun Bay, belonging to the period of emergence, towards the end of which the swamp peat was formed.

(G) Resorted Boulder Clay. This deposit was derived from the boulder clay probably during the erosion cycle of Boreal times. It is made up of broken and striated stones tightly packed in a matrix of reddish clay. No human artifacts came from this horizon.

(H) Laminated Clay. As a large extra-glacial lake was formed in Glendun during the Late-Glacial Period (see p. 277), it seems certain that this deposit was laid down at that time. Fossils, plant remains and diatoms are completely absent, although a few rounded pebbles occur. The clay is composed of fine particles, indicating that its sedimentation took place in still water.

(I) BOULDER CLAY. During Late-Glacial times Glendun was invaded by the Scottish Readvance Ice (see p. 51), therefore it is probable that this deposit, which is the typical boulder clay of the coast of North-East Ireland, dates from this stage in the glaciation of this region.

The above section is extraordinarily complete, and it reveals the geological history of the area from the close of the Late-Glacial Period to the end of Atlantic times. Following the retreat of the ice the Cushendun region was invaded by the Late-Glacial Sea, as proved by the 50-foot terrace which flanks the valley (Richardson, 1940, p. 12). There next occurred a period of erosion during which the land rose above its present level with respect to the sea. On a comparative basis this may be dated to the Boreal Period, and it seems likely that human settlement began during this phase, when the climate was favourable. In Atlantic times the land was submerged to the 25-foot level, warm, moist conditions of the Post-Glacial climatic optimum prevailed, and a terrace, 25·60 feet above high-water level at the site, or +35·65 feet O.D., was built up during the transgression of the Litorina Sea. The deposits of this terrace contain three horizons of Mesolithic material in secondary position, whereas the humus, which has accumulated on the surface, has yielded a fourth which is Post-Larnian in age. Horizon 1 is Early Larnian, found in Deposit E (the lower lagoon silt), which dates from the Late Boreal–Early Atlantic Transition Period; Horizon 2 is also Early Larnian, found in Deposit D (the upper gravel), laid down by the sea during the submergence; Horizon 3 is Late Larnian, found in Deposit B (the upper gravel), which was formed during the time of the maximum of the submergence and during the emergence; and Horizon 4, which is Neolithic in age, is found in Deposit A, the surface humus which overlies the Litorina raised beach. Sealing in Horizon 2 is a layer of lagoon silt, Deposit B, which may be dated palaeobotanically to Zone V*b*; it was laid down in comparatively shallow water.

B. GLENARM, COUNTY ANTRIM

This site, excavated in 1934 by the Harvard Archaeological Expedition to Ireland (Movius, 1937), is situated at The Cloney, immediately north of the town of Glenarm, and 36 miles north of Belfast on the County Antrim coast (Fig. 15). The surface topography along this portion of the foreshore, which runs from north-north-west to south-south-east, is marked by a gentle rise inland from the modern beach to an approximate elevation of 50 feet above

O.D. At the base of this low hill a Litorina raised beach was found banked against, and resting on, the Late-Glacial Boulder Clay of which the hill is formed. The highest point attained by the raised beach is approximately +37 feet O.D.; it slopes off on the seaward side to +20·2 feet O.D., and at this point it has been disturbed by the modern coast road. Thus the average height may be taken as about 28·6 feet above O.D., or almost 19 feet above average high-water level in Glenarm Bay. A typical section through the deposits (Plate III and Fig. 19) is as follows:

(A) Humus	(Horizon 2) . . .	35 cm.
(B) Litorina Raised Beach .	(Horizon 1) . . .	1·85 m.
(C) Boulder Clay		Thickness undetermined

(A) HUMUS. This consists of dark loamy soil and some pebbles, which form the superficial deposit throughout the vicinity, and it has been disturbed by ploughing. At the base of the hill the thickness increased to 65 cm., probably as the result of erosion. Animal remains in Deposit A consist of Cattle, Sheep and Pig; also the following shells occur: *Patella vulgata*, *Littorina littorea* and *Ostrea edulis*. Flint implements from this layer are very prolific, display a light, reddish-brown patination, and are sharp and unrolled, in contrast to the heavily rolled, chalky white material from the lower deposit. The ochreous upper series (Horizon 2) is therefore distinctive; it represents a similar industry to that found in Horizon 1 at Cushendun.

(B) LITORINA RAISED BEACH. Directly below the humus a deposit of tightly packed, heavily rolled pebbles is present, which are egg-shaped, round, or oval. These pebbles are piled up in inclined beds, which dip towards the sea at a slope of 15–20°, and they comprise a typical storm beach built up by wave action during the emergence. At an average depth of 1·4 m., and 80 cm. above the top of the boulder clay, the character of the deposit in the lower (seaward) portion of the beach changes. Here the upper 40 cm. is composed of small pebbles and sand dipping towards the coast at angles between 15° and 20°; the lower portion is sandy and contains many large boulders worn smooth as a result of wave action and sand polish. As will be made clear when the underlying boulder clay is discussed, this lower part of the beach dates from the maximum of the Litorina submergence. Throughout Deposit C, large, coarse, heavily rolled implements occur, of Late Larnian type (Horizon 1). Remains of Red Deer (*Cervus elaphus*)

GLENARM, COUNTY ANTRIM

Upper General view of the site, showing the upper end of the Litorina raised beach.
Lower Typical section through the deposits.

and Cow have been recorded, but since the latter is represented only by a small tooth fragment, it is not possible to identify it with a definite species, either wild or domestic (Allen, 1937, p. 216). Shells are rare and in all cases badly worn, a fact which suggests a deposit accumulated at high-water mark. The following species are included: *Littorina littorea*, *Dosina exoleta* (both common locally in a recent state) and *Cyprina islandica* (McMillan, 1937, p. 216). The latter is extremely rare as a Litorina fossil, but has been recorded at other raised beach sites in Ireland. This characteristically northern species points to the return to colder conditions in Late Atlantic times after the climatic optimum.

(C) BOULDER CLAY. This is composed of blue boulder clay containing natural flints and boulders with glacial striae. On the surface a brown oxidized zone, 10 cm. thick, indicates a weathering horizon formed during the maximum of the transgression. At this time the large boulders found at the base of Deposit C were eroded out of the boulder clay by wave action, and a low scarp ± 1·15 m. high was formed at the base of the hill. Deposits of the submergence are, therefore, absent at this site.

Since polleniferous deposits are absent at Glenarm, the Early Post-Glacial sequence must be reconstructed on the basis of the geological evidence. Whereas at Cushendun several deposits occur, laid down while the land was sinking, this period at Glenarm is represented only by an erosion cycle, which removed a portion of the boulder clay at the bottom of the hill, leaving a low scarp and residual boulders on the surface of Deposit C. The small pebbles and sand found at the base of the beach were probably laid down during the maximum of the submergence. However, the major portion of the beach is composed of inclined beds of pebbles typical of a storm-beach accumulation thrown up by the waves during the emergence. This is in accord with the evidence of the marine fauna, which includes one form indicative of the return of cooler conditions after the climatic optimum of Early Atlantic times had passed. The Litorina raised beach at this site, therefore, represents a true storm beach formed during the Late Atlantic Period. The archaeological material from this layer, Horizon 1, is Late Larnian, and in secondary position. Horizon 2 is Neolithic in age; implements of this phase are prolific in the humus formed on top of the beach after the emergence. Thus it may be concluded that Deposits A and B at Glenarm can be correlated with Deposits A and B at Cushendun. At both sites the geological stratigraphy is confirmed by the archaeological evidence.

C. Curran Point, Larne, County Antrim

The classic site of the Irish Stone Age at Larne, County Antrim, approximately 20 miles north of Belfast (Fig. 15), has been known since 1867, and a selected bibliography is given on p. 317. The work of the Belfast Naturalists' Field Club in 1890 and of Coffey and Praeger in 1904 represents the most thorough stratigraphic studies of the deposits; the other papers are mainly based on surface collections, with the exception of the small section cleared by Miss Layard in 1909. In 1935 a further excavation was carried out by the Harvard Archaeological Expedition to Ireland, in order to check the pre-existing data. The detailed report covering the results of this excavation will be published by the Royal Irish Academy. Litorina deposits have an extensive distribution in the vicinity of Larne, but the raised beach gravels at Curran Point are by far the most prolific of human artifacts manufactured from local flint. During the 1935 season over 15,000 were recovered. Curran Point is a long, tapering, sickle-shaped spit (Plate IV: upper), which forms an extension of the coast southward into Larne Lough from the west side of its narrow entrance. It rises from 10 to 20 feet above the present sea-level, and is approximately three-quarters of a mile long. Near high-water mark in these Post-Glacial deposits remains of Whale, associated with a derived and worn Mammoth bone, have been found (Grainger, 1874, p. 75; Moran, 1889). At the excavated site, which consisted of a pit 5 m. square, the Litorina raised beach has an elevation of 30 feet above O.D., or approximately 16 feet above average high-water level. The section is shown in Plate IV: lower; the following deposits occur in descending order:

(A) Surface Accumulation	0–40 cm.
(B) Storm Beach Material	40 cm.–1·30 m.
(C) Inclined Beds of Gravel and Sand . . .	1·30–4·25 m.
(D) Fine Reddish-Brown Sand	4·25–4·80 m.
(E) Hard Grey Sand	4·80–5·00 m.
(F) Fine Reddish-Brown Sand	5·00–5·15 m.
(G) Dark Blue Sand	5·15–6·00 m.
(H) Estuarine Clay*	6·00 —

* Total thickness undetermined. Dug to a depth of 8·10 m. and bored a further 2·90 m. (total depth = 11·00 m.) without any material change in the deposit.

High-tide level coincides approximately with the surface of Deposit E, so that the presence of water prevented the base of the estuarine clay being

LARNE, COUNTY ANTRIM

Upper Larne Lough, Island Magee and Curran Point showing the location of the site.

Lower The stratigraphy of the excavated pit.

reached. However, this layer overlies Late-Glacial deposits elsewhere in the vicinity (Coffey and Praeger, 1904, pp. 168–71), and it seems safe to assume that it does so here; at what depth this occurs in the section it was impossible to determine. A brief summary of the above deposits is as follows:

(A) Surface Accumulation. This is comparatively recent fill. It contains many modern objects in addition to abundant, heavily rolled, flint implements of Late Larnian type. The general appearance of the deposit, the characteristics of the flints, and the nature of the molluscs establish definitely that it is mainly derived material from Deposit B.

(B) Storm Beach Material. The material in this layer consists of tightly packed, round limestone pebbles. The nature of the bedding reveals that Deposit B is obviously a storm beach laid down by wave action during the emergence of the land, and this is confirmed by Mrs McMillan's conclusions regarding the molluscs. All are species which occur on the present coast of North-East Ireland, and represent a typical littoral fauna characteristic of a deposit close to high-water level. Flint implements are very numerous in the storm beach; large, crudely worked types predominate, for the most part heavily rolled, although a few unrolled forms are present. These are typical of the Late Larnian culture.

(C) Inclined Beds of Gravel and Sand. At the base of the storm beach the character of the deposit changes abruptly to inclined beds of very coarse, clean sand and gravel, containing boulders up to 30 cm. in diameter. These beds dip from north-east to south-west at an angle of 8–10°. Deposit C is clearly a series of beds laid down under conditions of a sinking coastline, accompanied by extensive and rapid erosion, as evidenced by the slightly rolled nature of some of the material. During this period, Curran Point probably formed a submerged spit or gravel bar near the mouth of Larne Harbour, which was exposed only at low tide. The storm-beach material, Deposit B, thrown up later as the land rose in Late Atlantic times, connected the Curran to the mainland. Throughout the inclined beds of gravel and sand, especially in the beds of coarser material, flint implements were abundant. These are characteristic of the Late Larnian, and for this phase of the Irish Mesolithic, Larne is the type site. Every degree of rolling of the archaeological material can be observed, from forms on which the flake facets have been entirely removed, to thin sharp blades, absolutely unrolled; in general the large implements exhibit the greatest degree of wear. Presumably the material was derived by the waves from the old land surface, as well as from the neighbouring headlands and foreshore, where extensive occupation sites must have provided the source of flint implements. This interpretation of the deposit is confirmed by the fauna, only one species of which is *in situ*, according to Mrs McMillan's report. Shells are plentiful throughout—fifty-four species of mollusca and five species of foraminifera occur—but with only a single exception they are all derived, some probably from deeper water outside the lough. All are worn. In the basal layers of Deposit C stones are present with Barnacles (*Balanus balanoides*) adhering to them. Since these are unworm and *in situ*, their presence indicates that this portion of the deposit is tidal. The occurrence of the Razor Clam (*Phacoides borealis*) points to the same conclusion, substantiating the geological evidence. Immediately prior to the maximum of the submergence, therefore, a sandy beach was laid down, over which sands and gravels were deposited during the final period of sinking, until as the land rose, a storm beach (Deposit B) was thrown up. The shells and foraminifera suggest that a climate not unlike the present then existed.

(D) Fine Reddish-Brown Sand. Approximately twenty-five flint implements, both rolled and unrolled forms, were found in this bed. These are of Late Larnian type. The fauna identified by Mrs McMillan from this horizon demonstrate that beach conditions and a climate very similar to the present obtained when Deposit D was laid down.

(E) Hard Grey Sand. This layer yielded several unrolled implements, including a core and a small utilized blade. The condition of deposition, a sandy foreshore exposed at low water, is proved by the fauna, described by Mrs McMillan. All the forms, which comprise nine species of mollusca, and thirty-four species of foraminifera, are *in situ*. The prevailing climate was fairly cool, in short very like the present.

(F) Fine Reddish-Brown Sand. In all respects this is identical with Deposit D, except that its clay content is somewhat higher. At the base of the layer there is an abrupt change in the sediments. One trimming flake patinated a dark greyish brown colour occurred in Deposit F.

(G) Dark Blue Sand. No implements were found in the dark blue sand. The conditions at the time of deposition have been established by Mrs McMillan from the fauna, which is characteristic of a sea bottom composed of muddy sand. The assemblage, comprising sixty-four species of mollusca and sixty-eight of foraminifera, shows that climatic conditions were somewhat warmer than those of the present day. That the Post-Glacial warmth maximum had passed, and the climate was gradually deteriorating, is proved by the fact that *Rissoa albella* is being replaced by *Rissoa parva*. The former is not present in Deposit F. This bed was laid down in shallow water—low-water level to a depth of one fathom.

(H) Estuarine Clay. This deposit includes some fine micaceous sand, but is mainly composed of very consistent, tough, sticky, greasy clay which is very coarsely laminated. Five human flints of indeterminate age, three of them patinated a dark blue, were found. The marine fauna, according to Mrs McMillan, proves that the deposit accumulated in shallow water between low-water level and 2–3 fathoms deep. The forms represent molluscs, foraminifera, ostracods, and calcareous algae; all are in unanimous agreement that warmer conditions prevailed at this time. *Rissoa albella*, a southern mollusc, is abundant. Therefore this portion of the deposit at Larne shows that the Post-Glacial climatic optimum does not correspond exactly with the maximum of the Litorina transgression. Although numerous palaeobotanical samples were taken throughout this deposit, their pollen frequency was unfortunately too low for determining the age of Deposit H on this basis. However, Professor Jessen has dated the corresponding layer, Deposit C, at Island Magee to Zone VI in Ireland (see p. 137), which agrees with the evidence from Cushendun and elsewhere that the maximum of the submergence occurred subsequently to Zone V*b*.

The Post-Glacial history of the Larne region as revealed by the above section on Curran Point is reasonably clear. The estuarine clay, Deposit H, was laid down between low-tide mark and a depth of 2–3 fathoms of water during a late stage of the Litorina transgression. At this time the Post-Glacial climatic optimum was attained. Deposit G was formed in shallow water, and in the upper part of this bed the comparative rarity of *Rissoa albella* points to a deterioration in the climate. Above this there is an abrupt break between the dark blue sands and clays to the light-coloured, ferruginous sands and gravels, and Deposit F marks the transition. Deposit E represents a sandy tidal flat, at which time the climate was similar to the present. On top of this, Deposit D, a beach formed between tide marks, was laid down. Up to this point, there is no indication of a change in the mutual relations of land and sea following the submergence represented by the estuarine clay. It seems probable, therefore, that after the latter movement had occurred, the land was stable for a brief interval, although it is impossible to determine what part the eustatic rise in sea-level played in moulding the history of this series of deposits. Beach conditions prevail into the base of Deposit C, but throughout the rest of the layer the nature of the beds and the character of the contained fauna shows that it was laid down immediately prior to the maximum of the submergence at a period when the land was sinking for the last time. As this movement intensified, the gravel spit which forms Curran Point was built southward into Larne Lough, the shape of which was determined by the tidal currents. The inclined beds of gravel and sand of which this spit is formed were deposited *in tempo* with the final phase of the submergence. Thus, the above section suggests that the sinking of the land during this period has been interrupted by a period of stagnation in the movement, accounting for the littoral deposits at the base of and underlying Deposit C. The storm beach, formed during the emergence, is represented by a shallow layer, Deposit B, at the site; farther inland this occurs up to a height of 26 feet above high-water level (Coffey and Praeger, 1904, p. 168). Deposit A at Curran Point is modern surface accumulation. The archaeological material recovered at the site is throughout characteristic of the Late Larnian phase of the Irish Mesolithic.

D. Island Magee, County Antrim

On the west side of Island Magee, directly opposite Larne, but separated from Curran Point by the narrow entrance of the lough (Pl. IV: upper), an important Post-Glacial section has been recorded by Mr Burchell (1930[*b*]; 1931, pp. 270–81; 1932, 1933[*a*], 1934). The marine fauna from this locality was studied by Dr Baden-Powell (1937), and Professor Jessen has determined the age of one of the layers on the basis of palaeobotany. The conclusions of these authorities are incorporated in the summary presented below, since these data are of importance for purposes of establishing the stratigraphy of the Irish Stone Age. Although no measurements of the individual beds are available, the section is recorded as follows:

(A) Raised Beach Gravels	Horizon 3
(B) Black Sand	
(C) Estuarine Clay	Horizon 2
(D) Black Sand	Horizon 1
(E) Subangular Black Gravel and Sand	Horizon 1
(F) Fine Black Sand	Horizon 1
(G) Subangular Black Gravel and Sand	Horizon 1
(H) Land Surface (Submerged Peat)	
(I) Boulder Clay	

The surface of the boulder clay occurs at 1 foot 6 inches below low-water level; the overlying layers (G–B inclusive) are 10 feet thick, and high-water level corresponds approximately with the surface of Deposit C. Archaeological material was covered from three horizons as indicated: Horizon 1 is Early Larnian, and Horizons 2 and 3 are Late Larnian. The fauna from Deposits C, F and G has been thoroughly recorded, and Deposit C has been assigned to Zone VI (Late Atlantic) in Ireland by pollen analysis. This evidence makes it possible to compare the Island Magee section with that from Larne, described above.

Deposits A, B and C correspond to those recorded at Curran Point, Deposits B to H inclusive. A yields archaeological material identical with the Late Larnian of the sands and gravels on the opposite side of the lough (Deposits B–F); B probably has its counterpart in the dark blue sand (Deposit G); the fauna and the depth of water at the time of deposition prove that C corresponds to Deposit H at the Curran site. The molluscs and foraminifera from this level at Island Magee indicate slightly warmer conditions than those at present. On the whole forms found on the modern coasts of North-East Ireland predominate, but the presence of *Modiolaria costulata* and *Tapes* (*Paphia*) *decussatus*, both of which have a normal southern range, point to somewhat more equable conditions, according to Dr Baden-Powell. The pollen frequency in Deposit C at Island Magee is low, nevertheless Professor Jessen has placed this layer in the beginning of Zone VI (Late Atlantic) in Ireland, since high amounts of Pine and Alder are found. As previously stated, this horizon has yielded implements typical of the Late Larnian. Deposit C in the above section was laid down in a depth of not more than 2–3 fathoms of water, which indicates that it is comparable in age with the Intermediate Estuarine Clays of the coastal sequence (Baden-Powell, 1937, pp. 95–6). The fauna from the lower levels (Deposits F and G), however, point to littoral conditions. Thus the lower portion of Burchell's section was accumulated between tide marks, and Baden-Powell concludes that it corresponds with the Lower Estuarine Clay—*Scrobicularia* Zone—in Dr Praeger's sequence (see p. 122). Since Burchell (1934, p. 369) records Birch, Pine, Elm, Alder, Oak, a high frequency of Hazel, and traces of Willow from this horizon at Island Magee, it seems probable that it may be assigned to the Early Atlantic Period—the upper part of Jessen's Zone V*b*. Now the implements collected by Mr Burchell from Horizon 1 are unrolled, patinated dull blue to black, and are of Early Larnian type, comparable to

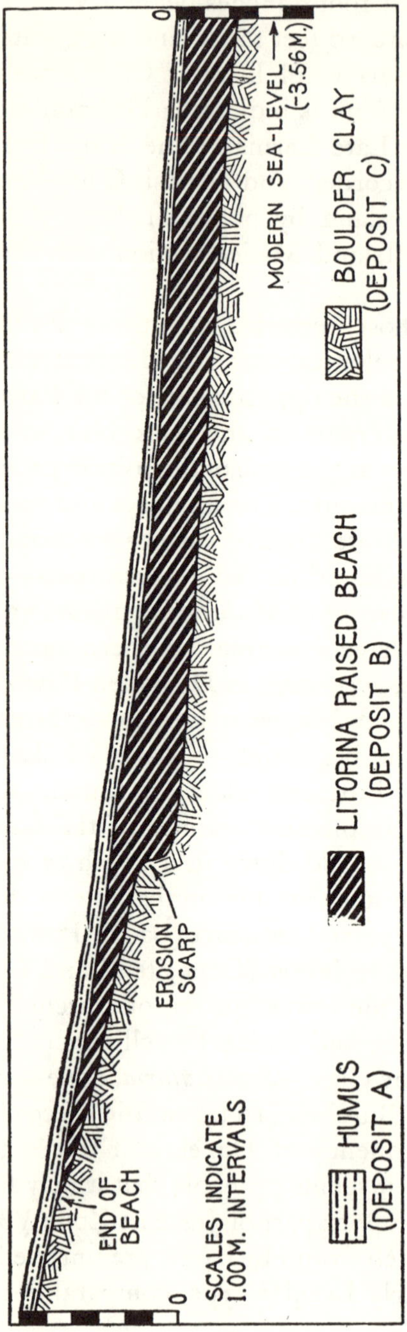

Fig. 19. Section through the Deposits at The Cloney, Glenarm, County Antrim.

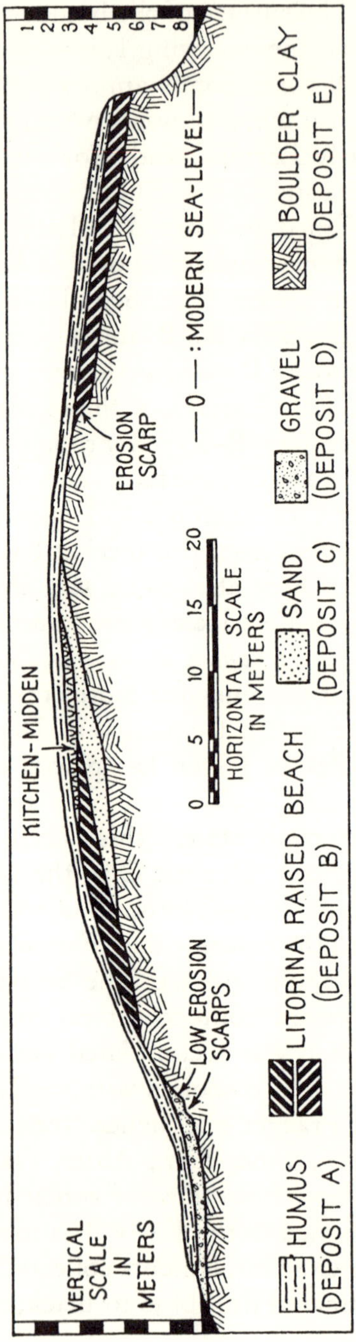

Fig. 20. Section showing the Early Post-Glacial Deposits at Rough Island, County Down

Horizons 1 and 2 at Cushendun. The archaeological material therefore confirms the palaeobotanical and palaeontological evidence that Deposits D–G, alternating layers of sands and gravels, date from the beginning of the Litorina transgression. The old land surface shown in Deposit H has its counterpart in the swamp peat layer at Cushendun; it presumably dates from the commencement of the Atlantic Period in Ireland. Thus on the basis of the above data it is possible to complete that portion of the Early Post-Glacial history of the Larne area which is not represented by the Curran Point section. The Island Magee site is also important, since it reveals the stratigraphical relation of the early and late phases of the Larnian, and makes it possible to tie these in with the established coastal sequence of North-East Ireland on the one hand, and with Jessen's system of zoning the Irish pollen diagrams on the other.

E. Rough Island, County Down

A site on this small island, situated in Strangford Lough midway between Newtownards and Comber, County Down (Fig. 15), was excavated in 1936 by the Harvard Archaeological Expedition to Ireland (Movius, 1940[*a*]). The island itself (Plate V: upper) is formed of a small drumlin with a boulder clay core, and is connected with the mainland during low tide by a narrow causeway approximately a quarter of a mile long. The maximum height of the drumlin is 30·5 feet above high-water level; on its slopes below the 18-foot contour are deposits of the Litorina Sea. The following section occurred (Fig. 20 and Plate V: lower):

(A) Humus	(Horizon 2)	20 cm.	(average thickness)
(B) Coarse Sand and Gravel	(Horizon 1)	50 cm.	,, ,,
(C) Dark Yellow Sand		40 cm.	,, ,,
(D) Loose Sandy Gravel		12 cm.	,, ,,
(E) Boulder Clay: Thickness undetermined			

(Deposits C and D both overlie E, but are not associated with each other.)

(A) Humus. This forms a deposit of dark, greyish-brown, sandy loam which covers the entire island. It is badly disturbed as a result of ploughing, and a mixed series of flint implements and shells is present. The former include both Early Larnian (derived from Deposit B) and typically later material probably Neolithic in age. These may be easily differentiated by their patination, since the former are a rich chalky white, and the latter vary from grey-black to a deep ochreous colour. Many of the artifacts are calcined as a result of heat; characteristic Neolithic forms, completely absent in the lower levels, predominate. On the slopes of the island, between Deposits C and D, the surface humus rests directly on boulder clay.

(B) COARSE SAND AND GRAVEL. The lower end of this deposit, which is similar in many respects to Deposit D at Cushendun, is ±13 feet above high-water level, whereas the upper end is at approximately +18 feet. It is a raised beach, composed of roughly inclined beds which dip towards the sea at an angle corresponding to the slope of the hill. Charcoal fragments consisting mainly of Hazel but including Oak, Yew and Hawthorn (?) were obtained in this deposit. One Ox tooth (Aurochs?) was recovered at a depth of 26 cm. The shells include *Littorina littorea*, *L. littoralis*, *Ostrea edulis*, *Cardium edule*, *Paphia decussata*, and five other forms which call for no special comment. No foraminifera or organic remains were found in the washing samples. According to Mrs McMillan (1940[*a*]), the marine fauna represents a typical assemblage found in the estuarine clays and raised beaches of Counties Antrim and Down; however, the comparative abundance of *Paphia decussata*, a southern form, suggests slightly warmer conditions. In North-East Ireland this species has only so far been found at present in Strangford Lough, and it is rare. Only small unrolled flake implements of Early Larnian type, which display a chalky white patina, occur in Deposit B. This sand and gravel layer was laid down during the Litorina submergence.

(C) DARK YELLOW SAND. The summit of the island is covered with fine sand which is archaeologically sterile. Although no fossils were obtained in this layer, it seems certain that it is the result of Late-Glacial outwash. During the Post-Glacial marine transgression the surface of the sand was eroded; in fact it was entirely removed in certain areas. In the northern portion of the island part of the raised beach overlies Deposit C.

(D) LOOSE SANDY GRAVEL. Deposit D, which is composed of rolled material, occurs only at the base of the hill on the north side of the island. It is likewise devoid of archaeological material, a fact which indicates that it was probably laid down subsequently to the marine transgression. The absence of a cold fauna and the abundance of *Ostrea edulis* prove that this deposit dates from the Post-Glacial Period. It probably was formed during a late stage in the recovery of the land.

ROUGH ISLAND, STRANGFORD LOUGH, COUNTY DOWN

Upper The Island at high tide.

Lower Section through the deposits: (A) Deposit A; (B) Deposit B; Sand, Deposit C.

(E) Boulder Clay. As mentioned above, the core of the island is composed of boulder clay; all the flints in it are natural. Two low erosion scarps, each approximately 25 cm. high, have been cut into this deposit near the base of the hill by the sea. Since Deposit D overlies these in both cases, they probably date from a late phase of the Litorina Sea, and are old strand-lines formed during the emergence.

Along the northern portion of the island, immediately below its summit, a large kitchen-midden[1] was found, which is composed of a layer of tightly packed shells, lying more or less horizontally. This layer averages 25 cm. thick; throughout charcoal and ash are abundant, consisting mainly of Oak and some Hazel. Most of the shells are large thick oysters (95 per cent), but *Littorina littorea*, *Cardium edule*, *Paphia decussata*, *Paphia aurea*, *Patella vulgata*, *Buccinum undatum*, *Mytilus edulis*, and six other marine forms, as well as *Cepaea nemoralis*, a land snail, are present. As Mrs McMillan points out (1940[*a*]), all are edible species; the assemblage strongly suggests that this material was accumulated during a period when the climate was slightly warmer than at present. In the midden a hearth, 1·5 m. in diameter and 12 cm. thick, which rested on a rough pavement of beach pebbles, was found. In addition to Oak, this yielded some Hawthorn charcoal, and in a small pocket in the surface of the sand below the midden, fragments of Yew were recovered. According to Professor Jessen, these trees were all present in Ireland during Atlantic times. The archaeological material from this deposit is very disappointing: only a few trimming flakes were found, none of which shows signs of use. However, since several implements of Mesolithic type came from the surface of the sand directly below the midden, and since a Neolithic industry is abundant in Deposit A directly above, this stratum is probably of Atlantic age. This is substantiated by the evidence of the molluscs and the charcoal. Stratigraphically the midden is later than the beach, the upper end of which is directly overlain by this occupation layer, which proves that it dates from a period subsequent to the maximum of the Litorina transgression.

The site at Rough Island definitely establishes the Early Larnian, of the County Antrim coast, in the Strangford Lough region of County Down. As

[1] It should be emphatically pointed out that the use of the term Kitchen-Midden in this context refers to a type of refuse mound composed of shells accumulated during a period of human occupation. This is merely indicative of a particular mode of life and does not imply a cultural connection with the well-known kitchen-midden or Ertebølle culture of the Baltic (likewise of Late Mesolithic age) where similar mounds are typical.

at Cushendun (Horizon 2) and Island Magee (Horizon 1), this material is in secondary position in Litorina gravels (Deposit B), which were laid down in relatively quiet water during the submergence. No polleniferous horizons are present, so that the age of these gravels must be determined on the basis of stratigraphy, the marine fauna, and the contained artifacts. All point to the Early Atlantic Period, and this is supported by the fact that Deposit B is directly overlain by an occupation layer dating from the time of the emergence. Since during the height of the submergence, this low island must have been almost if not completely covered by the sea, the midden may be placed immediately subsequent to the transgression maximum. No marine deposits referable to the period of the maximum of the submergence were found; therefore the Litorina gravels, Deposit B, probably belong to the early stages of this event. Late Larnian material is absent at Rough Island, although the kitchen-midden seems to date from Late Mesolithic times. This occupation must have been only temporary, as the associated archaeological material is very poor and scanty. Nevertheless, it is the only primary site of the Atlantic Period so far recorded in Ireland, and its importance lies in the fact that it throws some light on the manner of living at a time after the Post-Glacial climatic optimum. The comparatively warm climate which still obtained is reflected by the presence of abundant remains of oysters. When the emergence was well under way, a later industry, Rough Island 2, similar to Glenarm 2 and Horizon 4 at Cushendun, appeared in the Strangford Lough region. At Rough Island this is found in Deposit A, where this distinctive and comparatively fresh material is mixed with Early Larnian types, derived from Deposit B, as a result of disturbance. The two may be easily differentiated, however, on the basis of both typology and patination.

3. CHRONOLOGY

The stratigraphy of the five archaeological sites described above furnishes the key to the Mesolithic sequence of North-East Ireland. Geological, palaeobotanical and palaeontological evidence in each case provides the basis for establishing this sequence, and for synchronizing it with the composite section presented at the beginning of this chapter. A synthesis of the evidence, as revealed by excavation, is given below; it is incorporated on the chart, Table 7, p. 143. The approximate position of the Lough Neagh

TABLE 7. The Post-Glacial Chronology and Archaeological Sequence in North-East Ireland

TENTATIVE DATES (based on De Geer)	CLIMATIC PHASES: SCANDINAVIA (Blytt and Sernander)		CLIMATIC PHASES: IRELAND (K. Jessen)		LAND MOVEMENTS AND TEMPERATURE		COASTAL DEPOSITS IN NORTH-EAST IRELAND (Praeger)	STRATIGRAPHY OF EXCAVATED SITES	ARCHAEOLOGY	
B.C.	SUB-BOREAL (Continental climate)		VI		EMERGENCE	Cold and dry	CONDITIONS AS AT PRESENT	Cushendun—Deposit A Glenarm—Deposit A Rough Island—Deposit A	NEOLITHIC: Cushendun—Horizon 4 Glenarm—Horizon 2 Rough Island—Horizon 2	
2500	ATLANTIC (Oceanic climate)	LATE	VI		EMERGENCE	Cooler at end Fauna as in present seas Warmer at beginning	RAISED STORM BEACHES	Cushendun—Deposit B (upper) Glenarm—Deposit B Larne—Deposit B Island Magee—Deposit A (upper)	*Implements in Secondary Position* LATE LARNIAN Cushendun—Horizon 3 Glenarm—Horizon 1 Larne—Curran Deposits Island Magee—Horizons 2 and 3	MESOLITHIC
3000					MAXIMUM OF SUBSIDENCE					
	ATLANTIC (Oceanic climate)	LATE	VI		SUBMERGENCE: LITORINA TRANSGRESSION	POST-GLACIAL CLIMATIC OPTIMUM (Maximum of Southern Forms) Warm and Moist Fauna as in present seas Cooler in beginning	UPPER ESTUARINE CLAY (±5 fathoms)	Cushendun—Deposit B (lower) Glenarm—Erosion Surface Larne—Deposits C–G Island Magee—Deposit A (lower) and Deposit B		
4000							INTERMEDIATE CLAYS (±2–3 fathoms)	Larne—Deposit H Island Magee—Deposit C		
4500 5000		EARLY	V*b*	LATE			LOWER ESTUARINE CLAYS (Littoral)	Cushendun—Deposits C–E Island Magee—Deposits D–G Rough Island—Deposit B	*Implements in Secondary Position* EARLY LARNIAN Cushendun—Horizons 1 and 2 Island Magee—Horizon 1 Rough Island—Horizon 1	
5600	BOREAL (Continental climate)	LATE	V*b*	EARLY	EMERGENCE	EMERGENCE OF IRISH SEA BASIN TO ±20 FATHOM LINE PARTIAL LAND-BRIDGE BETWEEN BRITAIN AND IRELAND	SUBMERGED PEATS FORMING IN NORTH-EAST IRELAND	Cushendun—Deposit F Island Magee—Deposit H Lough Neagh—Deposit B	EARLY LARNIAN (*in situ*) Lough Neagh, near Toomebridge	
6000		EARLY	V*a*					Cushendun—Deposit G		
6800	PRE-BOREAL (Transition from Late-Glacial conditions)		IV		LATE-GLACIAL SEA		OUTWASH SANDS AND GRAVELS, ARCTIC MARINE DEPOSITS	Rough Island—Deposit C Lough Neagh—Deposit C Cushendun—Deposit H		

section, described in the last chapter, will be indicated in terms of the coastal succession.

(A) The oldest deposit is the boulder clay of the last ice-sheet, and this underlies all of the sections. In addition several other Late-Glacial horizons are present. Deposit H at Cushendun, a coarsely laminated clay, was laid down in an extra-glacial lake formed in Glendun during the last advance of the Scottish Ice into North-East Ireland (see p. 277). At Rough Island, Deposit C, a Late-Glacial outwash sand, belongs to the final retreat of the ice-sheet from that area. It is probable that Deposit C at Lough Neagh, dark greenish-grey sand, also dates from this period.

(B) The emergence of the land in Early Post-Glacial times is indicated by Deposit G at Cushendun, an old land surface composed of resorted boulder clay formed during an erosion cycle. At this time much of the present Irish Sea was dry land. This resulted in the rapid increase and spread of new forest genera, and the first colonization of Ireland by man. The surface of the Lough Neagh sand, Deposit C, yields definite evidence of settlement referable to this period, since the occupation layer is overlain by Late Boreal–Early Atlantic peat, Deposit B, which may be assigned to Jessen's Zone V*b*. Submerged peats were formed at many sites along the coast during this period of uplift. At Cushendun, Deposit F, which definitely belongs to Zone V*b*, was formed, and it appears probable that the peat layer recorded at Island Magee, Deposit H, is of a comparable age.

(C) The next event, the transgression of the Litorina Sea, was responsible for the deposition of three zones of estuarine clays in the bays and estuaries of North-East Ireland. An attempt will be made to synchronize these with the stratigraphy of the archaeological sites described in this chapter, based on the present evidence.

(1) *Lower Estuarine Clay* (*Scrobicularia Zone*). This clay, which is littoral in character, may be assigned to pollen-diagrammatical Zone V*b*, according to Professor Jessen. At Cushendun, Deposit E, the lower lagoon silt, accumulated during an early phase of the submergence, and Deposit D, the lower gravel which is overlain by the upper lagoon silt, Deposit C, may be equated with this horizon. The latter bed is referable to the upper part of Zone V*b*; both it and the lower gravel were laid down during the sinking of the land. In the Island Magee section, Deposits G–D, alternating layers of gravel and fine sand, also belong with this series, on the evidence of pollen

analysis and the marine fauna. The thin gravel layer at Rough Island, Deposit B, may be correlated with the Lower Estuarine Clay, since it dates from the early part of the submergence. Throughout, the deposits of this zone have yielded Early Larnian implements.

(2) *Intermediate Clay Zone.* At Curran Point, Larne, Deposit H, and at Island Magee, Deposit C, this zone, which was laid down in water up to 2–3 fathoms deep, has been identified. At the former locality the Post-Glacial climatic optimum was attained during the period represented by this deposit. At Island Magee, the Intermediate Estuarine Clay, Deposit C, belongs to the beginning of Zone VI, and at this locality Late Larnian artifacts occur in the layer.

(3) *Upper Estuarine Clay* (*Thracia Zone*). This deposit was formed during the maximum of the submergence in approximately 5 fathoms of water; the upper part of this horizon belongs to the middle portion of Zone VI. At Cushendun the inclined beds forming the lower part of Deposit B are of this period, and at Glenarm there is an erosion surface on top of the boulder clay which may be placed here.[1] The Deposits D–G at Larne, a series of shallow water, tidal flat, and beach deposits, and Deposit B, at Island Magee, a layer of black sand, accumulated under conditions of relative stability, provide evidence for a slight pause in the sinking, following the deposition of the Intermediate Clays. At both localities, however, this was probably of very short duration, and at Curran Point, Larne, it was followed by a further submergence when the inclined beds of sand and gravel, Deposit C, were accumulated. Likewise the lower portion of Deposit A, raised beach gravels, at Island Magee was formed during the final stages of the sinking. The deposits of this period yield abundant material of the Late Larnian culture.

(D) Raised Storm Beaches. The storm beaches, which overlie the deposits of the marine transgression, were formed partly during the maximum of the subsidence and partly during the recovery of the land in Late Atlantic times. Contemporary with the emergence and the approach of the cold, dry, Continental climate, conditions seem to have deteriorated somewhat, since northern forms invaded the sea and the warmth-loving

[1] Undoubtedly the formation of the erosion surface at Glenarm commenced soon after the beginning of the Litorina transgression, but it was not completed until the maximum of the submergence. It is so placed on Table 7 that it immediately precedes the following cycle, which was one of deposition. Furthermore, although the point is impossible to prove, the lowermost portion of the Deposit B beds at Cushendun probably should be assigned to the "Intermediate Clay Zone"; the bulk of the deposit, however, was laid down during the maximum of the sinking.

mollusca are rare. To this horizon may be assigned the upper portion of Deposit B at Cushendun, the pebble beach at Glenarm, Deposit B, the storm beach at Larne, Deposit B, and the upper part of Deposit A at Island Magee. In all cases heavily rolled, Late Larnian implements are typical. In the recent deposits overlying this layer at Cushendun, Glenarm, and Rough Island, Neolithic material occurs above the raised beach. This will be described in a later chapter.

The above synthesis of the Early Post-Glacial stratigraphy of North-East Ireland shows the firm establishment of the Stone Age sequence by several allied sciences. Thus the Early Larnian occurs in deposits of pollen-diagrammatical Zone V*b*, which are geologically the age of the Lower Estuarine Clays. On the coast it is found in layers of gravel and sand laid down during the early part of the submergence. Late Larnian material, on the other hand, comes from horizons referable to Zone VI, and these may be correlated with the Intermediate and Upper Estuarine Clays, formed prior to the maximum of the subsidence. The latter event appears to correspond to the middle portion of Zone VI. Raised storm beaches, built up by the sea mainly during the emergence of the land, also contain Late Larnian implements.

One fact above all others is of paramount importance for an understanding of the Irish Mesolithic: *All the material recovered from the excavated coastal sites is secondary, and it dates from a period prior to the maximum of the Litorina submergence.* Up to the present the kitchen-midden on Rough Island is the only possible exception to this rule, but no implements were found in the occupation layer. The inland site on Lough Neagh, near Toomebridge, described in the last chapter, is sealed below Late Boreal–Early Atlantic peat of Zone V*b*, which proves that Ireland was inhabited during Boreal times, when a partial land connection with Scotland was in existence (see p. 82). Hazel was dominant in the Irish forests; Pine was increasing, and Elm and Oak were coming in at the time of the first settlement. On the coast it is almost certain that there were extensive occupation sites associated with deposits on the Early Post-Glacial land surface. But these were destroyed during the marine transgression, when the sea inundated large areas of the then-existing coastal lowlands. The archaeological material was transported inland by strong currents and incorporated into the submerged gravel and sand deposits which were formed along the present coast. Therefore, the mode of life during Early Larnian times can only be deciphered from a study of the implements themselves. Since these are essentially adapted for forest-hunting pursuits, contemporaneity with a period when a greater extent of land existed in the region of the North Channel is inferred. This will be fully discussed when the material itself is described. Another important point which militates in favour of an Early Larnian occupation on the old land surface during the period of emergence is the fact that this culture is also found in Scotland (see p. 178); however, after the submergence, when the area of the present Irish Sea was formed, a marked divergence took place. This resulted in local specialization in the two areas. Therefore, there is archaeological confirmation for assigning the Early Larnian to the Boreal Period.

When the marine transgression began, it became necessary for the occupants of North-East Ireland to adapt themselves to new conditions. The greater extent of the sea; the rise in mean annual temperature; the gradual change in forest forms; and the coming in of new edible species of shell-fish, were all important factors contributing to a new cultural development. As the land sank in relation to the sea, it was constantly necessary to shift the location of dwelling sites, since new portions of the foreshore were continually being inundated by the water. During the submergence erosion was active along the coast, and under these conditions, when the sea instead of the land was the dominant factor in this area, the Late Larnian was evolved. The material from the dwelling sites, which were invaded by the ocean, was incorporated into deposits that can be dated to Zone VI in Ireland, but the material itself is older than the horizons in which it is found. With the emergence of the land towards the close of the Atlantic Period, present-day conditions were partially restored; erosion became less active on the foreshore, and instead deposition in the form of storm beaches began. Thus the only contemporary material incorporated into these layers was that lost either directly on the beaches or within reach of the waves along nearby portions of the strand. In other words, the Late Larnian implements in the storm beaches were derived from coastal sites by marine erosion during the submergence and built into these deposits by the waves during the uplift. Above the line of the maximum extent of the Litorina Sea, there undoubtedly are undisturbed settlement sites of the Larnian culture; it is probable that in them the ultimate development of the Irish Mesolithic will be traced. The Rough Island midden is at present the only indication of the existence of such settlements, but, as stated above, this shell heap did not produce any implements, and it does not contribute to our knowledge of the cultural sequence.

Its great importance, however, lies in the fact that it throws some light on the mode of life at this time; it affords some confirmation of the implication that the Late Larnian people were primarily dependent on the sea for subsistence.

The stratigraphy of the Irish Mesolithic, as revealed by the excavated coastal stations, may be summarized as follows:

(A) *Early Larnian:*

(1) *Cushendun.* Horizon 1 (Deposit E): Lower Lagoon silt. Horizon 2 (Deposit D): Lower gravel.

(2) *Island Magee.* Horizon 1 (Deposits D–G): Alternating layers of gravel and sand.

(3) *Rough Island.* Horizon 1 (Deposit B): Coarse sand and gravel.

(B) *Late Larnian:*

(1) *Cushendun.* Horizon 3 (Deposit B): Upper gravel (raised beach).

(2) *Glenarm.* Horizon 1 (Deposit B): Raised beach.

(3) *Larne.* Deposits G to D: Sand series at base of gravel. Deposit C: Inclined beds of gravel and sand. Deposit B: Storm Beach.

(4) *Island Magee.* Horizon 2 (Deposit C): Estuarine clay. Horizon 3 (Deposit A): Raised beach.

4. ARCHAEOLOGICAL MATERIAL

A. Early Larnian

The most prominent feature of the Early Larnian flint-work is the overwhelmingly high proportion of finely struck blade implements. For the most part these are sharp and unrolled, a fact which suggests that some of this material is *in situ*, and that Mesolithic settlements or chipping sites were once actually located on the surface of the coastal deposits at the time of the Litorina submergence. This possibility, however, is precluded by the evidence of the sediments—Cushendun (Deposits D and E), Island Magee (Deposits D to G), and Rough Island (Deposit B)—all of which are composed of materials laid down between low-water mark and a depth of a few fathoms. Furthermore, there is no indication of occupation at any level in these horizons. It must be concluded therefore that the nature of the submergence was such that the layers, which yield Early Larnian implements, were laid down in a manner which protected them from excessive wear. Under conditions of a sinking coastline, circumstances would be favourable: erosion, both on the headlands and on the old land surface which had been transgressed by the sea, would be rapid as new areas were continually brought within reach of the waves. There would be a constant supply of sands and gravels being transported, together with archaeological material, to new positions farther inland. Along the then-existing coastline beaches of aggression were rapidly built up, and each successive layer in them was buried by more material, thereby protecting it from extensive wear. On the other hand, many of the implements from the abandoned occupation sites must have been lost during the submergence. Probably the only material preserved was that from localities situated either in the paths of strong long-shore currents, or at the mouths of valleys or estuaries, where it was borne inland by the sea. Thus refuse from chipping sites as well as that from settlements is present in confusion, which possibly accounts to a certain degree for the very small percentage of retouched forms. The circumstances pertaining at the time of deposition have been important factors, therefore, in determining the selection of the implements.

Typologically the Early Larnian may be considered under the following headings:

(1) *Primary blades showing signs of use* (Figs. 21 and 22) comprise over 95 per cent of the industry. The most outstanding fact about the Early Larnian blades is that, although found in secondary deposits, they appear strikingly fresh. Presumably some of the edge-chipping is a result of sea action, but nevertheless the majority of these artifacts show signs of use, as cutting tools, scrapers, or points. In some cases (Fig. 21, nos. 12 and 14) the original cortex of the flint has not been removed, but such examples are rare, and careful preparation of the core by skilful flaking is usual. Throughout the striking platform is plain and makes an angle with the long axis of the blade just exceeding 90°. The form varies from broad, oval, leaf-shaped points to narrow, parallel-sided blades which may or may not be pointed. Asymmetrical points (Fig. 21, no. 6; Fig. 22, no. 8) from Horizon 2 at Cushendun, and Horizon 1 at Island Magee, are distinctive. Size varies from large blades 10 cm. long (Fig. 21, no. 5) to small examples 3 cm. in length (Fig. 22, nos. 23 and 25); the average are ±6 cm. The presence of core-dressing flakes (Fig. 22, no. 13) suggests that some of the material has been derived from chipping sites. Often the upper surface of the bulbar end of the blades is chipped in an effort to reduce the thickness, possibly for hafting (Fig. 21, nos. 5–7, 11, 14; Fig. 22, nos. 1, 3–6, 11 and 12). The specimens shown in Fig. 22, nos. 1–5, not only display this feature, with the

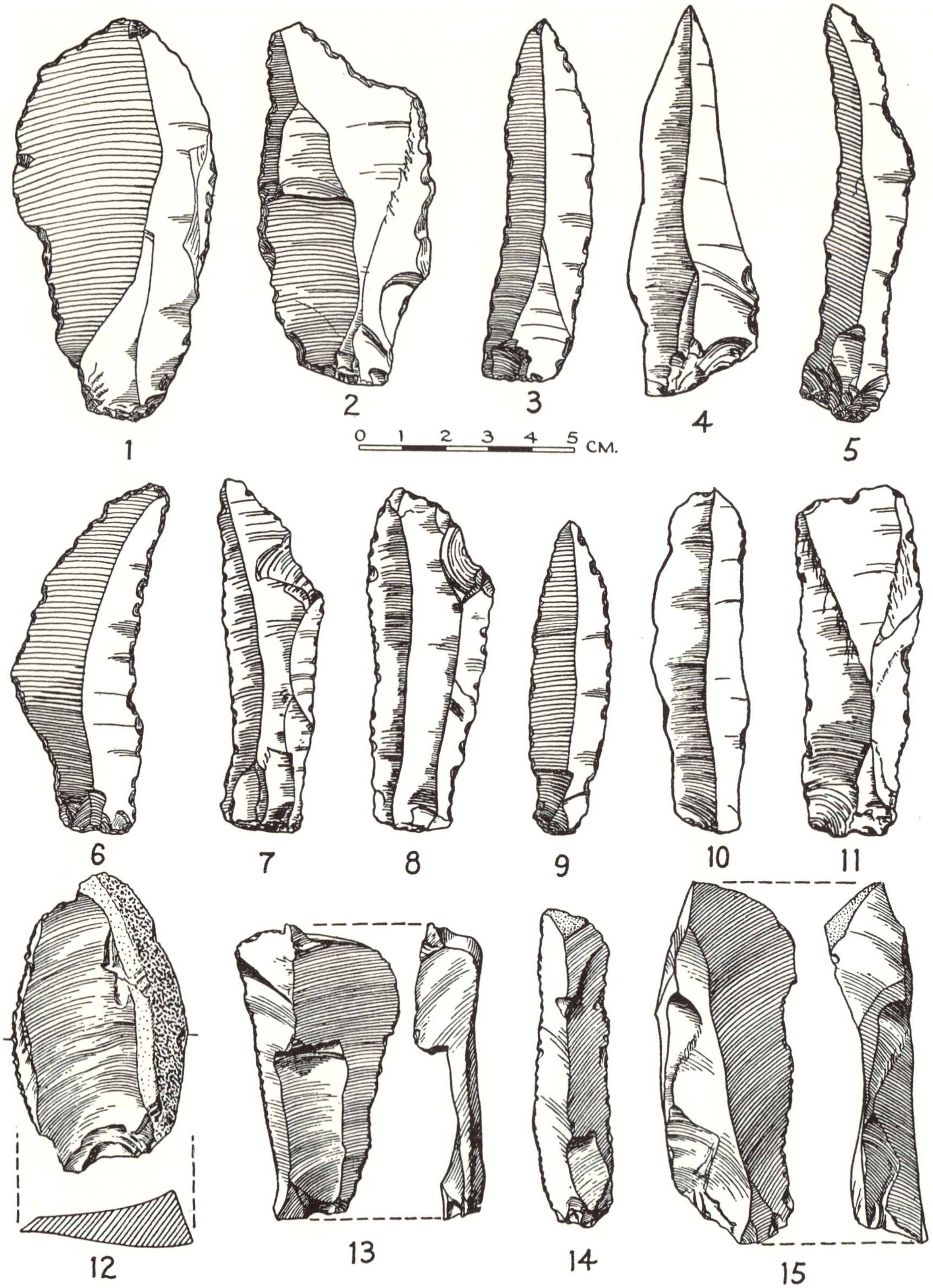

Fig. 21. Early Larnian Flints from Cushendun—Horizon 1 (nos. 1, 4, 10), Cushendun—Horizon 2 (nos. 2, 3, 5–9, 11), Island Magee—Horizon 1 (nos. 12–15). (Nos. 12–15 after Burchell.) Scale: 2/3.

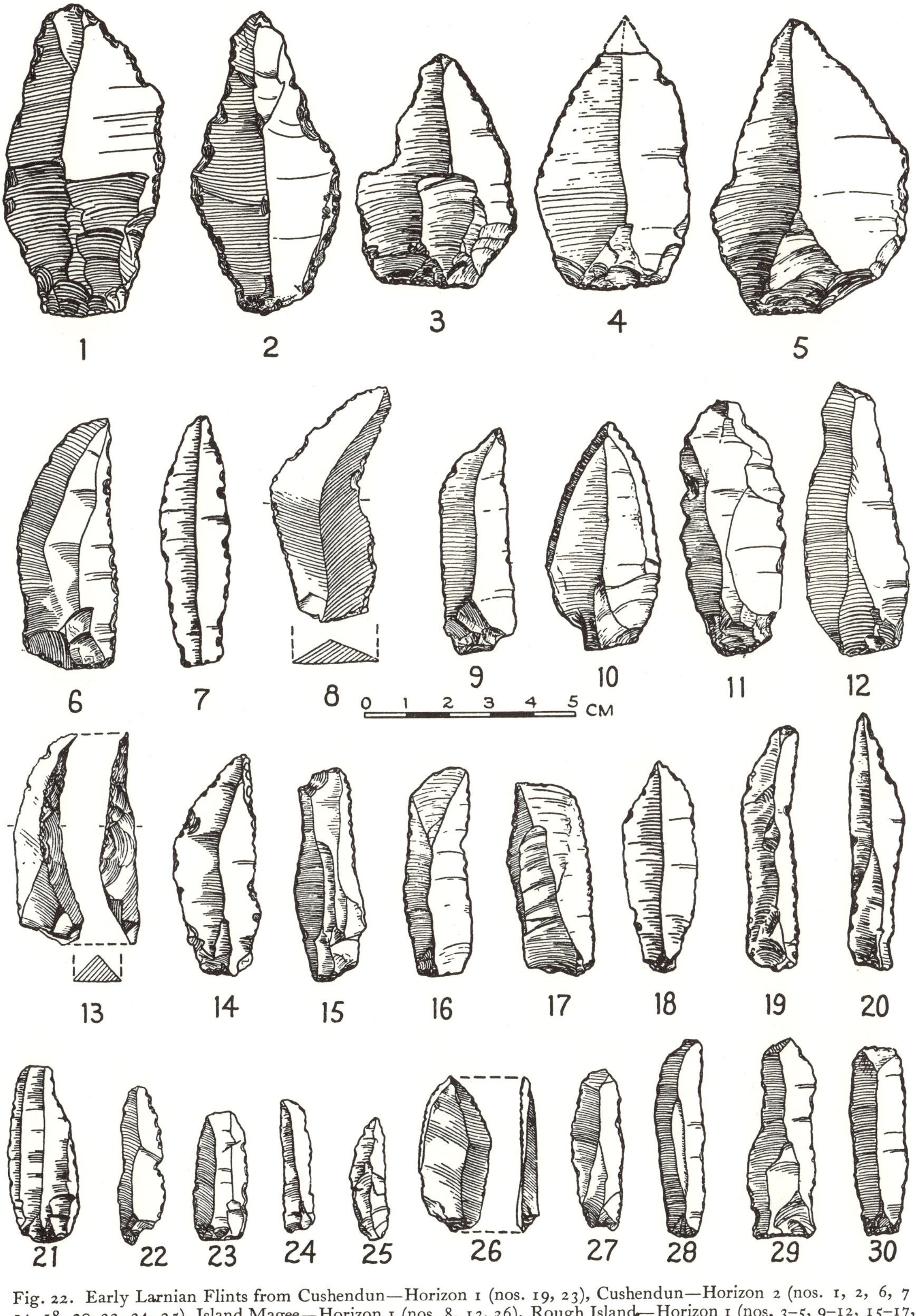

Fig. 22. Early Larnian Flints from Cushendun—Horizon 1 (nos. 19, 23), Cushendun—Horizon 2 (nos. 1, 2, 6, 7 14, 18, 20–22, 24, 25), Island Magee—Horizon 1 (nos. 8, 13, 26), Rough Island—Horizon 1 (nos. 3–5, 9–12, 15–17, 27–30). (Nos. 8, 13 and 26 after Burchell.) Scale: 2/3.

exception of no. 2, but they are chipped along both sides for a short distance away from the striking platform as well. Nos. 3 and 5 are especially good examples of this technique, which indicates that these implements were probably used as spear heads. However, regardless of purpose, similar points are very characteristic of the Neolithic culture of the Lower Bann Valley (Movius, 1936, p. 26), and it is, therefore, important to note their presence in the Early Larnian of the coast.

(2) *Small Blades with* Dos Rabattu *Trimming* (Fig. 23, nos. 1–4) are rare. Although three of the examples are from Horizon 2 at Cushendun (nos. 2–4), one was found in Horizon 1 at Rough Island (no. 1), proving that this type is not limited in distribution to the former locality. Nos. 2 and 3, a small point and a semi-lunate shaped implement respectively, are shown enlarged by $\frac{1}{3}$ (*a*) and at the same scale as nos. 1 and 4 by the outline drawings (*b*). The point of no. 4 is broken, but it displays fine trimming along the back, which has been executed from the bulbar surface. On the opposite edge extensive chipping from use is present. No. 1 is a small *dos rabattu* blade typical of Upper Palaeolithic deposits; its edge, in common with that of no. 3, shows no signs of use.

(3) *Side Scrapers* are extraordinarily rare, and the two examples shown (Fig. 23, nos. 5 and 9) are the only ones found thus far in the Early Larnian levels of North-East Ireland. No. 5, a large flake with cortex adhering to its upper surface, is only worked along one edge. The three sides of no. 9 have all been used, and on the left inverse chipping is apparent. The comparative absence of side scrapers is surprising, but it is in keeping with the limited occurrence of retouched forms.

(4) *End Scrapers* (Fig. 23, nos. 7 and 8). No end-of-blade scrapers are present in the Early Larnian in spite of the fact that blades are prolific. Indeed true end scrapers occur very sporadically, and the two illustrated specimens reveal the range from short, square-ended forms (no. 7) to small, steep, nosed types (no. 8). However, thumb-nail end scrapers of small, irregular shape, but with a decided tendency to be ovate or discoidal in outline (Fig. 23, nos. 15–21), are common. These scrapers are all made on the broken-off portions of fairly thick flakes, which have been carefully retouched. The illustrated specimens are from Rough Island (Horizon 1) and Cushendun (Horizon 2). Whereas thumb-nail end scrapers are particularly characteristic of the Early Larnian, they are also present in the later phase of this culture (see p. 164).

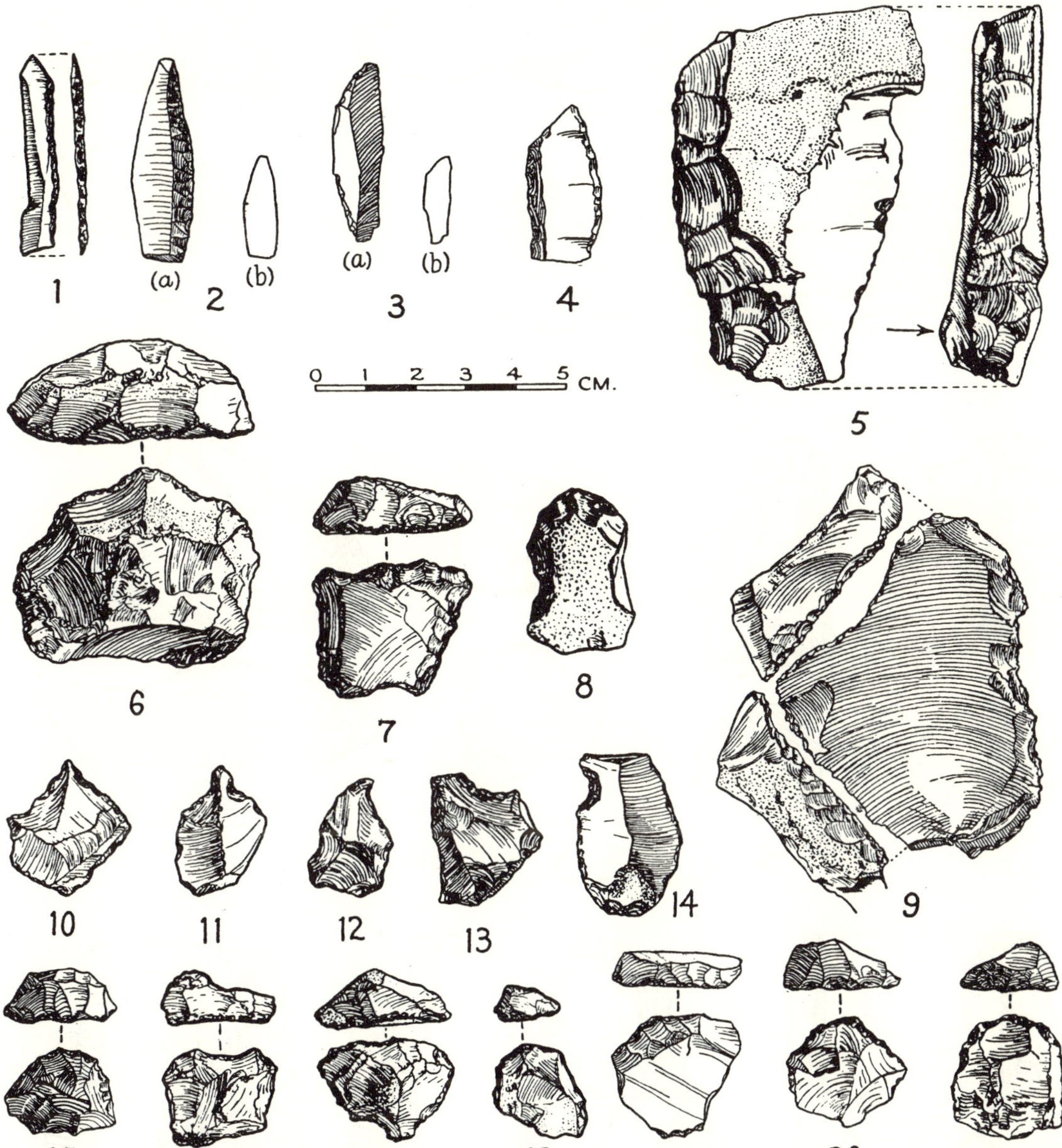

Fig. 23. Early Larnian Flints from Cushendun—Horizon 1 (no. 8), Cushendun—Horizon 2 (nos. 2–5, 12, 19–21), Island Magee—Horizon 1 (no. 9), Rough Island—Horizon 1 (nos. 1, 6, 7, 10, 11, 13–18). (Nos. 3 and 9 after Burchell.) Scale: 2/3.

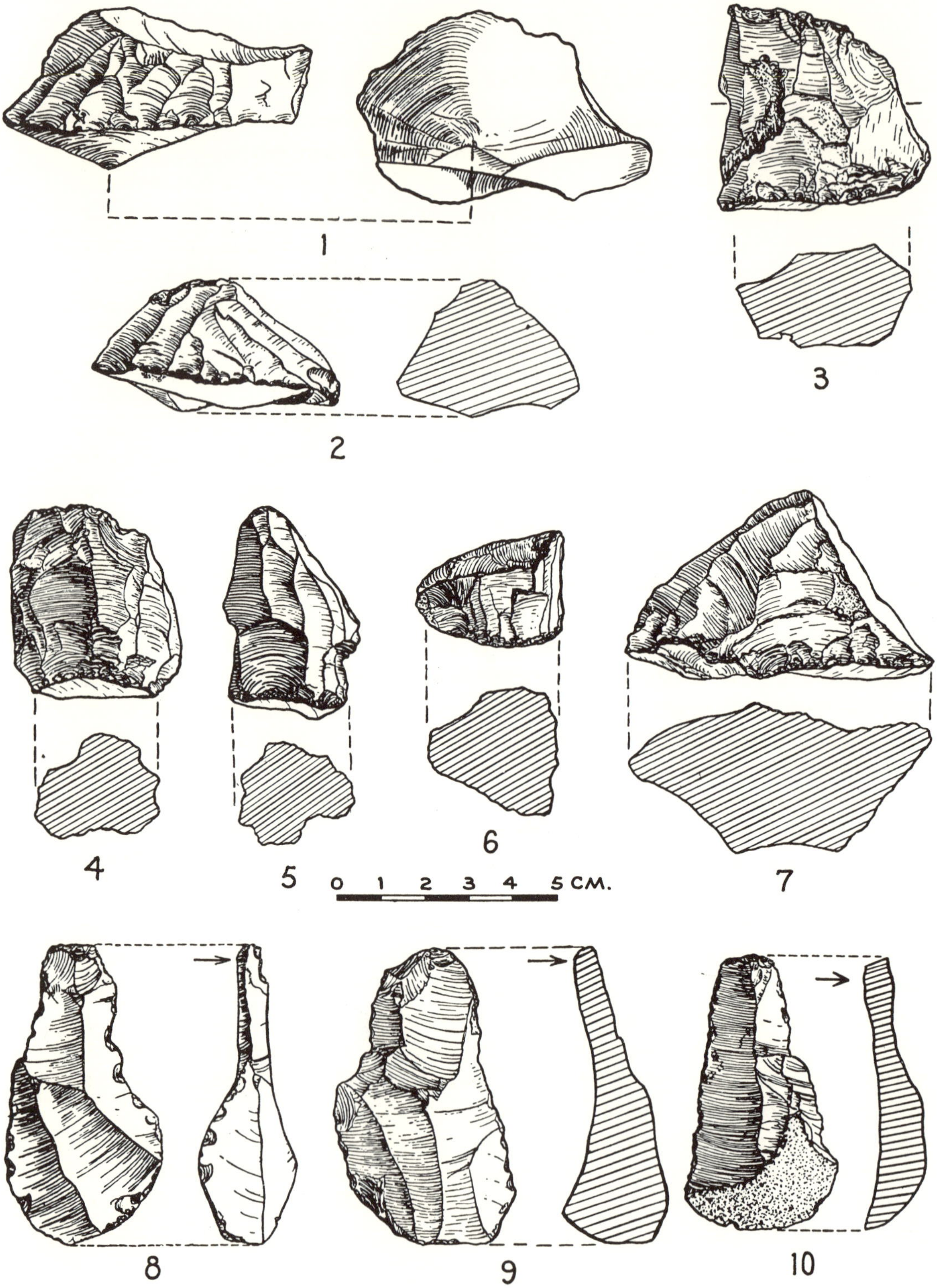

Fig. 24. Early Larnian Flints from Cushendun—Horizon 2 (nos. 1, 2, 8), and Rough Island—Horizon 1 (nos. 3–7 9, 10). Scale: 2/3. N.B. The arrows in nos 8–10 indicate the location of the bulb rather than the direction of the force applied to remove the flake. This convention is used throughout the book, except in the case of gravers.

(5) *Steep or Core Scrapers* (Fig. 24, nos. 1–7) form a noteworthy component of the industry. The relative abundance of the type, which is fairly characteristic of Aurignacian deposits, suggests that small blades were in common use, but these implements are not always made on cores, since nos. 1 and 2 are both short thick flakes. In most cases the face inclines gently upward, but very steep (nos. 4 and 5), or even vertical (no. 6) angles, occur. In contrast to cores, which display no evidence of utilization with the exception of the points of impact delivered for the purpose of flake removal, these implements show signs of use, often along more than one edge (nos. 3 and 6). It is probable that steep or core scrapers were employed as planes or perhaps as adzes.

(6) *Notched Scrapers* (Fig. 23, nos. 13 and 14). Notches resulting from use are a common feature of the blade implements, but purposely notched implements also occur. These may have served for scraping wooden shafts or bone points. The retouched concavity may be either on the end (no. 13) or the side (no. 14) of the blade; forms in this category are all small.

(7) *Perforators or Awls* (Fig. 23, nos. 10–12) are not infrequent. They are usually made on small flakes or chips which have been retouched for use as small boring tools. The figured specimens from Rough Island (Horizon 1) and Cushendun (Horizon 2) show the range from thick squat forms (no. 12) to types with a more tapering point (no. 10) or with a distinct neck (no. 11). The implements may have been used for perforating hides.

(8) *Choppers* are not common. A small example of an implement in this category is illustrated by Fig. 23, no. 6. It is a rough oval in shape, and the edge has been produced by alternate flaking.

(9) *Plunging Flakes* (Fig. 24, nos. 8–10) are rare in the Early Larnian, but as the type implement of the Late Larnian—the Larne pick (see p. 166)—is made by this technique, a few examples are shown. None of the figured specimens have been extensively used, although the core has been carefully prepared prior to detachment. Not infrequently a small area of cortex adheres to the end opposite the striking platform. The peculiar feature of these implements is the fact that the bulbar end is the one intended for use. These implements are the prototype of the Larne pick.

(10) *Rostrate Implements* (Fig. 25, no. 1). It has been mentioned elsewhere that typical rostro-carinates were present in the Irish Mesolithic, and in this connection it would be difficult to find a better example from deposits of any age than the illustrated specimen. It was found *in situ* in Horizon 2

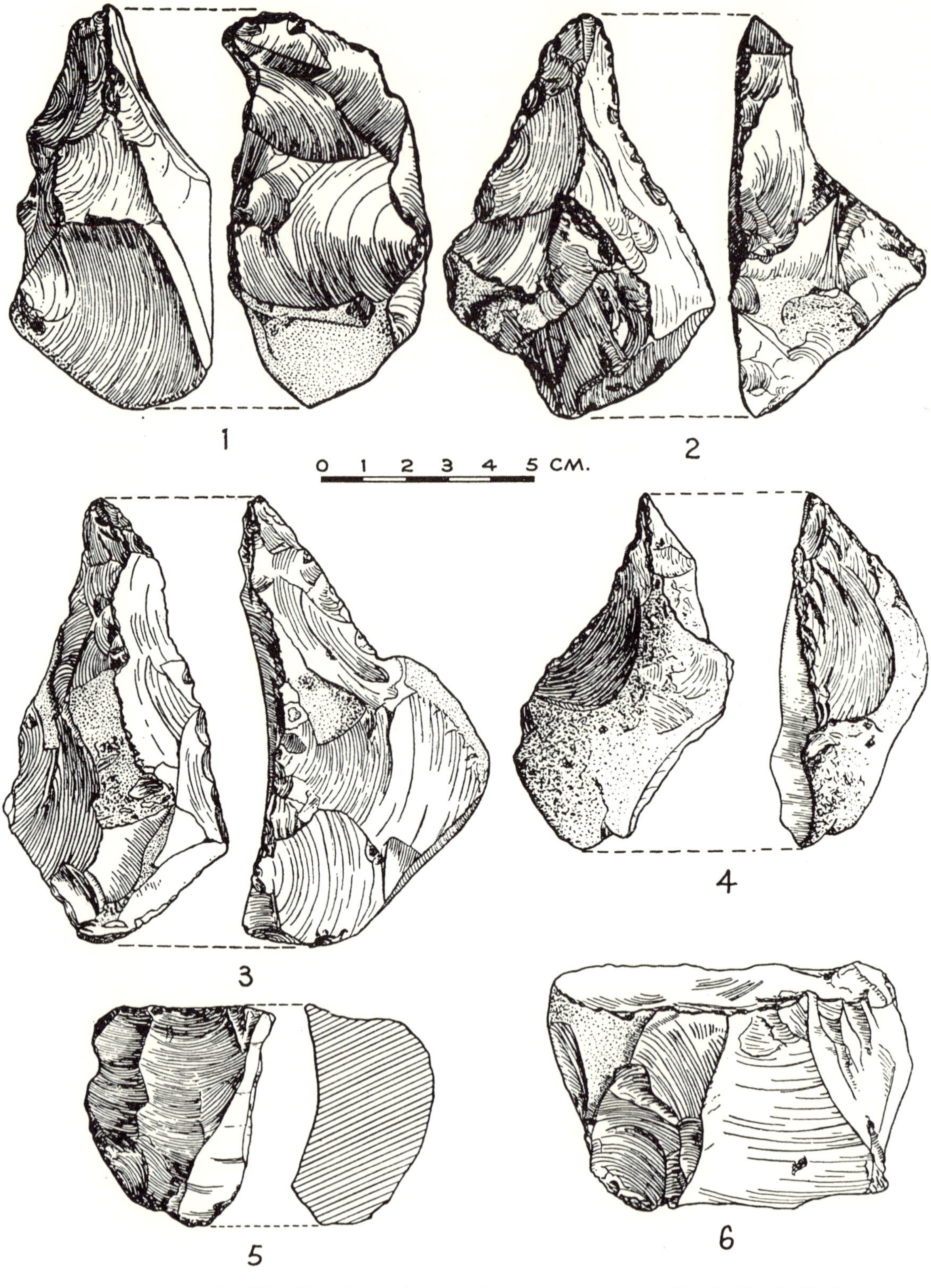

Fig. 25. Early Larnian Flints from Cushendun—Horizon 2 (nos. 1–3, 6), and Rough Island—Horizon 1 (nos. 4 and 5). Scale: 2/3.

(Deposit D) at Cushendun, and is sharp and almost unrolled. Furthermore, it is made on a core carefully flaked to produce a keel-like cutting edge. There is no doubt that this implement is part of the Early Larnian complex, and that it represents a tool developed in response to the need for heavy artifacts in the changing environment of the Early Post-Glacial Period. The possibility of either a Lower or a Pre-Palaeolithic ancestry seems very remote.

(11) *Cushendun Picks* (Fig. 25, nos. 2–4). In a sense these are also rostrate implements; no. 4 especially may be considered a crude example of the specimen described above, and a large area of cortex adheres to its upper surface. The point, ventral keel, and both edges show signs of utilization. Nos. 2 and 3 display careful core preparation, and they are typical of the massive flake implements characteristic of the Larnian culture. Possibly no. 2 is a large borer, but no. 3 is unmistakably a pick; the pointed end of both implements is triangular in section. The butt of these massive artifacts is chipped in such a way as to afford a convenient grip; it seems reasonably clear that they are hand tools.

(12) *Cores* (Fig. 25, nos. 5 and 6) occur in great numbers in the Early Larnian deposits at Cushendun and Rough Island. The striking platform is usually plain, but that of no. 6 displays several facets. Both show numerous flake scars, and in no. 5 the surface of impact is at an angle of less than 90° to the axis of the detached flakes: a feature which is found throughout the Mesolithic in Ireland. Late Larnian cores are of the same type as those described above.

Considering the typology of the Early Larnian flint implements from the coastal stations of North-East Ireland, the extraordinarily small proportion of purposely retouched forms is difficult to understand. Those that have been recovered are well made and reflect the workmanship of a race of skilled artificers of flint tools. One would normally expect gravers in association with this complex, but none have as yet been identified from the localities described above. Nor has any worked bone been discovered in the Early Larnian deposits. The points, blades and scrapers of various types suggest an economy based primarily on hunting, but until actual occupation sites are documented, which were not disturbed during the marine transgression, one can only speculate on the mode of life. The origins of this culture, which lie fundamentally in the Upper Palaeolithic of Britain, will be discussed in the next chapter.

B. Late Larnian

The implements depicted as typical of the Irish Mesolithic infer that massive, crudely worked and very heavily rolled forms comprise an overwhelming majority of the industry. Actually this is not the case. The Late Larnian levels which have been investigated—Cushendun (Deposit B), Glenarm (Deposit B), Larne (Deposits B and C) and Island Magee (Deposits A and C)—reveal that there is a considerable mixture of types exhibiting all degrees of rolling and including specimens which are absolutely unrolled and as fresh as when they were struck. Mr Whelan (1928, p. 188) has called attention to this fact with reference to the Curran deposits at Larne—the type station for the late phase of the Irish Mesolithic and by far the richest site in North-East Ireland. To account for the mixture at this locality several possibilities are open: (*a*) the more heavily rolled specimens represent an older industry, since they are coarser and more weathered; (*b*) the question of degree of rolling is determined by the location of the sites themselves—material from those farthest removed from the deposit would thus have been subject to the greatest amount of sea erosion; (*c*) the unrolled material was lost directly on the "beaches", or lay immediately in the path of the tidal currents and hence was not transported far; and (*d*) the sea itself has played the dominant role in sorting the material. Actually the first possibility, while apparently the more plausible, must be dismissed on the following grounds: (1) the coarse forms, which are *always* heavily rolled, represent an evolved industry peculiar to Ireland, and are part of the Late Larnian complex; (2) whereas all the coarse forms are rolled, some of the most heavily rolled types in the entire series are small tools identical with absolutely fresh material; and (3) the coarse implements are rare in the sand deposits, proving that the material has been sorted. A combination of (*b*), (*c*) and (*d*) must be considered, therefore, as the probable solution; all of these possibilities seem necessary to account for the situation, especially at Curran Point. At this site all the coarse implements are rolled, since they were too heavy to be transported directly by the sea and had to be rolled along the bottom of the lough. Consequently a great deal of this material was incorporated into the storm beach, Deposit B, at a time when wave action appears to have been severe. Some of the smaller material is unrolled, due to the proximity of the sites—the farther removed the site the greater the degree of rolling.

The question of the type of sediments composing a given horizon at the same or at different localities must be also considered. Late Larnian tools from the estuarine clay (Deposit C) at Island Magee display a comparatively fresh appearance in contrast to the rolled forms which predominate in the overlying raised beach gravels (Deposit A). In the pebble beach at Glenarm (Deposit B), all the implements have been badly worn by wave action. Furthermore, large forms are rare at this locality, which reflects the character of the beach itself: the pebbles are seldom larger than 4–5 cm. in diameter, the approximate size of a hen's egg. Deposits composed mainly of sand, such as Cushendun (Deposit B), yield very few artifacts except in the coarser layers of gravel and stones. Late Larnian tools are not abundant at this site, and sand polish is present on many of the flints. Because of the influence of local conditions controlling deposition at various localities, it is difficult to make direct comparisons of the archaeological material. Thus it is impossible to distinguish between variations which have resulted from local development and those caused by natural selection on the part of the sea. Before this distinction can be made, a detailed study of individual collections from deposits composed of similar material and containing Late Larnian artifacts at various sites on the Antrim and Down coasts will be necessary. Even more accurate results will be obtained if undisturbed occupation sites with primary stratigraphy can be found. Admittedly subdivisions of this culture exist, but for the present the implements, which have been derived from numerous settlements covering a time interval of perhaps two and a half millennia, must be considered as a whole.

Typologically the Late Larnian falls into the following groups:

(1) *Massive Flake Implements* (Fig. 26, nos. 1–10) are very characteristic of the Late Mesolithic in Ireland. As previously stated, these forms are generally heavily rolled, although the flake facets on nos. 3 and 5, both from Cushendun (Horizon 3), are more clearly defined than those exhibited by the other illustrated specimens. Careful retouching is rarely found; the edge chipping in most cases has resulted from use and from battering by the sea. Some of the implements in this series have served as end scrapers (nos. 5 and 10), but usually the end is blunt and displays a portion of the original cortex of the flint. Notches indicating use as hollow scrapers (no. 9) are frequent. Such specimens as nos. 1, 2 and 4, each over 3 cm. thick, are probably choppers.

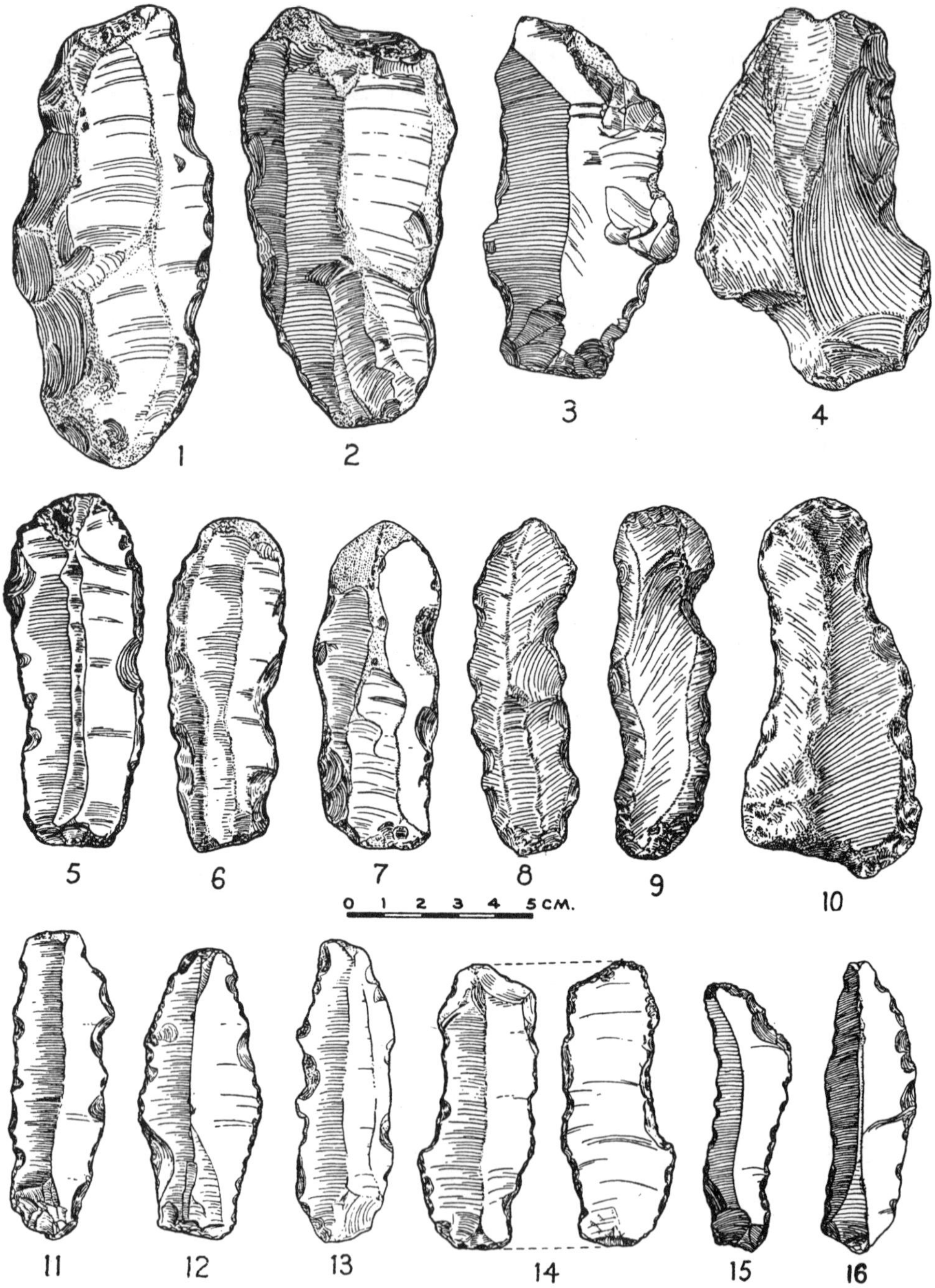

Fig. 26. Late Larnian Flints from Cushendun—Horizon 3 (nos. 3, 5, 15, 16), Glenarm—Horizon 1 (nos. 4, 8–10), Larne—Curran Deposits (nos. 1, 2, 6, 7, 11–14). Scale: 1/2.

(2) *Primary Blades showing signs of use* (Fig. 26, nos. 11–16; Fig. 27, nos. 10–22) are of much the same type as those found in the Early Larnian horizons, but they tend to be thicker and not as skilfully struck. Thus Late Larnian blades are coarse and clumsy, as if the industry, which originally was characterized by thin delicate blades, had lost its vitality to a certain degree. Although small blade tools occur (Fig. 27, nos. 10–20), they are never abundant, and *dos rabattu* trimming is absent. One of the most pronounced differences between the early and late phases of the Larnian culture may be detected in the blade technique, as a comparison of the present series with that previously illustrated (Figs. 21 and 22) will reveal. It seems evident that with the approach of the more clement conditions of the climatic optimum, the Larnian culture degenerated—the tools are coarser and more generalized. Doubtless peripheral isolation was an important factor contributing to this development, for in Stone Age times Ireland was only an indirect recipient of the new influences which penetrated South-East Britain from the Continent. Likewise the material effect of the Litorina transgression cannot be overlooked. When the forested lowlands of the Boreal Period were transgressed by the sea, Mesolithic settlers along the coast were gradually forced to adopt a new mode of life patterned to meet the exigencies of marine conditions. Under these circumstances it is not surprising to find a change in the typology and technique of the flint implements.

(3) *Points.* Superficially tanged, leaf-shaped points (Fig. 27, nos. 1–7), which carry on the tradition of the Early Larnian (compare Fig. 22, nos. 1–5), are present. The illustrated specimens, which come from Cushendun (Horizon 3), Glenarm (Horizon 1), and Larne (Deposits B and C), have been trimmed on the upper surface of, as well as along both sides away from, the bulbar end. Fig. 27, nos. 8 and 9, two definitely tanged examples from the estuarine clay (Deposit C) at Island Magee, are important. Although no. 9 is made on a side-blow flake, it is an excellent example of a well-known Upper Palaeolithic form. The pointed end of no. 8 is broken; it belongs to the same class as no. 9. This series demonstrates that the protypes of the Neolithic Bann points are found in the Larnian, a fact which strongly suggests that the later culture of the interior of North-East Ireland and the Isle of Man (see pp. 239–51) was founded primarily on Mesolithic survivals of the Antrim coast.

(4) *Side Scrapers* (Fig. 28, nos. 1 and 2) are not common. Doubtless many of the massive flake implements described above were used for scraping

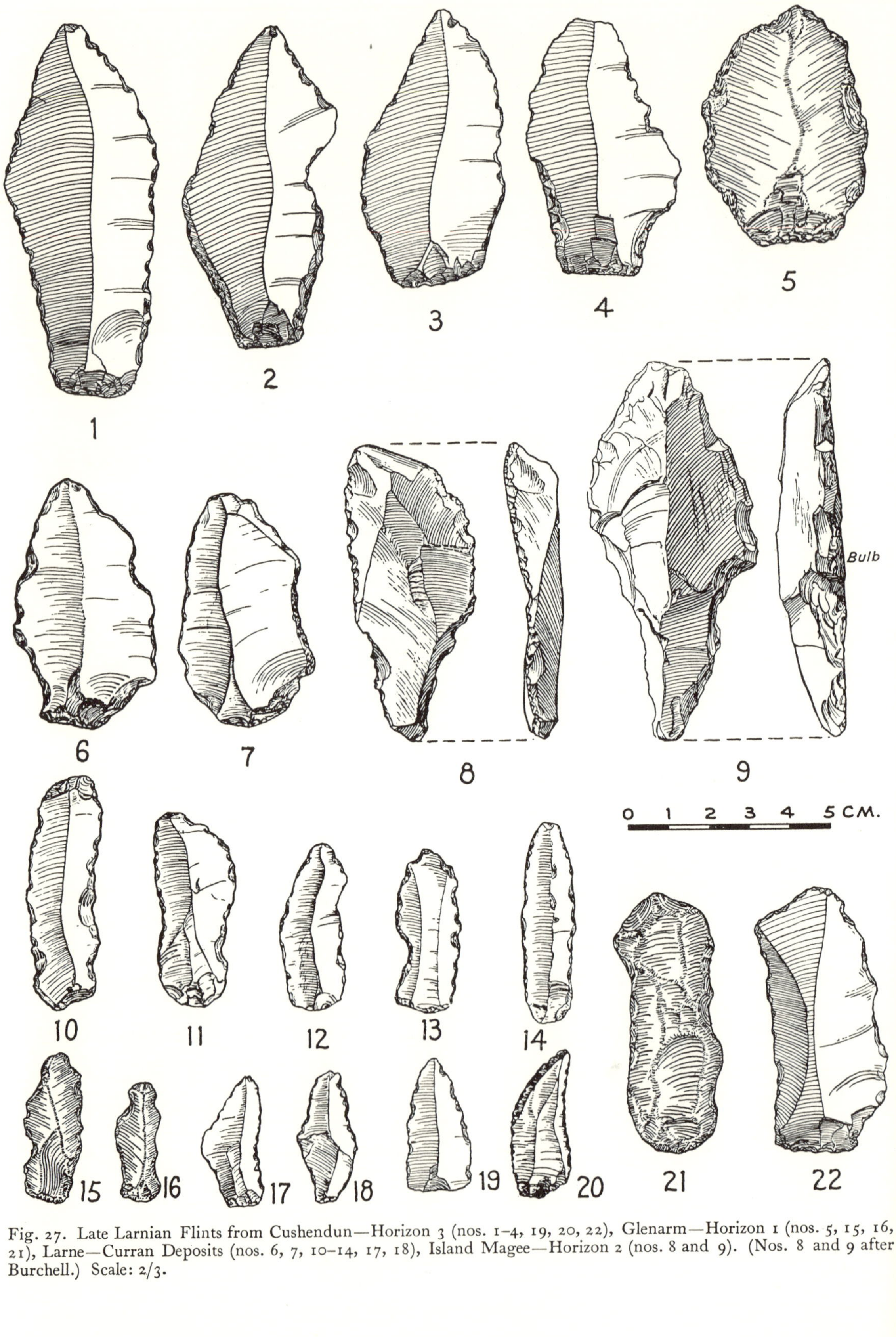

Fig. 27. Late Larnian Flints from Cushendun—Horizon 3 (nos. 1–4, 19, 20, 22), Glenarm—Horizon 1 (nos. 5, 15, 16, 21), Larne—Curran Deposits (nos. 6, 7, 10–14, 17, 18), Island Magee—Horizon 2 (nos. 8 and 9). (Nos. 8 and 9 after Burchell.) Scale: 2/3.

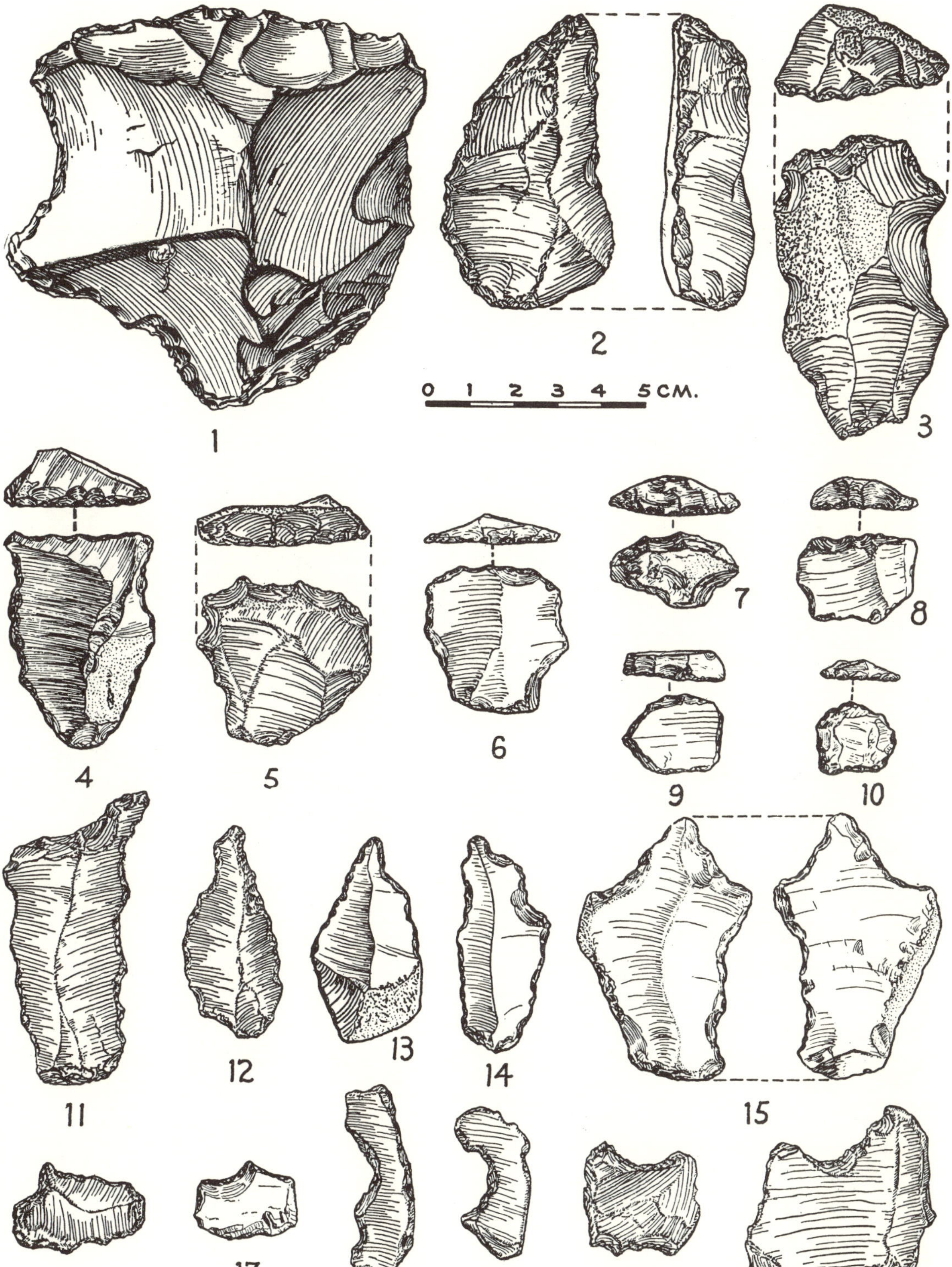

Fig. 28. Late Larnian Flints from Glenarm—Horizon 1 (nos. 2, 3, 5, 11, 12, 16, 18–21), Larne—Curran Deposits (nos. 4, 6–10, 13–15, 17), Island Magee—Horizon 2 (no. 1). (No. 1 after Burchell.) Scale: 2/3.

among other purposes, although very few clearly defined types occur. The large square-ended and hollow scraper or boring tool (no. 1) is typical of the generalized artifacts which may be classified in this category. Smaller examples, such as no. 2, made on thick flakes are more numerous; the retouching is always irregular. A fine series of Late Larnian side scrapers has been illustrated by Knowles (1914, Figs. 18–30).

(5) *End Scrapers.* A few, very crude end-of-blade scrapers (Fig. 28, nos. 3 and 4) are typical. As the illustrated specimens show, these may be either of the steep (no. 3) or square-ended (no. 4) variety. Nos. 5 and 6 are rough discoidal scrapers which are fairly common. Thumb-nail end scrapers (Fig. 28, nos. 7–10) are survivals from the Early Larnian (compare Fig. 23, nos. 15–21); no. 10 is reminiscent of forms characteristic of the sand-hill settlements of Northern Ireland.

(6) *Perforators or Awls* are mainly made on short pointed blades (Fig. 28, nos. 11–15). The working end is usually defined by a short neck, and inverse retouching (no. 15) is frequent. Fig. 28, no. 11, is an obliquely pointed blade with a projection for drilling on the right side at an approximate angle of 45° to the long axis of the blade. Small forms (Fig. 28, nos. 16 and 17) are very characteristic; in some cases they seem to be combination tools and to have been used as hollow thumb-nail scrapers as well as perforators.

(7) *Notched Scrapers.* Large examples of implements of this type have been previously noted (Fig. 26, no. 9); however, small blades with well-defined notches (Fig. 28, nos. 18 and 19) are also found. Concave end scrapers (Fig. 28, nos. 20 and 21) may be included here. In all instances the secondary working has been executed from the under side of the flake.

(8) *Choppers* (Fig. 29, nos. 1–4) are very characteristic of the Late Larnian culture. No. 2 is a typical example made on a massive flake with a steeply worked side, and a large area of cortex present on the butt. Smaller, and in some cases more extensively worked choppers, are often made on thick, medium-sized flakes, or cores (nos. 3 and 4). In the Curran deposits at Larne, approximately one-third of the archaeological material, exclusive of blades, consists of choppers, or other heavy implements presumably connected with woodworking. Fig. 29, no. 1, is an excellent example of a massive combination tool used as a spokeshave and a chopper. It is manufactured from a very crude flake and was collected on the foreshore at Curran Point. It is the only illustrated specimen which was not found in direct

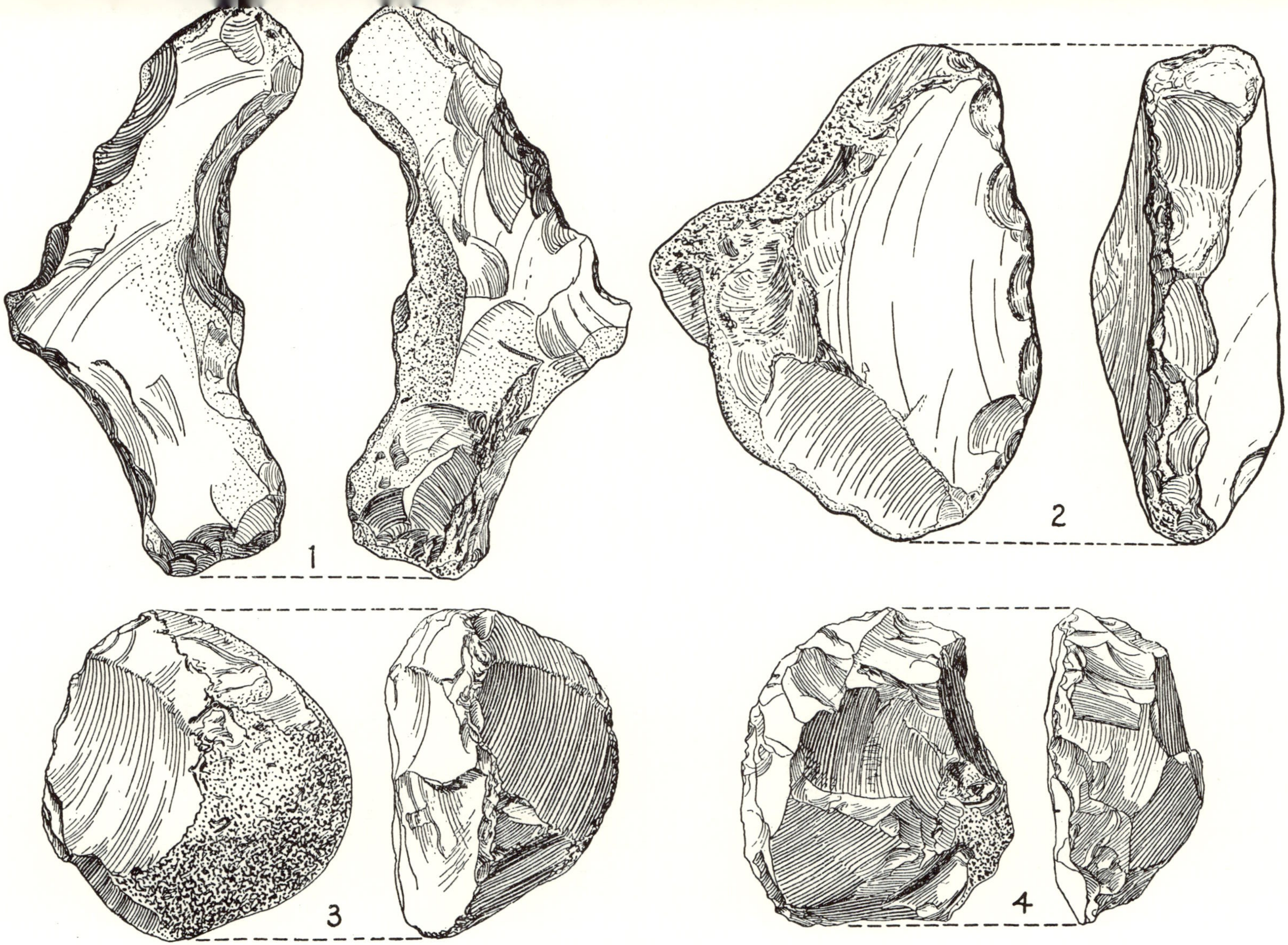

Fig. 29. Late Larnian Flints from Larne—Curran Deposits (nos. 1 and 2), and Island Magee—Horizon 2 (nos. 3 and 4). (Nos. 3 and 4 after Burchell.) Scales: no. 1, 3/8; nos. 2–4, 1/2.

association with the Litorina raised beach, although there is no doubt that it belongs to the Late Larnian series.

(9) *Larne Picks* (Fig. 30; Fig. 31, nos. 1–5) are the type implements of the Irish Mesolithic. They occur in profusion in Late Larnian deposits, especially at Larne and Island Magee, and characterize a cultural development strictly indigenous to Ireland. The figured specimens have been selected to show the variations in type and size, which range from huge forms over 14 cm. long (Fig. 30, no. 1), to small examples with an average length of 6 cm. (Fig. 31, nos. 3–5). In all cases the core has been carefully prepared prior to detaching these peculiar implements, which, it should be pointed out, are very difficult to manufacture intentionally. As they have been extensively used, they are not merely "core rejuvenation flakes". What distinguishes the Larne pick from other tool families, known from elsewhere, is the fact that the bulbar end is the one which is intended for use. The proximal end has been intentionally left thick, a feature which is often accentuated by the plunging method employed in delivering the blow for the removal of the implement from the core. Fig. 30, no. 6, is an excellent example of this technique. The large specimen (Fig. 30, no. 1) may have served as a crude adze, but usually the narrow end terminates in a thick point. Very rarely is the bulb of percussion not in evidence, and in some cases (Fig. 30, no. 7) the striking platform is intact. Actually the term pick may be a misnomer, as indicated by the extensive signs of use along the sides, but such examples as Fig. 31, no. 1, are certainly hand implements of the pick variety. The purpose of these tools is, however, difficult to determine, but a definite need for them must have existed judging by their frequent occurrence. As previously mentioned (see p. 155) the prototype of the Larne pick is present in the Early Larnian levels at Cushendun and Island Magee. Although the Cushendun pick (Fig. 25, nos. 2–4) is a more massive implement with a ventral keel, it is also made on a flake and may be ancestral to this family of late Larnian tools (compare Fig. 31, no. 1).

(10) *Axes* (Fig. 31, nos. 6–8; Fig. 32) have hitherto been considered a predominant form in the industry contained in the Litorina raised beaches of North-East Ireland, but this idea may have been a result of selective collecting. The fact that not a single axe was found in a series of over 5000 implements, excavated at Curran Point, Larne, in 1935, gives reason to believe that their occurrence must be extremely sporadic. Whereas these implements have been reported from localities on Island Magee and around

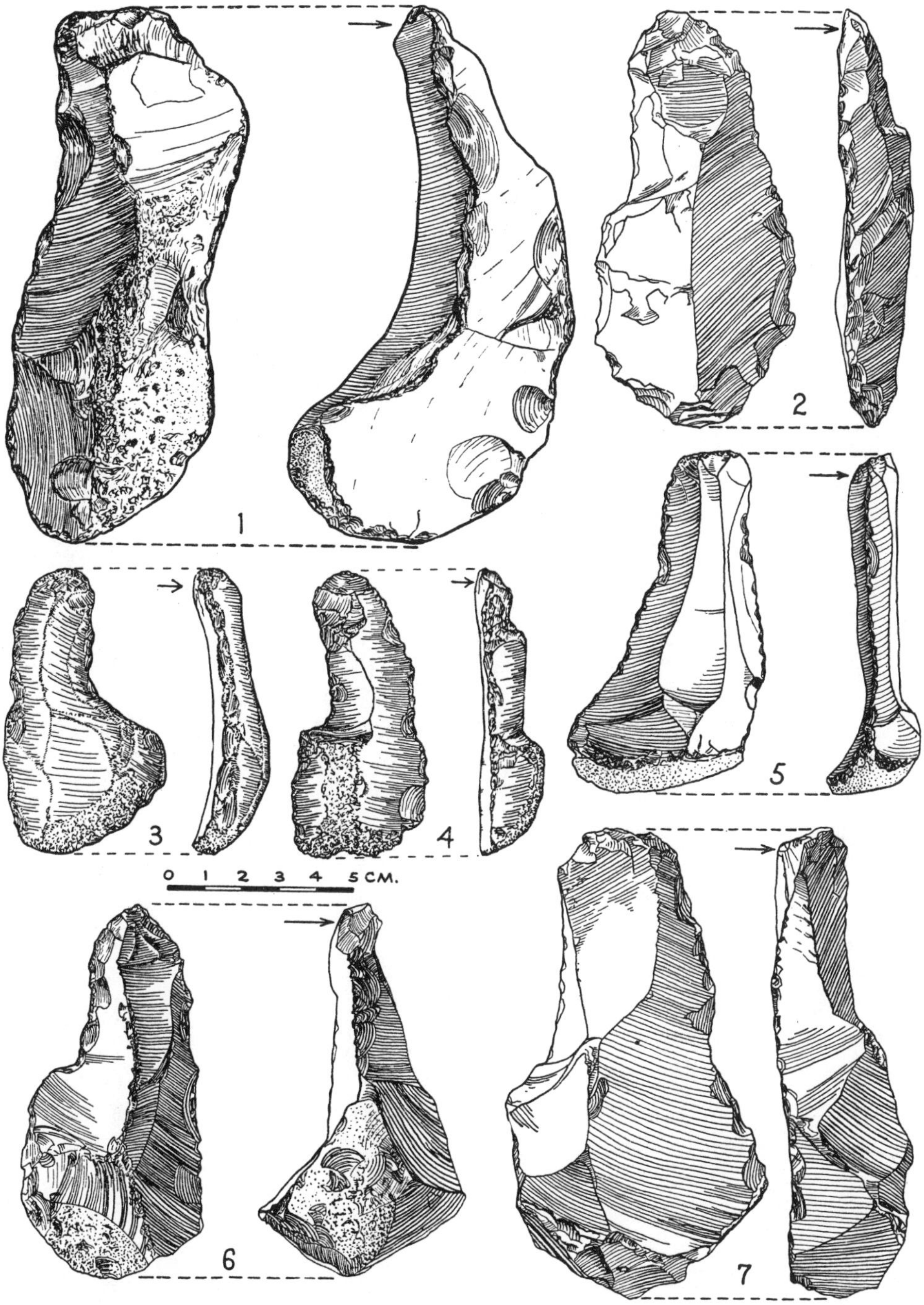

Fig. 30. Late Larnian Flints from Cushendun—Horizon 3 (no. 5), Glenarm—Horizon 1 (nos. 3 and 4), Larne—Curran Deposits (no. 1), Island Magee—Horizon 2 (nos. 2, 6, 7). (Nos. 2 and 7 after Burchell.) Scale: 1/2.

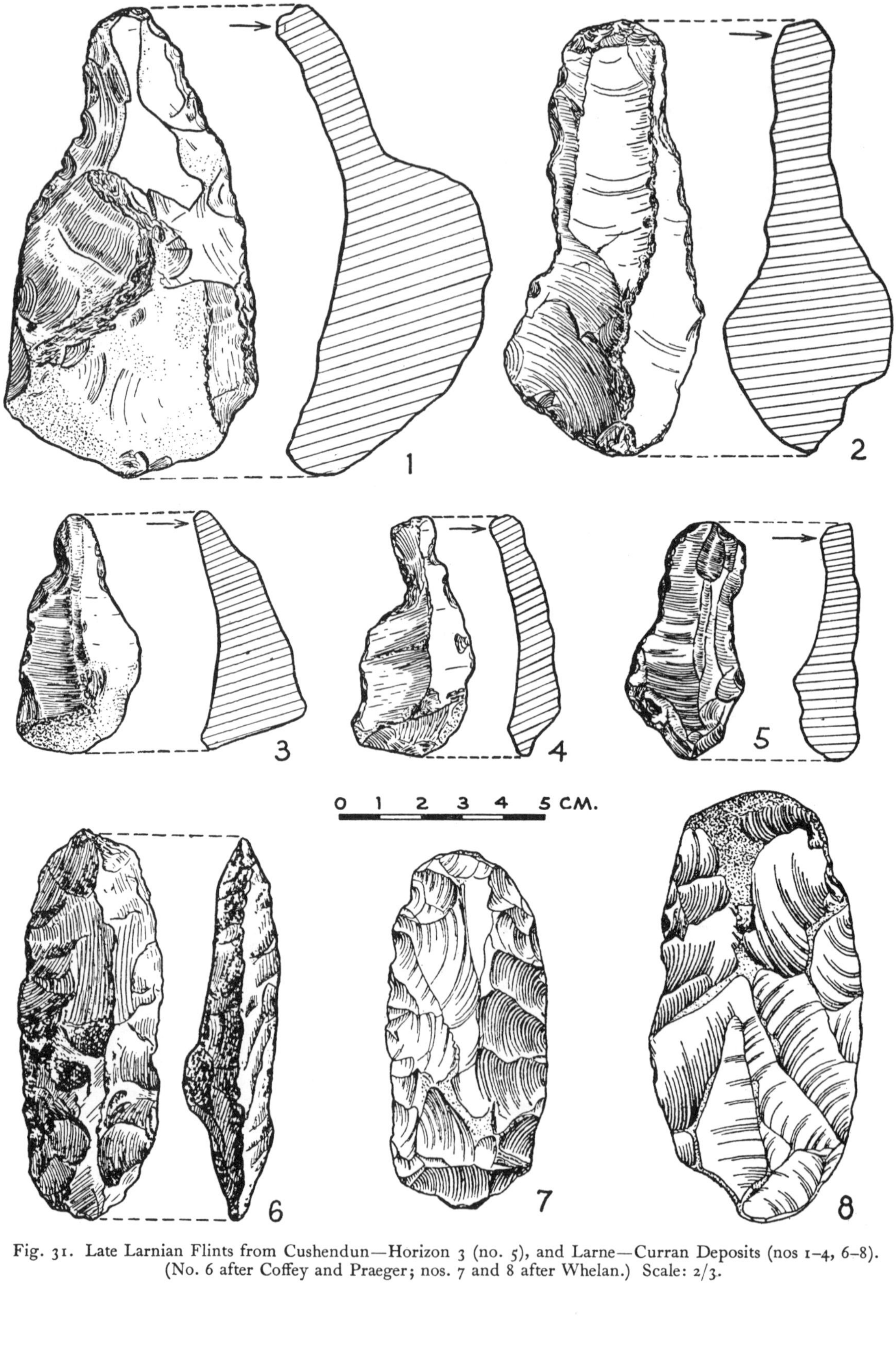

Fig. 31. Late Larnian Flints from Cushendun—Horizon 3 (no. 5), and Larne—Curran Deposits (nos 1–4, 6–8). (No. 6 after Coffey and Praeger; nos. 7 and 8 after Whelan.) Scale: 2/3.

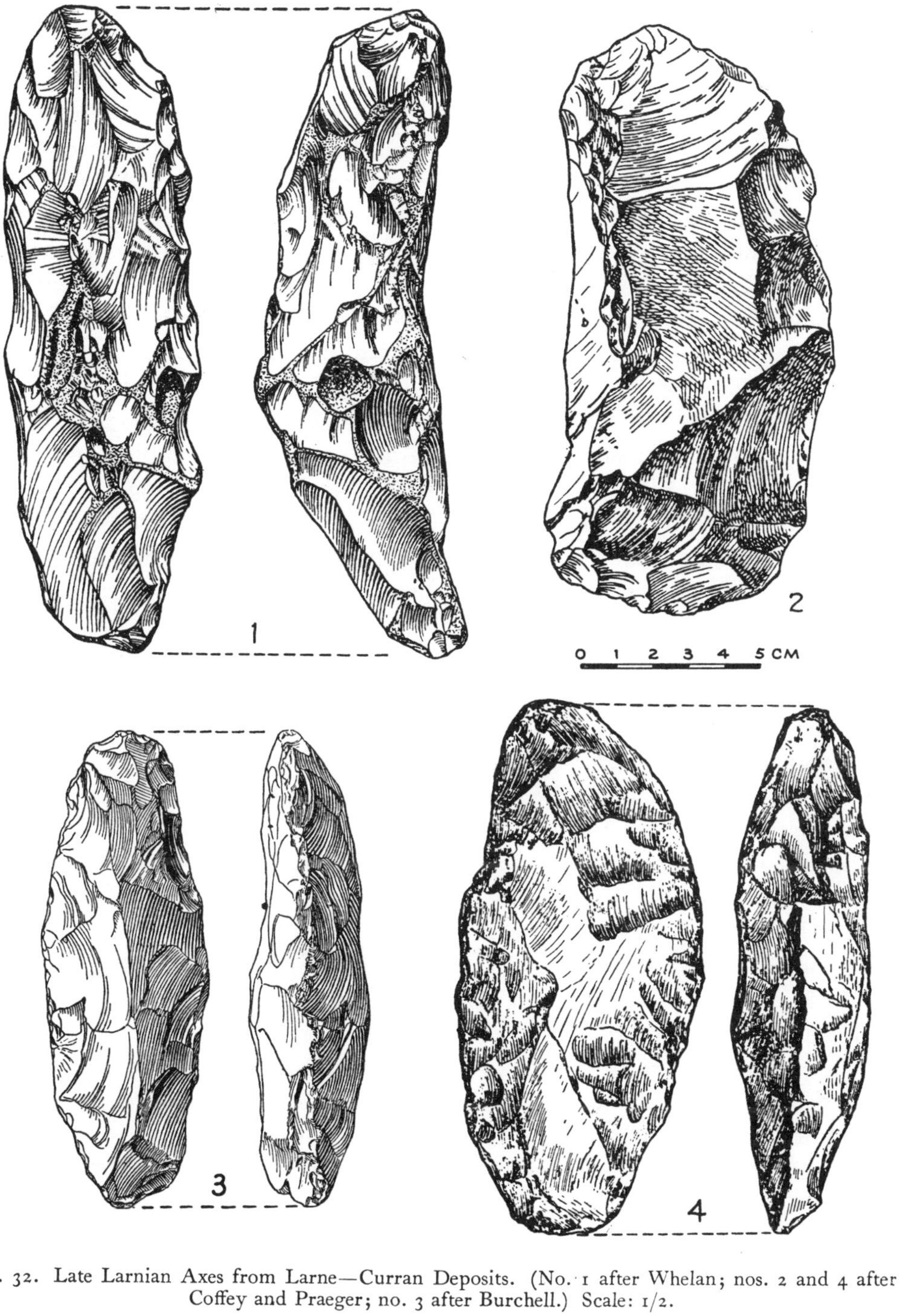

Fig. 32. Late Larnian Axes from Larne—Curran Deposits. (No. 1 after Whelan; nos. 2 and 4 after Coffey and Praeger; no. 3 after Burchell.) Scale: 1/2.

Belfast Lough (Gray, W., 1893, p. 614; Knowles, 1893, pp. 140–2), they are all surface finds, and one cannot be certain of their age. Typologically there is very little difference between axes of the Larnian culture and later examples (Neolithic and Early Metal Age). However, the *tranchet*, or flake axe, was not introduced into Ireland until Neolithic times. Only the core axe is present, but well-documented examples are rare. The illustrated specimens were all found *in situ* at Larne: Fig. 31, no. 6, comes from the base of a sand layer, 11 feet below the surface; Fig. 32, no. 2, at a depth of 5 feet; and Fig. 32, no. 4, at "a considerable depth in the gravels" (Coffey and Praeger, 1904, p. 183). Fig. 31, nos. 7 and 8, and Fig. 32, no. 1, were collected by Mr Whelan at Curran Point. The latter specimen is actually a large, shoe-shaped adze (Whelan, 1935), chipped on both sides; Fig. 30, no. 1, illustrates a crude example of a flake implement of comparable type. The excellent core axe (Fig. 32, no. 3) found by Mr Burchell (1931, p. 288) is very reminiscent of an unsharpened "Thames pick" of the Late Mesolithic of South-East England. As the illustrations show, there is no uniformity as to shape among the larger specimens; however, the small axes, or celts (Fig. 31, nos. 6–8), agree fairly well in type. No. 7 has been sharpened in characteristic manner by the removal of a flake transverse to the main axis of the implement. The presence of axes in the Late Larnian demonstrates that a definite influence from the Mesolithic Forest cultures of Northern and Western Europe penetrated Ireland during Atlantic times.

The data presented above clearly show that essentially the Late Larnian is a flake culture, which developed with certain modifications from the Early Mesolithic of Ireland. However, core tools—choppers, axes and celts chipped from flint nodules—do occur. As yet it is impossible to subdivide this phase of the Irish Mesolithic, since primary stratigraphy is lacking, and local conditions determining the type of sedimentation at the various localities have been important in sorting the material. One fact is clear, in the Litorina raised beaches of North-East Ireland, degree of rolling is no criterion of age. Therefore, until undisturbed settlement sites of this period have been discovered, it will be difficult to trace the cultural development. Although the Late Mesolithic kitchen-midden on Rough Island proved sterile, similar sites elsewhere will unquestionably repay excavation. In them some trace of organic remains should be expected as well as a possible clue to the use of the Larne pick.

5. SUMMARY AND CONCLUSIONS

In the absence of primary occupation sites yielding Larnian implements, it is difficult to make any definite statements concerning the nature of Irish Mesolithic settlements. Although direct proof is lacking, a study of the archaeological material indicates that the culture of this period was based on a primitive hunting economy, as elsewhere in Northern and Western Europe. Thus fowling, fishing, hunting and collecting formed the basis of subsistence. A study of natural phenomena reveals that at the time of the first occupation an equable climate prevailed with a summer temperature approximately the same as at present, but the winters were probably colder, and the rainfall was definitely lower than it is now. With the approach of the climatic optimum, there was a steady increase of warm conditions, and a correspondingly heavier precipitation. The earth movements, submergence followed by emergence, during this latter phase, the Atlantic, were events of major geographical importance, therefore occupation along the coast would have been hazardous to some extent, especially during the time of the Litorina transgression when the land was sinking. Contemporary dwelling-sites must have been continually inundated by the sea, and their contents, washed away by wave action, were incorporated into the coastal marine deposits, subsequently elevated to their present height. Unfortunately very few bone implements have been preserved, and our knowledge of the Irish Mesolithic is limited almost solely to a study of the flint tools; nevertheless, bone and antler must have been used. Henry Holme (1912) records three "prickers", made from Deer ulnae, found at the base of a raised beach near Holywood, County Down, in association with chipped and rolled flints. At a depth of 15 feet in the estuarine clays of Belfast Lough, near Belfast, Robert Young (1877, p. 19) discovered a Deer antler and rib, both of which had been cut, presumably by a flint implement; these came from a gravelly stratum in the clay which contained an immense accumulation of bone, horn and antler (Deer and Ox), as well as trunks and branches of small trees. Likewise in the raised beach at Glenarm (Movius, 1937, p. 198; Fig. 6, no. 36) a fragment of a Cow's rib (Aurochs?) was recovered. This scanty list, which includes only three recognizable implements, covers all the published finds of worked bone and antler from Litorina deposits in Ireland.

As previously stated, the Early Larnian developed on the lowlands which existed during the period of the Early Post-Glacial emergence off the present coasts of North-East Ireland. The implement types include an overwhelming proportion of blade tools, a fact which suggests a complex fundamentally based on a hunting economy and of ultimate Upper Palaeolithic origin. This culture probably evolved on a Boreal land surface, now under the sea, but in Early Post-Glacial times characterized by swampy, fresh-water fens. It must also have supported both forests and open grasslands, where game was plentiful. It is certain that Irish Elk, Red Deer, Wolf and Wild Boar roamed about in the region during this period, but contemporary evidence from elsewhere (*e.g.* Inchnadamff, see p. 72) suggests that additional forms, including wild fowl, must have been extant. Although separated by the Irish Channel River, communication with Scotland was comparatively easy, and Antrim flint was exported at least as far as Campbeltown, Argyll. This implies that boats were included in the material culture, a point which will be further discussed in the next chapter. With the Litorina submergence, the old land surface was inundated by the sea, and the material from these sites is found in coastal deposits of Zone V*b* in Ireland, contemporary with the Lower Estuarine Clays. This event, the marine transgression, played an important role in effecting a cultural change. Whereas many types common to the earlier phase continued in use, new tool forms were evolved to meet the needs conditioned by the changed environment. After the submergence the sea in place of the land seems to have been of primary concern. The hunting culture represented by the Early Larnian diverged along lines adapted to marine pursuits, in which fishing and collecting edible molluscs probably formed the basis of subsistence. Present evidence demonstrates that settlement was concentrated on the coast, where the invasion of the pre-existing valleys and lowlands by the ocean transformed the landscape relatively suddenly, and marine erosion began on a wide scale. The contemporary rise in temperature led to the growth of more extensive forests, and heavy tools, apparently specialized for woodworking, form a notable component of the Late Larnian. Material referable to this phase of the Irish Mesolithic occurs in deposits of the early and middle portion of Zone VI in Ireland, which corresponds in age with the Intermediate and Upper Estuarine Clays. No abrupt break took place between the Early and Late Larnian phases, although the gradual transformation clearly reflects the changing mode of life induced by the Litorina transgression. In addition a new influence penetrated Ireland at this time (see pp. 202–3).

It seems reasonably clear that the Early Larnian may be assigned to the Boreal Period, while the Late Larnian definitely belongs to that part of Atlantic time which antedates the maximum of the Litorina subsidence. This chronology is strongly implied by the secondary position of the implements. There is as yet no material in Ireland, with the exception of the midden on Rough Island and a few Late Larnian flints from the superficial layers of the raised beach at Glenarm, which may be assigned to the end of the Atlantic phase. Hence the final development of the Larnian is virtually unknown. Future research, especially around the shores of such relatively quiet bodies of water as Larne Lough, Belfast Lough and Strangford Lough, and below peats on portions of the foreshore not invaded by the Litorina Sea, should reveal undisturbed occupation sites. Likewise it is probable that caves, cut by the Litorina Sea during the maximum of the submergence, contain Mesolithic occupation layers contemporary with the emergence. In such sites it should be possible to establish Irish Mesolithic chronology by more direct evidence than that afforded by the sites described in this chapter. These yield comparatively few well-worked flint implements, which together with the almost complete absence of bone artifacts, makes the roots of the Irish Mesolithic difficult to trace. However, the Larnian hunters and fishermen were expert at making blade tools, and in certain deposits the forms are preserved in an almost perfectly fresh condition. In general this applies to the Early Larnian, but nearly all the implements of the later phase are badly rolled, sometimes almost beyond recognition. Secondary chipping is often obliterated as a result of wave action, or the edges are far too battered to enable a differentiation to be made between what is of human origin and what is not. The comparative scarcity of retouched forms, however, is surprising. Possibly this resulted from the fact that the almost unlimited flint supply in North-East Ireland enabled the Mesolithic inhabitants to strike fresh blade tools whenever they wished. It was therefore unnecessary to rework the blunted edges of used implements, which may account for the abundance of comparatively sharp or only slightly used flakes in a normal Larnian series. A summary of the leading forms is given below:

Early Larnian. Typical: small to medium-sized blades showing signs of use; steep or core scrapers; thumb-nail scrapers; perforators; microliths with *dos rabattu* trimming; and Cushendun picks. Present but rare: end scrapers; points; leaf-shaped points with trimmed butts; rostrate implements; choppers; side scrapers; and concave end scrapers.

Late Larnian. Typical: coarse, heavy flake and blade implements; choppers; rostrate implements; notched or concave scrapers; leaf-shaped points with trimmed butts; tanged points; Larne picks; and core axes (rare but found *in situ* at Larne). Survivals: thumb-nail scrapers; perforators; end scrapers; side scrapers (rare); points (rare); and small to medium-sized blades. Absent: Steep or core scrapers; and microliths with *dos rabattu* trimming.

At the inland station on the northern shore of Lough Neagh, described on pp. 117–20, an Early Larnian industry occurs *in situ*. The leading types include: steep or core scrapers (typical); small utilized blades; end scrapers; perforators; picks; and gravers. The latter implement is conspicuously absent at the coastal sites; in the entire series of over 20,000 implements excavated in 1934–6 by the Harvard Archaeological Expedition, not one single authentic graver was found, although a few *burins de fortune* occur. This is surprising in view of the marked Upper Palaeolithic facies of the Larnian and the presence of this type at Lough Neagh. Nevertheless the industry from below the Late Boreal–Early Atlantic peat at the latter site definitely belongs to the same cultural tradition as the Early Larnian of the Antrim and Down coasts. In the next chapter will be traced the distribution of this culture, whose roots apparently lie in the Upper Palaeolithic (Creswellian) of Britain, and the Azilian of Southern France. The Upper Palaeolithic types, microliths with *dos rabattu* trimming and steep or core scrapers, are characteristic of earlier deposits in the south of Britain. The thumb-nail end scraper is the only Azilian form present in the Irish Mesolithic. But in Scotland, where a similar culture exists, other characteristic bone and antler implements are found, indicating a definite influence from France. These are also present in the Late Larnian; but the Upper Palaeolithic types, with the single exception of tanged points, are absent in this complex, which indicates the degree of specialization which took place. In general heavy woodworking tools are characteristic, including choppers, notched or concave scrapers (some probably used as spokeshaves) and the Larne pick, an implement peculiar to Ireland and the type fossil of the Irish Mesolithic. In the Curran deposits at Larne, core axes occur sporadically, which indicates an influence from the Forest cultures of North-West Europe coming via Britain. Cushendun is the type site for the Early Larnian, and provides the key for the Early Post-Glacial archaeological sequence, whereas Larne is the classic site for the fully developed Irish Mesolithic.

Chapter III

THE ORIGIN AND AFFINITIES OF THE LARNIAN CULTURE

1. INTRODUCTION

The final retreat of the last ice-sheet and the rapid spread of the Early Post-Glacial forests came at a period when the culturally homogeneous North European Plain extended as far as England, then separated from Ireland by only a narrow arm of the sea, the Irish Channel River. The Upper Palaeolithic settlers from Creswell Crags and other sites in Southern Britain began to move north and west and a new Mesolithic culture, the Larnian, was developed. This movement had already reached Scotland in Late-Glacial times, as suggested by the occupation layers in the caves near Inchnadamff, Sutherland, and by the flake implement found near Comrie, Perthshire, previously described (see pp. 48 and 71–3). Present evidence, however, does not indicate that Ireland was permanently settled until Mesolithic times. Sporadic hunting parties may have crossed on the ice or on former land-bridges at an earlier period, but there is no proof as yet that this occurred. As the name implies, the Larnian was centred in North-East Ireland. Here it is richly represented, especially on the coast, where the flint supply is almost inexhaustible, and to trace its development an understanding of environmental factors is necessary. Typologically the Early Larnian, which corresponds to Dr Clark's Period II (1936, p. 31), is much closer to the Creswellian (Upper Palaeolithic) of Britain than is its descendant, the Late Larnian, of Clark's Period III, a fact which reflects geographical conditions. At best timber was always scarce in the steppe-tundra country of the Late Glacial Period, hence woodworking tools are rare in cultures which flourished under the prevailing Arctic-Alpine conditions. As the climate became more equable, however, heavy implements were evolved, and the steep or core scrapers of the Early Larnian possibly represent early forms of adzes. Later as the forests increased there is a noticeable tendency towards larger and heavier implements; the approach of the climatic optimum is reflected in the Late Larnian by the occurrence of massive tools which are presumably woodworking implements.

It seems very likely that the inundation by the sea of huge tracts of land was directly responsible for a complete reorganization of the mode of life. From an economy apparently based on forest hunting activities, a coastal type of existence seems to have been adopted. As a result of this change, as well as the prevailing warmer conditions, signs of degeneration in the flint technique are apparent: the workmanship is crude, well-struck blades are rare and the implements, though abundant, are coarse. This reflects not only climatic conditions but also the presence of rich flint quarries; life was easy with a ready supply of shell-fish in the Litorina Sea, and new implements could be made almost at will. In certain respects the situation parallels the evidence in the Baltic during Periods II and III. Just as a "strand-looper" type of existence superseded a more vigorous hunting economy in the case of the Maglemose–Ertebølle transition in Northern Europe, a close study of the Larnian suggests that a similar transition took place in Ireland. But while the Baltic received exotic influences enriching the local cultures, the Irish development was more strictly indigenous. Nevertheless, both were subject to remarkably similar environmental influences which, in addition to provoking a similar response, had a profound effect on the basic pattern of cultural development in the two areas. Whereas in the early period Ireland and Scotland formed one continuous culture area with identical traits, the two countries were permanently separated by the North Channel and its Litorina extensions in Atlantic times. It is not surprising therefore to find that a marked divergence in the cultural development in the two regions took place. Before tracing the ultimate roots of the Larnian, the Scottish Mesolithic will be summarized, but, owing to lack of scientific excavation of Stone Age sites in the latter region, many of the geological data have not been recorded. The locations of all the sites mentioned in this chapter are shown on the map, Fig. 33.

2. THE MESOLITHIC OF SCOTLAND

As indicated above, North-East Ireland was the focus of settlement throughout Early Post-Glacial times, but influences from this region penetrated South-West Scotland, which, only separated by a few miles of water from Ireland, formed part of the same province. The distribution of sites as known at present favours the view that the centre of this Mesolithic development lay in Counties Antrim and Down, and the evidence suggests

• EARLY LARNIAN SITES

1 — *CUSHENDUN*
2 — *ISLAND MAGEE*
3 — *ROUGH ISLAND*
3′— *CAMPBELTOWN*

∘ OBANIAN SITES

● SETTLEMENT SITES
∘ STRAY FINDS

4 — *RISGA ISLAND*
5 — *ORONSAY : CAISTEAL-NAN-GILLEAN*
CNOC SLIGEACH
CROCH SLIGACH
CROCH RIACH
6 — *OBAN : MACARTHUR CAVE*
DRUIM VARGIE
7 — *INCHKEITH*
8 — *RIVER IRVINE*
9 — *RIVER DEE*
10 — *WHITBURN*

★ AZILIAN SITE

11 — *VICTORIA CAVE*

• TARDENOISEAN SITES IN SCOTLAND

12 — *ARDEER*
13 — *SHEWALTON*
14 — *STRANRAER*
15 — *STONEYKIRK*
16 — *GLENLUCE*
17 — *SELKIRK*
18 — *DRYBURGH MAINS*
19 — *EARLSTON*
20 — *GULLANE*
21 — *BANCHORY*

+ MAGLEMOSEAN SITES

+ ONE OR TWO OBJECTS
+ SITES AND GROUP FINDS

22 — *BLAIR DRUMMOND*
23 — *MEIKLEWOOD*
24 — *AIRTHREY*
25 — *CAUSEWAYHEAD*
26 — *KINCARDINE*
27 — *WEST HARTLEPOOL*
28 — *SKIPSEA*
29 — *HORNSEA*
30 — *KELLING*
31 — *LEMAN AND OWER BANKS*
32 — *ROYSTON*
33 — *COLNE VALLEY*
34 — *BROXBOURNE*
35 — *UXBRIDGE*
36 — *WANDSWORTH*
37 — *BATTERSEA*
38 — *THATCHAM*

▪ LATE MESOLITHIC SITES

(MICROLITHIC — *Tranchet* AXE-PICK INDUSTRIES)

39 — *LOWER HALSTOW*
40 — *SELMESTON*
41 — *HASSOCKS*
42 — *PEACEHAVEN*
43 — *FARNHAM*
44 — *WEST HEATH*
45 — *WERRAR*

▲ CONTINENTAL SITES

46 — *REMOUCHAMPS*
47 — *ZONHOVEN*
48 — *FRÈRE-EN-TARDENOIS*
49 — *LE CAMPIGNY*
50 — *SPIENNES*

Fig. 33. Map showing the Location of Sites mentioned in the text.

that this area was fairly intensively populated by Upper Palaeolithic survivors, judging from the wealth of material derived from contemporary sites and incorporated in the Litorina deposits. The reason is clear: Western Scotland possesses no ready supply of flint, and the North-East Irish coast is abundantly productive of it. According to Professor Charlesworth (1926, p. 8), the sporadic occurrence of flint in both the raised and modern beaches of Wigtownshire and South Ayrshire is a result of the advancing ice, which scooped up great quantities of Cretaceous chalk from the sea floor between Arran and the Rhinns of Galloway, and transported it, together with marine shells and erratics from Ailsa Craig, to its present position. Even so, flint was a rare commodity throughout the Stone Age in Scotland, a fact which is confirmed by archaeology. Thus at Campbeltown, Kintyre, Argyllshire, three large flint nodules were found in a raised beach, associated with a series of Early Larnian implements (Gray, A., 1893, pp. 270–4). It is generally agreed (Breuil, 1922, p. 265) that this material is of Irish origin since it is identical in colour, and there is also absolutely no doubt that the specimens (which are now in the Campbeltown Museum) did come from County Antrim. They have no scratches, display no evidence of erosion, and are perfectly fresh, which precludes the possibility of transport by ice or, as has been suggested, by floating seaweed. It is therefore highly probable that they were brought in as raw material by man in Early Post-Glacial times. Dr Clark (1929, p. 53) cites additional information in this regard, demonstrating that the practice of trade in this commodity was not uncommon. According to him, near Portpatrick, Luce Bay, Wigtownshire, two hoards of flakes made of Antrim flint—one of 77, the other of 156—were found tightly packed beneath peat. The age of the peat, however, was not determined.

The only site thus far discovered in Scotland, which seems to be referable to the Boreal Period, is the one at Millknowe, Campbeltown, mentioned above. The implements were only briefly described by the discoverer, but they may be definitely assigned to the Early Larnian culture. They come from raised beach gravels approximately a quarter of a mile from the present coast, 30 feet above sea-level, and several feet below the surface. As at Cushendun, these flints were apparently derived from the old land surface and washed inland, during the early part of the Litorina transgression. Associated with the flints, a tooth of the Great Grey Seal (*Halichoerus gryphus*) was found, but other remains of fauna and bone implements were absent. On the whole the Campbeltown implements are small, but in all respects—form, technique, degree of rolling, patination, etc.—there is no basis for disassociating this industry from that contained in the lower gravel (Horizon 2) at Cushendun, a scanty 25 miles away on the opposite side of the North Channel. A small series, illustrated by Breuil (1922, pp. 262 and 264), is shown in Fig. 34. As in the Early Larnian of Ireland, well-struck, small to medium-sized blades showing signs of use (nos. 3, 6–9, 14 and 15) predominate, and the upper surface of the bulbar end is often slightly worked in characteristic fashion. In spite of the fact that Ireland was almost directly accessible by land at this period, the rarity of large blades (nos. 7 and 14–16) reflects the scarcity of flint. Other characteristic implements include: microliths with *dos rabattu* trimming (nos. 1, 2 and 11); points (nos. 4 and 5); leaf-shaped examples of the same type with partial trimming of the butt-end (no. 12); perforators (no. 16); end scrapers (nos. 10 and 21); steep or core scrapers (nos. 17–20); and small scaled flakes showing signs of use (no. 13). Thumb-nail scrapers; the Cushendun pick; rostrate implements; choppers; side scrapers (rare in Ireland) are not present. The absence of small scrapers is surprising, but the fact that no large pick, choppers, etc. occur at Millknowe, is consistent with the tendency towards small implements. Recent excavations at Campbeltown by Dr W. J. McCallien have yielded the only Early Larnian graver thus far recorded; it displays a chisel-like edge, and is made on a quartz pebble (Lacaille, 1938, p. 186).[1] The material clearly demonstrates, as Professor Breuil points out (1922, p. 261), the strong resemblance between the Early Mesolithic of Scotland and a poor Upper Palaeolithic series, consisting in the main of flakes with a Magdalenian aspect.

During the period of the Litorina submergence, there is only indirect evidence that Scotland was inhabited, since caves formed at this time were not occupied until after the land began to rise. Also extensive kitchen-midden settlements of the Late Mesolithic are found on top of the raised beaches, which points to the same conclusion. In both cases the basic forms seem to be derived from the Early Larnian (Period II) culture. In these so-called Scottish "Azilian" sites bone has fortunately been preserved, but the stone implements show a marked degree of divergence from the Late Larnian, which after the beginning of the Litorina transgression of the

[1] For further remarks concerning Dr McCallien's interesting site, located at Albyn Distillery, Campbeltown, see *addendum*, p. 319.

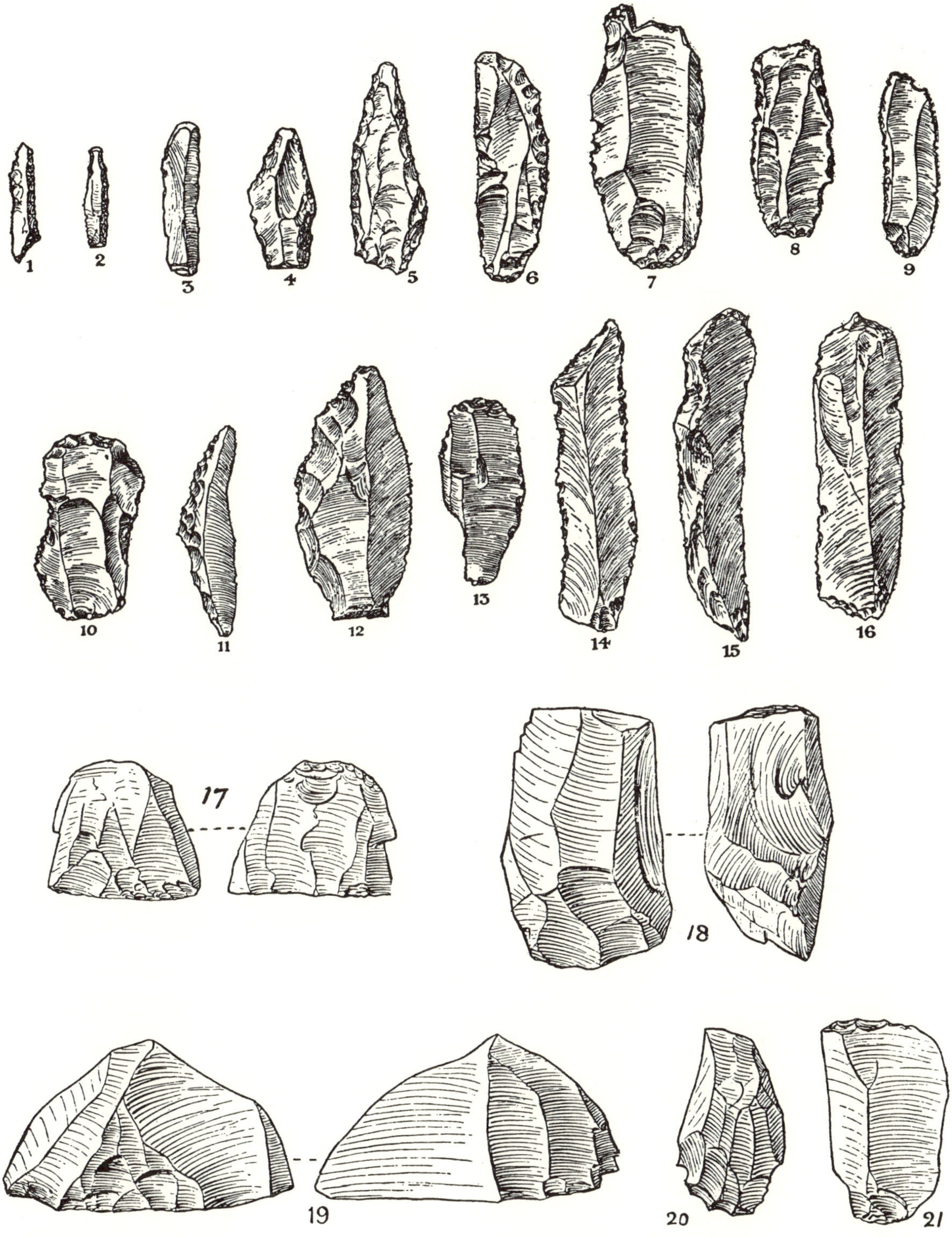

Fig. 34. Early Larnian Flints from the Litorina Raised Beach at Campbeltown. (After Breuil.) Scale 3/4.

Early Atlantic was developed in Ireland. The material from the "Azilian" sites, most of which are situated on the west coast, dates from the end of Atlantic times, a period which is a veritable lacuna in Irish archaeology. It is, therefore, difficult to compare the two regions—the Rough Island midden (see p. 141) reveals that the mode of life was similar, and that shell-fish formed a staple component of diet—however, none of the actual forms of the Late Larnian have been recorded to date in Scotland. On the basis of the present Irish evidence, it seems reasonable to assume that an evolved facies of the Late Larnian survived into Metal Age times, forming the basis of the Bann culture of Ireland and that represented in the sand dunes of the north and east (see pp. 239 and 252). Scotland was now cut off from Ireland by the sea, and became even more difficult of access as the continual deepening and widening of the North Channel by marine erosion and tidal scour made sea traffic between the two regions more hazardous. Here a completely different development took place. The Litorina Sea extended far up the Clyde and Forth Valleys (Fig. 11, p. 79), separating Northern Scotland from the rest of Great Britain except for a narrow isthmus (Jamieson, 1865, p. 163; Erdtman, 1928, p. 181). Undoubted Maglemosean and Tardenoisean influences from the south and east of Scotland were felt by these survivors on the west coast, who clung to a fundamentally Early Larnian tradition probably well into the Neolithic Period, in a region almost barren of flint. With the changing environment certain new forms were evolved to meet the new needs, but lack of flint or other easily worked rocks hampered cultural progress. It is proposed to call this culture the Obanian, after the type site in Argyllshire. As previously stated, the Obanian is well known as the "Azilian" of Scotland, but it seems necessary to reclassify it on the basis of present knowledge.

The Obanian was discovered in 1879 by Symington Grieve (1883) at Caisteal-nan-Gillean, a large kitchen-midden 150 feet in diameter on the Island of Oronsay, Argyllshire. This small island is joined to Colonsay at low tide, and on it three other large middens have also been reported: Cnoc Sligeach (Bishop, 1914, p. 52); Croch Sligach (Anderson, 1898, p. 311); and Croch Riach (Anderson, 1898, pp. 312–13). At Caisteal-nan-Gillean a large series of stone, bone and antler implements was found, typical of the Obanian culture, in addition to two harpoons, one with the barbs opposite each other and the other with alternating barbs (compare Wright and Peach, 1911, p. 167; Anderson, 1898, p. 306). Cnoc Sligeach yielded similar material, including shell beads with double perforations, polishers of red deer antler and seven harpoons. All are open-air camp sites along or above the Litorina raised beach, which is at a height of 22–24 feet above high-water level on Oronsay. The refuse layers are up to 4½ feet thick, and in some cases are interrupted by thin layers of blown sand. Cnoc Sligeach had been disturbed by wave action, therefore the occupation must be contemporary with the time of uplift, since it is on top of the Litorina beach, and high above the maximum reach of present-day storm waves. On the top of this mound six holes for stakes, 7 inches in diameter, were observed penetrating the heap, probably to support a crude shelter (Childe, 1935, p. 14).

On the mainland the same culture has been reported by Dr J. Anderson (1895, pp. 211–30) at MacArthur Cave, Oban, a site which opens on to the Litorina raised beach, and after which the culture has been named. On the cave floor, 30 feet above high-water level, was 4 feet of beach gravel, and above this and partly intercalated with it was the refuse of occupation, including shells, hearths and charcoal. The cave was apparently formed during the maximum of the submergence, so that re-elevation must have begun before the site was occupied. The sea could not then have receded very far, as Professor Childe points out (1935, p. 14), since in a storm the waves could still carry material into the cave mouth, whereas to-day the shore is over 100 yards away. The archaeological material from this site includes: a few small flint cores; small flakes without secondary chipping; 140 large implements of stone, bone and horn; three bone pins; three awls; and seven deer-horn harpoons, two of which are complete. These implements will be described presently. A second site, the large rock shelter of Druim Vargie, was excavated at Oban in 1898 also by Dr Anderson (1898, pp. 298–306), but it looks towards a marsh rather than the sea. The occupation layer was, therefore, undisturbed by wave action, and it was buried in talus at the base of the cliff. The nature of this layer reveals a similar culture to that at MacArthur Cave, since the following objects were found: large implements, four of which were made of water-worn pebbles; bone points; flint flakes; and two bone harpoons, barbed on one side only.

The fauna is similar at all the sites, and the following forms are represented: *Mollusca*: Oysters, Limpets, Periwinkles, Mussels, Razor Clams, Cockles, Whelks (all large shells), and *Cyprina islandica* (a northern form indicating that the climatic optimum had passed); *Fish*: Wrasse, Grey Mullet, Skate and Dogfish; *Crustacea*: Crab (big claws); *Mammals*: Grey

Seal, Common Seal, Red Deer (most common in the lower levels), Roe Deer, Wild Pig, Badger, Otter, and Wild Cat; *Birds*: Small Wild Fowl, Guillemot, and the Great Auk (now extinct). From Caisteal-nan-Gillean there is a recent-looking sheep bone, and from MacArthur Cave some bones were identified as *Bos longifrons* (Childe, 1935, p. 15), but this may be Aurochs (see p. 91). It is claimed that the dog was present, since gnawed bones are common at all sites. No actual dog remains are, however, reported. It is clear that the Obanians were Late Mesolithic food gatherers, living in caves, rock shelters and camps in the open. Hunting, fishing and collecting comprised their basic economy, and navigation is suggested by the presence of seal bones. For hunting and fishing the harpoons or barbed bone points (Lacaille, 1939, p. 50) were doubtless used. The characteristic implements of the Obanian, as described by Breuil (1922, pp. 265–81), are as follows:

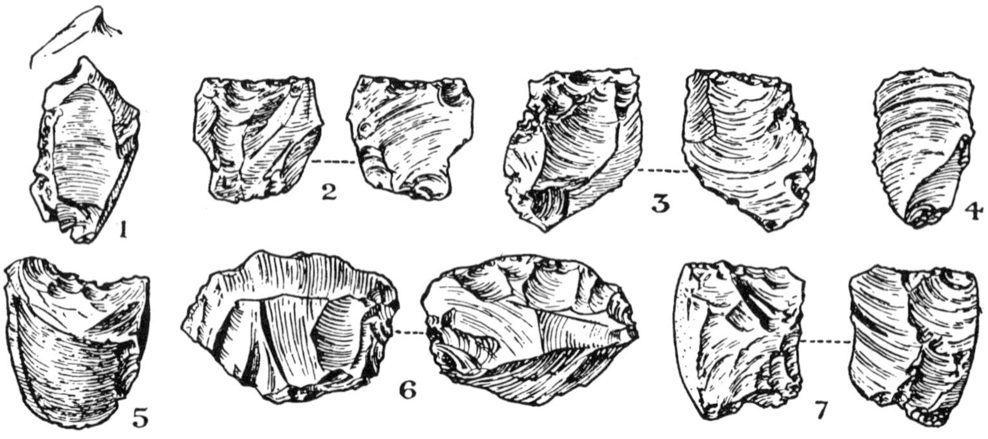

Fig. 35. Obanian Flints from the Caisteal-nan-Gillean Kitchen-Midden, Oronsay. (After Breuil.) Scale: 1/1.

1. Flint. "What characterizes nearly all the flints gathered from the kitchen-middens and contemporary littoral caves of Scotland is that we are not faced with a normal outfit of tools, but with the residue of tools used to such a degree that they were no longer capable of further service" (Breuil, 1922, p. 265). The forms are not characteristic of any special horizon or industry, but consist of amorphous shapes, produced by a people cut off from a dependable flint supply. It is probable that the flake technique represents a survival from the Early Larnian of Campbeltown, where only flint implements occur, as previously described. Three implements are still

recognizable, a small micro-graver (Fig. 35, no. 1) with Tardenoisean affinities, made on a small flake with a notched beak and a graver facet on the opposite side, a small ovoid scraper (no. 6) and a hollow end scraper (no. 5). Nos. 2, 3, 4 and 7 are all typical squamous flakes, scaled or splintered by use almost beyond recognition. In no case, except possibly no. 4, is the original shape discernible. This series, all from Caisteal-nan-Gillean, Oronsay, illustrates how the meagre flint supply, consisting of erratics from the glacial drift was utilized to the utmost, in some cases possibly only as strike-a-lights.

2. STONE. The original claim that these implements, shown in Fig. 36, were for detaching limpets from the rocks was strongly opposed by Breuil (1922, p. 267), who suggests instead that they are flakers used in the fabrication of flint. As Clark points out (1932, p. 15), such an idea seems far from satisfactory, since the most abundant types from the sites of the Obanian culture can hardly be recorded as no more than auxiliary tools. Furthermore, flint is present in such a limited quantity that there was virtually nothing to be flaked. It does not seem unreasonable therefore to suggest that some of the large stone implements represent a comparable development in Scotland with the Late Larnian of Ireland, where the tendency is, as previously noted, towards heavy woodworking tools. Nevertheless Grieve's original statement (1883, pp. 485–7) that they are stone hammers for knocking limpets off the rocks must be reconsidered. Doubtless certain of the stone tools did actually serve this purpose, since the limpet shells from Caisteal-nan-Gillean frequently exhibit holes caused by a sharp blow, and the modern fishermen of Oronsay often use similar stones for collecting limpets for bait. In fact when shown the tools in question, these people assumed that they had been used for this purpose. The series is all made on naturally elongated water-worn pebbles of schist and consists of two types:

(A) *Rubbers* (Fig. 36, nos. 2 and 5–9). These are probably for the preparation of seal skins for shelters or clothing, and the abrasion may be caused by sand sprayed on the skins to assist in the process. It is also possible that they have been used as grinders for crushing seeds or nuts. Either one or both ends are rounded and show evidence of hard use. Nos. 2, 6 and 9 seem to have been struck at one end.

(B) *Heavy Chisels or Adzes* (Fig. 36, nos. 1, 3 and 4). The ends as well as the sides of these implements are usually battered by violent use, suggesting that they were held against something and struck by a blow from a heavy hammer (Breuil, 1922, p. 269). The average size is 5 cm. long and

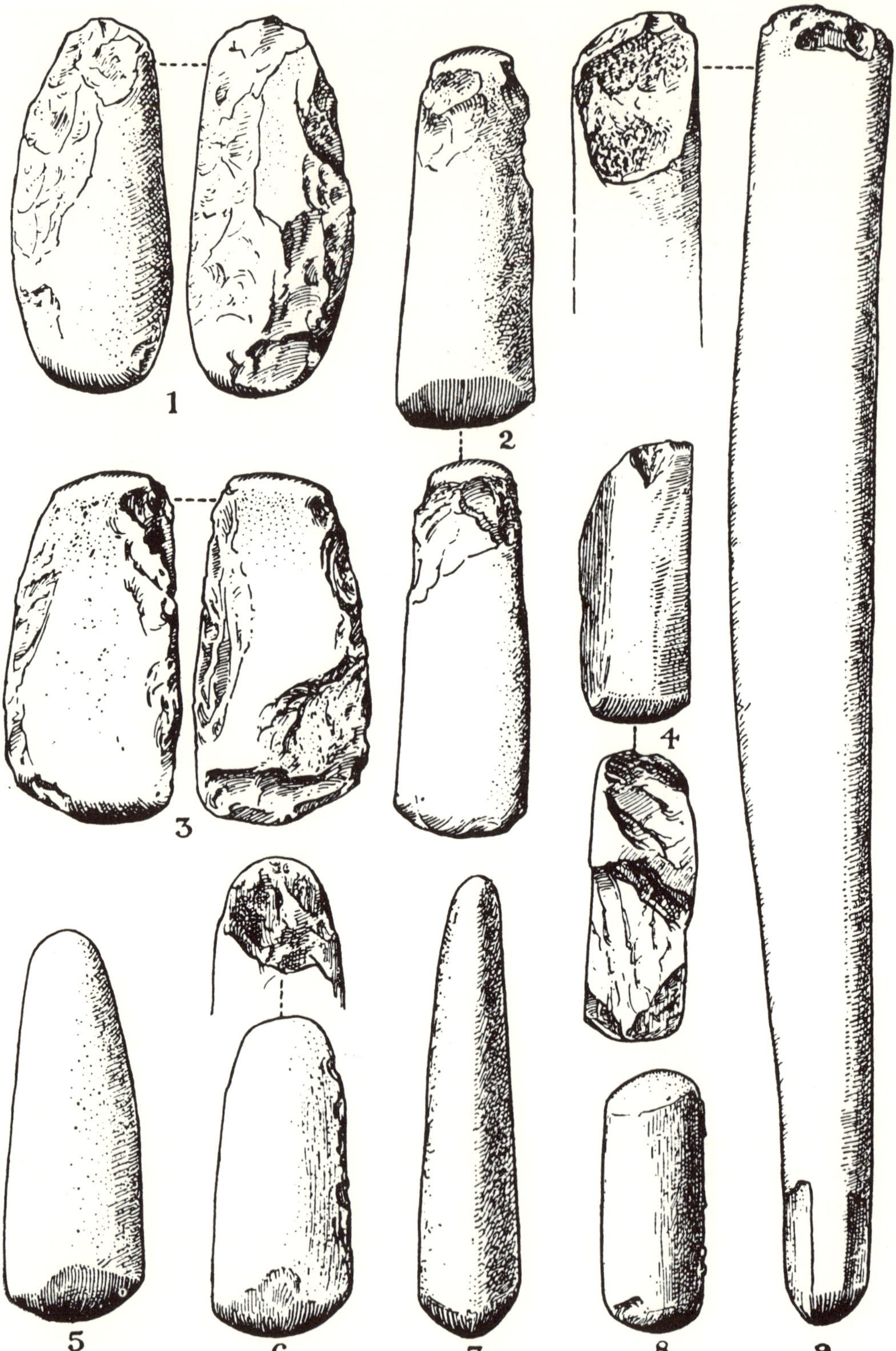

Fig. 36. Obanian Stone Implements from the Caisteal-nan-Gillean Kitchen-Midden, Oronsay. (After Breuil.) Scale: 1/1.

2·5 cm. wide, one end or the side is crudely sharpened, and most of the flakes seem to be removed by use. It seems likely that some of these heavy tools were used for woodworking, thus apparently fulfilling a function not unlike those typical of the Late Larnian in Ireland. Others, however, undoubtedly served for collecting limpets for purposes of subsistence, whereas one definitely resembles a large knife (Grieve, 1922).

(C) *Hammerstones*. Hammerstones of round or oval form are common at all sites (Childe, 1935, p. 16).

3. Bone (Fig. 37). In addition to bone points, awls and pins, a large series of crude bone implements occurs. These are morphologically the same as stone types A and B above, and in some cases deer horn was used for the same purpose (Breuil, 1922, p. 267). Nos. 1 and 5 are fragments of heavy long bones, probably deer, split and used as chisels; nos. 2 and 4 are polishers or rubbers; and nos. 3, 6 and 7 are combination tools probably used for both purposes.

4. Harpoons (Fig. 38). The harpoons of the Late Mesolithic deposits of Scotland agree in general with those which characterize the Azilian of South France and Northern Spain except that they are commonly made of bone and not deer horn (Breuil, 1922, p. 279). In addition they are longer than Azilian forms, but they are far too characteristically Azilian to be the result of independent invention (Childe, 1935, p. 15). However, the types from Northern Britain as a group are later and more evolved than those of the Continent. With the exception of the seven from MacArthur Cave, Oban, and one of the seven from Cnoc Sligeach, Oronsay, which are of deer horn, all are made of bone. The two from the rock shelter of Druim Vargie, Oban (nos. 2 and 3), are atypical in that they are barbed on one side only, but all the others have double rows of barbs. One from MacArthur Cave, Oban, is pierced with a small slit near the butt for the attachment of the line (no. 1). No. 9, from Cnoc Sligeach, is of antler and has a round stem from which the barbs stand out like thorns (Childe, 1935, p. 15). This has no parallels in Azilian deposits, according to Professor Childe, while its closest analogies exist with Danish types of the Early Atlantic Period. The resemblance seems almost too close to be accidental (compare Childe, 1931, Fig. 2, no. 9, p. 331).[1]

[1] Recent information from Mr A. D. Lacaille discloses the interesting fact that in the Hunterian Museum, Glasgow, there is a perforated antler axe-head from one of the Oronsay middens, precisely like the Meiklewood specimen shown in Fig. 42 (p. 192). This piece further confirms the presence of a Baltic influence in the Obanian, discussed on p. 193.

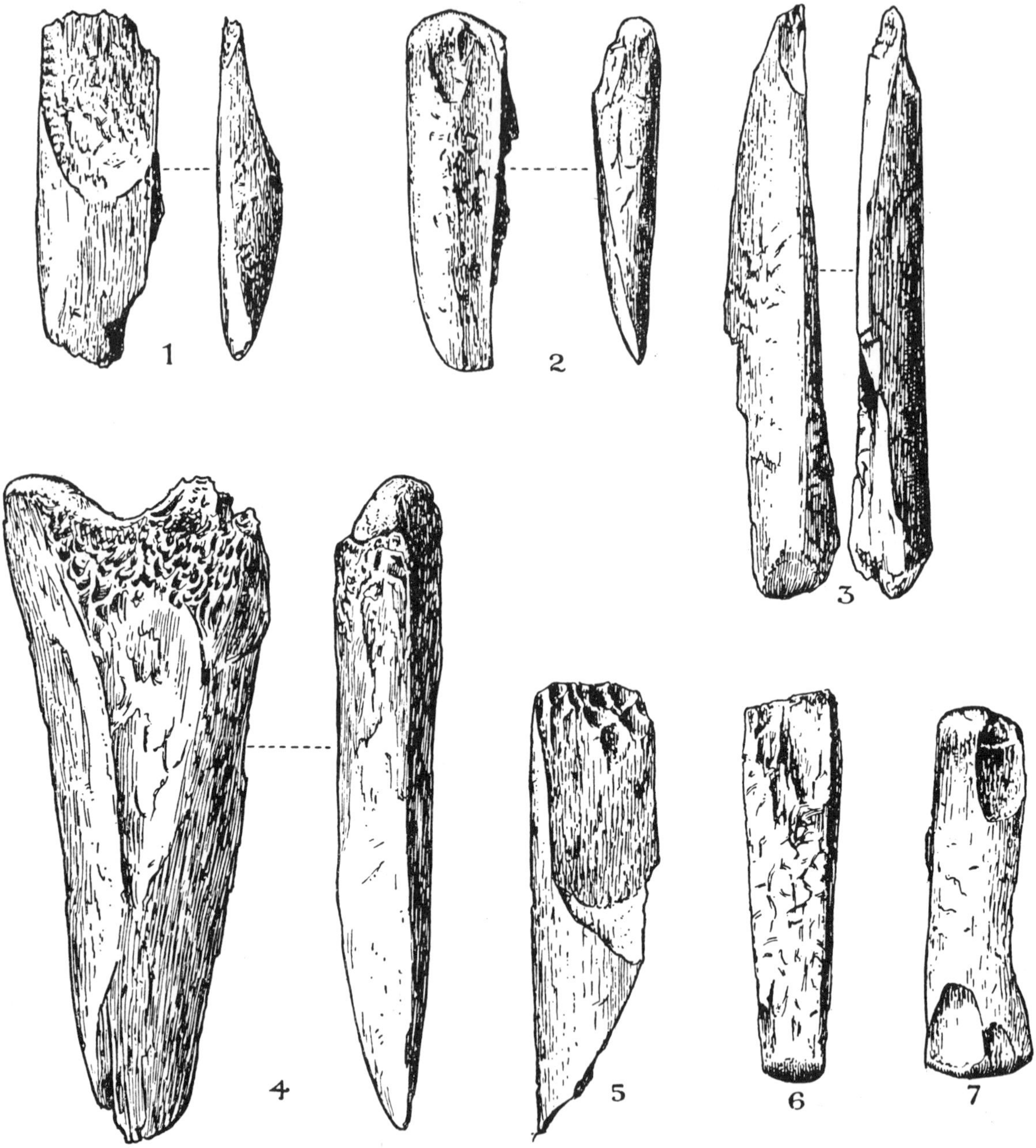

Fig. 37. Obanian Bone Implements from the Caisteal-nan-Gillean Kitchen-Midden, Oronsay. (After Breuil.) Scale: 1/1.

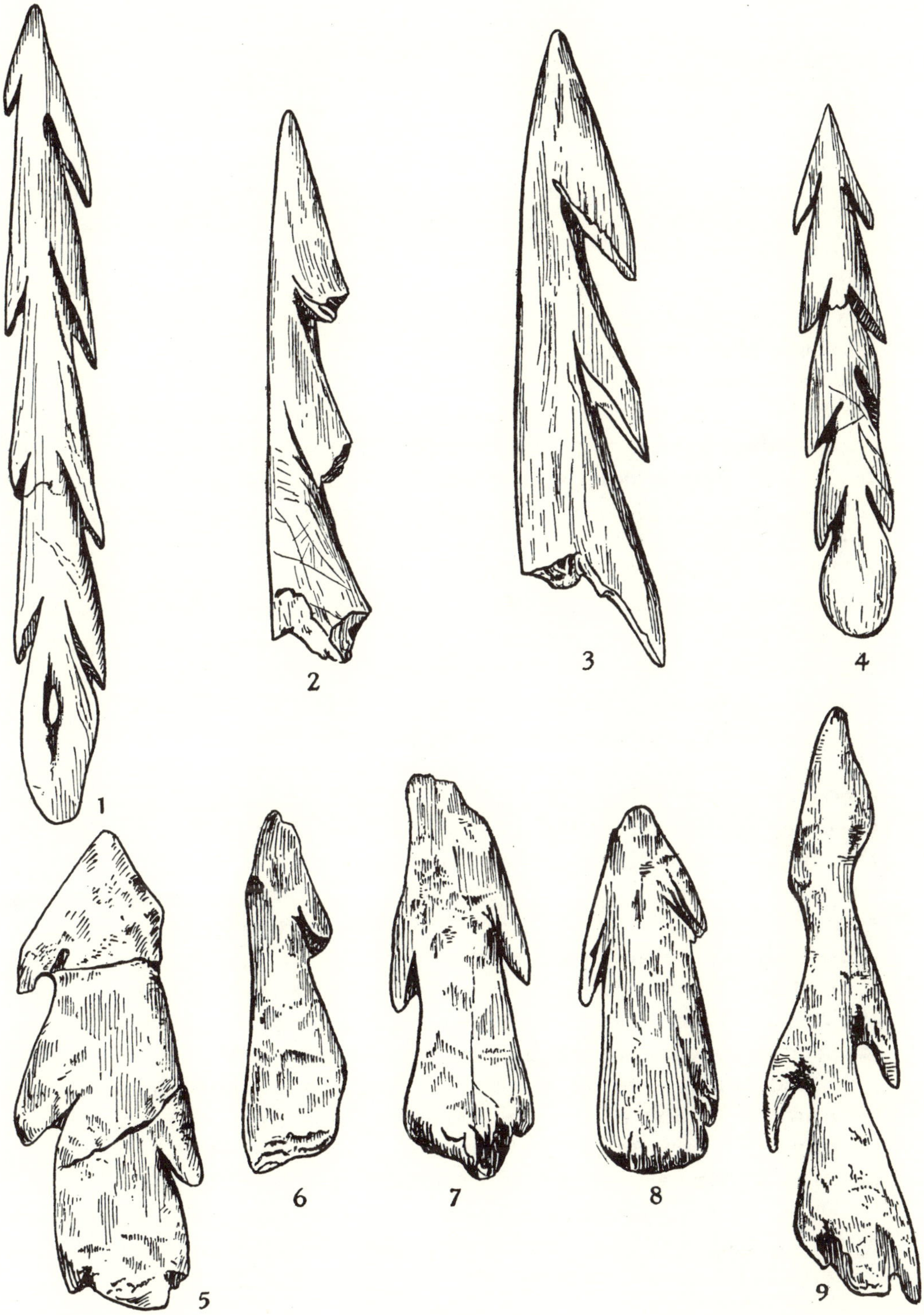

Fig. 38. Obanian Harpoons of Bone (nos. 2, 3, 5–8) and Horn (nos. 1, 4, 9) from MacArthur Cave, Oban (nos. 1 and 4); Druim Vargie Rock-Shelter, Oban (nos. 2 and 3); Cnoc Sligeach Kitchen-Midden, Oronsay (nos. 5–9). (After Breuil.) Scale: 1/1.

In addition to the above sites, the Obanian is known from the Island of Risga on Loch Sunart, where a large midden has been excavated by Mr Ludovic Mann (unpublished: material in the Kelvingrove Museum, Glasgow; mentioned by Callander, 1929, p. 317). This shell heap is on top of the raised beach and is similar in all respects to those at Oronsay. In addition to a typical fauna, the following implements were found: squamous flint flakes, stone chisels and rubbers, bone and horn smoothers, three complete bone harpoons, and two fragments. An interesting harpoon, or bilaterally barbed point, has recently been recovered by Mr Lacaille from the bed of the River Irvine, at Shewalton, Ayrshire (Lacaille, 1939, pp. 48–50; Childe, 1938, p. 323). This specimen resembles very closely Fig. 38, no. 1, from MacArthur Cave, Oban, with the exception that the bevelled base exhibits no perforation, it is slightly more elongated (length, 19·4 cm.), and on both sides of the pronounced midrib there is a groove near the point to facilitate penetration. In appearance it suggests Azilian derivation, although somewhat influenced from Maglemosean sources, which possibly accounts for the midrib, and the elongation as well as the rounding of the extremity. A stray bone harpoon has also been recorded from the bed of the River Dee, near Kircudbright (Childe, 1935, p. 14; Lacaille, 1939, p. 49 and Pl. XXIV, 4). This completes the distribution of the Obanian in Western Scotland, although it is possible that the midden found by Bryce (1903, pp. 43–4) below the Glecknabae Cairn, Island of Bute, belongs to this complex. However, this deposit yielded no archaeological material. In the east only one occupation site, a kitchen-midden, on the Island of Inchkeith, in the Firth of Forth, near Edinburgh, has been recorded (Anderson, 1898, p. 304; Munro, 1908, p. 230). Besides many broken and split bones and shells, the archaeological material includes the same blunt chisel-like tools, as well as rubbers or fabricators of bone and deer horn, characteristic of Oban and Oronsay. In spite of the fact that it is impossible to arrive at a satisfactory conclusion regarding the age of this site on the basis of the published data, it seems probable that it dates from Late Mesolithic times.

In order to complete the distribution of the Obanian as well as to consider the evidence for the Azilian influence discernible in the Mesolithic developments of Scotland and Ireland, it is necessary to turn to Northern England. In Durham one bone harpoon, with a perforated butt and two rows of barbs, was picked up in 1852 on the shore at Whitburn near Newcastle-on-Tyne (Munro, 1908, p. 230), but the strong Azilian influence, which persisted in Scotland during the Late Atlantic Period, is best represented in Northern Britain at Victoria Cave, near Settle, Yorkshire (Breuil, 1922, pp. 275–8). The deposit was badly disturbed during Celtic times by man and burrowing animals[1] (Burkitt, 1925, pp. 35–6); however, Breuil identified a

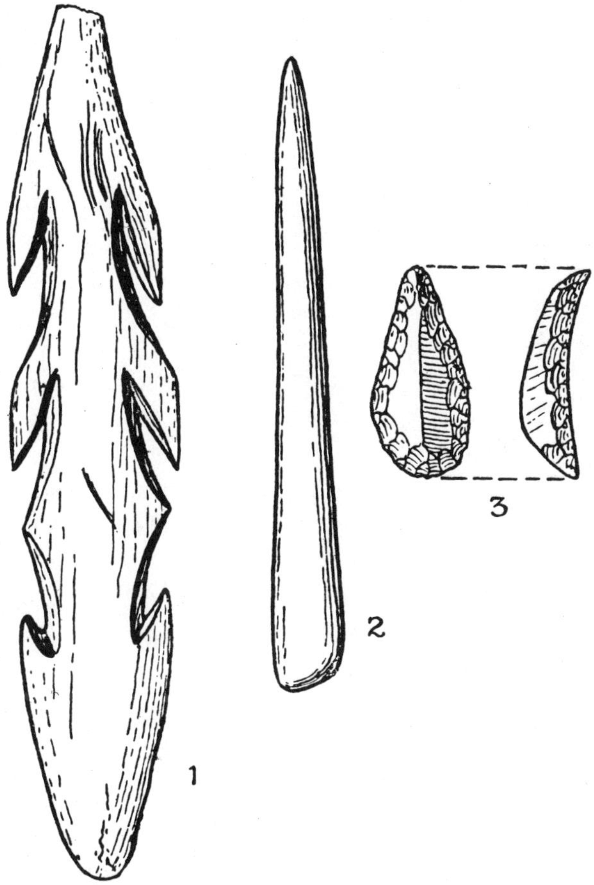

Fig. 39. Azilian Implements from Victoria Cave, near Settle, Yorkshire. (After Breuil.) Scale: slightly reduced.

partly fossilized reindeer-antler harpoon of characteristic Azilian form (Fig. 39, no. 1), a bone borer (no. 2), and a flint implement (no. 3), all from the same level which is believed to be Early Mesolithic. In addition a collection

[1] Fossilized bones of cave bear were found in the Romano-British layer, whereas a typical bone bead of this period is described by W. Boyd Dawkins (1874, p. 111) from the Late Mesolithic horizon.

of objects made of sandstone and schist (Fig. 40) was recognized as typically Azilian by the same authority. These probably belong to the period of the harpoon, and represent a kit of tools of a manufacturer of ochreous colours.

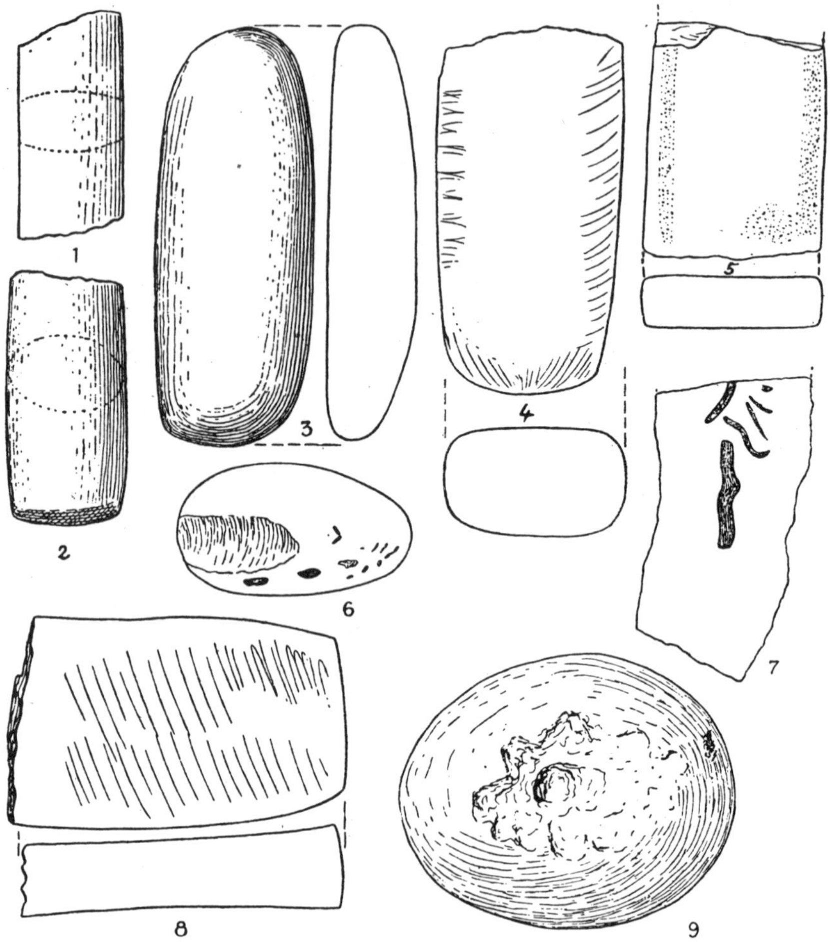

Fig. 40. Implements of Sandstone and Schist, probably Azilian, from Victoria Cave, near Settle, Yorkshire. (After Breuil.) Scale: 1/2.

They include the following: rubbing-stones and pounders for pulverizing ochre (nos. 1–4); plaques on which to mix ochreous colours with grease (nos. 5, 7 and 8); a hammerstone for grinding red and black colouring matter (no. 9); and a chipped pebble with traces of ochre on it (no. 6). This material was all from the upper cave earth and was associated with recent objects, probably Iron Age in date. More ancient implements apparently from a lower layer of grey clay also occur, however, and these include two cylindrical rods of reindeer horn (Fig. 41, nos. 1 and 2), whose surfaces are very lustrous, and which are completely fossilized (Breuil, 1922). A bone borer (Fig. 41, no. 3), in similar condition, seems to belong with this series. As these three implements are strongly suggestive of an Upper Palaeolithic occupation, there is some indication here that Creswellian hunters occupied the cave in Late Glacial times (see p. 71), a fact which is also inferred by many splintered and incised bones from the lower levels. The bone rods have terminal bevelling and are almost exactly parallel to some from Pin Hole Cave, Creswell Crags (Armstrong, 1925, p. 168). This site is, therefore, of great importance, because it not only indicates that Upper Palaeolithic people occupied the new land in Northern England after the ice began to melt, and the steppe and tundra fauna to withdraw to new regions along its margin, but also it demonstrates that Azilian influences from Southern France and the Cantabrian region of Northern Spain were felt in England at an early period, possibly as early as Pre-Boreal. The fact that the Victoria harpoon is made of Reindeer antler, and that remains of this animal are not found in the Obanian deposits of Scotland, suggests that at this Yorkshire site we are dealing with a very early spread of Azilian culture. The harpoon is, furthermore, typologically earlier than the Scottish examples, since it has two downward curving notches near the but-end for hafting. These are never found in the Obanian. Furthermore, as Professor

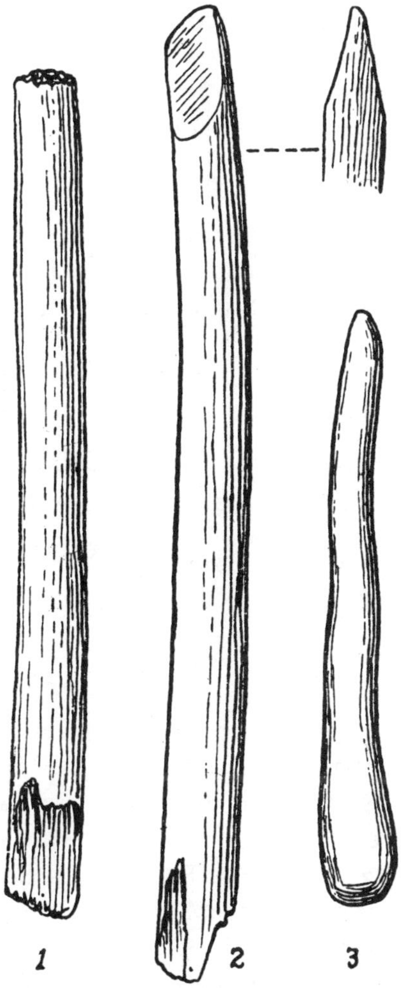

Fig. 41. Implements of Horn (nos. 1 and 2) and Bone (no. 3), probably Magdalenian, from Victoria Cave, near Settle, Yorkshire. (After Breuil.) Scale: 1/1.

Breuil points out, this type is Early Azilian in France, and is always made of Reindeer antler (1922, pp. 278–9). The small flint end scraper and perforator (Fig. 39, no. 3), also typical of the Early Azilian of France, is significant, since it is the only implement of this type represented in Britain and datable to this period. It is apparently the prototype of the thumb-nail scrapers which are typical of the Early Larnian, and which occur in great numbers in the Litorina gravels of Ireland. The absence of this implement in Scotland is not explicable on the basis of present evidence.

In addition to the debased Upper Palaeolithic and Azilian influences present in Scotland in the Early Post-Glacial Period, Professor Childe has drawn attention to several stray finds, suggesting that the Forest cultures of

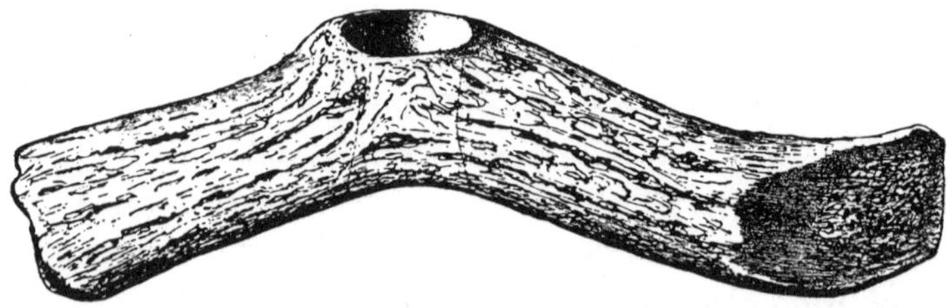

Fig. 42. Perforated Antler Axe-Hammer from Meiklewood Estate, near Stirling. (After Munro.) Scale: 1/3.

the North European Plain actually penetrated the Forth Valley in the eastern portion of the area (1931, pp. 332–3; 1935, pp. 17–18). Whereas in Eastern and South-Eastern England the Maglemosean of the Baltic (Period II) is present in and below peats of the Boreal climatic phase (Clark, 1932, pp. 16–18), there is no evidence of influence from this source in Scotland before Atlantic times. Thus near Kincardine and in the vicinity of Causewayhead, perforated pieces of antler have been found in the Carse of Stirling associated with remains of Whale (Childe, 1935), and on Meiklewood estate an antler axe-hammer (Fig. 42) has been recorded from the same deposit (Munro, 1898, pp. 271–2; 1908, pp. 226–7). This latter implement was found with a portion of the wooden handle in the hole resting on the skull of a Whale. It is a type similar to those found in Baltic sites of Period II (Clark, 1936, p. 111). Other examples are quoted by Jamieson (1865, p. 190) and Sir Archibald Geikie (1862, pp. 225–6), who mention fragments of stag's horns, each one with a hole bored through it, found with Whale skeletons at Blair Drummond and Airthrey. No actual Mesolithic settlement sites have yet been excavated in the Stirling region; however, it is possible that the extensive kitchen-middens in the valley of the Firth of Forth, where the River Avon enters the Forth carse lands (Wright, 1914, p. 386), date from this period. These sites, which have never been satisfactorily dated and may be Obanian, occur on the bluff which borders the carse, or just at its base, "as if, when it was the limit of high-water, the people who formed the middens, after searching the shores during low-water, had retreated thither to enjoy their feast while the tide covered their hunting ground" (quoted by Wright, 1914, p. 386, from A. M. Peach, *Memoirs of the Geological Survey of Scotland*, 1879).[1] One of these middens, near Kinneil, was investigated by Callander (1929, pp. 314–16); in addition to numerous molluscs, it yielded several Red Deer antlers which had been cut. Further, a Baltic influence has been noted in one of the harpoons from Cnoc Sligeach, Oronsay (see p. 185), and Breuil has suggested that the use of bone instead of antler in the manufacture of other harpoons from Oban, Oronsay, and Kircudbright, may be a result of influence from the same source (1922, p. 279). In Ireland the core axes from Larne almost certainly were derived from Maglemosean types of South-East Britain, hence it is not surprising to find that Scotland likewise received echoes of the same culture. It may be concluded, therefore, that the Forest culture of the North European Plain arrived in Scotland, in Early Atlantic times, during the period of the Litorina transgression, and that similar influences were diffused ultimately into the Late Larnian culture of Ireland.

During the Early Post-Glacial Period a third culture penetrated Scotland, the Tardenoisean. All the sites of this complex, with one exception in the Dee Valley, Kincardineshire, are limited to Southern Scotland, south of a line between the Firth of Forth and the Firth of Clyde. Thus it is possible that the presence of the Obanian in the north and west caused a concentration of Tardenoisean in the south, and prevented its infiltration into the Highlands except on the east. Doubtless lack of flint or other easily worked rocks, and the greater extension of sea during Atlantic times, were additional factors contributing to this distribution, although in the vicinity of Peterhead, Aberdeenshire, derived flint pebbles are abundant in the glacial gravels

[1] This reference was not available to the writer.

(Anderson, 1896, p. 348). However, influences penetrated as far as Oronsay (e.g. the micro-burin from Caisteal-nan-Gillean),[1] but there is no evidence for actual Tardenoisean settlement in this region. The sites, shown on the map (Fig. 33), are distributed as follows (Lacaille, 1931, p. 310):

1. Sites in the Tweed Basin, Berwickshire and Roxburghshire.
   (A) Earlston.
   (B) Dryburgh Mains (Corrie, 1916; Callander, 1927).
   (C) Selkirk (Mason, 1931).
2. Sands around Glenluce, Stoneykirk (B.R.G. [*k*], p. 94), and Stranraer, Wigtownshire.
3. Sites at the mouth of the Irvine River, Ayrshire:
   (A) Ardeer.
   (B) Shewalton (Lacaille, 1929).
4. Gullane, East Lothian.
5. Banchory, Dee Valley, Kincardineshire (Paterson, 1913; Paterson and Lacaille, 1936).

Dating evidence is scanty, but at Stranraer, and other localities in Southern Scotland (Lacaille, 1931, p. 309; McCallien, 1937, p. 202), implements have been found in dunes above the Litorina raised beach, which indicates that this culture did not reach Scotland until very Late Atlantic times. All the settlements are on sandy waste lands, which is the usual distribution of English Tardenoisean stations. In most cases the flints are associated with Neolithic, or even Bronze Age material (compare Lacaille, 1937); this fact makes it exceedingly difficult to determine whether the Scottish Tardenoisean persisted a long time or whether the later types are simply stray objects lost on earlier habitation layers (Paterson and Lacaille, 1936, p. 424). On the whole the material from the Tweed Valley sites and from the Banchory region represents a relatively early and pure form of the Tardenoisean, whereas the Ayrshire group seems to be somewhat more recent[2] (Paterson and Lacaille, 1936, p. 423). Microliths of various types are

[1] Recently Dr W. J. McCallien has found several micro-burins, associated with a small pick of Forest Culture type, in an evolved Early Larnian context at Albyn Distillery, Campbeltown (see *addendum*, p. 320).
[2] An extensive surface station on the 50-foot raised beach, yielding a typically Middle Tardenoisean assemblage, has recently been reported from near Ballantrae, Ayrshire (Edgar, 1939).

common (Fig. 43): small flakes with *dos rabattu* trimming (nos. 8–10); scalene triangles (no. 1); equilateral triangles (nos. 2–5); trapezes (nos. 6 and 7); sub-triangular points (no. 11); and crescents (nos. 14–16). In addition the following non-geometric forms are present: awls (nos. 12 and 25); blades blunted obliquely (no. 13), or down one side (nos. 17, 18 and 23); slug-

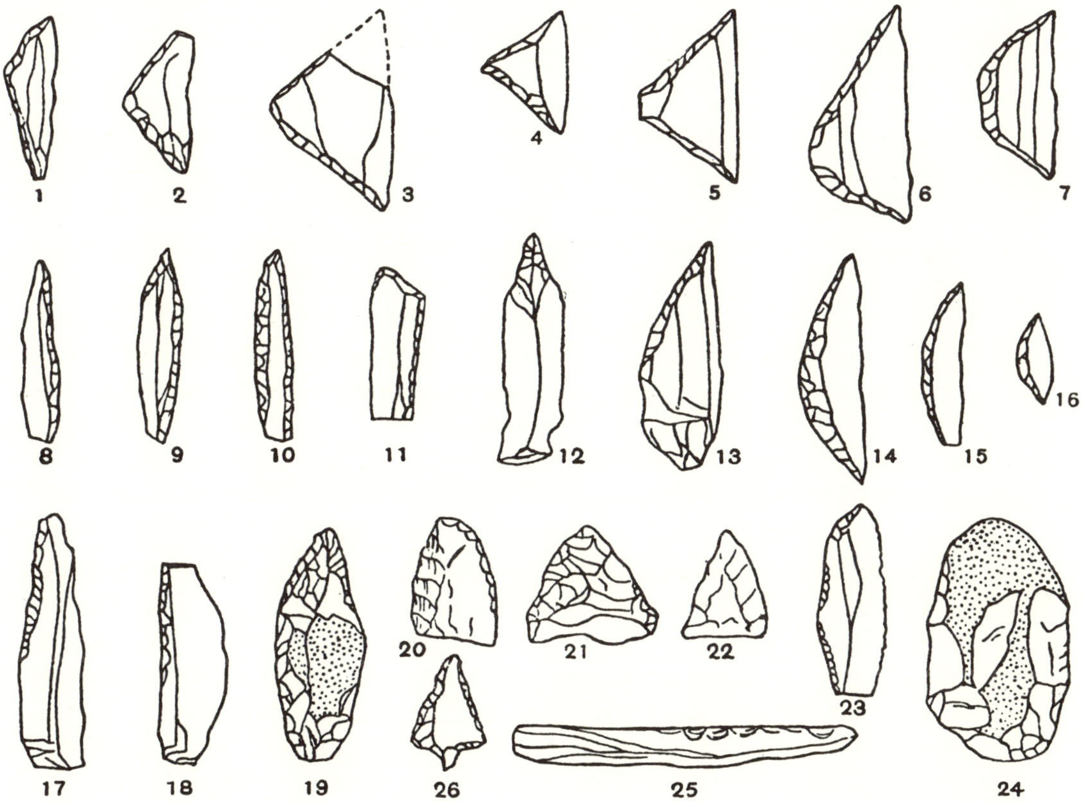

Fig. 43. Tardenoisean Flints from Shewalton Moor, Ayrshire. (After Lacaille and Clark.) Scale: 1/1.

shaped flints or fabricators (no. 19); triangular arrowheads (nos. 20–22); tanged arrowheads (no. 26); and small side and end scrapers (no. 24). In the above series from Shewalton (Lacaille, 1929; Clark, 1932, pp. 50–1), the micro-burin is absent. This form is rare at most Scottish stations, but it occurs at Dryburgh Mains and Banchory[1] (Lacaille, 1935; Paterson and

[1] On the other hand, Edgar (1939, p. 184) states that at the new Ballantrae locality micro-burins are frequent.

Lacaille, 1936), where its presence is suggestive of an earlier dating for these stations. In addition other types of gravers of simple angle form are found (Lacaille, 1938). Recent excavations at Banchory in the Dee Valley have disclosed that the occupation layer was on top of sand which rested on the low terrace of the river (Paterson and Lacaille, 1936). The series from this site includes not only the same forms as Shewalton, with the exception of arrowheads and fabricators, but also many fine steep or core end scrapers, as well as occasional blade implements. Whereas at most of the southern stations the tools are made of chert, chalcedony, jasper, and even quartz, the Banchory artifacts are an excellent quality of flint. This reflects the distribution of flint in Scotland, since it only occurs in quantities of a tractable nature in a small belt in Aberdeenshire, north of the Dee Valley (Lacaille, 1932, p. 99). This source was not discovered by the Obanian peoples, however, who were mainly concentrated on the west coast.

The tanged arrowhead and slug-like flints from Shewalton indicate that the Tardenoisean survived late in South-West Scotland, probably until the Bronze Age (Clark, 1932, p. 51), and the comparative scarcity of the microburin, except in the east and south-east, supports this conclusion. The situation parallels Continental evidence, since in Central and Western Europe it has been shown that the Tardenoisean overlapped well into the Neolithic Period (Clark, 1936, pp. 216–17). In Ireland what appears to be a very late Tardenoisean influence has been detected by Mr Whelan (1933, p. 1214; 1933[*a*]; 1938, pp. 133–5) at a small surface station near Belfast in the Castlereagh Hills, County Down, but since only occasional flints from this locality present traces of intentional working, it is difficult to express an opinion on the age of the culture layer (compare Schleicher, 1932). Tardenoisean forms are completely lacking in the Larnian and later Neolithic cultures of Ireland, a fact which indicates an extremely late date for the Castlereagh material. Influences from this source were, however, felt in the Obanian of Scotland, suggesting that the Tardenoisean culture arrived here towards the close of Atlantic time, and the stratigraphic position of the finds, immediately above the Litorina raised beach, bears out this contention.

To sum up the Scottish Mesolithic: three independent cultures are present—(1) Debased Upper Palaeolithic mixed with Azilian; (2) Maglemosean Forest culture ultimately from the Baltic; and (3) Tardenoisean. The earliest evidence of the first group is from Victoria Cave, Yorkshire, an important site, since it indicates that Upper Palaeolithic hunters advanced northwards as the ice melted, and that Azilian influences were felt in England during the Early Post-Glacial Period. A combination of these two increments produced the Early Larnian, which was centred in North-East Ireland, and which is represented in Scotland at Campbeltown in the Litorina raised beach. At this period Ireland and Scotland formed a single culture province. With the submergence in Early Atlantic times, however, Ireland and Scotland were separated, which led to the development of the two independent cultures referable to Clark's Period III: the Late Larnian in Ireland, and the Obanian in Scotland. With the exception of one site—Inchkeith—and several undated stray finds—Kircudbright, the River Irvine at Shewalton, and Whitburn—the Obanian is concentrated in the west, north of the Midland Valley of Scotland. Lack of an available flint supply in this region led to a local specialization of the industry, in which, as in the Early Larnian, heavy tools predominate. Small game was supplemented by shell-fish, seal, and wild fowl, in the diet of these people, and seal skins appear to have been used for clothing. This fact is suggested by the numerous rubbers and smoothers, probably for preparing skins, found in Obanian sites, as well as by the harpoons and bone pins and awls for sewing. The Obanians seem to have been slightly influenced both by the Maglemosean survivors in the Firth of Forth, and by the Tardenoisean cultures of the South of Scotland. Their sites are on top of the Litorina raised beaches, and hence belong to the end of the Atlantic Period.

The Maglemosean is unrepresented by actual occupation sites, although several middens in the Forth Valley may belong to this culture. Perforated antler axe hammers, characteristic of the Baltic, have been found at five localities in the carse clays, in direct association with whale skeletons. Furthermore, certain Obanian harpoons have pronounced Maglemosean affinities. In Late Atlantic times, the Middle Tardenoisean of Britain penetrated into Southern Scotland, where the meagre supply of flint, various cherts, jasper, etc. was exploited. These sites are restricted to the open sandy regions, as elsewhere. The Tardenoiseans spread north into the Eastern Highlands, where the only abundant supply of native flint occurs, and their culture is well developed at Banchory. At Shewalton, a tanged arrowhead of Bronze Age form, but executed in Tardenoisean style, proves that this culture survived well into later periods. In North-East Ireland a similar very debased industry has been described, but it seems to have played a very minor role in the Stone Age sequence of that region.

The entire Mesolithic development in Scotland was impaired by the lack, or comparative rarity, of flint. The region is important, however, because of its bone tools, which have been preserved, and for the development of an independent Late Mesolithic culture, the Obanian. It seems probable to the writer that the Azilian harpoons, characteristic of this culture, represent a development from the Early Azilian influence at Victoria Cave, reinforced by later arrivals from Southern France. In any case Azilian types survived far longer in the Scottish Obanian than at the type station, Mas d'Azil, where the culture is presumably of Boreal age. One may infer that, were bone implements preserved in the Larnian of Ireland, similar harpoons would doubtless be represented, especially as typically Azilian thumb-nail scrapers occur. The Maglemosean, which penetrated north into Scotland in Atlantic times, parallels the evidence in Ireland, where core axes appear sporadically in the Late Larnian.

As yet the Late Larnian has not been identified in Britain, but it seems probable that its presence will eventually be established in the coastal regions of England and Scotland bordering on the northern section of the Irish Sea and the North Channel. Tonks (*M.G.S.* England and Wales, 1926, p. 79) has already drawn attention to surface finds of flint implements from the Solway District of Cumberland at New Mawbray, near Silloth, but there is no proof that they come from the Litorina raised beach, and their age is uncertain. However, according to information received from Mr A. D. Lacaille, coarse, heavy, rolled implements, typologically comparable with Irish examples, are found in association with the raised beach near Stranraer and on the west coast of Arran. Thus scientific investigation in this area may yet definitely establish the presence of the Late Larnian of the rich coastal stations of Antrim and Down in North-West England and South-West Scotland.

3. THE MESOLITHIC OF ENGLAND

Already in Late-Glacial times Upper Palaeolithic people were occupying the new regions in Northern England, now freed from ice, and this fact is demonstrated by the presence of certain implements previously noted from Victoria Cave, Settle (see pp. 190–1). However, the British Upper Palaeolithic sequence differs somewhat from that of the Continent in that no predominantly Solutrean or Magdalenian horizons have yet been detected at any of the cave sites (Garrod, 1926; Burkitt, 1932, pp. 11–13). The sequence from Pin Hole Cave (see p. 46) and Mother Grundy's Parlour, Creswell Crags, Derbyshire, is complete from the Mousterian through to the Mesolithic, and reveals the development of a specialized and extended Upper Aurignacian culture, lasting on into Magdalenian times and showing Magdalenian influences. This culture is known as the Creswellian. The Late Mousterian sequence of Pin Hole Cave is underlain by a sterile layer indicative of the Arctic conditions of the Old Drift Glaciation (Upper Chalky Boulder Clay = Würm I), as discussed on p. 47. The overlying Aurignacian levels, however, contain the temperate fauna of the Interstadial Period between the last two glaciations, and in the upper levels of red cave earth, in which Creswellian implements are found associated with a cold fauna (Armstrong, 1931), there is definite evidence for a recrudescence of a cold glacial climate (Period of the New Drift = Würm II). Other sites of this period are shown on the map (Fig. 5, p. 42), and their distribution, south of the York Line (see p. 47), reveals that they are contemporary with the last glacial maximum.

At Mother Grundy's Parlour, the Creswellian is characterized in the basal and lower middle zones of cave earth by small *dos rabattu*, and other types of points; end scrapers of blade, disc, carinated, or steep form; gravers; bone or ivory implements; engraved fragments of bone; *dos rabattu* blades; and shouldered points (Armstrong, 1925, pp. 155–72; Garrod, 1926, pp. 140–5). These latter implements together with bevel-based bone points, typical of the French Magdalenian, demonstrate that the Creswellian survived until the end of the Late-Glacial Period in England. In the next zone of cave earth, the middle, the cold fauna disappears, even the Reindeer is absent except for a single fragment near the base, and *Bos primigenius* is present. Forest forms—Horse, Bison, Red Deer and Wild Pig—are characteristic at this time. The flint industry is not well represented: it shows a continuity of the Creswellian tradition, but is poorer and has a more Azilian aspect (Garrod, 1926, p. 145). In the upper middle zone a new element, the Tardenoisean, appears, and numerous small implements including micro-burins (Armstrong, 1925, Fig. 9) indicate the presence of this culture. The local industry at this time shows a decided tendency to become microlithic, and, as Dr Clark points out, "it would appear that the Tardenoisean influence intervened upon a Post-Pleistocene survival of the provincial Aurignacian, which already on its own account was showing a decided geometric tendency" (1932, p. 20). This site is also important, since it demonstrates the presence of the Creswellian in Post-Glacial times as revealed by the middle zone, probably Pre-Boreal or Early Boreal in age.

Whereas three main subdivisions of the Tardenoisean have been identified on the Continent, in Britain the upper or final phase seems to be absent (Clark, 1936, p. 212), and the English Late Tardenoisean resembles more the Middle Tardenoisean of Belgium. In the main, sites of this complex are concentrated in regions of sandy soils showing the control of geographical factors over the spread of the culture (Clark, 1936, pp. 190–5); in the North of England all the stations are on high ground ±1000 feet above sea-level, with the exception of eleven on the coast. These sites have been studied by Raistrick (1933[*b*] and [*c*]), who, in agreement with Clark (1932, pp. 21–8), recognizes two phases:

1. A non-geometric broad-blade industry which used white flint or chert, and is related to the Early Tardenoisean of Zonhoven in Belgium. The leading types include: the "broad blade point"; lunates; micro-bruins; typical small scrapers (thumb-nail end scrapers); steep or core scrapers; and very occasional geometric points. Sites referable to this phase are concentrated in the North Pennines and on the coast (Raistrick, 1933[*b*], p. 151).

2. A later geometric narrow-blade industry which uses brown or amber-coloured flint, and which is in part a local development combined with Middle Tardenoisean influence which came into Southern and Central England from the Continent. Typical sites belonging to this phase are distributed in the Southern Pennines; they are rarer northward along the ridges as far as Wharfedale, and have not been distinguished on the coast (Raistrick, 1933[*b*], p. 151), although several sites are known in the Cleveland Hills (Elgee, 1930, pp. 26–31).

Certain of the upland sites occur below peat, which was investigated at Warcock Hill, near Marsden, Yorkshire, by Erdtman (1928, p. 131), and assigned to the Atlantic Period. Recent finds of Neolithic and Early Bronze Age material at the base of this peat, however, together with the fact that the characteristic Early Post-Glacial indices are absent, suggest a Sub-Boreal dating (Godwin and Clark, 1934). This also applies to other sites in the upland region, which indicates that the Tardenoisean may have survived very late in this area. Likewise Raistrick's argument for the age of the coastal sites between Hartlepool and Banborough (1933[*c*], p. 197) seems inconclusive, since direct proof that the culture layer is contemporary with Boreal–Atlantic peat found at Newbiggin Carr is lacking (Godwin and

Clark, 1934). The age of the Pennine Mesolithic must therefore be left open. But notwithstanding the exact chronological position of the material in question, it is a fact that certain forms in the stations yielding the broad blade industry, notably steep or core scrapers, thumb-nail scrapers, broad blade implements and points, bear a striking similarity to the Early Larnian of North-East Ireland. It would seem, on the basis of this evidence, that this non-geometric industry owes more to the survival of Creswellian and other elements than is generally admitted, although the presence of lunates and micro-burins indicates undeniable Tardenoisean introductions. Continental analogies support this view. In the Early Tardenoisean level at Zonhoven (Clark, 1932, p. 24), which overlies an Early Mesolithic (Period I) layer showing affinities with Remouchamps (Clark, 1936, pp. 59–62), a "broad blade" industry is present. According to Dr Clark, this non-geometric complex in Belgium resulted from a strong Tardenoisean influence in the surviving culture, which was fundamentally Upper Palaeolithic in ancestry. Thus the non-geometric Tardenoisean industries of Northern England are comparable with the corresponding level at Zonhoven, but they seem to represent a parallel development, originating from an intrusion of Early Tardenoisean culture on the local Upper Palaeolithic survivals during Early Post-Glacial times, rather than a direct cultural influence from the Continent. This point is made clear only when the ultimate derivation of the Early Larnian, found north and west of the Pennines, is traced. But since the Tardenoisean only contributes in an indirect way to the Stone Age of Ireland, a full account of it is outside the scope of this book. The above material is, nevertheless, significant, as it illustrates the strong effect of Creswellian survivals on the Early Mesolithic of Northern Britain. The Larnian is an independent development, which evolved from the Creswellian under pressure from Azilian sources; the fact that microlithic influences were not felt on this culture indicates that the descendants of the Upper Palaeolithic hunters were probably well established in Ireland before Late Boreal times, when the Tardenoisean appeared in England (Clark, 1935[*a*], p. 319). Also the close degree of parallelism between certain Early Larnian forms, i.e. small blades with *dos rabattu* trimming (compare Armstrong, 1925, Fig. 7, no. 8), tanged points (Burkitt, 1932, Fig. 3, no. 4; Moir, 1930, Fig. 17), steep or core scrapers (Moir, 1917, Figs. 29–31), and Upper Palaeolithic types in England is in accord with this conclusion. However, the cultural development during the Late-

Glacial and Early Post-Glacial Periods in the region between North-East Ireland and Britain south of the end-moraines of the New Drift is so little understood that it is impossible to fill in the gaps at present. Further knowledge concerning sites similar to Victoria Cave and Inchnadamff, both within the area covered by ice during the last major glacial episode, is of urgent necessity in this respect, before the complete picture of the survival of the British Upper Palaeolithic along the margin of the retreating ice-sheets is completed. It is possible that influences from the reindeer-hunting cultures of North Germany, as suggested by Clark (1938[*a*]) and recently discovered in the Ebbsfleet Valley on the right bank of the Lower Thames (Burchell, 1938), were felt upon these local survivals, which may account for the presence of the tanged point in the Larnian of Ireland.

Definitely Azilian elements also appeared at this time (compare Breuil, 1937[*a*], p. 73), and presumably some of the forms associated with the "broad blade" industries of Northern England can be traced to this source. Thumb-nail scrapers in Ireland and harpoons in Scotland undoubtedly reveal contact with Southern France and the Cantabrian region of Northern Spain. It may be suggested that the Azilian came along the present west coast of England during Boreal times, where there was a far greater extent of land at that period than at present. As Clark points out (1932, pp. 38, 45, 47 and 49), typical Obanian heavy tools of the so-called "limpet-scoop" type have been found in South-West England, Cornwall and Wales (compare Cantrill, 1915, pp. 179–89, 196–203; Wheeler, 1925, p. 46), but, if this culture was distributed in Boreal times along the west coast, most of the material would have been lost as a result of the Litorina transgression and the secondary sinking of the land in Post-Atlantic times. The absence of Azilian sites in South-East England makes this hypothesis of an Irish Sea route of diffusion seem likely, though this is only negative evidence. In any case, regardless of how it got there, a strong influence from Southern France certainly made itself felt on the Mesolithic cultures of North-East Ireland and South-West Scotland, and present data indicate that it came from the south, probably via Cornwall.

The presence of occasional core axes in the Late Larnian has led to considerable misapprehension concerning the Irish Mesolithic. When these axes were first found they were considered to be Neolithic (Coffey and Praeger, 1904, pp. 186–7). Later Erdtman pointed out Baltic parallels for these implements with the Nøstvet culture of South Sweden (1928, p. 163).

This brought the culture more nearly into its proper perspective, since the Nøstvet is an extension of the Ertebølle (Period III) culture and it is associated with the Tapes (Litorina) shore-lines of Scandinavia (Shetelig and Falk, 1937, pp. 42–3). More recently, however, it has been demonstrated that the Forest cultures of the Baltic, as worked out by Professor Childe (1931, pp. 325–48), are present in England. Thus in Period II (Maglemosean) times, direct influences were felt on the east and south-east coast, and Maglemose harpoons from Yorkshire (Skipsea and Hornsea) as well as the specimen from the Leman and Ower Banks in the North Sea, may be dated pollen statistically to Boreal times (Godwin, H. and M. E., 1933). Other harpoon finds from the Thames at Battersea and Wandsworth (London), and Royston (Cambridgeshire), belong to this period (Clark, 1932, p. 18), in addition to core axes which are frequent at Maglemosean stations.

The whole question of the Maglemosean in England has recently received its merited attention due to the discovery at Broxbourne in the Lea Valley, Hertfordshire (see Fig. 33, facing p. 176), of a settlement site sealed under Late Boreal peat (Warren, Clark, Godwin, and Macfadyen, 1934, pp. 101–28). The implements include primary flakes, some showing signs of use; obliquely blunted points and blades with *dos rabattu* trimming; microburins; cores and core scrapers; core dressings or trimmings; flake scrapers; burins or gravers; core axes; and hammerstones. Typologically therefore Broxbourne falls into that group of axe, microburin and non-geometric microlith industries of South-East England, which represents an extension of Period II culture into England. The same industry is also present at Kelling on the Norfolk coast (Clark, 1932, pp. 54–7), Thatcham, Berkshire in the Thames Valley, Uxbridge, Middlesex, by the River Colne, and in the Colne Valley, Essex (Clark, 1932, pp. 59–67). Thus its distribution is mainly in East Anglia from the Thames to the Norfolk coast, but isolated finds occur in Yorkshire (Skipsea and Hornsea) as well as in Durham. Here at West Hartlepool a typical Maglemosean site with flint implements including a core axe has been described (Trechmann, 1936, pp. 161–8), but in a somewhat later context presumably of Early Atlantic date. In addition there are five isolated finds from near Edinburgh, mentioned on p. 192, which are also from deposits of the Atlantic Period. Thus after its introduction in Boreal times via the land connection between Great Britain and the Continent, the Maglemosean survived in the north and east of Britain well into the period of the Litorina transgression, after the Baltic connection had been severed. A comparison of the core axes from Broxbourne and from Holderness with the Larne types accounts for the origin of the latter forms. They are absent in Scotland, but their presence in the Late Larnian is clearly attributable to an influence from the Forest cultures of South-East England.

During Period III (Atlantic) the Late Tardenoisean flourished in England and it penetrated north into Scotland (see p. 193) and west into Wales (Clark, 1932, pp. 46–50; 1938[*b*]) and the Isle of Man (Clark, 1935, pp. 71–4). It did not reach Ireland, however, at this time, and it is not until the Late Neolithic or Early Bronze Age that an extremely debased Tardenoisean industry seems to have appeared in County Down. The sites in South-East England reveal a strong tendency towards Baltic types, since the majority of them in this area have yielded microlithic industries in addition to flake axes and picks (Clark, 1932, Chapters IV and V). At three of them: Selmeston (Clark, 1934) and Hassocks (Clark, 1936, p. 198) in Sussex, and Farnham (Clark, 1937; 1938[*c*], p. 316) in Surrey, pit-dwellings have been reported. Other important sites in South-East England: West Heath and Peacehaven; and in the Isle of Wight: Werrar (Poole, 1936; Clifford, 1936), are shown on the map (Fig. 33). These have all yielded material belonging to a late phase of the Mesolithic Forest culture tradition, resembling the industry recovered from Lower Halstow, Kent (Burchell, 1925, 1927, 1928), which may be considered the British counterpart of the Ertebølle (Period III) culture of Denmark (Clark, 1936, p. 158). At this site a flint industry was found below peat, pollen analysed by Erdtman, and dated to the Late Atlantic Period. Whereas Lower Halstow is analogous to Ertebølle, it differs more definitely from its Baltic counterpart than Broxbourne does from the Maglemosean (Clark, 1936, p. 160). The implements include the "Thames pick", a special form of the core axe; microliths of simple form; scrapers (rare); gravers (rare); flake axes (rare); and one quartzite pebble with counter-sunk hollows, which is a Forest culture type (Childe, 1931, p. 343). In Danish sites of this period core axes are rare, evolved microliths are common, and scrapers, flake axes and gravers are all characteristic (Clark, 1936, pp. 142–8), which indicate the local divergences that took place. Whereas in Period II the closeness in relationship between British and Danish industries is borne out by the existence of a direct land connection, this was non-existent in Period III after the marine transgression. Thus, as Dr Clark remarks, this geographical event is reflected in the cultural tendencies of the time.

To sum up the British evidence: the Creswellian (an evolved Aurignacian culture lasting into Magdalenian times) survived into the Early Post-Glacial Period at Creswell Crags, and other Upper Palaeolithic sites in Southern and Central England. Partly under pressure from the Forest culture, which came in during the Boreal phase, and partly as a result of environmental factors, these hunting peoples migrated north into the now ice-free regions of Northern Britain. Here meagre traces of their presence have been discovered at Victoria Cave in Yorkshire, but their principal focus of settlement was North-East Ireland, which was at this period nearly accessible by land, and where there was an excellent flint supply. An Azilian influence from Southern France seems also to have reached Northern Britain and Ireland early in the Post-Glacial Period via the west coast of Great Britain. This played an important role in the development of the local culture. In the Pennines the "broad blade" Early Mesolithic industry is probably a result of contact between this persisting Upper Palaeolithic tradition and a Tardenoisean immigration from Belgium. South-East England formed part of the North European Plain at this time, the Dogger Bank being dry land, and the Maglemosean (Period II) culture of the Baltic is richly represented in that region. This industry spread north and reached the Durham coast in Northern England and Scotland early in the Atlantic phase. Local specialization took place in the Thames Valley, where picks are common, and at Lower Halstow the effect of the marine transgression on the Forest culture development of Britain can be easily detected. Although, in the early period, the material is homogeneous in the two regions, in later times close contact ceased, and a specialized form of Period III culture developed in England. The diffusion of the core axe into Ireland in Late Mesolithic times reveals that Baltic influence was felt even on the outermost periphery of Western Europe. Here an Upper Palaeolithic people had evolved an indigenous culture, the Larnian, and had perfected several new stone implements to meet the new needs conditioned by the changing environment. In both Great Britain and Ireland these cultures persisted, even after the introduction of the Early Neolithic.

4. OTHER CONSIDERATIONS

The claim has been put forward that the Irish Mesolithic was related to the Asturian, of the Cantabrian province of Asturias (Oviedo), North-West Portugal (Ancora), and South-West France (Biarritz), where it is found mainly in caves and rock shelters along the coast (Bremer, 1928; 1928[*a*], p. 7; Whelan, 1930, 1932). Deposits in which this culture occurs usually consist of shell heaps which overlie Azilian deposits (Obermaier, 1925, pp. 354–5; Burkitt, 1923), and which may be assigned to the period of the Post-Glacial warmth maximum. Mr Whelan considers that the technique of manufacture of the Larne pick "represents a somewhat crude translation of the Iberian quartzite implement into flint" (1930, p. 184). In Professor Obermaier's opinion this apparent similarity is a result of convergence, and not of contact between the two regions (1932, p. 544; 1933, p. 1288); a fact which is substantiated by the northern limit of distribution of the Asturian culture, and by its total absence in England (Burkitt, 1932, p. 16; Movius, 1937, p. 196). Furthermore, the Larne pick is a flake implement struck from a previously prepared core, whereas the Asturian examples are core tools made on water-worn quartzite pebbles, as Burchell and Moir have pointed out (1931). Perhaps in both Ireland and Iberia these tools served comparable purposes, but it is impossible to trace any genetic connection between them. Therefore the question of an Asturian origin for the Irish Mesolithic must be ruled out.

5. MESOLITHIC NAVIGATION

As yet there is no proof that navigation was practised during Palaeolithic times, but abundant evidence exists indicating that this art was widely spread in the Mesolithic Period. Suggestions made elsewhere in this book that certain heavy implements in the Larnian and the Obanian were woodworking tools, possibly for boatbuilding among other purposes, are not entirely without foundation. Although no boats of this period have as yet been discovered in Ireland, in Scotland eighteen dug-out canoes were found in the silts and sands of the Litorina raised beach near Glasgow during the last century (Geikie, A., 1865, p. 324), and similar finds are recorded in the Forth region (Jamieson, 1865, p. 190; Munro, 1898, p. 272). But the circumstances of discovery are somewhat obscure in certain cases and a few of these boats may belong to a much more recent period, according to information received from Mr A. J. H. Edwards, F.S.A. (Scot.), Keeper of the National Museum of Antiquities of Scotland (compare Geikie, A., 1862, p. 222). Nevertheless, it does not necessarily follow that none of the early finds are Mesolithic in age. At least one authentic boat of this period is known from the Tay Valley at Friarton brickworks, near Perth (Geikie, J., 1879; 1895, p. 292). This specimen, recently described by Clark (1936[*c*], p. 146), rested on the submerged peat below 10 feet of carse clay, an estuarine sediment of the Atlantic Period (Erdtman, 1928, pp. 131–2). In England there is also one well-documented example. Dredging in 1935 at Sewardstone near Chingford, Essex, revealed a large dug-out boat, which may be assigned on fairly satisfactory evidence to Boreal times, or at the latest to a date not far advanced in the succeeding Atlantic phase (Phillips, 1936, pp. 144–5). In Northern Europe (Clark, 1936[*c*], p. 146) additional proof of Mesolithic navigation exists. In Ireland the very presence of the Larnian implies that boats were known; these would have been necessary to negotiate a passage in Boreal times because of the deep Irish Channel River which separated Ireland and Britain when Ireland was first occupied. The existence of an intensive Obanian settlement on the Island of Oronsay may also be cited as proof of marine traffic at a somewhat later date.

It is clear, therefore, that navigation was widely spread in Northern and Western Europe during the Early Post-Glacial Period, but it was probably never practised on a large scale. Had this been the case Irish flint would have been exported to Scotland during the period of the Litorina Sea, and the Obanian and the Late Larnian would not have tended to develop independently of Continental Mesolithic cultures, as the Boreal climate gave way to that of the Atlantic, if the land connection had not been more important than navigation for the interchange of ideas at that date. The fact of the existence of this form of transport is significant, however, since it helps to explain such interrelations of Mesolithic cultures as the discontinuous distribution of the Azilian, and the diffusion of Maglemosean core axes to the Late Larnian of Ireland.

6. THE EARLIEST SETTLERS IN IRELAND

The existence of a partial land-bridge between Great Britain and Ireland, during the Boreal climatic phase of Early Post-Glacial time, made the rich flint region in Counties Antrim and Down accessible to peoples of Upper Palaeolithic tradition. These people, mainly Creswellians, spread from Southern England, where they had survived the last glaciation, and they were reinforced by Azilians from Southern France and Northern Spain, who probably migrated, under pressure from the south exerted by Late Capsian and Early Tardenoisean groups, via the region of the present Irish Sea, along the west coast of England. From the point of view of physical type the Creswellians were fundamentally long-headed, although a round-headed element was also present (Keith, 1931, pp. 407–21; Clark, 1932, p. 107). A Mediterranean strain may have come in during Early Post-Glacial times with the spread of the Azilian, but as this culture even in South France is predominately of Upper Palaeolithic heritage, it is unlikely that this increment could have ever been very strong. As yet no skeletons definitely associated with the Early Post-Glacial deposits of Ireland have been discovered. One badly broken adult male skull was found in 1922 at Castle Market, Belfast, in a stratum of estuarine clay (Martin, 1935, pp. 55–6), which may possibly date from Late Atlantic times. However, the evidence for the age of this specimen is unsatisfactory. It is high, very narrow, and of the river-bed type; Martin estimates the cephalic index at 70. In Scotland, the remains of two individuals were found during excavations at MacArthur's Cave, Oban, in the last century (Turner, 1895; 1915, pp. 211–14). Whereas the age of one of these burials is uncertain, the other actually lay in the Obanian (Late Mesolithic) horizon at this site (see p. 181). Dr Coon states (1939, p. 75) that this individual, Skull B, is "typical of the purely long-headed variety of the Upper Palaeolithic European racial group", and represents the Upper Palaeolithic type of the British Isles in all respects.[1] The implications of Dr Coon's statement are of extreme importance in view of the archaeological evidence, as it has been shown that the Scottish Mesolithic was ultimately derived from Upper Palaeolithic sources. If we assume with Professor Walmsley and Dr Mogey (1938, p. 97) that the earliest immigrants into Ireland were of this same fundamental type, we materially strengthen the argument for Palaeolithic survivals in the Larnian culture. This assumption is in strict accord with anthropological data on the modern Irish: the predominant strain in certain sections of Western and Southern Ireland to-day, especially Counties Kerry and Cork, is basically of the Upper Palaeolithic type (Coon, 1939, pp. 376–84). According to Dr Coon this group was pushed into the west and south of Ireland by later immigrants during Neolithic, Bronze and Iron Age times. These people probably

[1] In addition there are the two Early Post-Glacial burials found at the Reindeer Cave at Inchnadamff, near Assynt, Sutherland, mentioned on pp. 72–3; one of these is stated to be a dolichocephalic individual (Callander, Cree and Ritchie, 1927, p. 171), but further details are lacking.

represent the descendants of the original Mesolithic settlers who arrived during the Early Post-Glacial Period (compare Hooton, 1940, p. 248; 1940 [*a*], pp. 171–2). As the ice melted, new land was available for settlement in the north, where the game, on which the Upper Palaeolithic peoples largely depended for their food supply, was retreating. It is not surprising, therefore, that of their own volition the Creswellians migrated to a different region with the changing environment, and made an obvious effort to stay as long as possible in the steppe-tundra conditions of the Late-Glacial Period, to which their economy was adapted.

A few settlers remained in the highland regions of Northern England, where they came in contact with Tardenoisean influences which penetrated England during the Boreal phase, and which contributed to the local Palaeolithic survivals. A portion of the Creswellian stock traversed the Highland Zone, however, and occupied Ireland, where new conditions led to a cultural adaptation, and a new Mesolithic industry, the Larnian, was evolved. Since in Ireland the Early Larnian is free from any Tardenoisean or Maglemosean influence, this spreading out most probably occurred early in the Post-Glacial Period. On the coast the sites were inundated by the sea during the Litorina transgression, hence the material is all found in secondary position in deposits of a later period. It is therefore impossible to fix with certainty the actual date of the first settlement, but one inland site has yielded material sealed below Late Boreal peat. Thus it is probable that the first settlers arrived somewhat earlier, perhaps in the seventh millennium B.C., at the beginning of Post-Glacial times. At this time the region of the Irish Sea must have been similar to the Dogger Bank, both supporting forests which were favourable to settlement. The regions were dissimilar in one respect however: the English-Irish land-bridge was broken by the Irish Channel River (see p. 89), whereas the North Sea connection was complete. Tidal scour has, of course, altered the marine contours to such an extent that one can only surmise what the early conditions were, but it seems probable that many sites existed on the floor of the present Irish Sea between Ireland and Scotland which were completely destroyed by the Litorina Sea of the Atlantic climatic phase.

The Highland Zone of Britain, which follows the Pennines north into Scotland from the Cambrians of Wales and which is formed by Palaeozoic rocks (Fox, 1938, p. 27), shut off the region of North-East Ireland and South-West Scotland from the rest of Britain. The two areas formed a single culture-province in Early Mesolithic times, but diverged after the marine transgression, when the Late Larnian developed in Ireland and the Obanian in Scotland, both based on similar prototypes. These cultures owe little to the innovations which were coming into the Lowland Zone of the south and east. As previously stated, the main factor which controlled the development of culture within this "province" in Early Post-Glacial times was environment, but in Scotland both a faint Tardenoisean echo and a stronger Maglemosean influence are present in the Obanian, and in Ireland the core axe was diffused ultimately from the Maglemosean in the Atlantic Period. As one would expect, there is a considerable time-lag on the periphery, proved by the fact that at the centre of its distribution the Maglemosean is of Boreal date. Thus, while Northern and Western Europe received influences from the south and east enriching the local Mesolithic cultures, very few new ideas were diffused into the region of the Irish Sea and the North Channel during Early Post-Glacial times. As Fox points out (1938, p. 41), there is a tendency in this area to form a "cultural pool", which is furthered by the physical isolation of the west coast of Britain from the Eastern Lowlands. While this statement is especially applicable to the later periods, it is also true of the Mesolithic.

Chapter IV

POST-LARNIAN DEVELOPMENTS

1. INTRODUCTION

The change in climate at the end of the warm moist Atlantic Period witnessed the arrival of two new influences in Ireland: one from the south-west by sea and the other from Northern France via Britain. The introduction of Megalithic culture into Ireland was the chief contribution from the south-western source; from Northern France came an industry with definite Campignian affinities. As yet there is no evidence to prove which of these new influences reached Ireland first. Present data strongly suggest that they arrived more or less contemporaneously during the second half of the third millennium B.C. It should be made clear at the outset that it is not the writer's intention to examine in detail the question of the origin and development of the Megalithic culture which, as stated above, was the main south-western contribution. Whereas some of the megaliths in Ireland are admittedly Neolithic, the practice of constructing these monuments reached its peak with the first appearance of metal and is outside the scope of this book. Here it is proposed to consider only those Stone Age industries directly related to the Campignian of Southern Britain and Northern France, and to discuss the question of the continuity of Larnian tradition in Northern Ireland. In certain instances these were strongly influenced as a result of contact with the Megalithic complex from the south-west. Where this is found to be the case the nature of these influences will be examined.

The scope of this chapter as defined above presents certain difficulties. These arise from the fact that, in addition to the survival of indigenous Mesolithic (Larnian) tradition, the Campignian itself represents a basically Mesolithic heritage in the Western Neolithic complex, as indicated by Clark (1936, p. 160) and Mahr (1937, p. 402). In Britain and France the Campignian seems to be an industrial rather than a cultural manifestation of Western Neolithic culture, but as yet so few occupation sites of this period have been scientifically excavated in Ireland that it is difficult to cite any very convincing proof in this regard. The bulk of the evidence is from axe factories, workshops and open surface stations which will be described below. Therefore the term "Campignian" is used here with reference to those industries the roots of which can be traced directly to Mesolithic antecedents in Northern and Western Europe, but which comprise a highly specialized industrial phenomenon which developed during Neolithic times and persisted in certain regions as long as flint and stone tools were used. Data from Ireland support the view that the Campignian was not a chronological stage as inferred by the term "Proto-Neolithic". Rather the Campignian is to be regarded as a Mesolithic survival in Western Europe. On its arrival in Ireland it superseded the indigenous Mesolithic and took possession of the fertile coastal lowlands of the north-east.

The focus of settlement continued to be Counties Antrim and Down, because, like its predecessor, the Campignian was dependent on stone tools, and the Cretaceous chalk contained the best available supply in the form of flint. There is no evidence as to what form of basic economy was practised at this time. The major Campignian activity was the manufacture of stone implements, an industrial development associated with the Western Neolithic, as stated above. Since this latter complex was based on food production in place of food gathering, and was no longer dependent wholly upon hunting and collecting as a means of subsistence, it seems probable that a primitive form of agriculture should be likewise attributed to those groups who manufactured Campignian tools. The same applies to domestic animals. Analogy with other areas in Northern and Western Europe where Campignian industries are found suggests that possibly stock-raising was introduced at this time. As to material culture, certain Larnian elements were absorbed by the newcomers for which their equipment provided no innovations in the form of improved or more satisfactory implements, and for which there was still a definite need. On the whole, however, in Ireland the change is abrupt, and there is no indication of a gradual transition. The introductions far outnumber the older elements and include *tranchet* (flake) axes, abundant core axes, polished stone tools, arrowheads and pottery. With the exception of the core axe, of which the Mesolithic examples are less developed and of sporadic occurrence, no evidence for the presence of any of these traits is found in the Larnian culture of the Litorina raised beach. The Campignian is therefore distinctive as far as the Northern Irish sites are concerned. At the time of its introduction the extensive and dense forests of late Zone VI existed, containing Oak, Elm, Pine, Birch and an abundance of Alder. Hazel was comparatively rare. The emergence of the land was completed during the time covered by the upper portion of Zone VI, a phase which may be identified with a recrudescence of the comparatively cold and dry Continental climate of the Sub-Boreal Period. There is some indication that severe storms were infrequent, and that the prevailing winds came from the east or north-east in place of the strong moisture-bearing westerlies of Atlantic times (Brooks, 1927, p. 417). Therefore although the optimum climate of the Post-Glacial warmth maximum had passed, conditions for ocean travel were extremely favourable. This is reflected in the extensive traffic along the Atlantic seaboard, resulting in increased contacts between the more vigorous Mediterranean centres and the peripheral regions of Northern and Western Europe. Climatic conditions thus led to an acceleration in the diffusion of culture and induced fresh migrations of people into Ireland.

In addition to the innovations which appeared in Ireland at the end of Atlantic times, it is necessary to consider in this chapter the Bann and Sand Hill cultures which developed out of the indigenous Irish Mesolithic stem of the coast--the Larnian. Sooner or later these complexes were absorbed, or on their own account they may have taken up agriculture. In neither case are there any data concerning whether or not crops were grown. But, judging from the evidence of the sites themselves, in spite of the fact that both the Bann and the Sand Hill cultures were strongly influenced as a result of contact with Neolithic, Megalithic and other elements, there is every indication that the occupants were basically food gatherers. For this reason it is proposed to call them EPI-MESOLITHIC. Both are Larnian survivals: the Bann culture of the interior is a direct outgrowth of the earlier coastal complex, and in the sand-hill sites of Northern Ireland a predominantly food-gathering economy seems to have lasted as late as the Early Christian Period. Thus the Post-Larnian developments in Ireland which are to be discussed here include:

(*a*) *The Campignian Complex*—ultimately derived from Mesolithic sources but of *foreign* introduction.

(*b*) *The Epi-Mesolithic Bann and Sand Hill Cultures*—directly descended from the Larnian and of *indigenous* origin.

The industries with Campignian affinities will be described first.

2. THE CAMPIGNIAN SITES

The stone tools classed as Campignian represent at least in the technique of their manufacture a powerful link with the old food-gathering past, but as indicated above the Campignian itself cannot be regarded as a culture. It is intimately connected with the Western Neolithic, of which it forms an important industrial aspect. It is found most highly developed precisely in those regions—Northern France, South-East England and North-East Ireland—where flint is readily obtainable in large nodules. It also occurs associated with extensive axe factories in Wales and Ulster. In Counties Antrim and Down numerous localities have yielded Campignian material, which in each case is thoroughly different from the earlier Larnian culture of the Litorina raised beaches. In contrast with the latter it is *in situ*, and at several sites it has been found directly above the beach deposits. Each station is strongly individualistic, therefore the evidence of the main sites will be summarized, since it is as yet impossible to treat this phase of Irish archaeology as a whole.

A. Glenarm, County Antrim

The Glenarm stratigraphy is given on p. 130. Horizon 1, which belongs to the Late Larnian, is overlain by Horizon 2, which contains material with Campignian[1] affinities of which the *tranchet* axe and various types of scrapers are typical. No traces of ash or charcoal were found in the culture layer, so that it is probable that the site had been a workshop rather than an actual habitation. The sharp, unrolled forms, typical of this horizon, display a characteristic ochreous patination, although a few light chalky grey, dark bluish-grey, and mottled dark green specimens are present. In marked contrast to the Mesolithic material from the underlying raised beach, the Campignian series contains many retouched forms. Well-struck blade implements (Fig. 44, nos. 1–3) are very typical, and include forms which have been chipped by use (no. 1), as well as specimens with deep notches on one or both edges (no. 3). Leaf-shaped points (Fig. 44, no. 2) with the upper surface of the butt-end flaked and slight retouching of the edges on each side of the bulb are found. These are reminiscent of earlier examples

[1] Elsewhere (Movius, 1937, pp. 210–14) the archaeological material in this horizon has been referred to the Neolithic Period. This attribution still holds, but, in order to distinguish between Neolithic culture as a whole and the industrial manifestation which accompanied it, the term Campignian, as defined on p. 212, has been employed.

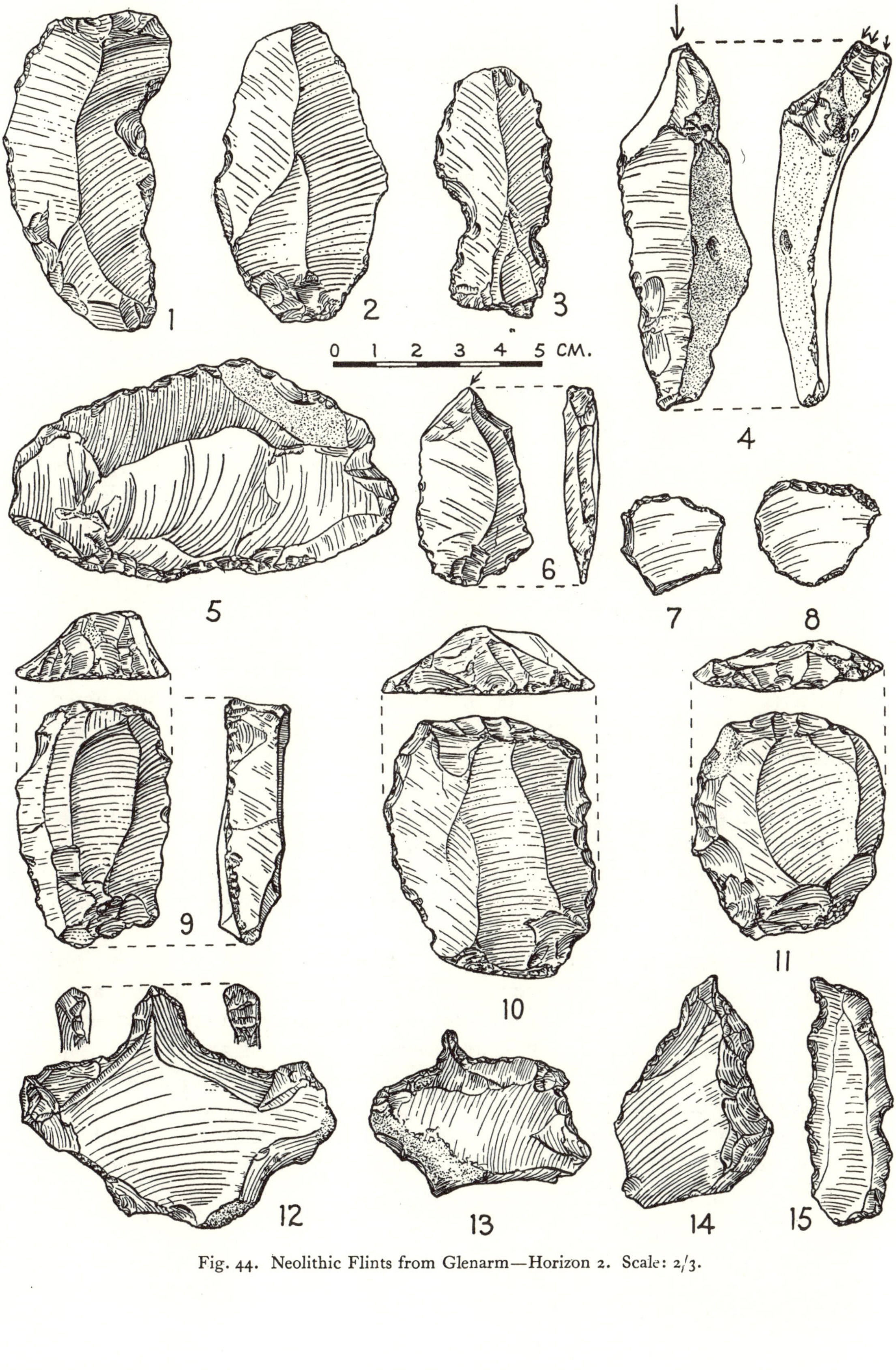

Fig. 44. Neolithic Flints from Glenarm—Horizon 2. Scale: 2/3.

(Fig. 27, nos. 1–7), which are the prototypes of the Bann point (see p. 251). Gravers (Fig. 44, nos. 4 and 6) and side scrapers (Fig. 44, no. 5) are rare. The former are of the ordinary angle variety, while the latter are made on broad, oval flakes, technically similar to Levallois flakes. End scrapers (Fig. 44, nos. 7–11) are very common, and they include the small thumb-nail forms (nos. 7 and 8), which also occur in both the early and late phases of the Irish Mesolithic. The illustrated specimens (Fig. 44, nos. 9–11) are typical examples of the Glenarm end scrapers, all of which display the careful retouching characteristic of the series. True end-of-blade scrapers, made on long parallel-sided blades, are not represented.

The fish-tail scraper (Fig. 45, nos. 1, 2 and 4), a form identified by Octobon (1931, p. 174) from examples found at the French site of Champlat, Aisne, is very typical of the Irish Campignian. This implement, a variant of the flake axe, is made on a broad flake with a transverse cutting edge. Fig. 45, no. 1, which is the shape of a fish's tail, is an excellent example of this class of scraper. The worked edge is usually slightly concave and chipped as a result of use; retouched forms are rare. At Glenarm a series of large flakes, broken at right angles to the axis of the blade so as to leave one-half to one-third of the butt-end remaining (Fig. 45, no. 8), are very common. In some cases these have been used as scrapers. Trimming flakes with faceted butts (Fig. 45, no. 3) illustrate the pseudo-Levalloisean tradition noted throughout. Perforators (Fig. 44, nos. 12–15) comprise a large series and several distinct types occur. The most common form (no. 12) is a broad boring or reaming tool, but finer examples (no. 13), as well as perforators made on blades (nos. 14–15), are also found. Two peculiarly shaped implements in the form of a broad Y (Fig. 46, no. 2) are known from Glenarm. Possibly these are boring or reaming tools, although each of the three concave edges could serve for scraping. In the Peabody Museum of Harvard University there is an identical French specimen from Grand Pressigny.

Numerous *tranchets*, or flake axes (Fig. 45, nos. 6, 9 and 10), in addition to smaller examples probably used as chisels (Fig. 45, nos. 5 and 7), are a feature of the Glenarm industry. The cutting edge has been produced in the usual fashion, by removing a flake transversely to the long axis of the implement, in all cases, except no. 9. This specimen is interesting in that the unfaceted striking platform is at right angles to the edge, and it exhibits a double bulb of percussion. In comparison with flake axes from elsewhere, the Glenarm series is characterized by the small size of these implements.

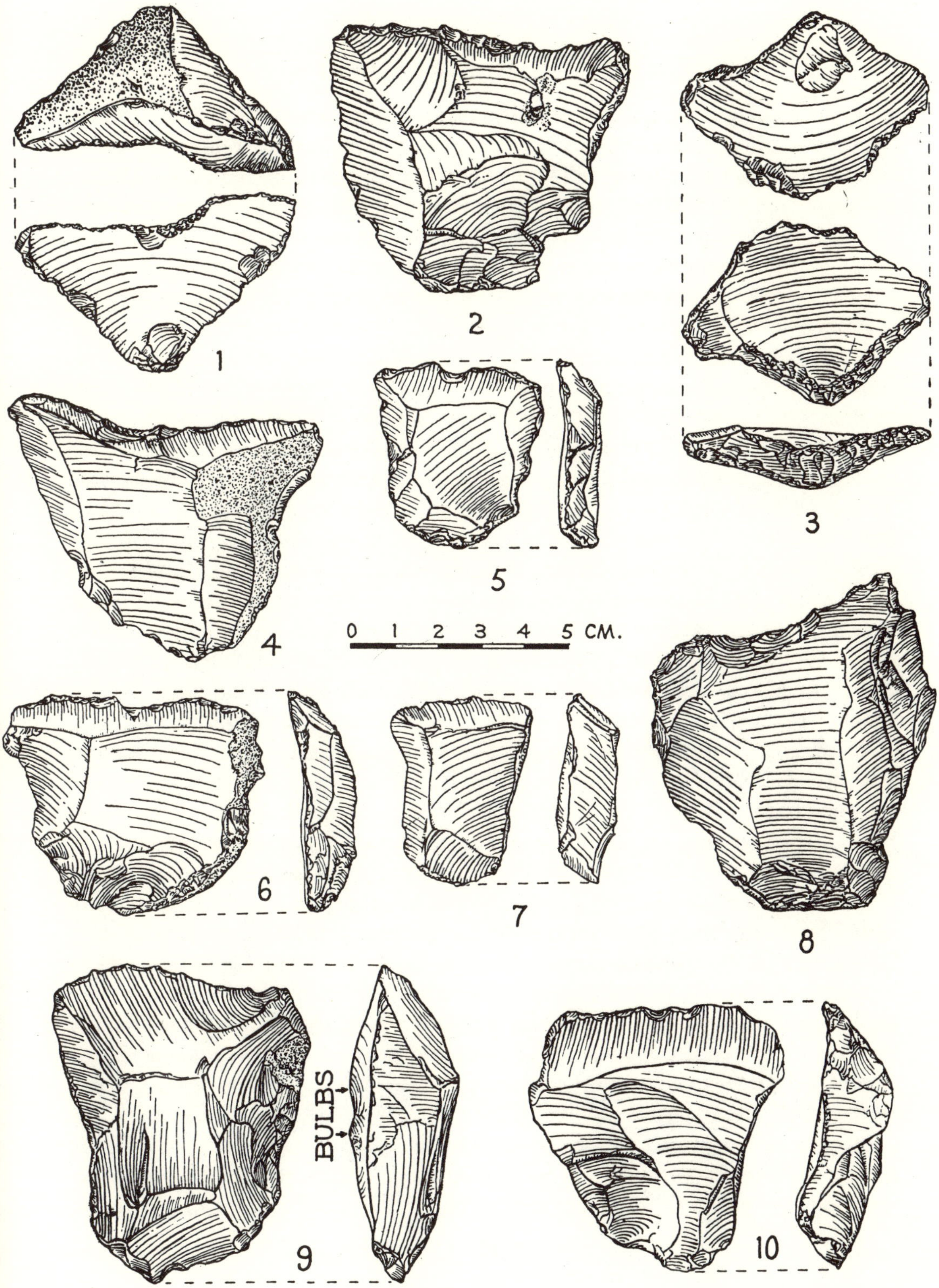

Fig. 45. Neolithic Flints from Glenarm—Horizon 2. Scale: 2/3.

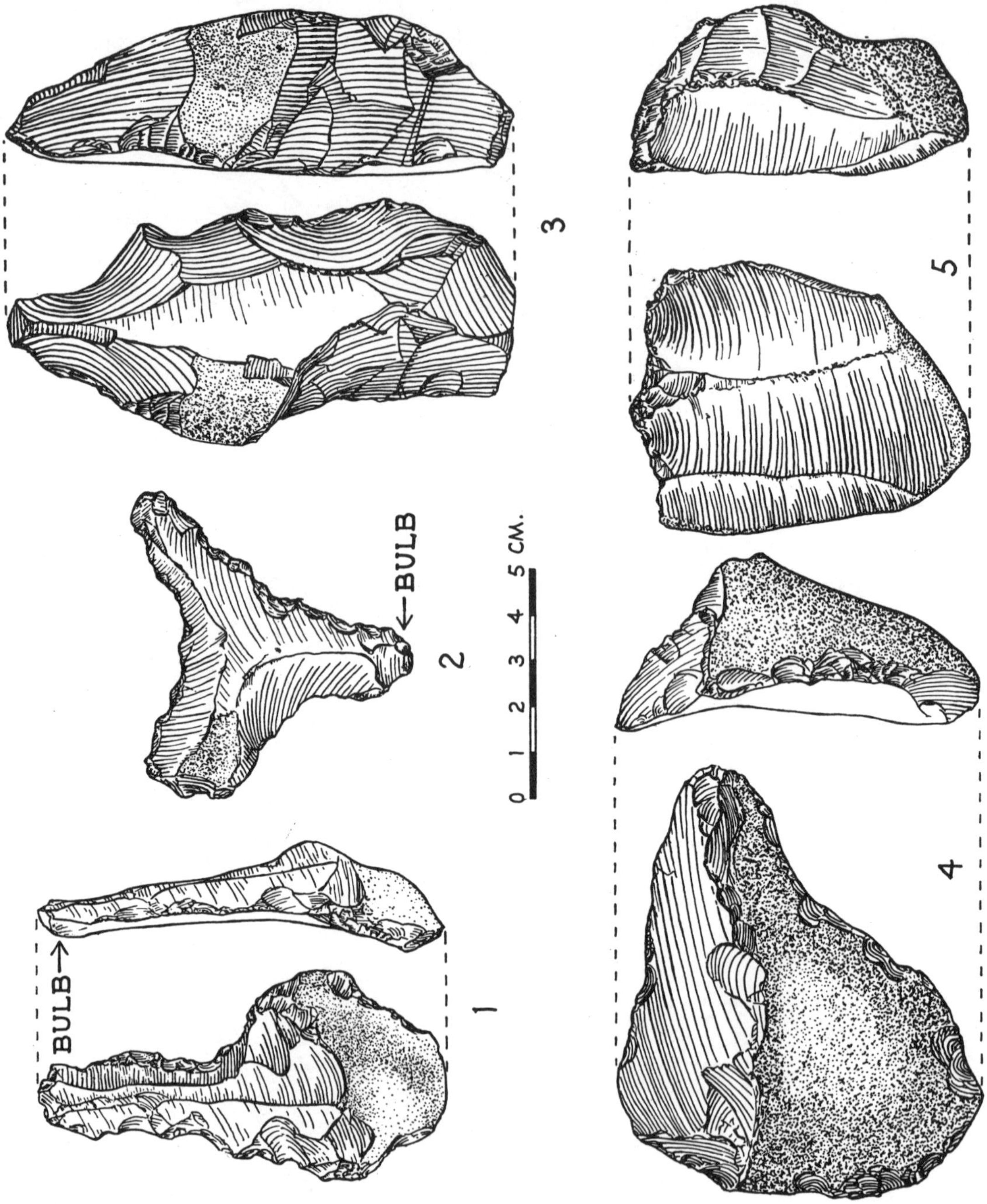

Fig. 46. Neolithic Flints from Glenarm—Horizon 2. Scale: 2/3.

This may be the result of intensive use, as constant resharpening of the edge would tend to reduce the length. No core axes have been recorded at this station, but picks made on cores are known (Whelan, 1938, Fig. 5, no. 1). Flake examples of this type of implement (Fig. 46, no. 3) are also present, in addition to a few specimens of the Larne pick (Fig. 46, no. 1), which is described on p. 166. The illustrated object is smaller, better made, and more extensively used than the early types, but nevertheless it suggests a survival from the earlier culture. Choppers, often made on coarse trimming flakes, are common. Fig. 46, no. 4, is a typical example, and it displays the transverse cutting edge which is characteristic of the industry. Cores are very numerous. In many cases the striking platform has been prepared (Fig. 46, no. 5), and a few tortoise types are also found.

B. Cushendun, County Antrim

Overlying the Litorina raised beach (Deposit B) at this site there is a layer of humus (Deposit A), which contains a similar industry to that found at Glenarm (Movius, 1940, p. 63). A few of the flints from this layer, archaeological Horizon 4 in the Cushendun sequence (see p. 126), were found in association with a large hearth 2·5 m. in diameter and 7 cm. thick. Otherwise no indication of occupation exists, but as the percentage of retouched forms is high, it is improbable that the site is that of a workshop. The implements exhibit a dull to dark grey patination, and are sharp and absolutely unrolled. Leaf-shaped and triangular points (Fig. 47, nos. 1 and 2) with extensive trimming on the upper surface of the bulbar end are present. As previously pointed out, these implements are Mesolithic survivals, and point to a definite link between the inland culture of the Lower Bann Valley and the earlier Larnian complex of North-East Ireland. As at Glenarm, end scrapers are common; steep ended, horse-shoe forms (Fig. 47, nos. 3 and 4), which display careful working, are characteristic. Other Glenarm types include side scrapers (Fig. 47, no. 7), which are rare, and small flakes with transversely sharpened cutting edges (Fig. 47, no. 6), probably used as chisels. The most interesting single specimen from Horzion 4 at Cushendun is a derivative of the transverse arrowhead illustrated in Fig. 47, no. 5. It is 5·5 cm. long and is made on a blade, the sides of which have been worked in such a way that an elongated triangular form has been produced. A shoulder has been fashioned on the upper surface by the intentional removal of a flake by hinge fracture, possibly to assist in hafting.

On the left-hand corner of the transverse edge there is a sharp point; it appears likely that a similar prong was once present on the opposite corner, but it was subsequently broken. Implements of this type are found in England and Scotland (Clark, 1934[*a*]) from the first occupation of Windmill Hill (Neolithic A) until the early part of the Bronze Age when flint was

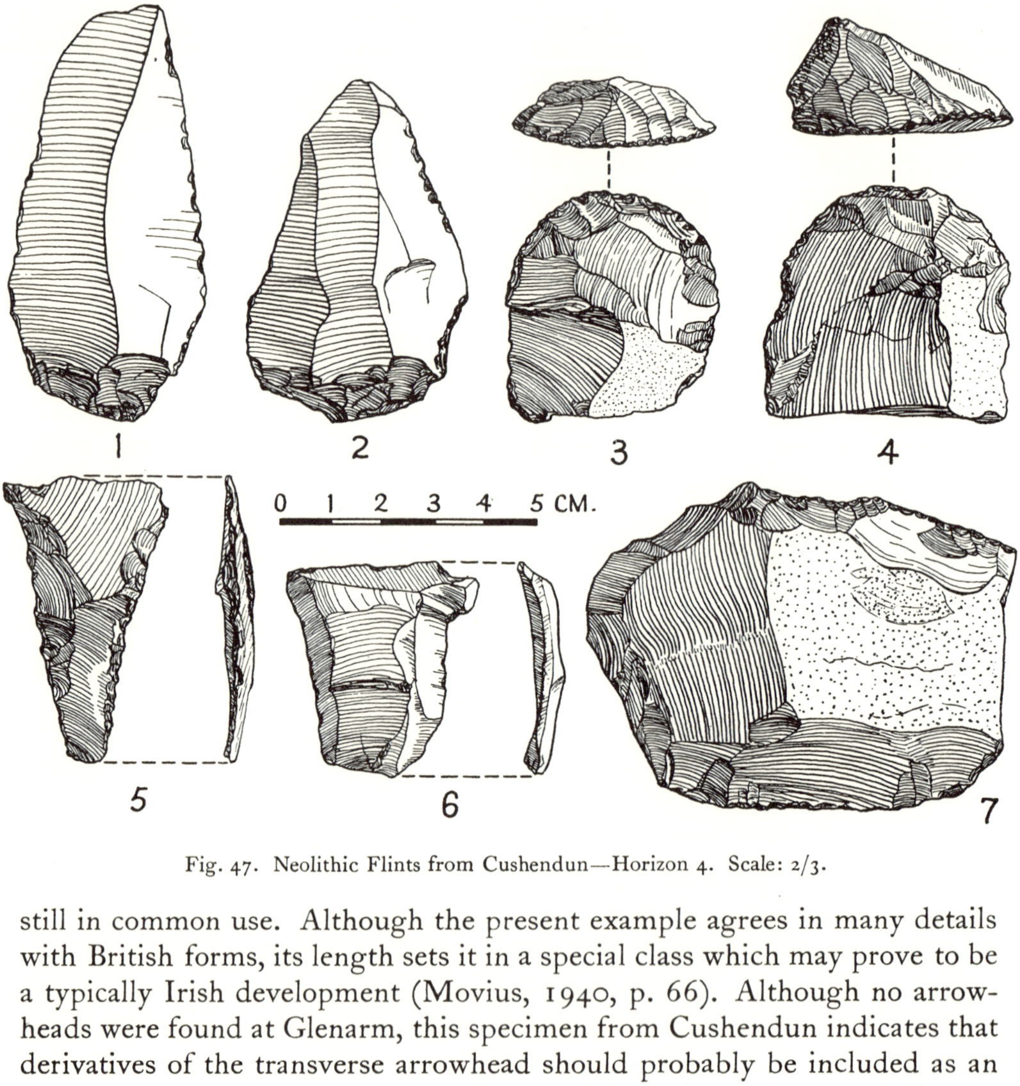

Fig. 47. Neolithic Flints from Cushendun—Horizon 4. Scale: 2/3.

still in common use. Although the present example agrees in many details with British forms, its length sets it in a special class which may prove to be a typically Irish development (Movius, 1940, p. 66). Although no arrowheads were found at Glenarm, this specimen from Cushendun indicates that derivatives of the transverse arrowhead should probably be included as an element of the culture which brought the flake-axe complex into Ireland.

C. Rough Island, County Down

The Campignian series from this site contrasts sharply with the Early Larnian material of the Litorina raised beach, and it occurs in the humus (Deposit A) immediately above (see p. 139). Although implements of both

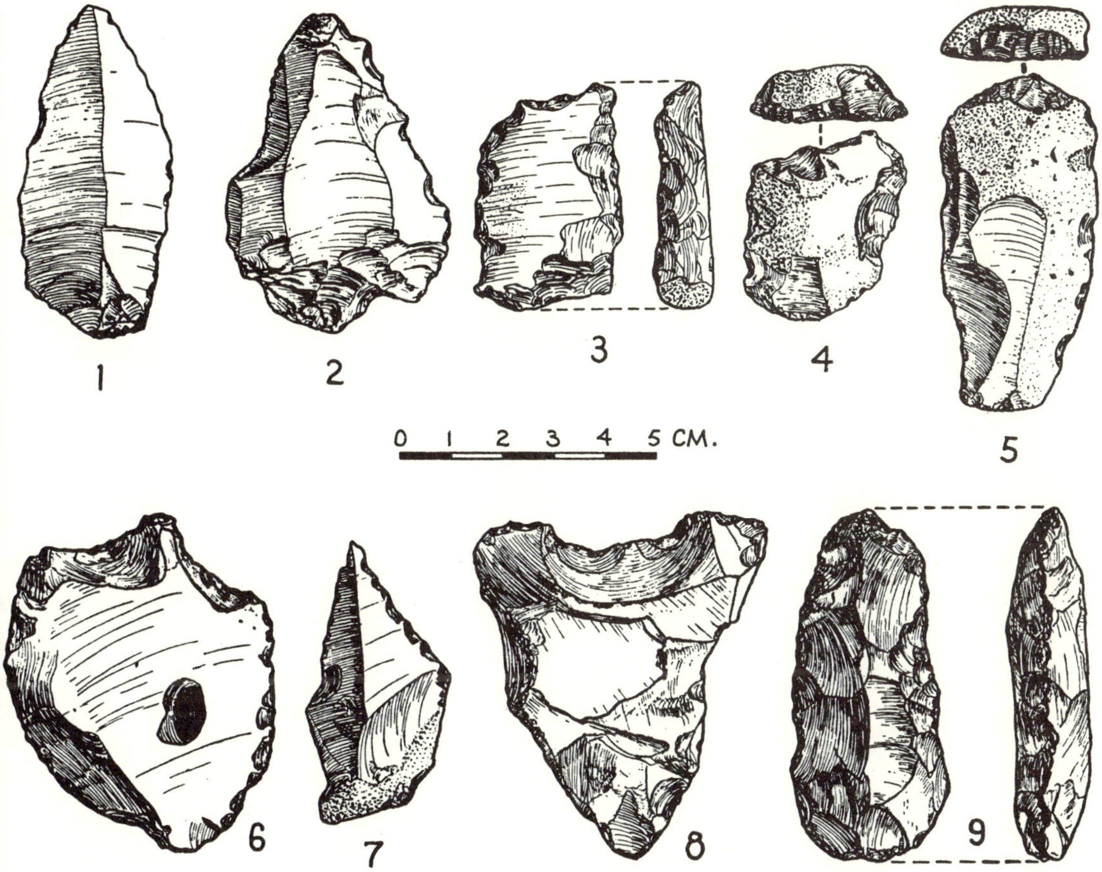

Fig. 48. Neolithic Flints from Rough Island—Horizon 2. Scale : 2/3.

cultures occur in this upper layer, as a result of disturbances due to ploughing, the industry of Deposit A, or Horizon 2, is easily recognizable. The typical patination is grey, but white flints with "rust stains" and others of deep ochreous colour are also present. In a great many cases earlier material from the beach was reworked during the later occupation of the site in

Post-Mesolithic times. The flaking technique displayed by the implements from Horizon 2 at Rough Island is cruder than either Glenarm 2 or Cushendun 4; however, well-struck, pointed blades (Fig. 48, no. 1) are present. Although only one tanged point (Fig. 48, no. 2) was found during the excavation, Mr Hugh Kirk of Newtownards, the discoverer of the site, has several in his collection from this locality. The illustrated specimen is made on a pointed triangular flake, the butt-end of which has been worked into a short tang. Small side and end scrapers (Fig. 48, nos. 3 and 4), end-of-blade scrapers (Fig. 48, no. 5), and fish-tail scrapers (Fig. 48, no. 8), the latter similar to Glenarm examples, are all typical of the Campignian series from Rough Island. No. 8 may be a crude flake axe, but its transverse edge is concave, and it appears to have been used for scraping. Perforators made either on pointed blades (Fig. 48, no. 7), or rough trimming flakes (Fig. 48, no. 6), are common. No. 6 is a crude example of a type found also at Glenarm (compare Fig. 44, no. 12). Core implements include small chipped celts of flint (Fig. 48, no. 9) and picks (Whelan, 1938, Fig. 4, no. 1). In addition to the above types, Mr Kirk has found leaf-shaped arrowheads and *tranchets* or flake axes at this site. The presence of leaf arrowheads suggests that the industry of Horizon 2 at Rough Island is possibly slightly later than either Glenarm 2 or Cushendun 4.

D. Tievebulliagh, near Cushendall, County Antrim

The sites of many extensive axe factories were discovered in Ballyemon Glen near Cushendall, County Antrim, by Mr W. J. Knowles of Ballymena, in the early part of this century (Knowles, 1903, 1906, 1906[*a*]). Two of these, Tavnagharry and Clougheen, are surface stations found by ploughing, but near the summit of Tievebulliagh Mountain important stratigraphy exists. On the almost perpendicular eastern face of this mountain (shown in Fig. 15, p. 110), which is formed of basalt and rises to a height of 1346 feet, is a large outcrop of fine-grained bluish rock, discovered in 1934, and it is from this material that the implements from the Ballyemon sites were manufactured. This rock has been identified as an altered form of diorite, called aphanite (Knowles, 1903, pp. 363–4) or a hornfelsed sediment (Whelan, 1934, p. 135); in any case it fractures in a similar way to quartzite, but since it is finer-grained, the bulb of percussion is well marked, and the edges more clearly defined. Axes made from this material are superior to flint examples; the rock is harder and less friable than flint, hence a better and more lasting cutting edge can be produced. The Tievebulliagh outcrop was extensively exploited in Late Stone Age times, and Mr Knowles records several sites in the vicinity of Ballyemon, as well as in the neighbouring regions of Glendun and Glenariff. The main archaeological horizon is at the base of the mountain peat which covers much of Tievebulliagh, and which directly overlies the boulder clay. It is hard and black, typical forest peat, and at the time of its formation Scotch Fir grew on the uplands. Stumps of this tree occur in the deposit, and human implements are sometimes found associated with them. Although some material is actually in the peat, the principal concentration is at its juncture with the boulder clay. Occasional artifacts are also present in the superficial layers of the clay, which is very hard, unweathered, and of a light blue colour. It seems probable that the base of the peat is of Sub-Boreal age, but the results of Professor Jessen's palaeobotanical investigations at this site have not as yet been published.

All the localities described by Mr Knowles are similar, and they have been the factories where stone implements were made. The area is usually a rough oval where axes and picks—both finished and unfinished or broken—flakes, chips and hammerstones occur in great numbers. On Tievebulliagh the material lies *in situ*, but elsewhere it has been disturbed, and Mr Knowles records his observations on a large sector of the mountain-side, completely denuded of the surface peat, which had slipped down, exposing several undisturbed chipping sites. Here the objects were concentrated, and the whole process of the manufacture of axes and picks was plainly revealed. Since most of the implements were broken or only partly worked, very few fine specimens were recovered. It is probable, therefore, that the finished articles were taken to the settlement sites in the valley, either for use or for further working, such as grinding and polishing. In addition to the types mentioned above, there are many flake implements, including points and scrapers. Sites of this type exist all over the mountain; even on the almost perpendicular east face there are ledges with chipping refuse on them, and the talus at the foot is also full of material from this huge Late Stone Age factory-site. There are, however, no potsherds, shells or bones, either in or below the peat, to suggest evidence of occupation on Tievebulliagh.

Mr Knowles collected over 2500 crudely worked axes with coarse chipping from the Tievebulliagh district, in addition to the butt or edge portions of many broken specimens. These illustrate the entire range of the process of manufacture, from partly chipped rocks to a few finished implements. Some display either pecking or local polishing, but completely polished axes are rare. Furthermore no grindstones were found, although sandstone is abundant in the region. Although the majority of the axes represent core types, occasionally they are made on flakes, and a few *tranchets* (flake axes) are present (Knowles, 1903, Pl. XXXVI, no. 22). The average length is 15 cm., but examples up to 37 cm. long occur (Knowles, 1906, p. 386). The shape of the edge varies from semicircular or elliptical to straight; a few specimens display expanded edges. Fig. 49, no. 1, is an unfinished implement from which only a few chips have been removed; no. 2, a more nearly completed specimen, is still in a rude state; nos. 3–5 are all completed axes, as finely finished as possible by chipping, and they illustrate the type which was manufactured at the site. Actually a large proportion of the implements classified as crude or unfinished axes from Tievebulliagh are probably picks; one with a transverse edge is shown by Mr Knowles (1903, Pl. XXXIV, no. 9). Crude implements like hand axes also occur (Fig. 50, nos. 1, 2, 4 and 5), which are dressed to a point on the end opposite the heavy butt. These bifacial tools may have been used as either picks or choppers.

As for the flake tools, there is no evidence to suggest that the fine-grained blue rock from Tievebulliagh was used like flint for procuring flakes solely for implements of this type. No nuclei are present, and all the flake artifacts seem to be made on trimming flakes or chips, produced by the thousand in the manufacture of axes, picks and other bifacial implements. As a rule they are short and broad, with projecting wings on each side of the bulb of percussion; resolved flaking is common, and long, well-struck types are usual. Since flint was readily obtainable in the vicinity, it was probably used mainly for implements of this class, and some flint tools were found at the site. The flake implements of rock include disc scrapers (Fig. 50, no. 3); side scrapers, in some cases used as end scrapers as well (Fig. 50, no. 6; Fig. 51, nos. 3–7); short thick points (Fig. 51, no. 2) and leaf-shaped points (Fig. 51, no. 1). All are carefully retouched flake implements, in some cases (e.g. Fig. 51, nos. 1, 6 and 7) made on blades, and they reveal great technical skill, as the rock is very hard and difficult to flake. Round or oval hammerstones with abrasion scars on the surface are frequent at the chipping sites. Although no implements from this locality have been recorded at Glenarm, several typical Tievebulliagh axes have been found in Deposit A of the 35-foot terrace at Cushendun. Thus the Cushendall axe factories were in part contemporary with the camp site, found above the Litorina raised beach in archaeological Horizon 4 at Cushendun.

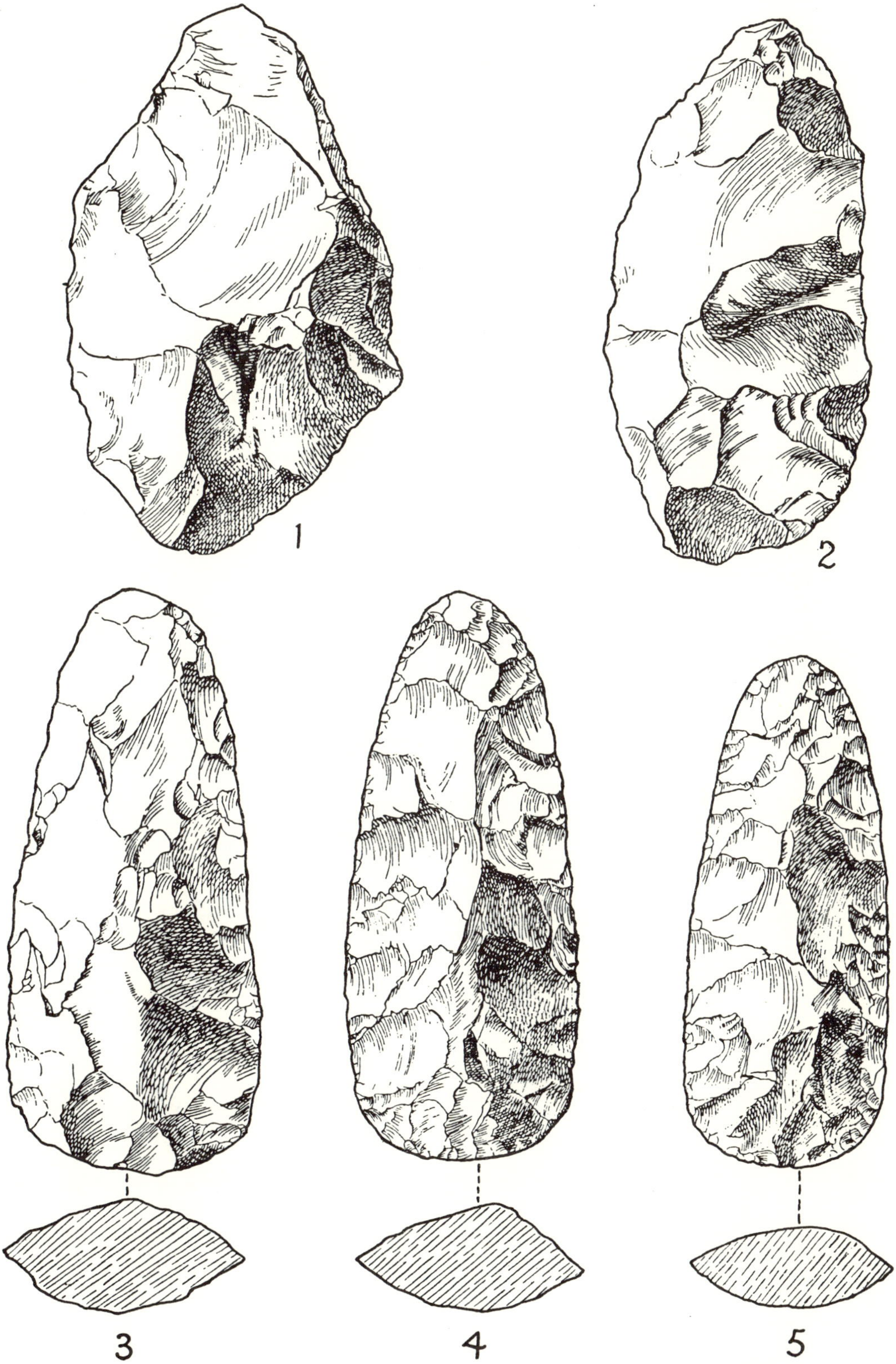

Fig. 49. Neolithic Stone Axes from Tievebulliagh, near Cushendall. (After Knowles.) Scale: 1/2.

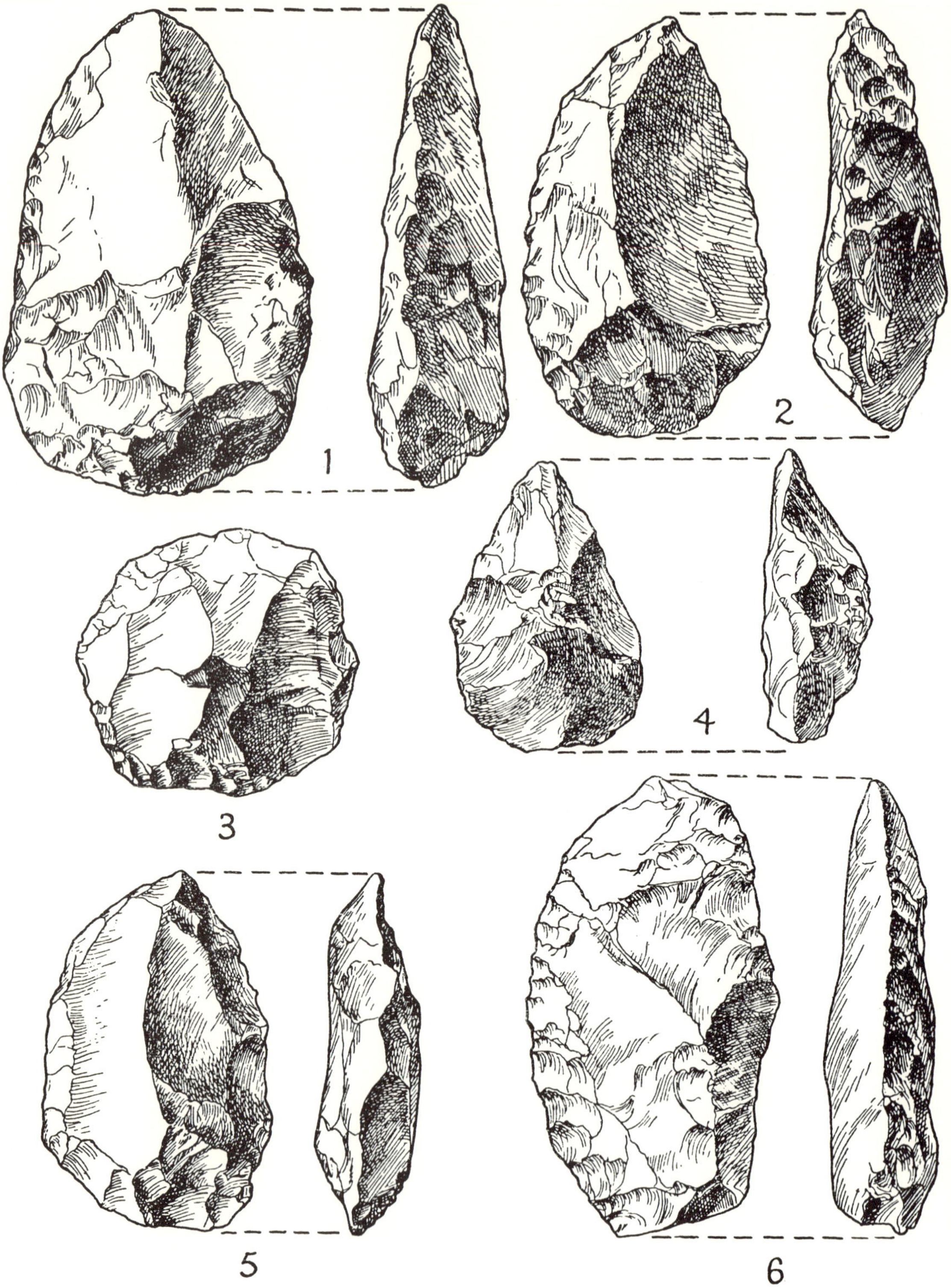

Fig. 50. Neolithic Stone Implements from Tievebulliagh, near Cushendall. (After Knowles.) Scale: 1/2.

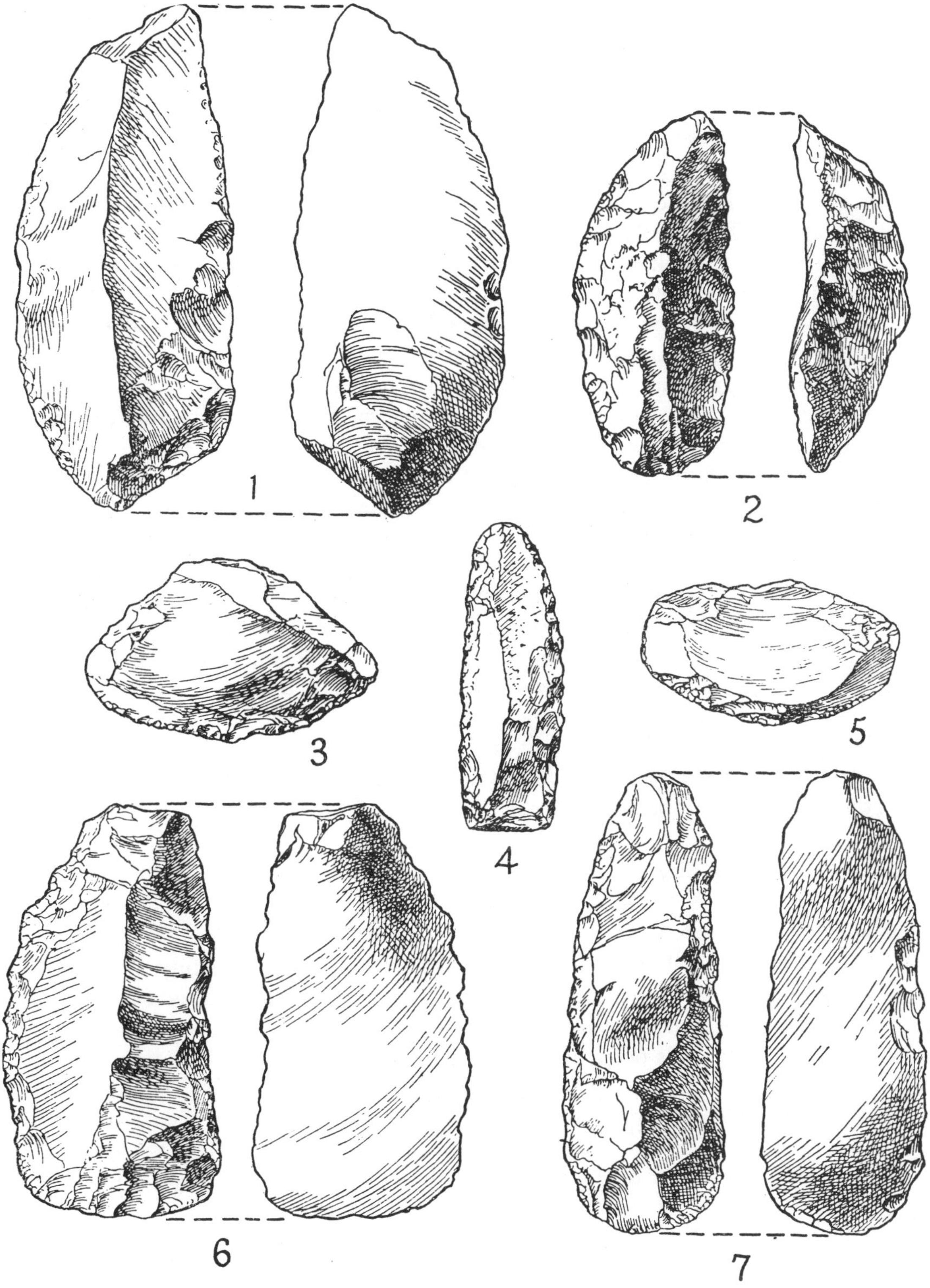

Fig. 51. Neolithic Stone Implements from Tievebulliagh, near Cushendall. (After Knowles.) Scale: 1/2.

E. Ballynagard, Rathlin Island, County Antrim

Rathlin, a small island 6 miles from the north coast of Ireland (Fig. 15, p. 110), and 12 miles from Kintyre, Scotland, is formed of Cretaceous chalk overlain by Tertiary basalt, and was extensively occupied during the Late Stone Age. At Brockley in the western part of the island there is an outcrop in the basalt of the same fine-grained bluish rock (alphanite or hornfelsed sediment) that appears on Tievebulliagh, and near which there is likewise an axe factory, although not as extensive as at the Cushendall site. Two elongated axes, one chipped and the other partially polished, and a cordate hand axe, similar to Fig. 50, no. 1, from Tievebulliagh, have been described from Rathlin Island (Baudouin and Whelan, 1931; Whelan, 1935[*a*]); all are made of the fine-grained rock found at Brockley. Near the centre of Rathlin, on the townland of Ballynagard, Mr C. B. Whelan (1934) has discovered an important settlement site, which is situated on the northern side of a large glacial cirque approximately 350 feet above sea-level (Whelan, 1934, Fig. 2). In 1933 Mr Whelan, in co-operation with the Harvard Archaeological Expedition to Ireland, excavated at this site, which yielded significant results. A trench 72·2 m. long and 2 m. wide (Whelan, 1934, Fig. 1) was dug through the area of the maximum concentration of surface material. In the eastern portion of the trench the humus (average thickness = 20 cm.) rested directly on glacial till, but at the western end, in a shallow depression between two rock ridges where the trench was expanded to a width of 4 m., the following section was recorded (Whelan, 1934, Fig. 10):

(A) Humus	16 cm.
(B) Loamy Clay	18 cm.
(C) Red Glacial Till	35 cm.
(D) Bed Rock	Thickness undetermined

(A) Humus. This consisted of dark brown to black loamy clay with occasional small to medium stones, and has been disturbed as a result of ploughing. A mixed series of types was found; Late Bronze Age–Early Iron Age potsherds occur in this deposit near the excavated site.

(B) Loamy Clay. Below the humus, in the western part of the trench only, a deposit of tough, consistent, dark reddish-brown clay occurred. This was archaeologically sterile, and it was probably laid down in the shallow depression by water during a period when the level of the small bog, now present on Ballynagard, had a higher water table.

(C) Red Glacial Till. On the surface of the till, immediately below Deposit B, an extensive occupation site was discovered. Here many implements of both flint and the local blue rock were recovered, in association with two small oval hearths, and a large area of ash spread (Whelan, 1934, Fig. 10, plan). Below the hearths the surface of the red clay was burned a dull orange colour, and a few artifacts were found trampled into the clay. Deposit C, which was hard and contained striated stones and boulders, rested immediately upon bed rock.

The archaeological horizon therefore is completely sealed by the loamy clay, Deposit B, although no direct dating evidence was secured at the site. But since the Rathlin industry is similar in many respects to Tievebulliagh and Glenarm, it can be provisionally assigned to the Sub-Boreal Period on typological grounds. Definite proof of this point can only be established by palaeobotany. In the occupation layer thirty-three artifacts (21 of local rock, and 12 of flint) were found associated with the hearths described above. The stone types include: choppers, side scrapers, flakes showing signs of use (Fig. 52, no. 10), a notched flake and a hammerstone. The following flint implements are listed (Whelan, 1934, p. 138): a square-ended scraper, a hollow-ended scraper, a nose scraper, three knives, a flake implement of pseudo-Levallois type (Fig. 52, no. 14) and five blades—two showing signs of use. The flints from this level are patinated an ochreous or chestnut colour and may be easily recognized when compared with the grey or brown series from the surface. The two most important objects from the occupation layer are: (1) the broken portion of a stone celt 7 cm. long with a semicircular cutting edge which is ground and polished (Fig. 15, no. 15); and (2) a potsherd (Fig. 15, no. 16). The character of this sherd, which is the undecorated rim portion of a large globular vessel, clearly shows that the pot had a marked incurve. The lip itself is pronounced and is raised above the sides of the vessel both internally and externally. The colour is dull red; the texture is coarse with conspicuous grits. Professor Childe and Mr Piggott each examined the sherd and are in complete agreement that it represents typical British Neolithic A ware. In fact Mr Piggott points out that comparable examples are known from Windmill Hill, Wiltshire, and Maiden Bower, Bedfordshire (Whelan, 1934, p. 141).

Both these objects were found near one of the small hearths on the surface of the glacial till. Thus their association with the Ballynagard industry is indisputable, and it demonstrates a Neolithic age for this level. The

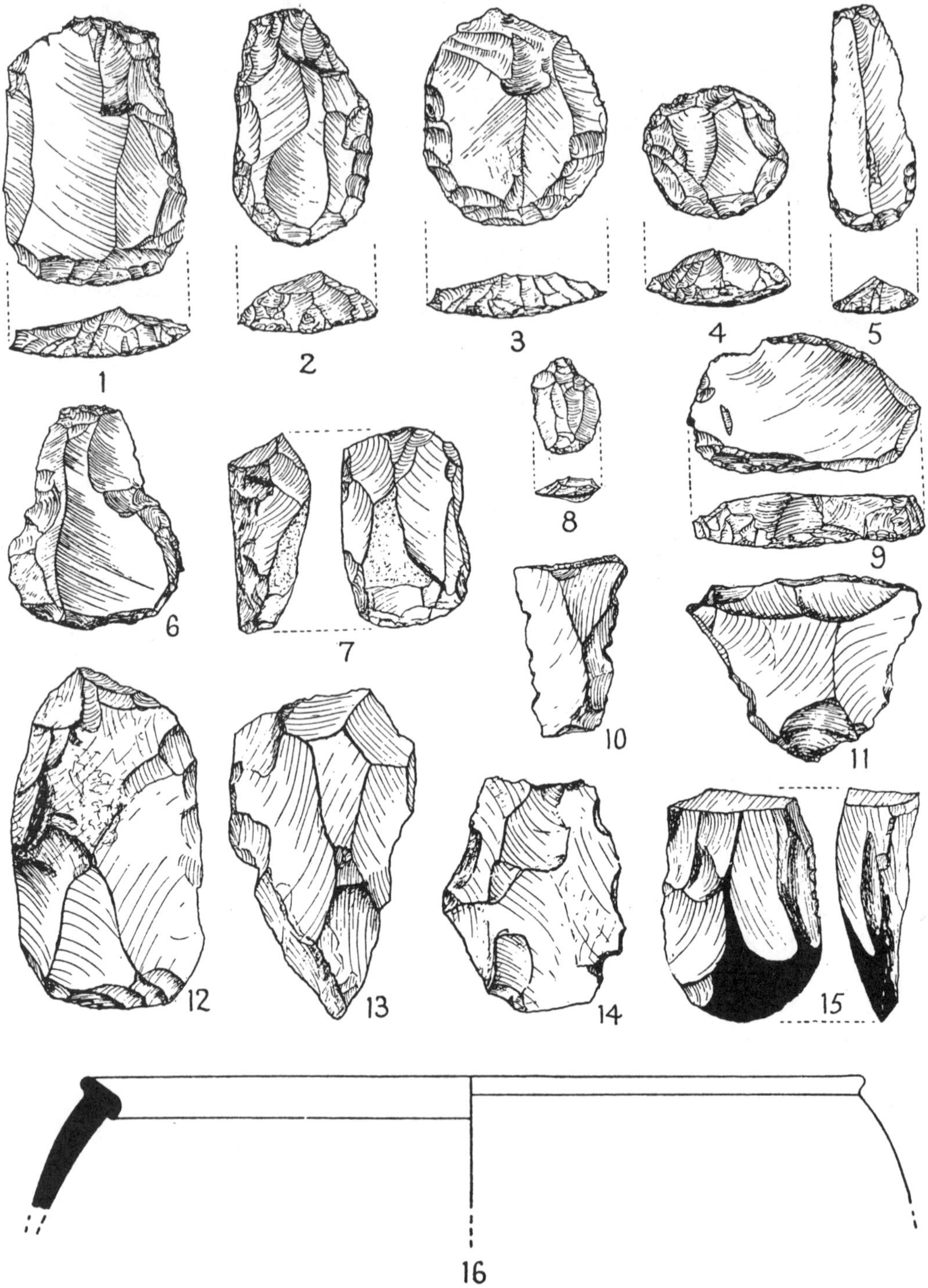

Fig. 52. Neolithic Implements of Flint and Stone (nos. 1–15) and Pottery (no. 16) from Ballynagard, Rathlin Island. Nos. 10, 14, 15 and 16 from the occupation layer sealed below Deposit B. (After Whelan.) Scale: 2/3.

surface industry is mixed, but it proves that there was a continuum of Stone Age tradition throughout the later periods during which time the same stone types survived. In addition to blades showing signs of use, the industry from the humus (Deposit A) consists of end scrapers (Fig. 52, nos. 1–6 and 8), as well as a few side scrapers (Fig 52, no 9), fish-tail scrapers of the local fine-grained rock (Fig. 52, no. 11), side and end scrapers of both flint and rock (Fig. 52, no 7), and hollow or notched forms. As at Glenarm, leaf-shaped points (some with faceted butts) and perforators form a notable component of the industry. The core implements include stone axes of Tievebulliagh type, often displaying traces of local polish, choppers (Fig. 52, no. 12), and picks with finely worked delicate points (Fig. 52, no. 13). It does not seem probable therefore that picks were used at Ballynagard as flint-mining tools, which is generally considered to be their normal function elsewhere. Although a few small flake axes or *tranchets* occur, they are rare. As Mr Whelan points out (1934, p. 129), arrowheads are absent at Rathlin as at Glenarm and Tievebulliagh. Further excavations carried out by Mr Whelan near the site revealed a curious structure of stone chambers, which contained hearths, the Ballynagard industry, and Late Bronze Age–Early Iron Age pottery (Whelan, 1934[*a*]). The island was therefore apparently occupied for at least two thousand years by Stone Age people, who persisted in the Campignian tradition, and who only received faint echoes from the centres of Bronze and Iron Age civilizations on the mainlands of Ireland and Scotland. Ballynagard illustrates the extreme need for caution with regard to typological dating of surface material in Ireland, as the same stone industry survived until almost the end of prehistoric times.

Perhaps the most significant point established by the Ballynagard excavation is that the stone tools from the culture layer are of Tievebulliagh type, whereas the flint implements from the same horizon recall a normal series from Glenarm. This fact supports the view that the workshops where flint artifacts were manufactured, such as Glenarm, and the stone-axe factories found at Tievebulliagh and on Rathlin Island, belong to one and the same complex. This association of the flint and stone industries of the Irish Campignian with Windmill Hill pottery, polished stone and hearths indicates that Ballynagard must be considered an occupation site related to the Western Neolithic culture. In fact it probably represents a camp site connected with the axe factory at Brockley in the western part of the island. It is therefore an important locality in that it demonstrates the introduction of Western Neolithic elements into Ireland along with the appearance of the Campignian. For this reason Ballynagard may be considered a peripheral development of the Western Neolithic.

3. THE AGE AND CULTURAL AFFINITIES OF THE IRISH CAMPIGNIAN

The sites discussed thus far all yield different local aspects of the same fundamental Stone Age industry, which has also been recorded at several localities in the vicinity of Belfast. At one of these, Greenoge, Dunmurry, County Antrim (Whelan, 1928[*a*], 1932), material possessing features reminiscent of Glenarm has been found associated with typical British Neolithic A pottery (Whelan, 1938, p. 130). A second site, Black Mountain,[1] has yielded flint implements of similar type, but no pottery (Whelan, 1938, pp. 131–2), whereas at Squires Hill, Mr Angus MacDonald has excavated a rich station containing flint artifacts in addition to worked blades and fragments of polished stone axes made of material from Tievebulliagh and a few potsherds (Evans, 1938, p. 322). Dr Evans' site at Lyle Hill, 8 miles north-west of Belfast (Evans, 1938), is probably later, as leaf and lozenge arrowheads occur, which do not form part of the complex under discussion. Nevertheless the presence of polished axes of Tievebulliagh stone demonstrates that the Late Stone Age factory sites near Cushendall were still exploited. According to Evans, it is probable that Lyle Hill is to be dated to the Early Metal Age.

Reviewing the evidence as a whole, it is definite that the presence or absence of pottery at the localities described above is without significance for dating purposes. Regarding the pottery, all one can say is that it demonstrates an extension of the Western Neolithic into Ireland. But the most widespread contribution from this source, as far as the present Irish evidence is concerned, was the great industrial development known as the Campignian. No sherds have yet been found either at any of the stations overlying the raised beaches or at the factory site of Tievebulliagh. Pottery is also absent at the Black Mountain workshops, although it occurs elsewhere in direct association with slightly different facies of the same lithic industry present at these localities. The precise chronological position of this culture is, however, as difficult to establish in Ireland as elsewhere. The data from Glenarm,

[1] Bell, Robert, *Proc. Belfast Nat. Field Club* (1922–3). This volume was not available to the writer.

Cushendun and Rough Island, where Campignian material is found directly overlying the Litorina raised beach, proves that a new influence penetrated North-East Ireland during the period of the emergence, which must have been well advanced by the end of the third millennium B.C. The evidence to be discussed presently shows that the newcomers, who possessed a superior culture, took possession of the fertile coastal lowlands, forcing the earlier Mesolithic occupants to seek refuge in the interior and in the less favourable sandy sections of the foreshore. What complicates the picture is that, once the Campignian appeared in Ireland, it gave rise to a development which survived well into Metal Age times. This is made clear by the evidence from Ballynagard, Rathlin Island. Here an undisturbed occupation floor containing typical Campignian implements is sealed below a deposit of sterile loamy clay. In the overlying humus Late Bronze Age–Early Iron Age sherds are found in association with flint and stone types identical with those from the lower levels. Whereas all periods of Irish archaeology are characterized by the fact that older elements have persisted into comparatively recent times, this doctrine of survival is particularly applicable to the Stone Age.

The cultural affinities of the Irish sites are with Western Europe, as stated at the outset of this chapter. Numerous surface stations containing material of the same type have been recorded in England, but for the most part they are very poorly documented. The main concentrations are in the flint regions of the Central Lowlands, East Anglia and the South Downs; one station has been recorded in Yorkshire (Bowler-Kelley, 1935, p. 6). Flake axes (which are present but rare), picks, end scrapers, disc scrapers and fish-tail scrapers are characteristic (Smith, R. A., 1931, pp. 1–8 and 16–19). Y-shaped implements, found at Glenarm (see p. 216), are also common at sites in Norfolk, Suffolk, Middlesex, Kent, Sussex, Dorset, the Isle of Wight, and Oxfordshire (Bowler-Kelley, 1935, pp. 5–7). Core axes, sometimes with local polish, picks, and British Neolithic A pottery are also found at stations in the same area (Smith, R. A., 1931, pp. 30–6). In Wales the great stone-axe factory, discovered in 1919 in Carnarvonshire on the seaward slopes of Penmaenmawr, above Craig Lwyd farm (Warren, 1919, 1921, 1922; Wheeler, 1925, pp. 46–52), provides an analogy with Tievebulliagh, although typologically the axes from the Welsh site differ from those of North-East Ireland. In both cases, however, a Post-Mesolithic dating seems definite (compare Glenn, 1935), and it is interesting to note that during this period rocks other than flint were apparently sought after for purposes of axe manufacture: the Craig Lwyd axes are hewn from the local igneous rock, and a similar material was used at Tievebulliagh.

Apparently the flint technique of the Neolithic settlement sites of the Lowland Zone of Britain is derived from the same source as that of the surface stations, but the lithic material has not yet been adequately studied. Huge collections of flint implements, which seem to be associated with the same complex, have also come from the flint mines—Grimes Graves, Cissbury, etc.—and they were formerly regarded as having Palaeolithic affinities (Smith, R. A., 1911; Armstrong, 1920, 1923, 1924, 1926). More recently, however, the pottery from these sites has been intensively studied (Piggott and Clark, 1933). There is absolutely no doubt that on the basis of the pottery alone the flint mines are Neolithic in age, and that they are associated with St Gertrude, Spiennes, Clermont, Grand Pressigny and other well-known flint mines on the Continent, as pointed out by Piggott and Clark. The Campignian aspect of this industry is undeniable, and the occurrence of flake axes, characteristic of Le Campigny, makes it necessary to consider the results of the excavation done in 1896 at this site.[1]

Le Campigny is situated on a hill, 1 mile north-west of Blagny on the Bresle River, Seine Inférieure, in North-West France (see Fig. 33, facing p. 176). The hill is 80 m. high, and the site, where a series of pits was excavated, occupies an easily defensible position on its summit (Salmon, du Mesnil and Capitan, 1898). A typical section of one of the pits, which was oval in shape (4·30 m. long and 1·65 m. deep), is as follows (Salmon *et al.* 1898, Fig. 42):

A.	Humus	20–25 cm.
B.	Loamy Yellowish Clay	1 m. 20 cm.
C.	Hearth (cinders and charcoal)	45 cm.

This pit had been dug into glacial gravels containing remains of *Elephas primigenius*, underlying which (1·15 to 1·50 m. below the base of the pit) Cretaceous chalk with flint occurs. In the humus polished stone implements were recovered, but in the pits (Deposits B and C) only chipped forms were recognized by the excavators. On the basis of this evidence, it has been claimed that proof of a Late Mesolithic culture was secured at the site. The

[1] Actually Le Campigny was discovered in 1872 by Jacques de Morgan's father, Eugène de Morgan, but it was not until 1886 that P. Salmon proposed to create an "*époque campignienne*" (De Morgan, 1921, p. 82).

following critical facts make such a contention seem improbable: (1) Whereas pit-dwellings are not entirely unknown in the Mesolithic (see p. 204), a series of large oval types, associated with numerous hearths such as those at Le Campigny, suggests a later date. They are in fact similar to Danubian dwellings of the Early Neolithic of Central Europe (Childe, 1929, p. 42). (2) The contained fauna includes Ox and Horse (Salmon *et al.* 1898, p. 375), which indicates that stock-raising was practised. (3) Agriculture is demonstrated by several large mill-stones or querns from the base of one of the pits (Salmon *et al.* 1898, pp. 398–9), as well as by a potsherd with a barley impression from the same horizon. (4) Charcoal from the hearths includes Oak and Ash (Salmon *et al.* 1898, p. 275); according to Dubois (1932, p. 288), Ash did not appear in France until the Sub-Boreal Period. (5) The position of the site itself, on a hill-top, is highly suggestive of a Neolithic occupation. (6) Pottery was found throughout the culture layer at Le Campigny, and over fifty vessels are represented (Salmon *et al.* 1898, p. 377), although none have been reconstructed. The colour and texture is variable; the paste is coarse with conspicuous grits of shell and quartz. True handles and horizontally pierced lugs (Fig. 53, nos. 10–11) are present, and incised geometric ornament occurs on some of the finer black ware (Salmon *et al.* 1898, p. 402). The forms include bowls with flat rims up to 12–15 cm. in diameter, which are often decorated with zones of cross-hatched incised lines (Fig. 53, no. 9). In every respect this pottery is separate and distinct from the Late Mesolithic kitchen-midden ware of the Baltic described by Clark (1936, pp. 152–3), and it is very reminiscent of the Neolithic ware from Camp de Chassey (Déchelette, 1908, pp. 554–64).

Flint implements, found in abundance in the pits, include the following characteristic forms (Fig. 53): end scrapers, single or double (no. 1); disc scrapers (no. 2); fish-tail scrapers (no. 3); perforators; both large and small picks (nos. 5 and 6); flake axes or *tranchets*, with transverse cutting edge (nos. 7, 8 and 12); notched scrapers; points (no. 4, including forms reminiscent of Abri Audi); beaked implements; and flakes showing signs of use as knives or scrapers. Excavations at the site carried out by Professor Breuil prove that polished stone axes must be added to the list of material from the pit-dwellings at Le Campigny (unpublished).[1] Although transverse arrowheads

[1] Furthermore, Jacques de Morgan (1921, p. 84), who regarded the Campignian as a Mesolithic holdover surviving into the Neolithic and being strongly influenced by it, states that he once found a polished flint axe, reworked by chipping but not repolished, at the base of one of the pits at Le Campigny.

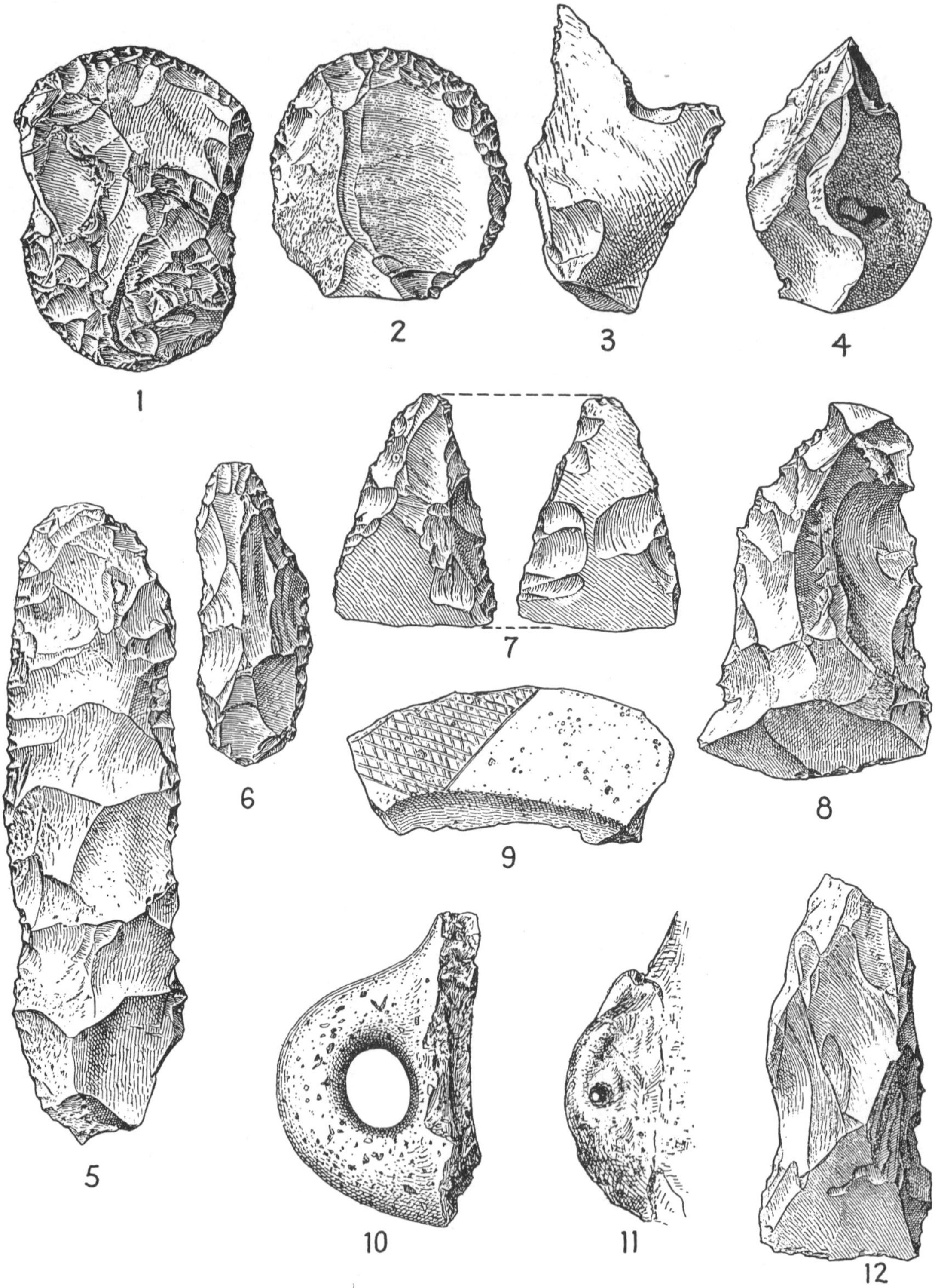

Fig. 53. Neolithic Flints and Pottery from Le Campigny, Seine-Inférieure. (After Salmon, Du Mesnil and Capitan.) Scale: 2/3.

are present, types with bifacial pressure flaking have never been found at this site. Cores are rare, a fact which suggests that the flint working was done at a workshop removed from the settlement. Whereas antler implements were not found at this locality, they occur in the region associated with the same industry.

It is reasonably clear from the published data that the culture which has been called Campignian after the type site of Le Campigny, described above, is Neolithic rather than Mesolithic, as pointed out in 1925 by Professor Childe, since it is based on a food-producing economy (Childe, 1925, p. 18). Certain Mesolithic traits, such as flake axes ultimately derived from the Period II (Maglemosean) culture of Northern Europe, are, however, present. During Boreal times this culture was widely diffused over the North European Plain, and at seven sites in Northern France and Belgium Maglemosean bone objects have been recorded (Clark, 1936, pp. 231–7). It is therefore probable that Late Mesolithic influences from Ertebølle (Period III) also penetrated south along the coastal region of the North Sea, but that the sites dating from this period south of the 0-isobase of the Litorina strand-lines, which runs from North-West Jutland through the Island of Falstar (see Fig. 3, p. 10), have disappeared as a result of Post-Litorina sinking. In the Kiel Museum there is a collection of Ertebølle material from the Kiel and Flensburg Fjords, which has been discovered by dredging below present sea-level, and near Oldesloe in Schleswig-Holstein a typical kitchen-midden pot associated with antler and bone objects has been recovered from the bed of the Trave River (Lonke, 1935, p. 251). Thus it appears probable that the North European Forest cultures had a more extensive southern distribution than is indicated by the present evidence, and that the flake axes of Le Campigny were derived from this source. This contention is strengthened by the evidence of typology and distribution, for the forms are identical in both areas, and flake axes do not seem to occur in either Central or Southern Europe.

The source of the main elements at Le Campigny—pottery, agriculture and pit-dwellings—are very difficult to establish for the reason that the Neolithic in Western Europe has never been satisfactorily worked out. It is probable, however, that these traits are Danubian offshoots, which were modified by contact with the Cortaillod culture of the Swiss Lakes and the Michelsberg culture of Switzerland and the Rhine Valley (Hawkes, J.,

1936, p. 127).[1] Farther north a purer expression of Danubian I, locally known as Omalian, with shoe-last celts penetrated the Belgian province of Liége (De Puydt, 1909, pp. 23–4) and Southern Holland (Childe, 1929, pp. 58–9). In both cases the associated flint types are identical with those from Le Campigny; in fact, as Professor Childe points out, Spiennian or Campignian flints have actually been found overlying Omalian hearths.

The Campignian stone industry associated with the Neolithic of Western Europe is almost impossible to trace to its place of origin on the basis of typological comparisons. Its distribution covers an area stretching from North Germany and Poland (Kosłowski, 1926, p. 65) to the Near East (Neuville, 1930), and includes Italy, Slovakia, Hungary, Transylvania, Russia and the Urals (Menghin, 1931, pp. 211–15). Picks, which are always associated with the Campignian, are considered to be hoes by Professor Menghin (1931, p. 213), and indeed this suggestion seems extremely likely if one admits agriculture as a component of this complex. In Western Europe Campignian picks are generally considered to be flint-mining tools, but as the edges are quite fresh on most specimens, it seems unlikely that this is always the case. In the flint mines themselves antlers were commonly used for this purpose (Piggott and Clark, 1933, pp. 4–5); moreover flint and stone picks are not restricted to the flint-mining regions. It therefore seems likely that at least some of the Campignian picks are in reality hoes, and that certain features of the complex represent manifestations of the Neolithic civilization of Europe. This as a whole was ultimately inspired from the early centre of the development of food producing located somewhere in the Near East. On the periphery of Western Europe new elements, such as the flake axe, were adopted from the indigenous Mesolithic inhabitants whose food-gathering communities were disbanded by the invasion of the newcomers. Following this line of approach it is impossible at the moment to be more definite.

The above survey is by no means exhaustive, but one fact seems to be firmly established: the term Campignian must be considered obsolete with reference to a chronological stage; whatever else it is the Campignian is not

[1] Professor Childe (1939, p. 288) assigns Le Campigny to the same Western Neolithic complex as Camp de Chassey (Saône-et-Loire), Fort Harrouard (Eure-et-Loire) and Michelsberg (Baden). Following Professor Menghin (1931, p. 401), Childe (1939, p. 272) has recently suggested that this complex, to which the Neolithic of the Swiss Lakes also belongs, is derived from North Africa and spread northward via the Iberian Peninsula and around the Pyrenees. This, however, throws no light on the question of the origin of the flint and stone industry (Campignian) with which the culture as a whole is associated in Western Europe.

Late Mesolithic or Proto-Neolithic. Nor is the Campignian itself a culture, and hence strictly speaking it cannot be considered Neolithic. Although the main roots of the Campignian are Mesolithic, the real development began in Neolithic times. The situation is further complicated by the fact that the Campignian technique persisted well into the Metal Age, especially in the rich flint regions of Northern France, South-East England and North-East Ireland. As it does not seem desirable to abandon the term, it may as well be retained but given a more precise definition. Thus it seems to the writer that the Campignian represents a basic substratum or heritage from the Mesolithic which forms an important and highly specialized aspect of those Western European cultures which continued to use flint and stone tools after the introduction of agriculture. It is an important component of the Western Neolithic culture but not until after this had been introduced into the area under discussion, and the change of economy from food gathering to food production had been effected by the diffusion of new ideas and by the movement of new peoples into Europe. In France and Britain the Western Neolithic is well documented, and the relationship of the Campignian to the higher culture is clear. In Ireland, however, no well-defined Neolithic of pure Western European origin has been recognized as yet. Nevertheless the occurrence of Windmill Hill pottery and other elements of "western" origin at several stations associated with Campignian tools may be regarded as indicating a peripheral development of the Western Neolithic in this region during Post-Larnian times. At the Irish sites of Glenarm, Cushendun and Rough Island, where stratigraphic association with the Litorina raised beach has been demonstrated, the second half of the third millennium B.C. seems a likely date for the arrival of this new influence in Counties Antrim and Down.

4. THE BANN CULTURE

The Bann culture arose when some of the Mesolithic occupants of the coast of North-East Ireland penetrated the interior with the advent of the Post-Larnian immigrants from Western Europe, who settled in the favourable lowlands bordering on the North Channel.[1] The main centre of this new

[1] It is possible that a Late Mesolithic development, comparable to the Late Larnian and the forerunner of the Bann culture, will eventually come to light in the Lower Bann Valley. But present evidence strongly suggests that the main Late Mesolithic settlements were along the coasts, and that the uplands of County Antrim as well as the valley itself were not intensively occupied until after the regression of the Litorina Sea. In spite of the fact that one Early Larnian site of the Boreal Period exists on Lough Neagh (see pp. 117–20, and p. 174), there is no proof that this region was reinhabited until Late Atlantic–Early Sub-Boreal times. Furthermore, as discussed on p. 251, the basic roots of the Bann culture lie in the Late Larnian of the coast.

development was in the valley of the Lower Bann River, which separates Counties Antrim and Londonderry and flows north from Lough Neagh to the Atlantic Ocean some 4 miles below Coleraine. Almost as far as Kilrea the valley is broad and flat and is covered by a deposit of diatomaceous earth which extends on both banks to an average depth of 3 to 4 feet, the maximum depth being 6 feet. In places it is overlain by a thick layer of peat and rests for the most part on peat averaging 2 to 3 feet in thickness. Under the lower peat is a fine grey sand below which are deposits of glacial origin. Since 1857 (see bibliography, p. 318) this region has been known to collectors as a prolific area for Stone Age antiquities. Until 1927, however, when Dr G. Erdtman examined the peat below the diatomite from a palaeobotanical point of view (1928, pp. 162–3), no conclusions regarding the age of the deposit had been reached, and no thorough geological or archaeological work had been done. In 1934 the Harvard Archaeological Expedition to Ireland excavated an area 30 feet square at Newferry, County Londonderry (Fig. 15, p. 110), in the meadow adjoining the outlet of the Bann from Lough Beg (Movius, 1936). At this point the surface of the ground is approximately 60 feet above O.D., and the top of the diatomite 7 feet 3 inches above the surface of the water in the lough. The following section was established (Plate VI):

(A) Modern Surface Accumulation	23 cm.
(B) Humus	22 cm.
(C) Diatomite	89 cm.
(D) Mixed Ash Deposit (Archaeological Horizon)	14 cm.
(E) Lacustrine Silt	15 cm.
(F) Peat (Jessen's Layers F and G)	82 cm.
(G) Sand (Jessen's Layers H and J)	Thickness undetermined

(A) MODERN SURFACE ACCUMULATION. This consists of small angular lumps of white diatomite, which has accumulated as a result of commercial activities on the site.

(B) HUMUS. On top of the diatomite occurs a deposit of greyish-brown clay representing the original surface of the section.

(C) DIATOMITE. The diatomite, a clear fresh-water deposit, is a dull bluish-grey colour with a brownish tinge. It dries almost a pure white, and is either exploited commercially as insulator material or mixed with clay and used locally for the manufacture of bricks. It is composed of silica and contains little or no sand. One of the commonest diatoms in this deposit is

NEWFERRY, COUNTY LONDONDERRY

Upper General view of the excavated site.

Lower Section through the deposits, showing two large hearths associated with Deposit D and projecting into the base of the Diatomite.

Tabellaria fenestrata, a plankton species dominant at the present day in Lough Neagh and Lough Beg. This fact indicates that former conditions must have been very similar to those prevailing at present in the shallow waters of the valley. The occurrence of numerous hearths actually stratified in this deposit, as well as the existence of the culture layer (Deposit D), gives

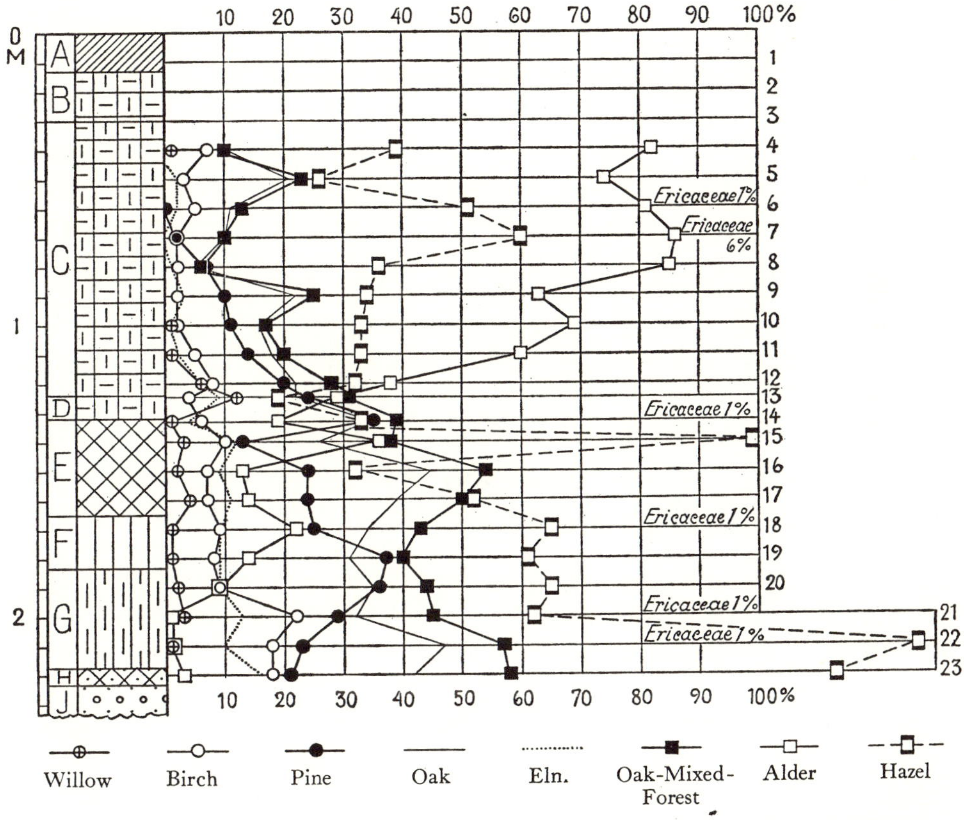

Fig. 54. Pollen Diagram from the Excavated Site at Newferry, County Londonderry. The Zone border V/VI falls at Sample 21. (After Jessen.)

further evidence for the manner in which the diatomite formation took place, and compels the conclusion that great areas of the valley have lain dry during certain seasons of the year. This must have been in the summer when the river would have followed confined channels. During the other seasons the water from Lough Beg flooded the area, and only at this time were the conditions for the sedimentation of the diatomite created. According to the pollen diagram (Fig. 54) this deposit was formed during Sub-Boreal times

(Jessen, 1936, p. 36); it may be assigned to the upper part of Zone VI in Ireland (Jessen, 1938, with Farrington, p. 256).

(D) Mixed Ash Deposit. The main archaeological horizon, of which a detailed description has been given elsewhere (Movius, 1936, pp. 21–2), occurs in this deposit. Palaeobotanically the age is Late Atlantic–Early Sub-Boreal, or subsequent to the maximum of the Litorina submergence of the coast. Thus the Bann culture may be placed in the upper part of Zone VI, as Professor Jessen points out (with Farrington, 1938, p. 256); the pollen spectrum reveals a rise in the Pine and Alder curves, and a corresponding decrease in the curves for Hazel and the Oak-Mixed-Forest. Fluctuating lacustrine conditions are indicated by the nature of this deposit, which is composed of stratified bands of coarse and fine grey sand, peaty material, silt and diatomite, between which much ash and charcoal (Willow, Alder and Oak) are found.

(E) Lacustrine Silt. This thin layer suggests a slight rise of the water-level which led to the deposition of a true lake mud or silt on top of the peat (Deposit F).

(F) Peat. Abundant remains of *Phragmites communis* (Common Reed) and *Cladium mariscus* (Prickly Twig-Rush) suggest that Deposit F was formed in a very shallow lake, presumably a branch of Lough Neagh, of which Lough Beg may be considered the last remnant. The upper 18 cm. (Jessen's layer F) are somewhat stratified, but yielded no archaeological material. At sample 21, which was taken in the middle of the lower part of this deposit (Jessen's layer G) the zone border (V/VI) has been established (Jessen, 1938, with Farrington, p. 256). Therefore, the peat and the overlying lacustrine silt may be assigned to the Late Atlantic Period in Ireland and are synchronous with the maximum of the Litorina submergence on the coast.

(G) Sand. The surface of this deposit corresponds in height with the water-level in the lake. It is a dark grey-blue, rather fine, sub-angular sand, evidently a lacustrine deposit, and in it a few small natural flints occur.

It is evident, from the facts relating to the archaeological horizon and to the overlying diatomite, that the site could only have been in use during the dry summer period when the lake level was low. In the wet season the region was covered with water which dispersed the ashes forming the culture layer and laid down lacustrine deposits. These fluctuating conditions prevailed throughout the entire period of diatomite formation, as proved by the hearths found up to within 39 cm. of the surface of this deposit, and by the occurrence of thin bands of peat as high as 14 cm. below the top. Furthermore, the site never served as a place of permanent habitation, as (*a*) no trace of any construction whatsoever was found; (*b*) for a settlement site

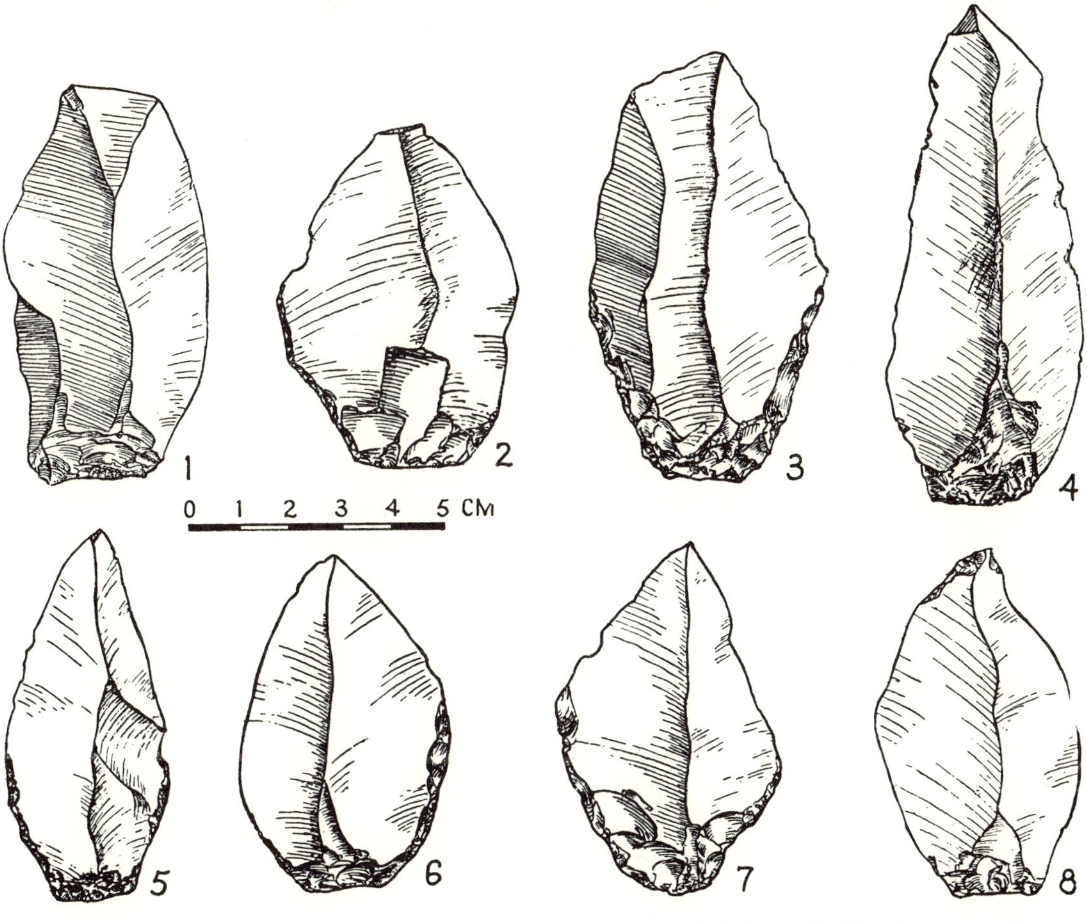

Fig. 55. Flint Implements typical of the Bann Culture from the Sub-Diatomite Hearths excavated at Newferry, County Londonderry. Scale: 2/3.

there are too many contemporary hearths concentrated in a very small area; and (*c*) in spite of perfect conditions for preservation no refuse of any sort occurs. A total of 198 blade implements of flint was found in the excavated area, and these display a uniform light chestnut-brown patination. All the blades have plain unretouched striking platforms; in most cases the upper surface of the bulbar end has been chipped in an effort to reduce the thickness, presumably for hafting. Leaf-shaped points (Fig. 55, nos. 1–8) are characteristic of the culture. Usually either one or the other, or both sides of the blade are retouched for approximately one-third of the distance towards the point, which may be regarded as a tendency to produce a sort of tang (compare Fig. 55, no. 7). At the excavated site, however, no well-defined tanged types were found.

Clusters or group finds of unworked primary flakes are common. In Deposit D three clusters consisting of up to six blades came to light, and in the vicinity of Toome a similar find of ten blades has been recorded by Whelan (1930[*b*]). It is possible that these clusters may be rough blades brought to the site from a workshop for manufacture into implements, but it is more likely that several of them were hafted together to form some sort of multi-pronged fishing implement. Such implements made of iron were used until recently in the region for spearing eels (Movius, 1936, p. 24), and there is an example of one from the Bann Valley in the collection of the National Museum, Dublin.[1] Nevertheless, hoards or group finds of unworked flakes are known. One containing 164 flakes accompanied by a worked pebble was discovered near a former strand-line of Lough Beg (Parker, 1938); it seems probable that this is a case of raw material which had been brought to the valley for manufacture into implements, as flint is not found in the immediate vicinity. Nearby, however, there is an abundant supply, since flint is found on Slieve Gallion (Stanford's, 1913, p. 173) and near Maghera (*M.G.S.* Ireland, 1882, p. 11), both in County Londonderry. Its good quality is attested by the excellent workmanship displayed by the implements, which represent a very advanced flint technique.

In addition to leaf-shaped points with superficially tanged butts, the excavated site yielded several boring or reaming tools (Fig. 56, no. 1) with inverse retouching, a few long tapering points (Fig. 56, no. 5), carinated implements of triangular section (Fig. 56, no. 4), one short thick scraper with steep sides (Fig. 56, no. 2), and a small rough disc-shaped scraper (Fig. 56, no. 3). These implements are all of flint. The stone types include: three petaloid celts made of polished basalt (Fig. 56, nos. 6–8), several sharpening stones (Fig. 56, no. 9) and one stone polisher made of lithomarge. Although not actually found at the excavation, the sherds of a nearly complete bowl (Fig. 57) were recovered from the base of the diatomite

[1] Multi-pronged eel-spears of iron have also been found in Early Christian crannogs at Strokestown, County Roscommon (Wood-Martin, 1886, p. 144, and Pl. XXXVI, Nos. 1 and 2).

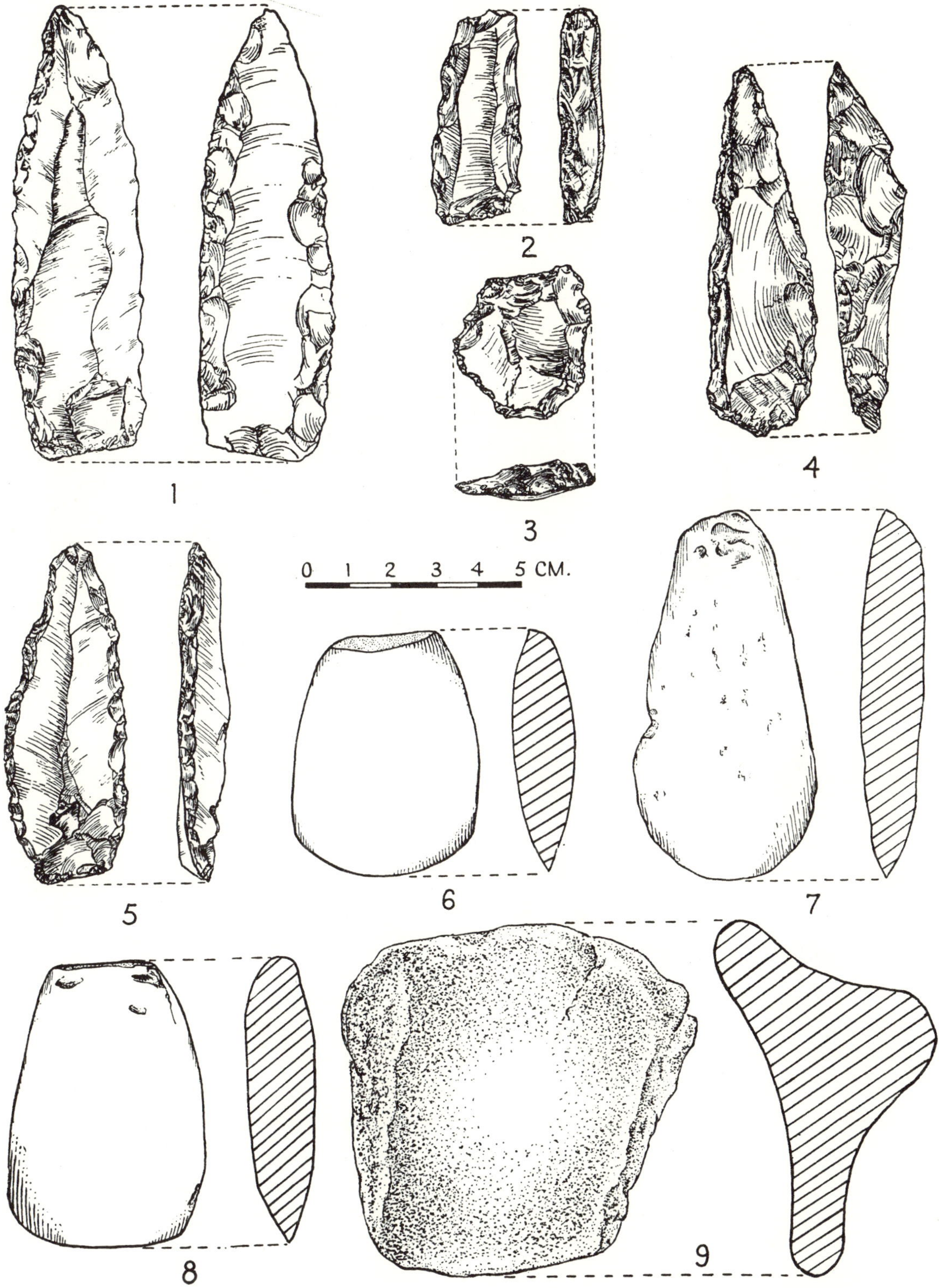

Fig. 56. Flint and Stone Implements typical of the Bann Culture from the Sub-Diatomite Hearths excavated at Newferry, County Londonderry. Scale: 2/3.

in the immediate vicinity. These were associated with a large hearth yielding flints identical with those described above. The horizon of the pottery is definite, therefore, and it is of great importance in demonstrating the affinities of the Bann culture.

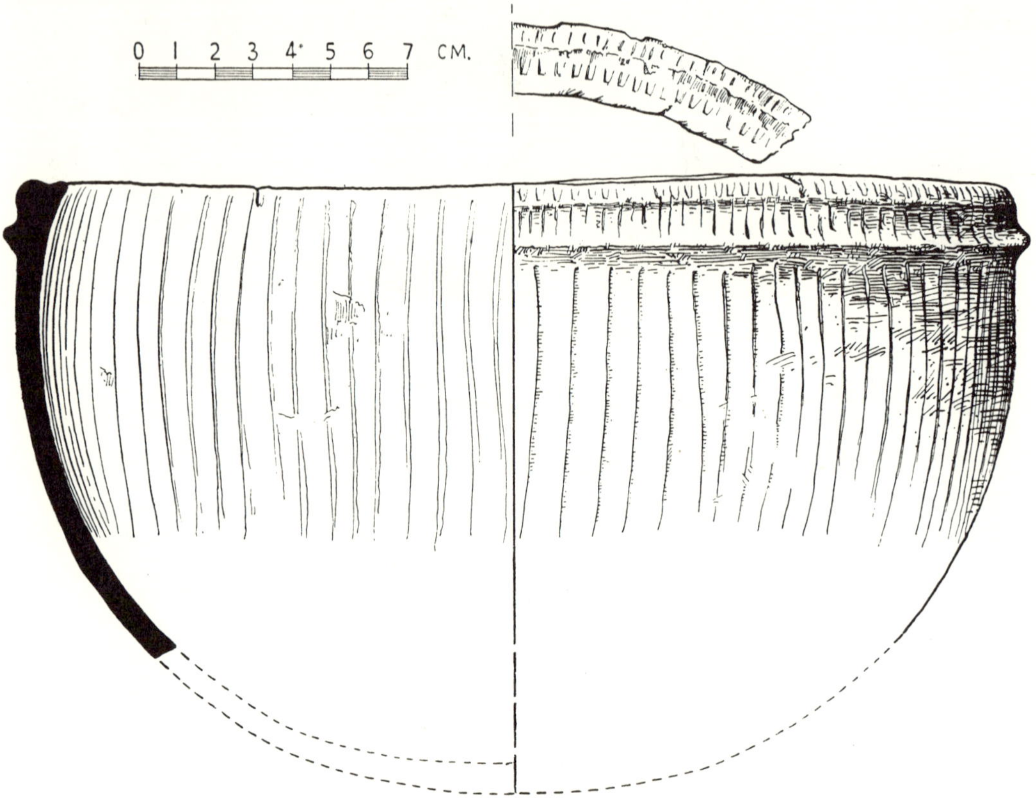

Fig. 57. Neolithic Pot from the Base of the Diatomite at Newferry, County Londonderry. Scale: ½.

According to Professor Childe (1936, pp. 37–40), the vessel had an internal diameter of 12·5 cm. at the mouth. No sherds belonging unambiguously to the base were recovered, but the surviving contour points definitely to a rounded base. A reconstruction on this assumption would give a vessel 15·8 cm. high. The rim is thickened and flat on top. It is definitely incurved and has been flattened downward and outward in order to leave a groove just outside the lip. Approximately 1·2 cm. below the rim a narrow horizontal moulding about 4 mm. high has been applied. This

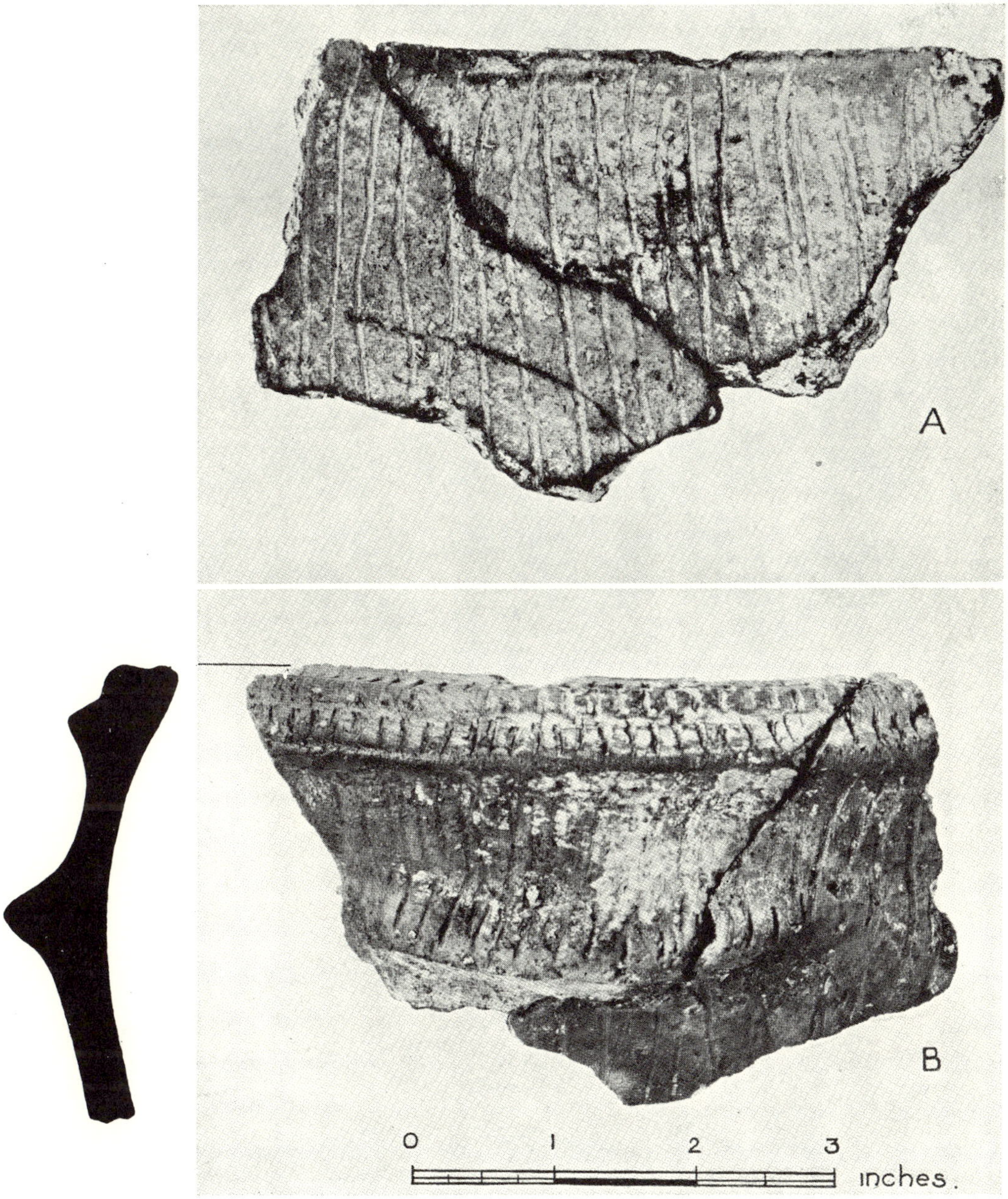

NEWFERRY, COUNTY LONDONDERRY

Sherds from the base of the Diatomite: A, interior; B, exterior showing horizontal lug. Scale: $\frac{3}{4}$.

encircles the exterior of the vessel. Below this a broad flat lug (described by Mr Whelan, 1936, p. 39) projects horizontally (Pl. VII), and apparently another occurred opposite this, but it has not survived. The rim is decorated by deep oblique jabs made with a rough, slightly tapering, narrow, square-ended implement, almost certainly of wood. These are arranged in three rows—on the slightly concave top of the rim, on its outer edge, and between the rim and the moulding. Both the interior and the exterior below the moulding are incised with irregularly spaced vertical or radial strokes or scorings, probably executed with the same implement. These are more lightly applied, and more irregular on the inside. They descend only to a vertical depth of 8·5 cm. below the rim on both interior and exterior of the vessel.

The moulding below the rim is not paralleled in England, but analogies exist among the sherds from Eilean an Tighe, North Uist, in Scotland (Childe, 1936, p. 39), which is closely allied to the Unstan class of Orkney and Caithness. This Scottish group of ceramics is confined to the areas in which passage graves occur (Childe, 1935, p. 67); in Ireland a few sherds of Unstan type published by Childe (1935[*a*]) from Carn R2 at Loughcrew (Slieve na Cailllighe) are, therefore, not without significance, as this site is likewise a passage grave. Mrs Hawkes has recently pointed out (1938, p. 150) that the Unstan bowls decorated with the stab-and-drag, as opposed to the channelled (Beacharra) technique, have affinities with Iberia and Brittany. Thus the Neolithic pottery from Newferry is of extreme importance in that it indicates the presence of a Megalithic influence on the development of the Bann culture.

Whereas the site excavated in 1934 provided important dating evidence, only a small range of the total implement series is illustrated by the material recovered. However, leaf- and lozenge-shaped arrowheads (Fig. 58, nos. 9 and 10), perforators, well-developed tanged points often with inverse retouch (Fig. 58, nos. 1–5), picks, flake axes or *tranchets* (Fig. 58, no. 6), large stone axes, and small spiky points with *dos rabattu* trimming also occur in the diatomite which overlies the main archaeological horizon in the Lower Bann Valley. In the same region lanceolate spear points (Fig. 58, no. 7) have been reported; one found in the bog at Derrytagh North on the southern end of Lough Neagh is referable on palaeobotanical evidence to the Early Sub-Boreal Period (Jessen, 1936, p. 36). The perforated stone battle-axe (Fig. 58, no. 8) was dredged from the bed of the Bann at Kilrea, County Londonderry (Hawkes, C., 1937), and although an undated find, can

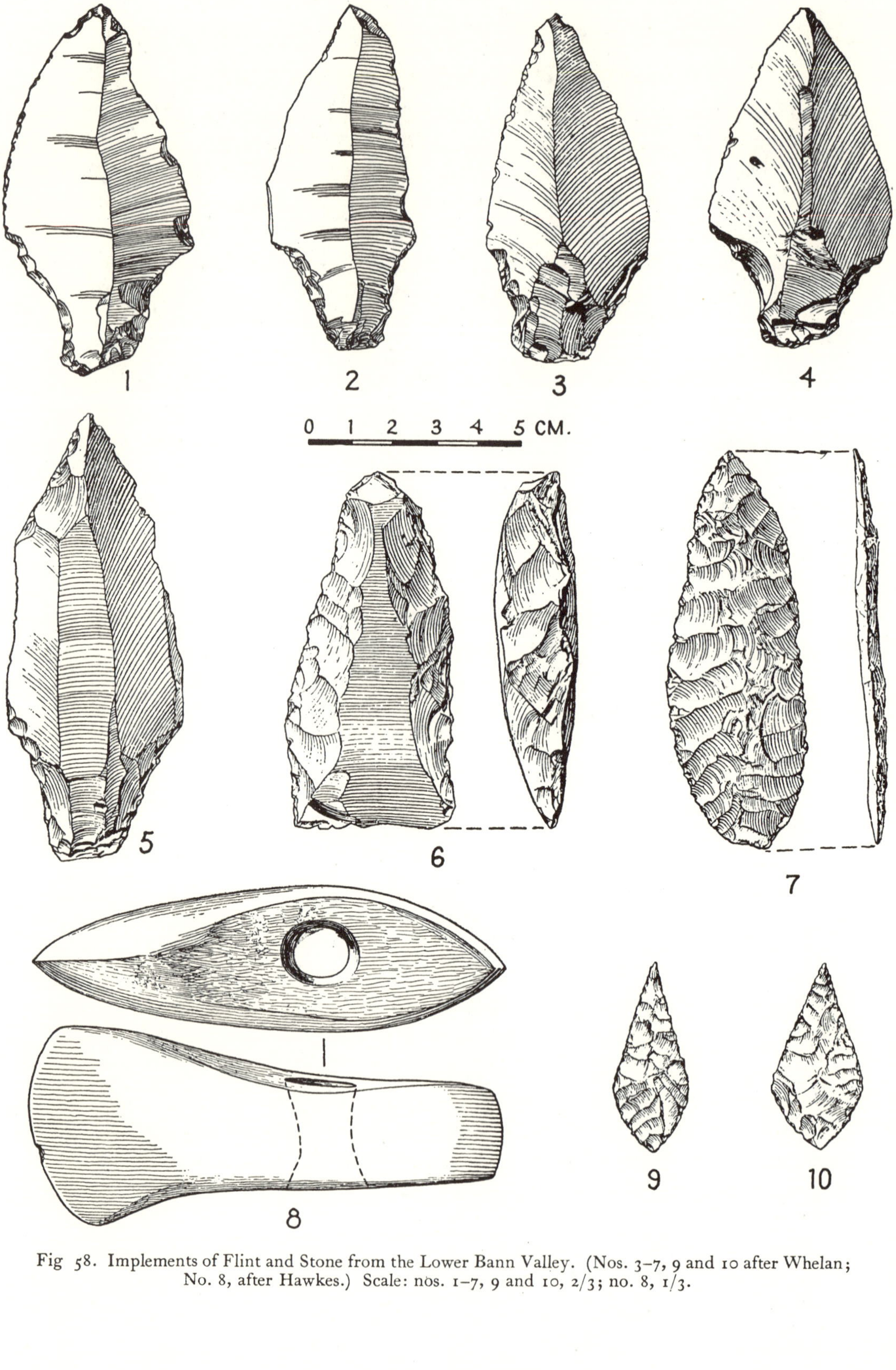

Fig 58. Implements of Flint and Stone from the Lower Bann Valley. (Nos. 3–7, 9 and 10 after Whelan; No. 8, after Hawkes.) Scale: nos. 1–7, 9 and 10, 2/3; no. 8, 1/3.

probably be regarded as forming part of the Bann complex. This specimen is of interest, since, as pointed out by Hawkes, the governing idea in its development is an antler prototype with the blade at the broad end. Recently several group finds of rather heavy bone points 3 to 8 inches long, most of which were dredged from the Bann in the vicinity of Coleraine, County Antrim, have been reported (May, 1939). Although dating evidence is lacking, these finds were associated with flint implements similar to those from the subdiatomite hearths at Newferry. May suggests (1939, p. 155) that, as the points occurred in clusters in the bed of the river, they perhaps formed entrance guides for wooden traps used in fishing. But as pliable wood would be infinitely more effective for this purpose, it seems more likely that they were hafted and used as multi-pronged eel spears, similar to the Early Christian and modern examples mentioned on p. 244. On this basis both flint and bone appear to have been used in this region during prehistoric times for the same purpose. Picks and flake axes from the Bann are of flint or basalt (Knowles, 1912, pp. 206–8), and they are similar to examples from Tievebulliagh and other coastal Campignian sites. Parallels also exist with Ballynagard on Rathlin Island. From the latter site a triangular polished stone axe with sawn edges has been published (Whelan, 1932, p. 96, Fig. 3), which is identical with one from the diatomite at Culbane, County Londonderry (Jackson, 1909, p. 12 and Pl. III, no. 7). The small spiky points with *dos rabattu* trimming (Knowles, 1912, p. 202; Batty, 1938) have parallels in the Early Larnian of Cushendun and Rough Island (Fig. 23, nos. 1 and 2). Comparable forms are also known in Orkney (Lacaille, 1935[*a*]), but in neither the Bann Valley nor in Northern Scotland have these implements been definitely dated.

The large stone axes of the Bann are among the most extraordinary features of the Late Stone Age of Ireland. Possibly not all the finds are authentic, but at least two examples, both discovered by competent observers, are genuine. Knowles (1912, p. 214) found one specimen, almost 14 inches long, at Culbane below 2 feet of diatomite and standing upright; a second axe, 17 inches long, described by Jackson (1909, p. 12), is recorded as having come from a depth of 3 feet below the surface of this deposit. Axes up to 16 inches long are common, according to Knowles, and in the collection of Dr J. B. Stewart, Portglenone, County Antrim, recently published by Dr Mahr (1937, p. 294, and Pl. XX), there is one 28 inches in length. However, this find is undocumented. The typical forms are round to oval in section and sharp at one end. They are ground all over and are of a hard clay slate. As they weigh up to 20 pounds and over, it is difficult to regard them as either cutting implements or stone clubs, although the latter do occur in the Bann complex (compare O'Laverty, 1857). They seem, instead, more like some sort of ceremonial objects, which were introduced by the megalith builders. Supporting evidence for this explanation is forthcoming from Brittany, where considerable numbers of large, pointed-butted, greenstone axes occur in Southern Morbihan (Forde, 1930, p. 86). Often these are found in hoards, but several examples have been recorded in association with large closed chambers, passage dolmens and galleries. Three examples, illustrated by Professor Forde (1930, Fig. 34) from Mané-er-Hröek, are over 15 inches long, and are very similar in type to the Irish examples. These have connections with Iberia, as large specimens of similar form are known from Algarve in Southern Portugal, as well as from El Garcel and Los Millares in the south-eastern portion of the peninsula (Forde, 1930). It is not improbable that the Irish, Breton and Iberian examples are to be connected with some sort of an "axe cult", since sculptured figures of axes occur in many of the French dolmens and burial caves of the Neolithic and Early Bronze Age Periods (MacCurdy, 1916, pp. 311–13). We must therefore reject Professor Mahr's theory that the large stone axes of the Bann are in reality clubs, and that they indicate a "Riverford culture". Indeed whether or not any such thing as "Riverford culture" exists in Ireland cannot be proved; certainly the Bann complex is an entity of its own, not as yet demonstrably related to the material dredged from the Shannon and other rivers in Éire.

As revealed by the Newferry excavation, the major occupation of the people responsible for the Bann culture appears to have been fishing. Thus the hearths, only available during the dry summer season when the lake waters receded, are probably the remains of smudge fires for smoking and drying fish, and the tanged or partially tanged blades would have served as points for fish spears. We are therefore dealing primarily with a typical food-gathering complex, since these people repaired to the same site many years in succession for fishing. These hearths rested on lacustrine silts, and it has been established that they may be assigned to the upper part of Zone VI in Ireland, which is Early Sub-Boreal in terms of the Continental climatic sequence. This evidence suggests the end of the third millennium B.C. for the beginning of the main Bann development.

The Bann culture has recently been reported from twenty-one surface stations on the Isle of Man (Clark, 1935, pp. 74–5), but no satisfactory stratigraphy is present. Tanged points, often with inverse retouch, and identical with those from Ireland, occur, but Dr Clark states that at the two most important Manx stations—Cronk y Chule and Kirkill (shown on the map, Fig. 15, p. 110)—the association of the Bann culture with Tardenoisean forms is not altogether clear. In Man pottery and polished stone are not represented at the tanged point sites, a fact which suggests that a direct invasion of Mesolithic people occurred from the Irish coast before the indigenous inland development of this culture began in Ireland. Clark favours the view that the Baltic was the ultimate centre of diffusion of the tanged point tradition (Clark, 1936[*d*], p. 243), but the Irish evidence makes it seem almost certain that we are dealing here with a case of convergence. In spite of the strong typological similarity which exists, it is not at all necessary to invoke a connection with the Pre-Boreal tanged point cultures of the Baltic, nor with the coastal Fosna and Komsa cultures of Norway, which probably persisted into Bronze Age times (Clark, 1936, pp. 66–73) for the origins of this form. Such a connection was originally suggested by Mr H. J. E. Peake and Professor H. J. Fleure (1927, pp. 105–14, 118 and Fig. 65*b* and *c*), and it was accepted in Ireland (Whelan, 1933[*a*], p. 150; 1934, 1938), but in the light of present knowledge this view is no longer tenable. One has only to turn instead to the Larnian culture of the Litorina raised beaches of Ireland to find prototypes for the fully developed Bann points. In all cases—Cushendun, Glenarm, Larne and Rough Island—leaf-shaped points with trimmed butts exist in the Late Larnian, evidently evolved from the earlier phase. These persist throughout the Campignian industries of the coast; in fact a true tanged point occurs in Horizon 2 (Neolithic) at Rough Island (Fig. 48, no. 2), which is very similar to examples from the Bann. Whereas the flake axes and picks are of Campignian derivation, the pottery and large stone axes are directly traceable to the Megalithic civilization, as demonstrated by the fact that both are found in megalithic tombs in Brittany and Iberia. The obvious conclusion is that the Bann culture was developed by the indigenous Mesolithic survivors, who were pushed inland by invading Late Stone Age groups and persisted in a basic food-gathering economy. However, they were strongly influenced by, and probably even mixed with, the more powerful food-producing newcomers, as well as being in receipt of Megalithic ideas. As suggested by Dr Evans and Miss Gaffikin (1935,

p. 245), it is probable that sooner or later these people learned the new art of crop cultivation. Nevertheless, this inland fishing culture maintained the earlier coastal tradition in an almost purer form than did the sand-hill sites of Northern Ireland. In the case of the latter, the Mesolithic tradition seems to have persisted longer, but it is probable that more absorption took place.

5. THE SAND HILLS

The sand-hill settlements of Northern Ireland, which have an extensive distribution and which are found in the sand-dune regions of the coast, are open-air camp sites. They are characterized by one or more "black layers", composed of ashes, charcoal, shells, implements and other refuse of everyday life separated by sterile layers of sand. A few caves yielding material of similar type have been investigated (Jackson, 1933, p. 233; 1934, p. 108; 1936[*a*], pp. 32–6; 1938, p. 112; May, A., 1934). Of the numerous localities recorded (see p. 318 for bibliography), the most important ones are open stations at Maghera, County Donegal (D'Evelyn, 1933); Portstewart, County Londonderry (Knowles, 1879, 1879[*a*]; Coffey and Praeger, 1904, pp. 195–8); White Park Bay, County Antrim (Knowles, 1885; Davison, Orr, Stelfox and Stendall, 1927); and Dundrum Bay, County Down (Knowles, 1881, 1898). Southward along the coast they gradually fade out, the main concentration being in the north and north-west (Knowles, 1889, 1891, 1895, 1901; Brunicardi, 1914; Ó'Ríordáin, 1935, pp. 183–7; Hewson, 1935, 1936). In the west and the south a considerable number have been reported, but they are not so numerous (Brunicardi, 1914, map facing p. 185) and very few have been thoroughly investigated except in Counties Galway (Knowles, Patterson, Praeger and Bigger, 1899) and Clare (Knowles, 1901, p. 335). Contact with Campignian, Megalithic, Bronze and Iron Age, in addition to Early Christian sources, is proved by the frequent occurrence of picks, flake axes, arrowheads of the hollow-based and tanged varieties (Whelan, 1928, p. 188; 1932; 1938, p. 135; May, R., 1939), pottery (Knowles, 1895, pp. 659–61; 1901, pp. 384–8; Hassé, 1890, 1894; Buick, 1891, pp. 440–2; Coffey and Praeger, 1904, p. 197; D'Evelyn, 1933, p. 98; Hewson, 1936, pp. 161–72) and bronze pins and brooches (Knowles, 1891, p. 621; 1901, p. 387; Hassé, 1890; D'Evelyn, 1933, p. 98; Ó'Ríordáin, 1935, pp. 184–5). Furthermore, glass beads are very common and several of the dumb-bell type (Knowles, 1894, p. 245;

Hassé, 1890, p. 131), which are likewise of Early Christian type in Ireland (Hencken, 1938, p. 40), have been reported from a few localities. One tracked stone was found at Dundrum, County Down (Knowles, 1888, p. 500), of identical form to a series dated to the first century A.D. in Scotland (Childe, 1936[*a*]). The Reverend G. R. Buick (1891) and Mr L. Hassé (1894) were firmly of the opinion that the sand hills were occupied as late as the Early Christian Period, as demonstrated by material which they excavated in the "black layer" at many sites. Nevertheless, in spite of the overwhelming mass of data favouring this contention, Mr Knowles (1894) bitterly criticized his colleagues and stated that all the metal and glass as well as much of the pottery could be dismissed on the grounds that these objects were "chance finds". In Mr Knowles' opinion all the sand hills were Neolithic and represented not only a Late Stone Age culture in a pure form but also a definite chronological stage of development—a view which in reality is a half-truth. The culture is basically Stone Age, but it survived until absorption took place during the Early Christian Period, as Buick (1891), Hassé (1894), Coffey and Praeger (1904, p. 191), and recently Ó'Ríordáin (1935, pp. 183–4) have contended. Associated with the assemblage enumerated above there occur: bones of domestic animals, implements of antler and bone, beautifully made hollow scrapers (Knowles, 1894[*a*]) of a type commonly found in the Megalithic tombs of Northern Ireland, small thumb-nail scrapers and various blades, points, side scrapers, etc., which in a few instances, as at White Park Bay, have been made on reworked Larnian flakes (Mahr, 1937, p. 337). Certain of the antler implements are of interest. Knowles (1885, p. 119, Pl. IX, Fig. 91) records a perforated antler hammer 7½ inches long, and made from the basal portion of a Red Deer's antler. This specimen is from the "black layer" at White Park Bay.[1] It is strikingly like Mesolithic examples of the Baltic and, except for its blunt end, to the antler axes from the Carse of Stirling in Scotland (see p. 192) as well. Since Forest culture influences reached Ireland via Scotland during Atlantic times (Movius, 1940, pp. 72–3), the antler hammer from White Park Bay unquestionably represents a survival of the Mesolithic tradition which is only too apparent when other aspects of the sand hills are considered. As suggested on p. 247, the perforated stone

[1] Mr A. D. Lacaille has kindly informed the writer that in the Knowles Collection at the Wellcome Historical Medical Museum, London, there are two similar antler implements, perforated in the best Baltic manner, both from "the black layer at White Park Bay". The larger measures 18 cm. by 7·5 cm. and the smaller, actually a tine, 10·3 cm. by 2·5 cm.

battle-axe dredged from the Bann at Kilrea was probably derived from a similar antler implement which had a sharp rather than a blunt end.

The very scanty evidence available at present indicates that the sand hills played an almost completely negative role with regard to the actual development of the Late Stone Age in Ireland. During Late Stone Age times as well as in the later periods the inhabitants of these sites seem to have been recipients rather than contributors of material culture traits. But before any definite statements can be made the whole complex must be systematically studied, as Professor Mahr (1937, p. 336) has emphasized. Unfortunately almost nothing approaching stratigraphy has been reported by the investigators of these interesting stations; the only site where a sequence was observed—White Park Bay (Davison, Orr *et al.* 1927)—is referable to the Bronze Age. It is therefore difficult to arrive at any very satisfactory conclusions concerning this phase of Irish archaeology. Nevertheless, one fact not likely to be seriously modified by future research may be deduced: no single chronological stage is represented by the sand hills. Whereas some sites are undoubtedly early (Neolithic, Megalithic or Early Bronze Age in date), as a group they suggest a continuum of Late Larnian tradition which was influenced by that particular culture which was dominant in the vicinity at any given time. In other words, a mode of life based primarily on food gathering persisted in regions of isolation, and in the sand-dune areas of the coast, in spite of contact with more advanced sources. Eventually absorption took place and the sand hills were no longer occupied; whether this occurred before these people had commenced the actual practice of agriculture cannot be determined on the basis of present evidence. In any case the heritage of the Old Stone Age seems to have been perpetuated in Ireland at least as late as the beginning of the Christian Era.

6. SUMMARY

The data discussed above are shown diagrammatically on the chart, Fig. 59. It has been demonstrated that a new influence from Western Europe penetrated Ireland prior to the beginning of the Bronze Age. The evidence also suggests that more or less simultaneously a new culture, ultimately of Mediterranean origin, was introduced from the south-west, but there is no proof as to which if either was the earlier. The Western European elements came from France via Britain. In Ireland they represent a peripheral development of the Western Neolithic, a culture whose associated flint and stone industries may be regarded as forming a Mesolithic tradition known as the Campignian. Many stations in Counties Antrim and Down, some of which directly overlie Larnian deposits, have yielded implements of Campignian type—material which is distinctive as compared with the earlier series. Whereas in

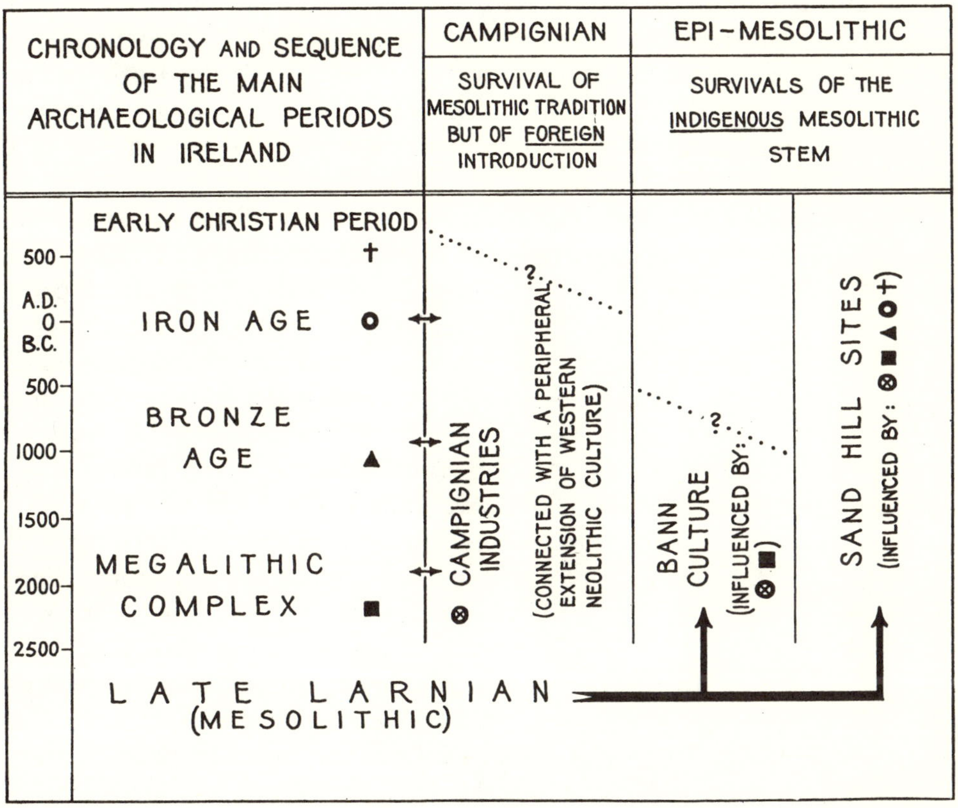

Fig. 59. Chart showing the Post-Larnian Developments in Ireland and their Relationship (indicated by symbols and arrows) to the Megalithic and Metal Age Cultures during the Sub-Boreal and Early Sub-Atlantic Periods.

England and on the Continent the practice of mining flint is an important component of the Campignian, in Ireland this was not necessary, as an almost inexhaustible supply was readily available in the Cretaceous limestone of the north-east coast. Doubtless this fact attracted the newcomers, as attested by the numerous workshops and two centres of axe manufacture which have thus far been discovered. Very few settlement sites may be assigned to this phase: Ballynagard, Rathlin Island (an occupation layer containing Neolithic A pottery sealed below a sterile clay deposit), Cushendun (hearth in Deposit A superimposed on the raised beach), and Dunmurry (an open hearth associated with flint implements and Neolithic A pottery), but future research should amplify the meagre list. Since the flint technique introduced at this time persisted well into the Metal Age, absolute dating of the Irish sites is difficult. Nevertheless, the evidence from the coastal stations, where Campignian material is found directly overlying the Litorina raised beach, proves that the new elements arrived when the emergence was well under way; this suggests an approximate dating of the second half of the third millennium B.C.

Perhaps the most striking fact revealed by a study of the Post-Mesolithic Period in Ireland is that cultures based on food gathering survived as late as Early Christian times, although strongly modified as a result of contact with more advanced groups. In this regard the cultural evidence supports Dr Coon's conclusions (1939, pp. 376–84), based on anthropometric data collected by Wesley Dupertius of the Harvard Irish Survey, that in the west and south-west of Ireland to-day the predominant racial type is of Upper Palaeolithic ancestry. As Professor Hooton suggests (1940, p. 248; 1940 [*a*], pp. 171–2), these people are apparently the descendants of the original settlers who came into Ireland during Early Post-Glacial times and developed the Larnian culture. At the beginning of the Sub-Boreal Period they were driven from the fertile coastal lowlands of Counties Antrim and Down to refuge areas in the interior and along the sandy waste lands of the coast (see p. 208). In the Lower Bann Valley a culture based primarily on the Late Mesolithic of the coast, but possessing elements of both Campignian and Megalithic origin, was evolved. In spite of the fact that it is also found in the Isle of Man, the Bann culture is distinctively Irish and represents an indigenous development free of direct Baltic influence, although subject to the same Megalithic contacts which are common to both regions. In the sand-dune areas of the coasts of Northern and Western Ireland, Larnian survivors clung on to a basically food-gathering economy until the Early Christian Period. As proved by the collections from the sand hills, this coastal complex is not indicative of any given cultural stage; furthermore, no new contributions emanated from this source.

Chapter V

CONCLUSIONS

Throughout Part II of this book an attempt has been made to show that the Stone Age cultures of Ireland can be neither correctly interpreted nor properly understood except in terms of the natural surroundings to which they were adapted. It seems evident that the prehistorian can no longer deal in the abstract with humanity and fail to connect material culture traits with the environment in which they were produced. As Tallgren has stated (1937, p. 159), culture must be regarded as a product of man and not of nature. It is only when the sum total of the evidence is examined and synthesized that it is possible to offer an interpretation, since cultures, whether prehistoric or modern, cannot be dealt with as dead groups of fossils but must be treated as living functioning organisms. In other words, the archaeologist must regard traits functionally and not fall into the pitfall of the typologist, who observes them as isolated abstractions. An attempt should be made to demonstrate why tools were evolved, what they were used for, whether and how they were hafted, and to study them collectively, not only from a typological viewpoint, but also as artifacts made by man to assist him in his control over nature. By employing this approach Stone Age archaeology takes on a new and more comprehensive character, and falls in with the human sciences, disassociating itself from the more definitely subjective approach of the taxonomic disciplines. Research into various fields covered by the natural sciences whether taxonomic or not is, however, essential for the establishment of prehistoric cultures in their proper chronological perspective, and for providing the data for a reconstruction of the natural conditions pertaining at a given period. Nevertheless, for synthesizing this material and bringing the net results to bear on the problem of man's development archaeology stands alone.

In order to reconstruct the environment of early Ireland, it was necessary at the outset of Part I to review the evidence from Northern Europe, where the study of prehistory began over a century ago, and where a synthesis of scientific method has been brought to bear on archaeology, which has profoundly altered field technique. Although the facts relating to the Late-

Glacial and Early Post-Glacial Periods in Great Britain and Ireland are far less complete than in the Baltic, it was found that sufficient material already existed on which to base a tentative time correlation between the two areas. This is substantiated by archaeology, as the introduction of the Aurignacian culture into Western Europe fixes the lower limit, while the upper limit is dated to within a reasonable figure by the advent of the Neolithic. Likewise in Post-Glacial time the two areas have been subject to very similar geological changes, and these can be synchronized with a comparable climatic sequence, which has been established in both regions. During the last glaciation the temperature in the British Isles was lowered as a result of the general cooling effect of the Fennoscandian ice-sheet; at this period Northern and Western Europe must have had almost the same relationship as that which exists to-day between Greenland and Baffin Land. Whereas in Britain and Ireland the ice was far less extensive than in Scandinavia, direct exposure to Atlantic storms from the west resulted in the formation of snowfields of considerable magnitude, and a comparatively small but active ice-sheet, whose behaviour during the recession seems to have been a duplication of the established Scandinavian sequence. Geochronology has provided a reliable time-scale in the latter area, which makes it possible to estimate with reasonable certainty the earliest date when human settlement could have been effected in North-East Ireland. Up to the present, only one serious attempt has been made at Dunning, Perthshire, to date the varve clays of the British Isles with relation to Northern Europe, the results of which are in complete accord with our correlation. This method, applied more generally, should yield significant results, thereby establishing an absolute chronology for the retreat of the last ice-sheets. A start has also been made in Ireland, but there are as yet insufficient data to establish the age of the diagrams in terms of dated sequences elsewhere. In this connection the formation of a National Quaternary Research Committee in England to work on the problem of geochronology and Pleistocene correlations, as proposed by Hawkes (1937[*a*], pp. 52–5), would undoubtedly lead to conclusions of the utmost importance.

There is no proof as yet that Ireland was occupied before the Boreal Period. At this time the amelioration of the Early Post-Glacial climate and the rise to dominance and rapid spread of forest forms witnessed the first occupation of the area by a people of basically Upper Palaeolithic stock, reinforced by Early Mesolithic (Azilian) arrivals from Southern France and

Northern Spain.[1] The new conditions by their control over the climate and fauna played a leading part in the northward expansion of these food-gathering peoples. The rich flint area of North-East Ireland attracted the newcomers, and the regions of Counties Antrim and Down formed the focus of settlement. Based predominantly on Upper Palaeolithic tradition but with elements from the Azilian, a new Mesolithic culture developed in this area, and for it the name LARNIAN has been proposed. It is a strictly indigenous development, and, as it is entirely free of Tardenoisean influence (see p. 201), an early date for its first phase is indicated. The classic station, the site from which the Irish Mesolithic is named, is at Larne in County Antrim, but Cushendun some 25 miles farther north on the coast provides the key for the Mesolithic succession. The Larnian was evolved in an area isolated from the rest of Britain by the Highland Zone, which acted as a partial barrier to new influences,[2] and which formed together with South-West Scotland and North-West England a single province in Early Post-Glacial times. The fact that during the Boreal Period these regions were brought closer together by the existence of a nearly complete land-bridge led to homogeneity, and a true Epi-Palaeolithic complex existed in what may be termed a "cultural pool" on the very periphery of Western Europe. With the transgression of the Litorina Sea, however, independent development in Ireland and Scotland led to the Late Larnian on the one hand and the OBANIAN on the other, in spite of the proximity of the two areas and the existence of boats.

The distribution of Mesolithic sites in Great Britain and Ireland shows at a glance the peripheral retardation of new influences, as well as the importance of geographical factors in the spread of culture. During Early Post-Glacial time England and the Baltic formed one continuous area in which the Forest culture flourished: the Maglemosean hunters extended their activities from Denmark to East Anglia and the Yorkshire coast. At the same time Tardenoisean people invaded Britain from Belgium, occupying the open sandy areas and exposed regions of high altitudes. Their distribution reflects the fact that their equipment was adapted to open grasslands, and

[1] Direct connections with Iberia appear improbable. Although Azilian culture is well developed in Northern Spain, especially in the Cantabrian region, it seems likely that the Azilian influences which reached Britain early in the Post-Glacial Period came from France. In any case, as far as the Iberian Peninsula is concerned, the question of an influence from the Asturian being felt in Ireland during Mesolithic times must be ruled out (see pp. 205–6).

[2] Eventually both the Tardenoisean and the Maglemosean cultures penetrated the Highland Zone, but not until after the Larnian had become well established in the region of the North Channel (see pp. 201 and 209).

that they were unable to cope with forest conditions. After the inundation of the North Sea bed by the Litorina Sea in Late-Boreal–Early Atlantic times, England progressed in comparative independence of the Baltic. One Forest culture element—the core axe—was taken over by the Tardenoiseans, and it was developed into the "Thames Pick". In South-Eastern England the Lower Halstow culture evolved out of the Maglemosean, and this reveals the degree of divergence from the contemporary North European kitchen-middens of the Ertebølle phase that took place. At the same time the Maglemosean also spread north and reached Durham (West Hartlepool) and East Scotland (the Carse of Stirling) in Early Atlantic times. The only apparent external influence on the Larnian came from this source, as core axes occur sporadically in Irish Late Mesolithic deposits. For the bone implements of this period, we must rely on the Obanian of Scotland, since in the Litorina gravels of Counties Antrim and Down bone is only very occasionally preserved, and very few tools have thus far been discovered. The harpoons associated with the Obanian of Scotland are Azilian in type, but show strong influence from the Forest culture area. The tendency in the Late Larnian to develop heavy tools is also present in the Scottish Mesolithic and chisels or adzes of stone and bone possibly for working wood are also included in this food-gathering complex. Flint tools are rare because after the submergence the Irish supply was not available; an occasional micro-burin discloses a faint Tardenoisean influence. The Obanian was evolved therefore in relative isolation after the submergence, since at this time the sea extended far up the Scottish Midland Valley, and the country was separate from the rest of Britain except for a narrow isthmus. In the main the Tardenoisean sites are south of this line, but the finds at Banchory in the Dee Valley show how in the one region in the whole of Scotland where flint occurs in quantities of a tractable nature a Tardenoisean settlement was effected.

One of the most important points established by a study of the Early Larnian is that it is now possible to trace back, from the periphery in North-East Ireland to the centre of distribution in South England, those traits in contemporary industries which have their roots in the Upper Palaeolithic and to separate them from those which are innovations. It thus appears probable that the Early Tardenoisean "broad blade" industries of the Pennines were partly derived from the earlier Creswellian, suggesting that in this, as well as in other cases, the local variations revealed by intrusive cultures are undoubtedly often the result of survivals from older native elements. Furthermore, the well-established principles of diffusion are clearly substantiated by the distribution of Mesolithic settlements in England and Ireland. On the periphery influences arrived late, and, due to the proximity of the Continent, South-Eastern England was farther advanced than Ireland and Scotland, which, isolated by the Highland Zone of Britain, received new ideas at a later date.

Other factors, both climatological and geological, were operative, and, in so far as they affected either mode of life or facilities for movement, they must be considered by the archaeologist. These also were of importance in the diffusion of new ideas. Unless there was a definite need resulting from such a major cause as environmental conditions, traits would probably fail to diffuse. Or in the absence of suitable raw materials specialized developments might occur after the introduction of an idea by diffusion. In other cases where the changing conditions presented a definite need for a new type of implement and where diffusion was slow, special forms were developed; locally these often led to highly individualistic industries. In this way the Early Post-Glacial cultures seem to conform to a series of sloping horizons, the lower end of which is earlier in the time-scale, and nearer to the centre of origin, and the upper, or more retarded end, on the periphery. Thus, at the time of the Al'Ubaid culture in Mesopotamia, Ireland was still virtually in an evolved Upper Palaeolithic stage of development.

The principle of sloping horizons is further demonstrated by a study of certain Post-Larnian developments. During Early Sub-Boreal times two new influences, one from the south-west and the other from Western Europe, arrived in Ireland. The Megalithic culture, diffused from the south-western source, is of only indirect concern to the main subject-matter of this book. The other influence may be regarded as a peripheral development of the Western Neolithic complex, but is thus far principally documented in Counties Antrim and Down by surface stations which yield material of Campignian type. Now the Campignian has been defined as an industrial heritage from the Mesolithic of Northern and Western Europe; it represents a survival of an older tradition which persisted after the introduction of food producing as long as flint and stone continued in use. Nevertheless, it was fully developed in the Neolithic Period and is the stone and flint industry of the Western Neolithic complex. As far as Ireland is concerned the arrival of the Campignian seems to mark an invasion of new peoples: a few settlement sites are known which have been assigned to the Western Neolithic culture; the workshops and axe factories yield material which is thoroughly distinctive in comparison with a normal Larnian series.

As in earlier times, the North Channel was the line of approach used by the newcomers, who, possessing superior equipment, forced the Larnian food collectors inland and to the infertile sand dune areas of the coast, and occupied the rich flint region of Counties Antrim and Down. In addition to a new stone and flint technique, core axes were introduced for a second time, along with flake axes, pottery, and probably domestic animals as well as the rudiments of agriculture. Certain fine-grained rocks were apparently found to be superior to flint in the manufacture of axes, since at two localities the remains of great factory sites have been discovered. The date of the arrival of this complex cannot as yet be fixed with respect to the earliest megaliths, but at several sites it has been found directly overlying the Litorian raised beaches. This evidence suggests the second half of the third millennium B.C., when the emergence was well advanced, as the lower limit for its introduction; it survived into late prehistoric times.

The Larnian survivors persisted in an economy which was based on food gathering, although sooner or later they must have learned how to grow crops. Two Epi-Mesolithic cultures, both derived from the indigenous Mesolithic stem, have been recognized: the Bann culture and the culture of the Sand Hill sites. The Bann culture of the interior can be dated to the Early Sub-Boreal Period, but its precise upper limit is unknown. It was strongly influenced not only from Campignian centres along the coast but also by the Megalithic culture of the uplands. Petaloid celts, leaf- and lozenge-shaped arrowheads, large stone axes and a distinctive type of pottery came in from this latter (south-western) source, which diffused from the Mediterranean area via the Atlantic sea-board of Western Europe into the Irish Sea and as far as the Baltic, utilizing for the first time the direct oceanic route. The Epi-Mesolithic culture of the sand-hill sites survived until Early Christian times, although strongly modified by later introductions. The sand-hill dwellers themselves were recipients rather than contributors of new cultural traits. Strictly speaking, the objects from the sand hills, which have an extensive distribution in Northern Ireland and the north-western counties of Éire, are not representative of one homogeneous culture. Rather they are to be regarded collectively as a survival of the old food-gathering tradition which was brought under the influence of whatever higher culture was dominant in the region during a given period. Thus in insular isolation on the outermost periphery of Western Europe the doctrine of survival, which is so outstandingly applicable to the later periods, pertains with equal force to the original settlers.

Appendices I–VI

Appendix I

PART I: CHAPTER II, SECTION 3

THE RAISED BEACH OF THE THIRD INTERGLACIAL PERIOD

As mentioned in the text (see p. 29), a raised beach dating from the Third Interglacial (Riss-Würm) Period is found in Britain and Ireland south of a line shown on the map (Fig. 7, p. 58). In Ireland it extends from Achill Island, County Mayo[1] (Wright, 1934, p. 34; 1937, p. 120), down the west coast (Wright, 1911, p. 98; Charlesworth, 1930, p. 364), along the entire southern coast, where it is especially clearly defined in County Cork (Wright and Muff, 1904, pp. 274–300), on the east coast (Martin, 1930, pp. 500–6), in the Dublin area (Farrington, 1929, p. 169), and at Ardglass, Killough Bay, County Down (Charlesworth *et al.* 1935, p. 480; Martin, 1930). It is present in the Isle of Man (Wright, 1911, p. 98), Wales (George, 1932, p. 292; Jones, 1934, pp. 304–6), the south coast of England (Pengelly, 1867; Dewey, 1913; Jones, 1934, p. 307), with the exception of the Chalk region of Dover, and it appears again in Yorkshire (Wright, 1914, pp. 94 and 96). In the Channel Islands it is well marked, and at numerous localities along the coasts of Normandy and Brittany it has been identified (Wright, 1914, pp. 94–5), especially important sections existing in the vicinity of Calais (Day, 1866, p. 111).

In the Gower Peninsula of Southern Wales there are two raised beaches older than Würm—the Neritoides beach and the Patella beach (George, 1932, p. 317). The latter is older and is associated with a cold fauna, whilst the former may be correlated with the bone deposits at Minchen Hole, which have yielded warm interglacial forms. The Neritoides beach is overlain by Old Drift, which indicates that its age is probably Third Interglacial, although it may be older. Certainly a Third Interglacial dating is suggested by the fauna of Minchen Hole (compare Wheeler, 1925, p. 18; *B.R.G.*[*e*], p. 109), as well as by the fact that the Gower Peninsula was ice-free during the period of the New Drift Glaciation (George, 1933, p. 208). On the opposite side of the Bristol Channel the counterpart of the Neritoides beach has been identified at several localities (Day, 1866[*a*], p. 116; Palmer, 1931, pp. 346–52; *B.R.G.*[*c*], p. 85). In the Severn and Avon Valleys terraces occur at heights corresponding to these coastal marine platforms (Wills, 1938, pp. 232–3; Tomlinson, 1935, pp. 456–9). In Southern England, Ireland and Northern France, the Interglacial raised beach occurs at a fairly constant height of 10–12 feet above high-water level, although on the west coast of Ireland—Achill Island—it rises to 20 feet above the sea (Wright, 1937, p. 120), and in the Channel

1 This feature has not been recorded in County Sligo, although Wright (1937, Fig. 127, p. 369) shows the 0-isobase passing north of Sligo Bay.

Islands the same platform may occur at 25 feet above mean-tide level, according to information received from Dr Zeuner. In County Mayo, County Down, the Isle of Man, and Northern Yorkshire, however, it is only slightly above present high-water level. It seems probable that this Interglacial raised beach of Britain and Ireland is the equivalent of the Tyrrhenian phase of the Mediterranean Basin, assigned by Zeuner to the Riss-Würm Interglacial (1938[*a*], pp. 400–1). This phase was followed by the Flandrian transgression (Blanc, 1936, pp. 138–40; 1937, pp. 625–8), the three stages of which are synchronous with the Würm I, II and III stages of glaciation (Zeuner, 1938[*a*]).

Appendix II

PART I: CHAPTER II, SECTION 5

DEPOSITS OF THE INTERSTADIAL PERIOD BETWEEN THE OLD AND THE NEW DRIFT GLACIATIONS (W_1/W_2) IN ENGLAND AND SCOTLAND

During the period between the retreat of the Old Drift Ice-Sheets and the subsequent New Drift advance interstadial deposits were formed in Britain and Ireland. In many cases these consist only of sands and gravels which contain very few organic remains, but in addition peat and clay beds, yielding such valuable climatic indicators as pollen and molluscs, occur. "Interval" deposits of this period are known in East Anglia—at Ipswich and The Traveller's Rest Pit, Cambridge (Fig. 4, p. 35)—where interglacial soils overlie the Upper Chalky Boulder Clay (MacClintock, 1933, pp. 1047–9). In the north of England, in the Brampton district, Trotter and Hollingworth (*M.G.S.* England and Wales, 1932, p. 146) have established the presence of sands, gravels and laminated clays above the boulder clay of the Early Scottish Glaciation, and in Northumberland (Woolacott, 1921, p. 25) and West Yorkshire (Raistrick, 1933, p. 264) similar deposits are reported. The same is true of North-East Scotland (Bremner, 1934[*a*], p. 55), North-East Ireland (Dwerryhouse, 1923, p. 421) and the coastal portion of County Wicklow (Farrington, 1931, p. 218). In addition to these deposits there is along the coast of Eastern England from Norfolk to Durham abundant evidence demonstrating a marine transgression during the period under discussion (Harrison, 1935). This is known as the March-Nar submergence. At several localities important data have been secured. In the peat layer, Deposit 4, at Kirmington (Fig. 4, p. 35; for section see p. 31), Dr G. Erdtman has identified the following flora: *Alnus*, *Betula*, *Pinus*, *Picea*, *Quercus*, *Ulmus*, *Tilia*, *Ilex*, *Fraxinus* (?) and *Corylus*, indicating a temperate climate at the time of formation of this bed of no greater severity than that of Lincolnshire to-day (Burchell, 1935, p. 327). Overlying the peat, at a height of 70–80 feet above O.D., are silts and clays, Deposit 5, containing *Scrobicularia piperata*, *Rissoa ulvae*, *Tellina balthica*,

Cardium edule, Mactra subtruncata and *Mytilus edulis* in an undisturbed condition (Wright, 1937, p. 87). Thus during this period the sea transgressed this portion of the east coast, and since there is a layer of Hessle Boulder Clay above, these deposits must surely date from the interval between the Old and the New Drift. The Kirmington evidence is substantiated in County Durham. At Easington (Fig. 4, p. 35) a raised beach, 60 feet above present sea-level and containing a temperate marine fauna, has been recorded (Woolacott, 1922, p. 66; Trechmann, 1931); overlying the raised beach is a reassorted boulder clay the equivalent of the Hessle (Harrison, 1935, p. 258). In the Trent Valley, 3 miles south of Derby, river gravels of this period have yielded abundant remains of Hippopotamus, associated with *Elephas* sp., Rhinoceros, beetle and plant remains. These indicate a moist temperate climate (Arnold-Bembrose and Deeley, 1896, pp. 499–500), not unlike that inferred from the Kirmington peat (Harrison, 1937, p. 246). On the Norfolk coast, raised beach gravels at Morston (Fig. 4, p. 35) ± 20 feet above present sea-level, banked against the Cromer Ridge and overlaid by Hessle Boulder Clay (Solomon, 1932, p. 251), fix the southern limit to which these marine deposits have been traced in the region bordering on the North Sea. Inland there are extensive deposits at March, Cambridgeshire (Fig. 4, p. 35), showing that marine conditions pertained in the Fens during this Interstadial Period (Baden-Powell, 1934, pp. 194–5). Besides the molluscs listed above from Kirmington, Baden-Powell (1934, pp. 198–210) records the following as typical forms from March: *Tellina balthica, Tellina calcarea, Corbicula consobrina* (*fluminalis*), *Pholas dactylus, Ostrea edulis* (found also at Easington), *Cyprina islandica, Astarte borealis* and *Astarte montagui*. In addition *Littorina littorea, Littorina obtusata* and *Patella vulgata* are commonly found in the Easington beach (Woolacott, 1922). In the March area the foraminifera indicate no colder conditions than those of the present day, but the marine molluscs from the Cambridgeshire localities point to Southern Norway or Denmark for a modern climatic equivalent. The Upper Barnwell Village Beds, near Cambridge, which lie at a height of + 54 feet O.D. and which represent the fluviatile equivalent of the March-Nar submergence (Harrison, 1935, p. 258), have yielded the following fossils: *Elephas primigenius, Cervus elaphus* and *Cervus capreolus* (Marr, 1919, p. 222), and to this list *Bos* sp. and *Equus caballus*, recorded by Baden-Powell (1934, p. 211) from the March region, may be added.

The equivalent of this submergence is not recorded in the southern portion of the Irish Sea Basin. But it is probable that the lower cave earth at Victoria Cave, near Settle, Yorkshire (Fig. 4, p. 35), may be correlated with these interstadial deposits. *Hyaena, Canis vulpes, Ursus ferox, Ursus arctos, Elephas antiquus, Rhinoceros leptorhinus, Hippopotamus* (probably derived), *Cervus elaphus* and *Bos primigenius* have been identified from this layer (Garrod, 1926, p. 118). Indeed the overlying stratum of stiff grey clay containing laminated patches at various depths is stated by the excavators to be of glacial origin (*Rep. Brit. Ass.* 1873, p. 250).[1] Since the site lies within the area covered by the

[1] See also the following *Reports of the British Association for the Advancement of Science*: 1872, pp. 178 and 179; 1874, p. 133; 1875, p. 166; 1876, p. 115; 1877, p. 215; and 1878, p. 377.

New Drift Ice-Sheets, and since in the vicinity there is abundant evidence of extensive and severe glaciation, the bone layer presumably belongs to the Interstadial Period (W_1/W_2), although some of the bones are undoubtedly derived. In Scotland a marked recession of the ice is demonstrated by the deposits which occur between the Early Scottish Glaciation (Old Drift) and the next glacial episode. To this period the fossiliferous beds at Kilmaurs, near Kilmarnock, Ayrshire, and Cadder, Dumbartonshire, shown in Fig. 4, p. 35, have been assigned (McCallien, 1937, p. 184). The former locality at Woodhill Quarry, 90 feet above sea-level, was discovered in 1816. The following section is based on J. Bryce (1865, p. 216), Young and Craig (1869, pp. 313–19) and the *Memoirs of the Geological Survey of Scotland* (1930, pp. 325–30):

7. Surface Soil	—
6. Upper Drift	20 ft.
5. Reddish-Brown Boulder Clay	16 ft.
4. Coarse Sand	6–18 in.
A marine deposit which contains shells (*Pecten islandicus*, *Tellina calcarea* and *Leda oblongata*), as well as foraminifera and ostracods indicating Arctic conditions	
3. Fine Dark-Blue Clay	9 in.
A freshwater deposit, probably laid down at the mouth of a river; it contains the remains of Mammoth and Reindeer, plants (*Potamogeton*, *Ranunculus* and *Hippuris*), in addition to the beetle (*Notiophilus aquaticus*)	
2. Hard Gravel and Clay	2 ft.
1. Carboniferous Sandstone	—

There seems to be little question that the glacial beds (Nos. 5 and 6) are deposits of the New Drift Glaciation. On the basis of the evidence of the coarse sand layer (Bed 4), it appears probable that preceding this advance of the ice an Arctic sea invaded this part of Ayrshire, and that it reached a height in excess of 100 feet at this locality (*M.G.S.* Scotland, 1930, p. 329). The underlying clay (Bed 3) is of freshwater origin; it contains a cold fauna and flora, and the beetle remains point to moist conditions. Bed 2 probably represents an old land surface. According to Young and Craig (1869, pp. 315–16) interstadial deposits, similar to those recorded at Woodhill Quarry, have an extensive distribution in the vicinity of Kilmaurs. The above section is also important in that it proves the appearance of Mammoth and Reindeer in Scotland during the period under discussion. Woolly Rhinoceros (*Rhinoceros antiquitatis*), very scarce in Scotland, has been identified from interstadial beds overlain by New Drift deposits at Cadder, just north of Glasgow (Swinton, 1927, p. 395). At a third Scottish locality, Cowdon Burn, Ayrshire (Fig. 4, p. 35), lacustrine sediments up to 60 feet thick intercalated between two boulder clays and containing sand, fine gravel, clay and peat, have yielded abundant remains (*M.G.S.* Scotland, 1930, pp. 330–1). These include: *Bos primigenius*, *Cervus megaceros*,[1] *Cervus elaphus*, *Equus caballus*, diatoms, beetle remains, ostracods, mosses, sedges and leaves; at Croftamie, near the Cowdon Burn site, *Rangifer tarandus* has been found (Gregory, 1927, p. 372). From the peat, which varies from 6 inches to 2 feet thick, *Betula alba*, *Salix alba*, *Calluna vulgaris*, *Pinus sylvestris*, in addition to twenty-seven other plants and trees, have been identified. To this list may be added *Corylus*, known from an interstadial clay bed at Beith, Ayrshire (*M.G.S.* Scotland, 1930, p. 332), as well as *Betula nana*, described by Dunlop (1888, p. 314) from a contorted peat layer 17 inches thick at Airdrie, Lanark. The Airdrie peat occurs between two boulder clays; it has yielded insects and mosses, but tree remains are stated to be almost completely absent, according to Dunlop (1888, pp. 313–14). At Chappel Hall, near Airdrie, marine shells, including *Tellina calcarea* and *Cyprina islandica*, have been reported from a layer of fine clay between two boulder clays (Crosskey, 1865, p. 220), and hence is presumably of the same interstadial period as the contorted peat bed. This affords further proof of a transgression of the sea, but unfortunately the elevation of the marine clay at Airdrie is not recorded.

In Eastern Scotland, Campbell (1934) has described an extremely important section in the Burn of Benholm, Kincardineshire (Fig. 4, p. 35). Here a deposit of peat was found above the basal grey (Old Drift) boulder clay, which is associated with dark shelly drift (see p. 28), and this is overlain in turn by the red boulder clay of the New Drift or Strathmore Ice-Sheet. The peat is sometimes contorted up to 6 inches thick, and indicative of marshy conditions (Campbell, 1934[*a*]). Pollen analysis reveals that *Pinus* and *Betula* are the most important forest forms—*Pinus* being dominant (up to 60–80 per cent) in the lower layer, whereas the situation is reversed in the upper part of the section, where *Betula* yields values of over 60 per cent. In addition "*Alnus* and *Quercus* occur throughout the profile, and in the upper layers *Ulmus* and *Corylus* are also found" (Campbell, 1934[*a*], p. 314). The above evidence from Eastern Scotland strongly favours the view that the ice had receded into the Highlands at this stage, and that the equable, temperate conditions of a cool Interstadial Period prevailed along this portion of the coast. Derived peat, found at two places in the moraines of the Strathmore (New Drift) Ice-Sheet in the Aberdeen District (Bremner, 1934, p. 18), affords further proof that the ice must have retreated well into the Highland Valleys during the period under consideration.

[1] Gregory and Currie (1928, p. 18) state that Irish Elk (*Cervus megaceros*) is absent at this site, and that the bones of Red Deer (*Cervus elaphus*) were incorrectly identified as "Elk".

Appendix III

PART I: CHAPTER II, SECTION 6

THE NEW DRIFT GLACIATION

The end-moraine of the New Drift Glaciation, as described by Charlesworth (1929, pp. 335–7), seems to be essentially correct (compare Wright, 1937, pp. 93–4). It is known as the "York Line", and its most southerly link is on the north coast of Norfolk where the ice was not sufficiently powerful to override the earlier Cromer Ridge deposits (Solomon, 1932, p. 269). The line continues north of the Wash to the south end of the Lincolnshire Wolds, and flanks the eastern slopes of the Wolds to the Humber at South Ferriby. From the plain north of Holderness it extends near the eastern side of the York Wolds into the Vale of Pickering, and thence to York, where it is clearly defined by a double terminal moraine at York and Escrick (MacClintock, 1933, p. 1042). Thus oscillations occurred along the ice-front during this glaciation, which probably explains the gravel band intervening between the Upper and Lower Hessle Clays near Hull, described by Bisat (1933, p. 441), since, at the type section, interstadial deposits underlie the Hessle Clays. Marginal phenomena are likewise apparent in the Cleveland Hills, which were unglaciated during this period (Kendall, 1902, pp. 498–513), as well as in the Vale of York (Edwards, 1937, p. 103). In both these regions huge ice-dammed lakes were formed as a result of the blocking of the mouth of the Humber by Hessle Ice under pressure from Scandinavian Ice in the North Sea (compare *B.R.G.* [*h*], pp. 70–1). In the Pennines the local ice-sheets were strongly influenced by glaciers from Western England which extended through the valleys and across the chain as far as the eastern lowlands (Raistrick, 1931; 1933[*a*], p. 199). In Nidderdale one of these glaciers met the Vale of York Ice near Ripley (Tillotson, 1933, p. 233). At the time of the maximum advance of the New Drift Glaciation, the extent of the ice in the Pennine Valleys is marked by lateral moraines developed in the eastern part of the region; the flow was roughly radial from a centre over the Mallerstang area (Raistrick, 1933, p. 264). In Airedale and Wharfedale there are well-defined moraines, but the southern extension of the Pennines was apparently unglaciated at this stage. On the west side of the chain the margin of the New Drift has been followed around the Rossendale Uplands (Jowett, 1914, p. 212), and south of Rossendale it adjoins the western slopes of the Southern Pennines (Charlesworth and Jowett, 1929, p. 316). Irish Sea Ice occupied part of Northern Wales (*B.R.G.* [*f*], pp. 81–2) and most of the Cheshire and Shropshire Basin, according to Wright, extending into Eastern Staffordshire, north-west of Wolverhampton (*B.R.G.* [*g*], pp. 78–80), and as far south as the Ironbridge Gorge in the Upper Severn Valley (*M.G.S.* England and Wales, 1928, pp. 186–99; Wills, 1937, p. 995). Here the line swings westward to Marton Pool, near Montgomery; thence south to Hereford it has been followed by Dwerryhouse and Miller (1930, p. 125), and from there to Usk,

Monmouthshire, its course is given by Pocock and Whitehead (*B.R.G.* [*d*], p. 75). Whereas there is much detailed work still to be done on the remaining 200 miles in Southern Wales as far as the Irish Sea, the limits of the New Drift as shown on the map, Fig. 6, p. 52, seem to be essentially correct (compare Charlesworth, 1929, pp. 338–49; George, 1933, p. 208; Griffiths, 1939; *B.R.G.* [*e*], pp. 103–7). In the Severn Valley it is possible that this stage, known as the Welsh Readvance (Wills, 1937, p. 1039), and correlated with the Worcester Terrace—no. 5 in the Severn sequence (Wills, 1938, p. 206)—is the age of the New Drift Glaciation. As discussed on p. 281, however, the evidence for the date of the Welsh Readvance is not conclusive. On the basis that terrace no. 1 in the Avon Valley is probably Post-Glacial, Avon Terrace no. 2 (Tomlinson, 1935, pp. 443 and 459) seems to be the equivalent of the Worcester stage in the Severn, but this area was not glaciated by the last ice-sheet.

In Wales (Charlesworth, 1929) the moraines, which are so conspicuous a feature connected with this glaciation elsewhere in Britain and Ireland, are poorly developed. Marginal drainage features give the only clue as to the former position of the ice-front. At the maximum the nine principal local Welsh Glaciers were confluent; these, together with the Irish Sea Ice which covered Cardigan Bay and invaded the coastal portions of Cardigan and Pembroke from Fishguard to Aberystwyth, were the source of the ice in this region (compare Jehu, 1904). Everywhere the heavily weathered Old Drift lies outside the area of the New Drift (Charlesworth, 1929, pp. 349–50; George, 1933; Griffiths, 1939). From Usk the ice-front passes southward through Cardiff, then goes westward to Swansea, pursues a sinuous line northward to Aberystwyth, via Tregaron, and becomes confluent with the Irish Sea Ice on the Cardiganshire coast (Charlesworth, 1929, Pl. XXI; *B.R.G.* [*e*], Fig. 27, p. 104).

In Northern England the deposits of the last main ice-advance, Episode 2 (see p. 31), are the equivalent of the Hessle Boulder Clay of Yorkshire, the Cheviot and Western Clays of Northumberland and Durham, and the clays of the Main Glaciation in the Lake District and adjoining areas (Trotter and Hollingworth, 1932, p. 376). The main centres of ice-dispersal were the Southern Uplands of Scotland and the Tweed-Cheviot area (*B.R.G.* [*i*], p. 67); Irish Sea Ice invaded the western section, whereas Highland Ice from the Firth of Forth was an important component on the east coast (Woolacott, 1921, p. 26). At the time of maximum advance the Lake District Ice was deflected into an easterly stream which flowed into Northumberland and Durham via the Tyne Valley and the Stainmore Gap, and a westerly stream which flowed into the Solway Basin after establishing contact with ice from the Southern Uplands (Hollingworth, 1931, p. 292). In addition the Southern Uplands Ice-Sheet was confluent with the large glacier which moved east across the northern end of the Pennine Chain (Dwerryhouse, 1902, p. 606). This major easterly flow was maintained to a point near the coast, where the presence of Scandinavian Ice in the North Sea, together with the pressure from Cheviot Ice on the north, diverted the composite glacier and caused it to move southward (Woolacott, 1921, p. 26). Thus had it not been for the influence exerted by the North European Ice-Sheet on the British Ice, it is very unlikely that the east coasts of Yorkshire and Lincolnshire and the north coast of Norfolk would have been glaciated (compare Fig. 6, p. 52). During this stage the local Pennine Ice was sufficiently strong to keep the ice from Northern England from invading the area (Raistrick, 1933, p. 264).

The most important centre of ice-dispersal in Britain and Ireland during Late-Glacial times was in the Scottish Highlands. Factors connected with wind direction and precipitation in this region caused the ice-centre to be situated somewhat east of the present watershed and the ice, which attained a maximum thickness of ± 3000 feet, covered the entire area, leaving only the highest peaks as unglaciated nunataks (*B.R.G.* [*n*], p. 91). Another important centre of ice-dispersal lay in the Southern Uplands of Scotland (*B.R.G.* [*j*], p. 89), and the Midland Valley was invaded from this as well as from the Highland source (*B.R.G.* [*k*], p. 82). This glaciation is referred to by some geologists as the stage of confluent glaciers (*B.R.G.* [*n*], p. 94). In Western Ross-shire this ice moved in a general north-westerly direction (*B.R.G.* [*n*], p. 91), which is confirmed by the evidence in Mull, Skye, Colonsay, Islay (*B.R.G.* [*m*], p. 110), and the Outer Hebrides (Jehu and Craig, 1926, p. 487; 1933, p. 868). In addition to the ice from the mainland, there was local ice in Mull and Skye which altered the course of the powerful Highland Ice-Sheet. It seems probable that this stage in Western Scotland and the Hebrides is the equivalent of the Strathmore Glaciation of Eastern and Northern Scotland (*B.R.G.* [*n*], p. 92).

The course of the Strathmore Ice-Sheet, whose centre was south of the Moray in the Central Highlands, is marked by deposits of red boulder clay (Bremner, 1934 [*a*], pp. 50–1). Whereas the earlier ice-sheet in this region was actually confluent with the Scandinavian Ice on the east and consequently moved from north to south (see p. 32), during this later glacial stage the two were not in direct contact. Rather the Scandinavian Ice advanced only to a line off the coast and strongly influenced the direction of the local ice-flow in such a way that the path of the earlier glaciation was reversed (Fig. 6, p. 52), and the Strathmore Ice moved from south to north, crossing the Moray and extending into Caithness as proved by the distribution of "shelly" drift containing a marine fauna on the Caithness Plain (Bremner, 1934, p. 18). This northerly movement in Northern and Eastern Scotland is proved not only by striae, but also by erratics from the Ochil Hills (between Stirling and Perth) which are found as far north as the Orkneys, and by shelly boulder clay from the Moray Basin found in Sutherland and Caithness (Bremner, 1934 [*a*], pp. 51–2). The relation of these deposits is shown at Leavad, near Thurso (Tait, 1909, 1910); it is apparent that the north-westerly moving ice in this region is an extension of the Strathmore Ice-Sheet of the east coast (*B.R.G.* [*n*], p. 91). In the Burn of Benholm, Kincardineshire, the Red Strathmore Boulder Clay containing southern erratics overlies the peat layer described on p. 269, and the evidence from this locality, together with Bremner's detailed work (1915, 1920 and 1934 [*c*]) on the east coast, makes it possible to follow with accuracy the extent of this glaciation.

In North-East Ireland the Scottish Ice from the Firth of Clyde was not as powerful as it was during the Old Drift Glaciation. It deployed as far as the extreme north-eastern tip of County Donegal and swept over the major portions of Counties Antrim and Down as far as the valley of the Main River (Dwerryhouse, 1923, p. 420). Many sections exist such as the one south of Newtownbreda, County Down, given by Dwerryhouse (1923, p. 397), which clearly show the relationship of the Old Drift with Scottish and northern erratics, and the New Drift with slate and grit from County Tyrone. During the earlier period the direction of ice-flow was from the north-east, whereas later, when the Ivernian Ice extended east to Scarva, County Down, it was from the north-west (Charlesworth *et al.* 1935, p. 482; Charlesworth, 1939, pp. 256–60). At the time of the New Drift Glaciation the Scottish Ice reached the sea at Newcastle, County Down (Dwerryhouse, 1923, Fig. 13, p. 420), and in the south it formed the northern component of the Irish Sea Ice invading a narrow strip of the eastern seaboard of the Central Plain. South of Dublin it advanced upon the coastal plain of Counties Wicklow and Wexford. The extent of the main ice-advance during this period in Ireland has been established by Professor Charlesworth (1928). In general the line (Fig. 5, p. 42) begins near Wexford, follows the east coast around the northern flank of the Wicklow Hills and the southern outskirts of the City of Dublin and continues from there to Baltinglass, County Wicklow. In the Dublin region it attains its maximum elevation, 1250–1275 feet O.D. (Charlesworth, 1928, pp. 295–300, compare Farrington, 1939, pp. 340–1). From Baltinglass it continues south across Counties Carlow and Kilkenny to the Slieve Ardagh Hills; it then curves west to County Tipperary, and thence to the north face of the Galtee Mountains. Sweeping across the Glen of Aherlow to County Limerick, it runs on west to Newcastle. Near Ardagh it comes against the hills and rises 300–400 feet O.D., but its elevation steadily decreases westward. On the south side of the Shannon River it swings west as far as the vicinity of Ballylongford, while north of the Shannon it runs via Kilrush and Kilkee, in County Clare, to the coast.

Appendix IV

PART I: CHAPTER II, SECTION 8

THE RECESSION OF THE LAST ICE-SHEETS

At the time of the maximum advance of the last ice-sheets, minor oscillations occurred along the margin of the ice-front, as shown by the York and Escrick moraines and the overriding of sands and gravels by boulder clay near Hull, mentioned on p. 270. According to Charlesworth (1928, pp. 295–300) this also happened in Ireland. The melt-water escaped via the principal river valleys, into which flowed streams heavily loaded with sediments. The material was ultimately discharged in the form of outwash fans and trains, spread over the valleys, and subsequently carved into terraces and redeposited by Late-Glacial and Early Post-Glacial rivers. Marginal drainage channels and other recessional phenomena existed everywhere along the edge of the waning ice. In many cases the melt-water was impounded and extra-glacial lakes formed, but it would be impossible to describe these within the limits of the present book. The reader, especially if he be interested in investigating the possibility of establishing a geochronological time-scale for the recession, is referred to the bibliography where innumerable exposures of Late-Glacial laminated or varved clays are recorded. Similarly the writer does not intend to discuss minor stages in the recession established in many areas; these were formed during the early stages of the recession when the ice began to melt. As the melting advanced the retreat was accelerated, but it was not a steadily progressive withdrawal. Instead it was interrupted by prolonged halts and periods of readvance which are of great importance for purposes of chronology. Only the major stages, therefore, which broke up the recession into several clearly defined periods, are of immediate concern.

In Ireland, when actual retreat began, the Irish Sea Ice withdrew northwards in such a way that its western edge curved over the coastal plain and out to sea (Charlesworth, 1937, pp. 32–4). West of the Wicklow Hills, which acted as a pivot for the melting Ivernian Ice, the sinuous margin fell away in a series of tangential curves, and the moraines, which are festooned between Wicklow and the west coast, show clearly the early history of the ice-retreat in this area (Charlesworth, 1928, p. 326). In the Central Plains extensive eskers and large wall-like moraines, formed during the period of retreat, occur in great numbers. The distribution of these recessional features clearly shows that the most important centre of ice-dispersal was in North-West Ireland. On the northern portion of the east central coast, in Counties Meath and Louth, an almost moraineless tract exists, so that it is impossible to establish the mode of separation of the Irish Sea and Ivernian Ice in this area, according to Charlesworth (1928, p. 337). The few small moraines that do exist indicate that the ice withdrew from here at an early period. The moraines of the Carlingford Readvance, recently identified by Charlesworth (1939, pp. 267–72), have been drawn on the map (Fig. 6, p. 52). The position of these, with respect to the line marking the limit of the Scottish and Ivernian Ice in Ireland during the New Drift Glaciation, suggests that they represent a well-defined oscillation at an early stage of the retreat. But until the southern extent of this readvance is traced, it is not possible to determine its precise position in the Late-Glacial sequence. Nevertheless, the fact that the chief component of the Carlingford Glacier was ice from North-West Ireland indicates that this oscillation occurred soon after the maximum of the last advance, when the Ivernian Ice in this region was still very powerful. Possibly the solution to this problem will be revealed by the varved clays. Those counted by Charlesworth in Silent Valley (1939, p. 270; see Fig. 9, p. 66) cover a period of 120 years, and display a considerable variation in thickness. When diagrams from other parts of the country are available, comparisons of the curves may show the exact age of the Carlingford Readvance regarding the dissolution of the New Drift Ice-Sheets.

The first halt in the retreat was in the northern part of the Central Plain, where a complex system of drumlins, eskers and moraines occur. At first these appear to be chaotic, but Charlesworth's careful mapping (1928, Pl. XXIII) has revealed that the ice was at this time deployed in three confluent lobes which issued from the mountains of

Counties Donegal, Leitrim and Galway, respectively, as shown in Fig. 6. The general line of this tripartite division stretches with marked sinuousity from Virginia, Kells and Navan in County Meath to Kinnegad, County Kildare, Tyrrellspass, County Westmeath, the Shannon Valley north-west of Cloghan, County Offaly, and thence to the head of Galway Bay (Charlesworth, 1928, pp. 337–41). In places, especially around Enfield and Navan, County Meath, the eskers, ridges and moraines form a belt over 10 miles wide, and the lakes of the Central Plain are a result of these features. In the western part of County Meath, Charlesworth has found evidence suggesting that the Central Plains Moraines are probably the produce of a readvance of the ice.

During the recession of the ice from Northern England the major directions of retreat appear to have been towards the north and west (Raistrick, 1931, pp. 286–9). In Lancaster a westerly recession has been traced by Charlesworth and Jowett (1929, pp. 316–34), and a similar phenomenon is recorded in the Pennine region south of the River Tyne (Raistrick 1933[*a*], pp. 207–11). At this time the Pennine Ice split off from the Northern Ice and it receded up the Pennine Valleys. On the east coast the movement was north, and the stages in the retreat of the Hessle Ice have been described by Raistrick (1933[*a*], p. 212). The first ice to leave Durham and Northumberland was that from South-West Scotland and following this the Cheviot Ice withdrew to the north and west (Woolacott, 1921, pp. 27–9); it split off from the Lake District–Southern Uplands Glacier from south to north (Trotter and Hollingworth, 1932, p. 376). This glacier retreated to the west, and the complex series of recessional stages of the Lake District Ice in Western Edenside have been mapped by Hollingworth (1931, pp. 302–56). In the Brampton district (*M.G.S.* England and Wales, 1932, pp. 147–8) the north-westerly retreat of the Southern Uplands Ice is clearly defined by drainage pattern and the extensive drumlins formed on the Carlisle Plain (see also Trotter, 1929, pp. 550–600). Details of the recession in South-Western Cumberland and the bipartition of the Irish Sea and Lake District Ice-Sheets have been worked out by Bernard Smith (1932, pp. 60–74). It seems evident that the Scandinavian Ice withdrew from the vicinity of the North Sea coast of Britain at this time, since its influence was not felt on the local ice during subsequent stages of glaciation.

The retreat stage described above represents part of Episode 2 in the Late-Glacial sequence of Northern England (see p. 31), and at this time sands, gravels and lacustrine sediments were deposited along the front of the melting ice. Following its withdrawal from this area, however, the ice from the Southern Uplands of Scotland readvanced on to the Carlisle Plain and laid down an upper boulder clay on top of these marginal accumulations. This is Episode 3, or the Scottish Readvance—the British counterpart of the Pomeranian phase in North Germany and Würm III in the Alps (Boswell, 1936, p. 159; Zeuner, 1937, p. 139). As compared with the earlier glacial stages this occupation of the area by ice was short and not severe (*M.G.S.* England and Wales, 1932, p. 155), in fact the ice failed to override ground + 450 feet O.D., and the drumlins formed during the preceding period are almost unaltered (Trotter and Hollingworth, 1932, p. 378). According to Trotter, a readvance of ± 12 miles is indicated (1929, pp. 600–2). On the south this ice is known to have impinged on the coast at St Bees, but the exact limit of its extent beyond this point is not definitely fixed (*M.G.S.* England and Wales, 1931, p. 234). But the Cumbrian Mountains were not affected, and the line swings around their northern flanks, extends along the edge of the Carlisle Plain to north of Brampton; as indicated in Fig. 6, however it has not been traced beyond this point (Trotter, 1929, and Pl. XXXIII). No moraines mark this readvance in the Carlisle region, hence it is necessary to fix the extent of the glaciated area by tracing the upper boulder clay and South Upland erratics. At St Bees (Fig. 9, p. 66), the upper boulder clay overlies a peat bed, which was contorted and folded as a result of the pressure of the ice during the readvance; the peat is underlain in turn by sands, gravels and boulder clay of Episode 2 (*M.G.S.* England and Wales, 1931, pp. 244–5). Cool temperate conditions are indicated by this bed, in fact the contained flora is not unlike that found in the Lake District to-day. This peat, together with the extensive interstadial deposits on the Carlisle Plain, suggests that there was a considerable time-interval between the retreat of the main ice-sheet and the Scottish Readvance (Trotter, 1929). A marked climatic oscillation at this period is registered at Holmpton (Fig. 9), on the Holderness coast (Harrison, 1937, p. 239). Here a peat bed resting on Hessle Boulder Clay has yielded a temperate flora in its lower layer of probably the same age as the St Bees peat. In the Holmpton section the temperate zone is overlain by an Arctic bed, which demonstrates that the Scottish Readvance stage had an important cooling effect on the climate of North-East England, and that more equable conditions pertained during the preceding retreat stage.

At several localities in Northern England laminated clays laid down in extra-glacial lakes[1] and actually overlain by deposits of the Scottish Readvance have been found (*M.G.S.* England and Wales, 1926, pp. 50–8, 66–7; 1931, p. 234). This clay is frequently contorted as a result of ice-pressure, but nevertheless Baron de Geer, to whom samples collected at Botcherby, near Carlisle (Fig. 9), were sent, has identified the laminae as true varves (*M.G.S.* England and Wales, 1932, pp. 162–3). According to de Geer (1935, pp. 337–8), thirty varves, averaging 2–5 cm. thick, are present, but it is not possible to correlate them with Sweden where no Pre-Gotiglacial varves are known. This evidence agrees with the correlation of the Scottish Readvance with the Pomeranian or Baltic End-Moraine stage of North Germany, since the Gotiglacial Retreat began after the withdrawal of the Scandinavian Ice from this moraine (see p. 4). Further investigations of the varved clays in Northern Britain would certainly produce significant results.

From the South Cumberland coast the margin of the Scottish Readvance Ice curves out to sea, but it appears again on the northern plain of the Isle of Man (Fig. 6) where it overlies deposits of the same age as the New Drift Glaciation of Northern Britain (Smith, 1930, p. 23).[2] The ice invaded only the low ground in the northern portion of the island to a line between Ramsey and Ballaugh (compare Slater, 1931), and it deposited the

[1] See Carruthers (1939) for an aberrant explanation.

[2] Lamplugh, G. W., "Geology of the Isle of Man", *Mem. Geol. Surv.* England and Wales, 1903. This reference was not available to the writer.

morainic belt of the Bride Hills. The front curved around to the south in the Irish Sea on each side of the island. Thus during the first retreat stage in the recession of the New Drift Ice-Sheets, the Isle of Man appears to have been ice-free, but as a result of the subsequent readvance, Irish Sea Ice overrode the northern lowlands. A similar sequence is revealed in North-East Ireland where, at the time of the retreat of the Ivernian Ice to the Navan-Galway line, the Scottish Ice seems to have withdrawn completely from the country. During the period of the Scottish Readvance, however, ice from Scotland impinged on the coastal sections of Counties Antrim and Down. As shown on the map (Fig. 6), this did not establish contact with the Ivernian Ice, whose front extended at this stage from west of Lough Neagh, south of the city of Londonderry and thence into County Donegal (Charlesworth, 1924, pp. 235–94). The line of the Scottish Readvance in North-East Ireland is marked by an enormous moraine which may be traced from Holywood along the north coast via Larne, Glenarm and Cushendun to Ballycastle on the north (Charlesworth, 1926[*a*], pp. 45–7; 1939, pp. 280–7). From there it continues in a south-westerly direction into the Bann Valley, west of Ballymoney, and then north-west forming a lake in the mouth of the Foyle Estuary (Charlesworth, 1924, pp. 294–9). All the Antrim Glens seem to have contained lakes at this stage, especially important ones being in Glendun (Charlesworth *et al.* 1935, p. 483) and the Belfast area (*M.G.S.* Ireland, 1904, pp. 50–1, 72–3). Varved clays, formed during this period, have been counted by Charlesworth (1939, p. 270) at Martin's Brickyard, Belfast (Fig. 9, p. 66), but as yet comparative material is lacking in Ireland, except the older diagram from Silent Valley previously mentioned. At the time of this advance, the ice cut off the land drainage and caused the formation of a greatly enlarged Lough Neagh which drained into the sea at Carlingford Lough (Charlesworth, 1924, pp. 294–9). Although direct proof is lacking, it seems very probable that the Galway-Offaly-Meath-Tyrone Moraines are to be correlated with the Antrim-Down-Manx-Cumberland stage, as Charlesworth has suggested (1928, p. 341), since in both cases a readvance of the ice-sheet is indicated. On this basis the Central Plains Moraines delimit the extent of the Ivernian Ice-Sheets at the time of the Scottish Readvance of North-East Ireland and North-West England.

In North-East England this stage has not been recorded in Northumberland, Durham or the Pennines (Trotter and Hollingworth, 1932, pp. 377–8). In the Cheviots there is no evidence for a readvance of the local ice, and no boulder clay of this age is known in the region (Woolacott, 1921, pp. 28–9 and 61). Thus as far as Northern England was concerned this glaciation affected only Cumberland, and the ice all came from the Southern Uplands of Scotland. But north of Brampton the extent has not been fixed. It is therefore necessary to trace the limits of the Highland Ice, and in this respect we may conclude from present evidence that South-East Scotland was ice-free at this period. On the north the Southern Uplands Ice was confluent with the Highland Ice (Fig. 6), since moraines are absent in that section of Ayrshire where the two ice-sheets must have merged (compare Charlesworth, 1926[*a*], p. 44). Commencing in the hills near Cumnock, continuing north-west to Muirkirk and the River Clyde above Lanark, west via the northern slopes of the Moorfoot and Lammermuir Hills, and the east coast south of St Abbs Head, the line of the readvance of the Highland Ice has been traced by Charlesworth (1926[*a*], pp. 27–44). This appears to be contemporaneous with the Scottish Readvance. After a break in South Ayrshire, the moraines marking this line occur again at Stranraer and the Rhinns of Galloway. Further research in the latter region will probably reveal that the ice from the Southern Uplands was absent here at this period, and whereas Southern Uplands Ice reached the Isle of Man, it was only Highland Ice from the region of the Clyde which impinged on the coast of North-East Ireland. Likewise one may assume, if the above interpretation is correct, that the region immediately north of the Southern Uplands was deglaciated at this period, but the exact extent of the Southern Uplands Ice between New Cumnock and Brampton is unknown. The direction of the drumlin trends, mapped by Gregory (1926, p. 437), suggests that the readvance of the Southern Uplands Ice was probably not extensive in this area. Nevertheless the southern limit of the Highland Ice, marked by the Lammermuir-Stranraer Moraine, indicates a readvance of considerable magnitude. That this ice-sheet was still very powerful is evidenced by the fact that it overrode the Pentland Hills at an altitude of over 1000 feet, as well as the highest limit of the marginal channels, which occur up to 1000 feet O.D. (Charlesworth, 1926[*a*], pp. 27 and 44; Kendall and Bailey, 1907, pp. 17–20). It is therefore proposed that the Lammermuir-Stranraer Readvance Moraine represents a stage which is the equivalent of the Scottish Readvance and, as will be discussed below, both are synchronous with the Highland Glaciation of Scotland.

At this period a strong glacier from the Valley of the Forth must have issued out to sea in a general easterly direction, although most of Eastern Fifeshire was ice-free. The Ochil, Lomond and Cleish Hills supported local ice, but this did not join the powerful confluent glaciers which emanated from the Highlands via the valleys and straths (Charlesworth, 1926[*a*], p. 43; Simpson, 1933). West of the River Tay the ice extended to a line between Crieff and Methven during this phase (Fig. 6), and it was actually in contact with the Late-Glacial Sea in the Earn and Tay Valleys (Simpson, 1933, pp. 635 and 639). That the sea had transgressed this section of the coast prior to the readvance is proved by the section at Almond where laminated clays, overlain by drift and resting on boulder clay, have been recorded by Simpson at a height of ± 90 feet above present sea-level (1933, pp. 639–40). On the basis of evidence from other parts of the British Isles the so-called Perth Readvance almost certainly represents a portion of the Highland Glaciation. In Eastern Scotland the ice moved in a general easterly direction at this time, but it did not everywhere reach the coast (Bremner, 1934[*a*], p. 54; 1934[*c*]). The end-moraines of this ice-sheet, which deposited an ochreous boulder clay (Bremner, 1936, p. 378), are close to the Highland Boundary Fault from Glenesk to Stonehaven (Bremner, 1920; 1934[*a*], p. 54). According to Bremner (1920), it follows the coast north to the Dee Valley, passes out to sea between Aberdeen and the Ythan Valley, and then goes along the coast as far as Fraserburg (1934, p. 18). This line is shown on the map (Fig. 6). In the Moray district the ice was made up of four components, the most important of which emanated from the region north and west of the Great Glen, and flowed eastward into the sea, impinging upon the coast on both sides of the Moray Firth which was filled with mainland ice at this period (Bremner, 1934[*a*], p. 19). This ice was confluent with local ice-sheets from the Grampian Highlands; details of the movements in North-East Scotland at this stage are given by Fraser (1868) and Bremner (1934[*a*], pp. 18–22). Thus the extent of the Highland Glaciation is clearly defined on the east coast and similar evidence also occurs in the north. Here a glaciation, during which one-half of the Caithness Plain was covered with ice and which is later than the Strathmore Glaciation, has been proved (Bremner, 1934[*a*], p. 54). Moraines in the vicinity of Thurso (Gregory, 1926[*a*]) are probably referable to this stage, which is marked in the Orkneys by local ice-sheets in Hoy and Mainland (Bremner, 1934[*a*]). Scottish Ice, flowing in a general westerly direction from the Northern Highlands, overrode Western Ross-shire and extended out to sea (*B.R.G.* [*n*], p. 92). In the Outer Hebrides local ice covered portions of Lewis and Harris (Jehu and Craig, 1933, p. 870), and it seems probable that the mountains of Skye and Mull likewise nourished local glaciers (*B.R.G.* [*n*], p. 92; *ibid.* [*m*], p. 110), although absolute proof that these were contemporary with the Highland Glaciation is lacking. Since Scottish Ice overrode the coast of North-East Ireland during this stage, as described on p. 277, it seems very probable that the Western Isles of Scotland, unglaciated during the previous retreat period, were covered with ice at this time. Thus the so-called "Pre-Glacial" raised beaches of these islands, described by Wright (1911), probably represent a phenomenon of the Late-Glacial Sea (see p. 57), and hence they fall in the period between the New Drift Glaciation and the Scottish Readvance–Highland Glaciation stages. This is confirmed by the evidence in Cumberland which indicates a considerable time-interval between these stages (Trotter, 1929, pp. 600–2), as well as by the fact that, had they been formed during the preceding Interstadial Period (W_1/W_2), their features would not be so clear-cut and well preserved as they are to-day (compare Wright, 1911, Pl. VI). Rather they would be almost completely obliterated, due to severe erosion in this area during the New Drift Glaciation.

The second retreat period in Ireland witnessed the final withdrawal of the Scottish Ice from the north-east coast, as well as the splitting up of the Donegal, Leitrim and Galway lobes during the recession of the Ivernian Ice from the moraines of the Central Plains to the mountains of North-West Ireland, Mayo and Connemara. In the Sperrin Mountains five stages in the retreat have been determined which are associated with glacial lakes up to 33 square miles in surface extent (Charlesworth, 1924, pp. 237–60, Pl. VIII). The sediments in these old lake beds, provided they are laminated, should be of great importance along with the many other Late-Glacial lakes formed during the retreat of the last ice in establishing a geochronological time-scale for the recession in Ireland. The Donegal Ice got thinner as it receded and split up into eleven local glaciers (Charlesworth, 1924). At this period similar conditions probably existed in the Sligo Mountains. In Mayo the ice withdrew from the north-western part of the area to a clearly defined line running from Ballycastle to Glenco, North Achill Island and the Curraun Peninsula. The recession to this line may be correlated with the first retreat to the Central Plain Moraine (Charlesworth, 1928[*a*], p. 112), and a temporary readvance of ice from the south which flowed into Clew Bay at this time is suggested by the evidence from Clare Island (Hallissy, 1914, pp. 10–14). The second retreat left the major portion of the area ice-free, with only small corrie glaciers in the Ox Mountains (Charlesworth, 1928[*a*], p. 114). In Galway (Charlesworth, 1929[*a*], p. 106), the ice, which withdrew in two lobes, was centred in four mountain groups in Connemara, and evidence for a slight readvance after the retreat from the Central Plain exists here. This represents the Valley Glaciation of North-West Ireland, as shown in Fig. 6, p. 52.

In addition local glaciation affected the mountains of Southern Ireland at this time, indicated by the sequence in the Wicklow Mountains. Here as a result of Farrington's intensive work (1934) it has been conclusively proved that the local ice attained its maximum at a time subsequent to the withdrawal of the main ice-sheet from the Central Plains. Therefore it seems reasonable to consider that this local phase is roughly the equivalent of the Late-Glacial stage under discussion. The precise limit of the last local glaciation of County Wicklow (Fig. 6) is difficult to determine; Charlesworth (1937, p. 31) suggests that it extended approximately to the 2000-foot contour line. Recent work has revealed that the average snow-line at this time was $\pm$ 1650 feet (Farrington, 1938, p. 208), but on the north and east it was higher than on the west and south (Charlesworth, 1937, p. 30), which implies that the prevailing wind was from the west (Farrington, 1934, pp. 204–5). Nowhere did the local ice reach the sea. But according to Farrington, marginal drainage channels, some of which end on the coast at a height of 50 feet O.D., show the extent to which the Wicklow coast was submerged. The only region where this ice established contact with the moraines of the New Drift Glaciation was on the north near Dublin (Farrington, 1934, p. 199), and all available evidence indicates that while the main ice-sheet was invading the slopes, the mountains themselves were unglaciated. The reason for this is connected with the climatic conditions existing on the periphery of an ice-mass, as demonstrated by present-day parallels in Greenland. In spite of the absence of direct proof there seems to be no valid reason for not considering the local glaciation of Wicklow the same age as the Valley Glaciation of North-West Ireland. Palaeöbotanical evidence confirming the correlation is discussed in Chapter II, Section 11.

The last glaciation of South-West Ireland, centred in County Kerry (Fig. 6), consisted in the main of corrie and valley glaciers which in many cases united to form extensive piedmont masses (Charlesworth, 1928, pp. 302–4). The main centre of ice-dispersal was not in the highest mountains, whose summits were unglaciated, but somewhat to the south of Macgillicuddy's Reeks in the Valley of the Kenmare River (*M.G.S.* Ireland, 1927, pp. 53–9). From here the ice poured through the mountain passes on to the plain to the north, the main movement being deflected around the ranges. On the south the ice extended from the Kenmare region into the Bantry Bay District, and the south-eastern extent has been traced by Farrington (1936, pp. 345–7), from Skibbereen to the Pass of Keimaneigh in the western part of County Cork. To the east-north-east an exceedingly powerful lobe of the Kenmare Ice extended up the Roughty Valley (*M.G.S.* Ireland, 1927, p. 53). Charlesworth states (1928) that the low Kerry Hills supported firn ice-caps at this time, and he estimates that a total of approximately 800 square miles was covered by ice in the Dingle Peninsula, the Kenmare-Bantry Bay region, and the local ranges. These ice-sheets, which were the last to invade the district (Farrington, 1936, p. 359), are probably the same age as the Local Glaciation of the Wicklow Mountains (Charlesworth, 1928, p. 316), and this is confirmed by Dr Wright (1937, p. 97). Wright points out that the remarkable freshness of the Kerry Moraines, as compared with those of the New Drift Glaciation farther north, is proof that the former ice-sheets were comparatively late and in this respect resemble the moraines of the last Wicklow Glaciation. This conclusion regarding the age of the local ice in the mountains of Southern Ireland is reinforced by Farrington's recent work in County Wexford (1938[*a*]; 1939, pp. 242–3). Both Mount Leinster and Blackstairs Mountain supported ice during the Late-Glacial Period, and an average snow-line of ± 1650 feet O.D. is indicated. As in Wicklow and Kerry there is clear evidence here that the prevailing wind was from the west, which supports Farrington's view that the local ice in this region was the same age as the last Wicklow Ice. In addition to Counties Wicklow, Wexford and Kerry, minor ice-centres were also present in the Comeragh, Knockmealdown and Galtee Mountains which nourished corrie glaciers, as well as Boggeragh Mountain and Slievenamon, where a small amount of ice was present (Charlesworth, 1928, p. 304). Some 78 square miles were covered in these and the Wexford ranges, making a total of about 1400 square miles of ice in Southern Ireland at this time. This figure includes Charlesworth's estimated total of 530 square miles for the Wicklow area and 800 square miles for South-West Ireland. The small local glaciers in the Mourne Mountains, described by Charlesworth (1939, pp. 287–9), may also belong to the Valley Glacier stage.

Since the mountains of Wales lie at roughly the same latitude as the Southern Irish Mountains, it seems very probable that they were also covered by local ice at this period. Wright states (1937, p. 94) that the Shropshire Plain as far as Shrewsbury is covered by local Welsh drift which appears to be distinctly later than that of the New Drift Glaciation; possibly this is the Welsh Readvance shown by Wills (1937, p. 995, Fig. 1, and p. 1039). On the basis of present data, however, it is impossible to arrive at a satisfactory conclusion in this matter, therefore it is necessary to leave this point open until further work has been done in the area. One would expect that the Welsh Mountains still supported extensive local glaciers at this date on the basis of recent palaeobotanical results from the bogs near Tregaron, Cardiganshire (Godwin and Mitchell, 1938). No Late-Glacial polleniferous horizons were found in these bogs. This fact suggests that the region was still covered by ice, since, had the situation been otherwise, the sequence would probably have commenced earlier than the Early Post-Glacial Period as it did in Ireland (see p. 67). In Wales there is an urgent need for further mapping of the limits of the ice at this stage in the retreat of the New Drift Glaciation.[1]

In Northern England and Southern Scotland the Second Retreat stage witnessed the recession of the Scottish Readvance Ice from the Cumberland Plain. In the Southern Uplands of Scotland this ice split up into nine local glaciers (Charlesworth, 1926, pp. 9–17), and five minor stages have been established for their retreat. In the standard sequence as established in the Cree Valley one of these, known as the Kircowan stage

[1] According to information received from Professor P. G. H. Boswell (April 1940) this is in progress.

(Fig. 6), is important since it marks a slight readvance, according to Charlesworth (1926, pp. 20–2). The counterpart of this minor oscillation is documented in the region north of the Southern Uplands by the well-developed Pentland-Carstairs-Maybole Moraine, the location of which is shown on the map. This was formed by northern ice of Highland origin during the retreat following the Lammermuir-Stranraer Readvance (Charlesworth, 1926[*a*], pp. 35–8).[1] The line marking the extent of the ice-sheet during this stage can be traced across the Esk Valley, east of Edinburgh, along the northern slopes of the Pentland Hills to Carstairs (compare Macgregor, 1927, p. 495), and via the valleys of the Avon and Irvine to near Galston. It reappears after a break, which indicates the union of the Highland Ice with the local glaciers in the Southern Uplands, in the Girvan Valley near Maybole, and along the Ayrshire coast whence the ice-front curved out to sea (Charlesworth, 1926[*a*], pp. 35–9 and p. 50). Following this stage, the Highland Ice broke up into the Forth and Clyde Glaciers which receded down their respective Firths, leaving moraines and drainage channels and impounding the melt-water in the Midland Valley (Charlesworth, 1926[*a*], pp. 39–42; *M.G.S.* Scotland, 1925, p. 233). Thus in Northern Britain, as in Ireland, the second stage in the retreat of the ice witnessed a number of minor oscillations along the ice-front as it receded stepwise into the main mountain centres of glaciation.

At Corstorphine, near Edinburgh (Fig. 9, p. 66), an Arctic plant bed yielding a Late-Glacial fauna has been recorded in the laminated sediments of an ice-dammed lake (Tait, 1934[*a*], pp. 110–13). This layer is overlain by outwash gravels, proving that the lake was formed during the retreat of the ice from the Carstairs Moraine. According to Tait (1934[*a*], p. 119), as well as Peach and Horne (1917, p. 342), the fauna includes *Cervus megaceros* (Irish Elk) and Arctic Lemming; *Betula nana*, *Salix polaris*, *Salix herbacea*, *Salix reticulata*, *Dryas octopetala* and *Oxyria digyna* are among the plants thus far identified. In marine deposits at Portobello, also near Edinburgh and east of Corstorphine (Fig. 9, p. 66), remains of Wolf (*Canis lupus*) have been found (see p. 287). De Geer, who visited this locality, stresses its importance for geochronological purposes (1935, p. 338). The Corstorphine deposits would likewise repay further investigation for the same reason, as well as for a thorough analysis of the polleniferous layer.

North of the Midland Valley of Scotland the ice retreated into the valleys following the Highland Glaciation. In the Perth region the movement was in a general westerly direction (Simpson, 1933, pp. 635–7), and simulataneously with this the land rose, since marginal deposits laid down by the glaciers overlie marine sediments, demonstrating a transgression of the sea at the time of the Perth Readvance (Simpson, 1933, pp. 639–40; see p. 278). The retreat phenomena of the Highland Glaciation have been studied in

[1] Whereas Charlesworth (1926[*a*], pp. 47–8) suggests that the Kircowan stage is the equivalent of the Lammermuir Readvance, the writer feels, on the basis of the published evidence, that this is improbable, since the Lammermuir-Stranraer Moraines indicate the limits of the Highland Ice at the time of the Scottish Readvance, as previously discussed. This question, however, needs further intensive field investigation and mapping in the region east of the Southern Uplands. At present it appears that the Kircowan stage and Pentland-Carstairs-Maybole Moraine should be considered synchronous.

Glenesk (Bremner, 1936, pp. 380–2); during this stage the ice withdrew from the Moray Firth, and the confluent glaciers of North-East Scotland receded into the Highland Valleys (Bremner, 1934[*a*], pp. 17–37). Doubtless wherever the ice moved inland from the coast the land was transgressed by the Late-Glacial Sea, but data on this point are very meagre, especially in the North of Scotland. In the Scottish Highlands the effects of the last glacial episode are very marked. This stage is known as the Valley, District, or Morainic Glaciation of Scotland; the term Valley Glaciation, which seems most appropriate, is used in this book. Terminal and lateral moraines in every Highland glen and strath mark the limits of the ice during this period (*B.R.G.* [*n*], p. 95) when a halt or even a minor readvance of the Highland Ice occurred, as shown in Fig. 6. The distribution of the ice during the Valley Glaciation was controlled by the topography (*B.R.G.* [*l*], p. 73) and nearly all the land bordering on the main Highland mass above 1250 feet O.D. appears to have been covered by ice, which descended to lower levels in the valleys (McCallien, 1937, p. 189). Nowhere did the ice extend far south of the Highland Border, where there are abundant moraines marking its limits (Gregory, 1927, p. 354). These have been studied in detail by Simpson in the Loch Lomond depression and the Upper Forth Valley (1933, pp. 641–5); in both cases a readvance of the ice-front is indicated. The limits of the Loch Lomond Glacier have been accurately established by tracing the distribution of a shelly drift. During the previous retreat stage this loch, ±90 feet above O.D., had been an arm of the sea, and the ice transported the shelly marine deposits, which had formed the sea floor, as low as 50 feet above O.D. when it reoccupied this area. Similarly the Upper Forth Glacier returned to the region north-west of Stirling, where its front was in contact with the Late-Glacial Sea at a height of 65 feet above present sea-level. Simpson concludes from a study of the marginal drainage channels that the Loch Lomond and Upper Forth Valley Glaciations were contemporaneous. In Gare Loch, Dr McCallien (1937[*a*], pp. 386–8) has recorded a re-advance moraine overlying laminated clays of the Late-Glacial Sea, and it seems probable that this is the same age as the Loch Lomond Readvance. In Glenesk (1936, pp. 381–2), the Dee Valley (1921, pp. 62–3), the Spey Valley (1934[*a*], p. 26) and the Abernethy region (1934[*b*]), Bremner has worked out the limits of the ice at this stage, which marks a distinct advance following a period of retreat. In the south-eastern part of the Highlands the ice does not appear to have extended across the Highland Boundary Fault. There are no published data covering this stage in Northern Scotland, but on the west coast several regions have been mapped. These will be discussed in the next section, since the moraines have been mainly studied with relationship to the Late-Glacial Sea. The evidence in this area is unanimous in demonstrating the contemporaneity of the Valley Glaciation and the formation of the 100- and 50-foot Late-Glacial raised beaches. It is possible that local valley or corrie glaciers were present at this time in the higher mountains of Skye, Mull and North Arran (*B.R.G.* [*m*], p. 110). In the Southern Uplands local corrie glaciers were present (Charlesworth, 1926, p. 20) and these indicate a slight readvance (Kendall and Bailey, 1907, p. 22) which seems to be contemporary with Lewis' second Arctic peat bed (1907, p. 59).

In Ireland the final retreat stages of the Donegal (1924, pp. 304–10), Mayo-Sligo (1928[*a*]), and Galway (1929[*a*]) Ice-Sheets have been worked out by Charlesworth—only the Galway Ice shows evidence of a readvance at the time of the Valley Glaciation. This is the probable age of Jessen's second solifluction layer in the Late-Glacial horizons of the Irish bogs (Jessen, with Farrington, 1938, p. 246). The retreat of the Highland Ice in Scotland following the Valley Glaciation is recorded by the stepped levels of the lateral and terminal moraine barriers at intervals along the valleys (*B.R.G.* [*n*], p. 95). During the final waning of the ice there was pronounced erosion of corries, which were probably occupied by ice until very late times; they represent the final stage of active ice (*B.R.G.* [*n*], p. 95). In Glenesk and the Abernethy region the final recession of the valley glaciers has been investigated by Bremner (1936, pp. 381–2; 1934[*b*]). Late-Glacial ice-dammed lakes of this period are numerous in the Highlands; Glen Roy was occupied by one of these lakes, the successive strand-lines of which correspond with cols which controlled the particularly well-defined lake levels (*B.R.G.* [*l*], p. 73). The small local corrie glaciers in the South Uplands and the principal ranges of Wales and Southern Ireland rapidly disappeared, and the Post-Glacial forests became established at an early stage during this retreat in Britain and Ireland.

Appendix V

PART I: CHAPTER II, SECTION 9

DEPOSITS OF THE LATE-GLACIAL SEA

Deposits of the Late-Glacial Sea are better developed in Scotland than elsewhere in Britain and Ireland. In South-Western Ayrshire—in the Rhinns of Galloway and near Kircudbright—and on the east coast of St Abbs Head, 50-foot raised beaches have been reported, while in the former region between Girvan and Ballantrae, and at Dunbar, Haddingtonshire, this feature occurs at 75 feet above O.D. (Kendall and Bailey, 1907, p. 31; Charlesworth, 1926, pp. 21–2; *B.R.G.* [*j*], p. 92). This marks the southern limit of this Late-Glacial phenomenon in Northern Britain, although traces of it exist on the Northumbrian and Durham coasts (Woolacott, 1921, p. 68). In the region of the other great centre of the last ice—North-West Ireland—the extent of these marine platforms is very little known except in the northern part of County Donegal. Brooks (1917, p. 332) records a shelf at 70 feet above present water-level on Horn Head, and high-level beaches exist at 50, 75 and 100 feet in Inishowen (Praeger, 1895, pp. 282–3). In North Wales a Late-Glacial raised beach at ± 50 feet O.D. has been reported (Matley, 1936), and on the coast of County Wicklow in Ireland a Late-Glacial 50-foot marine platform is likewise present (Farrington, 1934, p. 204). In both cases contemporaneity with the recession of the local ice has been demonstrated. It seems probable that the Heatherslade raised beach of the Gower Peninsula in Southern Wales (George, 1932, p. 316) also belongs to this period. In North-East Ireland the effects of marine erosion, following the recession of the last ice in this region, have been observed at an approximate level of 50 feet O.D. at a few localities on the County Antrim coast. Thus at Red Bay there are caves at this height near the town of Waterfoot (*M.G.S.* Ireland, 1876, p. 36), and a wave-cut platform, a cave, as well as a 50-foot terrace, were found on the north side of Cushendun Bay near the 50-foot level (Richardson, 1940, p. 13). The 100-foot beach in Southern Scotland is extensively developed on the North Ayrshire coast (*M.G.S.* Scotland, 1930, pp. 342–3) and west of Glasgow (*M.G.S.* Scotland, 1925, p. 231). In the Forth Valley above Stirling the Late-Glacial Sea was in contact with the ice of the Valley Glaciation (Simpson, 1933, p. 644); in this region important information regarding the uplift has been secured (Dinham, 1927, p. 488). At the head of the valley the raised beach rises to 155 feet above present water-level and slopes off to 100 feet near Stirling. This fact demonstrates clearly that the greatest amount of uplift has occurred in the Highland region towards the centre of ice-dispersal. Near Stonehaven, Kincardineshire, the 100-foot raised beach is a well-marked feature (Bremner, 1920, p. 39); and in North-Eastern Inverness the deposits of this beach overlie the worn edge of a kame (Gregory, 1926[*a*], pp. 410–11). North of Dornoch Firth, at Brora and Helmsdale, the beach gradually loses elevation and falls off to ± 75 feet O.D. (*B.R.G.* [*n*], p. 95). This accords with the evidence in the extreme North of Scotland, where in Caithness the Late-Glacial raised beach is absent (*B.R.G.* [*n*], p. 96), as in the case with the Orkney and Shetland Islands (Flett, 1920, p. 49). Hence the evidence indicates that the 0-isobases should be drawn through this region; immediately north of this line the land has been sinking since Late-Glacial times (see Fig. 7, p. 58).

The association between the Late-Glacial Sea and the Valley or Moraine Glaciation of the Highlands in Loch Lomond and Gare Loch has already been mentioned in Appendix IV (see p. 283). The classic work on the relation between these factors has been done in the region of the Inner Sound between Skye and the mainland, where the distribution of moraines with respect to the high-level strand-lines is well established (Wright, 1937, pp. 371–3, and Fig. 128). McCallien points out that in Lochs Don and Spelve the 100-foot raised beach is absent, due to the existence of valley glaciers, but during a later stage in the recovery of the land, following the retreat of the ice, a raised beach was cut at a height of 85 feet in the outer face of the moraines (1937, p. 189). In Glen Thraill moraines have actually been noted on top of the Late-Glacial beach (*B.R.G.* [*n*], p. 96), and at Strome Ferry, Loch Carron, a Late-Glacial, outwash fan overlies the 100-foot raised beach and extends down to 60 feet above high-water level (Wright, 1937, p. 373). Many instances have been recorded where the highest strand-lines are absent in the upper reaches of the Western Scottish lochs, due to the presence of ice. This is well illustrated in Mull—Loch Ba and Glen Forsa—and in Loch Linnhe (Wright, 1937, pp. 373–4), as well as in Lochs Hourn and Duich (*B.R.G.* [*n*], p. 95). Similarly in the Kyle of Sutherland, Eastern Ross-shire, the presence of a valley glacier resulted in the exclusion of the sea. But before the final retreat of the ice, the land had risen, since fluvio-glacial deposits, which could not have formed under water, extend as low as 30 feet above O.D. in Glen Forsa (*B.R.G.* [*m*], p. 111). Thus as the ice receded from the fjords, beaches marking stages in the isostatic uplift of the land were formed at lower levels. These are later, as they occur below the others and penetrate the fjords, ice-free at this period, where the higher beaches are absent. They are also later than the 50- and 75-foot beaches formed in the peripheral part of the area, which seem to correspond to the highest beaches farther north. Below the 50-foot level data on the recovery of the land, as recorded by strand-lines, are lacking; this may indicate a sudden uplift or extensive Post-Glacial marine erosion. For the most part the beaches of the Late-Glacial Sea are composed of sands and gravels, but on Black Isle, in Eastern Ross-shire, raised beach deposits consisting of silt and clay have been recorded (*B.R.G.* [*n*], p. 95).

In addition to the raised beaches, evidence for the Late-Glacial Sea is afforded by the presence of marine clays yielding an Arctic marine fauna. These are not to be confused with the shelly drifts whose distribution is shown by Wright (1937, p. 66, Fig. 36), and which were derived from the sea bottom by the advancing ice and deposited, especially along the coastal portions of Britain and Ireland bordering on the Irish Sea, by the Scottish Ice-Sheet. They are seldom found far inland except in Cheshire. These beds of drift are not all the same age, since they were formed during at least two major glaciations. In County Mayo, Western Ireland (Charlesworth, 1928[*a*], pp. 113–14), they are found on the north coast east of Belderg and were laid down during the last main ice-advance by the Mayo and Sligo Ice skirting the coast from the south and south-east. In the East of Scotland and on the Lincolnshire and Norfolk coasts the shelly drift is an important criterion for early Scandinavian Ice on the coast, and in Caithness for much later northward-moving ice from the Moray region (see pp. 28 and 272). Charlesworth (1926[*a*], p. 47) suggests that its presence in Ayrshire, where it is found at altitudes up to 1061 feet O.D., may represent interstadial deposits of the sea preceding the last ice advance, but it is generally accepted that the Scottish Ice was responsible for its being thrust up from the depths of the Firth of Clyde and dumped upon the hills of Ayr during the last advance (*M.G.S.* Scotland, 1930, p. 321).

During Late-Glacial times, however, the sea and not the ice was the responsible agent of deposition of extensive clay beds. Typical molluscs from marine sediments of this period include: *Chlamys* (*Pecten*) *islandicus*, *Cyprina islandica*, *Astarte borealis*, *Astarte compressa*, *Yoldia norvegica*, *Tellina* (*Macoma*) *calcarea* (Brown, 1867, p. 627). Extensive Late-Glacial clays are found in the Clyde region, on the Island of Bute and in Argyllshire (Wright, 1937, p. 369), and an important section has been described at Paisley on the Clyde (Wright, 1937, pp. 369–71). Here the clay, whose surface is at 40 feet above present sea-level, is finely laminated and tenacious. It abounds in shells of a distinctly Arctic type. That these are *in situ* is proved by the fact that in many cases the valves are still united, and their delicacy and state of preservation point to the same conclusion. The nature of the deposit reveals that quiet, fairly deep-water conditions prevailed over great tracts of Southern Scotland in Late-Glacial times. In addition to the fauna, Arctic conditions are clearly indicated by the presence of large boulders, which must have been transported by great masses of floating ice, since the deposits are far removed from any high ground. Lines on the boulders and shells on their surfaces show that they once stood in mud on the shore before being transported by the ice to deeper water where they were incorporated into the marine deposits. At this period therefore the Clyde Estuary was more extensive, with icebergs floating about in it during the summer. Supporting evidence is forthcoming from other regions of Scotland. At Bankhead and near Drummuir, Ayrshire, thick deposits of finely laminated clay yielding an Arctic marine fauna have been reported at a height of 80–90 feet above present sea-level, and the Bankhead section, which is 40 feet thick, is overlain by fluvio-glacial gravels, proving contemporaneity with the recession of the ice in this region (*M.G.S.* Scotland, 1930, pp. 342–3). Jamieson (1865, p. 175) records striated stones which were dropped in the clay by the ice at Errol, Perthshire, and Dinham (1927, p. 486) points out that the laminated clays in the Stirling district are folded and contorted in places as a result of the stranding of storm-blown bergs and pack-ice. Near Grangemouth, Stirling, the bones of an Arctic Seal were found in this deposit (Dinham, 1927); Seal remains are also reported from Springfield Brickyard, Fifeshire (Jamieson, 1865, p. 171). Howden (1868, pp. 140–2) states that the Late-Glacial marine clay containing Arctic mollusca is never found at a greater elevation than 40 feet above present high-water level in the estuary of the South Esk. At Portobello Brickyards, near Edinburgh (Jamieson, 1865, p. 169; Tait, 1934, pp. 62–3), and at other sites in the vicinity (Tait, 1934, pp. 65–71), extensive deposits of laminated clay occur. A portion of the jaw of a Wolf (*Canis lupus*) has been found in the Portobello brick clays, which at this locality are overlain by deposits of the Early Post-Glacial Sea (Tait, 1930, p. 319). Marine sediments of Late-Glacial age have thus far been reported at several sites in North-East Ireland; they are especially well developed at Cushendun, County Antrim (see p. 129).

In South-West Scotland river valleys with terraces corresponding in height with the Late-Glacial raised beach platforms have been described. These are situated in the Lower Tweed Valley (*B.R.G.* [*j*], p. 93), and the valley of the North Calder Water (*M.G.S.* Scotland, 1925, p. 233). Further study in other valleys which were ice-free at the time of the Late-Glacial Sea should reveal similar terrace formations which can be associated with the raised beaches and laminated clays of the coast. This period of submergence has its counterpart in the Yoldia Sea of the Baltic, but in comparison with it the Late-Glacial Sea of Northern Britain was relatively small (Fig 2, p. 9; Wright, 1937, Pl. XVIII). In both areas high-level strand-lines were formed by these seas which are synchronous with the later stages in the retreat of the ice.

Appendix VI

PART I: CHAPTER III, SECTION 2

SUBMERGED FORESTS AND RAISED BEACHES IN BRITAIN AND IRELAND

Comparatively few of the important Early Post-Glacial localities along the coasts of Britain and Ireland have been adequately studied. None the less, numerous sections exist which afford abundant evidence for a period of relative emergence after the retreat of the ice-sheets. This was followed by a period of relative submergence when there was a transgression of the sea along the coast accompanied by a phase during which the climate was warmer than at present. Since the submergence the evidence proves that the land in the north has risen, whereas the sinking has continued in the south. Until more regions have been palaeobotanically investigated, however, it is difficult to make more than tentative suggestions as to the probable age of a given horizon at certain type localities. But on the basis of data already published, as well as the published material from other regions, especially in Northern Europe where very similar deposits are found, it is possible to outline the Early Post-Glacial history of Britain and Ireland as presented in Chapter III of Part I of this book. In this Appendix a somewhat more detailed account of the sites will be found.

A. ENGLAND AND WALES. At Pentuan, Cornwall (Austen, 1851, p. 120), peat has been recorded 50 feet below high-water level, and in the overlying clay remains of whale have been found. In addition to submerged peats (Pengelly, 1865, p. 30), valleys cut to ± 100 feet below present sea-level on the South Devon coast (Reid, 1913, p. 88; Jones, 1934, p. 308) indicate the extent of the former emergence in this area. In the region of the Bristol Channel, submerged peats have been found at several localities (Palmer, 1931, pp. 355–7); that the land formerly stood at least 100 feet higher here is proved by a buried channel in the Lower Severn Valley (Wills, 1938, pp. 216–17). Many important sections in South Wales (*B.R.G.* [*e*], pp. 110–12) indicate intermittent periods of submergence, and the evidence from this region, in addition to that from the south coast of England, proves that the last movement has been a sinking of the land. In fact Jones (1934, p. 306) has recorded a buried channel in the valley of the Tawe River at a depth of ± 150 feet, showing that a considerable sinking has taken place in Post-Glacial time, following a period of uplift. The famous section at Barry, Glamorganshire (Strahan, 1896), reveals three peat beds indicating at least three pauses in the submergence. As Godwin has shown (1935, p. 212), one of these has occurred since the Late Boreal Period, on the basis of the analysis of samples from a layer 50 feet below high-water level at Swansea. It seems probable that Anglesey was joined to the mainland during Boreal times (*B.R.G.* [*f*], p. 87), judging by the distribution of submerged peats in North Wales. Oscillations in the submergence also occurred in Flintshire (Neaverson, 1936, p. 45), as well as in Cheshire and Lancashire, where there are many excellent sections in the vicinity of the Dee and Mersey Estuaries (De Rance, 1870; Mellard Reade, 1871, 1883, 1896; Double, 1932; Boswell, 1937, p. 165; *B.R.G.* [*h*], p. 73). According to Mellard Reade (1900, p. 103), the marine beds which separate the upper and lower peats in this region contain a "warm" fauna. In Heysham Harbour, Lancashire, Reid (1913, p. 50) has recorded a peat bed at 52 feet below present sea-level, and in Workington Harbour, Cumberland, 58½ feet of estuarine deposits overlie the old land surface (*M.G.S.* England and Wales, 1931, p. 260). The Post-Glacial raised beach occurs in the Silloth district of the Solway Firth at a maximum height of 15 feet 6 inches (*M.G.S.* England and Wales, 1931, p. 257), but farther south its elevation is less, until in North-West Wales it approaches sea-level where, as indicated in Fig. 11 (p. 79), its 0-isobase has been established (Wright, 1937, Fig. 127, p. 369). Marine clays, or warps, and raised beaches, at an average height of 12 feet above high-water level, are found in the Silloth district overlying submerged peats (*M.G.S.* England and Wales, 1926, pp. 76–9).

In Eastern England the 0-isobase of the Post-Glacial raised beach, shown in Fig. 11, p. 79, occurs near Sunderland in Durham, according to Wright (1937, Fig. 127). Excellent sections have been reported in the Thames Valley (Reid, 1913, pp. 13–19; *B.R.G.* [*b*], pp. 57–9; King and Oakley, 1936, p. 70), in the Medway Valley (Burchell, 1931, pp. 296–9), and in the Fenland, where Godwin and Clifford (1938, p. 400) have intensively studied the successive stages of forest development in connection with changes in the mutual relations of land and sea (see also Godwin, 1940, pp. 285–302). The Humber Estuary (Reid, 1913, pp. 13–19) affords additional data for Post-Glacial changes of level; at Grimsby, Lincolnshire, submerged peat is found 35–52 feet below mean high-water mark (Wood and Rome, 1868, pp. 156–7), and at Hull these authorities describe a peat bed 20–37 feet below high-water level (compare Erdtman, 1928, pp. 147–8; Wright, 1937, p. 378). On the Durham coast, in Northern England, Trechmann (1936, pp. 161–4) states that submerged peat deposits extend for approximately 3 miles in the vicinity of West Hartlepool. Similar evidence from other localities in England and Wales proves conclusively that the greatest Post-Glacial submergence has occurred in the south of Britain. Here the coastline has been intermittently sinking since the Early Post-Glacial Period, which closely parallels the situation in the Baltic region south of a line from North-West Jutland to the Island of Falstar. That this sinking in the British Isles has been taking place in comparatively recent times may be shown by the presence of submerged peats, often associated with archaeological material, at several localities. Thus on the Essex coast Late Mesolithic, Neolithic and Bronze Age remains occur on a submerged land surface (Warren, Piggott *et al.* 1936). Swinnerton (1931) has reported a similar sequence on the coast of Lincolnshire, where archaeological horizons are associated with superimposed layers of peats and clays. At Rhyl, Flintshire, in Western Britain, two peat layers separated by Early Post-Glacial Clays have been described (Neaverson, 1936). The upper bed, which is Late Atlantic–Sub-Boreal (Erdtman, 1928, p. 136), has yielded polished stone axes from Penmaenmawr (see p. 233), bone and flint implements, as well as several bronze objects; Tardenoisean artifacts occur in the lower peat (Smith, F. G., 1925, p. 120). The Post-Glacial deposits along the Lancashire and Cheshire coasts have likewise yielded prehistoric remains (De Rance, 1870, p. 659; Mellard Reade, 1896). In Cardiganshire—Borth and Ynylas—peat beds found between tide-marks may be tentatively assigned to the Atlantic Period (Godwin and Newton, 1938). In Southern Britain sites which have yielded archaeological material, and which would repay investigation, have been reported in Pembrokeshire (Cantrill, 1915; Leach, 1913, 1918), Devon (Ellis, 1867; Rogers, 1908), and elsewhere in the region of the Bristol Channel (compare Fox, 1938, pp. 24–5). A peat layer 44 feet below mean sea-level at Southampton has yielded flint implements, a bone needle, a perforated stone hammer or mace, in addition to a rich mammalian fauna (Shore and Elwes, 1889). Since Atlantic peats are found in the South of England just below high-water mark (Erdtman, 1928, p. 151), it seems apparent that the sea along the entire coast of Southern Britain has been slowly encroaching upon the land as a result of secondary movements in Post-Atlantic times. In fact the Scilly Isles are very much smaller at present than they were during the Early Metal Age (Hencken, 1932, pp. 31–3). The exact fulcrum, south of which there has been land sinking subsequent to the submergence, permitting the invasion of the Dogger Bank by the North Sea and the lowering of the old Pre-Boreal–Boreal land surface, has never been accurately fixed. Nevertheless, it probably coincides in the main with the maximum extent of the Litorina raised beach in the British Isles shown in the map (Fig. 11, p. 79). It is a significant fact that this line corresponds in general with the northern extension of the raised beaches which are earlier than the first advance of the last ice-sheet in Britain and Ireland (Fig. 7, p. 58).

B. Scotland. In Southern Scotland submerged peats, raised beaches and associated deposits are found at many localities (*B.R.G.* [*j*], pp. 92–3; *M.G.S.* Scotland, 1930, pp. 343–4), and Glasgow and Edinburgh are partly built on the "25-foot" marine terrace (*B.R.G.* [*k*], p. 85). In the vicinity of Edinburgh there is an important section which shows Late-Glacial clays overlain by later clays, also known as "carse" deposits, of the Early Post-Glacial Period (Tait, 1934). As mentioned on pp. 80–1, the latter are widely distributed in the Forth and Tay Valleys. In the region of the Forth the carse clays are found between 25 and 30 feet above sea-level, whereas towards the north of Scotland the elevation of these deposits decreases (Jamieson, 1865, pp. 189–90). Raised beaches of this period are found on the shores of the Moray Firth (Wallace, 1868; Steers, 1937), but on the west coast of Scotland they attain their maximum development. Excellent exposures are found in South-West Jura (Ting, 1936, p. 187), Central Mull (*B.R.G.* [*m*], p. 111), the Treshnish Isles (Wright, 1911, p. 106), and between Loch Linnhe and the Firth of Clyde the Post-Glacial raised beach is found at a maximum height of just over 40 feet (McCallien, 1937, p. 198). This confirms the evidence from the east coast and shows that the greatest uplift has occurred in the upper reaches of the Scottish lochs and firths which border on the Grampian Highlands. Thus in the Tay Valley, overlying a submerged peat layer (Fleming, 1822), marine and estuarine deposits of this period are found up to the 50-foot contour (Geikie, J., 1881, p. 383; Simpson, 1933, p. 640), and in the Upper Forth Valley the evidence is particularly clear as a result of Dinham's investigation (1927, p. 490). At the head of the valley above Stirling the Post-Glacial marine terrace occurs at a height of 49 feet above sea-level, at Carnock it slopes down to + 40 feet, but on approaching the carse lands of the Forth it rapidly loses elevation until reaching the 25-foot level. Therefore the greatest amount of recoil has been in the regions proximal to the centre of ice-dispersal in Late-Glacial times.

Submerged peats are found in Sutherland, Caithness and the Orkneys (*B.R.G.* [*n*], p. 96; Jamieson, 1865, p. 187), as well as at several localities in the Outer Hebrides (Lewis, 1907, p. 49; Jehu and Craig, 1926, p. 474). The distribution of the Post-Glacial fauna suggests that during this period of emergence the Orkneys formed part of the mainland (Flett, 1920, p. 48). North of the Tay district on the east coast the Post-Glacial raised beach occurs at lower levels (Geikie, J., 1881, p. 418); in the Orkneys and Shetlands it is entirely absent (Flett, 1920, p. 49). In the west it is found at 10 feet above high-water level in North Uist (Stewart, 1937), and in Lewis it reaches the present sea-level (McCallien, 1937, p. 198). A shelf at + 15 feet has been recorded in Eastern Ross-shire and Sutherland where extensive deposits occur in Dornoch Firth (*B.R.G.* [*n*], p. 96). The level falls in Caithness to between 8 and 5 feet above sea-level (*B.R.G.* [*n*], p. 96). Therefore in the North of Scotland the 0-isobase, marking the limits of this feature (see Fig. 11, p. 79), approximates that of the Late-Glacial raised beach, as shown in Fig. 7, p. 58.

The age of this submergence has been established for Northern Britain by Erdtman (1928, pp. 181–2), who investigated sections of the carse clays in Eastern Scotland. Whereas no pollen has actually been obtained from them, peat containing a high pollen frequency exists both above and below the carse deposits. At Ochtertyre Moss, north-north-west of Stirling, the lower peat is of Boreal age, and a study of the upper *Sphagnum* peat overlying 14 feet of carse clay has shown it to be of Late Sub-Boreal–Sub-Atlantic age. It is probable that a time interval separates the upper clay from the *Sphagnum* peat, since a bronze cauldron was found in the surface of the clay nearby at Kincardine Moss (Erdtman, 1928, p. 181). All except the upper part of the clay was therefore formed previous to the Late Sub-Boreal Period. Likewise at Forgandenny, south of Perth, Erdtman records a peat that is of Boreal age below 12 feet of carse deposits. This peat was tightly compressed and yielded Hazel, Willow, Birch, Pine, Oak and Elm. In Southern Scotland at the Moss of Cree, Wigtownshire, and at Lochar Moss, Dumfriesshire (Erdtman, 1928, pp. 173 and 175), peats which may be assigned to the Sub-Boreal Period overlie the "25-foot" raised beach. It may be stated that these investigations prove beyond reasonable doubt the age of the Post-Glacial marine and estuarine deposits described above as of the Atlantic Period. The submergence which they represent is the British counterpart of the Litorina transgression of the Baltic. It is probable that the submerged peat corresponds to the Lewis' Upper Forest Bed (1905, p. 715), but this cannot be proved as yet.

C. IRELAND. As far as North-East Ireland is concerned a summary of the Early Post-Glacial stratigraphy is presented on pp. 82–85, whereas in Chapter II of Part II a very much more detailed discussion of the evidence will be found. South of Counties Antrim and Down along the east coast of Ireland the Early Post-Glacial raised beach has been reported at numerous localities (Martin, 1930, pp. 494–500; Hull, 1872). It is well developed in Carlingford Lough (Praeger, 1896, pp. 31–2), Dundalk Bay (Martin, 1930, p. 495), and traces of it occur at several places along the coasts of Counties Louth and Meath. The Dublin region has been intensively studied (*M.G.S.* Ireland, 1903, pp. 41–56; Farrington, 1933); at Clontarf estuarine clays are found (Praeger, 1892, p. 242), and on the north side of Bray Harbour these deposits overlie a bed of submerged peat (Praeger, 1895 [*a*], pp. 155–6). Southward the elevation of the raised beach steadily decreases, but indications of it occur in Wexford Harbour (Kinahan, 1873), where the 0-isobase has been drawn (Fig. 11, p. 79). As Kinahan points out, the south coast of Ireland has been sinking subsequently to the uplift following the formation of the raised beach. The submerged peats in this region (Kinahan, 1873, p. 63) show that the situation is complex, and that the movement has been interrupted by several halts and oscillations, which parallels the situation in South Wales and the Bristol district (see p. 288). In Ireland this is confirmed by the evidence from other localities. At Tramore Bay, County Waterford, Hardman (1873) records three superimposed land surfaces separated by deposits formed during periods of submergence. But the most striking evidence for a sinking of the south coast is mentioned by Hallissy (1914, p. 21). At Dunworley Bay, County Cork, there is a peat bog, the surface of which approximates high-water level, and which was bored to a depth of 50 feet without reaching the base. This evidence, together with the Rostellon Dolmen, County Cork, and the Ardmore Crannog, County Waterford (Ussher, 1903), both submerged at high tide, affords almost conclusive proof that the south coast of Ireland has been sinking in comparatively recent times. On the basis of Hallissy's map (1914, Pl. V), it is probable that, during the period of the Early Post-Glacial emergence, many of the western islands of Ireland were joined to the mainland and that much of Galway Bay was dry land. Pre-Boreal–Boreal peats in Ballyconnell Bay, County Sligo (Burchell, 1934, pp. 367–9), also demonstrate a greater extension of land in this region at this time. As with the case of the south coast, the west coast of this country south of Sligo Bay seems to have been sinking, since raised beaches of the Early Post-Glacial Period are apparently absent in Counties Mayo, Galway, Clare and Kerry. At Rosses Point, County Sligo, there is a deposit of marine shells ± 8 feet above high-water level (see p. 109), and in the west of County Donegal this feature has been reported by Wright at a height of ± 5 feet (1928, p. 100). Thus the 0-isobase, marking the southern limits of the Early Post-Glacial raised beach, may be drawn through the south-western part of County Sligo and connected with the line passing through County Wexford, as shown on the map (Fig. 11, p. 79). In Northern Donegal, Praeger (1895) has recorded raised beaches at 25 feet above high-water level in the Inoshowen Peninsula; in Lough Foyle it is similarly well developed (*M.G.S.* Ireland, 1908, pp. 66–7).

D. Isle of Man. The presence of a Post-Glacial raised beach has been recorded here by Lamplugh (*M.G.S.* England and Wales, 1903)[1] at an altitude of 10–12 feet above high-water level. In Ayr, at the north of the island, it is best developed and attains a width of over 1½ miles. Below it the submerged forest occurs, indicating a period of relative land elevation (Clark, 1935, p. 70), but this deposit has not been studied by a palaeobotanist. Near Strandhall, in the south of the island, a submerged forest at or near sea-level was investigated by Erdtman (1928, p. 170), and evidence for the later land surface of the Atlantic Sub-Boreal Transition Period secured. This accords with other evidence in Ireland, Wales and Southern England of a secondary sinking of the land in comparatively recent times.

[1] Work not available.

REFERENCES
CITED IN THE TEXT

The bibliographical references in this book have been designed in such a way as to eliminate footnotes in so far as possible. In the text the works which have been consulted are documented in parentheses. The author's name and date of publication provide the key to the references, as well as the title of the work cited, which is given below. Small letters have been used to distinguish between several works by the same author in a given year, although no letter accompanies the date of the first publication listed (e.g. 1936, 1936[*a*], 1936[*b*]). In the case of two or more authors with the same name, their first initial is given in the text.

Since some of the *Memoirs of the Geological Survey* have been written by as many as six joint authors, no attempt has been made to refer to the sections written by a given specialist, except in a few isolated instances. The abbreviation *M.G.S.* has been used throughout for these memoirs, and the name of the country (e.g. England and Wales, Scotland, Ireland), as well as the date of publication, provide the key; the names of the authors will be found in the list. A modification of this convention has been adopted for documenting the *British Regional Geology* series, published by the Geological Survey of Great Britain. In order that these would appear consecutively in the list, each is designated by a small letter.

LIST OF ABBREVIATIONS

Amer. Anth.	*The American Anthropologist.*
Ann. Rep. Smith. Inst.	*Annual Report of the Smithsonian Institution.*
Antiq. Jour.	*Antiquaries Journal* (Journal of the Society of Antiquaries of London).
Arch. Camb.	*Archaeologia Cambrensis.*
Arch. Jour.	*Archaeological Journal* (Journal of the Royal Archaeological Institute of Great Britain and Ireland).
Archiv f. Anth.	*Archiv für Anthropologie.*
B.G.S.A.	*Bulletin of the Geological Society of America.*
B.R.G.	*British Regional Geology.* Department of Scientific and Industrial Research. Geological Survey and Museum, London.
B.S.P.F.	*Bulletin de la Société Préhistorique Française.*
Geog. Jour.	*The Geographical Journal.*
Geol. Förens. Förh.	*Geologiska Föreningens i Stockholm Förhandlingar.*
Geol Mag.	*Geological Magazine.*
I.N.J.	*Irish Naturalists' Journal.*
J.K.A.S.	*Journal of the Kilkenny Archaeological Society.*
J.R.A.I.	*Journal of the Royal Anthropological Institute of Great Britain and Ireland.*
J.R.G.S., Ireland.	*Journal of the Royal Geological Society of Ireland.*
J.R.H.A.A.I.	*Journal of the Royal Historical and Archaeological Association of Ireland.*
J.R.S.A.I.	*Journal of the Royal Society of Antiquaries of Ireland* (formerly *J.R.H.A.A.I.*)
L'Anth.	*L'Anthropologie.*

LIST OF ABBREVIATIONS

M.G.S.	*Memoirs of the Geological Survey of Great Britain and Ireland.* Department of Science and Industrial Research. England and Wales: Published in London. Scotland: Published in Edinburgh. Ireland: Published in Dublin. (Department of Education.)
P.B.S.S.	*Proceedings of the University of Bristol Spelaeological Society.*
Proc. Geol. Ass.	*Proceedings of the Geologist's Association.*
P. 1st I.C.	*Proceedings of the First International Congress of Prehistoric and Protohistoric Sciences.* London, 1932. (Published, Oxford, 1934.)
P.L.G.S.	*Proceedings of the Liverpool Geological Society.*
P.P.S.	*Proceedings of the Prehistoric Society* (formerly *P.P.S.E.A.*).
P.P.S.E.A.	*Proceedings of the Prehistoric Society of East Anglia.*
P.R.I.A.	*Proceedings of the Royal Irish Academy.*
P.R.P.S., Edin.	*Proceedings of the Royal Physical Society of Edinburgh.*
P.R.S., Edin.	*Proceedings of the Royal Society of Edinburgh.*
P.R.S., London	*Proceedings of the Royal Society of London.*
P.S.A., Scot.	*Proceedings of the Society of Antiquaries of Scotland.*
P.T.R.S., London	*Philosophical Transactions of the Royal Society of London.*
P.Y.G.S.	*Proceedings of the Yorkshire Geological Society.*
Q.J.G.S.	*Quarterly Journal of the Geological Society of London.*
Q.J.M.S.	*Quarterly Journal of the Meteorological Society.*
Rep. Brit. Ass.	*Report of the British Association for the Advancement of Science.*
R. XVI I.G.C.	*Report of the XVIth Session of the International Geological Congress.* Washington, 1933. (Published in 1936.)
R. and P. Bel. N.F.C.	*Annual Report and Proceedings of the Belfast Naturalists' Field Club.*
R. and P. Bel. N.H. and P.S.	*Reports and Proceedings of the Belfast Natural History and Philosophical Society.*
S.P.R.D.S.	*Scientific Proceedings of the Royal Dublin Society.*
S.T.R.D.S.	*Scientific Transactions of the Royal Dublin Society.*
Trans. Devon. Ass.	*Transactions of the Devonshire Association for the Advancement of Science.*
T.E.G.S.	*Transactions of the Edinburgh Geological Society.*
T.G.S., Glasgow	*Transactions of the Glasgow Geological Society.*
Trans. R.I.A.	*Transactions of the Royal Irish Academy.*
T.R.S., Edin.	*Transactions of the Royal Society of Edinburgh.*
U.J.A.	*Ulster Journal of Archaeology.*

LIST OF WORKS

ADAMS, A. L. 1881. (With Kinahan, G. H. and Ussher, R. J.) Explorations in the Bone Cave of Ballynamintra, near Cappagh, County Waterford. *S.T.R.D.S.* I (1881), 177–226.

ALLEN, G. M. 1937. The Animal Remains from Glenarm. Appendix I to Movius, H. L., Jr. (1937). *J.R.S.A.I.* LXVII (1937), 216.

ANDERSON, J. 1895. Notice of a Cave Recently Discovered at Oban. *P.S.A., Scot.* XXIX (1895), 211–30.

—— 1896. Notes on a Deposit of Flints found at Bulwark, Old Deer, Aberdeenshire. *P.S.A., Scot.* XXX (1896), 346–51.

—— 1898. Notes on the Contents of a Small Cave or Rock Shelter at Druim Vargie, Oban; and of Three Shell-Mounds in Oronsay. *P.S.A., Scot.* XXXII (1898), 298–313.

ANTEVS, ERNST. 1928. *The Last Glaciation.* New York, 1928.

—— 1929. Maps of the Pleistocene Glaciations. *B.G.S.A.* XL (1929). 631–770.

ARMSTRONG, A. L. 1920. Flint-Crust Engravings and Associated Implements from Grimes Graves, Norfolk. *P.P.S.E.A.* III (1920), 434–43.

—— 1923. Discovery of a New Phase of Early Flint Mining at Grimes Graves, Norfolk. *P.P.S.E.A.* IV (1923), 113–25.

LIST OF WORKS

ARMSTRONG, A. L. 1924. Percy Sladen Memorial Fund Excavations, Grimes Graves, Norfolk, 1924. *P.P.S.E.A.* IV (1924), 182–202.

—— 1925. Explorations at Mother Grundy's Parlour, Creswell Crags, Derbyshire. *J.R.A.I.* LV (1925), 146–78.

—— 1926. The Grimes Graves Problem in the Light of Recent Researches. *P.P.S.E.A.* V (1926), 91–136.

—— 1931. Excavations in the Pin Hole Cave, Creswell Crags, Derbyshire. *P.P.S.E.A.* VI (1931), 330–4.

—— 1931[*a*]. A Late Upper Aurignacian Station in North Lincolnshire. *P.P.S.E.A.* VI (1931), 335–9.

—— 1932. An Upper Aurignacian Station on the Lincolnshire Cliff. *P. 1st I.C.*, London, 1932, pp. 74–5.

—— 1932[*a*]. North of England Notes. Upper Palaeolithic and Mesolithic Stations in North Lincolnshire. *P.P.S.E.A.* VI (1932), 130–1.

ARNOLD-BEMBROSE, H. H. and DEELEY, R. M. 1896. Discovery of Mammalian Remains in the Old River-Gravels of the Derwent, near Derby. *Q.J.G.S.* LII (1896), 497–510.

AUSTEN, R. A. C. 1851. On the Superficial Accumulations of the Coasts of the English Channel, and the Changes they indicate. *Q.J.G.S.* VII (1851), 118–36.

BADEN-POWELL, D. W. F. 1934. On the Marine Gravels at March, Cambridgeshire. *Geol. Mag.* LXXI (1934), 193–219.

—— 1937. On the Holocene Marine Fauna from the Implementiferous Deposits of Island Magee, County Antrim. *Jour. of Animal Ecology*, VI (1937), 86–97.

BATTY, J. 1938. Pigmy Flints from the Lower Bann Valley. *U.J.A.* I (1938), 90–4.

BAUDOUIN, M. and WHELAN, C. B. 1931. Deux Haches en Diorite taillée et polie, d'Irland. *B.S.P.F.* XXVIII (1931), 428–34.

BISAT, W. S. 1933. Field Meeting to the Holderness Coast. *Proc. Geol. Ass.* XLIV (1933), 441–2.

BISHOP, A. H. 1914. An Oronsay Shell-Mound. *P.S.A., Scot.* XLVIII (1914), 52–101.

BLANC, A. C. 1936. La Stratigraphie de la Plaine Cotière de la Basse-Versilia (Italie) et la Transgression Flandrienne en Méditerranée. *Revue de Géographie Physique et de Géologie Dynamique*, IX (1936), 129–62.

—— 1937. Low Levels of the Mediterranean Sea during the Pleistocene Glaciation. *Q.J.G.S.* XCIII (1937), 621–51.

BOSWELL, P. G. H. 1931. The Stratigraphy of the Glacial Deposits of East Anglia in Relation to Early Man. *Proc. Geol. Ass.* XLII (1931), 87–108.

—— 1932. The Contacts of Geology: the Ice Age and Early Man in Britain. *Rep. Brit. Ass.* 1932, pp. 57–88.

—— 1935. Geology and Early Man in East Anglia. *Rep. Brit. Ass.* 1935, pp. 366–9.

—— 1936. Problems of the Borderland of Archaeology and Geology in Britain. *P.P.S.* Presidential Address, II (1936), 149–60.

—— 1937. The Geology of the New Mersey Tunnel. *P.L.G.S.* XVII (1937), 160–91.

BOWLER-KELLEY, Mrs A. 1935. Silex énigmatiques de Grande Bretagne. *B.S.P.F.* XXXII (1935), 1–7.

BREMER, WALTHER. 1928. Notes on Some Objects in the National Collection of Irish Antiquities. *P.R.I.A.* XXXVIII (1928), 21–30.

—— 1928[*a*]. *Ireland's Place in Prehistoric and Early Historic Europe*. Dublin, 1928.

BREMNER, ALEX. 1915. Problems in the Glacial Geology of North-East Scotland and some Fresh Facts bearing on them. *T.E.G.S.* X (1915), 334–47.

—— 1920. The Glacial Geology of the Stonehaven District. *T.E.G.S.* XI (1920), 25–39.

LIST OF WORKS

BREMNER, ALEX. 1921. Limits of Valley Glaciation in the Basin of the Dee. *T.E.G.S.* XI (1921), 61–8.

—— 1928. Further Problems in the Glacial Geology of North-eastern Scotland. *T.E.G.S.* XII (1928), 147–64.

—— 1934. The Surface Geology of the Aberdeen District. *Brit. Ass. Adv. Sci.* A Scientific Survey of Aberdeen and District, London, 1934, pp. 16–19.

—— 1934[*a*]. The Glaciation of Moray and Ice Movements in the North of Scotland. *T.E.G.S.* XIII (1934), 17–56.

—— 1934[*b*]. The Glaciation of Abernethy Forest. *T.E.G.S.* XIII (1934), 1–16.

—— 1934[*c*]. Meltwater Drainage Channels and other Glacial Phenomena of the Highland Border Belt from Cortachy to the Bervie Water. *T.E.G.S.* XIII (1934), 174–5.

—— 1935. Glacial and Postglacial Geology. *T.E.G.S.* XIII (1935), 260–70.

—— 1936. The Glaciation of Glenesk. *T.E.G.S.* XIII (1936), 378–82.

BREUIL, H. 1922. The Pre-Neolithic Industries of Scotland. *P.S.A., Scot.* LVI (1922), 261–81.

—— 1937. Objects of Palaeolithic Type Found near Comrie, Perthshire, Scotland. *P.P.S.* III (1937), 463–4, Pl. XXIX.

—— 1937[*a*]. Les Subdivisions du Paléolithique Supérieur et Leur Signification. *Congrès International d'Anthropologie et d'Archéologie Préhistoriques.* Compte Rendu de la XIVe Session. Genève, 1912 (2nd edition, 1937).

B.R.G. [*a*] CHATWIN, C. P. East Anglia and Adjoining Areas. 1937.
[*b*] SHERLOCK, R. L. London and Thames Valley. 1935.
[*c*] WELCH, F. B. A. and CROOKALL, R. Bristol and Gloucester District. 1935.
[*d*] POCOCK, R. W. and WHITEHEAD, T. H. The Welsh Borderland. 1935.
[*e*] PRINGLE, J. and GEORGE, T. N. South Wales. 1937.
[*f*] SMITH, BERNARD and GEORGE, T. N. North Wales. 1935.
[*g*] OAKLEY, K. P. and EDMUNDS, F. H. The Central England District. 1936.
[*h*] WRAY, D. A. The Pennines and Adjacent Areas. 1936.
[*i*] EASTWOOD, T. Northern England. 1935.
[*j*] PRINGLE, J. The South of Scotland. 1935.
[*k*] MACGREGOR, M. and MACGREGOR, A. G. The Midland Valley of Scotland. 1936.
[*l*] READ, H. H. The Grampian Highlands. 1935.
[*m*] RICHEY, J. E. Scotland—The Tertiary Volcanic Districts. 1935.
[*n*] PHEMISTER, J. Scotland—The Northern Highlands. 1936.

BROOKS, C. E. P. 1917. The Correlation of the Quaternary Deposits of the British Isles with those of the Continent of Europe. *Ann. Rep. Smith. Inst.* 1917, pp. 277–375.

—— 1927. The Climate of Prehistoric Britain. *Antiquity*, I (1927), 412–18.

—— 1931. Changes of Climate in the Old World during Historic Times. *Q.J.M.S.* LVII (1931), 13–30.

BROWN, T. 1867. On the Arctic Shell-Beds of Elie and Errol, viewed in connection with our other Glacial and Recent Deposits. *T.R.S., Edin.* XXIV (1867), 617–34.

BRUNICARDI (Mrs). 1914. The Shore Dwellers of Ancient Ireland. *J.R.S.A.I.* XLIV (1914), 185–213.

BRYCE, JAMES. 1865. On the Occurrence of Beds in the West of Scotland beneath the Boulder Clay. *Q.J.G.S.* XXI (1865), 213–18.

BRYCE, T. H. 1903. On the Cairns and Tumuli of the Island of Bute: A Record of Explorations during the Season of 1903. *P.S.A., Scot.* XXXVIII (1903), 17–81.

BUICK, Rev. G. R. 1891. Fresh Facts about Prehistoric Pottery. *J.R.S.A.I.* I (1891), 433–42.

LIST OF WORKS

Burchell, J. P. T. 1925. The Shell-Mound Industry of Denmark as Represented at Lower Halstow, Kent. *P.P S.E.A.* v (1925), 73–8.

—— 1927. Further Report on the Epi-Palaeolithic Factory Site at Lower Halstow, Kent. *P.P.S.E.A.* v (1927), 217–21.

—— 1927[*a*]. Discovery of Stone Implements of Lower Palaeolithic Age in Ireland. *Nature,* 120 (1927), 260–1.

—— 1928. A Final Account of the Investigations carried out at Lower Halstow, Kent. *P.P.S.E.A.* v (1928), 288–96.

Burchell, J. P. T., Moir, J. Reid and Dixon, E. E. L. 1929. Palaeolithic Man in North-West Ireland. Occasional Paper, No. 1, *Prehist. Soc. E.A.* (1929), pp. 1–15.

Burchell, J. P. T. 1930. Upper Palaeolithic Implements from beneath the Uppermost Boulder Clay of Flamborough Head. *Antiq. Jour.* x (1930), 359–83.

—— 1930[*a*]. Upper and Lower Palaeolithic Man in East Yorkshire. *P.P.S.E.A.* vi (1930), 226–30.

—— 1930[*b*]. Palaeolithic Man in North-East Ireland. *Nature,* 126 (1930), 352.

—— 1931. Early Neanthropic Man and his Relation to the Ice Age. *P.P.S.E.A.* Presidential Address, vi (1931), 253–303.

—— 1931[*a*]. Palaeolithic Implements from Kirmington, Lincolnshire, and their Relation to the 100-foot Raised Beach of Late Pleistocene Times. *Antiq. Jour.* xi (1931), 262–72.

Burchell, J. P. T. and Moir, J. Reid. 1931. The Asturian Industry of Northern Ireland. *Man,* xxxi (1931), 170–2.

Burchell, J. P. T. 1932. Implements of Late Magdalenian Age Underlying the Raised Beach at Larne, County Antrim. *Nature,* 129 (1932), 726.

Burchell, J. P. T. and Moir, J. Reid. 1932. The Evolution and Distribution of the Hand-Axe in North-East Ireland. *P.P.S.E.A.* vii (1932), 18–34.

Burchell, J. P. T. 1933. The Ice Age and Early Man in Yorkshire and North Lincolnshire. *Geol. Mag.* lxx (1933), 285–6.

—— 1933[*a*]. Flint Implements of Early Magdalenian Age from Deposits Underlying the Lower Estuarine Clay at Island Magee, County Antrim. *Nature,* 132 (1933), 860.

—— 1934. Some Littoral Sites of Early Post-Glacial Times, Located in Northern Ireland. *P.P.S.E.A.* vii (1934), 366–72.

—— 1935. Some Pleistocene Deposits at Kirmington and Crayford. *Geol. Mag.* lxxii (1935), 327–31.

Burchell, J. P. T. and Moir, J. Reid. 1935. Diminutive Flint Implements of Pliocene and Pleistocene Age. *Antiq. Jour.* xv (1935), 119–33.

Burchell, J. P. T. 1938. Two Mesolithic "floors" in the Ebbsfleet Valley of the Lower Thames. *Antiq. Jour.* xviii (1938), 397–401.

Burkitt, M. C. 1923. A Newly-Discovered Transition Culture in North Spain. *P.P.S.E.A.* iv (1923), 42–5.

—— 1925. *Prehistory.* Cambridge, 1925.

—— 1932. *A Handbook of the Prehistoric Archaeology of Britain.* Oxford, 1932. Chapter 1: The Palaeolithic and Mesolithic Periods, pp. 1–16.

—— 1933. *The Old Stone Age.* Cambridge, 1933.

Burkitt, M. C. and Childe, V. G. 1932. A Chronological Table of Prehistory. *Antiquity,* vi (1932), 185–205.

Callander, J. G. 1927. A Collection of Tardenoisean Implements from Berwickshire. *P.S.A., Scot.* lxi (1927), 318–27.

LIST OF WORKS

Callander, J. G. 1929. Land Movements in Scotland in Prehistoric and Recent Times. *P.S.A., Scot.* LXIII (1929), 314–22.

Callander, J. G., Cree, J. E. and Ritchie, James. 1927. Preliminary Report on Caves Containing Palaeolithic Relics, near Inchnadamph, Sutherland. *P.S.A., Scot.* LXI (1927), 169–72.

Campbell, R. 1934. On the Occurrence of Shelly Boulder Clay and Interglacial Deposits in Kincardineshire. *T.E.G.S.* XIII (1934), 176–82.

—— 1934[*a*]. (With Robertson, I. M.) Glacial and Interglacial Deposits at Benholm, Kincardineshire. *Rep. Brit. Ass.* 1934, pp. 313–14.

Cantrill, T. C. 1915. Flint Chipping-Floors in South-West Pembroke. *Arch. Camb.* XV (1915), 157–210 (6th series).

Carruthers, R. G. 1939. On Northern Glacial Drifts: Some Peculiarities and their Significance. *Q.J.G.S.* XCV (1939), 299–333.

Charlesworth, J. K. 1924. The Glacial Geology of the North-West of Ireland. *P.R.I.A.* XXXVI (1924), 174–314.

—— 1926. The Glacial Geology of the Southern Uplands of Scotland, West of Annandale and Upper Clydesdale. *T.R.S., Edin.* LV (1926), 1–23.

—— 1926[*a*]. The Readvance, Marginal Kame-Moraine of the South of Scotland, and some Later Stages of Retreat. *T.R.S., Edin.* LV (1926), 25–50.

—— 1928. The Glacial Retreat from Central and Southern Ireland. *Q.J.G.S.* LXXXIV (1928), 293–344.

—— 1928[*a*]. The Glacial Geology of North Mayo and West Sligo. *P.R.I.A.* XXXVIII (1928), 100–15.

—— 1929. The South Wales End-Moraine. *Q.J.G.S.* LXXXV (1929), 335–55.

—— 1929[*a*]. The Glacial Retreat in Iar Connacht (Galway). *P.R.I.A.* XXXIX (1929), 95–106.

Charlesworth, J. K. and Jowett, A. 1929. The Glacial Geology of the Derbyshire Dome and the Western Slopes of the Southern Pennines. *Q.J.G.S.* LXXXV (1929), 307–34.

Charlesworth, J. K. 1930. The Origin of Irish Fauna and Flora. *P.R.I.A.* XXXIX (1930), 358–90.

Charlesworth, J. K. and Macalister, R. A. S. 1930. The Alleged Palaeolithic Implements of Sligo: A Summary. *P.R.I.A.* XXXIX (1930), 18–32.

Charlesworth, J. K. 1931. A Tentative Reconstruction of the Successive Margins of the Quaternary Ice-Sheets in the Region of the North Sea. *P.R.I.A.* XL (1931), 67–83.

—— 1932. The Distribution of the Irish Peats. *I.N.J.* IV (1932), 37–9.

Charlesworth, J. K., McCallien, W. J., Hartley, J. J., Reynolds, D. L., Richey, J. E. and Tomkeieff, S. I. 1935. The Geology of North-East Ireland. *Proc. Geol. Ass.* XLVI (1935), 441–86.

Charlesworth, J. K. and Erdtman, G. 1935. Post-Glacial Section at Milewater Dock, Belfast. *I.N.J.* V (1935), 234–5.

Charlesworth, J. K. 1936. Geomorphology of the Irish Sea Basin. *Nature*, 138 (1936), 1040–1.

—— 1937. A Map of the Glacier Lakes and the Local Glaciers of the Wicklow Hills. *P.R.I.A.* XLIV (1937), 29–36.

—— 1939. Some Observations on the Glaciation of North-East Ireland. *P.R.I.A.* XLV (1939), 255–95.

Childe, V. G. 1925. *The Dawn of European Civilization.* London, 1925 (1st edition).

—— 1929. *The Danube in Prehistory.* Oxford, 1929.

—— 1931. The Forest Cultures of Northern Europe: A Study in Evolution and Diffusion. *J.R.A.I.* LXI (1931), 325–48.

—— 1935. *The Prehistory of Scotland.* London, 1935.

LIST OF WORKS

CHILDE, V. G. 1935[a]. Some Sherds from Slieve na Caillighe. *J.R.S.A.I.* LXV (1935), 320–4.

—— 1936. Report on Neolithic Pottery from Newferry, County Londonderry. Appendix II to Movius, H. L., Jr. (1936). *P.R.I.A.* XLIII (1936), 37–9.

—— 1936[a]. Scottish Tracked Stones and their Significance. *P.P.S.* II (1936), 233–6.

—— 1936[b]. Changing Methods and Aims in Prehistory. *P.P.S.* Presidential Address, I (1936), 1–15.

—— 1938. Notes on Excavations in Scotland during 1938. *P.P.S.* IV (1938), 314–25.

—— 1939. *The Dawn of European Civilization.* London, 1939 (3rd edition).

CLARK, J. G. D. 1929. Discoidal Polished Flint Knives—Their Typology and Distribution. *P.P.S.E.A.* VI (1929), 41–54.

—— 1932. *The Mesolithic Age in Britain.* Cambridge, 1932.

—— 1934. A Late Mesolithic Settlement Site at Selmeston, Sussex. *Antiq. Jour.* XIV (1934), 134–58.

—— 1934[a]. Derivative Forms of the *petit tranchet* in Britain. *Arch. Jour.* XCI (1934), 32–58.

—— 1935. The Prehistory of the Isle of Man. *P.P.S.* I (1935), 70–92.

—— 1935[a]. Report on Recent Excavations at Peacock's Farm, Shippea Hill, Cambridgeshire. *Antiq. Jour.* XV (1935), 284–319.

—— 1936. *The Mesolithic Settlement of Northern Europe.* Cambridge, 1936.

—— 1936[a]. The Separation of Britain from the Continent. *P.P.S.* II (1936), 239.

—— 1936[b]. Upper Palaeolithic Man in Ireland? *P.P.S.* II (1936), 241–2.

—— 1936[c]. Early Navigation in North-Western Europe. *P.P.S.* II (1936), 146.

—— 1936[d]. The Bann River Culture of Northern Ireland. *P.P.S.* II (1936), 243.

—— 1937. Mesolithic Pit-Dwellings. *Antiquity,* XI (1937), 476–8.

—— 1938. The Reindeer Hunting Tribes of Northern Europe. *Antiquity,* XII (1938), 154–71.

—— 1938[a]. Reindeer Hunters' Summer Camps in Britain? *P.P.S.* IV (1938), 229.

—— 1938[b]. Microlithic Industries from Tufa Deposits at Prestatyn, Flintshire, and Blashenwell, Dorset. *P.P.S.* IV (1938), 330–4.

—— 1938[c]. Notes on Excavations in England during 1938. *P.P.S.* IV (1938), 316–32.

—— 1939. *Archaeology and Society.* London, 1939.

CLIFFORD, M. H. 1936. A Mesolithic Peat in the Isle of Wight. *Proc. Isle of Wight Nat. Hist. and Arch. Soc.* II (1936), 582–94.

COFFEY, G. and PRAEGER, R. LL. 1904. The Antrim Raised Beach: A Contribution to the Neolithic History of the North of Ireland. *P.R.I.A.* XXV (1904), 143–200.

COLEMAN, A. P. 1929. *Ice Ages Recent and Past.* New York, 1929.

COLLINS, E. R. 1932. Palaeolithic Implements of Nidderdale, Yorkshire. *P. 1st I.C.* London, 1932, pp. 76–8.

—— 1933. Upper Palaeolithic Site in Nidderdale. *P.P.S.E.A.* VII (1933), 185–7.

COON, C. S. 1939. *The Races of Europe.* New York, 1939.

CORRIE, J. M. 1916. Notes on Some Stone and Flint Implements found near Dryburgh, in the Parish of Mertoun, Berwickshire. *P.S.A., Scot.* L (1916), 307–13.

CREE, J. E. 1927. Palaeolithic Man in Scotland. *Antiquity,* I (1927), 218–21.

CROSSKEY, Rev. H. W. 1865. On the *Tellina Calcarea* Bed at Chappel Hall, near Airdrie. *Q.J.G.S.* XXI (1865), 219–21.

DALY, R. A. 1934. *The Changing World of the Ice Age.* New Haven, 1934.

DAVISON, A. H., ORR, JAMES, STELFOX, A. W. and STENDALL, J. A. S. 1927. Excavation of White Park Bay Kitchen-Midden Site. *I.N.J.* I (1927), 280–2.

DAWKINS, W. BOYD. 1874. *Cave Hunting.* London, 1874.

—— 1880. *Early Man in Britain and His Place in the Tertiary Period.* London, 1880.

Day, E. C. H. 1866. On an Ancient Raised Beach and Submerged Forest, near Wissant. *Geol. Mag.* III (1866), 109–15.

—— 1866[*a*]. On a Raised Beach and other Recent Formations, near Weston-super-Mare. *Geol. Mag.* III (1866), 115–19.

Déchelette, J. 1908. *Manuel d'Archéologie Préhistorique, Celtique, et Gallo-Romaine.* Paris, 1908, t. I: Archéologie Préhistorique.

De Geer, G. 1910. A Geochronology of the Last 12,000 Years. *International Geological Congress,* XIe Session, Stockholm, Fasc. 1 (1910), 241–57.

—— 1927. Schwankungen der Sonnenstrahlung seit 18,000 Jahren. *Geologische Rundschau,* XVIII (1927), 417–54.

—— 1928. Geochronology Based on Solar Radiation, and its Relation to Archaeology. *Antiquity,* II (1928), 308–18.

—— 1935. Dating the Ice Age in Scotland. *T.G.S.* Glasgow, XIX (1935), 335–9.

—— 1935[*a*]. Dating of Late-Glacial Clay Varves in Scotland. *P.R.S., Edin.* LV (1935), 23–6.

De Morgan, J. 1921. *L'Humanité Préhistorique.* Paris, 1921.

De Puydt, M. 1909. Considérations Générales sur les Fonds de Cabanes Néolithiques de la Hesbaye. *Annales de la Fédération archéologique et historique de Belgique.* Congrès de Liège, 1909, XXIe Session, pp. 1–50.

De Rance, C. E. 1870. On the Post-Glacial Deposits of Western Lancashire and Cheshire. *Q.J.G.S.* XXVI (1870), 655–68.

D'Evelyn, A. M. 1933. A Sandhill Settlement, Maghera, County Donegal. *J.R.S.A.I.* LXIII (1933), 88–100.

Dewey, H. 1913. The Raised Beach of North Devon: its relation to others and to Palaeolithic Man. *Geol. Mag.* X (1913), 154–63.

Dinham, C. H. 1927. The Geology of the Stirling District. *Proc. Geol. Ass.* XXXVIII (1927), 470–94.

Dixon, R. B. 1928. *The Building of Cultures.* New York, 1928.

Double, I. S. 1932. On Some Recent Sections in the Post-Glacial Deposits in the Neighbourhood of Liverpool, with Petrographical Notes. *P.L.G.S.* XVI (1932), 66–87.

Dubois, G. 1932. L'Analyse Pollinique des Tourbes et son Application à l'Étude du Quaternaire et de la Préhistoire. *L'Anth.* XLII (1932), 269–89.

Dunlop, R. 1888. Note on a Section of Boulder Clay Containing Peat. *T.G.S., Glasgow,* VIII (1888), 312–15.

Du Noyer, G. V. 1869. On Flint Flakes from Carrickfergus and Larne. *Q.J.G.S.* XXV (1869), 48–50.

—— 1869[*a*]. On the Flint Flakes of Antrim and Down. *J.R.G.S., Ireland,* II (1869), 169–71.

Dwerryhouse, A. R. 1902. The Glaciation of Teesdale, Weardale, and the Tyne Valley, and their Tributary Valleys. *Q.J.G.S.* LVIII (1902), 572–608.

—— 1923. The Glaciation of North-East Ireland. *Q.J.G.S.* LXXIX (1923), 352–422.

Dwerryhouse, A. R. and Miller, A. A. 1930. The Glaciation of Clun Forest, Radnor Forest, and Some Adjoining Districts. *Q.J.G.S.* LXXXVI (1930), 96–128.

Edgar, Rev. William. 1939. A Tardenoisean Site at Ballantrae, Ayrshire. *Trans. Glasgow Arch Soc.* lx–3 (1939), 184–8.

Edwards, W. 1937. A Pleistocene Strand-Line in the Vale of York. *P.Y.G.S.* XXIII (1937), 103–18.

Elgee, Frank. 1930. *Early Man in North-East Yorkshire.* Gloucester, 1930.

Ellis, H. S. 1867. On Some Mammalian Bones and Teeth, found in the submerged Forest at Northam. *Trans. Devon. Ass.* II (1867), 162–3.

ERDTMAN, G. 1924. Studies in Micro-Palaeontology. II Moorlog from the Dogger Bank. pp. 677–8. *Geol. Förens. Förh.* XLVI (1924), 676–8.

—— 1927. Traces of the History of the Forests of Ireland. *I.N.J.* I (1927), 242–5.

—— 1927[*a*]. Literature on Pollen-Statistics Published Before 1927. *Geol. Förens. Förh.* XLIX (1927), 196–211.

ERDTMAN, G. 1928. Studies in the Postarctic History of the Forests of Northwestern Europe. *Geol. Förens. Förh.* L (1928), 123–92.

—— 1929. Some Aspects of the Post-Glacial History of British Forests. *Jour. of Ecology*, XVII (1929), 112–26.

—— 1931. The Boreal Hazel Forests and the Theory of Pollen Statistics. *Jour. of Ecology*, XIX (1931), 158–63.

—— 1932. Some Indications of the Character of Climate and Vegetation in North-Western Europe during the Mesolithic Age. *P. 1st I.C.*, London, 1932, pp. 105–7.

EVANS, E. E. and GAFFIKIN, Miss M. 1935. Belfast Naturalists' Field Club Survey of Antiquities: Megaliths and Raths. *I.N.J.* V (1935), 242–52.

EVANS, E. E. 1938. Notes on Excavations in Northern Ireland during 1938. *P.P.S.* IV (1938), 322–3.

FARRINGTON, A. 1929. The Pre-Glacial Topography of the Liffey Basin. *P.R.I.A.* XXXVIII (1929), 148–70.

—— 1931. Glacial Sands at Greystones, County Wicklow. *I.N.J.* III (1931), 218.

—— 1932. Origin of the Irish Fauna and Flora. *I.N.J.* IV (1932), 66–8.

—— 1933. Raised Beaches near Dublin. *I.N.J.* IV (1933), 211–12.

—— 1934. The Glaciation of the Wicklow Mountains. *P.R.I.A.* XLII (1934), 173–209.

—— 1936. The Glaciation of the Bantry Bay District. *S.P.R.D.S.* XXI (1936), 345–61.

FARRINGTON, A. (and JESSEN, K.) 1938. The Bogs at Ballybetagh, near Dublin, with Remarks on Late-Glacial Conditions in Ireland. *P.R.I.A.* XLIV (1938), 205–60.

FARRINGTON, A. 1938[*a*]. The Local Glaciers of Mount Leinster and Blackstairs Mountain. *P.R.I.A.* XLV (1938), 65–71.

—— 1939. The Glacial Geology of South-Eastern Ireland. *Proc. Geol. Ass.* L (1939), 337–44.

FLEMING, JOHN. 1822. On a Submarine Forest in the Firth of Tay, with Observations on the Formation of Submarine Forests in General. *T.R.S., Edin.* IX (1822), 419–31.

FLETT, J. S. 1920. The Submarine Contours Around the Orkneys. *T.E.G.S.* XI (1920), 42–9.

FORDE, C. D. 1930. Early Cultures of Atlantic Europe. *Amer. Anth.* XXXII (1930), 19–100.

FOX, Sir CYRIL. 1933; 1938. *The Personality of Britain*—Its Influence on Inhabitant and Invader in Prehistoric and Early Historic Times. Cardiff, 2nd edition, 1933; 3rd edition, 1938.

FRASER, JAMES. 1868. The Recent Formations and Glacial Phenomena of Strathnairn. *T.E.G.S.* I (1868), 55–66.

—— 1869. First Notice on a Post-Tertiary Shell Bed at Clava, in Nairnshire, Indicating an Arctic Climate, and a Sea Bed at a height of 500 feet. *T.E.G.S.* I (1869), 136–40.

GAMS, H. 1938. Die bisherigen Ergebnisse der Mikrostratigraphie für die Gliederung der letzten Eiszeit und des Jungpaläolithikums in Mittel- und Nordeuropa. *Quartär*, I (1938), 75–96.

GARROD, D. A. E. 1926. *The Upper Palaeolithic Age in Britain.* Oxford, 1926.

—— 1938. The Upper Palaeolithic in the Light of Recent Discovery. *P.P.S.* IV (1938), 1–26.

GEIKIE, Sir ARCHIBALD. 1862. On the Date of the Last Elevation of Central Scotland. *Q.J.G.S.* XVIII (1862), 218–32.

—— 1865. *The Scenery of Scotland.* London, 1865.

GEIKIE, JAMES. 1879. Discovery of an Ancient Canoe in the Old Alluvium of the Tay at Perth. *Scottish Naturalist*, V (1879), 1–7.

GEIKIE, JAMES. 1881. *Prehistoric Europe*. London (Edward Stanford), 1881.

—— 1895. *The Great Ice Age and Its Relation to the Antiquity of Man*. New York, 1895 (3rd edition).

GEORGE, T. N. 1932. The Quaternary Beaches of Gower. *Proc. Geol. Ass.* XLIII (1932), 291–324.

—— 1933. The Glacial Deposits of Gower. *Geol. Mag.* LXX (1933), 208–32.

GLENN, T. A. 1935. Distribution of the Graig Lwyd Axe and its Associated Cultures. *Arch. Camb.* XC (1935), 189–218.

GODWIN, H. and M. E. 1933. British Maglemose Harpoon Sites. *Antiquity*, VII (1933), 36–48.

GODWIN, H. 1934. Pollen Analysis: an outline of the problems and potentialities of the method. *New Phytologist*, XXXIII (1934), 278–305, 325–58.

GODWIN, H. and CLARK, J. G. D. 1934. The Age of the Pennine Peats. *Man*, XXXIV (1934), 53–5.

GODWIN, H. 1935. (With Reid, E. M., Boswell, P. G. H., Chandler, M. E. J., Wilmott, A. J. and Salisbury, E. J.) Discussion on the Origin and Relationship of the British Flora. *P.R.S., London*, CXVIII (1935), 197–241.

GODWIN, H. and CLIFFORD, M. H. 1938. Studies of the Post-Glacial History of British Vegetation. I. Origin and Stratigraphy of Fenland Deposits near Woodwalton, Hunts. II. Origin and Stratigraphy of Deposits in Southern Fenland. *P.T.R.S. London*, CCXXIX (1938), 323–406.

GODWIN, H. and MITCHELL, G. F. 1938. Stratigraphy and Development of Two Raised Bogs near Tregaron, Cardiganshire. *New Phytologist*, XXXVII (1938), 425–54.

GODWIN, H. and NEWTON, L. 1938. The Submerged Forest at Borth and Ynyslas, Cardiganshire. *New Phytologist*, XXXVII (1938), 333–44.

GODWIN, H. 1940. Studies of the History of British Vegetation. III. Fenland Pollen Diagrams. IV. Post-Glacial Changes of Relative Land- and Sea-Level in the English Fenland. *P.T.R.S., London*, CCXXX (1940), 239–303.

GRAINGER, Rev. JOHN. 1874. On the Fossils of the Post-Tertiary Deposits of Ireland. *Rep. Brit. Ass.* 1874, pp. 73–6.

GRAY, ALEXANDER. 1893. Notice of the Discovery of a Cinerary Urn, etc.; also of an Old Flint Working Place in the 30-foot Raised Beach at Millknowe, Campbeltown. *P.S.A., Scot.* XXVIII (1893), 263–74.

GRAY, WILLIAM. 1880. The Character and Distribution of the Rudely Worked Flints of the North of Ireland, Chiefly in Antrim and Down. *J.R.H.A.A.I.* V (1879–1882), 109–43.

—— 1890. The Antiquarian Aspects of the County Antrim Raised Beaches. *J.R.S.A.I.* I (1890), 388–90.

—— 1893. Worked Flints: Ancient and Modern. *R. and P. Bel. N.F.C.* III (1892–93), 548–69.

GREGORY, J. W. 1926. Scottish Drumlins. *T.R.S., Edin.* LIV (1926), 433–40.

—— 1926[*a*]. The Scottish Kames and their Evidence on the Glaciation of Scotland. *T.R.S., Edin.* LIV (1926), 395–432.

—— 1927. The Moraines, Boulder Clay and Glacial Sequence of Southwestern Scotland. *T.G.S., Glasgow*, XVII (1927), 354–76.

GREGORY, J. W. and CURRIE, E. D. 1928. The Vertebrate Fossils from the Glacial and Associated Post-Glacial Beds of Scotland in the Hunterian Museum, University of Glasgow. *Monographs of the Geological Department of the Hunterian Museum, Glasgow University*, II (1928), 1–25.

GREGORY, J. W. *et al.* 1930. (With Ritchie, Jas., Kennedy, W. G. and Leitch, Duncan.) Some Caves and a Rock-Shelter at Lock Ryan and Portpatrick, Galloway. *P.S.A., Scot.* LXIV (1930), 247–64.

GRESSWELL, R. K. 1936. (With Charlesworth, J. K., Greenly, E., Miller, A. A. and Hollingworth, S. E.) Discussion on the Geomorphology of the Irish Sea Basin. *Rep. Brit. Ass.* 1936, pp. 346–9.

GRIEVE, SYMINGTON. 1883. Notice of the Discovery of Remains of the Great Auk or Garefowl (*Alca impennis*) on the Island of Oronsay, Argyllshire. *Jour. of the Linn. Soc., Zoology*, XVI (1883), 479–87.

—— 1922. A Remarkable Stone Implement Resembling a Knife found at Caisteal-nan-Gillean, Oronsay. *P.S.A., Scot.* LVI (1922), 164–8.

GRIFFITHS, J. C. 1939. The Mineralogy of the Glacial Deposits of the Region between the Rivers Neath and Towy, South Wales. *Proc. Geol. Ass.* L (1939), 433–62.

GRIMES, W. F. 1932. Prehistoric Archaeology in Wales since 1925. *P.P.S.E.A.* VII (1932), 82–106.

GROSS, HUGO. 1938. Auf den ältesten Spuren des Menschen in Altpreussen. *Preussia*, XXXII (1938), 84–139.

HALLISSY, T. 1914. Clare Island Survey. Geology. *P.R.I.A.* XXXI, Pt. 7 (1914), 1–22.

HARDMAN, E. 1873. Note on a Small Raised Estuarine Beach at Tramore Bay, showing traces of several oscillatory movements during the Recent Period. *J.R.G.S., Ireland*, XIV (1873), 31–6.

HARDY, E. M. 1939. Studies of the Post-Glacial History of British Vegetation. V. The Shropshire and Flint Maelor Mosses. *New Phytologist*, XXVIII (1940), 364–96.

HARRISON, K. 1935. The March-Nar Sea. *Geol. Mag.* LXXII (1935), 257–62.

—— 1937. Solar Radiation and the Ice Age in Britain. *North Western Naturalist, Arbroath, Scotland*, XII (1937), 235–51.

HASSÉ, LEONARD. 1890. Objects from the Sandhills at Portstewart and Grangemore, and their Antiquity. *J.R.S.A.I.* I (1890), 130–8.

—— 1894. Objects from the Sandhills at Dundrum and their Antiquity. *J.R.S.A.I.* IV (1894), 1–13.

HAWKES, C. F. C. 1937. A Stone Battle-Axe from Northern Ireland. *Antiq. Jour.* XVII (1937), 72–3.

—— 1937[*a*]. Current British Archaeology: A Survey of Aims and Needs. *Institute of Archaeology of the University of London, First Annual Report*, 1937, pp. 47–69.

HAWKES, JACQUETTA. 1936. The Place of Origin of the Windmill Hill Culture. *P.P.S.* I (1936), 127–9.

—— 1938. The Significance of Channelled Ware in Neolithic Western Europe. *Arch. Jour.* XCV (1938), 126–73.

HENCKEN, H. O'N. 1932. *The Archaeology of Cornwall and Scilly.* London, 1932.

—— 1938. Cahercommaun: A Stone Fort in County Clare. *Royal Society of Antiquaries of Ireland*, Extra Volume, 1938.

HEWSON, Rev. L. M. 1935. Notes on Irish Sandhills. *J.R.S.A.I.* LXV (1935), 231–44.

—— 1936. Notes on Irish Sandhills (*cont.*). *J.R.S.A.I.* LXVI (1936), 154–72.

HINTON, M. A. C. 1926. The Pleistocene Mammalia of the British Isles and their Bearing upon the Date of the Glacial Period. *P.Y.G.S.* XX (1926), 325–48.

HOLLINGWORTH, S. E. 1931. The Glaciation of Western Edenside and the Adjoining Area, and the Drumlins of the Edenside and Solway Basin. *Q.J.G.S.* LXXXVII (1931), 281–359.

HOLME, HENRY. 1912. Worked Flints obtained from "the 25-foot Raised Beach" near Holywood, County Down. *Nature*, 90 (1912), 361.

HOOTON, E. A. 1940. Stature, Head Form, and Pigmentation of Adult Male Irish. *Amer. Journ. Physical Anth.* XXVI (1940), 229–49.

—— 1940[*a*]. *Why Men Behave like Apes and Vice Versa.* Princeton, 1940.

HOPWOOD, A. T. 1936. Earth Movements, Ice Ages, and Faunas. *Geol. Mag.* LXXIII (1936), 185–8.

HOWDEN, J. C. 1868. On the Superficial Deposits of the Estuary of the South Esk. *T.E.G.S.* I (1868), 140–50.

HULL, EDWARD. 1866. The Raised Beach of Cantyre (Kintyre). *Geol. Mag.* III (1866), 5–10.

—— 1872. On the Raised Beach of the North-East of Ireland. *Rep. Brit. Ass.* 1872, pp. 113–14.

JACKSON, J. W. 1909. On the Diatomaceous Deposit of the Lower Bann Valley, Counties Antrim and Derry, and Prehistoric Implements found therein. *Memoirs and Proceedings of the Manchester Literary and Philosophical Society*, LIII (1909), 3–18.

—— 1933. Preliminary Report on Excavations at the Caves of Ballintoy, County Antrim. *I.N.J.* IV (1933), 230–5.

—— 1934. Further Excavations at Ballintoy Caves, County Antrim. *I.N.J.* V (1934), 104–9.

—— 1936. Review of Kilgreany Cave, County Waterford. *I.N.J.* VI (1936), 56.

—— 1936[*a*]. Excavations at Ballintoy Caves, County Antrim. Third Report. *I.N.J.* VI (1936), 31–42.

—— 1938. Excavations at Ballintoy Caves, County Antrim. Fourth Report. *I.N.J.* VII (1938), 107–12.

JAMIESON, T. F. 1865. On the History of the Last Geological Changes in Scotland. *Q.J.G.S.* XXI (1865), 161–203.

JEHU, T. J. 1904. The Glacial Deposits of Northern Pembrokeshire. *T.R.S., Edin.* XLI (1904), 53–87.

—— 1909. The Glacial Deposits of Western Carnarvonshire. *T.R.S., Edin.* XLVII (1909), 17–56.

JEHU, T. J. and CRAIG, R. M. 1926. Geology of the Outer Hebrides. Part III—North Uist and Benbecula. *T.R.S., Edin.* LIV (1926), 467–89.

—— 1933. Geology of the Outer Hebrides. Part IV—North Harris and Lewis. *T.R.S., Edin.* LVII (1933), 839–74.

JESSEN, K. and MILTHERS, V. 1928. Stratigraphy and Palaeontological Studies of Interglacial Fresh-Water Deposits in Jutland and North-West Germany. *Denmarks geologiske Undersøgelse*, No. 48, København, 1928.

JESSEN, K. 1935. (With Jonassen, H.) The Composition of the Forests in Northern Europe in Epipalaeolithic Time. *Det Kgl. Danske Videnskabernes Selskab. Biologiske Meddelelser*, XII (1935), 3–64.

—— 1935[*a*]. Archaeological Dating in the History of North Jutland's Vegetation. *Acta Archaeologia*, V (1935), 185–214.

—— 1936. Palaeobotanical Report on the Stone Age Site at Newferry, County Londonderry. Appendix I to Movius, H. L., Jr. (1936). *P.R.I.A.* XLIII (1936), 31–7.

JESSEN, K. (and FARRINGTON, A.) 1938. The Bogs at Ballybetagh, near Dublin, with Remarks on Late-Glacial Conditions in Ireland. *P.R.I.A.* XLIV (1938), 205–60.

JESSEN, K. 1938[*a*]. Some West Baltic Pollen Diagrams. *Quartär*, I (1938), 124–39.

—— 1940. Geological and Palaeobotanical Report on an Early Post-Glacial Archaeological Site at Cushendun, County Antrim. *P.R.I.A.* XLVI (1939), 38–51.

JONES, C. B. 1932. The Origin and Development of British Cattle. *P. 1st I.C.*, London, 1932, pp. 151–4.

JONES, O, T. 1934. Some Observations on Recent Geological Movements of the British Coastline. *Antiquity*, VIII (1934), 303–9.

JONES, O. T. and BOSWELL, P. G. H. 1928. Geological Features of the Sites of the Sligo Implements. *Nature*, 121 (1928), 861–2.

JOWETT, ALBERT. 1914. The Glacial Geology of East Lancashire. *Q.J.G.S.* LXX (1914), 199–231.
KEITH, Sir ARTHUR. 1931. *New Discoveries Relating to the Antiquity of Man.* New York, 1931.
KENDALL, P. F. 1902. A System of Glacier Lakes in the Cumberland Hills. *Q.J.G.S.* LVIII (1902), 471–571.
KENDALL, P. F. and BAILEY, E. B. 1907. The Glaciation of East Lothian South of the Garleton Hills. *T.R.S., Edin.* XLVI (1907), 1–31.
KINAHAN, G. H. 1873. The Estuary of the River Slaney, County Wexford. *J.R.G.S., Ireland,* XIV (1873), 60–9.
KING, W. B. R. and OAKLEY, K. P. 1936. The Pleistocene Succession in the Lower Parts of the Thames Valley. *P.P.S.* II (1936), 52–76.
KNOWLES, W. J. 1879. Portstewart and other Flint Factories in the North of Ireland. *J.R.A.I.* IX (1879–80), 320–8.
—— 1879[*a*]. Excavations at Porstewart, and Elsewhere in the North of Ireland. *Rep. Brit. Ass.* 1879, pp. 171–5.
—— 1881. Prehistoric Implements found in the Sandhills of Dundrum, County Down. *P.R.I.A.* II (1881), 105–13.
—— 1885. Whitepark Bay, County Antrim. *J.R.H.A.A.I.* VII (1885), 104–25.
—— 1888. Tracked Stones. *J.R.H.A.A.I.* VIII (1888), 497–502.
—— 1889. Report on the Prehistoric Remains from the Sandhills of the Coast of Ireland. *P.R.I.A.* I (1889), 173–87.
—— 1891. Second Report on the Prehistoric Remains from the Sandhills of the Coast of Ireland. *P.R.I.A.* I (1891), 612–25.
—— 1892. On the Occurrence of Flint Flakes in the Glacial Gravels of Ballyrudder, near Larne, County Antrim. *R. and P. Bel. N.F.C.* III (1891–92), 410–14.
—— 1893. Irish Stone Axes and Chisels. *J.R.S.A.I.* III (1893), 140–63.
—— 1894. Prehistoric Pottery from the Sandhills, and its Antiquity. *J.R.S.A.I.* IV (1894), 243–55.
—— 1894[*a*]. Irish Flint Saws. *J.R.S.A.I.* IV (1894), 341–8.
—— 1895. The Third Report on the Prehistoric Remains from the Sandhills of the Coast of Ireland. *P.R.I.A.* III (1895), 650–63.
—— 1897. Survivals from the Palaeolithic Age among Irish Neolithic Implements. *J.R.H.A.A.I.* VII (1897), 1–18.
—— 1898. Irish Flint Scrapers. *J.R.S.A.I.* VIII (1898), 367–91.
KNOWLES, W. J., PATTERSON, W. H., PRAEGER, R. LL. and BIGGER, F. J. 1899. Investigation of the Prehistoric Settlements near Roundstone, Connemara. *P.R.I.A.* V (1899), 433–40.
KNOWLES, W. J. 1901. The Fourth Report on the Prehistoric Remains from the Sandhills of the Coast of Ireland. *P.R.I.A.* VI (1901), 331–89.
—— 1903. Stone Axe-Factories near Cushendall, County Antrim. *J.R.A.I.* XXXIII (1903), 360–6.
—— 1906. Stone Axe-Factories near Cushendall. *J.R.S.A.I.* XVI (1906), 383–94.
—— 1906[*a*]. Stone Age Axe-Factories near Cushendall. *R. and P. Bal. N.F.C.* V (1906), 421–3.
—— 1912. Prehistoric Stone Implements from the River Bann and Lough Neagh. *P.R.I.A.* XXX (1912), 195–222.
—— 1914. The Antiquity of Man in Ireland, Being an Account of the Older Series of Irish Flint Implements. *J.R.A.I.* XLIV (1914), 83–121.
KOSŁOWSKI, L. 1926. L'Epoque Mésolithique en Pologne. *L'Anth.* XXXVI (1926), 47–74.

LACAILLE, A. D. 1929. Mesolithic Implements from Ayrshire. *P.S.A., Scot.* LXIV (1929), 34–48.
—— 1931. Silex Tardenoisiens de Shewalton. *B.S.P.F.* XXVIII (1931), 301–12.
—— 1932. A Survey of the Scottish Tardenoisean Industries. *P. 1st I.C.*, London, 1932, pp. 99–100.
—— 1935. The Tardenoisean Micro-Burin in Scotland. *P.S.A., Scot.* LXIX (1935), 443–5.
—— 1935[*a*]. The Small Flint Knives of Orkney. *P.S.A., Scot.* LXIX (1935), 251–62.
—— 1937. The Microlithic Industries of Scotland. *Trans. Glasgow Arch. Soc.* ix–1 (1937), 56–74.
—— 1938. Scottish Gravers of Flint and Other Stones. *P.S.A., Scot.* LXXII (1938), 180–92.
—— 1939. A Barbed Point of Deer-Antler from Shewalton, Ayrshire. *P.S.A., Scot.* LXXIII (1939), 48–50.
LA TOUCHE, C. J. 1936. Occurrence of Pollen of *Carpinus* (Hornbeam) in Irish Peat. *Nature*, 137 (1936), 949.
LAYARD, Miss N. F. 1909. The Older Series of Irish Flint Implements. *Man*, IX (1909), 81–5.
LEACH, A. L. 1913. Stone Implements from Soil-Drifts and Chipping-Floors, etc. in South Pembroke. *Arch. Camb.* XIII (1913), 391–432 (6th series).
—— 1918. Flint-Working Sites on the Submerged Land (Submerged Forest) Bordering the Pembrokeshire Coast. *Proc. Geol. Ass.* XXIX (1918), 46–67.
LEASK, H. G. 1934. Notes on Excavations in the Irish Free State during 1934. *P.P.S.E.A.* VII (1934), 410–11.
—— 1938. Notes on Excavations in Éire during 1938. *P.P.S.* IV (1938), 314–15.
LEVERETT, F. 1929. Pleistocene Glaciations of the Northern Hemisphere. *B.G.S.A.* XL (1929), 745–60.
LEWIS, F. J. 1905. The Plant Remains in the Scottish Peat Mosses. Part I, The Scottish Southern Uplands. *T.R.S., Edin.* XLI (1905), 699–723.
—— 1906. The Plant Remains in the Scottish Peat Mosses. Part II, The Scottish Highlands. *T.R.S., Edin.* XLV (1906), 335–60.
—— 1907. The Plant Remains in the Scottish Peat Mosses. Part III, The Scottish Highlands and the Shetland Islands. *T.R.S., Edin.* XLVI (1907), 33–70.
—— 1910. The Plant Remains in the Scottish Peat Mosses. Part IV, The Scottish Highlands and Shetland, with an Appendix on the Icelandic Peat Deposits. *T.R.S., Edin.* XLVII (1910), 793–833.
LONKE, A. 1935. Tagung des Nordwestdeutschen Verbandes für Altertumsforschung in Lüneburg vom 23.–25. April, 1935. Wissenschaftliche Jahresberichte. *Praehistorische Zeitschrift*, XXVI (1935), 251–4.
MACALISTER, R. A. S. 1928. *The Archaeology of Ireland.* London, 1928.
MACCLINTOCK, P. 1933. Interglacial Soils and the Drift Sheets of Eastern England. *R. XVI I.G.C.* 1933, pp. 1041–53.
MACCURDY, G. G. 1916. *The Cult of the Ax.* Holmes Anniversary Volume. Washington, 1916, pp. 301–15.
MACGREGOR, M. 1927. The Geology of the Carstairs District. *Proc. Geol. Ass.* XXXVIII (1927), 495–8.
MAHR, A. 1937. New Aspects and Problems in Irish Prehistory. *P.P.S.* Presidential Address, III (1937), 262–436.
MANN, L. McL. 1936. Antiquities in Shetland. *Nature*, 138 (1936), 512.
MARR, J. E. 1919. The Pleistocene Deposits around Cambridge. *Q.J.G.S.* LXXV (1919), 204–44.

Martin, C. P. 1930. The Raised Beaches of the East Coast of Ireland. *S.P.R.D.S.* xix (1930), 491–511.
—— 1935. *Prehistoric Man in Ireland.* London, 1935.
Mason, W. D. 1931. Prehistoric Man at Tweed Bridge, Selkirk. *P.S.A., Scot.* lxv (1931), 414–17.
Matley, C. A. 1936. A 50-foot Coastal Terrace and Other Late-Glacial Phenomena in the Lleyn Peninsula. *Proc. Geol. Ass.* xlvii (1936), 221–33.
Maxwell, J. H. 1934. Chronology of Scottish Caves. *Nature,* 134 (1934), 316.
May, A. McL. 1934. Excavations in Caves at Port Braddon, County Antrim. *I.N.J.* v (1934), 56–8.
—— 1939. Some Pointed Bones. Flints and Stone Discs from the Lower River Bann. *J.R.S.A.I.* lxix (1939), 152–61.
May, R. L. 1939. Javelin- and Arrow-heads from the Lower Bann Valley. *U.J.A.* ii (1939), 104–9.
McCallien, W. J. 1935. Ice Age Dating in Britain. *Science Progress,* xxx (1935), 67–71.
—— 1937. Late-Glacial and Early Post-Glacial Scotland. *P.S.A., Scot.* lxxi (1937), 174–206.
—— 1937[*a*]. Rhu (Row) Point—A Readvance Moraine. *T.G.S., Glasgow,* xix (1937), 385–9.
McMillan, Mrs N. F. 1937. The Molluscan Remains from Glenarm. Appendix II to Movius, H. L., Jr. (1937) (by Miss Nora Fisher). *J.R.A.S.I.* lxvii (1937), 216–17.
—— 1938. A Kitchen-Midden at Greenisland. *U.J.A.* i (1938), 226–7.
—— 1938[*a*]. Evidence of a Change in the Relative Levels of Land and Sea at Greenisland, County Antrim. *I.N.J.* vii (1938), 89.
—— 1940. Report on the Fauna from and Early Post-Glacial Archaeological Site at Cushendun, County Antrim. *P.R.I.A.* xlvi (1940), 34–8.
—— 1940[*a*]. Report on the Marine Fauna from Rough Island, Strangford Lough, County Down. *J.R.S.A.I.* lxx (1940), 138–41.
Menghin, O. 1931. *Weltgeschichte der Steinzeit.* Wien, 1931.
M.G.S. England and Wales. 1926. Dixon, E. E. L., Maden, J., Trotter, F. M., Hollingworth, S. E. and Tonks, L. H. The Geology of the Carlisle, Longtown, and Silloth District, 1926.
1928. Whitehead, T. H., Robertson, T., Pocock, R. W. and Dixon, E. E. L. The Country between Wolverhampton and Oakengates. 1928.
1931. Eastwood, T., Dixon, E. E. L., Hollingworth, S. E. and Smith, Bernard. The Geology of the Whitehaven and Workington District.
1932. Trotter, F. M. and Hollingworth, S. E. The Geology of the Brampton District. 1932.
M.G.S. Scotland. 1925. Bailey, E. B., MacGregor, M., Dinham, C. H. and Anderson, E. M. The Geology of the Glasgow District. 1925.
1930. Bailey, E. B., Richey, J. E., Anderson, E. M. and MacGregor, A. G. The Geology of North Ayrshire. 1930.
M.G.S. Ireland. 1876. Hull, Edward and Baily, W. H. The Country around Antrim, Larne, and Carrickfergus. 1876.
1892. Egan, F. W. Explanatory Memoir to Accompany Sheet 19 of the Maps (Southern Section of the Lower Bann Valley). 1892.
1903. Lamplugh, G. W., Kilroe, J. R., McHenry, A., Seymour, H. J. and Wright, W. B. The Geology of the Country around Dublin. 1903.
1904. Lamplugh, G. W., Kilroe, J. R., McHenry, A., Seymour, H. J., Wright, W. B. and Muff, H. B. The Geology of the Country around Belfast. 1904.

M.G.S. Ireland. 1908. Wilkinson, S. B., McHenry, A., Kilroe, J. R. and Seymour, H. J. The Geology of the Country around Londonderry. 1908.

1927. Wright, W. B., Cole, G. A. J. and Hallissy, T. The Geology of Killarney and Kenmare., 1927.

Mitchell, G. F. 1940. Studies in Irish Quaternary Deposits: Some Lacustrine Deposits near Dunshaughlin, County Meath. *P.R.I.A.* xlvi–B (1940), 13–37.

Moir, J. Reid. 1917. On Some Human and Animal Bones, Flint Implements, etc., Discovered in Two Ancient Occupation Levels in a Small Valley near Ipswich. *J.R.A.I.* xlvii (1917), 367–412.

—— 1920. On the Occurrence of Flint Implements of Man in the Glacial Chalky Boulder Clay of Suffolk. *J.R.A.I.* l (1920), 135–52.

—— 1930. Flint Implements of Upper Palaeolithic Types from Glacial Deposits in Norfolk. *Antiq. Jour.* x (1930), 359–71.

—— 1931. Further Discoveries of Flint Implements in the Brown Boulder Clay of North-West Norfolk. *P.P.S.E.A.* vi (1931), 306–15.

Moran, John. 1889. Mammoth's Tooth recently found in the Drift Gravels at Larne Harbour. *R. and P. Bel. N.H. and P.S.* (1888–89), pp. 35–7.

Movius, H. L., Jr. 1935. Kilgreany Cave, County Waterford. (With Appendices by Stelfox, A. W., Roche, Miss G. and Maby, J. C.) *J.R.S.A.I.* lxv (1935), 254–96.

—— 1936. A Neolithic Site on the River Bann. (With Appendices by Jessen, Professor K., Childe, Professor V. G. and Whelan, C. B., Esq.) *P.R.I.A.* xliii (1936), 17–40.

—— 1937. A Stone Age Site at Glenarm, County Antrim. (With Appendices by Allen, Professor G. M., Fisher (McMillan), Miss N. and Richardson, F. L. W., Jr.) *J.R.S.A.I.* lxvii (1937), 181–220.

—— 1940. An Early Post-Glacial Archaeological Site at Cushendun, County Antrim. (With Reports by Jessen, Professor K., McMillan, Mrs N. F. and Richardson, F. L. W., Jr.) *P.R.I.A.* xlvi (1940), 1–84.

—— 1940[*a*]. Report on a Stone Age Excavation at Rough Island, Strangford Lough, County Down. *J.R.S.A.I.* lxx (1940), 111–42.

Munro, R. 1898. The Relation between Archaeology, Chronology and Land Oscillations in Post-Glacial Times. *Arch. Jour.* lv (1898), 259–85.

—— 1908. On the Transition between the Palaeolithic and Neolithic Civilizations in Europe. *Arch. Jour.* lxv (1908), 205–44.

Neaverson, E. 1936. Recent Observations on the Post-Glacial Peat Beds around Rhyl and Prestatyn (Flintshire). *P.L.G.S.* xvii (1936), 45–63.

Neuville, R. 1930. The Stone Industries of the Bronze Age. *Jour. of the Palestine Oriental Society*, x (1930), 199–216.

Obermaier, H. 1906. Beiträge zur Kenntnis des Quartärs in den Pyrenäen. *Archiv f. Anth.* iv. (1906), 299–310; v (1906), 244–62.

—— 1925. *Fossil Man in Spain.* New Haven, 1925.

—— 1932. Le Premier Congrès International des Sciences Préhistoriques, Londres, 1932 (by Vaufrey, R.). Excursion d'Irland (pp. 543–4): Section dealing with the Irish Stone Age based on notes from Obermaier, H. *L'Anth.* xlii (1932), 544.

—— 1933. Der Diluviale Mensch auf der Pyrenäenhalbinsel. *R. XVI I.G.C.* 1933, pp. 1275–89.

Octobon, M. E. 1931. Documents pour servir à l'étude du Néolithique. Le Pré-Campignian ou Campignian I. Station Pré-Campignian de Champlat. Hameau de Boujacourt (Aisne). *B.S.P.F.* xxviii (1931), 172–84.

O'LAVERTY, Rev. JAMES. 1857. Relative Antiquity of Stone and Bronze Weapons. *U.J.A.* v (1857), 122–7.

Ó'RÍORDÁIN, S. P. 1935. Recent Acquisitions from County Donegal in the National Museum. *P.R.I.A.* XLII (1935), 145–91.

OSBORN, J. F. and REEDS, C. A. 1922. Old and New Standards of Pleistocene Division in Relation to the Prehistory of Man in Europe. *B.G.S.A.* XXXIII (1922), 411–90.

PALMER, L. S. 1931. On the Pleistocene Succession of the Bristol District. *Proc. Geol. Ass.* XLII (1931), 345–61.

PARKER, D. 1938. Flints from the Shore of Lough Beg. *U.J.A.* I (1938), 107.

PATERSON, H. M. L. 1913. Pigmy Flints in the Dee Valley. *Man*, XIII (1913), 103–5.

PATERSON, H. M. L. and LACAILLE, A. D. 1936. Banchory Microliths. *P.S.A., Scot.* LXX (1936), 419–34.

PATTERSON, W. H. 1896. A Recent Discovery of Worked Flints in Submerged Peat at Portrush. *R. and P. Bel. N.H. and P.S.* (1896–97), pp. 32–4.

—— 1896[*a*]. On a Find of Worked Flints in Submerged Peat at Portrush, County Antrim. *J.R.S.A.I.* XXVI (1896), 383–4.

PEACH, B. N. and HORNE, J. 1917. The Bone Cave in the Valley of Allt-nan-Uamh, near Inchnadamff, Assynt, Sutherland. *P.R.S., Edin.* XXXVII (1917), 327–49.

PEAKE, H. J. E. and FLEURE, H. J. 1927. *The Corridors of Time.* II, Hunters and Artists. New Haven, 1927.

PEAKE, H. J. E. and CLARK, J. G. D. 1938. The Separation of Britain from the Continent. *P.P.S.* IV (1938), 230–1.

—— 1938[*a*]. The Final Insulation of Britain. *P.P.S.* IV (1938), 343–4.

PENCK, A. and BRÜCKNER, E. 1909. *Die Alpen in Eiszeitalten*, Bds I–IV. Leipzig, 1909.

PENGELLY, W. 1865. The Submerged Forests of Torbay. *Trans. Devon. Ass.* I (1865), 30–42.

—— 1867. The Raised Beaches in Barnstaple Bay, North Devon. *Trans. Devon. Ass.* II (1867), 43–56.

PHILLIPS, C. W. 1936. A Dug-Out Boat from the Lea Valley. *P.P.S.* II (1936), 144–5.

PIGGOTT, STUART and CLARK, J. G. D. 1933. The Age of the British Flint Mines. *Antiquity*, VII (1933), 2–19.

POST, L. VON. 1937. The Geographical Survey of Irish Bogs. *I.N.J.* VI (1937), 210–27.

POOLE, H. F. 1936. An Outline of the Mesolithic Flint Cultures of the Isle of Wight. *Proc. Isle of Wight Nat. Hist. and Arch. Soc.* II (1936), 551–81.

PRAEGER, R. LL. 1888. On the Estuarine Clays at the New Alexandra Dock, Belfast. *R. and P. Bel. N.F.C.* Appendix II, Vol. II (1888), 29–51.

—— 1890. Report of a Committee of Investigation on the Gravels and Associated Beds of the Curran, at Larne, County Antrim. *R. and P. Bel. N.F.C.* III (1889–90), 198–210.

—— 1892. Report on the Estuarine Clays of the North-East of Ireland. *P.R.I.A.* II (1892), 212–89.

—— 1893. Marine Shells at Ballyrudder. *P. Bel. N.F.C.* III (1893), 518–25.

—— 1895. The Raised Beaches of Inishowen. *The Irish Naturalist*, IV (1895), 278–85

—— 1895[*a*]. A Submerged Pine-Forest. *The Irish Naturalist*, V (1895), 155–60.

—— 1896. Report on the Raised Beaches of the North-East of Ireland with Special Reference to their Fauna. *P.R.I.A.* IV (1896), 30–54.

—— 1896[*a*]. A Bibliography of Irish Glacial and Post-Glacial Geology. *R. and P. Bel. N.F.C.* IV (1896), 239–316 (Appendix).

—— 1904. Round About Belfast Lough. *The Irish Naturalist*, XIII (1904), 141–7.

—— 1928. Ireland and Europe In and Since the Ice Age. *I.N.J.* II (1928), 100–1.

LIST OF WORKS

PRAEGER, R. LL. 1934. Recent Views Bearing on the Problem of the Irish Fauna and Flora. *P.R.I.A.* XLI (1934), 125–45.
—— 1935. The Belfast Post-Glacial Section. *I.N.J.* V (1935), 291.
PRAEGER, R. LL., FARRINGTON, A., JESSEN, K., WHELAN, C. B., MAHR, A. and CLARK, J. G. D. 1934. The Committee for Quaternary Research in Ireland and Its Work. *I.N.J.* V (1934), 126–52.
RAISTRICK, A. 1931. The Glaciation of Northumberland and Durham. *Proc. Geol. Ass.* XLII (1931), 281–91.
—— 1933. The Glacial and Post-Glacial Periods in West Yorkshire. *Proc. Geol. Ass.* XLIV (1933), 263–9.
—— 1933[*a*]. The Correlation of Glacial Retreat Stages across the Pennines. *P.Y.G.S.* XXII (1933), 199–214.
—— 1933[*b*]. The Distribution of Mesolithic Sites in the North of England. *Yorks. Arch. Jour.* XXXI (1933), 141–54.
—— 1933[*c*]. Mesolithic Sites of the North-East Coast of England. *P.P.S.E.A.* VII (1933), 188–98.
READ, H. H., BREMNER, ALEX., CAMPBELL, ROBT. and GIBB, A. W. 1923. Records of the Occurrence of Boulders of Norwegian Rocks in Aberdeenshire and Banffshire. *T.E.G.S.* XI (1923), 230–1.
READE, T. MELLARD. 1871. The Geology and Physics of the Post-Glacial Period, as shown in the Deposits and Organic Remains in Lancashire and Cheshire. *P.L.G.S.* II (1871), 36–88.
—— 1883. On a Section of the Formby and Leasowe Marine Beds and Superior Peat Bed, Disclosed by the Cuttings for the Outlet Sewer at Hightown. *P.L.G.S.* IV (1883), 269–77.
—— 1896. Oscillations in the Level of the Land as shown by the Buried River-Valleys and Later Deposits in the Neighbourhood of Liverpool. *Geol. Mag.* III (1896), 488–92.
—— 1900. A Contribution to Post-Glacial Geology: Foraminifera of the Formby and Leasowe Marine Beds. *Geol. Mag.* VII (1900), 97–105.
REID, CLEMENT. 1913. *Submerged Forests.* London, 1913.
RICHARDSON, F. L. W., Jr. 1940. Physiographical Report on an Early Post-Glacial Archaeological Site at Cushendun, County Antrim. *P.R.I.A.* XLVI (1940), 10–24.
RITCHIE, JAMES. 1929. The Fauna of Scotland during the Ice Age (Presidential Address, 1928). *P.R.P.S., Edin.* XXI (1929), 185–94.
ROGERS, INKERMANN. 1908. On the Submerged Forest at Westward Ho! Bideford Bay. *Trans. Devon. Ass.* XL (1908), 249–59.
SALMON, P., DU MESNIL, D'A. and CAPITAN, L. 1898. Le Campignien. *Revue Mensuelle de l'École d'Anthropologie de Paris,* VIII (1898), 365–408.
SANDFORD, K. S. 1932. The Pleistocene Succession in England. *Geol. Mag.* LXIX (1932), 1–18.
—— 1933. Recent Researches on Fossil Man in England and Wales. *R. XVI I.G.C.* 1933, pp. 1185–7.
—— 1933[*a*]. The Quaternary Glaciation of England and Wales. *Nature,* 132 (1933), 863–4.
—— 1935. Geological Relations of Early Man in East Anglia. *Nature,* 136 (1935), 502–3.
SCHARFF, R. F. 1926. The "Irish Elk". *I.N.J.* I (1926), 109–12.
SCHLEICHER, CH. 1932. Quelques petits silex recueillis dans les environs de Castlereagh (Compté Down, Irland). *B.S.P.F.* XXIX (1932), 227.
SHETELIG, H. and FALK, H. 1937. *Scandinavian Archaeology.* London, 1937.
SHORE, T. W. and ELWES, J. W. 1889. The New Dock Excavation at Southampton. *Papers and Proceedings of the Hampshire Field Club,* I (1889), 43–56.

SIMPSON, J. B. 1933. The Late-Glacial Readvance Moraines of the Highland Border West of the River Tay. *T.R.S., Edin.* LVII (1933), 633–46.
SIMPSON, W. J. 1889. On Worked Flints found on a Raised Beach at Portrush. *P.R.I.A.* I (1889), 76–7.
SLATER, G. 1931. The Structure of the Bride Moraine, Isle of Man. *P.L.G.S.* XV (1931), 284–96.
SMITH, BERNARD. 1930. Borings through the Glacial Drifts of the Northern Plain of the Isle of Man. *Mem. Geol. Surv.* Summary of Progress for 1930, Part III, pp. 14–23.
—— 1932. The Glacier-Lakes of Eskdale, Miterdale and Wasdale, Cumberland: and the Retreat of the Ice during the Main Glaciation. *Q.J.G.S.* LXXXVIII (1932), 57–83.
SMITH, Rev. F. 1909. *The Stone Age in North Britain and Ireland.* London, 1909.
SMITH, F. G. 1925. Some Evidences of Early Man Within and Near to the Northern Portion of the Vale of Clwyd. *P.L.G.S.* XIV (1925), 117–22.
SMITH, R. A. 1911. On the Date of Grimes Graves and Cissbury Flint-Mines. *Archaeologia,* LXIII (1911), 109–58.
—— 1931. *The Sturge Collection.* British Museum, London, 1931.
SOLOMON, J. D. 1931. Palaeolithic and Mesolithic Sites at Morston, Norfolk. *Man,* XXXI (1931), 275–8.
—— 1932. The Glacial Succession on the North Norfolk Coast. *Proc. Geol. Ass.* XLIII (1932), 241–71.
STANFORD'S. 1913. *Geological Atlas of Great Britain and Ireland.* London, 1913 (4th edition).
STEERS, J. A. 1937. The Culbin Sands and Burghead Bay. *Geog. Jour.* XC (1937), 498–528.
STELFOX, A. W. 1927. An Arctic Peat Bed in Ireland. *Nature,* 119 (1927), 781.
—— 1934. The Problem of the Irish Elk. *I.N.J.* V (1934), 74–6.
—— 1937. On the Former Occurrence of a Species of Lynx in Ireland. *I.N.J.* VI (1937), 251.
—— 1938. Did the Giant Deer Survive the Last Glaciation in Ireland? *I.N.J.* VII (1938), 70–1.
STEWART, M. 1937. Raised Beaches in the Outer Hebrides. *Geol. Mag.* LXXIV (1937), 192.
STEWART, S. A. 1871. The Latest Fluctuations of the Sea-Level on our own Coasts. *8th Annual R. and P. Bel. N.F.C.* 1871, pp. 55–7.
STRAHAN, A. 1896. On Submerged Land-Surfaces at Barry, Glamorganshire. *Q.J.G.S.* LII (1896), 474–89.
SWINNERTON, H. H. 1931. The Post-Glacial Deposits of the Lincolnshire Coast. *Q.J.G.S.* LXXXVII (1931), 360–72.
SWINTON, W. E. 1927. Note on a Rhinoceros Bone from the Glacial Sands of Cadder. *T.G.S., Glasgow,* XVII (1927), 395.
TAIT, DAVID. 1909. On the Occurrence of Cretaceous Fossils in Caithness. *T.E.G.S.* IX (1909), 318–21.
—— 1910. On a Large Glacially Transported Mass of Lower Cretaceous Rock at Leavad in the County of Caithness. *T.E.G.S.* X (1910), 1–9.
—— 1930. Excavations under the Sea at Portobello. *T.E.G.S.* XII (1930), 313–20.
—— 1934. Braid Burn, Dunnington, and Portobello Excavations, 1929–31. *T.E.G.S.* XIII (1934), 61–71.
—— 1934[*a*]. Excavations in the Old Lake Deposits at Corstorphine during 1930–32. *T.E.G.S.* XIII (1934), 110–25.
TALLGREN, A. M. 1937. The Method of Prehistoric Archaeology. *Antiquity,* XI (1937), 152–61.
TILLOTSON, ERNEST. 1933. The Glacial Geology of Nidderdale. *P.Y.G.S.* XXII (1933), 215–28.
TING, S. 1936. Beach Ridges and other Shore Deposits in South-West Jura. *Scottish Geog. Mag.* LII (1936), 182–7.

TOMLINSON, M. E. 1935. The Superficial Deposits of the Country North of Stratford-on-Avon. *Q.J.G.S.* XCI (1935), 423–62.

TRATMAN, E. K. 1928. Excavations at Kilgreany Cave, County Waterford. *P.B.S.S.* III (1928), 109–53.

—— 1937. Observations on Kilgreany Cave, County Waterford. *J.R.S.A.I.* LXVII (1937), 120–4.

TRECHMANN, C. T. 1931. The 60-Foot Raised Beach at Easington, Co. Durham. *Proc. Geol. Ass.* XLII (1931), 295–6.

—— 1936. Mesolithic Flints from the Submerged Forest at West Hartlepool. *P.P.S.* II (1936), 161–8.

TROTTER, F. M. 1929. The Glaciation of Eastern Edenside, the Alston Block, and the Carlisle Plain. *Q.J.G.S.* LXXXV (1929), 549–609.

TROTTER, F. M. and HOLLINGWORTH, S. E. 1932. The Glacial Sequence in the North of England. *Geol. Mag.* LXIX (1932), 364–80.

TURNER, Sir WILLIAM. 1895. The Human Remains from the Oban Caves. *P.S.A., Scot.* V (1895), 410–38.

—— 1915. The Craniology of the People of Scotland. *T.R.S., Edin.* LI (1915), 209–17.

ULLYOTT, P. 1936. A Note on the Zoogeographical History of North-West Europe. *P.P.S.* II (1936), 169–77.

USSHER, R. J. 1903. The Crannog at Ardmore, County Waterford. *J.R.S.A.I.* XXXIII (1903), 387–8.

WALLACE, T. D. 1868. Recent Geological Changes on the Moray Firth. *T.E.G.S.* I (1868), 40–54.

WALMSLEY, THOMAS and MOGEY, J. M. 1938. The Peoples of Northern Ireland: An Anthropometric Survey. *U.J.A.* I (1938), 89–97.

WALTON, J. 1933. The Survival of Vegetation Through the Ice Age in Ireland. *I.N.J.* IV (1933), 142–3.

WARREN, S. H. 1919. A Stone-Axe Factory at Graig-Lwyd, Penmaenmawr. *J.R.A.I.* XLIX (1919), 342–65.

—— 1921. Excavations at the Stone-Axe Factory of Graig-Lwyd, Penmaenmawr. *J.R.A.I.* LI (1921), 165–99.

—— 1922. The Neolithic Stone Axes of Graig-Lwyd, Penmaenmawr. *Arch. Camb.* II (1922), 1–36, (7th series).

WARREN, S. H., CLARK, J. G. D., GODWIN, M. E. and MACFADYEN, W. A. 1934. An Early Mesolithic Site at Broxbourne sealed under Boreal Peat. *J.R.A.I.* LXIV (1934), 101–28.

WARREN, S. H., PIGGOTT, S., CLARK, J. G. D., BURKITT, M. C. and GODWIN, M. E. 1936. Archaeology of the Submerged Land-Surface of the Essex Coast. *P.P.S.* II (1936), 178–210.

WELCH, R. J. 1928. Beach at Rosses Point, County Sligo. *I.N.J.* II (1928), Plate IV.

WHEELER, R. E. M. 1925. *Prehistoric and Roman Wales.* Oxford, 1925.

WHELAN, C. B. 1928. The Implementiferous Raised Beach Gravels of South-East Antrim. *Man,* XXVIII (1928), 186–9.

—— 1928[*a*]. A Prehistoric Hearth at Greenoge, Dunmurry, County Antrim. *I.N.J.* II (1928), 94–8.

—— 1930. The Flint Industry of the Northern Irish (25-Foot) Raised Beach: A Preliminary Study of its Relation to the Asturian Industry of Portugal. *J.R.A.I.* LX (1930), 169–84.

—— 1930[*a*]. News of the Societies. *I.N.J.* III (1930), 95.

—— 1930[*b*]. The Tanged Flake Industry of the River Bann, County Antrim. *Antiq. Jour.* X (1930), 134–8.

WHELAN, C. B. 1932. Notes on Northern Irish Prehistory. *I.N.J.* IV (1932), 95–7.
—— 1933. The Palaeolithic Question in Ireland. *R. XVI I.G.C.* (1933), 1209–18.
—— 1933[*a*]. Post-Glacial Prehistory in Northern Ireland: Three Recent Chronological Indications. 1. Lough Neagh, *I.N.J.* IV (1933), 149–50; 2. Castlereagh, *ibid.* pp. 201–2; 3. The Industry of the Raised Beach, *ibid.* p. 215.
—— 1934. Studies in the Significance of the Irish Stone Age: The Campignian Question. *P.R.I.A.* XLII (1934), 121–43.
—— 1934[*a*]. Further Excavation at Ballynagard, Rathlin Island, County Antrim. *R. and P. Bel. N.F.C.* (1933–34), pp. 107–11.
—— 1935. An Implement from the Larne Raised Beach. *Antiq. Jour.* XV (1935), 465–6.
—— 1935[*a*]. A Cordate Hand-Axe of Chalcolithic Age. *Antiq. Jour.* XV (1935), 194–5.
—— 1936. Report on Neolithic Pottery from Newferry, County Londonderry. Appendix III to Movius, H. L., Jr. (1936). *P.R.I.A.* XLIII (1936), 39–40.
—— 1938. Studies in the Significance of the Irish Stone Age: The Culture Sequence. *P.R.I.A.* XLIV (1938), 115–36.
WILLIAMS, K. E. 1927. The Glacial Drifts of Western Cardiganshire. *Geol. Mag.* LXIX (1927), 205–27.
WILLS, L. J. 1937. The Pleistocene History of the West Midlands. *Nature,* 140 (1937), 995–7, 1036–9.
—— 1938. The Pleistocene Development of the Severn from Bridgenorth to the Sea. *Q.J.G.S.* XCIV (1938), 161–242.
WOOD, S. V., Jr. and ROME, J. L. 1868. On the Glacial and Postglacial Structure of Lincolnshire and South-East Yorkshire. *Q.J.G.S.* XXIV (1868), 146–84.
WOOD-MARTIN, W. G. 1886. *The Lake-Dwellings of Ireland.* Dublin, 1886.
WOOLACOTT, D. 1921. The Interglacial Problem and the Glacial and Post-Glacial Sequence in Northumberland and Durham. *Geol. Mag.* LVIII (1921), 21–32, 60–9.
—— 1922. On the 60-foot Raised Beach at Easington, County Durham. *Geol. Mag.* LIX (1922), 64–74.
WRIGHT, W. B. and MUFF, H. B. 1904. The Pre-Glacial Raised Beach of the South Coast of Ireland. *S.P.R.D.S.* X (1904), 250–324.
WRIGHT, W. B. 1911. On a Pre-Glacial Shore-line in the Western Isles of Scotland. *Geol. Mag.* VIII (1911), 97–109.
WRIGHT, W. B. and PEACH A. M. 1911. The Neolithic Remains of Colonsay. *Geol. Mag.* VIII (1911), 164–75.
WRIGHT, W. B. 1912. Submerged Forests in certain Inland Lakes in Donegal. *Geol. Mag.* IX (1912), 115–20.
—— 1914. *The Quaternary Ice Age.* London, 1914.
—— 1925. Three Short Papers on Isostasy: I, The Isostatic Lag; II, The Wave-Like Progress of the Emergence; III, The Azilians of Oban. *Geol. Mag.* LXII (1925), 227–34.
—— 1928. The Raised Beaches of the British Isles. *First Report of the Commission on Pliocene and Pleistocene Terraces* (edited by Sandford, K. S.), 1928, pp. 99–106.
—— 1934. The Isokinetic Theory of Glacially-Controlled Shorelines. *Congrès International de Géographie, Varsovie.* Comptes Rendus, 1934, pp. 33–52. (Published in 1936.)
—— 1937. *The Quaternary Ice Age.* London, 1937 (2nd edition).
YOUNG, JOHN and CRAIG, ROBERT. 1869. Notes on the Occurrence of Seeds of Freshwater Plants and Arctic Shells along with the Remains of the Mammoth and Reindeer, in Beds under the Boulder Clay at Kilmaurs. *T.G.S., Glasgow,* III (1869), 310–21.

Young, Robert. 1877. Some Questions in which Recent Researches in Science are Tending to Modify the Opinions of Geologists. *R. and P. Bel. N.H. and P.S.* Presidential Address (1877–78), pp. 1–21.

—— 1894. A Recent Find of Irish Elk Bones in Belfast. *R. and P. Bel. N.H. and P.S.* (1893–94), pp. 76–8.

Zeuner, F. E. 1935. The Pleistocene Chronology of Central Europe. *Geol. Mag.* lxxii (1935), 350–76.

—— 1937. A Comparison of the Pleistocene of East Anglia with that of Germany. *P.P.S.* iii (1937), 136–57.

—— 1937[*a*]. Report of the Department of Geochronology for 1937. *First Annual Report; Inst. of Arch. of the Univ. of London*, 1937, pp. 29–46.

—— 1937[*b*]. The Climate of the Countries adjoining the Ice-Sheet of the Pleistocene. *Proc. Geol. Assoc.* xlviii (1937), 379–95.

—— 1938. Die Chronologie des Pleistozäns. *Académie Royale Serbe. Bulletin de l'Académie des Sciences Mathématiques et Naturelles*, No. 4, Belgrade, 1938, pp. 1–79.

—— 1938[*a*]. The Chronology of the Pleistocene Sea-Levels. *Annals and Magazine of Natural History*, i (1938), 389–405.

Additional references which appeared too late for comsideration in the text

Childe, V. G. 1940. *Prehistoric Communities of the British Isles.* London and Edinburgh, 1940.

Lacaille, A. D. 1940. Some Scottish Core-Tools and Ground-Flaked Implements of Stone *P.S.A., Scot.* lxxiv (1940), 6–13.

CLASSIFIED LIST OF REFERENCES TO CAVE RESEARCH AND STONE AGE ARCHAEOLOGY IN IRELAND

I. CAVE RESEARCH

A. General

Adams, A. L., *P.R.I.A.* III (1877), 89–100; Forrest, H. E., *I.N.J.* I (1925–27), 112–14, 152–3, 171–4, 215–19, 228, 234–6, 259–62, 284–5; Praeger, R. Ll.; *The Irish Naturalist*, V (1896), 123–4; Scharff, R. F., *ibid.* IV (1895), 57–9.

B. Ballynamintra Cave, Cappagh, County Waterford

Adams, A. L., Kinahan, G. H. and Ussher, R. J., *S.T.R.D.S.* I (1881), 177–226.

C. Castlepook Cave, Doneraile, County Cork

Scharff, R. F., Seymour, H. J. and Newton, E. T., *P.R.I.A.* XXXIV (1918), 33–72; Ussher, R. J. *P.R.I.A.* XXV (1904), 1–5; Ussher, R. J., Seymour, H. J., Newton, E. T. and Scharff, R. F., *Rep. Brit. Ass.* 1908, p. 697.

D. Edenvale and Newhall Caves, County Clare

Scharff, R. F., Ussher, R. J., Cole, G. A. J., Newton, E. T., Dixon, A. F. and Westrop, T. J., *Trans. R.I.A.* XXXIII (1906), 1–76.

E. Kesh Caves, County Sligo

Scharff, R. F., Coffey, George, Cole, G. A. J., Ussher, R. J. and Praeger, R. Ll., *Trans. Roy. Irish Acad.* XXXII (1903), 171–214.

F. Kilgreany Cave, County Waterford

Boule, M., *L'Anth.* XXXIX (1929), 575–6; Clark, J. G. D., *P.P.S.* II (1936), 241–2; Jackson, J. W., *I.N.J.* VI (1936), 56; Keith, Sir Arthur, *New Discoveries Relating to the Antiquity of Man*, 1931, pp. 426–31; Mahr, Adolf, *P.P.S.* Presidential Address, III (1937), 281–2; Movius, H. L., Jr. (with Stelfox, A. W., Roche, Miss G. and Maby, J. C.), *J.R.S.A.I.* LXV (1935), 254–96; Ó'Ríordáin, S. P., *Antiquity*, V (1931), 360–2; Id. *Art and Archaeology*, XXXIII (1932), 101–2; Stelfox, A. W., *I.N.J.* III (1930), 118–23; Id. *I.N.J.* VI (1937), 251; Tratman, E. K. (with Jackson, J. W. and Fawcett, E.), *P.B.S.S.* III (1928), 109–53; Tratman, E. K., *J.R.S.A.I.* LXVII (1937), 120–4; Vaufrey, R., *L'Anth.* XLII (1932), 641–2.

G. Killavullen Caves, County Cork (Preliminary Notes)

Leask, H. G., *P.P.S.E.A.* VII (1934), 410; Ó'Ríordáin, S. P., *Discovery*, April 1935.

H. Knockmore Caves, County Fermanagh

Plunkett, Thos., *J.R.G.S., Ireland*, XIV (1873–77), 131–40; Pringle, Alex., *I.N.J.* I (1927), 208.

I. Oonaglour, Carrigmhuirish, and The Brothers Cave, Cappagh, County Waterford (Description of Dr Forsayeth's excavations)

Power, Rev. P., *I.N.J.* I (1927), 188; II (1928), 98–100, 122–3.

J Red-Cellar Cave, Lough Gur, County Limerick (Preliminary Notes)

Leask, H. G., *P.P.S.* IV (1938), 31S–5.

K. Shandon Cave, Dungarvan, County Waterford

Adams, A. L., *Trans. Roy. Irish Acad.* XXVI (1875), 187–230; Brenan, E., *J.R.D.S.* 1859.

CLASSIFIED LIST OF REFERENCES

II. STONE AGE ARCHAEOLOGY (NORTH-EAST IRELAND)

A. General

Bremer, W., *P.R.I.A.* xxxviii (1928), 21–30; Gray, W., *J.R.H.A.A.I.* v (1879–82), 109–43; Knowles, W. J., *P.R.I.A.* ii (1883), 209–13; Id. *P.R.I.A.* ii (1885), 436–44; Id. *R. and P. Bel. N.F.C.* ii (1886), 539–42; Id. *P.R.I.A.* i (1889), 188–9; Id. *J.R.A.I.* xliv (1914), 83–121; Macalister, R. A. S., *Ireland in Pre-Celtic Times*, 1921, pp. 52–110; Id. *The Archaeology of Ireland*, 1928, pp. 29–50; Id. *Ancient Ireland*, 1935, pp. 1–15; Whelan, C. B., *B.S.P.F.* xxviii (1931), 348–51; Id. *R. XVI I.G.C.* 1933, pp. 1209–18; Id. *I.N.J.* iv (1933), 215; Id. *P.R.I.A.* xlii (1934), 121–9; Id. *P.R.I.A.* xliv (1938), 115–37.

B. Mesolithic Sites

1. Cushendun, County Antrim

Burchell, J. P. T., *P.P.S.E.A.* vi (1931), 282–7; Dwerryhouse, A. R., *Q.J.G.S.* lxxix (1923), 364–6; Movius, H. L., Jr. (with Jessen, K., McMillan, Mrs N. F. and Richardson, F. L. W., Jr.), *P.R.I.A.* xlvi (1940), 1–84.

2. Glenarm, County Antrim

Movius, H. L., Jr. (with Allen, G. M., Fisher, Miss N. (Mrs McMillan) and Richardson, F. L. W., Jr.), *J.R.S.A.I.* lxvii (1937), 181–220; Whelan, C. B., *J.R.A.I.* lx (1930), 178–9; Id. *P.R.I.A.* xliv (1938), 125–7.

3. Island Magee, County Antrim

Baden-Powell, D. F. W., *Jour. of Animal Ecology*, vi (1937), 86–97; Burchell, J. P. T., *P.P.S.E.A.* vi (1931), 270–81; Id. *P.P.S.E.A.* vii (1932), 31–4; Id. *Nature*, 132 (1933), 860; Id. *P.P.S.E.A.* vii (1934), 366–72; Common, R. H., *I.N.J.* iv (1933), 139–40.

4. Curran Point, Larne, County Antrim

Burchell, J. P. T., *P.P.S.E.A.* vi (1931), 287–94; Coffey, G. and Praeger, R. Ll., *P.R.I.A.* xxv (1904), 143–200; Gray, W., *J.R.S.A.I.* i (1890), 388–90; Layard, Miss N. F., *Man*, ix (1909), 81–5; Praeger, R. Ll., *R. and P. Bel. N.F.C.* iii (1889–90), 198–210; Whelan, C. B., *J.R.A.I.* lx (1930), 169–84; Id. *Antiq. Jour.* xv (1935), 465–6.

5. Lough Neagh, County Londonderry

Erdtman, G., *P. 1st I.C.* 1932, pp. 105–7; Whelan, C. B., *I.N.J.* iii (1930), 95; Id. *I.N.J.* iv (1933), 149–50; Id. *P.R.I.A.* xliv (1938), 128–9.

6. Rough Island, County Down

Movius, H. L., Jr. (with McMillan, Mrs N. F., Maby, J. C. and Stelfox, A. W.), *J.R.S.A.I.* lxx (1940), 111–42; Seymour, H. J., *M.G.S., Ireland*, 1904, pp. 117–18; Whelan, C. B., *R. XVI I.G.C.* 1933, p. 1216; Id. *P.R.I.A.* xliv (1938), 124–5.

C. Neolithic and Later Sites

1. Coastal Stations Associated with the Litorina Raised Beach—Glenarm, and Cushendun, County Antrim; Rough Island, County Down—see references listed above.

2. Tievebulliagh, near Cushendall, County Antrim

Knowles, W. J., *J.R.A.I.* xxxiii (1903), 360–6; Id. *J.R.S.A.I.* xvi (1906), 383–94; Id. *R. and P. Bel. N.F.C.* v (1906), 421–3.

CLASSIFIED LIST OF REFERENCES

3. BALLYNAGARD, RATHLIN ISLAND, COUNTY ANTRIM

Whelan, C. B., *P.R.I.A.* XLII (1934), 121–43; Id. *R. and P. Bel. N.F.C.* 1933–34, pp. 107–11.

RATHLIN ISLAND—MISCELLANEOUS

Whelan, C. B., *I.N.J.* III (1930), 18–19; Baudouin, M. and Whelan, C. B., *B.S.P.F.* XXVIII (1931), 428–34; Whelan, C. B., *I.N.J.* IV (1932), 96–7; Id. *Antiq. Jour.* XV (1935), 194–5.

4. DUNMURRY, COUNTY ANTRIM

Whelan, C. B., *I.N.J.* II (1928), 94–8; Id. *I.N.J.* IV (1932), 95; Id. *P.R.I.A.* XLIV (1938), 130–3.

5. BLACK MOUNTAIN, NEAR BELFAST

Bell, Robert, *R. and P. Bel. N.F.C.* 1922–23 (this reference was not available to the writer).

6. LOWER BANN VALLEY

Batty, J., *U.J.A.* I (1938), 90–4; Clark, J. G. D., *P.P.S.* II (1936), 243; Day, Robert, *J.K.A.S.* V (1867), 227–8; Erdtman, G., *I.N.J.* I (1927), 245; Id. *Geol. Förens. Förh.* L (1928), 162–3; Id. *Jour. of Ecology*, XVII (1929), 112–26; Evans, Sir John, *Archaeologia*, XLI (1868), 397–408; Hawkes, C. F. C., *Antiq. Jour.* XVII (1937), 72–3; Jackson, J. W., *Mem. and Proc. Manchester Lit. and Phil. Soc.* LIII (1909), 3–18; Id. *I.N.J.* IV (1933), 213–14; Knowles, W. J., *J.R.A.I.* X (1880), 150–4; Id. *P.R.I.A.* XXX (1912), 195–222; Lawlor, H. C., *I.N.J.* IV (1932), 77–9; Mahr, A., *P.P.S.* Presidential Address, III (1937), 289–95; Movius, H. L., Jr. (with Jessen, K., Childe, V. G. and Whelan, C. B.), *P.R.I.A.* XLIII (1936), 17–40; O'Laverty, Rev. Jas., *U.J.A.* V (1857), 122–7; Parker, Dehra, *U.J.A.* I (1938), 107; Peake H. and Fleure, H. J., *The Corridors of Time*, Vol. II, 1927, pp. 105 and 114; Whelan, C. B., *Antiq. Jour.* X (1930), 134–8; Wilde, W. R., *Catalogue of Antiquities*, Dublin, 1857, pp. 10–12.

7. SANDHILL SITES

Bigger, F. J., *P.R.I.A.* III (1896), 727–31; Brunicardi (Mrs), *J.R.S.A.I.* XLIV (1914), 185–213; Buick, Rev. G. R., *J.R.S.A.I.* I (1891), 433–42; Coffey, G. and Praeger, R. Ll., *P.R.I.A.* XXV (1904), 190–8; Davison, A. H., Orr, Jas., Stelfox, A. W. and Stendall, J. A. S., *I.N.J.* I (1927), 280–2; D'Evelyn, A. M., *J.R.S.A.I.* LXIII (1933), 88–100; Hassé, L., *J.R.S.A.I.* I (1890), 130–8; Id. *J.R.S.A.I.* IV (1894), 1–13; Hewson, Rev. L. M., *J.R.S.A.I.* LXV (1935), 231–44; Id. *J.R.S.A.I.* LXVI (1936), 154–72; Knowles, W. J., *J.R.A.I.* VI (1876), 485–7; Id. *J.R.A.I.* VII (1877), 202–5; Id. *J.R.A.I.* IX (1879), 320–8; Id. *Rep. Brit. Ass.* 1879, pp. 171–5; Id. *P.R.I.A.* II (1881), 105–13; Id. *J.R.H.A.A.I.* VII (1885), 104–25; Id. *P.R.I.A.* I (1889), 173–87; Id. *P.R.I.A.* I (1891), 612–25; Id. *J.R.S.A.I.* IV (1894), 243–55; Id. *J.R.S.A.I.* IV (1894), 341–8; Id. *P.R.I.A.* III (1895), 650–63; Id. *J.R.S.A.I.* VIII (1898), 367–91; Id. *P.R.I.A.* VI (1901), 331–89; Knowles, W. J., Paterson, W. H., Praeger, R. Ll. and Bigger, F. J., *P.R.I.A.* V (1899), 433–40; May, A. McL., *I.N.J.* V (1934), 56–8; May, R. L., *U.J.A.* II (1939), 104–9; Ó'Ríordáin, S. P., *P.R.I.A.* XLII (1935), 183–7; Whelan, C. B., *Man*, XXVIII (1928), 188; Id. *I.N.J.* IV (1932), 95–7; Id. *P.R.I.A.* XLIV (1938), 135–7.

ADDENDUM

Although received too late to be included in the text of this book, brief mention should be made of the important site at Albyn Distillery, Campbeltown, Argyllshire, excavated by Dr W. J. McCallien. This information was kindly supplied by the authors of the excavation report, and the writer wishes to take this opportunity of thanking Dr McCallien and Mr A. D. Lacaille for generously furnishing not only a copy of their manuscript but also a complete set of photographs of the illustrations of the archaeological material. At the site of the excavation the raised beach attains a height of + 32 ft. 2 in. O.D. and the artifacts, most of which are sharp and unrolled, were found in a layer 3 in. thick overlying the beach, as well as in the upper portion of the beach gravels. Almost all the material is made of flint imported from Ireland, but local rocks—quartz and schistose grit—were also used. The industry is definitely comparable with the Early Larnian, but in certain respects it is more advanced than Cushendun (Horizons 1 and 2), Island Magee (Horizon 1), Rough Island (Horizon 1), or Mr A. Gray's collection from the nearby site at Millknowe, described on pp. 177–8 of this book. In the first place, as at Millknowe, the forms are smaller than in a normal Early Larnian series, reflecting the lack of a readily available flint supply in this region. Secondly, the presence of micro-burins and obliquely truncated flakes, both absent in Ireland, demonstrates a penetration of Tardenoisean influence into Scotland at a period which may be somewhat earlier than hitherto suspected. Thus, as Mr Lacaille points out, the material from Albyn Distillery contains forms met with in the upper layers at Creswell Crags, but not in the Early Larnian stations of Counties Antrim and Down. Thirdly, one small chisel-edged pick of quartz was found, which, in spite of the absence of bone, is a definite indication of an infiltration of Forest culture ideas. Although the latter are absent in Ireland until Late Larnian times, the new Campbeltown industry is certainly not Late Larnian. Therefore, on purely typological grounds, it appears likely that we have to deal here with a more developed facies of the Early Larnian than has yet been documented in North-East Ireland or Scotland. Mr Lacaille has informed the writer that his and Dr McCallien's excellent report on the Albyn Distillery site will be published shortly in the *Proceedings of the Society of Antiquaries of Scotland*, probably during 1941.

INDEX

Aberdeen, 278; Aberdeenshire, 44, 193
Abernethy region, 283–4
Aberystwyth, 271
Abri Audi type points, 235
Acer platanoides, 20
Achill Island, Co. Mayo, 265, 279
Adams, A. L., 114
adzes, 22, 155, 166, 170, 175, 183, 260
Africa, North, 237
agriculture, xxiii–xxiv, 212–13, 235, 237–9, 251, 254, 262
Aherlow, Glen of (Co. Limerick), 273
Ahrensburg culture, 18, 21, 64
Ailsa Craig, 177
Airdrie, Lanark, 36, 269
Airedale, 270
Airthrey, Stirling, 193
Albyn Distillery, Campbeltown, Argyllshire, 178, 194, 320 (*addendum*)
Alder (*Alnus*), 19–20, 34, 92, 93, 96, 99, 118, 123, 127, 137, 212, 241–2
Alexandra Dock, Belfast, 83
Algarve, Portugal, 250
Allen, G. M., 131
Allerød Period or Oscillation, 18, 21, 64, 68; deposits of, in Ireland, 67–70, in the Isle of Man, 64–5, in East Prussia, in North-West Germany, 64, unrecorded in England, 64
Almond, Perthshire, 278
Alnus glutinosa, 19
Alps, 4
Al'Ubaid culture, 261
amber, 115
anchors, stone, 114
Ancora, Portugal, 205
Ancylus fluviatilis, 13
Ancylus Lake, 13–14, 19
Anderson, J., 180–1, 188, 194
Anglesey, 89; land-bridge to in Post-Glacial Period, 288–9
animals, *see* fauna, domestic animals; style of art in Ireland, 116
Antarctica, 13
Antevs, E., 18, 25, 39
anthropometric data, Ireland, 208, 256
antler, implements of, 73, 171, 180 ff., 192–3, 236, 237, 253
Antrim, xxi, 129–30; Late-Glacial: sequence of, 32, raised beach in, 285, lakes in, 51, 277; glaciation of, 272, 277; Post-Glacial deposits of, 83, 99; flint from, in Scotland, 172, 177; alleged Palaeolithic from, 106; Mesolithic of, 117, 120, 124, 126 ff., 148 ff., 161, 174, 176, 239, 256, 259; Campignian in, 214 ff., 261–2; Neolithic of, 212, 239
aphanite, 222, 228
archaeology, xxii, 45, 64, 75, 94, 96, 102; archaeological material, transportation of, by ocean currents, 146, 158
Arctic climate, 18, 175
Ardagh, Co. Limerick, 273
Ardeer, Ayrshire, 194
Ardglass, Co. Down, 265
Ardmore Crannog, Co. Waterford, 85, 292
Argyllshire, 180, 286
Armagh, 37
Armstrong, A. L., 45–7, 199, 201, 234
Arnold-Bembrose, H. H., 267
Arran, Bute, 177, 198, 283
arrowheads, 195, 212, 219–20, 222, 231–2, 235, 247, 252, 262
Ash (*Fraxinus*), 20, 34, 99, 115, 235
ashes, 229, 242, 252
Aspen, 19
Astarte borealis, 60
Asturian culture, 205–6, 259
Asturias, Oviedo, 205
Atlantic Period, 14 ff., 20, 90, 93, 98–100, 102, 126, 171, 213; marine transgression of, 89, 95, 176, 209, 291 (*see also* Litorina Sea); deposits of, in England and Wales, 76 ff., 200, 203–4, 288 ff., in the Isle of Man, 293, in Scotland, 80 ff., 204, 290 ff., in Ireland, 83 ff., 118, 127, 131, 141, 208, 242, 292; cultural developments during, 22, 173, 178–80, 193, 197, 203, 205–6, 211, 253, 260
Atlantic–Sub-Boreal Transition Period, 100, 239, 242, 289, 293
Atlantic sea-board, 213, 262
Auk, great, 182
Aurignacian culture, 36, 45, 47, 61, 118, 155, 258; Upper, 199
"Aurignacian Oscillation", 33
Aurochs, 91, 140, 171, 182
Austin, R. A. C., 288
Auvergne district, France, 14
Aveline's Hole, Somerset, 47
Avon River, Scotland, 193, 282; England, 265, 271
awls, of bone, 72, 181, 185; of flint, 155, 164, 195 (*see also* perforators)
axes, 22, 222–4, 228; core, 166, 170, 174, 193, 198, 202–5, 207, 212, 223 ff., 231, 233, 260, 262; flake, 170, 204, 212, 214, 216, 222, 224, 231, 233–5, 237, 247, 249, 251–2, 262; hand, 106–7, 224, 228; large stone, 247, 249–51, 262; polished stone, 232, 235, 249, 289–90
"axe cult", 250

INDEX

axe-factories, 211, 214, 222 ff., 228, 231, 233–4, 255, 261–2
Ayr, Isle of Man, 293
Ayrshire, 53, 57, 59, 177, 277, 284–6
Azilian, 202, 205, 207; in Northern England, 188 ff., 191, 199; in Scotland, 178–9, 180, 185, 188, 196–8 (*see also* Obanian culture); in Ireland, xxiv, 174, 208, 258

backed blades, points, etc., see *dos rabattu* trimming
Baden-Powell, D. W. F., 33, 45, 136–7, 267
Badger, 182
Baffin Land, 258
Bailey, E. B., 278, 283–4
Bailieborough, Co. Cavan, 68
Balanus balanoides, 134
Ballantrae, Ayrshire, 194, 284
Ballaugh, Isle of Man, 65, 276
Ballinamintra Cave, Co. Waterford, 38, 114
Ballintoy, Co. Antrim, 125
Ballybetagh Bog, Co. Dublin, 65–8
Ballycastle, Co. Mayo, 279
Ballyconnell, Co. Sligo, 110 ff., 292
Ballyemon Glen, Co. Antrim, 222–3
Ballyholme Bay, Co. Down, 125
Ballylongford, Co. Limerick, 273
Ballymoney, Co. Antrim, 277
Ballynagard, Rathlin Island, Co. Antrim, 228 ff., 249, 256
Ballyrudder, Co. Antrim, 37, 105
Ballyvoy, Co. Antrim, 106–7
Baltic, water bodies in basin of, 11 ff.; changes in level of, 19–21; Ice-Lake, 12, 62, 101; End-Moraine, 4, 6–7, 12, 61 (*see also* Pomeranian End-Moraine); Stone Age cultures in the region of, 176, 235, 251, 253, 259, 262
Baltinglass, Co. Wicklow, 273
Banborough, Yorkshire, 200
Banchory, Kincardineshire, 194–6, 197, 260
Bankhead, Ayrshire, 287
Bann culture, 100, 152, 180, 213, 219, 240 ff., 251, 262; points, 161, 216, 251; pottery, 244–7
Bann River, xxi, 117, 121, 253; Valley, 33, 219, 239 ff., 256, 277
Bantry Bay, Co. Kerry, 280
barley, impression of, 235
Barnacles (*Balanus balanoides*), 134
Barry, Glamorganshire, 288
basalt, xxi, 107, 124, 222, 228, 244, 249
Battersea, Thames Valley, 203
battle-axe, 247, 254
Batty, J., 249
Baudouin, M., 228
beach, modern, 129; storm, 84, 127, 130–3, 145–7, 158 (*see also* raised beaches)
Beacharra ware, 247
beads, amber, 115; bone, 189; glass, 252
beaked implements, 235
Bear (*Ursus arctos*), 38; Cave, 72–4, 91, 114–15, 189
Beaver, 91
Beech (*Fagus*), 20, 95
beetles, remains of, 56, 68, 75, 83, 123, 268–9
Beith, Ayrshire, 36, 269
Belderg, Co. Mayo, 286
Belfast, 83, 125, 196, 232, 277; Lough, 91, 123, 125, 170, 171, 173
Belfast Municipal Museum and Art Gallery, 121, 125
Belgium, 98, 200, 237, 259
Bell, Robert, 232
Berwickshire, 194
Betula nana, 18; *Betula pubescens*, 18–19
Biarritz, 205
bifacial implements, 224
Bigger, F. J., 252
Billing, Mount, 12–13
Birch (*Betula*), 18–20, 34, 36, 76, 92, 96–9, 118, 123, 127, 137, 212; Period, 98; Birch-Pine Period, *see* Pre-Boreal Period
Birds, 72, 181–2
Bisat, W. S., 270
Bishop, A. H., 180
Bison, 199
Black Isle, Ross-shire, 286
Black Mountain, Belfast, 232
Blackstairs Mountain, Co. Wexford, 54, 281
blades, 118, 133–4, 149–52, 157, 173–4, 178, 195, 232, 253; implements made on, 148, 171, 173, 196, 214, 222, 243; with *dos rabattu* trimming, 152, 199, 201, 203; technique, 161
Blagny, Seine Inférieure, 234
Blair Drummond, Forth Valley, 80, 193
Blanc, A. C., 266
Blytt-Sernander climatic periods, 23, 89–90, 92, 102
Boar, wild (*Sus scrofa*), 83, 91, 123, 128, 172 (*see also* Pig, wild)
boats, 120, 172, 206–7, 259; tools for building, 206
Boggeragh Mountains, Co. Cork, 54, 281
bogs, 96, 98
bone, implements of, 171, 174, 178, 180 ff., 185, 191, 198–9, 237, 260, absent in Early Larnian, 157; points, 199; use of, for food, 114
Bone Cave, Inchnadamff, Sutherland, 72–3
Boreal Period, 14 ff., 19, 22, 96, 105, 203; emergence during, 94, 101, 172; partial land-bridge between England and Ireland during, 87 ff., 207; deposits of, in England and Wales, 76 ff., 203, 288, in Scotland, 80 ff., 177, 291, in Ireland, 83, 91, 99, 118, 123–4, 128, 209, 239; in Britain and Ireland, 90, 92–3, 98; cultural developments during, 22, 117 ff., 146–7, 161, 173, 192, 200, 204, 209, 237, 258–9
Boreal-Atlantic Transition Period, 96, 99–100, 123, 128, 144, 146, 174, 200, 206–7, 260
Boreal Hazel maximum (in Ireland), 98, 128
borers, of bone, 71, 189, 191; of flint, 157; boring tool, 155, 164, 216, 244

INDEX

Borth, Cardiganshire, 290
Bos longifrons, 91, 182 (*see also* Cattle); *Bos primigenius*, 199
Boswell, P. G. H., 26, 33, 41, 44, 46, 51, 60, 109, 111, 275, 281, 289
Botcherby, Cumberland (near Carlisle), 51, 276
Bowler-Kelley, (Mrs) A., 233
bowls, 235, 244–7 (*see also* potsherds, pottery)
Brampton, Cumberland, 53; district, 266, 275–6
Brandenburg End-Moraine, 4, 6, 34, 61
Bray Harbour, Co. Wicklow, 292
Bremer, W., 206
Bremner, A., 27–9, 32, 41, 44, 266, 269, 272, 278–9, 283–5
Bresle River, 234
Breuil, H., 48, 53, 71, 73, 177–9, 182–91, 193, 202
Brickey River, Co. Waterford, 114
bricks, 240
Bride Hills, Isle of Man, 277
Bristol Channel, 265, 288, 290; region, 77
Britain, ice movement and centres of ice-dispersal in, 41; Maglemosean harpoons in, 77; Campignian industries of, 211, 233–4; distribution of Mesolithic sites in, 259; Post-Glacial deposits in, 288 ff. (*see also* England)
British Association for the Advancement of Science, Report of, 267
British Isles, *see* England, Scotland, Ireland, Éire
British Regional Geology, [*a*], 26, 46; [*b*], 289; [*c*], 265; [*d*], 271; [*e*], 27, 265, 271, 288; [*f*], 45, 270, 288; [*g*], 270; [*h*], 270, 289; [*i*], 271; [*j*], 272, 284, 287, 290; [*k*], 194, 272, 290; [*l*], 41, 283–4; [*m*], 272, 279, 283, 285, 290; [*n*], 81, 272, 279, 283–6, 291
Brittany, 85, 247, 250, 251, 265
"broad blade" industries of the Pennines, 200 ff., 260
Brockley, Rathlin Island, Co. Antrim, 228, 231
Bronze Age, 20, 100, 115, 194, 196, 200, 204, 208, 220, 228, 231, 250–2, 254; Late Bronze Age–Early Iron Age, pottery of the, 228, 231, 233
Brooks, C. E. P., 18, 20, 37, 60, 100, 213, 284
Brown, T., 286
Broxbourne, Hertfordshire, 204
Brückner, E., 4, 6, 44
Brunicardi (Mrs), 252
Bryce, J., 268
Bryce, T. H., 188
Buccinum undatum, 141
Bühl Stadium, 6
Buick, (Rev.) G. R., 252–3
Burchell, J. P. T., 46, 80, 106–9, 111–13, 121, 125–6, 136–7, 150–1, 153, 162–3, 165, 167, 169–70, 202, 204, 206, 266, 289, 292
burials, human, 73, 114 ff., 208
buried river channels, 28 (*see also* drowned valleys)
burins, *see* gravers
Burkitt, M. C., 8, 47, 189, 198, 201, 206
Burn of Benholm, Kincardineshire, 36, 40, 269, 272
Bute, Island of, 188, 286

Cadder, Dumbartonshire, 36, 268
Cae Gwyn Cave, Flintshire, 45
Caisteal-nan-Gillean, Oronsay, 180, 182, 194
Caithness, glaciation of, 28, 53, 272, 279, 286; Late-Glacial raised beach absent in, 59–60, 285; Post-Glacial raised beach and submerged peats in, 81, 291; fauna in, 91; pottery from, 247
Callander, J. G., 71–2, 188, 193–4, 208
Cambrian Mountains, Wales, 209
Camp de Chassey, Saône-et-Loire, 235, 238
camp sites, 181, 252
Campbell, R., 36, 269
Campbeltown, Kintyre, Argyllshire, 28, 82, 172, 177–8, 182, 193, 197; Museum, 177
Campignian industries and sites, 211–12, 214 ff., 231–2, 234 ff., 238–9, 249, 251–2, 255–6, 261–2
Canis lagopus, 73
canoes, dug-out, 206
Cantabrian region, North Spain, 202, 259
Cantrill, T. C., 202, 290
Capitan, L., 234–6
Cappagh, Co. Waterford, 114
Cappoquin, Co. Waterford, 114
Capsian culture, 208
Cardiff, Wales, 271
Cardigan Bay, Wales, 88–9, 271
Cardium edule, 127–8, 140–1
Carey River, Co. Antrim, 106–7, 125
carinated implements, 244
Carlingford Lough, 121, 124, 292; district, 50; ice in region of, 274
Carlisle Plain, Cumberland, 51, 54, 275–6
Carlow, 273
Carncastle, Co. Antrim, 37
Carnlough, Co. Antrim, 125
Carnock, Stirling, 291
Carpinus, 20
Carrickfergus, Belfast Lough, Co. Antrim, 125
Carruthers, R. G., 276
Carse clay, *see* clay
Carstairs, Lanark, 282
Castle Market, Belfast, 208
Castlepook Cave, Co. Cork, 38
Castlereagh Hills, Co. Down, 196
Cat, wild, 182
Cattegat, 12–13
Cattle (*Bos longifrons*), 91, 130–1
Causewayhead, Kinross, 192
caves, 16, 22, 109, 205; in Ireland, 38, 74, 81, 114, 117, 125, 173, 252, 285; in Scotland, 71–3, 81, 178, 181–2 (*see also* MacArthur Cave); in England, 71 (*see also* Victoria Cave)
Celtic Period, 189

INDEX

celts, 170, 222, 229, 238, 244, 262
Central Plains of Ireland, glaciation of, 41, 50, 273–4; End-Moraine of, 53, 61, 68–9, 274–5, 277
Cepaea nemoralis, 141
cephalic index, 208
Ceremonial objects, 249
Cervus elaphus, 130
chalcedony, 196
chambers of stone, 231; for burial, 250
Champlat, Aisne, 216
Channel Islands, 265–6
channelled ornament, 247
channels, marginal drainage, 44, 67, 273, 280
Chappel Hall, Airdrie, Lanark, 36, 269
charcoal, 73, 115, 140, 181, 235, 242, 252
Charlesworth, J. K., 27, 33, 37–9, 41, 43–5, 49–51, 60, 67–8, 74, 83, 87, 89, 98, 109, 111, 177, 265, 270–1, 273–5, 277–84, 286
Cheddar, Somerset, 47
chert, 196, 200
Cheshire, 77, 87, 270, 289–90
Cheviot Hills, 53; ice-sheet from, and boulder clay of, 50, 271, 275
Childe, V. G., xxii–xxiii, 8, 181–2, 185, 188, 192, 203, 204, 229, 235, 238, 245, 247, 253
Chingford, Essex, 207
chisels, 183, 188, 216, 219, 260
choppers, 155, 159, 164, 170, 173–4, 219, 224, 229, 231; absence of, at Campbeltown, 178
Christian Period, Early, Reindeer from, 91; art object of, 116; crannogs of, 244; spears of, 249; survival of sand-hills (food-gathering economy) into, xxiv, 213, 252–4, 262
Christiana Valley, Sweden, 61
chronology, 7–8, 24, 120, 142 ff.
cirque, glacial, 228
Cissbury, Sussex, 234
Clactonian-type implements, 106
Cladium mariscus, 242
Clams, razor, 181
Clare, 114, 252
Clare Island, Co. Mayo, 279–80
Clark, J. G. D., xxii, 6–8, 14–19, 23–4, 48, 64, 76–7, 116, 175, 177, 183, 192, 195–6, 199–204, 207, 211, 220, 234–5, 237–8, 250–1, 293
Clava, Nairnshire, 28
clay, 11–12, 16, 18, 34, 36–7; carse, 80–2, 93, 192–3, 206, 253, 260, 290–1; estuarine, 83–4, 93, 117, 132, 135, 140, 144–5, 159, 161, 171, 208, Lower (*Scrobicularia*) Zone of, 84, 122–3, 144–5, 172, Intermediate Zone of, 122 ff., 137, 145, 172, Upper (*Thracia*) Zone of, 84, 122 ff., 145, 172; laminated clay (*see also* varves), 6–7, 31, 123, 128, 135, 144
Clermont, Meuse, 234
Cleveland Hills, 41, 200, 270
Clew Bay, Co. Mayo, 279–80
Clifford, M. H., 78, 94, 96, 204, 289
climate, 51; in Northern Europe, 17, 21–2; in Ireland, 49, 99, 134–5, 141, 171; oceanic, 14, 94–6; Continental, 14, 93, 102, 145, 213; effect of, on culture, 175–6, 213 (*see also* environment)
climatic optimum (Post-Glacial), 15, 19–20, 77, 84, 90–1, 93, 95, 98, 101–2, 122, 131, 135, 145, 161, 171, 175, 181, 213
Climatic Periods, in Northern Europe, 14 ff.; in Britain and Ireland, 89 ff.
climatology, 22, 94, 96, 261
Cloghan, Co. Offaly, 275
Cloney (The), Glenarm, Co. Antrim, 129
Clontarf, Co. Dublin, 292
Closeburn Bay, Co. Antrim, 125
Clougheen, Co. Antrim, 222
clubs, stone, 249–50
Clyde Valley, 180, 277; estuary, 28, 60, 86, 286–7; glacier, 282 (*see also* Firth of Clyde)
Cnoc Sligeach, Oronsay, 180–1, 185, 193
Cockles, 181
Codfish (*Gadus morrhua*), 128
Coffey, G., 121, 125, 132–3, 136, 168–70, 202, 252–3
Coleman, A. P., 25
Coleraine, Co. Antrim, 240, 248
Collins, E. R., 45
Colne Valley, Essex, 203
Colonsay, Argyllshire, 57, 180, 272
Comber, Co. Down, 139
Comeragh Mountains, Co. Waterford, 54, 281
Committee for Quaternary Research in Ireland, 98, 121
Comrie, Perthshire, 48, 53, 71
conchology, 15
Coney Island, Co. Sligo, 109 ff.
conifers, 20
Connemara, Co. Galway, 280
contours, 10 (*see also* isobases)
Coon, C. S., 208, 256
cores, 118, 134, 155, 157, 181 ff., 219, 235; implements made on, 155, 164, 170, 222; preparation of, 149, 157, 166; dressings or trimmings, 203; "core rejuvenation flakes", 166
Cork, 114, 208, 265
Corrie, J. M., 194
Corstorphine, near Edinburgh, 55, 282
Cornwall, 202
corries, erosion of, 284; corrie glaciers, 55, 280, 283
Cortaillod culture, 237
Corylus avellana, 19
Cow, *see* Cattle
Cowdon Burn, Ayrshire, 36, 268–9
Crabs, 11, 181 (*see also* Crustaceans)
Crag deposits, 26
Craig, R., 268
Craig, R. M., 272, 279, 291
Craig Lwyd Farm, Carnarvonshire, 233
crannog, 244

Cree, J. E., 71–2, 92, 208
Cree Valley, Southern Scotland, 281
crescents, 195
Creswell Crags, Derbyshire, 46, 191, 199, 205 (*see also* Mother Grundy's Parlour *and* Pin Hole Cave)
Creswellian culture, xxiv, 47, 174–5, 191, 199–201, 205; diffusion of, to Ireland, 207–9; physical type in Ireland, 208; distribution of sites, 46–7, 199
Cretaceous chalk, xxi, 124, 177, 212, 228, 234, 255
Crieff, Perthshire, 278
Croch Riach, Oronsay, 180
Croch Sligach, Oronsay, 180
Croftamie, Ayrshire, 36, 269
Cromer Ridge, 267, 270; gravels, 26
Cromerian-type flakes, 106
Cronk y Chule, Isle of Man, 251
Crosskey, (Rev.) H. W., 269
Crustaceans, 11, 181 (*see also* Crabs)
Culbane, Co. Londonderry, 249
Cultra, Co. Down, 125
"culture pool", 210, 259; province, 209–10; regional specialization of, 95
Cumberland, 51–3, 77–8, 275, 279; Plain, 281
Cumbrian Mountains, 276
Cumnock, Ayrshire, 277
Curran Point, Larne, Co. Antrim, 121, 125, 132 ff., 135–6, 158 ff., 164, 166 (*see also* Larne)
Curraun Peninsula, Co. Mayo, 279
Currie, E. D., 91, 269
Cushendun, Co. Antrim, 118, 121, 125, 126 ff., 128–9, 130, 143 ff., 148 ff., 158 ff., 174, 177–8, 219 ff., 224, 239, 249, 251, 256, 259, 277, 287; Bay, 128, 285
Cyprina islandica, 60, 131, 181

Daly, R. A., 4, 8, 23, 25
Daniglacial Period, 4, 6, 7
Danish Substage, 4; zone sequence (pollen-diagrams) extended into Ireland, 98–100
Danubian culture, in Western Europe, 238; pit-dwellings of, 234–5
Daun Stadium, 6
Davison, A. H., 252–3
Dawkins, W. Boyd, 77, 189
Day, E. C. H., 14, 265
Déchelette, J., 235
deciduous trees, 15, 19–20, 90, 96
Dee River, Flintshire, 87, 289; Dee Valley, Kincardineshire, 193–6, 260, 278, 283; Dee River, Kirkcudbright, 188
Deeley, R. M., 267
Deer, red (*Cervus elaphus*), 34, 36, 83, 91–2, 118, 123, 130, 172, 182, 199; use of bones and horns (antlers) of, for implements, 171, 185, 193, 253
De Geer, G., 4, 6–7, 21, 23, 63, 69–71, *Table* 6, 276, 282
delevelling, *see* level, changes of
De Morgan, E., 234
De Morgan, J., 234–5
Denmark, climate of, 267; glaciation of, 4; Late Mesolithic of, in England, 204; Maglemosean culture in, 77, 259, harpoon types of, in Scotland, 185, in England, 202–3; zoning of pollen-diagrams in, 18–20
De Puydt, M., 238
De Rance, C. E., 87, 289–90
Derby, Trent Valley near, 34, 267
Derrytagh North, Co. Armagh, bog at, 247
D'Evelyn, A. M., 252
Devon coast, Third Interglacial raised beach of 29; drowned valleys of, 288
Dewey, H., 29, 265
diatoms, 11–13, 240
diatomite, 239 ff.
Dingle Peninsula, Co. Kerry, 280
Dinham, C. H., 59, 81, 285, 287, 291
District Glaciation, *see* Valley Glaciation
disturbance, of cave deposits, 115–16, 188–9; due to ploughing, 130, 139, 221, 228
Dixon, E. E. L., 113
Dixon, R. B., xxii
Dog, 182
Dogfish, 181
Dogger Bank, 14, 75–6, 92, 209, 290
dolichocephalic skull, 72, 208
dolmens, 250
domestic animals, xxiii, 212, 253, 262
Donegal, glaciation of, 272, 277; ice from, 33, 41, 50, 274–5, retreat of, 279, 284; raised beaches in, Late-Glacial, 284, Post-Glacial, 292; sand-hill sites in, 252 ff.
Doneraille Cave, Co. Cork, 38
Dornoch Firth, Sutherland, 285, 291
Dorset, Campignian in, 233
dos rabattu trimming, 152, 173–4, 178, 195, 199, 201, 203, 247, 249; absence of, in Late Larnian, 161
Dosina exoleta, 131
Double, I. S., 289
Dover, chalk region of, 265
Down, glaciation of, 32, 272, 277; Third Interglacial raised beach in, 266; Post-Glacial deposits of, 83, 123, 139 ff.; Stone Age sites in, xxi, 117, 120, 124, 126, 203; Larnian culture in, 148 ff., 174, 176, 256, 259 ff.; Campignian in, 212, 214, 221 ff., 261–2; Neolithic introduced in, 239
Downpatrick, Co. Down, 83, 123
Downs, South, Campignian in, 233
drift, glacial, *see* boulder clay
drowned valleys, in England and Wales, 77, 288; in England and Ireland, 37, 87, 94; in Scandinavia, 11
Druim Vargie, Oban, 181, 185
Drumcliff Bay, Co. Sligo, 111
Drumfresky, Co. Antrim, 106–7

INDEX

drumlin, 139
Drummuir, Ayrshire, 287
Dryas octopetala, 18
Dryas Period, 18; clays of, 21; flora of, 64
Dryburgh Mains, Berwickshire, 194–5
Dublin area, glaciation of, 273; raised beaches of, Third Interglacial, 265, Post-Glacial, 292; partial land connection with Wales, 89
Dubois, G., 14, 235
Du Mesnil, D'A., 234–6
Dunlop, R., 36, 269
Du Noyer, G. V., 125
Dun River, Co. Antrim, 126
Dunbar, Haddington, 284
Dundalk Bay, Co. Louth, 292
Dundrum Bay, Co. Down, 123, 253
dunes (sand), microliths associated with, in Scotland, 194
Dungarvan, Co. Waterford, 114
Dunmurry, Co. Antrim, 232, 256
Dunning, Perthshire, varve clays at, 70–1, 258
Dunshaughlin, Co. Meath, 69
Dunworley Bay, Co. Cork, 292
Dupertius, Wesley, 256
Durham, boulder clay in, 271; Maglemosean culture in, 203, 205; raised beaches in, 34, 266–7, 284; retreat of ice from, 275; submerged peats on coast of, 78
dwelling sites, 147
Dwerryhouse, A. R., 32, 107, 126, 266, 271, 273

Earlston, Berwickshire, 194
Early Scottish Glaciation, 31, 266, 268
Earn River, Perthshire, 70; valley of, 278
Easington, Durham, 34, 267
East Anglia, Late-Glacial stratigraphy of, 26, 30–1; Interstadial (W_1/W_2) deposits in, 34, 266–7; glaciation of, 26–7, 41, 270; Maglemosean culture in, 203, 259; Campignian in, 233
Ebbsfleet Valley, Kent, 202
Edenside (Western), retreat of ice in, 275
Edenvale Cave, Co. Clare, 74
Edinburgh, Post-Glacial raised beach and marine deposits near, 81, 290; Forest culture from vicinity of, 203
Edwards, A. J. H., 206
Edwards, W., 270
Eem Sea, 34; submergence, 44
Eilean an Tighe, North Uist, 247
Éire, 250; Larnian culture in (Greenore), 124; sand-hill sites of, 262
Elephas primigenius, 234 (*see also* Mammoth)
Elfleda House, Cambridgeshire, 45
El Garcel, South-East Spain, 250
Elgee, F., 200
Elk (*Alces machlis*), 91
Ellis, H. S., 290
Elm (*Ulmus*), 15, 19–20, 34, 36, 92, 99, 118, 123, 127, 137, 146, 212
Elster Glaciation, 26
Elwes, J. W., 290
emergence, in Northern Europe (Post-Glacial), 8 ff., 13, 19; in Britain and Ireland: during Interstadial (W_1/W_2) Period, 38, 40; during Early Post-Glacial Period, 75, 101; effect of, on Irish Mesolithic development, 171; during Late Atlantic Period, 102; new elements in Ireland during, 233, 255
Enfield, Co. Meath, 275
England:
  Old Drift Glaciation of, 26–7
  Third Interglacial raised beach in, 29–30, 265–6
  Late-Glacial stratigraphy in, 26, 30–2
  Interstadial (W_1/W_2) Period, deposits of, 33 ff., 266 ff.
  New Drift Glaciation of, 41 ff., 270–2; age of, 44 ff.; cause of, 41, 61, 101, 271–2; recession of ice-sheets of, 49 ff., 61, 273 ff.; shelly drift of, 286
  Late-Glacial fauna of, 34, 267
  Late-Glacial Sea in, 57 ff., 284 ff.
  Post-Glacial Period in: deposits of, 75 ff., 288 ff.; climate of, 89 ff.; land connection with Ireland during, 87–9; Post-Atlantic submergence in south of, 80, 289–90
  Palaeobotany in, 92 ff., 95 ff.; zoning pollen-diagrams in, 98
  Upper Palaeolithic Period: date and distribution of sites, 45–7; occupation of north, 191; settlers migrate northward, 207–10
  Mesolithic Period, 198 ff., 204; sites and objects in Northern England, 188 ff.; Forest culture in, 203, 259; Tardenoisean culture in, 199 ff., 203; diffusion of Azilian into, 202; boats in, 206–7
  Campignian in, 233–4
English Channel, date of formation of, 76
environment, 75; dependence of food-gathering cultures on, xxii; cause of diffusion of ideas, 261; implement types change in response to, 108, 157, 205; influence of, on cultural developments, 22, 94–5, 161, 172, 175–6, 209–10; migrations as a result of changes in, 208, 213, 258–9
Eocene Period, 7
Eoliths, 106
Epi-Mesolithic cultures, 213, 262
"Epimiolithic", xxiii
"Epi-Palaeolithic", xxiii
Erdtman, G., 14, 16, 67, 76, 82–3, 118, 180, 200, 202, 207, 240, 266, 289–91, 293
erratics, glacial, 27–8, 32, 41, 177, 276
Errol, Perthshire, 80, 287
Ertebølle culture, 20, 22, 141, 176, 237, 260; counterpart of, in Sweden, 203, in England, 204 (*see also* Kitchen-Midden Culture)

INDEX

Escrick moraine, 270, 273
Esk, South (Forfar), estuary of, 287; Valley, Edinburgh, 282
Essex coast, submerged peats of, 94, 289; archaeological material from, 289
Esthonia, age of Maglemosean in, 77
estuarine deposits, 80 (*see also* clay)
ethnology, contributions from, xxii
Europe, central, 14, 196, 234–5; northern, 170, 207, 237; north-west, 174; western, 29, 196, 261–2
eustasy, 11, 13, 62, 75
Evans, E. E., 232, 251

fabricators, 183, 188, 195, 196
faceted butts, flakes with, 216, 231
Fagus, 20
Falk, H., 202
Falstar (Island of), Post-Glacial o-isobase in, 237, 289
Farnham, Surrey, 204
Farrington, A., 27, 39, 43, 65, 67–8, 92, 98, 265–6, 273, 280–1, 284, 292
fauna, 15–16, 22, 75; land, 15–16, 36 ff., 39, 40, 43, 61, 73–4, 90–2, 101, 105, 114 ff., 123, 130, 140, 181–2, 191, 198–9, 235, 265, 267–9, 282; marine, 15, 37, 40, 83–4, 101, 121–3, 128, 130–1, 133–4, 136 ff., 140, 145, 181, 289 (*see also* molluscs, shells)
fens, 75, 172
Fenland, 78, 80, 94, 267, 289
Fennoscandia, 4, 60 ff., 100 ff.
Fennoscandian Ice-Sheet, 4, 61, 101, 258; halt, 7; moraines, 4, 7, 18, 21, 62
Ffynnon Beuno Cave, Flintshire, 45
Finiglacial Period, 4, 6, 7, 8, 12, 13, 19, 21, 62
Finland, 4, 8, 13, 61
Finnmark, 13
Fir (*Albies*), absence of, in Britain and Ireland, 95; Scotch, 223
Firth of Clyde, 32, 81, 193, 272, 286, 290 (*see also* Clyde Valley or Estuary)
Firth of Forth, 271 (*see also* Forth Valley or Estuary)
fish, 11, 181; spears for, 244, 249; traps for, 249; catching of, as basis of subsistence, xxii, 172, 250
Fishguard, Pembrokeshire, 271
flags (marsh plants), 123
flakes, implements made on, 108 ff., 148 ff., 159 ff., 174, 181 ff., 188, 203, 223–4, 229, 235; miscellaneous types of, 106, 134, 141, 149, 155, 161, 183, 188, 194, 216, 219, 229, 253; facets or scars of, 107, 133, 157, 159; hoards of, 177, 243–4
Flamborough Head, Yorkshire, 46
Fläming End-Moraine, 34
Flandrian transgression, 266
flatworms, 76–7
Fleming, J., 290
Flensburg Fjord, 237
Flett, J. S., 81, 285, 291
Fleure, H. J., 251
flint, supply of, in Ireland and Scotland, xxi, 48, 106–8, 117, 124, 173, 175, 177, 193, 196, 212, 244, 259; Irish flint found in Scotland, 172, 177; mining of, 234, 255, tools for, 238; degeneration of technique 176
Flintshire, Post-Glacial deposits in, 77, 289
flora, 39, 55, 75–6, 266, 268–9, 282
food gathering or collecting of, xxii, xxiv, 212, 238–9, 250–1, 254, 256, 259–60, 262; production of, xxiii, xxiv, 212, 237, 238–9, 251, 261
foraminifera, 11, 15, 40, 84, 122–3, 134–5, 137, 140, 267
Forde, C. D., 250
Forest culture, xxiii, 170, 185, 192–3, 196–8, 202–5, 237, 253, 259–60 (*see also* Maglemosean culture)
forests, 90, 101
Forgandenny, Perthshire, 291
Formby coast, Lancashire, 87
Fort Harrouard, Eure-et-Loire, 238
Forth Valley, 55, 59, 81, 86, 180, 192–3, 206, 283, 290–1; estuary, 60; glacier, 282 (*see also* Firth of Forth)
Fosna culture, 251
Fowl, wild, 72, 172, 182
fowling, xxii
Fox, arctic (*Canis lagopus*), 38, 73
Fox, (Sir) Cyril, 76, 87–8, 91, 209–10, 290
Foyle Estuary, Northern Ireland, 277
fracture, conchoidal, 111
France, Palaeolithic of, 106, 199; Mesolithic of, 185, 191, 258–9, 237; Campignian of, 211, 234 ff.; Post-Glacial deposits of, 14; palaeobotany in, 14; Third Interglacial raised beach in, 265
Fraser, J., 28, 279
Fraserburg, Aberdeenshire, 278
Fraxinus, 20
Frenchpark, Co. Roscommon, 68–9
Friarton brickworks, Perth, 207

Gadus morrhua, 128
Gaffikin, (Miss) M., 251
Galtee Mountains, Co. Cork, 54, 273, 281
Galway, ice from, 41, 50, 274–5; retreat of ice in, 280, 284; Sand-Hill sites in, 252
Galway Bay, 37, 275, 292
Gams, H., 34, 64
Gare Loch, Dumbarton, 283, 285
Garrod, D. A. E., 45–7, 49, 71, 92, 198–9, 267
Gartmore, Perthshire, 82
Geikie, (Sir) A., 192, 207
Geikie, J., 80–1, 206, 291
geochronology, 6 ff., 20, 22, 69–71, 95, 101, 258, 274, 279, 282
geology, 22, 94, 96, 100, 142, 261

George, T. N., 265, 271, 284
German Substage, 4
Germany (north), geology of, 4, 12, 14, 64; Palaeolithic in, 64, 201–2; Mesolithic in, 77, 237; Campignian in, 238
Geschnitz Period, 6
Girvan, Ayrshire, 282, 284
Glamorganshire coast, 94
Glasgow, raised beach near, 81, 285, 290; dugout boats found near, 206
glass, 115, 252–3
Glecknabae Cairn, Island of Bute, 188
Glenariff, Co. Antrim, 37, 121
Glenarm, Co. Antrim, 121, 125, 129 ff., 143 ff., 148, 158 ff., 171, 173, 214 ff., 224, 229, 231–2, 239, 251, 277
Glenarm Bay, Co. Antrim, 130
Glenco, Co. Mayo, 279
Glendun, Cushendun, Co. Antrim, 106–7, 144, 223, 277
Glenesk, Kincardineshire, 278, 282–4
Glen Forsa, Mull, 285
Glen Roy, Inverness, 284
Glen Thraill, Ross-shire, 285
Glenluce, Wigtownshire, 194
Glenn, T. A., 233
Godwin, H., 16, 76–8, 80, 90, 94–8, 200, 203, 281, 288–90
Godwin, M. E., 77, 203
Göteborg, Sweden, 98
Gotiglacial Period, 4, 6–8, 12, 18, 61, 70
Götland, Sweden, 4
Gower, Glamorganshire, 87, 265, 284
Grainger, (Rev.) J., 132
Grampian Highlands, 279, 290
Grand Pressigny, Indre-et-Loire, 216, 234
Grangemouth, Stirling, 287
Grass Wrack (*Zostera marina*), 123
gravers, 118, 174, 178, 196, 199, 203–4, 216; absence of, in Early Larnian, 157
Gravettian culture, 47
Gray, A., 177
Gray, W., 121, 125, 166
Great Chalky Boulder Clay, 26
Great Glen, Scotland, 278
Greencastle, Belfast Lough, Co. Antrim, 125
Greenisland, Belfast Lough, Co. Antrim, 125
Greenland, 39, 49, 258, 280
Greenoge, Dunmurry, Co. Antrim, 232
Greenore, Co. Louth, 124
Gregory, J. W., 81, 91, 269, 278, 283, 285
grenzhorizont, 100
Gresswell, R. K., 87
Grieve, S., 180, 183, 185
Griffiths, J. C., 27, 33, 271
Grimes Graves, Norfolk, 234
Grimes, W. F., 47, 49
Grimsby, Lincolnshire, 289
grinders, 183
grinding, 223
Groomsport, Co. Down, 125
Gross, H., 18, 64
Guillemot, 182
Gullane, East Lothian, 194
Günz Glaciation, 26

Halichoerus gryphus, 177
Halling, Kent, 47
Hallissy, T., 280, 292
Hamburg area, archaeological succession in, 64
Hamburgian culture, 18, 64
hammerstones, 118, 183, 185, 190, 203, 223–4, 229
Hampshire coast, 94
hand axe, Chellean, 106; cordate, 228; rostrate, 106–7
hand tools, 157
handles, 235
Hardman, E., 292
Hardwick Hill, Lincolnshire, 45
Hardy, E. M., 98
harpoons, 77, 180 ff., 185, 188–9, 191, 198, 203, 260
Harrison, K., 27, 34, 44, 266–7, 276
Harris, Hebrides, 279
Harrisonian eoliths, 106
Hartlepool, Durham, 200
Harvard Archaeological Expedition to Ireland, 115, 121, 124–5, 126, 129, 132, 139, 228, 240
Harvard Irish Survey, 256
Hassé, L., 252–3
Hassocks, Sussex, 204
Hawkes, C. F. C., 247–8, 258
Hawkes, J., 238, 247
Hawthorn (?), 140–1
Hazel (*Corylus*), 19–20, 34, 36, 76, 92–3, 96–8, 115, 118, 123, 127–8, 137, 140–1, 146, 212, 242
hearths, 115, 127, 181, 219, 229, 231, 234, 238, 241–2, 244, 250, 256
Heatherslade beach, Wales, 284
Hebrides, glaciation of, 53, 279
Helmsdale, Sutherland, 285
Hencken, H. O'N., 252, 290
Hereford, glaciation of, 270
Hessle boulder clay, 31, 41, 51, 267, 270–1, 276; glaciation, 41; ice-sheet, 275 (*see also* Hunstanton *and* New Drift Glaciation)
Hewson, (Rev.) L. M., 252
Heysham Harbour, Lancashire, 289
Highland Boundary Fault, 278, 283
Highland Glaciation, 32, 48, 53, 57, 61–2, 71, 73, 277–8; ice-sheet, 28–9, 55, 271, 278, 284
Highland Zone of Britain, xxiii, 49, 117, 209, 259, 261
Highlands of Scotland, glaciation of, 41, 269, 272, 283–4; uplift of, 285; climate of, 40; Tardenoisean absent in, 193
Hinton, M. A. C., 43, 91
hoards, 177, 244, 250

INDEX

Hochmoor, *see* ombrogenous bogs
hoes, 238
Holderness, Yorkshire, 204, 270
Holland, 13, 238
Hollingworth, S. E., 31, 271, 275, 277
Holly (*Ilex*), 34
Holme, H., 125, 171
Holmpton, Yorkshire, 51, 64, 276
Holywood, Co. Down, 125, 171, 277
Hooton, E. A., 208, 256
Hopwood, A. T., 43
horn, implements of, 171, 181 ff., 190 ff.
Hornbeam (*Carpinus*), 20, 95
Horne, J., 72, 92, 282
hornfelsed sediment, *see* aphanite
Horn Head, Co. Donegal, 284
Hornsea, Yorkshire, 203
Horse, wild (*Equus caballus*), 34, 36, 91, 199; domestic, 235
Howden, J. C., 81, 287
Hoy (Orkneys), glaciation of, 279
Hoyles Mouth, Pembrokeshire, 47, 49
Hull, E., 81, 292
Hull, Yorkshire, 270, 273, 289
Humber Estuary, 46, 289; river, 270
Hungary, Campignian in, 238
Hunstanton (South), Norfolk, 46
Hunstanton boulder clay, 30, 41
Hunstanton-Hessle boulder clay, 26; glaciation, 44 (*see also* Hessle *and* New Drift Glaciation)
hunting economy, xxii, 157, 171 ff., 176
Hyaena, cave, 38

Iberia, 247, 250–1, 259; Iberian peninsula, 238, 259
ice-sheets, 100; in Britain and Ireland, 40, 49 ff., 105, 175, 273 ff.; in Northern Europe, 4–6, 19, 60–2; in the Alps, 4, 6; in the Pyrenees, 4; in North America, 13; in Antarctica, 13 (*see also* New Drift Glaciation)
igneous rock, 234
impact, point of, 112, 155; surface of, 157
Inchkeith (Island of), Firth of Forth, 188, 197
Inchnadamff (Sutherland), caves at, 72–3, 82, 92, 105, 175, 202
Inishowen Peninsula, Co. Donegal, 89, 284, 292
Inner Sound (between Skye and the mainland), Scotland, 285
insects, remains of, 36 (*see also* beetles)
insulator material, 240
Interglacial Period (Warthe-Weichsel), in Northern Europe, 34, 61 (for Third Interglacial, *see* Third)
Intermediate Zone of estuarine clay, Ireland, 122 ff., 137, 145, 172 (*see also* clay)
Interstadial Period (W_1/W_2), in Britain and Ireland, 33 ff., 40, 43, 45, 61, 199, 266 ff.
"Interval" deposits (W_1/W_2), 266
Inverness, 285
Ipswich, Suffolk, 45–6, 266
Ireland:
Old Drift Glaciation of, 27
Third Interglacial raised beach in, 29–30, 265–6
Late-Glacial stratigraphy in, 32–3
Interstadial (W_1/W_2) Period in, 37–8, 40, 73–4, 266
New Drift Glaciation of, 41 ff., 272–3; age of, 44; cause of, 61, 101; recession of ice-sheets of, 49 ff., 61, 273 ff.; shelly drift of, 286; flints from deposits of, 106–8
Late-Glacial fauna of, 38, 73–4, flora, 39
Late-Glacial Sea in, 57, 284 ff.
Post-Glacial Period in: deposits of, 82 ff., 121 ff., 142 ff., 292; climate of, 89 ff.; land connection with Britain during, 87–9, 172, 196; date of Litorina transgression of, 100, 144–5; caves formed during, 81; Post-Atlantic submergence in the south during, 80, 292; fauna of, 91, 123, 172
Palaeobotany in, 65 ff., 92 ff., 95 ff.; zoning pollen-diagrams in, 65 ff., 98 ff.
Mesolithic Period in (Larnian Culture): date of earliest occupation, xxiii–xxiv, 49, 73, 94–5, 105 ff., 117–20, 124, 144, 146–7, 171–2, 209, 258–9; distribution of Mesolithic sites, 121, 124–5, 176–7, 204–5, 259; earliest settlers of (physical type), 207–10, 256; Forest culture of, 170, 193, 202–3, 253, 260
Post-Larnian developments: Bann culture, 239 ff., 244–7, 256, 262; Sand-Hill sites, 252–4, 262; Tardenoisean, 196, 203–4; Campignian, 211 ff., 254, 261–2; Neolithic, 211, 239, 261–2; Megalithic, 211–13, 262
"Irish Channel River", 89, 172, 175, 207, 209
Irish Elk (*Cervus megaceros*), 36, 38, 55, 74, 83, 91–3, 114–15, 123, 172
Irish Mesolithic, stratigraphy of, 142 ff.; description of material, 148 ff.; summary and conclusions, 171 ff. (*see also* Larnian culture)
Irish Sea, 87, 92, 123, 147, 208, 209, 262; basin of, 93, 267–8; Ice-Sheet, 43–4, 50, 270–1, 274–5
iron, 115; oxide, 107; eel-spears of, 244
Iron Age, 20, 91, 190, 208, 252
Irvine River, Ayrshire, 188, 194, 197, 282
Island Magee, Co. Antrim, 107–8, 125, 136 ff., 143 ff., 148 ff., 158 ff.
Islay, 89, 272
Isle of Man, 32, 37, 51, 64–5, 88, 204, 251, 256, 265–6, 276–7, 293
Isle of Wight, 204, 233
isobases, 10–11, 57 ff., 78, 81–2, 85, 102, 237, 289, 291–2
isostasy, 9 ff., 62, 75, 85, 99; isostatic uplift, 37
isthmus, during Atlantic times between Scotland and England, 82, 89, 93, 180, 260
Italy, Campignian in, 238
Ivernian Ice-Sheet, 33, 41, 44, 49, 51, 53–4, 273–4, 277, 279
ivory, implements of, 199

INDEX

Jackson, J. W., 116, 125, 249, 252
Jamieson, T. F., 79–82, 91, 180, 192, 206, 287, 290–1
Jämtland, 4
jasper, use of, for implements, 196
Jehu, T. J., 27, 33, 271–2, 279, 291
Jessen, K., 13, 16, 18–21, 23, 34, 39, 44, 64–5, 67–70, 77, 83, 92, 98–100, *Table* 6, 118, 121, 127–8, 135–7, 139, 141, 144, 223, 242, 247, 284
John O'Groats, Caithness, 81
Jones, C. B., 91
Jones, O. T., 87, 109, 111, 265, 288
Jowett, A., 270, 275
Jura, Sound of, 89, 290
Jutland, 4, 13, 63–4, 237, 289

keel, ventral, 157
Keimaneigh, Pass of (Co. Cork), 280
Keith, (Sir) A., 116, 208
Kelling, Norfolk, 203
Kells, Co. Meath, 275
Kelvingrove Museum, Glasgow, 185
Kendall, P. F., 41, 270, 278, 283–4
Kenmara Valley, Co. Kerry, 280
Kent, Campignian in, 233
Kents Cavern, Devon, 47
Kerry, last glaciation of, 54, 62, 280–1; Upper Palaeolithic racial type in, 208
Kesh Cave, Co. Sligo, 74
Kiel, museum at, 237; fjord, 237
Kilchattan Brickyards, Island of Bute, 80
Kildare, 95
Kilgreany Cave, Co. Waterford, 38, 114 ff.; skeletons from, 115–16
Kilkee, Co. Clare, 273
Kilkenny, 273
Killavullen Caves, Co. Cork, 38
Killiney Bay, Co. Dublin, 105
Killough Bay, Co. Down, 265
Kilmaurs (near Kilmarnock), Ayr, 36, 268; section at Woodhill Quarry, 268
Kilrea, Co. Londonderry, 240, 247, 254
Kilroot (Belfast Lough), Co. Antrim, 125
Kilrush, Co. Clare, 273
Kilwaughter, Co. Antrim, 37
Kinahan, G. H., 292
Kincardine, Kinross, 192
Kincardine Moss, 291
King, W. B. R., 29, 43, 289
Kinnegad, Co. Kildare, 275
Kinnegar (Holywood), Co. Down, 125
Kinneil, Forth Valley, 193
Kintyre, Scotland, 177, 228
Kircowan Stage, 61, 281–2
Kircudbright, harpoon from, 188, 193, 197; Late-Glacial raised beach near, 284
Kirk, Hugh, collection of, 222
Kirkill, Isle of Man, 251
Kirmington, Lincolnshire, 31, 34, 40, 46, 266–7
Kitchen-Midden, culture of the Baltic, 20, 22, 260; pottery of, 235, 237; kitchen-middens in Ireland (Rough Island), 141–2, 146–7, 170, 173, 180, in Scotland, 178, 180 ff., 185, 188, 193
knives, of flint, 229, 235; of stone, 185
Knockmealdown Mountains, Co. Waterford, 54, 281
Knowles, W. J., 105–6, 125, 164, 166, 222–7, 249, 252; collection of, 253
Komsa culture, 251
Kosłowski, L., 238
Kyle of Sutherland, Scotland, 285

Lacaille, A. D., 178, 182, 185, 188, 194–6, 198, 249, 253
lacustrine deposits, 12–13, 36, 242, 250; conditions, 242
lagoon deposits, Cushendun, Co. Antrim, 126–8, 144
Lagore Bog, Co. Meath, 69
lakes, extra-glacial, 6–7, 123, 128, 144, 274, 284
Lake District Ice-Sheet, 50, 271, 275; climate of the Lake District, 276
Lambay Island, Ireland, 88
Lammermuir Hills, Scotland, 53, 277
Lammermuir-Stranraer Moraine, 53, 278, 281–2
Lamplugh, G. W., 276, 293
Lanark, 277
Lancashire, 87, 289–90
Lancaster, 275
land-bridge, between Denmark and Sweden (Post-Glacial), 12–13; between England and the Continent (Post-Glacial), 76, 92–3, 95–6, 203; between England and Ireland (W_1/W_2 Period), 37, 40; partial between England and Ireland (Post-Glacial), 87 ff., 96, 105, 124, 144, 146, 175–6, 207, 209, 259
land surface, Early Post-Glacial, 146–9, 172, 177
Larne, Co. Antrim, 37, 106–7, 132 ff., 143 ff., 148, 158 ff., 174, 193, 251, 259, 277 (*see also* Curran Point)
Larnian culture, 126, 143 ff., 146, 148, 171 ff., 175 ff., 192, 196, 202–3, 205–6, 207, 209, 211–14, 239, 251, 254, 256, 259 ff.; early, 127–9, 137, 139–40, 146–7, 148 ff., 173, 177, 196, 200–1, 249; late, 127, 129–30, 133 ff., 137, 146–8, 158 ff., 170, 173–4, 180, 193, 198, 210
Larne Lough, Co. Antrim, 125, 132, 173
Late-Glacial Period, 18, 21, 30 ff., 60 ff., 63 ff., 68–9, 75, 80, 98, 102, 124, 128–9, 257–8; occupation of Northern England during, 71, 191, 198, 208; occupation of Scotland during, 71–3, 175, 208
Late-Glacial Sea, 12, 55, 57 ff., 62, 83, 86–7, 99, 101, 120, 123, 129, 283, 284 ff.
La Touche, C. J., 95
Laufen Oscillation, 44

INDEX

Layard, (Miss) N. F., 132
Leach, A. L., 290
Leask, H. G., 74
Le Campigny, Seine Inférieure, 235 ff.
Lea Valley, Hertfordshire, 203
Leitrim, ice from, 41, 50, 68, 274–5
Leman and Ower Banks, North Sea, 203
Lemming, arctic, 21, 38, 55, 74, 91–2, 116
Levalloisean culture, 45; technique, 109; type flakes, 216, 229
Leverett, F., 61
Lewis, F. J., 65, 283, 291
Lewis, Hebrides, 279, 291
Liége, Belgium, 238
Lime (*Tilia*), 15, 19–20, 34, 93
Limerick, glaciation of, 273
limestone, implements of, 108 ff.
Limpets, 181; implements for detaching, 183, 185; "limpet-scoop", 202, 233–4
Lincolnshire, 31, 78, 271–2, 286, 289; Wolds, 270
Lisburn, Co. Down, 124
lithomarge, 244
Litorina Sea, 13, 15, 20, 86, 93, 102, 122, 144–5, 147, 173, 176, 180, 209, 239; deposits of, 86, 126–41, 176–7, 206; raised beach, *see* raised beach, Post-Glacial; submergence, 99, 101, 130, 140, 146, 148–9, 172–3, 178, 241–2; transgression of, xxiv, 13, 20, 82, 87, 90, 95, 100, 124, 126, 129, 135, 139, 161, 171, 177, 193, 202–3, 209, 259–60, 291 (*see also* marine deposits, marine transgression, etc., *or* submergence)
Little Eastern Glaciation, 26, 41
Littorina littorea, 13, 86, 128, 130–1, 140–1; *L. littoralis*, 128, 140; *L. saxatilis*, 128
Lleyn Peninsula, Wales, 89
Loch Ba, Mull, 285
Loch Don, Mull, 285
Loch Duich, Ross-shire, 285
Loch Hourn, Inverness, 285
Loch Linnhe, Argyllshire, 81, 86, 285, 290
Loch Lomond, Dumbartonshire, 55, 283, 285
Loch Spelve, Mull, 285
Loch Sunart, Argyllshire, 185, 188
Lochar Moss, Drumfries, 291
Lomond Hills, Fifeshire, 278
Londonderry, 239, 277
Lonke, A., 237
Los Millares, Spain, 250
Loughcrew, Co. Meath, 247
Lough Foyle, Northern Ireland, 292
Lough Gur, Co. Limerick, 74
Lough Neagh, Northern Ireland, xxi, 117 ff., 124, 142, 146, 174, 239–41, 247, 277
Louth, 274, 292
Lower Halstow, Kent, 80, 204–5; culture, 260
Lower Purple boulder clay, 31
Lowland Zone of Britain, xxiii, 210
Lowlands, Central (England), Campignian in, 233
Luce Bay, Wigtownshire, 177
lugs, pottery, 235, 246
lunates, microlithic, 201; semi-lunate shaped implement, 152
Lyle Hill, near Belfast, 232
Lyngby, Denmark, 71; culture, 19
Lynx, 73, 116

Macalister, R. A. S., 106, 109, 111, 115
MacArthur Cave, Oban, 181–2, 185, 188, 208
MacClintock, P., 27, 30–1, 41, 266, 270
MacCurdy, G. G., 250
MacDonald, Angus, 125, 232
Macfadyen, W. A., 203
Macgillicuddy's Reeks, Co. Kerry, 54, 280
Macgregor, M., 282
Magdalenian culture, xxiv, 47, 71, 199; implement types of, 178, 199
Maghera, Co. Donegal, 252
Maghera, Co. Londonderry, 244
Maglemosean culture, 20, 93, 176, 192, 202–3, 205, 207, 237, 259–60; influence of, in Scotland, 180, 188, 193, 196–7; absence of, in Early Larnian, 209 (*see also* Forest Culture)
Maghery (Belturbet), Co. Cavan, 37
Mahr, A., 99, 116, 211, 249–50, 254
Maiden Bower, Bedfordshire, 229
Main River, Co. Antrim, 272
Mainland, Orkneys, 279
Mallerstang area, Pennines, 270
Mammoth (*Elephas primigenius*), 34, 36–8, 40, 43, 132
Mané-er-Hroëk, Brittany, 250
Mann, L. McL., 48, 186
Maple (*Acer*), 20
March, Cambridgeshire, 34, 45, 267
March-Nar deposits, 34, 40, 266–7
marine deposits, 12, 36–7, 102, 171; erosion, 87, 147; transgression, 36, 40, 89, 93, 99–101, 122–3, 140, 145–9, 157, 266–7, effect of, on Irish Mesolithic development, 161, 171–2, 176 (*see also* submergence, Litorina Sea, Litorina submergence, etc.)
Marr, J. E., 45, 267
Martin, C. P., 124, 208, 265, 292
Martin's Brickyard, Belfast, 51, 277
Marton Pool, Montgomery, 270
Mas d'Azil, 198
Mason, W. D., 194
Matley, C. A., 284
Maxwell, J. H., 81
May, A. McL., 249, 252
May, R. L., 252
Maybole, Ayrshire, 91, 282
Mayo, ice from, 41, 50, retreat of, 279, 284; shelly drift in, 286; Third Interglacial raised beach in, 29, 266
McCallien, W. J., 27–9, 48, 57, 60, 69, 81, 86, 178, 194, 268, 283, 285, 290–1

INDEX

McMillan, (Mrs) Nora Fisher, 121, 125, 127–8, 131, 133–5, 140–1
Meath, glaciation of, 50, 274–5; Post-Glacial raised beach in, 292
Mediterranean, diffusion of culture from, 213, 262; physical type, 207; Tyrrhenian phase of, 266
Medway Valley, Kent, 289
Megalithic culture, 211 ff., 213, 247 ff., 251, 252–6, 261–2; megaliths, 251, 262
Meiendorf, near Hamburg, 64
Meiklewood estate, Stirling, 185, 192
Menghin, O., xxiii, 238
M.G.S., England and Wales, 31, 198, 266, 270, 275; Ireland, 244, 277, 280, 285, 292; Scotland, 57, 81, 268–9, 276, 282, 285–7, 289–90, 293
Mersey River, 87; estuary, 289
Mesolithic, 76, 259; definition of term, xxii–xxiii; dating of, xxiv; culture in the Baltic, 16, 18–22; in England, 198 ff.; in Scotland, 176 ff.; in Ireland, Chap. II (Pt. II)
Mesopotamia, 261
metal, 253
Metal Age, xxiv, 180, 239, 255; early, 76, 93, 170, 211, 232, 256
Methven, Perthshire, 278
Michelsberg, Baden, 238; culture, 238
micro-burins (gravers), 182, 193, 195–6, 199–201, 203, 260
microliths, 195, 199–201, 203–4; with *dos rabattu* trimming, 173–4, 178, 194
Middlesex, Campignian in, 233
Midland Valley of Scotland, 28, 40, 197, 260, 272, 282
Milankovitch's solar radiation curve, 7
Milewater Dock, Belfast, 83
mill-stones, 235
Miller, A. A., 271
Millknowe (Campbeltown), Argyllshire, 177–8
Milthers, V., 34, 44
Minchen Hole, South Wales, 265
Mindel Glaciation, 26
Mitchell, G. F., 69, 98, 281
modern objects, 115, 133
Modiolaria costulata, 137
Mogey, J. M., 208
Moir, J. Reid, 45–6, 106–7, 112–13, 201, 206
Molluscs, marine, 11–13, 15, 33–4, 40, 84, 90, 127, 133–5, 137, 193, 266–7, 268–9; warm forms of, 80, 145, cold forms of, 37, 60, 122, 286, edible forms of, 172, 181; freshwater, 13, 15; fluviatile, 33 (*see also* marine fauna, shells)
Monkton, Pembrokeshire, 47, 49
Montgomery, Wales, 270
Montrose, Forfar, 81
Moorfoot Hills, Scotland, 277
moorlog, 75–7
Morainic Glaciation, *see* Valley Glaciation
Moran, J., 132
Moray Firth, 53, 272, 278, 283, 286, 290
Morston, Norfolk, 30–1, 34, 40, 45, 267
Moss, 18, 36
Moss of Cree, Wigtownshire, 291
Mother Grundy's Parlour (Creswell Crags), Derbyshire, 199
Mount Leinster, Wexford, 54, 281
Mourne Mountains, Co. Down, 281
Mousterian culture, 29, 45, 199; type implements, 108 ff.
Movius, H. L., Jr., 115, 124–6, 129, 139, 152, 171, 206, 214, 219, 240, 242, 244, 253
Muff, H. B., 27, 265
Muirkirk, Ayrshire, 277
Mull, 57, 272, 279, 283, 285, 290
Mullerup culture, *see* Maglemosean culture
Mullet, grey, 181
multi-pronged spears, 244, 249
Munro, R., 85, 188, 192, 206
Munthe, H., 4
Mussels, 181
Myriophyllum alterniflorum, 18
Mytilus edulis, 141

National Museum of Antiquities of Scotland, 206
National Museum of Ireland, Dublin, 121, 244
National Quaternary Research Committee in England, 258
Navan, Co. Meath, 275
navigation, 206–7
Near East, Campignian in, 238
Neaverson, E., 289
Neolithic Period, 76, 196, 261; culture, xxiii–xxiv, 20, 94–5, 258; in Ireland, 100, 115–16, 122, 127, 129–30, 139–41, 146, 161, 166–70, 196, 202–3, 205, 208, 211, 213, 232–3, 244–7, 251, 253–5, 261; in Scotland, 180, 194, 196; in England, 200, 205, 229, 233–4; in the Isle of Man, 161, 250; in France, 234–7, 250; in Central Europe, 196, 234–5, 237; Western Neolithic culture, 211, 231–2, 237, 239, 254, 261
Neritoides beach, Wales, 265
Neuville, R., 238
Newbiggin Carr, Northumberland, 200
Newcastle, Co. Down, 83, 273
Newcastle, Co. Limerick, 273
Newcastle-on-Tyne, Durham, 188
New Drift Glaciation, 26–7, 39, 41 ff., 44 ff., 49 ff., 60–1, 199, 265–9, 270 ff., 273 ff.; boulder clay of, 36, 45 (*see also* Hessle *and* Hunstanton Glaciations)
Newferry, Co. Londonderry, 240 ff., 248
Newhall Cave, Co. Clare, 74
New Mawbray, Cumberland, 198
Newton, L., 290
Newtown Colliery, peat beds at, 37
Newtownards, Co. Down, 139
Newtownbreda, Co. Down, 273
Nidderdale, Yorkshire, 45, 270

INDEX

Norfolk, Interstadial (W_1/W_2) deposits in, 266–7; glaciation of, 270–2; shelly drift in, 286, Campignian in, 233
Normandy, 265
North America, ice-sheet in, 13
North Calder Water, Lanark, 287
North Channel, 176, 178, 180, 239, 262
North Sea, 12–13, 19, 75–6, 202, 237, 260, 267, 270, 275, 290; drift from, 26
North Uist, Hebrides, 291
Northumberland, 266, 271, 275, 284
Norway, 13, 27, 251, 267
Novaya Zemlya, 4
Nøstvet culture, 203
Nucella lapillus, 128
nunataks, 39

Oak (*Quercus*), 15, 19–20, 34, 36, 76, 92, 93, 99, 115, 118, 123, 127, 137, 140–1, 146, 212, 235
Oak-Mixed-Forest (OMF: Oak + Elm + Lime), 20, 76, 93, 96, 242
Oakley, K. P., 29, 43, 289
Oban, Argyllshire, 82, 188, 193
Obanian culture, 180 ff., 182, 193, 197–8, 206 ff., 210, 259–60
Obermaier, H., 4, 206
occupation sites, probable location of, during Irish Mesolithic, 148–9, 173 (*see also* settlement sites)
Ochil Hills, Scotland, 272, 278
ochre, use and preparation of, 189–90
Ochtertyre Moss, near Stirling, 291
Octobon, M. E., 216
O'Laverty, (Rev.) J., 250
Old Drift Glaciation, 26 ff., 29, 33, 39, 44, 199, 266–9; boulder clay of, 36, 265
Oldesloe, Schleswig-Holstein, 237
Omalian culture, 238
ombrogenous bogs, 16
"Opsimiolithic", xxiii
Ó'Ríordáin, S. P., 74, 252–3
Orkney Islands, glaciation of, 28, 53, 272, 279; raised beaches absent in, 59–60, 81, 285, 291; submerged peats in, 291; archaeological material from, 247, 249
ornament, geometric, 235
Oronsay, 180, 188
Orr, J., 252–3
Osborn, J. F., 60
oscillations during the retreat of the ice, 50; in Scotland, 54–5, 61–2, 282; in Ireland, 54, 62, 279; in Scandinavia, 4, 6, 61
ostracods, 135
Ostrea edulis, 128, 130, 140–1 (*see also* Oysters)
Otter, 182
Ox, wild (*Bos primigenius*), 34, 36, 91, 140, 171; domestic, 115–16, 235 (*see also* Cattle [*Bos longifrons*])
Ox Mountains, Co. Sligo, 280
Oxfordshire, Campignian in, 233
Oysters (*Ostrea edulis*), 181

Paisley, Renfrew, 286
palaeobotany, 16 ff., 21–2, 36, 76–7, 83, 93–5, 98, 100, 127–8, 136–7, 142, 223, 240–2, 247
Palaeolithic, question of, in Ireland, 48–9, 63, 105 ff., 111 ff., 114 ff., 116–17; implements in Scotland, 48, 53, 71; Lower or Pre-, 157, Mesolithic forms of, in Ireland, 105, 108; Upper, xxii–xxiii, 16, 18, 22, 45, 152, 157, 161, 172, 174, 178, 191, 204–5, 207–8, 260, hunters migrate northward, 175, 177, 196, 198, 207–10, 258, physical type in Ireland, 208, 256
palaeontology, 22, 94, 100, 142
Palaeozoic rocks, 209
Palmer, L. S., 265, 288
Paphia pullastra, 128; *P. decussata*, 128, 140–1; *P. aurea*, 141
Parker, D., 244
passage graves, 247
Patella beach, Wales, 265
Patella vulgata, 130, 141
Paterson, H. M. L., 194–6
patination, 107, 111, 118, 130, 134, 137, 140, 178, 214, 219, 221, 229, 242
Patterson, W. H., 125, 252
Peabody Museum of Harvard University, 216
Peacehaven, Sussex, 204
Peach, A. M., 180, 193
Peach, B. N., 72, 92, 282
Peake, H. J. E., 76, 251
peat, study of, in Northern Europe, 14 ff., 20, 63 ff., 75; in England, 31, 40, 51, 64, 276; in the Isle of Man, 65; in Scotland, 36, 40, 65, 269; in Ireland, 37, 65 ff., 98, 100, 223; *sphagnum* peat, 20, 94, 291
pebble, worked, 244
pecking technique, 224
Pembrokeshire, 271, 290
Penck, A., 4, 6, 44
Pengelly, W., 265, 288
Penmaenmawr, Carnarvonshire, 233, 289–90
Pennines, glaciation of, 270–2, 275; Tardenoisean in, 201–2, 205, 209, 260
Pentland Hills, 278, 282
Pentland-Carstairs-Maybole Moraine, 55, 61, 282
Pentuan, Cornwall, 288
perforators, 118, 155, 164, 173, 178, 216, 222, 231, 235, 247; and end scraper, 192
peripheral bulge, 8
Periwinkle (*Littorina littorea*), 13, 86, 181
Perth region, glaciation of, 282; Readvance, 57, 278
Peterhead, Aberdeenshire, 193
Phacoides borealis, 134
Phillips, C. W., 207
Phragmites communis, 128, 242
physiography, 121

INDEX

Pickering, Vale of, 270
picks, 118, 174, 178, 193, 204–5, 219, 222–4, 231, 233, 235, 238, 247, 249, 251–2; Cushendun, 157, 166, 173; Larne, 155, 166, 174, 206; Thames, 170
Pig, wild (*Sus scrofa*), 91–2, 182, 199; domestic, 130
Piggott, S., 229, 234, 238, 289
pins, bone, 72, 181, 185; bronze, 252
Pin Hole Cave (Creswell Crags), Derbyshire, 46–7, 191, 199
Pine (*Pinus*), 18 ff., 34, 36, 76, 90, 92–3, 96, 98–9, 118, 123, 127–8, 137, 146, 212, 241
Pinus sylvestris, 18–19
pit-dwellings, 204, 235, 237
Plain, North European, xxiii, 20, 22, 76, 94, 175, 193, 205, 237; North German, 14
planes, *see* steep scrapers
plaques, for mixing ochreous colours, 190
Pleistocene, 7, 25–6, 28, 114, 258
plunging technique, definition of, 166
Pocock, R. W., 271
points, 149, 157, 161, 173–4, 178, 195, 199–201, 203, 219, 223–4, 235, 244, 253; with *dos rabattu* trimming, 199, 247, 249; leaf-shaped, with trimmed butts, 149, 161, 173–4, 178, 214–16, 219, 231, 244, 250–1; tanged, 174, 201–2, 222, 247, 251; Reindeer antler, 71; bone, 181 ff., 185, 248–9; bilaterally barbed, 188
Poland, Campignian in, 238
polishers, of antler, 181 ff.; of bone, 185; of stone, 244
pollen, analysis of, 16 ff., 34, 75–6, 95–8, 100, 118, 122, 127–8, 203, 269; diagrams, 17, 98, 241; sequences, 102; spectra, 123; transportation of, 16 (*see also* zoning of pollen diagrams)
polleniferous deposits, 121
Pomeranian Stage, 6–8, 26, 51, 61, 71, 275–6; End-Moraine, 4, 6, 61 (*see* Baltic End-Moraine)
Ponders End Stage, 29
Poole, H. F., 204
Portglenone, Co. Antrim, 249
Portobello, near Edinburgh, 55, 282, 287
Portpatrick, Wigtownshire, 177
Portrush, Co. Antrim, 125
Portstewart, Co. Londonderry, 125, 252
Portugal, 250
Post, L. von, 16
Post-Glacial Period, 4, 6–7, 19–21, 62, 65, 84, 100 ff., 175, 258–9; climatic phases of, 14 ff., 98 ff.; deposits of, in Britain, 75 ff., 288 ff., in Ireland, 82 ff., 121 ff., 126–46, 292, in the Isle of Man, 293; fauna of, in Britain and Ireland, 90–2; forest development in Ireland, 98–100; occupation of Ireland during, 74, 120; warmth maximum (*see also* climatic optimum) of, 134–5, 205
Post-Larnian developments, 211 ff., 239, 254 ff., 261–2
potsherds, 229, 232, 244–7
pottery, xxiii, 115, 212, 235, 237, 250–3, 255, 262
Praeger, R. Ll., 37, 39, 82–4, 90–1, 98, 121–2, 124–5, 132–3, 136–7, 168–70, 202, 252–3, 284, 292
Pre-Boreal Period, 14 ff., 19, 21, 76 ff., 90, 92, 94, 98, 101, 120, 191, 200, 251; Pre-Boreal–Boreal Period, 290, 292
Prickly Twig-Rush (*Cladium mariscus*), 242
"Proto-Neolithic", xxiii, 212
Proto-Solutrean culture, 47
Prussia, East, 64
Purple Drift, 26; boulder clay, 31
Pyrenees, 4, 238

quarrying, scapling waste from, 114
quartz, implements of, 178, 196
quartzite, implements of, 108 ff., 204, 205–6; fracture of, 222
Quercus robur, 19–20
quern, 235

Ra Moraines, 4, 61
Ragunda, 4, 6–7, 19, 21, 62
rainfall, increase of in Ireland, 99–100
Raised Beaches, in Northern Europe, 8 ff., 12–13, 202; in Britain and Ireland, Third Interglacial, 29–30, 265–6, Interstadial Period (W_1/W_2), 34, 40, 266–7, Late-Glacial, 57 ff., 75, 279, 284 ff.
Post-Glacial (Litorina raised beaches) 85 ff., 93; nomenclature, 86, 122; in England and Wales, 75 ff., 288 ff.; in Ireland, 82 ff., 109, 122 ff., 260, 292, at Cushendun, 126 ff. at Glenarm, 129 ff., at Island Magee, 136 ff., at Larne, 132 ff., at Rough Island, 139 ff.; implements from, 106–8, 120, 158 ff., 171, 192, 212, 214, 251; Campignian found above, 219, 221–2, 232–3, 239, 255; in the Isle of Man, 293; in Scotland, 80 ff., 290 ff., at Campbeltown, 177 ff., at Oronsay, 180–1; Obanian occupation above, 178 ff.; Tardenoisean found above, 194, 196; sinking of land (Post-Atlantic) south of o-isobase of, 77, 102, 289, 292
raised bogs, *see* ombrogenous bogs
Raistrick, A., 31, 200, 266, 270, 272, 275
Ralaghan, Co. Cavan, 68–9
Ramsey, Isle of Man, 276
Rathlin Island, Co. Antrim, 228 ff., 249, 256
rational border, 19, 98–9; definition of, 19
Razor Clam (*Phacoides borealis*), 134
Read, H. H., 28
Reade, T. M., 289–90
reaming tools, *see* boring tools
recurrence surface (in Irish bogs), 99–100
Red Bay, Co. Antrim, 285
Red Cellar Cave, Co. Limerick, 74
Reed, common (*Phragmites communis*), 128, 242

INDEX

Reeds, C. A., 60
Reid, C., 65, 75–7, 288–9
Reindeer (*Rangifer tarandus*), 36, 38, 73–4, 91–3, 115, 199
Reindeer Cave (Inchnadamff), Sutherland, 55, 72–3
reindeer-hunting cultures, 202
Remouchamps, Belgium, 201
resolved flaking, 224
retouch, inverse, 152, 164, 244, 247, 250
Retreat Stages of the last ice-sheets in Britain and Ireland, 49 ff., 273 ff.
Rhinns of Galloway, Wigtownshire, 53, 177, 278, 284
Rhinoceros, woolly, 34, 36, 40, 43
Rhyl, Flintshire, 289–90
Ribble River, 87
Richardson, F. L. W., Jr., 121, 129, 285
Ripley, Yorkshire, 45, 270
Risby Warren, Lincolnshire, 47
Risga, Island of (Loch Sunart), 186–8
Riss Glaciation, 26
Riss-Würm Period, raised beach of the, 29 ff., 265–6
Rissoa albella, 135; *R. parva*, 135
Ritchie, J., 36, 71–2, 208
River-bed type, 208
"Riverford culture", 250
rock-cut platforms, *see* raised beaches
rock-shelters, in Ireland, 109; in Scotland, 181; Asturian found in, 205
rod, reindeer horn, 190–1
rodents, Arctic, 73
Roebuck (*Capreolus capreolus*), 34, 181
Rogers, I., 290
rolling, degree of, on flint implements, 108–9, 158 ff., 170, 173, 178
Roman Period, 91
Romano-British Period, 189
Rome, J. L., 289
Rossendale Uplands, 270
Rosses Point, Co. Sligo, 108 ff.
Ross-shire, glaciation of, 272, 279; Post-Glacial raised beach in, 291
Rostellon Dolmen, Co. Cork, 85, 292
rostro-carinates, 106–7, 155
rostrate implements, 155, 157, 173–4
Rough Island, Co. Down, 124, 139 ff., 141–2, 143 ff., 148 ff., 221 ff., 239, 249, 251; kitchen-midden at, 146–7, 170, 173, 180
Roughty Valley, Co. Kerry, 280
Roundstone, Co. Galway, 68–9
Roxburghshire (Scotland), Tardenoisean sites in, 194
Royal Irish Academy, Dublin, 132
Royston, Cambridgeshire, 203
rubbers, of stone, 183, 188; of bone, 185, 188; of horn, 188
rubbing-stones, 190
rushes, 123
Russia, Campignian in, 238
"rust stains", 221

Saale Glaciation, 26
St Abbs Head, Berwickshire, 53, 277–8, 284
St Bees, Cumberland, 51, 64, 276
St Gertrude, Holland, 234
Salix herbacea, 18
Salmon, P., 234–6
Salpausselkä moraines, 4, 61
Sand-Hill culture, 213, 256, 262; settlements, 164, 180, 252–4
Sandeel Bay, Co. Down, 125
Sandford, K. S., 25–6, 46
sandstone, 189, 224
Sauramo, M., 4
Scandinavia, 4, 7, 8 ff., 13, 19–20; ice-sheet from, 27–8, 32, 41, 44, 50, 270–2, 275, 286
Scanian Substage, 4; moraine, 4
Scarva, Co. Down, 273
Scharff, R. F., 74
schist, 183, 188
Schleicher, Ch., 196
Scilly Isles, 290
Scotland, Old Drift Glaciation of, 27–9; shelly drift of, 28, 269
"Pre-Glacial" deposits of, 28, 57, 279
Late-Glacial stratigraphy in, 32
Interstadial (W_1/W_2) Period, deposits of, 36–7, 266–9
New Drift Glaciation of, 41, 272; age of, 44, 272; sources of ice during, 43, 272; recession of ice-sheets of, 51–6, 273 ff.; shelly drift of, 272, 286
Late-Glacial fauna of, 36–7, 72–3, 268–9, 282, 287
Late-Glacial Sea in, 57, 59–60, 278–9, 284 ff.
Varve clays and geochronology in, 70–1, 258
Late-Glacial occupation of, 71–3, 175
Post-Glacial Period in, deposits of, 80 ff., 290–1; land connection with Ireland during, 89, 172, 196; date of Litorina transgression in, 82, 291; caves formed during, 81; fauna of, 91, 181–2
Palaeobotany in, 65, 82, 98, 269, 291
Mesolithic Period in, 124, 147, 176 ff., 196–8, 259–60; earliest period of permanent settlement, xxiii–xxiv, 95, 117; Forest culture in, 192–3, 203, 253, 260; Tardenoisean culture in, 193–6, 260; boats during, 206–7; flint, occurrence of, 177, 196, from Ireland, 172, 177; Mesolithic skeletons from, 72–3, 208; Neolithic pottery from, 247; Tracked stones in, 252
Scottish Ice-Sheet, 50, 54, 144, 272–4, 279, 286; Readvance, 26, 31–3, 51, 53, 57, 60–1, 64, 129, 275–7
Scrapers, 149, 157, 203, 214, 223; carinate, 199; concave, 164, 173–4; core, 155, 173, 175, 178, 195, 201, 203; discoidal, 152, 164, 199, 224, 233, 235, 244; double-ended, 235; end,

152, 159, 164, 173, 178, 192, 199, 216, 219, 231, 233, 235; end-of-blade, 118, 152, 164, 216, 222; fish-tail, 216, 222, 231, 233, 235; hollow, 159, 164, 183, 229, 231, 253; horse-shoe, 219; nose, 229; notched, 155, 174; ovate, 152, 164, 183; side, 152, 161–4, 173, 178, 203, 219, 224, 229, 231, 244, 253; side and end, 194, 222, 231; square-ended, 152, 164, 229; steep, 118, 155, 164, 173, 175, 178, 195, 199, 200–1, 219; thumb-nail, 152, 164, 173, 178, 192, 198, 201, 202–3, 253
Scrobicularia plana, 127
Scrobicularia Zone, 84, 122 ff., 144–5 (*see also* Lower Estuarine Clay)
sea, extent of during Litorina transgression, 147, 172
Seal, arctic, 60, 287; Grey (*Halichoerus gryphus*), 81, 177, 181; preparation of skins of, 183, 197
sedges, 123
seeds, 36
Selkirk, Scotland, 194
Selmeston, Sussex, 204
Settle, Yorkshire, 189
settlement sites, probable nature and location of in Irish Mesolithic, 146–7, 170–3 (*see also* occupation sites); on Rathlin Island, 228 ff.
Severn Valley, 265, 270–1, 288; river, 77
Sewardstone, Essex, 207
Shandon Cave, Co. Waterford, 38
Shannon River, 250, 273; valley, 275
sharpening stones, 244
Sheep, domestic, 115, 130, 182
Sheffield Hill, Lincolnshire, 47
shells, 122–3, 131, 139 ff., 177; from occupation sites, 181, 205, 252; beads of, 181 (*see also* marine fauna, molluscs)
shell-fish, 147, 180
shelly drift, 28, 286
Shetelig, H., 202
Shetland Islands, 28, 48, 285, 291
Shewalton, Ayrshire, 188, 194–5, 197
Shore, T. W., 290
Shrewsbury, Shropshire, 281
Shropshire, 270; Plain, 281
Silent Valley, Co. Down, 50, 274, 277
silica, 240
Silloth district, 289
silver-plated object, 116
Simpson, J. B., 57, 70, 81, 278, 282–3, 285, 291
Simpson, W. J., 125
Skibbereen, Co. Kerry, 280
Skye, 272, 279, 283
Skager Rack, 12
Skate, 181
skeletons, human, 72, 114 ff., 208
Skipsea, Yorkshire, 203
slate, 249
Slater, G., 276
Slieve Ardagh Hills, Cos. Kilkenny and Tipperary, 273
Slieve Gallion, Co. Londonderry, 244
Slieve na Caillighe, *see* Loughcrew
Slievenamon Mountain, Co. Kilkenny, 54, 281
Sligo, glacial deposits in, 111; ice from, 41, 286; retreat of ice in, 279, 284; raised beaches in, 85, 265; caves in, 114; sites in, 108 ff.; Bay, 109
Slovakia, Campignian in, 238
slug-shaped flints, 194, 196
Smith, B., 32, 37, 275–6
Smith, (Rev.) F., 105
Smith, F. G., 290
Smith, R. A., 106, 233–4
smoothers, bone and horn, 188
snail, land (*Cepaea nemoralis*), 141
soil analysis, 33
solar radiation, 7, 39, 90
solifluction, 18, 21, 30, 33, 46, 68, 284
soligenous bogs, 16
Solomon, J. D., 26, 31, 41, 45, 267, 270
Solutrean culture, 47, 198
Solway region, Cumberland, 78, 198, 271; Firth, 289
South Ferriby, Lincolnshire, 270
Southampton, 77, 96, 290
Southern Irish End-Moraine, 43, 49, 273
Southern Uplands of Scotland, 51, 53–5, 61, 63, 65, 271–2, 275, 277–8, 281–2, 284
Spain, 185, 191, 205, 250, 258–9
spear-heads, 152, 244, 247, 250
Sperrin Mountains, Co. Londonderry, 54, 279
Sphagnum peat, *see* peat
Spiennes, Belgium, 234
Spiennian, 238
Spitsbergen, 39
spokeshave, 164, 174
Springfield Brickyard, Fifeshire, 287
Spruce (*Picea*), 34, 95
Squires Hill, near Belfast, 232
stab-and-drag ornament, 247
Staffordshire, 270
Stainmore Gap, 271
stake holes, 181
stalagmite, 115
Stanford's, 244
Steers, J. A., 290
Stelfox, A. W., 67, 74, 116, 252
Stendall, J. A. S., 252
steppe-tundra environment, 175, 209
Stewart, M., 291
Stewart, S. A., 84
Stirling, 285, 291; region, 283 287; Carse of, 192–3, 253, 260
stone, implements of, 180 ff., 222 ff., 228 ff.; polished, xxiii, 212, 223–4, 231, 234, 250; with local polish, 231, 233; slabs of, 72
Stonehaven, Kincardineshire, 278, 285
Stoneykirk, Wigtownshire, 194
storm beaches, *see* beach

INDEX

Strahan, A., 288
Strandhall, Isle of Man, 293
strand-lines, high-level, *see* raised beaches
"strand-looper", 176
Strangford Lough, Co. Down, 124, 139 ff., 173
Stranraer, Wigtownshire, 53, 194, 198, 278
Strathmore Glaciation, 32, 272; ice-sheet, 36, 41, 44; boulder clay of, 269
strike-a-lights, 183
striking platform, 112, 149, 155, 157, 166, 242
Strokestown, Co. Roscommon, 244
Strome Ferry (Loch Carron), Ross-shire, 285
Sub-Atlantic Period, 14, 20, 94, 100
Sub-Boreal Period, 14, 20, 82, 90, 93–4, 100, 124, 213, 235, 239; archaeological material associated with deposits of, 223, 241, 247; cultural developments during, 95, 229, 250, 261–2
Sub-Boreal–Sub-Atlantic Period, 291
submerged forests or peats, 85, 87; in Scandinavia, 9 ff.; in England and Wales, 75 ff., 288 ff.; in Scotland, 80 ff., 290 ff.; in Ireland, 82 ff., 100, 123, 144, 292; in the Isle of Man, 293
submerged valleys, *see* drowned valleys
submergence, of Interstadial Period (W_1/W_2), 37–8, 40, 266–9; Late Glacial, 57–60, 284–7; Post-Glacial, in Britain, Ireland, and adjacent waters, 75 ff., 288 ff.; maximum of, in Ireland, 145; during Post-Atlantic times, 80, 87, 94, 95, 289–90, 292 (*see also* marine deposits, marine transgression, etc.; Litorina Sea, Litorina submergence, etc.)
summer, occupation, 242, 250; deposition during, 7
Sunderland, Durham, 78, 289
Sus scrofa, 128
Sussex, Campignian in, 233
Sutherland, 59, 272, 291
Swansea, Glamorganshire, 271, 288; Bay, 77
Sweden, 4, 7–8, 12–13, 27, 202
Swinnerton, H. H., 289
Swinton, W. E., 268
Swiss Lakes, Neolithic of, 237

Tabellaria fenestrata, 241
Tait, D., 272, 282, 287, 290
Tallgren, A. M., 257
Tanner, V., 4
Tapes decussatus, 13; *T.* (*Paphia*) *decussatus*, 137
Tapes raised beach, 203 (*see also* Litorina raised beach)
Tapes Sea, *see* Litorina Sea
Tardenoisean, 180, 182, 193–7, 199–201, 203–5, 208–9, 250, 259–60, 290
Tavnagharry, Co. Antrim, 222
Tawe River, Wales, 87, 288
Tay Valley, Scotland, 60, 81, 86, 207, 278, 290–1
Tellina calcarea, 60
terraces, 195; Late-Glacial, 29, 43, 129, 271, 287; Post-Glacial, 126, 129
Tertiary Period, 7; basalt of the, xxi, 107, 124, 228
Thames Valley, Late-Glacial terraces of, 29, 43; Mesolithic in, 202, 205; Post-Glacial deposits of, 80, 289
"Thames Pick", 204, 260
Thatcham, Berkshire, 203
The Wash, glaciation of, 270
Third Interglacial Period, 29–30, 102, 111, 265–6
Thracia convexa, 122
Thracia Zone, 84, 122 ff., 145 (*see also* Upper Estuarine Clay)
Thurso, Caithness, 272, 279
Tievebulliagh, Co. Antrim, 222 ff., 231; industry from, 229, 249; stone from, 232 (*see also* aphanite)
Tilia cordata, 19–20
Till, glacial, *see* boulder clay
Tillotson, E., 45, 270
timber, scarcity of during Late-Glacial Period, 175
time-scale (North European), extension of into Britain and Ireland, 60–3, 100–2
Ting, S., 290
Tipperary, glaciation of, 273
Tomlinson, M. E., 265, 271
Toome, Co. Antrim, 117, 244
topogenous bogs, 16
Tortoise, fresh-water, 16
tracked stones, 252
Tramore Bay (Co. Waterford), Post-Glacial deposits of, 292
tranchet, *see* flake axe
Transylvania, Campignian in, 238
trapezes, 194
Tratman, E. K., 114, 116
Trave River, Schleswig-Holstein, 237
Traveller's Rest Pit, Cambridge, 266
Trechmann, C. T., 203, 267, 289
Tregaron, Cardiganshire, 271, 281
Trent Valley, near Derby, 34, 267
Treshnish Isles, 57, 290
triangles, scalene and equilateral, 195
Trotter, F. M., 31, 271, 275–7, 279
tundra conditions, in Northern Europe, 18; in England, 27
Turner, (Sir) W., 208
Tweed Valley (Scotland), Tardenoisean sites in, 194; terraces in, 287
Tweed-Cheviot area, ice dispersal from, 271
Tyne Valley, glaciation of, 271, 275
Tyrone, ice movement from, 273
Tyrrhenian Phase, 266

Ullyott, P., 76
Ulmus glabra, 19–20
Ulster, Campignian in, 214

INDEX

Unstan pottery, 247
uplift, in Scandinavia, 8 ff.; in Scotland: occupation on Oronsay contemporaneous with, 181 (*see also* emergence)
Upper Barnwell Village Beds, Cambridge, 34, 267
Upper Chalky Boulder Clay (East Anglia), 26–7, 30, 44–5, 198, 266
Upper Diluvium, 60
Upper Purple Boulder Clay (Yorkshire), 31
Ural Mountains, 4; Campignian in, 238
Usk, Monmouthshire, 271
Ussher, R. J., 292
Uxbridge, Middlesex, 203

Valley Glaciation, in Ireland, 54, 62, 68, 279–80; occupation of Ireland after, 73; relation of, to Late-Glacial Sea, 57, 62, 285–6; in Scotland, 32, 55, 62, 283
valleys, invasion of, by Litorina Sea, 172
varves, 6–7, 50–1, 63 ff., 70–1, 75, 101, 258, 274, 276–7 (*see also* laminated clay)
Vener, Lake, 12
Vetter, Lake, 12
Victoria Cave, Yorkshire, 71, 92, 189 ff., 196–8, 202, 205, 267
Virginia (Co. Meath), moraines at, 275

Wales, axe-factory in, 233–4; Campignian in, 214; Glaciation of, 27, 54, 270–1, 273 ff., 281, 284; Late-Glacial raised beach in, 29, 284; "limpet-scoops" in, 233–4; Palaeozoic rocks in, 209; Post-Glacial deposits in, 75 ff., 288–290; Tardenoisean in, 204; zoning of pollen-diagrams in, 98
Wallace, T. D., 290
Walmsley, T., 208
Walton, J., 39
Wandsworth, Thames Valley, 203
Wangford Warren, Norfolk, 47
Warcock Hill, Marsden, Yorkshire, 200
Warren, S. H., 203, 233, 289
Warthe Glaciation, 26
Warthe-Weichsel Period, 34, 40
Waterfoot, Co. Antrim, 285
Waterford, caves in, 108, 114 ff.
wave-cut platforms, 57 (*see also* raised beaches)
weevils, 36
Weichsel Glaciation, 6, 26, 61; equivalent of, in Britain and Ireland, 44, 60–1
Welch, R. J., 109
Wellcome Historical Medical Museum, London, 253
Welsh Glaciers, 271; Readvance, 271, 281
Werrar, Isle of Wight, 204
West Hartlepool, Durham, 203, 260, 289
West Heath, 204
Western Boulder Clay (in Northern England), 271
Western Isles of Scotland, 57, 279, 285
Western Neolithic culture, 211, 231–2, 237, 239, 254, 261
Wexford, glaciation of, 273, 281
Wexford Harbour, 85, 292
Whale, remains of, 81, 132, 192, 288
Wharfedale, Yorkshire, 200, 270
Wheeler, R. E. M., 202, 233, 265
Whelan, C. B., 98, 117–19, 121, 124–6, 158, 168–70, 196, 206, 219–20, 222, 228–32, 244, 247, 248–9, 251–2
Whelks, 181
Whitburn, Durham, 188, 197
Whitehead, T. H., 271
White Park Bay, Co. Antrim, 125, 252–4
Wicklow, Irish Sea Ice in, 273; Interstadial (W_1/W_2) deposits in, 266; Late-Glacial raised beach in, 284; peat development in, 67 ff.; retreat of ice from, 50, 274
Wicklow Mountains, glaciation of, 43, 54, 62, 273, 280
Wigtownshire, flint in beaches of, 177
Williams, K. E., 27, 33
Willoughton, Lincolnshire, 47
Willow (*Salix*), 18, 36, 92, 98–9, 118, 123, 137, 242
Wills, L. J., 265, 270–1, 281, 288
Wiltshire, Neolithic A culture in, 229
Windmill Hill pottery, 115, 229, 231, 239; arrow-heads associated with, 220
Wirral coast, 87
Wolf (*Canis lupus*), 55, 73, 91, 92, 172, 287
Wolverhampton, Staffordshire, 270
Wood, S. V., Jr., 289
Wood-Martin, W. G., 244
woodworking tools, 164, 174–5, 183, 185, 206, 260
Woolacott, D., 266–7, 271, 275, 277, 284
Worcester Terrace (of the Severn Valley), 271
Workington Harbour, Cumberland, 289
workshops, 211, 214, 231, 255, 261
Wrasse, 181
Wright, W. B., 8, 12, 23, 25, 27–30, 41, 57–8, 60–1, 76, 78, 80, 86, 100–1, 180, 193, 265, 267, 270, 279, 281, 285–6, 287, 289–90, 292
Würm Glaciation, I, 26, 266; I–II, oscillation in the Alps, 40; II, 4, 6, 26, 44 (in Britain and Ireland), 61; III, 6, 7, 26, 32 (in Northern England), 51, 61, 275 (in Britain)

Y-shaped implements, 216, 233
Yew (*Taxus*), 140, 141
Ynylas, Cardiganshire, 290
Yoldia arctica, 12; *Y. norvegica*, 60
Yoldia Sea, 12, 19, 60, 62, 101; equivalent of, in Britain and Ireland, 83, 287
York Line, 41, 49, 60, 199, 270; moraine, 270, 273
Yorkshire, boulder clay of, 26; Campignian in, 233; cause of last glaciation in, 271–2; Inter-

INDEX

glacial raised beach in, 265–6; Interstadial (W_1/W_2) deposits of, 266; Maglemosean in, 203, 259; stratigraphy (Late-Glacial) in, 31; submerged peats of, 78
Young, J., 268
Young, R., 91, 125, 171
Ythan Valley, 278

Zealand, Maglemosean sites of, 77
Zeuner, F. E., 7, 26–7, 33, 47, 51, 60, 266, 275
Zonhoven, Belgium, 200–1
zoning of pollen-diagrams, in Denmark, 18–20, 63–4, 70; in England and Wales, 98; in Germany, 64, 70; in Ireland, 67–70, 98–100, 127–8, 135, 139, 144–7, 241–2, 284; in the Isle of Man, 65
zoogeography, 76
Zostera marina, 123